W9-BUN-453

EMMA GOLDMAN

LIVING MY LIFE

EMMA GOLDMAN

IN TWO VOLUMES

Vol. I

DOVER PUBLICATIONS, INC.

NEW YORK

This Dover edition, first published in 1970, is
an unabridged republication of the work originally
published in 1931 by Alfred Knopf, Inc., New York.

International Standard Book Number: 0-486-22543-7
Library of Congress Catalog Card Number: 74-105452

Manufactured in the United States of America
Dover Publications, Inc.
180 Varick Street
New York, N.Y. 10014

IN APPRECIATION

SUGGESTIONS THAT I WRITE MY MEMOIRS CAME TO ME WHEN I HAD barely begun to live, and continued all through the years. But I never paid heed to the proposal. I was living my life intensely — what need to write about it? Another reason for my reluctance was the conviction I entertained that one should write about one's life only when one had ceased to stand in the very torrent of it. " When one has reached a good philosophic age," I used to tell my friends, " capable of viewing the tragedies and comedies of life impersonally and detachedly — particularly one's own life — one is likely to create an autobiography worth while." Still feeling adolescently young in spite of advancing years, I did not consider myself competent to undertake such a task. Moreover, I always lacked the necessary leisure for concentrated writing.

My enforced European inactivity left me enough time to read a great deal, including biographies and autobiographies. I discovered, much to my discomfiture, that old age, far from ripening wisdom and mellowness, is too often fraught with senility, narrowness, and petty rancour. I would not risk such a calamity, and I began to think seriously about writing my life.

The great difficulty that faced me was lack of historical data for my work. Almost everything in the way of books, correspondence, and similar material that I had accumulated during the thirty-five years of my life in the United States had been confiscated by the Department of Justice raiders and never returned. I lacked even my personal set of the *Mother Earth* magazine, which I had published for twelve years. It was a problem I could see no solution for. Sceptic that I am, I had overlooked the magic power of friendship, which had so often in my life made mountains move. My staunch friends Leonard D. Abbott, Agnes Inglis, W. S. Van Valkenburgh, and others soon put my doubts to shame. Agnes, the founder of the Labadie Library in Detroit, containing the richest collection of radical and revolutionary material in America, came to my aid with her usual readiness. Leonard did his share, and Van spent all his free time in research work for me.

In the matter of European data I knew I could turn to the two best historians in our ranks: Max Nettlau and Rudolf Rocker. No further need to worry with such an array of co-workers.

Still I was not appeased. I needed something that would help me re-create the atmosphere of my own personal life: the events, small or great, that had tossed me about emotionally. An old vice of mine came to my rescue: veritable mountains of letters I had written. Often I had been chided by my pal Sasha, otherwise known as Alexander Berkman, and by my other friends, for my proclivity to spread myself in letters. Far from virtue bringing reward, it was my iniquity that gave me what I needed most — the true atmosphere of past days. Ben Reitman, Ben Capes, Jacob Margolis, Agnes Inglis, Harry Weinberger, Van, my romantic admirer Leon Bass, and scores of other friends readily responded to my request to send me my letters. My niece, Stella Ballantine, had kept everything I had written her during my imprisonment in the Missouri penitentiary. She, as well as my dear friend M. Eleanor Fitzgerald, had also preserved my Russian correspondence. In short, I was soon put into possession of over one thousand specimens of my epistolary effusions. I confess that most of them were painful reading, for at no time does one reveal oneself so much as in one's intimate correspondence. But for my purpose they were of utmost value.

Thus supplied, I started for Saint-Tropez, a picturesque fisher nest in the south of France, in company of Emily Holmes Coleman, who was to act as my secretary. Demi, as she is familiarly called, was a wild wood-sprite with a volcanic temper. But she was also the tenderest of beings, without any guile or rancour. She was essentially the poet, highly imaginative and sensitive. My world of ideas was foreign to her, natural rebel and anarchist though she was. We clashed furiously, often to the point of wishing each other in Saint-Tropez Bay. But it was nothing compared to her charm, her profound interest in my work, and her fine understanding for my inner conflicts.

Writing had never come easy to me, and the work at hand did not mean merely writing. It meant reliving my long-forgotten past, the resurrection of memories I did not wish to dig out from the deeps of my consciousness. It meant doubts in my creative ability, depression, and disheartenings. All through that period Demi held out bravely and by her faith and encouragement proved the comfort and inspiration of the first year of my struggle.

Altogether I was very fortunate in the number and devotion of friends who exerted themselves to smooth the way for *Living My Life.* The first to start the fund to secure me from material anxiety was Peggy Guggenheim. Other friends and comrades followed suit, giving without stint from their limited economic means. Miriam Lerner, a young American friend, volunteered to take Demi's place when the latter had to leave for England. Dorothy Marsh, Betty Markow, and Emmy Eckstein typed part of my manuscript as a labour of love. Arthur Leonard Ross, kindest and most lavish of men, gave me his untiring efforts as legal representative and adviser. How could such friendship ever be rewarded?

And Sasha? Many misgivings beset me when we began the revision of my manuscript. I feared he might resent seeing himself pictured through my eyes. Would he be detached enough, I wondered, sufficiently objective for the task? I found him remarkably so for one who is so much a part of my story. For eighteen months Sasha worked side by side with me as in our old days. Critical, of course, but always in the finest and broadest spirit. Sasha also it was who suggested the title, *Living My Life.*

My life as I have lived it owes everything to those who had come into it, stayed long or little, and passed out. Their love, as well as their hate, has gone into making my life worth while.

Living My Life is my tribute and my gratitude to them all.

EMMA GOLDMAN

Saint-Tropez, France
January 1931

ILLUSTRATIONS

(*Volume One*)

EMMA GOLDMAN
AT THE AGE OF SEVENTEEN, IN 1886

CHAPTER I

I T WAS THE 15TH OF AUGUST 1889, THE DAY OF MY ARRIVAL IN New York City. I was twenty years old. All that had happened in my life until that time was now left behind me, cast off like a worn-out garment. A new world was before me, strange and terrifying. But I had youth, good health, and a passionate ideal. Whatever the new held in store for me I was determined to meet unflinchingly.

How well I remember that day! It was a Sunday. The West Shore train, the cheapest, which was all I could afford, had brought me from Rochester, New York, reaching Weehawken at eight o'clock in the morning. Thence I came by ferry to New York City. I had no friends there, but I carried three addresses, one of a married aunt, one of a young medical student I had met in New Haven a year before, while working in a corset factory there, and one of the *Freiheit,* a German anarchist paper published by Johann Most.

My entire possessions consisted of five dollars and a small hand-bag. My sewing-machine, which was to help me to independence, I had checked as baggage. Ignorant of the distance from West Forty-second Street to the Bowery, where my aunt lived, and unaware of the enervating heat of a New York day in August, I started out on foot. How confusing and endless a large city seems to the new-comer, how cold and unfriendly!

After receiving many directions and misdirections and making frequent stops at bewildering intersections, I landed in three hours at the photographic gallery of my aunt and uncle. Tired and hot, I did not at first notice the consternation of my relatives at my unexpected arrival. They asked me to make myself at home, gave me breakfast, and then plied me with questions. Why did I come to New York? Had I definitely broken with my husband? Did I have money? What did I intend to do? I was told that I could, of course, stay with them.

"Where else could you go, a young woman alone in New York?"
Certainly, but I would have to look for a job immediately. Business
was bad, and the cost of living high.

I heard it all as if in a stupor. I was too exhausted from my wakeful
night's journey, the long walk, and the heat of the sun, which was
already pouring down fiercely. The voices of my relatives sounded distant, like the buzzing of flies, and they made me drowsy. With an
effort I pulled myself together. I assured them I did not come to im-
pose myself on them; a friend living on Henry Street was expecting
me and would put me up. I had but one desire — to get out, away from
the prattling, chilling voices. I left my bag and departed.

The friend I had invented in order to escape the " hospitality " of
my relatives was only a slight acquaintance, a young anarchist by the
name of A. Solotaroff, whom I had once heard lecture in New Haven.
Now I started out to find him. After a long search I discovered the
house, but the tenant had left. The janitor, at first very brusque, must
have noticed my despair. He said he would look for the address that
the family left when they moved. Presently he came back with the
name of the street, but there was no number. What was I to do?
How to find Solotaroff in the vast city? I decided to stop at every
house, first on one side of the street, and then on the other. Up and
down, six flights of stairs, I tramped, my head throbbing, my feet
weary. The oppressive day was drawing to a close. At last, when
I was about to give up the search, I discovered him on Montgomery
Street, on the fifth floor of a tenement house seething with humanity.

A year had passed since our first meeting, but Solotaroff had not
forgotten me. His greeting was genial and warm, as of an old friend.
He told me that he shared his small apartment with his parents and
little brother, but that I could have his room; he would stay with a
fellow-student for a few nights. He assured me that I would have no
difficulty in finding a place; in fact, he knew two sisters who were
living with their father in a two-room flat. They were looking for
another girl to join them. After my new friend had fed me tea and
some delicious Jewish cake his mother had baked, he told me about
the different people I might meet, the activities of the Yiddish anarchists, and other interesting matters. I was grateful to my host,
much more for his friendly concern and *camaraderie* than for the tea
and cake. I forgot the bitterness that had filled my soul over the cruel
reception given me by my own kin. New York no longer seemed the

monster it had appeared in the endless hours of my painful walk on the Bowery.

Later Solotaroff took me to Sachs's café on Suffolk Street, which, as he informed me, was the headquarters of the East Side radicals, socialists, and anarchists, as well as of the young Yiddish writers and poets. "Everybody forgathers there," he remarked; "the Minkin sisters will no doubt also be there."

For one who had just come away from the monotony of a provincial town like Rochester and whose nerves were on edge from a night's trip in a stuffy car, the noise and turmoil that greeted us at Sachs's were certainly not very soothing. The place consisted of two rooms and was packed. Everybody talked, gesticulated, and argued, in Yiddish and Russian, each competing with the other. I was almost overcome in this strange human medley. My escort discovered two girls at a table. He introduced them as Anna and Helen Minkin.

They were Russian Jewish working girls. Anna, the older, was about my own age; Helen perhaps eighteen. Soon we came to an understanding about my living with them, and my anxiety and uncertainty were over. I had a roof over my head; I had found friends. The bedlam at Sachs's no longer mattered. I began to breathe freer, to feel less of an alien.

While the four of us were having our dinner, and Solotaroff was pointing out to me the different people in the café, I suddenly heard a powerful voice call: "Extra-large steak! Extra cup of coffee!" My own capital was so small and the need for economy so great that I was startled by such apparent extravagance. Besides, Solotaroff had told me that only poor students, writers, and workers were the clients of Sachs. I wondered who that reckless person could be and how he could afford such food. "Who is that glutton?" I asked. Solotaroff laughed aloud. "That is Alexander Berkman. He can eat for three. But he rarely has enough money for much food. When he has, he eats Sachs out of his supplies. I'll introduce him to you."

We had finished our meal, and several people came to our table to talk to Solotaroff. The man of the extra-large steak was still packing it away as if he had gone hungry for weeks. Just as we were about to depart, he approached us, and Solotaroff introduced him. He was no more than a boy, hardly eighteen, but with the neck and chest of a giant. His jaw was strong, made more pronounced by his thick lips. His face was almost severe, but for his high, studious forehead and intelligent eyes. A determined youngster, I thought. Presently Berkman remarked to me: "Johann Most is speaking tonight. Do you want to come to hear him?"

How extraordinary, I thought, that on my very first day in New York I should have the chance to behold with my own eyes and hear the fiery man whom the Rochester press used to portray as the personification of the devil, a criminal, a bloodthirsty demon! I had planned to visit Most in the office of his newspaper some time later, but that the opportunity should present itself in such an unexpected manner gave me the feeling that something wonderful was about to happen, something that would decide the whole course of my life.

On the way to the hall I was too absorbed in my thoughts to hear much of the conversation that was going on between Berkman and the Minkin sisters. Suddenly I stumbled. I should have fallen had not Berkman gripped my arm and held me up. "I have saved your life," he said jestingly. "I hope I may be able to save yours some day," I quickly replied.

The meeting-place was a small hall behind a saloon, through which one had to pass. It was crowded with Germans, drinking, smoking, and talking. Before long, Johann Most entered. My first impression of him was one of revulsion. He was of medium height, with a large head crowned with greyish bushy hair; but his face was twisted out of form by an apparent dislocation of the left jaw. Only his eyes were soothing; they were blue and sympathetic.

His speech was a scorching denunciation of American conditions, a biting satire on the injustice and brutality of the dominant powers, a passionate tirade against those responsible for the Haymarket tragedy and the execution of the Chicago anarchists in November 1887. He spoke eloquently and picturesquely. As if by magic, his disfigurement disappeared, his lack of physical distinction was forgotten. He seemed transformed into some primitive power, radiating hatred and love, strength and inspiration. The rapid current of his speech, the music of his voice, and his sparkling wit, all combined to produce an effect almost overwhelming. He stirred me to my depths.

Caught in the crowd that surged towards the platform, I found myself before Most. Berkman was near me and introduced me. But I was dumb with excitement and nervousness, full of the tumult of emotions Most's speech had aroused in me.

That night I could not sleep. Again I lived through the events of

1887. Twenty-one months had passed since the Black Friday of November 11, when the Chicago men had suffered their martyrdom, yet every detail stood out clear before my vision and affected me as if it had happened but yesterday. My sister Helena and I had become interested in the fate of the men during the period of their trial. The reports in the Rochester newspapers irritated, confused, and upset us by their evident prejudice. The violence of the press, the bitter denunciation of the accused, the attacks on all foreigners, turned our sympathies to the Haymarket victims.

We had learned of the existence in Rochester of a German socialist group that held sessions on Sunday in Germania Hall. We began to attend the meetings, my older sister, Helena, on a few occasions only, and I regularly. The gatherings were generally uninteresting, but they offered an escape from the grey dullness of my Rochester existence. There one heard, at least, something different from the everlasting talk about money and business, and one met people of spirit and ideas.

One Sunday it was announced that a famous socialist speaker from New York, Johanna Greie, would lecture on the case then being tried in Chicago. On the appointed day I was the first in the hall. The huge place was crowded from top to bottom by eager men and women, while the walls were lined with police. I had never before been at such a large meeting. I had seen *gendarmes* in St. Petersburg disperse small student gatherings. But that in the country which guaranteed free speech, officers armed with long clubs should invade an orderly assembly filled me with consternation and protest.

Soon the chairman announced the speaker. She was a woman in her thirties, pale and ascetic-looking, with large luminous eyes. She spoke with great earnestness, in a voice vibrating with intensity. Her manner engrossed me. I forgot the police, the audience, and everything else about me. I was aware only of the frail woman in black crying out her passionate indictment against the forces that were about to destroy eight human lives.

The entire speech concerned the stirring events in Chicago. She began by relating the historical background of the case. She told of the labour strikes that broke out throughout the country in 1886, for the demand of an eight-hour workday. The centre of the movement was Chicago, and there the struggle between the toilers and their bosses became intense and bitter. A meeting of the striking employees of the McCormick Harvester Company in that city was attacked by police; men and women were beaten and several persons killed. To protest against the outrage a mass meeting was called in Haymarket Square on May 4. It was addressed by Albert Parsons, August Spies, Adolph Fischer, and others, and was quiet and orderly. This was attested to by Carter Harrison, Mayor of Chicago, who had attended the meeting to see what was going on. The Mayor left, satisfied that everything was all right, and he informed the captain of the district to that effect. It was getting cloudy, a light rain began to fall, and the people started to disperse, only a few remaining while one of the last speakers was addressing the audience. Then Captain Ward, accompanied by a strong force of police, suddenly appeared on the square. He ordered the meeting to disperse forthwith. " This is an orderly assembly," the chairman replied, whereupon the police fell upon the people, clubbing them unmercifully. Then something flashed through the air and exploded, killing a number of police officers and wounding a score of others. It was never ascertained who the actual culprit was, and the authorities apparently made little effort to discover him. Instead orders were immediately issued for the arrest of all the speakers at the Haymarket meeting and other prominent anarchists. The entire press and *bourgeoisie* of Chicago and of the whole country began shouting for the blood of the prisoners. A veritable campaign of terror was carried on by the police, who were given moral and financial encouragement by the Citizens' Association to further their murderous plan to get the anarchists out of the way. The public mind was so inflamed by the atrocious stories circulated by the press against the leaders of the strike that a fair trial for them became an impossibility. In fact, the trial proved the worst frame-up in the history of the United States. The jury was picked for conviction; the District Attorney announced in open court that it was not only the arrested men who were the accused, but that " anarchy was on trial " and that it was to be exterminated. The judge repeatedly denounced the prisoners from the bench, influencing the jury against them. The witnesses were terrorized or bribed, with the result that eight men, innocent of the crime and in no way connected with it, were convicted. The incited state of the public mind, and the general prejudice against anarchists, coupled with the employers' bitter opposition to the eight-hour movement, constituted the atmosphere that favoured the judicial murder of the Chicago anarchists. Five of them — Albert Parsons, August Spies, Louis Lingg, Adolph Fischer, and George Engel — were sentenced to die by hanging; Michael Schwab and Samuel Fielden were doomed to life imprisonment; Neebe received fifteen years' sentence. The innocent blood of the Haymarket martyrs was calling for revenge.

At the end of Greie's speech I knew what I had surmised all along: the Chicago men were innocent. They were to be put to death for their ideal. But what was their ideal? Johanna Greie spoke of Parsons, Spies, Lingg, and the others as socialists, but I was ignorant of the real meaning of socialism. What I had heard from the local speakers had impressed me as colourless and mechanistic. On the other hand, the papers called these men anarchists, bomb-throwers. What was anarchism? It was all very puzzling. But I had no time for further contemplation. The people were filing out, and I got up to leave. Greie, the chairman, and a group of friends were still on the platform. As I turned towards them, I saw Greie motioning to me. I was startled, my heart beat violently, and my feet felt leaden. When I approached her, she took me by the hand and said: " I never saw a face that reflected such a tumult of emotions as yours. You must be feeling the impending tragedy intensely. Do you know the men? " In a trembling voice I replied: " Unfortunately not, but I do feel the case with every fibre, and when I heard you speak, it seemed to me as if I knew them." She put her hand on my shoulder. " I have a feeling that you will know them better as you learn their ideal, and that you will make their cause your own."

I walked home in a dream. Sister Helena was already asleep, but I had to share my experience with her. I woke her up and recited to her the whole story, giving almost a verbatim account of the speech. I must have been very dramatic, because Helena exclaimed: " The next thing I'll hear about my little sister is that she, too, is a dangerous anarchist."

Some weeks later I had occasion to visit a German family I knew. I found them very much excited. Somebody from New York had sent them a German paper, *Die Freiheit,* edited by Johann Most. It was filled with news about the events in Chicago. The language fairly took my breath away, it was so different from what I had heard at the socialist meetings and even from Johanna Greie's talk. It seemed lava shooting forth flames of ridicule, scorn, and defiance; it breathed deep hatred of the powers that were preparing the crime in Chicago. I began to read *Die Freiheit* regularly. I sent for the literature advertised in the paper and I devoured every line on anarchism I could

get, every word about the men, their lives, their work. I read about
their heroic stand while on trial and their marvellous defence. I saw
a new world opening before me.

The terrible thing everyone feared, yet hoped would not happen,
actually occurred. Extra editions of the Rochester papers carried the
news: the Chicago anarchists had been hanged!

We were crushed, Helena and I. The shock completely unnerved
my sister; she could only wring her hands and weep silently. I was in
a stupor; a feeling of numbness came over me, something too horrible
even for tears. In the evening we went to our father's house. Everybody talked about the Chicago events. I was entirely absorbed in what
I felt as my own loss. Then I heard the coarse laugh of a woman. In
a shrill voice she sneered: "What's all this lament about? The men
were murderers. It is well they were hanged." With one leap I was at
the woman's throat. Then I felt myself torn back. Someone said:
"The child has gone crazy." I wrenched myself free, grabbed a pitcher
of water from a table, and threw it with all my force into the woman's
face. "Out, out," I cried, "or I will kill you!" The terrified woman
made for the door and I dropped to the ground in a fit of crying. I was
put to bed, and soon I fell into a deep sleep. The next morning I woke
as from a long illness, but free from the numbness and the depression
of those harrowing weeks of waiting, ending with the final shock. I had
a distinct sensation that something new and wonderful had been born
in my soul. A great ideal, a burning faith, a determination to dedicate
myself to the memory of my martyred comrades, to make their cause
my own, to make known to the world their beautiful lives and heroic
deaths. Johanna Greie was more prophetic than she had probably
realized.

My mind was made up. I would go to New York, to Johann Most.
He would help me prepare myself for my new task. But my husband,
my parents — how would they meet my decision?

I had been married only ten months. The union had not been happy.
I had realized almost from the beginning that my husband and I were
at opposite poles, with nothing in common, not even sexual blending.
The venture, like everything else that had happened to me since I had
come to America, had proved most disappointing. America, "the
land of the free and the home of the brave" — what a farce it now
seemed to me! Yet how I had fought with my father to get him to let
me go to America with Helena! In the end I had won, and late in

December 1885, Helena and I had left St. Petersburg for Hamburg, there embarking on the steamer *Elbe* for the Promised Land.

Another sister had preceded us by a few years, had married, and was living in Rochester. Repeatedly she had written Helena to come to her, that she was lonely. At last Helena had decided to go. But I could not support the thought of separation from the one who meant more to me than even my mother. Helena also hated to leave me behind. She knew of the bitter friction that existed between Father and me. She offered to pay my fare, but Father would not consent to my going. I pleaded, begged, wept. Finally I threatened to jump into the Neva, whereupon he yielded. Equipped with twenty-five roubles — all that the old man would give me — I left without regrets. Since my earliest recollection, home had been stifling, my father's presence terrifying. My mother, while less violent with the children, never showed much warmth. It was always Helena who gave me affection, who filled my childhood with whatever joy it had. She would continually shoulder the blame for the rest of the children. Many blows intended for my brother and me were given Helena. Now we were completely together — nobody would separate us.

We travelled steerage, where the passengers were herded together like cattle. My first contact with the sea was terrifying and fascinating. The freedom from home, the beauty and wonder of the endless expanse in its varying moods, and the exciting anticipation of what the new land would offer stimulated my imagination and sent my blood tingling.

The last day of our journey comes vividly to my mind. Everybody was on deck. Helena and I stood pressed to each other, enraptured by the sight of the harbour and the Statue of Liberty suddenly emerging from the mist. Ah, there she was, the symbol of hope, of freedom, of opportunity! She held her torch high to light the way to the free country, the asylum for the oppressed of all lands. We, too, Helena and I, would find a place in the generous heart of America. Our spirits were high, our eyes filled with tears.

Gruff voices broke in upon our reverie. We were surrounded by gesticulating people — angry men, hysterical women, screaming children. Guards roughly pushed us hither and thither, shouted orders to get ready, to be transferred to Castle Garden, the clearing-house for immigrants.

The scenes in Castle Garden were appalling, the atmosphere

charged with antagonism and harshness. Nowhere could one see a sympathetic official face; there was no provision for the comfort of the new arrivals, the pregnant women and young children. The first day on American soil proved a violent shock. We were possessed by one desire, to escape from the ghastly place. We had heard that Rochester was the " Flower City " of New York, but we arrived there on a bleak and cold January morning. My sister Lena, heavy with her first child, and Aunt Rachel met us. Lena's rooms were small, but they were bright and spotless. The room prepared for Helena and myself was filled with flowers. Throughout the day people came in and out — relatives I had never known, friends of my sister and of her husband, neighbours. All wanted to see us, to hear about the old country. They were Jews who had suffered much in Russia; some of them had even been in pogroms. Life in the new country, they said, was hard; they were all still possessed by nostalgia for their home that had never been a home.

Among the visitors there were some who had prospered. One man boasted that his six children were all working, selling newspapers, shining shoes. Everybody was concerned about what we were going to do. One coarse-looking fellow concentrated his attention on me. He kept staring at me all the evening, scanning me up and down. He even came over and tried to feel my arms. It gave me the sensation of standing naked on the market-place. I was outraged, but I did not want to insult my sister's friends. I felt utterly alone and I rushed out of the room. A longing possessed me for what I had left behind — St. Petersburg, my beloved Neva, my friends, my books and music. I became aware of loud voices in the next room. I heard the man who had enraged me say: " I can get her a job at Garson and Mayer's. The wages will be small, but she will soon find a feller to marry her. Such a buxom girl, with her red cheeks and blue eyes, will not have to work long. Any man will snatch her up and keep her in silks and diamonds." I thought of Father. He had tried desperately to marry me off at the age of fifteen. I had protested, begging to be permitted to continue my studies. In his frenzy he threw my French grammar into the fire, shouting: " Girls do not have to learn much! All a Jewish daughter needs to know is how to prepare *gefüllte* fish, cut noodles fine, and give the man plenty of children." I would not listen to his schemes; I wanted to study, to know life, to travel. Besides, I never would marry for anything but love, I stoutly maintained. It was really to escape my father's plans for me that I had insisted on going to America. Now attempts to marry me off pursued me even in the new land. I was determined not to be bartered: I would go to work.

Sister Lena had left for America when I was about eleven. I used to spend much time with my grandmother in Kovno, while my people lived in Popelan, a small town in the Baltic Province of Kurland. Lena had always been hostile to me, and unexpectedly I had discovered the reason. I could not have been more than six at the time, while Lena was two years older. We were playing a game of marbles. Somehow sister Lena thought I was winning too often. She flew into a rage, gave me a violent kick, and shouted: "Just like your father! He too cheated us! He robbed us of the money *our* father had left. I hate you! You are not my sister."

The effect of her outburst on me was petrifying. For a few moments I sat riveted to the ground, staring at Lena in silence; then the tension gave way to a fit of crying. I ran to sister Helena, to whom I carried all my childish woes. I demanded to know what Lena had meant when she said my father had robbed her, and why I was not her sister.

As usual Helena took me in her arms, tried to comfort me, and made light of Lena's words. I went to Mother, and from her I learned that there had been another father, Helena's and Lena's. He had died young and Mother had then chosen my father, mine and my baby brother's. She said that my father was also Helena's and Lena's, even if they were his stepchildren. It was true, she explained, that Father had used the money left to the two girls. He had invested it in business and failed. He had meant it for the good of all of us. But what Mother told me did not lessen my great hurt. "Father had no right to use that money!" I cried. "They are orphans. It is a sin to rob orphans. I wish I were grown up; then I could pay back the money. Yes, I must pay back, I must atone for Father's sin."

I had been told by my German nurse that whoever was guilty of robbing orphans would never get to heaven. I had no clear conception of that place. My people, while keeping Jewish rites and going to the synagogue on Saturdays and holidays, rarely spoke to us about religion. I got my idea of God and devil, sin and punishment, from my nurse and our Russian peasant servants. I was sure Father would be punished if I did not pay back his debt.

Eleven years had passed since that incident. I had long forgotten the hurt Lena had caused, but I by no means felt the great affection for her that I bore my dear Helena. All the way to America I had been anxious about what Lena's feelings might be towards me, but when I saw her, heavy with her first child, her small face pale and shrunken, my heart went out to her as if there had never been a shadow between us.

The day after our arrival we three sisters remained alone. Lena told us how lonely she had been, how she had longed for us and for our people. We learned of the hard life that had been hers, first as a domestic servant in Aunt Rachel's house, later as buttonhole-maker in Stein's clothing-factory. How happy she was now, with her own home at last and the joy of her expected child! "Life is still difficult," Lena said; "my husband is earning twelve dollars a week as a tin-smith, working on roofs in the beating sun and in the cold wind, always in danger. He had begun working as a child of eight in Berdichev, Russia," she added, "and he has been working ever since."

When Helena and I retired to our room, we agreed that we must both go to work at once. We could not add to the burden of our brother-in-law. Twelve dollars a week and a child on the way! Some days later Helena got a job retouching negatives, which had been her work in Russia. I found employment at Garson and Mayer's, sewing ulsters ten and a half hours a day, for two dollars and fifty cents a week.

CHAPTER II

I HAD WORKED IN FACTORIES BEFORE, IN ST. PETERSBURG. IN THE winter of 1882, when Mother, my two little brothers, and I came from Königsberg to join Father in the Russian capital, we found that he had lost his position. He had been manager of his cousin's dry-goods store; but, shortly before our arrival, the business failed. The loss of his job was a tragedy to our family, as Father had not managed to save anything. The only bread-winner then was Helena. Mother was forced to turn to her brothers for a loan. The three hundred roubles they advanced were invested in a grocery store. The business yielded little at first, and it became necessary for me to find employment.

Knitted shawls were then much in vogue, and a neighbour told my mother where I might find work to do at home. By keeping at the task many hours a day, sometimes late into the night, I contrived to earn twelve roubles a month.

The shawls I knitted for a livelihood were by no means master-pieces, but somehow they passed. I hated the work, and my eyes gave way under the strain of constant application. Father's cousin who had failed in the dry-goods business now owned a glove factory. He offered to teach me the trade and give me work.

The factory was far from our place. One had to get up at five in the morning to be at work at seven. The rooms were stuffy, unventilated, and dark. Oil lamps gave the light; the sun never penetrated the work-room.

There were six hundred of us, of all ages, working on costly and beautiful gloves day in, day out, for very small pay. But we were allowed sufficient time for our noon meal and twice a day for tea. We could talk and sing while at work; we were not driven or harassed. That was in St. Petersburg, in 1882.

Now I was in America, in the Flower City of the State of New York, in a model factory, as I was told. Certainly, Garson's clothing-works were a vast improvement on the glove factory on the Vassilev-sky Ostrov. The rooms were large, bright, and airy. One had elbow space. There were none of those ill-smelling odours that used to nauseate me in our cousin's shop. Yet the work here was harder, and the day, with only half an hour for lunch, seemed endless. The iron discipline forbade free movement (one could not even go to the toilet without permission), and the constant surveillance of the foreman weighed like stone on my heart. The end of each day found me sapped, with just enough energy to drag myself to my sister's home and crawl into bed. This continued with deadly monotony week after week.

The amazing thing to me was that no one else in the factory seemed to be so affected as I, no one but my neighbour, frail little Tanya. She was delicate and pale, frequently complained of headaches, and often broke into tears when the task of handling heavy ulsters proved too much for her. One morning, as I looked up from my work, I discovered her all huddled in a heap. She had fallen in a faint. I called to the foreman to help me carry her to the dressing-room, but the deafening noise of the machines drowned my voice. Several girls near by heard me and began to shout. They ceased working and rushed over to Tanya. The sudden stopping of the machines attracted the foreman's attention and he came over to us. Without even asking the reason for the commotion, he shouted: " Back to your machines! What do you mean stopping work now? Do you want to be fired? Get back at once! " When he spied the crumpled body of Tanya, he yelled: " What the hell is the matter with her? " " She has fainted," I replied, trying hard to control my voice. " Fainted, nothing," he sneered, " she's only shamming."

" You are a liar and a brute! " I cried, no longer able to keep back my indignation.

I bent over Tanya, loosened her waist, and squeezed the juice of an orange I had in my lunch basket into her half-opened mouth. Her face was white, a cold sweat on her forehead. She looked so ill that even the foreman realized she had not been shamming. He excused her for the day. " I will go with Tanya," I said; " you can deduct from my pay for the time." " You can go to hell, you wildcat! " he flung after me.

We went to a coffee place. I myself felt empty and faint, but all we had between us was seventy-five cents. We decided to spend forty on food, and use the rest for a street-car ride to the park. There, in the fresh air, amid the flowers and trees, we forgot our dreaded tasks. The day that had begun in trouble ended restfully and in peace.

The next morning the enervating routine started all over again, continuing for weeks and months, broken only by the new arrival in our family, a baby girl. The child became the one interest in my dull existence. Often, when the atmosphere in Garson's factory threatened to overcome me, the thought of the lovely mite at home revived my spirit. The evenings were no longer dreary and meaningless. But, while little Stella brought joy into our household, she added to the material anxiety of my sister and my brother-in-law.

Lena never by word or deed made me feel that the dollar and fifty cents I was giving her for my board (the car fare amounted to sixty cents a week, the remaining forty cents being my pin-money) did not cover my keep. But I had overheard my brother-in-law grumbling over the growing expenses of the house. I felt he was right. I did not want my sister worried, she was nursing her child. I decided to apply for a rise. I knew it was no use talking to the foreman and therefore I asked to see Mr. Garson.

I was ushered into a luxurious office. American Beauties were on the table. Often I had admired them in the flower shops, and once, unable to withstand the temptation, I had gone in to ask the price. They were one dollar and a half apiece — more than half of my week's earnings. The lovely vase in Mr. Garson's office held a great many of them.

I was not asked to sit down. For a moment I forgot my mission. The beautiful room, the roses, the aroma of the bluish smoke from Mr. Garson's cigar, fascinated me. I was recalled to reality by my employer's question: "Well, what can I do for you?"

I had come to ask for a rise, I told him. The two dollars and a half I was getting did not pay my board, let alone anything else, such as an occasional book or a theatre ticket for twenty-five cents. Mr. Garson replied that for a factory girl I had rather extravagant tastes, that all his "hands" were well satisfied, that they seemed to be getting along all right — that I, too, would have to manage or find work elsewhere. "If I raise your wages, I'll have to raise the others' as well and I can't afford that," he said. I decided to leave Garson's employ.

A few days later I secured a job at Rubinstein's factory at four dollars a week. It was a small shop, not far from where I lived. The house stood in a garden, and only a dozen men and women were employed in the place. The Garson discipline and drive were missing.

Next to my machine worked an attractive young man whose name was Jacob Kershner. He lived near Lena's home, and we would often walk from work together. Before long he began calling for me in the morning. We used to converse in Russian, my English still being very halting. His Russian was like music to me; it was the first real Russian, outside of Helena's, that I had had an opportunity to hear in Rochester since my arrival.

Kershner had come to America in 1881 from Odessa, where he had finished the *Gymnasium.* Having no trade, he became an " operator " on cloaks. He used to spend most of his leisure, he told me, reading or going to dances. He had no friends, because he found his co-workers in Rochester interested only in money-making, their ideal being to start a shop of their own. He had heard of our arrival, Helena's and mine — had even seen me on the street several times — but he did not know how to get acquainted. Now he would no longer feel lonely, he said brightly; we could visit places together and he would lend me his books to read. My own loneliness no longer was so poignant.

I told my sisters of my new acquaintance, and Lena asked me to invite him the next Sunday. When Kershner came, she was favourably impressed; but Helena took a violent dislike to him from the first. She said nothing about it for a long time, but I could sense it.

One day Kershner invited me to a dance. It was my first since I came to America. The very anticipation was exciting, bringing back memories of my first ball in St. Petersburg.

I was fifteen then. Helena had been invited to the fashionable German Club by her employer, who gave her two tickets, so she could bring me with her. Some time previously my sister had presented me with a piece of lovely blue velvet for my first long dress; but before it could be made up, our peasant servant walked off with the material. My grief over its loss made me quite ill for several days. If only I had a dress, I thought, Father might consent to my attending the ball. " I'll get you material for a dress," Helena consoled me, " but I'm afraid Father will refuse." " Then I will defy him!" I declared.

She bought another piece of blue stuff, not so beautiful as my velvet, but I no longer minded. I was too happy over the prospect of my first ball, of the bliss of dancing in public. Somehow Helena succeeded in getting Father's consent, but at the last moment he changed his mind. I had been guilty of some infraction during the day, and he categorically declared that I would have to stay home. Thereupon Helena said she also would not go. But I was determined to defy my father, no matter what the consequences.

With bated breath I waited for my parents to retire for the night. Then I dressed and woke Helena. I told her she must come with me or I would run away from home. "We can be back before Father wakes up," I urged. Dear Helena — she was always so timid! She had infinite capacity for suffering, for endurance, but she could not fight. On this occasion she was carried away by my desperate decision. She dressed and we quietly slipped out of the house.

At the German Club everything was bright and gay. We found Helena's employer, whose name was Kadison, and some of his young friends. I was asked for every dance, and I danced in frantic excitement and abandon. It was getting late and many people were already leaving when Kadison invited me for another dance. Helena insisted that I was too exhausted, but I would not have it so. "I will dance!" I declared; "I will dance myself to death!" My flesh felt hot, my heart beat violently as my cavalier swung me round the ball-room, holding me tightly. To dance to death — what more glorious end!

It was towards five in the morning when we arrived home. Our people were still asleep. I awoke late in the day, pretending a sick headache, and secretly I gloried in my triumph of having outwitted our old man.

The memory of that experience still vivid in my mind, I accompanied Jacob Kershner to the party, full of anticipation. My disappointment was bitter: there were no beautiful ball-room, no lovely women, no dashing young men, no gaiety. The music was shrill, the dancers clumsy. Jacob danced not badly, but he lacked spirit and fire. "Four years at the machine have taken the strength out of me," he said; "I get tired so easily."

I had known Jacob Kershner about four months when he asked me to marry him. I admitted I liked him, but I did not want to marry so young. We still knew so little of each other. He said he'd wait as long as I pleased, but there was already a great deal of talk about our being out together so much. "Why should we not get engaged?" he pleaded. Finally I consented. Helena's antagonism to Jacob had become almost an obsession; she fairly hated him. But I was lonely —

I needed companionship. Ultimately I won over my sister. Her great love for me could never refuse me anything or stand out against my wishes.

The late fall of 1886 brought the rest of our family to Rochester — Father, Mother, my brothers, Herman and Yegor. Conditions in St. Petersburg had become intolerable for the Jews, and the grocery business did not yield enough for the ever-growing bribery Father had to practise in order to be allowed to exist. America became the only solution.

Together with Helena I had prepared a home for our parents, and on their arrival we went to live with them. Our earnings soon proved inadequate to meet the household expenses. Jacob Kershner offered to board with us, which would be of some help, and before long he moved in.

The house was small, consisting of a living-room, a kitchen, and two bedrooms. One of them was used by my parents, the other by Helena, myself, and our little brother. Kershner and Herman slept in the living-room. The close proximity of Jacob and the lack of privacy kept me in constant irritation. I suffered from sleepless nights, waking dreams and great fatigue at work. Life was becoming unbearable, and Jacob stressed the need of a home of our own.

On nearer acquaintance I had grown to understand that we were too different. His interest in books, which had first attracted me to him, had waned. He had fallen into the ways of his shopmates, playing cards and attending dull dances. I, on the contrary, was filled with striving and aspirations. In spirit I was still in Russia, in my beloved St. Petersburg, living in the world of the books I had read, the operas I had heard, the circle of the students I had known. I hated Rochester even more than before. But Kershner was the only human being I had met since my arrival. He filled a void in my life, and I was strongly attracted to him. In February 1887 we were married in Rochester by a rabbi, according to Jewish rites, which were then considered sufficient by the law of the country.

My feverish excitement of that day, my suspense and ardent anticipation gave way at night to a feeling of utter bewilderment. Jacob lay trembling near me; he was impotent.

The first erotic sensations I remember had come to me when I was about six. My parents lived in Popelan then, where we children had no home in any real sense. Father kept an inn, which was constantly

filled with peasants, drunk and quarrelling, and government officials.
Mother was busy superintending the servants in our large, chaotic
house. My sisters, Lena and Helena, fourteen and twelve, were bur-
dened with work. I was left to myself most of the day. Among the
stable help there was a young peasant, Petrushka, who served as
shepherd, looking after our cows and sheep. Often he would take me
with him to the meadows, and I would listen to the sweet tones of his
flute. In the evening he would carry me back home on his shoulders,
I sitting astride. He would play horse — run as fast as his legs could
carry him, then suddenly throw me up in the air, catch me in his arms,
and press me to him. It used to give me a peculiar sensation, fill me
with exultation, followed by blissful release.

I became inseparable from Petrushka. I grew so fond of him that I
began stealing cake and fruit from Mother's pantry for him. To be
with Petrushka out in the fields, to listen to his music, to ride on his
shoulders, became the obsession of my waking and sleeping hours.
One day Father had an altercation with Petrushka, and the boy was
sent away. The loss of him was one of the greatest tragedies of my
child-life. For weeks afterwards I kept on dreaming of Petrushka, the
meadows, the music, and reliving the joy and ecstasy of our play.
One morning I felt myself torn out of sleep. Mother was bending over
me, tightly holding my right hand. In an angry voice she cried: "If
ever I find your hand again like that, I'll whip you, you naughty
child!"

The approach of puberty gave me my first consciousness of the
effect of men on me. I was eleven then. Early one summer day I woke
up in great agony. My head, spine, and legs ached as if they were
being pulled asunder. I called for Mother. She drew back my bed-
covers, and suddenly I felt a stinging pain in my face. She had struck
me. I let out a shriek, fastening on Mother terrified eyes. "This
is necessary for a girl," she said, "when she becomes a woman, as a
protection against disgrace." She tried to take me in her arms, but
I pushed her back. I was writhing in pain and I was too outraged for
her to touch me. "I am going to die," I howled, "I want the *Feldscher*
(assistant doctor). The *Feldscher* was sent for. He was a young
man, a new-comer in our village. He examined me and gave me something to put me to sleep. Thenceforth my dreams were of the *Feldscher*.

When I was fifteen, I was employed in a corset factory in the

Hermitage Arcade in St. Petersburg. After working hours, on leaving the shop together with the other girls, we would be waylaid by young Russian officers and civilians. Most of the girls had their sweethearts; only a Jewish girl chum of mine and I refused to be taken to the *konditorskaya* (pastry shop) or to the park.

Next to the Hermitage was a hotel we had to pass. One of the clerks, a handsome fellow of about twenty, singled me out for his attentions. At first I scorned him, but gradually he began to exert a fascination on me. His perseverance slowly undermined my pride and I accepted his courtship. We used to meet in some quiet spot or in an out-of-the-way pastry shop. I had to invent all sorts of stories to explain to my father why I returned late from work or stayed out after nine o'clock. One day he spied me in the Summer Garden in the company of other girls and some boy students. When I returned home, he threw me violently against the shelves in our grocery store, which sent the jars of Mother's wonderful *varenya* flying to the floor. He pounded me with his fists, shouting that he would not tolerate a loose daughter. The experience made my home more unbearable, the need of escape more compelling.

For several months my admirer and I met clandestinely. One day he asked me whether I should not like to go through the hotel to see the luxurious rooms. I had never been in a hotel before — the joy and gaiety I fancied behind the gorgeous windows used to fascinate me as I would pass the place on my way from work.

The boy led me through a side entrance, along a thickly carpeted corridor, into a large room. It was brightly illumined and beautifully furnished. A table near the sofa held flowers and a tea-tray. We sat down. The young man poured out a golden-coloured liquid and asked me to clink glasses to our friendship. I put the wine to my lips. Suddenly I found myself in his arms, my waist torn open — his passionate kisses covered my face, neck, and breasts. Not until after the violent contact of our bodies and the excruciating pain he caused me did I come to my senses. I screamed, savagely beating against the man's chest with my fists. Suddenly I heard Helena's voice in the hall. " She must be here — she must be here! " I became speechless. The man, too, was terrorized. His grip relaxed, and we listened in breathless silence. After what seemed to me hours, Helena's voice receded. The man got up. I rose mechanically, mechanically buttoned my waist and brushed back my hair.

Strange, I felt no shame — only a great shock at the discovery that the contact between man and woman could be so brutal and so painful. I walked out in a daze, bruised in every nerve.

When I reached home I found Helena fearfully wrought up. She had been uneasy about me, aware of my meeting with the boy. She had made it her business to find out where he worked, and when I failed to return, she had gone to the hotel in search of me. The shame I did not feel in the arms of the man now overwhelmed me. I could not muster up courage to tell Helena of my experience.

After that I always felt between two fires in the presence of men. Their lure remained strong, but it was always mingled with violent revulsion. I could not bear to have them touch me.

These pictures passed through my mind vividly as I lay alongside my husband on our wedding night. He had fallen fast asleep.

The weeks went on. There was no change. I urged Jacob to consult a doctor. At first he refused, pleading diffidence, but finally he went. He was told it would take considerable time to "build up his manhood." My own passion had subsided. The material anxiety of making ends meet excluded everything else. I had stopped work: it was considered disgraceful for a married woman to go to the shop. Jacob was earning fifteen dollars a week. He had developed a passion for cards, which swallowed up a considerable part of our income. He grew jealous, suspecting everyone. Life became insupportable. I was saved from utter despair by my interest in the Haymarket events.

After the death of the Chicago anarchists I insisted on a separation from Kershner. He fought long against it, but finally consented to a divorce. It was given to us by the same rabbi who had performed our marriage ceremony. Then I left for New Haven, Connecticut, to work in a corset-factory.

During my efforts to free myself from Kershner the only one who stood by me was my sister Helena. She had been strenuously opposed to the marriage in the first place, but now she offered not a single reproach. On the contrary, she gave me help and comfort. She pleaded with my parents and with Lena in behalf of my decision to get a divorce. As always, her devotion knew no bounds.

In New Haven I met a group of young Russians, students mainly, now working at various trades. Most of them were socialists and anarchists. They often organized meetings, generally inviting speakers from New York, one of whom was A. Solotaroff. Life was interesting and colourful, but gradually the strain of the work became too much for my depleted vitality. Finally I had to return to Rochester.

I went to Helena. She lived with her husband and child over their little printing shop, which also served as an office for their steamship agency. But both occupations did not bring in enough to keep them from dire poverty. Helena had married Jacob Hochstein, a man ten years her senior. He was a great Hebrew scholar, an authority on the English and Russian classics, and a very rare personality. His integrity and independent character made him a poor competitor in the sordid business life. When anyone brought him a printing order worth two dollars, Jacob Hochstein devoted as much time to it as if he were getting fifty. If a customer showed a tendency to bargain over prices, he would send him away. He could not bear the implication that he might overcharge. His income was insufficient for the needs of the family, and the one to worry and fret most about it was my poor Helena. She was pregnant with her second child and yet had to drudge from morning till night to make ends meet, with never a word of complaint. But, then, she had been that way all her life, suffering silently, always resigned.

Helena's marriage had not sprung from a passionate love. It was the union of two mature people who longed for comradeship, for a quiet life. Whatever there had been of passion in my sister had burned out when she was twenty-four. At the age of sixteen, while we were living in Popelan, she had fallen in love with a young Lithuanian, a beautiful soul. But he was a *goi* (gentile) and Helena knew that marriage between them was impossible. After a great struggle and many tears Helena broke off the affair with young Susha. Years later, while on our way to America, we stopped in Kovno, our native town. Helena had arranged for Susha to meet her there. She could not bear to go away so far without saying good-bye to him. They met and parted as good friends — the fire of their youth was in ashes.

On my return from New Haven Helena received me, as always, with tenderness and with the assurance that her home was also mine. It was good to be near my darling again, with little Stella and my young brother Yegor. But it did not take me long to discover the pinched condition in Helena's home. I went back to the shop.

Living in the Jewish district, it was impossible to avoid those one did not wish to see. I ran into Kershner almost immediately after my arrival. Day after day he would seek me out. He began to plead with me to go back to him — all would be different. One day he threatened suicide — actually pulled out a bottle of poison. Insistently he pressed me for a final answer.

I was not naïve enough to think that a renewed life with Kershner would prove more satisfactory or lasting than at first. Besides, I had definitely decided to go to New York, to equip myself for the work I had vowed to take up after the death of my Chicago comrades. But Kershner's threat frightened me: I could not be responsible for his death. I remarried him. My parents rejoiced and so did Lena and her husband, but Helena was sick with grief.

Without Kershner's knowledge I took up a course in dressmaking, in order to have a trade that would free me from the shop. During three long months I wrestled with my husband to let me go my way. I tried to make him see the futility of living a patched life, but he remained obdurate. Late one night, after bitter recriminations, I left Jacob Kershner and my home, this time definitely.

I was immediately ostracized by the whole Jewish population of Rochester. I could not pass on the street without being held up to scorn. My parents forbade me their house, and again it was only Helena who stood by me. Out of her meagre income she even paid my fare to New York.

So I left Rochester, where I had known so much pain, hard work, and loneliness, but the joy of my departure was marred by separation from Helena, from Stella, and the little brother I loved so well.

The break of the new day in the Minkin flat still found me awake. The door upon the old had now closed for ever. The new was calling, and I eagerly stretched out my hands towards it. I fell into a deep, peaceful sleep.

I was awakened by Anna Minkin's voice announcing the arrival of Alexander Berkman. It was late afternoon.

CHAPTER III

H ELEN MINKIN WAS AWAY AT WORK. ANNA WAS OUT OF A JOB just then. She prepared tea, and we sat down to talk. Berkman inquired about my plans for work, for activity in the movement. Would I like to visit the *Freiheit* office? Could he be of help in any way? He was free to take me about, he said; he had left his job after a fight with the foreman. "A slave-driver," he commented; "he never dared drive me, but it was my duty to stand up for the others in the shop." It was rather slack now in the cigar-making trade, he informed us, but as an anarchist he could not stop to consider his own job. Nothing personal mattered. Only the Cause mattered. Fighting injustice and exploitation mattered.

How strong he was, I thought; how wonderful in his revolutionary zeal! Just like our martyred comrades in Chicago.

I had to go to West Forty-second Street to get my sewing-machine out of the baggage-room. Berkman offered to accompany me. He suggested that on our way back we might ride down to Brooklyn Bridge on the Elevated and then walk over to William Street, where the *Freiheit* office was located.

I asked him whether I could hope to establish myself in New York as a dressmaker. I wanted so much to free myself from the dreadful grind and slavery of the shop. I wanted to have time for reading, and later I hoped to realize my dream of a co-operative shop. "Something like Vera's venture in *What's to be Done?*" I explained. "You have read Chernishevsky?" Berkman inquired, in surprise; "surely not in Rochester?" "Surely not," I replied, laughing; "besides my sister Helena, I found no one there who would read such books. No, not in that dull town. In St. Petersburg." He looked at me doubtfully. "Chernishevsky was a Nihilist," he remarked, "and his works are prohibited in Russia. Were you connected with the Nihilists? They

are the only ones who could have given you the book." I felt indignant. How dared he doubt my word! I repeated angrily that I had
read the forbidden book and other similar works, such as Turgeniev's
Fathers and Sons, and *Obriv* (*The Precipice*) by Gontcharov. My
sister had got them from students and she let me read them. " I am
sorry if I hurt you," Berkman said in a soft tone. " I did not really
doubt your word. I was only surprised to find a girl so young who had
read such books."

How far I had wandered away from my adolescent days, I reflected. I recalled the morning in Königsberg when I had come upon
a huge poster announcing the death of the Tsar, " assassinated by
murderous Nihilists." The thought of the poster brought back to
my memory an incident of my early childhood which for a time had
turned our home into a house of mourning. Mother had received a
letter from her brother Martin giving the appalling news of the
arrest of their brother Yegor. He had been mixed up with Nihilists,
the letter read, and he was thrown into the Petro-Pavlovsky Fortress
and would soon be sent away to Siberia. The news struck terror in us.
Mother decided to go to St. Petersburg. For weeks we were kept in
anxious suspense. At last she returned, her face beaming with happiness. She had found that Yegor was already on the way to Siberia.
After much difficulty and with the help of a large sum of money she
had succeeded in getting an audience with Trepov, the Governor-
General of St. Petersburg. She had learned that his son was a college
chum of Yegor and she urged it as proof that her brother could not
have been mixed up with the terrible Nihilists. One so close to the
Governor's own son would surely have nothing to do with the enemies
of Russia. She pleaded Yegor's extreme youth, went on her knees,
begged and wept. Finally Trepov promised that he would have the
boy brought back from the *étape.* Of course, he would put him under
strict surveillance; Yegor would have to promise solemnly never to go
near the murderous gang.

Our mother was always very vivid when she related stories of books
she had read. We children used to hang on her very lips. This time,
too, her story was absorbing. It made me see Mother before the stern
Governor-General, her beautiful face, framed by her massive hair,
bathed in tears. The Nihilists, too, I saw — black, sinister creatures
who had ensnared my uncle in their plotting to kill the Tsar. The
good, gracious Tsar — Mother had said — the first to give more

freedom to the Jews; he had stopped the pogroms and he was planning to set the peasants free. And him the Nihilists meant to kill! " Cold-blooded murderers," Mother cried, " they ought to be exterminated, every one of them! "

Mother's violence terrorized me. Her suggestion of extermination froze my blood. I felt that the Nihilists must be beasts, but I could not bear such cruelty in my mother. Often after that I caught myself thinking of the Nihilists, wondering who they were and what made them so ferocious. When the news reached Königsberg about the hanging of the Nihilists who had killed the Tsar, I no longer felt any bitterness against them. Something mysterious had awakened compassion for them in me. I wept bitterly over their fate.

Years later I came upon the term " Nihilist " in *Fathers and Sons*. And when I read *What's to be Done?* I understood my instinctive sympathy with the executed men. I felt that they could not witness without protest the suffering of the people and that they had sacrificed their lives for them. I became the more convinced of it when I learned the story of Vera Zassulich, who had shot Trepov in 1879. My young teacher of Russian related it to me. Mother had said that Trepov was kind and humane, but my teacher told me how tyrannical he had been, a veritable monster who used to order out his Cossacks against the students, have them lashed with *nagaikas,* their gatherings dispersed, and the prisoners sent to Siberia. " Officials like Trepov are wild beasts," my teacher would say passionately; " they rob the peasants and then flog them. They torture idealists in prison."

I knew that my teacher spoke the truth. In Popelan everyone used to talk about the flogging of peasants. One day I came upon a half-naked human body being lashed with the knout. It threw me into hysterics, and for days I was haunted by the horrible picture. Listening to my teacher revived the ghastly sight: the bleeding body, the piercing shrieks, the distorted faces of the *gendarmes,* the knouts whistling in the air and coming down with a sharp hissing upon the half-naked man. Whatever doubts about the Nihilists I had left from my childhood impressions now disappeared. They became to me heroes and martyrs, henceforth my guiding stars.

I was aroused from my reverie by Berkman's asking why I had become so silent. I told him of my recollections. He then related to me some of his own early influences, dwelling particularly on his beloved Nihilist uncle Maxim and on the shock he had experienced on learning that he had been sentenced to die. " We have much in common, haven't we? " he remarked. " We even come from the same city. Do you know that Kovno has given many brave sons to the revolutionary movement? And now perhaps also a brave daughter," he added. I felt myself turn red. My soul was proud. " I hope I shall not fail when the time comes," I replied.

The train was passing narrow streets, the dreary tenements so close by that I could see into the rooms. The fire-escapes were littered with dirty pillows and blankets and hung with laundry streaked with dirt. Berkman touched my arm and announced that the next station was Brooklyn Bridge. We got off and walked to William Street.

In an old building, up two dark and creaking flights, was the office of the *Freiheit*. Several men were in the first room setting type. In the next we found Johann Most standing at a high desk, writing. With a side-glance he invited us to sit down. " My damned torturers there are squeezing the blood out of me," he declared querulously. " Copy, copy, copy! That's all they know! Ask them to write a line — not they. They are too stupid and too lazy." A burst of good-natured laughter from the composing-room greeted Most's outburst. His gruff voice, his twisted jaw, which had so repelled me on my first meeting him, recalled to me the caricatures of Most in the Rochester papers. I could not reconcile the angry man before me with the inspired speaker of the previous evening whose oratory had so carried me away.

Berkman noticed my confused and frightened look. He whispered in Russian not to mind Most, that he was always in such a mood when at work. I got up to inspect the books which covered the shelves from floor to ceiling, row upon row. How few of them I had read, I mused. My years in school had given me so little. Should I ever be able to make up? Where should I get the time to read? And the money to buy books? I wondered whether Most would lend me some of his, whether I dared ask him to suggest a course of reading and study. Presently another outburst grated on my ears. " Here's my pound of flesh, you Shylocks! " Most thundered; " more than enough to fill the paper. Here, Berkman, take it to the black devils in there! "

Most approached me. His deep blue eyes looked searchingly into mine. " Well, young lady," he said, " have you found anything you want to read? Or don't you read German and English? " The harshness of his voice had changed to a warm, kindly texture. " Not English," I said, soothed and emboldened by his tone, " German." He told me I could have any book I wanted. Then he plied me with questions — where I hailed from and what I intended to do. I said I had come from Rochester. "Yes, I know the city. It has good beer. But the Germans there are a bunch of *Kaffern*. Why New York exactly?" he inquired; "it is a hard city. Work poorly paid, not easily found. Have you enough money to hold out?" I was deeply touched by the interest of this man in me, a perfect stranger. I explained that New York had lured me because it was the centre of the anarchist movement, and because I had read of him as its leading spirit. I had really come to him for suggestions and help. I wanted very much to talk to him. "But not now, some other time," I said, "somewhere away from your black devils."

"You have a sense of humour," — his face lit up — "you'll need it if you enter our movement." He suggested that I come next Wednesday, to help with expediting the *Freiheit,* to write addresses and fold the papers — "and afterwards we may be able to talk."

With several books under my arm and a warm handshake, Most sent me off. Berkman left with me.

We went to Sachs's. I had had nothing to eat since the tea Anna had given us. My escort, too, was hungry, but evidently not so much as the night before : he did not call for extra steak or extra cups of coffee. Or was he broke? I suggested that I was still rich and begged him to order more. He refused brusquely, telling me that he couldn't accept it from anyone out of a job who had just arrived in a strange city. I felt both angry and amused. I explained that I did not wish to hurt him; I believed that one always shared with a comrade. He repented his abruptness, but assured me that he was not hungry. We left the restaurant.

The August heat was suffocating. Berkman suggested a trip to the Battery to cool off. I had not seen the harbour since my arrival in America. Its beauty gripped me again as on the memorable day. But the Statue of Liberty had ceased to be an alluring symbol. How childishly naïve I had been, how far I had advanced since that day!

We returned to our talk of the afternoon. My companion expressed doubt about my finding work as a dressmaker, having no connexion in the city. I replied that I would try a factory, one for corsets, gloves, or men's suits. He promised to inquire among the Jewish comrades who were in the needle trade. They would surely help find a job for me.

It was late in the evening when we parted. Berkman had told me little about himself, except that he had been expelled from the *Gymnasium* for an anti-religious essay he had composed, and that he had left home for good. He had come to the United States in the belief that it was free and that here everyone had an equal chance in life. He knew better now. He had found exploitation more severe, and since the hanging of the Chicago anarchists he had become convinced that America was as despotic as Russia.

"Lingg was right when he said: 'If you attack us with cannon, we will reply with dynamite.' Some day I will avenge our dead," he added with great earnestness. "I too! I too!" I cried; "their death gave me life. It now belongs to their memory — to their work." He gripped my arm until it hurt. "We are comrades. Let us be friends, too — let us work together." His intensity vibrated through me as I walked up the stairs to the Minkin flat.

The following Friday, Berkman invited me to come to a Jewish lecture by Solotaroff at 54 Orchard Street, on the East Side. In New Haven Solotaroff had impressed me as an exceptionally fine speaker, but now, after having heard Most, his talk appeared flat to me, and his badly modulated voice affected me unpleasantly. His ardour, however, made up for much. I was too grateful for the warm reception he had given me on my first arrival in the city to allow myself any criticism of his lecture. Besides, everybody could not be an orator like Johann Most, I reflected. To me he was a man apart, the most remarkable in all the world.

After the meeting Berkman introduced me to a number of people, "all good active comrades," as he put it. "And here is my chum Fedya," he said, indicating a young man beside him; "he is also an anarchist, of course, but not so good as he should be."

The young chap was probably of the same age as Berkman, but not so strongly built, nor with the same aggressive manner about him. His features were rather delicate, with a sensitive mouth, while his eyes, though somewhat bulging, had a dreamy expression. He did not seem to mind in the least the banter of his friend. He smiled good-naturedly and suggested that we retire to Sachs's, "to give Sasha a chance to tell you what a good anarchist is."

Berkman did not wait till we reached the café. "A good anarchist," he began with deep conviction, "is one who lives only for the Cause and gives everything to it. My friend here " — he indicated Fedya —

" is still too much of a *bourgeois* to realize that. He is a *mamenkin sin* (mother's spoilt darling), who even accepts money from home." He continued to explain why it was inconsistent for a revolutionary to have anything to do with his *bourgeois* parents or relatives. His only reason for tolerating his friend Fedya's inconsistency, he added, was that he gave most of what he received from home to the movement. " If I'd let him, he'd spend all his money on useless things — ' beautiful,' he calls them. Wouldn't you, Fedya? " He turned to his friend, patting him on the back affectionately.

The café was crowded, as usual, and filled with smoke and talk. For a little while my two escorts were much in demand, while I was greeted by several people I had met during the week. Finally we succeeded in capturing a table and ordered some coffee and cake. I became aware of Fedya watching me and studying my face. To hide my embarrassment I turned to Berkman. " Why should one not love beauty? " I asked; " flowers, for instance, music, the theatre — beautiful things? "

" I did not say one should not," Berkman replied; " I said it was wrong to spend money on such things when the movement is so much in need of it. It is inconsistent for an anarchist to enjoy luxuries when the people live in poverty."

" But beautiful things are not luxuries," I insisted; " they are necessaries. Life would be unbearable without them." Yet, at heart, I felt that Berkman was right. Revolutionists gave up even their lives — why not also beauty? Still the young artist struck a responsive chord in me. I, too, loved beauty. Our poverty-stricken life in Königsberg had been made bearable to me only by the occasional outings with our teachers in the open. The forest, the moon casting its silvery shimmer on the fields, the green wreaths in our hair, the flowers we would pick — these made me forget for a time the sordid home surroundings. When Mother scolded me or when I had difficulties at school, a bunch of lilacs from our neighbour's garden or the sight of the colourful silks and velvets displayed in the shops would cause me to forget my sorrows and make the world seem beautiful and bright. Or the music I would on rare occasions be able to hear in Königsberg and, later, in St. Petersburg. Should I have to forgo all that to be a good revolutionist, I wondered. Should I have the strength?

Before we parted that evening Fedya remarked that his friend had mentioned that I would like to see something of the city. He was free the next day and would be glad to show me some of the sights. " Are you also out of work, that you can afford the time?" I asked. "As you know from my friend, I am an artist," he replied, laughing. "Have you ever heard of artists working?" I flushed, having to admit that I had never met an artist before. "Artists are inspired people," I said, "everything comes easy to them." "Of course," Berkman retorted, "because the people work for them." His tone seemed too severe to me, and my sympathy went out to the artist boy. I turned to him and asked him to come for me the next day. But alone in my room, it was the uncompromising fervour of the "arrogant youngster," as I mentally called Berkman, that filled me with admiration.

The next day Fedya took me to Central Park. Along Fifth Avenue he pointed out the various mansions, naming their owners. I had read about those wealthy men, their affluence and extravagance, while the masses lived in poverty. I expressed my indignation at the contrast between those splendid palaces and the miserable tenements of the East Side. "Yes, it is a crime that the few should have all, the many nothing," the artist said. "My main objection," he continued, "is that they have such bad taste — those buildings are ugly." Berkman's attitude to beauty came to my mind. "You don't agree with your chum on the need and importance of beauty in one's life, do you?" I asked. "Indeed I do not. But, then, my friend is a revolutionist above everything else. I wish I could also be, but I am not." I liked his frankness and simplicity. He did not stir me as Berkman did when speaking of revolutionary ethics; Fedya awakened in me the mysterious yearning I used to feel in my childhood at sight of the sunset turning the Popelan meadows golden in its dying glow, as the sweet music of Petrushka's flute did also.

The following week I went to the *Freiheit* office. Several people were already there, busy addressing envelopes and folding the papers. Everybody talked. Johann Most was at his desk. I was assigned a place and given work. I marvelled at Most's capacity to go on writing in that hubbub. Several times I wanted to suggest that he was being disturbed, but I checked myself. After all, they must know whether he minded their chatter.

In the evening Most stopped writing and gruffly assailed the talkers as "toothless old women," "cackling geese," and other appellations I had hardly ever before heard in German. He snatched his large felt hat from the rack, called to me to come along, and walked out. I followed him and we went up on the Elevated. "I'll take you to Terrace

Garden," he said; " we can go into the theatre there if you like. They are giving *Der Zigeunerbaron* tonight. Or we can sit in some corner, get food and drink, and talk." I replied that I did not care for light opera, that what I really wanted was to talk to him, or rather have him talk to me. " But not so violently as in the office," I added.

He selected the food and the wine. Their names were strange to me. The label on the bottle read: *Liebfrauenmilch.* " Milk of woman's love — what a lovely name! " I remarked. " For wine, yes," he retorted, " but not for woman's love. The one is always poetic — the other will never be anything but sordidly prosaic. It leaves a bad taste."

I had a feeling of guilt, as if I had made some bad break or had touched a sore spot. I told him I had never tasted any wine before, except the kind Mother made for Easter. Most shook with laughter, and I was near tears. He noticed my embarrassment and restrained himself. He poured out two glassfuls, saying: " *Prosit,* my young, naïve lady," and drank his down at a gulp. Before I could drink half of mine, he had nearly finished the bottle and ordered another.

He became animated, witty, sparkling. There was no trace of the bitterness, of the hatred and defiance his oratory had breathed on the platform. Instead there sat next to me a transformed human being, no longer the repulsive caricature of the Rochester press or the gruff creature of the office. He was a gracious host, an attentive and sympathetic friend. He made me tell him about myself and he grew thoughtful when he learned the motive that had decided me to break with my old life. He warned me to reflect carefully before taking the plunge. " The path of anarchism is steep and painful," he said; " so many have attempted to climb it and have fallen back. The price is exacting. Few men are ready to pay it, most women not at all. Louise Michel, Sophia Perovskaya — they were the great exceptions." Had I read about the Paris Commune and about that marvellous Russian woman revolutionist? I had to admit ignorance. I had never heard the name of Louise Michel before, though I did know about the great Russian. " You shall read about their lives — they will inspire you," Most said.

I inquired whether the anarchist movement in America had no outstanding woman. " None at all, only stupids," he replied; " most of the girls come to the meetings to snatch up a man; then both vanish, like the silly fishermen at the lure of the Lorelei." There was a roguish twinkle in his eye. He didn't believe much in woman's revolutionary zeal. But I, coming from Russia, might be different and he would help me. If I were really in earnest, I could find much work to do. "There is great need in our ranks of young, willing people — ardent ones, as you seem to be — and I have need of ardent friendship," he added with much feeling.

"You?" I questioned; "you have thousands in New York — all over the world. You are loved, you are idolized." "Yes, little girl, idolized by many, but loved by none. One can be very lonely among thousands — did you know that?" Something gripped my heart. I wanted to take his hand, to tell him that I would be his friend. But I dared not speak out. What could I give this man — I, a factory girl, uneducated; and he, the famous Johann Most, the leader of the masses, the man of magic tongue and powerful pen?

He promised to supply me with a list of books to read — the revolutionary poets, Freiligrath, Herwegh, Schiller, Heine, and Börne, and our own literature, of course. It was almost daybreak when we left Terrace Garden. Most called a cab and we drove to the Minkin flat. At the door he lightly touched my hand. "Where did you get your silky blond hair?" he remarked; "and your blue eyes? You said you were Jewish." "At the pigs' market," I replied; "my father told me so." "You have a ready tongue, *mein Kind.*" He waited for me to unlock the door, then took my hand, looked deeply into my eyes, and said: "This was my first happy evening in a long while." A great gladness filled my being at his words. Slowly I climbed the stairs as the cab rolled away.

The next day, when Berkman called, I related to him my wonderful evening with Most. His face darkened. "Most has no right to squander money, to go to expensive restaurants, drink expensive wines," he said gravely; "he is spending the money contributed for the movement. He should be held to account. I myself will tell him."

"No, no, you musn't," I cried. "I couldn't bear to be the cause of any affront to Most, who is giving so much. Is he not entitled to a little joy?"

Berkman persisted that I was too young in the movement, that I didn't know anything about revolutionary ethics or the meaning of revolutionary right and wrong. I admitted my ignorance, assured him I was willing to learn, to do anything, only not to have Most hurt. He walked out without bidding me good-bye.

I was greatly disturbed. The charm of Most was upon me. His remarkable gifts, his eagerness for life, for friendship, moved me deeply. And Berkman, too, appealed to me profoundly. His earnestness, his self-confidence, his youth — everything about him drew me with irresistible force. But I had the feeling that, of the two, Most was more of this earth.

When Fedya came to see me, he told me that he had already heard the story from Berkman. He was not surprised, he said; he knew how uncompromising our friend was and how hard he could be, but hardest towards himself. " It springs from his absorbing love of the people," Fedya added, " a love that will yet move him to great deeds."

For a whole week Berkman did not show up. When he came back again, it was to invite me for an outing in Prospect Park. He liked it better than Central Park, he said, because it was less cultivated, more natural. We walked about a great deal, admiring its rough beauty, and finally selected a lovely spot in which to eat the lunch I had brought with me.

We talked about my life in St. Petersburg and in Rochester. I told him of my marriage to Jacob Kershner and its failure. He wanted to know what books I had read on marriage and if it was their influence that had decided me to leave my husband. I had never read such works, but I had seen enough of the horrors of married life in my own home. Father's harsh treatment of Mother, the constant wrangles and bitter scenes that ended in Mother's fainting spells. I had also seen the debasing sordidness of the life of my married aunts and uncles, as well as in the homes of acquaintances in Rochester. Together with my own marital experiences they had convinced me that binding people for life was wrong. The constant proximity in the same house, the same room, the same bed, revolted me.

" If ever I love a man again, I will give myself to him without being bound by the rabbi or the law," I declared, " and when that love dies, I will leave without permission."

My companion said he was glad to know that I felt that way. All true revolutionists had discarded marriage and were living in freedom. That served to strengthen their love and helped them in their common task. He told me the story of Sophia Perovskaya and Zhelyabov. They had been lovers, had worked in the same group, and together they elaborated the plan for the execution of Alexander II. After the explosion of the bomb Perovskaya vanished. She was in hiding. She had every chance to escape, and her comrades begged her to do so. But she refused. She insisted that she must take the consequences, that she would share the fate of her comrades and die together with Zhelyabov. "Of course, it was wrong of her to be moved by personal sentiment," Berkman commented; "her love for the Cause should have urged her to live for other activities." Again I found myself disagreeing with him. I thought that it could not be wrong to die with one's beloved in a common act — it was beautiful, it was sublime. He retorted that I was too romantic and sentimental for a revolutionist, that the task before us was hard and we must become hard.

I wondered if the boy was really so hard, or was he merely trying to mask his tenderness, which I intuitively sensed in him. I felt myself drawn to him and I longed to throw my arms around him, but I was too shy.

The day ended in a glowing sunset. Joy was in my heart. All the way home I sang German and Russian songs, *Veeyut, vitri, veeyut booyniy,* being one of them. "That is my favourite song, Emma, *dorogaya* (dear)," he said. "I may call you that, may I not? And will you call me Sasha?" Our lips met in a spontaneous embrace.

I had begun to work in the corset factory where Helen Minkin was employed. But after a few weeks the strain became unbearable. I could hardly pull through the day; I suffered most from violent headaches. One evening I met a girl who told me of a silk waist factory that gave out work to be done at home. She would try to get me some, she promised. I knew it would be impossible to sew on a machine in the Minkin flat, it would be too disturbing for everybody. Furthermore, the girls' father had got on my nerves. He was a disagreeable person, never working, and living on his daughters. He seemed erotically fond of Anna, fairly devouring her with his eyes. The more surprising was his strong dislike of Helen, which led to constant quarrelling. At last I decided to move out.

I found a room on Suffolk Street, not far from Sachs's café. It was small and half-dark, but the price was only three dollars a month, and I engaged it. There I began to work on silk waists. Occasionally I would also get some dresses to make for the girls I knew and their friends. The work was exhausting, but it freed me from the factory and its galling discipline. My earnings from the waists, once I acquired speed, were not less than in the shop.

Most had gone on a lecture tour. From time to time he would send me a few lines, witty and caustic comments on the people he was meeting, vitriolic denunciation of reporters who interviewed him and then wrote vilifying articles about him. Occasionally he would include in his letters the caricatures made of him, with his own marginal comments: " Behold the wife-killer ! " or " Here's the man who eats little children."

The caricatures were more brutal and cruel than anything I had seen before. The loathing I had felt for the Rochester papers during the Chicago events now turned into positive hatred for the entire American press. A wild thought took hold of me and I confided it to Sasha. " Don't you think one of the rotten newspaper offices should be blown up — editors, reporters, and all? That would teach the press a lesson." But Sasha shook his head and said that it would be useless. The press was only the hireling of capitalism. " We must strike at the root."

When Most returned from his tour, we all went to hear his report. He was more masterly, more witty and defiant against the system than on any previous occasion. He almost hypnotized me. I could not help going up after the lecture to tell him how splendid his talk was. " Will you go with me to hear *Carmen* Monday at the Metropolitan Opera House ? " he whispered. He added that Monday was an awfully busy day because he had to keep his devils supplied with copy, but that he would work ahead on Sunday if I would promise to come. " To the end of the world ! " I replied impulsively.

We found the house sold out — no seats to be had at any price. We should have to stand. I knew that I was in for torture. Since childhood I had had trouble with the small toe of my left foot; new shoes used to cause me suffering for weeks, and I was wearing new shoes. But I was too ashamed to tell Most, afraid he would think me vain. I stood close to him, jammed in by a large crowd. My foot burned as if it were being held over a fire. But the first bar of the music, and the glorious singing, made me forget my agony. After the first act, when the lights went on, I found myself holding on to Most for dear life, my face distorted with pain. " What's the matter ? " he asked. " I must get off my shoe," I panted, " or I shall scream out." Leaning against him, I bent down to loosen the buttons. The rest of the opera I heard supported by Most's arm, my shoe in my hand. I could not tell whether my rapture was due to the music of *Carmen* or the release from my shoe !

We left the Opera House arm in arm, I limping. We went to a café, and Most teased me about my vanity. But he was rather glad, he said, to find me so feminine, even if it was stupid to wear tight shoes. He was in a golden mood. He wanted to know if I had ever before heard an opera and asked me to tell him about it.

Till I was ten years of age I had never heard any music, except the plaintive flute of Petrushka, Father's stable-boy. The screeching of the violins at the Jewish weddings and the poundings of the piano at our singing lessons had always been hateful to me. When I heard the opera *Trovatore* in Königsberg, I first realized the ecstasy music could create in me. My teacher may have been largely responsible for the electrifying effect of that experience: she had imbued me with the romance of her favourite German authors and had helped to rouse my imagination about the sad love of the Troubadour and Leonore. The tortuous suspense of the days before Mother gave her consent to my accompanying my teacher to the performance aggravated my tense expectancy. We reached the Opera a full hour before the beginning, myself in a cold sweat for fear we were late. Teacher, always in delicate health, could not keep up with my young legs and my frenzied haste to reach our places. I flew up to the top gallery, three steps at a time. The house was still empty and half-lit, and somewhat disappointing at first. As if by magic, it soon became transformed. Quickly the place filled with a vast audience — women in silks and velvets of gorgeous hue, with glistening jewels on their bare necks and arms, the flood of light from the crystal chandeliers reflecting the colours of green, yellow, and amethyst. It was a fairyland more magnificent than any ever pictured in the stories I had read. I forgot the presence of my teacher, the mean surroundings of my home; half-hanging over the rail, I was lost in the enchanted world below. The orchestra broke into stirring tones, mysteriously rising from the darkened house. They sent tremors down my back and held me breathless by their swelling sounds. Leonore and the Troubadour made real my own romantic fancy of love. I lived with them, thrilled and intoxicated by their passionate song. Their tragedy was mine as well, and I felt their joy and sorrow as my own. The scene between the Troubadour and his mother, her plaintive song "*Ach, ich vergehe und sterbe hier,*" Troubadour's response in "*O, teuere Mutter,*" filled me with deep woe and made my heart palpitate with compassionate sighs. The spell was broken by the loud clapping of hands and the new flood of light. I, too, clapped wildly, climbed on my bench, and shouted frantically for Leonore and the Troubadour, the hero and heroine of my fairy world. " Come along, come along," I heard my teacher say, tugging at my skirts. I followed in a daze, my body shaken with convulsive sobs, the music ringing in my ears. I had heard other operas in Königsberg and later in St. Petersburg, but the impression of *Trovatore* stood out for a long time as the most marvellous musical experience of my young life.

When I had finished relating this to Most, I noticed that his gaze was far away in the distance. He looked up as if from a dream. He had never heard, he remarked slowly, the stirrings of a child more dramatically told. I had great talent, he said, and I must begin soon to recite and speak in public. He would make me a great speaker — " to take my place when I am gone," he added.

I thought he was only making fun, or flattering me. He could not really believe that I could ever take his place or express his fire, his magic power. I did not want him to treat me that way — I wanted him to be a true comrade, frank and honest, without silly German compliments. Most grinned and emptied his glass to my " first public speech."

After that we went out together often. He opened up a new world to me, introduced me to music, books, the theatre. But his own rich personality meant far more to me — the alternating heights and depths of his spirit, his hatred of the capitalist system, his vision of a new society of beauty and joy for all.

Most became my idol. I worshipped him.

CHAPTER IV

THE 11TH OF NOVEMBER WAS APPROACHING, THE ANNIVERSARY of the Chicago martyrdoms. Sasha and I were busy with preparations for the great event of so much significance to us. Cooper Union had been secured for the commemoration. The meeting was to be held jointly by anarchists and socialists, with the co-operation of advanced labour organizations.

Every evening for several weeks we visited various trade unions to invite them to participate. This involved short talks from the floor, which I made. I always went in trepidation. On previous occasions, at German and Jewish lectures, I had mustered up courage to ask questions, but every time I would experience a kind of sinking sensation. While I was listening to the speakers, the questions would formulate themselves easily enough, but the moment I got up on my feet, I would feel faint. Desperately I would grip the chair in front of me, my heart throbbing, my knees trembling — everything in the hall would turn hazy. Then I would become aware of my voice, far, far away, and finally I would sink back in my seat in a cold sweat.

When I was first asked to make short speeches, I declined; I was sure I could never manage it. But Most would accept no refusal, and the other comrades sustained him. For the Cause, I was told, one must be able to do everything, and I so eagerly wanted to serve the Cause.

My talks used to sound incoherent to me, full of repetitions, lacking in conviction; and always the dismal feeling of sinking would be upon me. I thought everyone must see my turmoil, but apparently no one did. Even Sasha often commented on my calm and self-control. I do not know whether it was due to my being a beginner, to my youth, or to my intense feeling for the martyred men, but I never once failed to interest the workers I had been sent to invite.

Our own little group, consisting of Anna, Helen, Fedya, Sasha, and I, decided on a contribution — a large laurel-wreath with broad black and red satin ribbons. At first we wanted to buy eight wreaths, but we were too poor, since only Sasha and I were working. At last we decided in favour of Lingg: in our eyes he stood out as the sublime hero among the eight. His unbending spirit, his utter contempt for his accusers and judges, his will-power, which made him rob his enemies of their prey and die by his own hand — everything about that boy of twenty-two lent romance and beauty to his personality. He became the beacon of our lives.

At last the long-awaited evening arrived — my first public meeting in memory of the martyred men. Since I had read the accounts in the Rochester papers of the impressive march to Waldheim — the five-mile line of workers who followed the great dead to their last resting-place — and the large meetings that had since been held all over the world, I had ardently looked forward to being present at such an event. Now the moment had at last come. I went with Sasha to Cooper Union.

We found the historic hall densely packed, but with our wreath held high over our heads we finally managed to get through. Even the platform was crowded. I was bewildered until I saw Most standing next to a man and a woman; his presence made me feel at ease. His two companions were distinguished-looking people; the man radiated friendliness, but the woman, clad in a tight-fitting black velvet dress with a long train, her pale face framed in a mass of copper hair, seemed cold and aloof. She evidently belonged to another world.

Presently Sasha said: " The man near Most is Sergey Shevitch, the famous Russian revolutionist, now editor-in-chief of the socialist daily *Die Volkszeitung;* the woman is his wife, the former Helene von Dönniges." " Not the one Ferdinand Lassalle loved — the one he lost his life for ? " I asked. " Yes, the same; she has remained an aristocrat. She really doesn't belong among us. But Shevitch is splendid."

Most had given me Lassalle's works to read. They had impressed me by their profound thought, force, and clarity. I had also studied his manifold activities in behalf of the incipient workers' movement in Germany in the fifties. His romantic life and untimely death at the hands of an officer in a duel fought over Helene von Dönniges had affected me deeply.

I was repelled by the woman's haughty austerity. Her long train, the lorgnette through which she scrutinized everybody, filled me with resentment. I turned to Shevitch. I liked him for his frank, kindly face and the simplicity of his manner. I told him I wanted to put our wreath over Lingg's portrait, but it was hung so high that I would have to get a ladder to reach it. " I'll lift you up, little comrade, and hold you until you have hung your wreath," he said pleasantly. He picked me up as if I were a baby.

I felt greatly embarrassed, but I hung the wreath. Shevitch set me down and asked why I had chosen Lingg rather than some one of the other martyrs. I replied that his appeal was strongest to me. Raising my chin gently with his strong hands, Shevitch said: " Yes, he was more like our Russian heroes." He spoke with much feeling.

Soon the meeting began. Shevitch and Alexander Jonas, his co-editor on the *Volkszeitung,* and a number of other speakers in various languages told the story I had first heard from Johanna Greie. I had since read and reread it until I knew every detail by heart.

Shevitch and Jonas were impressive speakers. The rest left me cold. Then Most ascended the platform, and everything else seemed blotted out. I was caught in the storm of his eloquence, tossed about, my very soul contracting and expanding in the rise and fall of his voice. It was no longer a speech, it was thunder interspersed with flashes of lightning. It was a wild, passionate cry against the terrible thing that had happened in Chicago — a fierce call to battle against the enemy, a call to individual acts, to vengeance.

The meeting was at an end. Sasha and I filed out with the rest. I could not speak; we walked on in silence. When we reached the house where I lived, my whole body began to shake as in a fever. An overpowering yearning possessed me, an unutterable desire to give myself to Sasha, to find relief in his arms from the fearful tension of the evening.

My narrow bed now held two human bodies, closely pressed together. My room was no longer dark; a soft, soothing light seemed to come from somewhere. As in a dream I heard sweet, endearing words breathed into my ear, like the soft, beautiful Russian lullabies of my childhood. I became drowsy, my thoughts in confusion.

The meeting . . . Shevitch holding me up . . . the cold face of Helene von Dönniges . . . Johann Most . . . the force and wonder of his speech, his call to extermination — where had I heard that word before? Ah, yes, Mother — the Nihilists! The horror I had felt at her cruelty again came over me. But, then, she was not an idealist! Most was an idealist, yet he, too, urged extermination. Could idealists be cruel? The enemies of life and joy and beauty are cruel. They are relentless, they have killed our great comrades. But must we, too, exterminate?

I was roused from my drowsiness as if by an electric current. I felt a trembling, shy hand tenderly glide over me. Hungrily I reached for it, for my lover. We were engulfed in a wild embrace. Again I felt terrific pain, like the cut of a sharp knife. But it was numbed by my passion, breaking through all that had been suppressed, unconscious, and dormant.

The morning still found me eagerly reaching out, hungrily seeking. My beloved lay at my side, asleep in blissful exhaustion. I sat up, my head resting on my hand. Long I watched the face of the boy who had so attracted and repelled me at the same time, who could be so hard and whose touch was yet so tender. Deep love for him welled up in my heart — a feeling of certainty that our lives were linked for all time. I pressed my lips to his thick hair and then I, too, fell asleep.

The people from whom I rented my room slept on the other side of the wall. Their nearness always disturbed me, and now in Sasha's presence it gave me a feeling of being seen. He also had no privacy where he lived. I suggested that we find a small apartment, and he consented joyfully. When we told Fedya of our plan, he asked to be taken in. The fourth of our little commune was Helen Minkin. The friction with her father had become more violent since I had moved out, and she could not endure it. She begged to come with us. We rented a four-room flat on Forty-second Street and we all felt it a luxury to have our own place.

From the very first we agreed to share everything, to live like real comrades. Helen continued to work in the corset factory, and I divided my time between sewing silk waists and keeping house. Fedya devoted himself to painting. The expense of his oils, canvases, and brushes often consumed more than we could afford, but it never occurred to any one of us to complain. From time to time he would sell a picture to some dealer for fifteen or twenty-five dollars, whereupon he would bring an armful of flowers or some present for me. Sasha would upbraid him for it: the idea of spending money for such things, when the movement needed it so badly, was intolerable to him. His anger had no effect on Fedya. He would laugh it off, call him a fanatic, and say he had no sense of beauty.

One day Fedya arrived with a beautiful blue and white striped silk jersey, considered very stylish then. When Sasha came home and saw the jersey, he flew into a rage, called Fedya a spendthrift and an incurable *bourgeois,* who would never amount to anything in the movement. The two nearly came to blows, and finally both left the flat. I felt sick with the pain of Sasha's severity. I began to doubt his love. It could not be very deep or he would not spoil the little joys that Fedya brought into my life. True, the jersey cost two dollars and a half. Perhaps it was extravagant of Fedya to spend so much money. But how could he help loving beautiful things? They were a necessity to his artist's spirit. I grew bitter, and was glad when Sasha did not return that night.

He stayed away for some days. During that time I was a great deal with Fedya. He had so much that Sasha lacked and that I craved. His susceptibility to every mood, his love of life and of colour, made him more human, more akin to me. He never expected me to live up to the Cause. I felt release with him.

One morning Fedya asked me to pose for him. I experienced no sense of shame at standing naked before him. He worked away for a time, and neither of us talked. Then he began to fidget about and finally said he would have to stop: he could not concentrate, the mood was gone. I went back behind the screen to dress. I had not quite finished when I heard violent weeping. I rushed forward and found Fedya stretched on the sofa, his head buried in the pillow, sobbing. As I bent over him, he sat up and broke loose in a torrent — said he loved me, that he had from the very beginning, though he had tried to keep in the background for Sasha's sake; he had struggled fiercely against his feeling for me, but he knew now that it was of no use. He would have to move out.

I sat by him, holding his hand in mine and stroking his soft wavy hair. Fedya had always drawn me to him by his thoughtful attention, his sensitive response, and his love of beauty. Now I felt something stronger stirring within me. Could it be love for Fedya, I wondered. Could one love two persons at the same time? I loved Sasha. At that very moment my resentment at his harshness gave way to yearning for my strong, arduous lover. Yet I felt Sasha had left something untouched in me, something Fedya could perhaps waken to life. Yes, it must be possible to love more than one! All I had felt for the boy artist must have really been love without my being aware of it till now, I decided.

I asked Fedya what he thought of love for two or even for more persons at once. He looked up in surprise and said he did not know, he had never loved anyone before. His love for me had absorbed him to the exclusion of anyone else. He knew he could not care for another woman while he loved me. And he was certain that Sasha would never want to share me; his sense of possession was too strong.

I resented the suggestion of sharing. I insisted that one can only respond to what the other is able to call out. I did not believe that Sasha was possessive. One who so fervently wanted freedom and preached it so whole-heartedly could never object to my giving myself to someone else. We agreed that, whatever happened, there must be no deception. We must go to Sasha and tell him frankly how we felt. He would understand.

That evening Sasha returned straight from work. The four of us sat down, as usual, to our supper. We talked about various things. No reference was made to Sasha's long absence and there was no chance to speak to him alone about the new light that had come into my life. We all went to Orchard Street to a lecture.

After the meeting Sasha went home with me, Fedya and Helen remaining behind. In our flat he asked permission to come to my room. Then he began to talk, pouring out his whole soul. He said he loved me dearly, that he wanted me to have beautiful things; that he, too, loved beauty. But he loved the Cause more than anything else in the world. For that he would forgo even our love. Yes, and his very life.

He told me about the famous Russian revolutionary catechism that demanded of the true revolutionist that he give up home, parents, sweetheart, children, everything dear to one's being. He agreed with it absolutely and he was determined to allow nothing to stand in the way. " But I do love you," he repeated. His intensity, his uncompromising fervour, irritated and yet drew me like a magnet. Whatever longing I had experienced when near Fedya was silent now. Sasha, my own wonderful, dedicated, obsessed Sasha, was calling. I felt entirely his.

Later in the day I had to meet Most. He had spoken to me about a short lecture tour he was planning for me, but though I did not take it seriously, he had asked me to come to see him about it.

The *Freiheit* office was crowded. Most suggested a near-by saloon, which he knew to be quiet in the early afternoon. We went there. He began to explain his plans for my tour; I was to visit Rochester, Buffalo, and Cleveland. It threw me into a panic. " It is impossible! " I protested; " I don't know a thing about lecturing." He waved my objections aside, declaring that everybody felt that way in the beginning. He was determined to make a public speaker of me, and I would simply have to begin. He had already chosen the subject for me and he would help me prepare it. I was to speak on the futility of the struggle for the eight-hour workday, now again much discussed in labour ranks. He pointed out that the eight-hour campaigns in '84, '85, and '86 had already taken a toll far beyond the value of the " damned thing." " Our comrades in Chicago lost their lives for it, and the workers still work long hours." But even if the eight-hour day were established, there would be no actual gain, he insisted. On the contrary, it would serve only to distract the masses from the real issue — the struggle against capitalism, against the wage system, for a new society. At any rate, all I would have to do would be to memorize the notes he would give me. He was sure that my dramatic feeling and my enthusiasm would do the rest. As usual, he held me by his eloquence. I had no power to resist.

When I got home, away from Most's presence, I again experienced the sinking feeling that had come upon me when I had first tried to speak in public. I still had three weeks in which to read up, but I was sure I never could go through with it.

Stronger than my lack of faith in myself was my loathing for Rochester. I had completely broken with my parents and my sister Lena, but I yearned for Helena, for little Stella, now in her fourth year, and for my youngest brother. Oh, if I were really an accomplished speaker, I would rush to Rochester and fling my accumulated bitterness into the smug faces of the people who had treated me so brutally. Now they would only add ridicule to the hurt they had given me. Anxiously I waited for the return of my friends.

How great was my astonishment when Sasha and Helen Minkin grew enthusiastic about Most's plan! It was a marvellous opportunity, they said. What if I would have to work hard to prepare my talk? It would be the making of me as a public lecturer, the first woman speaker in the German anarchist movement in America! Sasha was especially insistent: I must set aside every consideration, I must think only of how useful I would become to the Cause. Fedya was dubious.

My three good friends insisted that I stop work to have more time for study. They would also relieve me of every domestic responsibility. I devoted myself to reading. Now and then Fedya would come with flowers. He knew that I had not yet spoken to Sasha. He never pressed me, but his flowers spoke more appealingly than anything he could have said. Sasha no longer scolded him for wasting money. " I know you love flowers," he would say; " they may inspire you in your new work."

I read up a great deal on the eight-hour movement, went to every meeting where the matter was to be discussed; but the more I studied the subject, the more confused I became. " The iron law of wages," " supply and demand," " poverty as the only leaven of revolt " — I could not follow it all. It left me as cold as the mechanistic theories I used to hear expounded in the Rochester Socialist local. But when I read Most's notes, everything seemed clear. The imagery of his language, his unanswerable criticism of existing conditions, and his glorious vision of the new society awakened enthusiasm in me. I continued to doubt myself, but everything Most said seemed irrefutable.

One thought took definite shape in my mind. I would never memorize Most's notes. His phrases, the flower and spice of his invective, were too well known for me to repeat them parrot-like. I would use his ideas and present them in my own way. But the ideas — were they not also Most's? Ah, well, they had become such a part of me that I could not distinguish how far I was repeating him or to what extent they had been reborn as my own.

The day of my departure for Rochester arrived. I met Most for a last talk; I came in a depressed mood, but a glass of wine and Most's spirit soon lifted the weight. He talked long and ardently, made numerous suggestions, and said I must not take the audiences too seriously; most of them were dullards, anyway. He impressed upon me the need of humour. " If you can make people laugh, sailing will be easy." He told me that the construction of my lecture did not matter much. I must talk in the way I related to him my impressions of my first opera. That would move the audience. " For the rest, be bold, be arrogant, I am sure you will be brave."

He took me to the Grand Central in a cab. On the way he moved close to me. He yearned to take me in his arms and asked if he might. I nodded, and he held me pressed to him. Conflicting thoughts and emotions possessed me; the speeches I was going to make, Sasha, Fedya, my passion for the one, my budding love for the other. But I yielded to Most's trembling embrace, his kisses covering my mouth as of one famished with thirst. I let him drink; I could have denied him nothing. He loved me, he said; he had never known such longing for any woman before. Of late years he had not even been attracted to anyone. A feeling of growing age was overcoming him, and he felt worn from the long struggle and the persecution he had endured. More depressing even was the consciousness that his best comrades misunderstood him. But my youth had made him young, my ardour had raised his spirit. My whole being had awakened him to a new meaning in life. I was his *Blondkopf,* his " blue eyes "; he wanted me to be his own, his helpmate, his voice.

I lay back with my eyes closed. I was too overpowered to speak, too limp to move. Something mysterious stirred me, something entirely unlike the urge towards Sasha or the sensitive response to Fedya. It was different from these. It was infinite tenderness for the great man-child at my side. As he sat there, he suggested a rugged tree bent by winds and storm, making one supreme last effort to stretch itself towards the sun. " All for the Cause," Sasha had so often said. The fighter next to me had already given all for the Cause. But who had given all for him? He was hungry for affection, for understanding. I would give him both.

At the station my three friends were already waiting for me. Sasha held out an American Beauty rose to me. " As a token of my love, *Dushenka,* and as a harbinger of luck on your first public quest."

Precious Sasha; only a few days before, when we went shopping on Hester Street, he had protested strenuously because I wanted him to spend more than six dollars for a suit and twenty-five cents for a hat. He would not have it. " We must get the cheapest we can," he reiterated. And now — what tenderness there was under his stern exterior! Like Hannes. Strange, I had never before realized how much alike they were. The boy and the man. Both hard; one because he had never yet tasted life, and the other because it had struck him so many blows. Both equally unyielding in their zeal, both so childlike in their need for love.

The train sped on towards Rochester. Only six months had passed since I had cut loose from my meaningless past. I had lived years in that time.

CHAPTER V

I HAD BEGGED MOST NOT TO GIVE THE TIME OF MY ARRIVAL TO THE German Union in Rochester, before which I was to speak. I wanted to see my beloved sister Helena first. I had written her about my coming, but not the purpose of my visit. She met me at the station and we clung to each other as if we had been separated for decades.

I explained to Helena my mission in Rochester. She stared at me open-mouthed. How could I undertake such a thing, face an audience? I had been away only six months; what could I have learned in such a brief time? Where did I get the courage? And in Rochester, of all cities! Our parents would never get over the shock.

I had never before been angry with Helena; there never had been occasion for it. In fact, it was always I who tried her patience to the breaking-point. But the reference to our parents made me wroth. It brought back Popelan, Helena's crushed young love for Susha, and all the other ghastly pictures. I broke out in a bitter arraignment of our people, especially picking out my father, whose harshness had been the nightmare of my childhood, and whose tyranny had held me even after my marriage. I reproached Helena for having allowed our parents to rob her of her youth. "They came near doing it to me, too!" I cried. I had finished with them when they joined the Rochester bigots and cast me out. My life was now my own, the work I had chosen more precious to me than my life! Nothing could take me from it, least of all consideration for my parents.

The pain in my darling's face checked me. I took her in my arms and assured her that there was nothing to worry about, that our family need not know about my plans. The meeting was to be only before a German union; no publicity would be connected with it. Besides, the Jews on St. Joseph's Street knew nothing about the advanced Germans, or about anything else, for that matter, outside of their own colourless, petty lives. Helena brightened up. She said that if my public speech was as eloquent as my arguments to her, I would make a hit.

When I faced the audience the next evening, my mind was a blank. I could not remember a single word of my notes. I shut my eyes for an instant; then something strange happened. In a flash I saw it — every incident of my three years in Rochester: the Garson factory, its drudgery and humiliation, the failure of my marriage, the Chicago crime. The last words of August Spies rang in my ears: " Our silence will speak louder than the voices you strangle today."

I began to speak. Words I had never heard myself utter before came pouring forth, faster and faster. They came with passionate intensity; they painted images of the heroic men on the gallows, their glowing vision of an ideal life, rich with comfort and beauty: men and women radiant in freedom, children transformed by joy and affection. The audience had vanished, the hall itself had disappeared; I was conscious only of my own words, of my ecstatic song.

I stopped. Tumultuous applause rolled over me, the buzzing of voices, people telling me something I could not understand. Then I heard someone quite close to me: " It was an inspired speech; but what about the eight-hour struggle? You've said nothing about that." I felt hurled down from my exalted heights, crushed. I told the chairman I was too tired to answer questions, and I went home feeling ill in body and mind. I let myself quietly into Helena's apartment and threw myself on the bed in my clothes.

Exasperation with Most for forcing the tour on me, anger with myself for having so easily succumbed to his influence, the conviction that I had cheated the audience — all seethed in my mind together with a new revelation. I could sway people with words! Strange and magic words that welled up from within me, from some unfamiliar depth. I wept with the joy of knowing.

I went to Buffalo, determined to make another effort. The preliminaries of the meeting threw me into the same nervous tension, but when I faced the audience, there were no visions to inflame my mind. In an endless, repetitious manner I made my speech about the waste of energy and time the eight-hour struggle involved, scoffing at the stupidity of the workers who fought for such trifles. At the end of what seemed to me several hours I was complimented on my clear and logical presentation. Some questions were asked, and I answered them with a sureness that brooked no gainsaying. But on the way home from the meeting my heart was heavy. No words of exaltation had come to me, and how could one hope to reach other hearts when one's own remained cold? I decided to wire Most the next morning, begging him to relieve me of the necessity of going to Cleveland. I could not bear to repeat once more the meaningless prattle.

After a night's sleep my decision seemed childish and weak. How could I give up so soon? Would Most have given up like that? Would Sasha? Well, I, too, would go on. I took the train for Cleveland.

The meeting was large and animated. It was a Saturday night, and the workers attended with their wives and children. Everybody drank. I was surrounded by a group, offered refreshments, and asked questions. How did I happen to come into the movement? Was I German? What was I doing for a living? The petty curiosity of people supposed to be interested in the most advanced ideas reminded me of the Rochester grilling on the day of my arrival in America. It made me thoroughly angry.

The gist of my talk was the same as in Buffalo, but the form was different. It was a sarcastic arraignment, not of the system or of the capitalists, but of the workers themselves — their readiness to give up a great future for some small temporary gains. The audience seemed to enjoy being handled in such an outspoken manner. They roared in some places, and in others vigorously applauded. It was not a meeting; it was a circus, and I was the clown!

A man in the front row who had attracted my attention by his white hair and lean, haggard face rose to speak. He said that he understood my impatience with such small demands as a few hours less a day, or a few dollars more a week. It was legitimate for young people to take time lightly. But what were men of his age to do? They were not likely to live to see the ultimate overthrow of the capitalist system. Were they also to forgo the release of perhaps two hours a day from the hated work? That was all they could hope to see realized in their lifetime. Should they deny themselves even that small achievement? Should they never have a little more time for reading or being out in the open? Why not be fair to people chained to the block?

The man's earnestness, his clear analysis of the principle involved in the eight-hour struggle, brought home to me the falsity of Most's position. I realized I was committing a crime against myself and the workers by serving as a parrot repeating Most's views. I understood why I had failed to reach my audience. I had taken refuge in cheap jokes and bitter thrusts against the toilers to cover up my own inner lack of conviction. My first public experience did not bring the result Most had hoped for, but it taught me a valuable lesson. It cured me somewhat of my childlike faith in the infallibility of my teacher and impressed on me the need of independent thinking.

In New York my friends had prepared a grand reception for me; our flat was spotlessly clean and filled with flowers. They were eager for an account of my tour and they felt apprehensive of the effect upon Most of my changed attitude.

The next evening I went out with Most, again to Terrace Garden. He had grown younger during my two weeks' absence: his rough beard was trimmed neatly and he wore a natty new grey suit, a red carnation in his buttonhole. He joined me in a gay mood, presenting me with a large bouquet of violets. The two weeks of my absence had been unbearably long, he said, and he had reproached himself for having let me go just when we had grown so close. But now he would never again let me go — not alone, anyhow.

I tried several times to tell him about my trip, hurt to the quick that he had not asked about it. He had sent me forth against my will, he had been so eager to make a great speaker of me; was he not interested to know whether I had proved an apt pupil?

Yes, of course, he replied. But he had already received the reports from Rochester that I had been eloquent, from Buffalo that my presentation had silenced all opponents, and from Cleveland that I had flayed the dullards with biting sarcasm. " What about my own reactions? " I asked. " Don't you want me to tell you about that? " " Yes, another time." Now he wanted only to feel me near — his *Blondkopf,* his little girl-woman.

I flared up, declaring I would not be treated as a mere female. I blurted out that I would never again follow blindly, that I had made a fool of myself, that the five-minute speech of the old worker had convinced me more than all his persuasive phrases. I talked on, my listener keeping very silent. When I had finished, he called the waiter and paid the bill. I followed him out.

On the street he burst out in a storm of abuse. He had reared a viper, a snake, a heartless coquette, who had played with him like a cat with a mouse. He had sent me out to plead his cause and I had betrayed him. I was like the rest, but he would not stand for it. He would rather cut me out of his heart right now than have me as a lukewarm friend. " Who is not with me is against me," he shouted; " I will not have it otherwise!" A great sadness overwhelmed me, as if I had just experienced an irreparable loss.

Returning to our flat, I collapsed. My friends were disturbed and did everything to soothe me. I related the story from beginning to end, even to the violets I had mechanically carried home. Sasha grew indignant. " Violets at the height of winter, with thousands out of work and hungry!" he exclaimed. He had always said that Most was a spendthrift, living at the expense of the movement. And what kind of a revolutionist was I, anyway, to accept Most's favours? Didn't I know that he only cared for women physically? Most of the Germans were that way. They considered women only as females. I would have to choose once for all between Most and him. Most was no longer a revolutionist; he had gone back on the Cause.

Angrily he left the house, and I remained bewildered, bruised, with my new-found world in debris at my feet. A gentle hand took mine, led me quietly into my room, and left me. It was Fedya.

Soon a new call came to me, of workers on strike, and I followed it eagerly. It came from Joseph Barondess, whom I had previously met; he was of the group of young Jewish socialists and anarchists who had organized the cloakmakers and other Yiddish unions. The aggregation numbered more informed men and abler speakers than Barondess, but he stood out by reason of his greater simplicity. There was no bombast about this attractive, lanky chap. His mind was not of a scholarly type; it was of a practical turn. He was just the man the workers needed to help them in their daily struggle. Barondess was now at the head of the union, directing the cloakmakers' strike.

Everybody on the East Side who was able to say a few words in public was drawn into the struggle. They were nearly all men, except Annie Netter, a young girl who had already made a name for herself by her untiring activity in the anarchist and labour ranks. She had been one of the most intelligent and indefatigable women workers in various strikes, including those of the Knights of Labor, an organization which had been for a number of years the storm-centre of the intense campaigns of the eighties. It had reached its zenith in the eight-hour fight led by Parsons, Spies, Fielden and the other men who had died in Chicago. It began its downward course when Terence V. Powderly, Grand Master of the Knights of Labor, had allied himself with the enemies of his comrades who were being rushed to their doom. It was well known that Powderly, in return for thirty pieces of silver, had helped to pull the strings that strangled the men in Chicago. Militant workers withdrew from the Knights of Labor, and it became a dumping-ground for unscrupulous job-hunters.

Annie Netter had been among the first to turn from the Judas organization. She was now a member of the Pioneers of Liberty, to which most of the active Jewish anarchists in New York belonged. An ardent worker, she gave unstintingly of her time and meagre earnings. In her efforts she was sustained by her father who had developed himself out of religious orthodoxy to atheism and socialism. He was a man of exceptional quality, a great scholar, of warm humanity, a lover of life and youth. The Netter home, behind their little grocery store, became the oasis for the radical element, an intellectual centre. Mrs. Netter kept open house: the *samovar* and a generous spread of *zakusky* were never off the table. We young rebels were appreciative, if not profitable, customers of the Netter grocery.

I had never known a real home. At the Netters' I basked in the sunny atmosphere of the beautiful understanding that existed between the parents and their children. The gatherings there were intensely interesting, the evenings spent in discussions, enlivened by the entertaining banter of our kindly host. Among the frequenters were some very able young men whose names were well known in the New York ghetto; among others, David Edelstadt, a fine idealistic nature, a spiritual petrel whose songs of revolt were beloved by every Yiddish-speaking radical. Then there was Bovshover, who wrote under the name of Basil Dahl, a high-strung and impulsive man of exceptional poetic gifts. Young Michael Cohn, M. Katz, Girzhdansky, Louis, and other young men of ability and promise used to meet at the Netters', all helping to make the evenings real intellectual feasts. Joseph Barondess often participated, and it was he who sent for me to help in the strike.

I threw myself into the work with all the ardour of my being and I became absorbed in it to the exclusion of everything else. My task was to get the girls in the trade to join the strike. For that purpose meetings, concerts, socials, and dances were organized. At these affairs it was not difficult to press upon the girls the need of making common cause with their striking brothers. I had to speak often and I became less and less disturbed when on the platform. My faith in the justice of the strike helped me to dramatize my talks and to carry conviction. Within a few weeks my work brought scores of girls into the ranks of the strikers.

I became alive once more. At the dances I was one of the most untiring and gayest. One evening a cousin of Sasha, a young boy, took me aside. With a grave face, as if he were about to announce the death of a dear comrade, he whispered to me that it did not behoove an agitator to dance. Certainly not with such reckless abandon, anyway. It was undignified for one who was on the way to become a force in the anarchist movement. My frivolity would only hurt the Cause.

I grew furious at the impudent interference of the boy. I told him to mind his own business, I was tired of having the Cause constantly thrown into my face. I did not believe that a Cause which stood for a beautiful ideal, for anarchism, for release and freedom from conventions and prejudice, should demand the denial of life and joy. I insisted that our Cause could not expect me to became a nun and that the movement should not be turned into a cloister. If it meant that, I did not want it. " I want freedom, the right to self-expression, everybody's right to beautiful, radiant things." Anarchism meant that to me, and I would live it in spite of the whole world — prisons, persecution, everything. Yes, even in spite of the condemnation of my own closest comrades I would live my beautiful ideal.

I had worked myself into a passion, my voice ringing out. I found myself surrounded by many people. There was applause, mingled with protests that I was wrong, that one must consider the Cause above everything. All the Russian revolutionists had done that, they had never been conscious of self. It was nothing but narrow egotism to want to enjoy anything that would take one away from the movement. In the hubbub Sasha's voice was the loudest.

I turned in his direction. He was standing near Anna Minkin. I had noticed their growing interest in each other long before our last altercation. Sasha had then moved out of our flat, where Anna used to be almost a daily visitor. It was now the first time in weeks that I had seen either of them. My heart contracted with yearning for my impetuous, headstrong lover. I longed to call him by the name he loved best, *Dushenka* — to stretch out my arms to him — but his face was set, his eyes full of reproach, and I checked myself. I danced no more that evening.

Presently I was called into the committee room, where I found Joseph Barondess and other strike leaders already at work. Next to Barondess I noticed Professor T. H. Garside, a Scotchman, formerly lecturer for the Knights of Labor, and now at the head of the strike. Garside was about thirty-five, tall, pale, and languid-looking. His manner was gentle and ingratiating, and he resembled somewhat the pictures of Christ. He was always trying to pacify conflicting elements, to smooth things over.

Garside informed us that the strike would be lost if we did not consent to a compromise. I disagreed with him and objected to his proposal. Several members of the committee upheld me, but Garside's influence prevailed. The strike was settled according to his suggestions.

The strenuous weeks of the strike now gave way to less arduous activities: lectures, evenings at the Netters' or at our flat, and efforts to secure employment again. Fedya had begun to work with crayons, enlarging photographs; he declared that he could not keep on wasting our money, Helen's and mine, on paints. He felt he would never become a great painter, anyway. I suspected it was something else: no doubt his desire to earn money so that he could relieve me of hard work.

I had not been feeling very well, especially during periods, on which occasions I always had to take to bed, in excruciating pain for days. It had been so since my great shock when Mother slapped my face. It grew worse when I caught a cold on our way from Königsberg to St. Petersburg. We had to be smuggled across the border, Mother, my two brothers, and I. It was in the latter part of 1881 and the winter was particularly severe. The smugglers had told Mother that we would have to wade through deep snow, even across a half-frozen brook. Mother worried about me because I was taken sick a few days earlier than my time, owing to the excitement of our departure from Königsberg. At five in the morning, shivering with cold and fear, we started out. Soon we reached the brook that separated the German and Russian frontiers. The very anticipation of the icy water was paralysing, but there was no escape; we had to plunge in or be overtaken and perhaps shot by soldiers patrolling the border. A few roubles finally induced them to turn their backs, but they had cautioned us to be quick.

We plunged in, Mother loaded with bundles and I carrying my little brother. The sudden chill froze my blood; then I felt a stinging sensation in my spine, abdomen, and legs, as if I were being pierced with hot irons. I wanted to scream, but terror of the soldiers checked me. Soon we were over, and the stinging ceased; but my teeth kept chattering and I was in a hot sweat. We ran as fast as we could to the inn on the Russian side. I was given hot tea with *maliny,* packed in hot bricks, and covered with a large feather bed. I felt feverish all the way to St. Petersburg, and the pain in my spine and legs was racking. I was laid up for weeks, and my spine remained weak for years afterwards.

In America I had consulted Solotaroff about my trouble, and he took me to a specialist, who urged an operation. He seemed surprised that I could have stood my condition so long and that I had been at all able to have physical contact. My friends informed me that the physician had said I would never be free from pain, or experience full sexual release, unless I submitted to the operation.

Solotaroff asked me whether I had ever wanted a baby. " Because if you have the operation," he explained, " you will be able to have a child. So far your condition has made that impossible."

A child! I had loved children madly, ever since I could remember. As a little girl I used to look with envious eyes on the strange little babies our neighbour's daughter played with, dressing them up and putting them to sleep. I was told they were not real babies, they were only dolls, although to me they were living things because they were so beautiful. I longed for dolls, but I never had any.

When my brother Herman was born, I was only four years old. He replaced the need of dolls in my life. The arrival of little Leibale two years later filled me with ecstatic joy. I was always near him, rocking and singing him to sleep. Once when he was about a year old, Mother put him in my bed. After she left, the child began to cry. He must be hungry, I thought. I remembered how Mother gave him the breast. I, too, would give him my breast. I picked him up in my arms and pressed his little mouth close to me, rocking and cooing and urging him to drink. Instead he began to choke, turned blue in the face, and gasped for breath. Mother came running in and demanded to know what I had done to Baby. I explained. She broke out into laughter, then slapped and scolded me. I wept, not from pain, but because my breast had no milk for Leibale.

My compassion for our servant Amalia had surely been due to the circumstance that she was going to have *ein Kindchen.* I loved babies passionately, and now — now I might have a child of my own and experience for the first time the mystery and wonder of motherhood! I closed my eyes in blissful day-dreaming.

A cruel hand clutched at my heart. My ghastly childhood stood before me, my hunger for affection, which Mother was unable to satisfy. Father's harshness towards the children, his violent outbreaks, his beating my sisters and me. Two frightful experiences were particularly fresh in my mind: Once Father lashed me with a strap so that my little brother Herman, awakened by my cries, came running up and bit Father on the calf. The lashing stopped. Helena took me to her room, bathed my bruised back, brought me milk, held me to her heart, her tears mingling with mine, while Father outside was raging: " I'll kill her! I will kill that brat! I will teach her to obey!"

Another time, in Königsberg, my people, having lost everything in Popelan, were too poor to afford decent schooling for Herman and myself. The city's rabbi, a distant relative, had promised to arrange the matter, but he insisted on monthly reports of our behaviour and progress at school. I hated it as a humiliation that outraged me, but I had to carry the report. One day I was given a low mark for bad behaviour. I went home in trembling fear. I could not face Father — I showed my paper to Mother. She began to cry, said that I would be their ruin, that I was an ungrateful and wilful child, and that she would have to let Father see the paper. But she would plead with him for me, although I did not deserve it. I walked away from her with a heavy heart. At our bay window I looked out over the fields in the distance. Children were playing there; they seemed to belong to another world — there never had been much play in my life. A strange thought came to me: how wonderful it would be if I were stricken with some consuming disease! It would surely soften Father's heart. I had never known him soft save on *Sukkess,* the autumnal holiday of rejoicing. Father did not drink, except a little on certain Jewish fêtes, on this day especially. Then he would grow jolly, gather the children about him, promise us new dresses and toys. It was the one bright spot in our lives and we always eagerly looked forward to it. It happened only once a year. As long as I could think back, I remembered his saying that he had not wanted me. He had wanted a boy, the pig woman had cheated him. Perhaps if I should become very ill, near death, he would become kind and never beat me again or let me stand in the corner for hours, or make me walk back and forth with a glass of water in my hand. " If you spill a drop, you will get whipped!" he would threaten. The whip and the little stool were always at hand. They symbolized my shame and my tragedy. After many attempts and considerable punishment I had learned to carry the glass without spilling the water. The process used to unnerve me and make me ill for hours after.

My father was handsome, dashing, and full of vitality. I loved him even while I was afraid of him. I wanted him to love me, but I never knew how to reach his heart. His hardness served only to make me more contrary. Why was he so hard, I was wondering, as I looked out of the bay window, lost in recollections.

Suddenly I felt a terrific pain in my head, as if I had been struck with an iron bar. It was Father's fist that had smashed the round comb I wore to hold my unruly hair. He pounded me and pulled me about, raging: "You are my disgrace! You will always be so! You can't be *my* child; you don't look like me or like your mother; you don't act like us!"

Sister Helena wrestled with him for my life. She tried to tear me away from his grip, and the blows intended for me fell upon her. At last Father became tired, grew dizzy, and fell headlong to the floor. Helena shouted to Mother that Father had fainted. She hurried me along to her room and locked the door.

All my love and longing for my father were turned to hatred. After that I avoided him and never talked to him, unless in answer. I did what I was told mechanically; the gulf between us widened with the years. My home had become a prison. Every time I tried to escape, I was caught and put back in the chains forged for me by Father. From St. Petersburg to America, from Rochester to my marriage, there were repeated attempts to escape. The last and final one was before I left Rochester for New York.

Mother had not been feeling well and I went over to put her house in order. I was on the floor scrubbing while Father was nagging me for having married Kershner, for having left him, and again for returning to him. "You are a loose character," he kept on saying; "you have always disgraced yourself in the family." He talked, while I continued scrubbing.

Then something snapped within me; my lone and woeful childhood, my tormented adolescence, my joyless youth — I flung them all into Father's face. He stood aghast as I denounced him, emphasizing every charge by beating my scrubbing-brush on the floor. Every cruel incident of my life stood out in my arraignment. Our large barn of a home, Father's angry voice resounding through it, his ill-treatment of the servants, his iron grip on my mother — everything that had haunted my days and terrorized my nights I now recalled in my bitterness. I told him that if I had not become the harlot he repeatedly called me, it was not his fault. I had been on the verge even of going on the street more than once. It was Helena's love and devotion that had saved me.

My words rushed on like a torrent, the brush pounding the floor with all the hatred and scorn I felt for my father. The terrible scene ended with my hysterical screams. My brothers carried me up and put me to bed. The next morning I left the house. I did not see Father again before I went to New York.

I had learned since then that my tragic childhood had been no exception, that there were thousands of children born unwanted, marred and maimed by poverty and still more by ignorant misunderstanding. No child of mine should ever be added to those unfortunate victims.

There was also another reason: my growing absorption in my new-found ideal. I had determined to serve it completely. To fulfil that mission I must remain unhampered and untied. Years of pain and of suppressed longing for a child — what were they compared with the price many martyrs had already paid? I, too, would pay the price, I would endure the suffering, I would find an outlet for my mother-need in the love of *all* children. The operation did not take place.

Several weeks' rest and the loving care of my friends — of Sasha, who had returned to the house, the Minkin sisters, Most, who called often and sent flowers, and, above all, the artist boy — gave me back to health. I rose from my sick-bed renewed in faith in my own strength. Like Sasha I now felt that I, too, could overcome every difficulty and face every test for my ideal. Had I not overcome the strongest and most primitive craving of a woman — the desire for a child?

During those weeks Fedya and I became lovers. It had grown clear to me that my feelings for Fedya had no bearing on my love for Sasha. Each called out different emotions in my being, took me into different worlds. They created no conflict, they only brought fulfilment.

I told Sasha about my love for Fedya. His response was bigger and more beautiful than I had expected. " I believe in your freedom to love," he said. He was aware of his possessive tendencies and hated them like everything else he had got from his *bourgeois* background. Perhaps if Fedya were not his friend, he might be jealous; he knew he had a large streak of jealousy in his make-up. But not only was Fedya his friend, he was his comrade in battle; and I was more to him than merely a woman. His love for me was intense, but the revolutionist and the fighter meant more to him.

When our artist friend came home that day, the boys embraced. Late into the night we talked of our plans for further activities. When we separated, we had made a pact — to dedicate ourselves to the Cause in some supreme deed, to die together if necessary, or to continue to live and work for the ideal for which one of us might have to give his life.

The days and weeks that followed were illumined by the glorious new light in us. We became more patient with each other, more understanding.

CHAPTER VI

M OST HAD TOLD ME THAT HE WAS PLANNING A SHORT LECTURE
tour through the New England States. Now he informed me
that he was about to leave, and he invited me to accompany him. He
said that I looked worn and thin and that a change of scene would do
me good. I promised to consider his invitation.

The boys urged me to go; Fedya stressed the need of getting away
from household duties, while Sasha said it would help me to get
acquainted with the comrades and open up a way for further activities.

Two weeks later I went with Most by the Fall River Line to
Boston. I had never before seen such a spacious, luxurious boat, such
cosy state-rooms; mine, not far from Most's, looked bright with a
bunch of lilacs he had sent. We stood on the deck as the boat steamed
out, and presently a beautiful green island came into view, with large
stately trees shading grey stone buildings. The sight was pleasing after
the endless tenement-houses. I turned to Most. His face was ashy,
his fist clenched. "What is it?" I cried in alarm. "That is Blackwell's Island Penitentiary, the Spanish Inquisition transferred to the
United States," he replied; "soon it will again hold me within its
walls."

Soothingly I placed my hand on his convulsed fingers. Gradually
they relaxed, and his hand stretched out in mine. We stood for a long
time, each absorbed in his thoughts. The night was warm, pungent
with the May air. Most's arm was around me as he related his experiences on Blackwell's Island, and of his early life and development.

He was, it seems, the offspring of a clandestine affair. His father
had at first led an adventurous life, later becoming a copyist in a lawyer's office. His mother had been a governess in a wealthy family. He
was born without legal, moral, or religious sanction; subsequently the
union was legalized.

It was his mother who had the most potent influence on him as a child. She taught him his first lessons and, most important of all, kept his young mind free from prevalent religious dogmas. His first seven years were care-free and happy. Then his great tragedy happened — the poisoning of his cheek and the consequent disfigurement of his face as the result of an operation. Perhaps if his beloved mother had remained alive, her affection would have helped him over the taunts his distorted appearance brought upon him, but she had died when he was only nine. Some time later his father married again. His stepmother turned the erstwhile joyous home into a purgatory for the child. His life became unbearable. At fifteen he was taken out of school and apprenticed to a bookbinder. That only changed one hell for another. His deformity pursued him like a curse and caused him untold misery.

He loved the theatre madly, and every pfennig he could save he used to invest in tickets. He became obsessed by a yearning to go on the stage. Schiller's plays, especially *Wilhelm Tell, Die Räuber,* and *Fiesco,* were his inspirations and he longed to play in them. Once he had applied to a manager of a theatre, but he was curtly told that his face was more fit for a clown than for an actor. The disappointment was crushing and made him still more sensitive about his affliction. It became the horror of his existence. It made him pathologically self-conscious, particularly in the presence of women. He wanted them passionately, but the harrowing thought of his deformity always drove him from them. For many years, until he was able to grow a beard, he could not overcome his morbid shyness. It came near driving him to end his life, when he was saved by his spiritual awakening. The new social ideas he had become acquainted with inspired him with a great purpose and made him hold on to life. Blackwell's Island revived his old horror of his appearance. They had there shaved his beard, and the sight of the hideous image looking back at him from a piece of mirror he had smuggled into his cell was more terrifying than the prison. He was sure that a great deal of his fierce hatred of our social system, of the cruelty and injustice of life, was due to his own maimed condition, to the indignities and maltreatment it had caused him.

He spoke with intense feeling. He had been married twice, he continued; both marriages were failures. Since then, he went on, he had given up hope for a great love — until he met me, when the old yearning came upon him again. But with it returned the monster of tormenting shyness. For months a great conflict had been raging within him. Fear that he was repellent to me haunted him. He became obsessed by one thought — to win me, to bind me to himself, to make himself indispensable to me. When he realized that I had talent and the making of a forceful speaker, he clutched at it as a means of reaching my heart. In the cab on the way to Forty-second Street his love had overcome his fears. He hoped that I also loved him, in spite of his affliction. But when I returned from my trip, he saw the change at once: I had awakened to independent thinking, I had slipped out of his reach. It made him frantic, roused bitter recollections, and drove him to attack the one he loved and wanted so much. Now, he concluded, he asked for nothing more than friendship.

I was stirred to my depths by the simple, frank confession of a tormented being. It was too overwhelming for speech. In silence I took Most's hand. Years of suppressed intensity crushed my body, cried out ecstatically, dissolving in me. His kisses mingled with my tears covering the poor mutilated face. It was beautiful now.

During the two weeks of our tour I saw Most alone only occasionally: for an hour or two during the day or while journeying from one city to another. The rest of the time he was busy with comrades. I marvelled how he could talk and drink until the last moment before going on the platform and then speak with such fire and abandon. He seemed oblivious of the audience, yet I was sure that he was aware of everything that went on around him. Most could, in the midst of an oratorical pitch, take out his watch to see if he had not spoken too long. Was his speech studied, I wondered; not at all spontaneous? It troubled me considerably. I hated to think that he did not intensely feel what he said, that his eloquence and his expressive gestures were conscious theatricality rather than inspiration. I was impatient with myself for such thoughts and I could not tell Most about them. Besides, the little time we could spend together was too precious: I was eager to hear about the social struggle in the various countries in which he had played an important part. Germany, Austria, Switzerland, and, later, England had all been Most's arena. His enemies had not been slow to understand the danger of the young, fiery rebel. They strove to crush him. Repeated arrests, years of imprisonment and exile, followed; even the customary immunity accorded to members of the German parliament was denied him.

Most had been elected to the Reichstag by a large Socialist vote, but unlike his colleagues he soon discovered what was going on behind the scenes of the " House of Marionettes," as he had nicknamed that legislative assembly. He realized that the masses had nothing to gain from that source. He lost faith in the political machinery. By August Reinsdorf, a very remarkable young German who was later executed for conspiracy against the life of the Kaiser, Most was introduced to anarchist ideas. Subsequently, in England, he definitely broke with his Social Democratic adherents and became the spokesman of anarchism.

Our two weeks together, or what we had of them alone, gave me more information about the political and economic struggle in European countries than years of reading could have done. Most had revolutionary history at his fingers' tips: the rise of socialism as sponsored by Lassalle, Marx, and Engels; the formation of the Social Democratic Party, originally imbued with revolutionary fire, but gradually absorbing political ambitions; the difference between the various social schools; the bitter struggle between social democracy and anarchism, as personified by Marx and Engels on one side and Michael Bakunin and the Latin sections on the other — a feud that finally broke the First International.

Most spoke interestingly of his past and he also wanted to know about my childhood and youthful life. All that had preceded my coming to New York seemed to me insignificant, but Most disagreed with me about it. He insisted that early environment and conditions are powerful factors in moulding one's life. He wondered whether my awakening to social problems was due entirely to the shock the Chicago tragedy had given me, or whether it was the flowering of what had its roots in myself, in the past and in the conditions of my childhood.

I related to him incidents of my recollections — some experiences of my schooldays, which seemed particularly to interest him.

When I was eight years of age, Father sent me to Königsberg to live with my grandmother and go to school there. Grandmother was the owner of a hairdressing parlour managed by her three daughters, while she herself continued to ply the trade of smuggler. Father took me as far as Kovno, where we were met by Grandmother. On the way he sternly impressed upon my mind what a sacrifice it was going to be for him to pay forty roubles a month for my board and schooling. I was going to be in a private school, as he would not permit his child in the *Volkschule*. He was willing to do anything for me if I would be a good girl, study hard, obey my teachers, grandmother, aunts, and uncles. He would never take me back if there should be any complaint against me and he would come to Königsberg to thrash me. My heart was heavy with fear of my father. I was even too miserable to care for Grandmother's loving reception. I had only one desire, to get away from Father.

Grandmother's quarters in Königsberg were cramped, consisting of only three rooms and a kitchen. The best room had been assigned to my aunt and uncle, while I had to sleep with my youngest aunt. I had always hated sharing my bed with anyone else. In fact, that was a constant bone of contention between my sister Helena and myself. Every night we would repeat the same argument: who should sleep next to the wall and who on the outside? I insisted always on the outside; it gave me the feeling of greater freedom. Now, too, the prospect of having to sleep with my aunt was oppressing me. But there was no other place.

From the very first I took a violent dislike to my uncle. I missed our large yard, the fields, and the hills. I felt stifled and alone in the world. Before long I was sent to school. I made friends there with the other children and began to feel a little less lonely. All went well for a month; then Grandmother had to go away indefinitely. Almost immediately my purgatory began. Uncle insisted that it was no use wasting money on my schooling, and that forty roubles were barely enough for my keep. My aunts protested, but to no purpose. They were afraid of the man who bullied them all. I was taken out of school and put to work in the house.

From early morning, when I had to fetch the rolls, milk, and chocolate for our breakfast, until late at night I was kept busy, making beds, cleaning boots, scrubbing floors, and washing clothes. After a while I was even put to cooking, but my uncle was never satisfied. His gruff voice shouting orders all day long would send cold shivers down my spine. I drudged on. At night I would weep myself to sleep.

I became thin and pale; my shoes were run down at the heels, my clothes were threadbare, and I had no one to go to for comfort. My only friends were the two old maids who owned our flat and lived below, and one of my mother's sisters, a noble soul. She was ill most of the time, and I could rarely get away to see her, but I was often taken in by the two dear ladies, fed on coffee, and treated to burnt almonds, my favourite delicacy. I used to see such sweets in the

Konditorei and look yearningly at them, but I never had ten pfennige to buy any. My two friends gave me all I wanted, as well as flowers from their lovely garden.

I never dared slip into their place until my uncle was away, but their friendly greeting was balm to my aching heart. It was always the same: "*Na, Emmchen, noch immer im Gummi?*" That was because I wore large rubbers, my shoes having become too worn out.

On the rare occasions when I could get away to see my aunt Yetta she insisted that my people must be written to and told to come and take me away. I would not listen to it. I had not forgotten Father's last words; besides, Grandmother was expected every day and I knew she would save me from my dreaded uncle.

One afternoon, after an especially hard day's work and endless errands, Uncle came into the kitchen to say that I would have to deliver one more parcel. I knew by the address that it was far away. Whether from fatigue or because I disliked the man so violently, I took the courage to say that I could not make the journey; my feet hurt me too much. He slapped me full in the face, shouting: "You are not earning your keep! You are lazy!" When he left the room, I went out into the corridor, sat down on the stairs, and began to cry bitterly. All of a sudden I felt a kick in the back. I tried to grab the banister as I rolled to the bottom, landing below in a heap. The clatter roused the sisters, who came running to see what had happened. "*Das Kind is tot!*" they screamed. "The scoundrel has killed her!" They took me to their room and I clung to them, beseeching them not to let me go back to my uncle. A doctor was called, who found no bones broken, but my ankle was sprained. I was put to bed, nursed and petted as I had never been before, except by my own Helena.

The elder of the two sisters, Wilhelmina, went upstairs, stick in hand. I don't know what she said to my uncle, but after that he never came near me again. I remained with my benefactors, basking in their garden and their love, and eating burnt almonds to my heart's content.

Soon my father and grandmother arrived. Aunt Yetta had telegraphed them to come. Father was shocked by my appearance; he actually took me in his arms and kissed me. Such a thing had not happened since I was four. There was a terrible scene between Grandmother and her son-in-law, which ended in his moving out of the house with his wife. Before long, Father took me back to Popelan.

I then discovered that he had been sending forty roubles regularly every month, and that my uncle had just as regularly been reporting to him that I was doing splendidly at school.

Most was deeply moved by my story. He patted my head and kissed my hands. "*Armes Aschenprödelchen*," he kept on saying; " your childhood was like mine after that beast of a stepmother came to our house." He was now more convinced than ever, he told me, that it was the influence of my childhood that had made me what I was.

I returned to New York much strengthened in my faith, proud of having the confidence and love of Johann Most. I wanted my young friends to see him as he appeared to me. In glowing colours I told them everything that had occurred during the two weeks on tour — everything except the episode on the boat. To do otherwise, I felt, would have meant to tear open Most's heart. I could not bear even the least reflection on anything he said or did.

We had moved to Thirteenth Street. Helen Minkin had gone back to live with her sister, as their father was no longer with them. Sasha, Fedya, and I shared our new flat. It became an oasis for Most from the bedlam of the *Freiheit* office. Often there would be verbal clashes between him and Sasha: nothing personal, it seemed, but about revolutionary consistency, methods of propaganda, the difference in zeal between the German and Russian comrades, and such matters. But I could not free myself from the feeling that underneath there might be something else, something concerning me. Their disputes used to make me uneasy, but as I always succeeded in diverting their particular arguments into general issues, the discussions ended in a friendly manner.

In the winter of that year (1890) the radical ranks were aroused over the report brought from Siberia by George Kennan, an American journalist. His account of the harrowing conditions of the Russian political prisoners and exiles moved even the American press to lengthy comments. We on the East Side had all along known of the horrors through underground messages. A year before, fearful things had taken place in Yakutsk. Politicals who had protested against the maltreatment of their comrades were lured into the prison yard and fired upon by guards; a number of prisoners were killed, among them women, while several others were subsequently hanged in the prison for " inciting an outbreak." We knew of other cases equally terrible, but the American press had kept silent on the inhumanities committed by the Tsar.

Now, however, an American had brought back authentic data and photographs, and he could not be ignored. His story aroused many public-spirited men and women, among them Julia Ward Howe, William Lloyd Garrison, Edmund Noble, Lucy Stone Blackwell, James Russell Lowell, Lyman Abbott, and others, who organized the first society of the Friends of Russian Freedom. Their monthly journal, *Free Russia,* initiated the movement against the proposed extradition treaty with Russia, and their activity and agitation brought splendid results. Among other things they succeeded in preventing the delivery of the famous revolutionist Hartmann into the clutches of the Tsarist henchmen.

When we first learned of the Yakutsk outrage, Sasha and I began discussing our return to Russia. What could we hope to achieve in barren America? It would require years to acquire the language thoroughly, and Sasha had no aspirations to become a public speaker. In Russia we could engage in conspiratorial work. We belonged to Russia. For months we went about nursing the idea, but the lack of necessary funds compelled us to give it up. But now, with George Kennan's *exposé* of the Russian horrors, our plans were revived. We decided to speak to Most about them. He became enthusiastic over the idea. " Emma is fast developing into a good speaker," he said; " when she will have mastered the language, she will become a force here. But you can do more in Russia," he agreed with Sasha. He would issue a confidential appeal for funds to some trustworthy comrades in order to equip Sasha for his trip and for his work afterwards. In fact, Sasha himself could help draw up the document. Most also suggested that it would be advisable for Sasha to learn the printing trade so as to enable him to start a secret press for anarchist literature in Russia.

I was happy to see Most become rejuvenated by his ardour over our plans. I loved him for his confidence in my boy, but my heart contracted with the thought that he did not want me to go also. He surely did not realize what it would mean to me to let Sasha go alone to Russia. No, that could never be, I decided inwardly.

It was agreed that Sasha should go to New Haven; in the printing shop of a comrade there he would familiarize himself with every aspect of the work. I, too, would go to New Haven to be near Sasha.

I would invite Helen and Anna Minkin to join us, and also Fedya. We could rent a house and there we would at last carry out my original purpose: start a co-operative dressmaking establishment. We could work for the Cause, too; organize lectures and invite Most and other speakers, arrange concerts and plays, and raise funds for the propaganda. Our friends welcomed the idea, and Most said he would be glad to have a home and friends to go to, a real place of rest. Sasha immediately left for New Haven. With Fedya I disposed of the household things we could not take with us, and the rest, together with my faithful sewing-machine, we carried to New Haven. Once there, we hung out a shingle: " Goldman and Minkin, Dressmakers," but we were soon compelled to realize that customers were not exactly standing in line on the corner and that it would be necessary at first to earn money by other means. I went back to the corset-factory where I had worked after my first separation from Kershner. Three years only had passed since then, but it seemed ages, my world had changed so completely, and I with it.

Helen joined me in the factory, while Anna remained at home. She was a good seamstress, but she was not able to cut or fit dresses. I prepared the work for her in the evening, so she could finish it in the day-time.

It was a great physical strain to run the machine all day in the factory, come home to prepare supper (no one else in our little commune could cook), then cut and fit dresses for the next day. But I had been in good health for some time and we had a great purpose. Then, too, there were our social interests. We organized an educational group, arranged lectures, socials, and dances. We hardly had time to think of ourselves; our lives were busy and full.

Most came for a series of lectures and visited with us. Solotaroff also, and we celebrated the event in memory of my first hearing him in New Haven. Our group became a centre for the progressive Russian, Jewish, and German elements. Our work, being carried on in foreign languages, did not arouse the attention of the press or police.

Gradually we built up a good clientele, which gave promise of my leaving the factory soon. Sasha was making great headway at the printer's. Fedya had gone back to New York because he could secure no work in New Haven. Our propaganda activities were bringing results. The lectures drew large crowds, much literature was sold, and many subscribers to the *Freiheit* gained. Our life was active and interesting, but presently it was disturbed. Anna, who had been ailing in New York, now grew worse, showing signs of consumption; and one Sunday afternoon, at the close of Most's lecture, Helen became hysterical. There seemed to be no particular cause for her attack, but the next morning she confided to me her love for Most, declaring that she would have to leave for New York, as she could not bear being away from where he was.

I myself had of late not been much with Most alone. He would come to us after his lecture, but there were always other visitors about, and in the evening he would take the train for New York. Occasionally I went to New York at Most's request, but our meetings there generally ended in a scene. He would urge closer contact, which I could not grant. Once he grew angry, declaring he didn't have to beg from me; he could " get Helen any time." I thought he was joking, until Helen's confession. Now I wondered if Most really loved the child.

The following Sunday he lunched at our place and we went out for a walk. I asked him to tell me about his feelings for Helen. " Ridiculous," he replied; " the girl simply needs a man. She thinks she loves me. I am sure any other man would do as well." I resented the insinuation, for I knew Helen; I knew she was not one who could give herself in the way he hinted. " She yearns for love," I replied. Most laughed cynically. " Love, love — it's all sentimental nonsense," he cried; " there is only sex! " So Sasha was right, after all, I thought. Most cared for women only as females. Probably he had also never wanted me for any other reason.

I had realized long before that Most's appeal to me was not physical. It was his intellect, his brilliant abilities, his peculiar, contradictory personality that fascinated me; the suffering and persecution he had endured melted my heart, even though I resented many of his traits. He would charge me with being cold, with not loving him. Once, while we were walking in New Haven, he became especially insistent. My refusal made him angry and he launched into a tirade against Sasha. He had known long ago, he said, that I preferred " that arrogant Russian Jew " who had dared to hold him, Most, to account; to tell him what was in keeping with revolutionary ethics. He had ignored the criticism of " the young fool who knew nothing of life." But he was tired of the whole thing, and that was why he was helping him go to Russia, far away from me. I would have to choose between him and Sasha.

I had been aware of the silent antagonism between the two, but Most had never spoken of Sasha before in such a manner. It stung me to the quick. I forgot Most's greatness; I was conscious only that he had dared to attack what was the most precious thing to me, my Sasha, my wild, inspired boy. I wanted Most and the very hills to know my love for this " arrogant Russian Jew." I cried it out, impulsively, passionately. I, too, was a Russian Jew. Was he, Most, the anarchist, an anti-Semite? And how dare he say that he wanted me all to himself? Was I an object, to be taken and owned? What kind of anarchism was that? Sasha had been right in claiming that Most was no longer an anarchist.

Most kept silent. Presently I heard a moan as of a wounded animal. My outburst came to an abrupt stop. He lay stretched on the ground, face downward, his hands clenched. Various emotions struggled within me — love for Sasha, mortification that I had spoken so harshly, anger with Most, intense compassion for him, as he lay like a child before me, crying. I lifted his head gently. I longed to tell him how sorry I felt, but words seemed banal. He looked up into my face and whispered: " *Mein Kind, mein Kind,* Sasha is a lucky dog to have such love. I wonder if he appreciates it." He buried his head in my lap and we sat in silence.

Suddenly voices broke upon our ears. " Get up, you two, get up! What do you mean making love in public? You are arrested for disorderly conduct." Most was about to raise himself. Cold terror clutched me, not for myself, but for him. I knew that if they recognized him they would take him to the station-house, and the next day the papers would again carry scurrilous stories about him. Quick as lightning the thought came to me to make up some yarn, anything that would prevent a scandal. " I am so glad you have come," I said; " my father had a sudden attack of dizziness. I was hoping someone would pass along so we could get a doctor. Won't one of you gentlemen do something? " The two broke out into loud laughter. " Father, huh, you shrew! Well, if your father will give us five bucks, we'll let you off this time." I fumbled in my purse nervously and got out the only five-dollar bill I owned. The men left, their suggestive laugh grating on my ears.

Most sat bolt upright, trying hard to suppress a chuckle. " You are clever," he said; " but I can see now that I shall never be anything else to you but a father." That evening, after the lecture, I did not go to the station to see Most off.

Early next morning I was torn out of sleep by Sasha. Anna had had a hæmorrhage of the lungs. The physician, hurriedly summoned, said the case was serious and ordered Anna to a sanatorium. Some days later Sasha took her to New York. I remained in New Haven to wind up our affairs. My great plan of a co-operative venture had gone to smash.

In New York we rented a flat on Forsythe Street. Fedya continued to make crayon enlargements whenever he was lucky enough to get orders. I again took up piece-work. Sasha worked as compositor on the *Freiheit,* still clinging to the hope that Most would enable him to go to Russia. The appeal for funds, composed by Most and Sasha, had been sent out, and we anxiously awaited the results.

I spent much time in the *Freiheit* office, where the tables were piled high with European exchanges. One of them particularly attracted my attention. It was *Die Autonomie,* a German anarchist weekly published in London. While not comparable with the *Freiheit* in force and picturesqueness of language, it nevertheless seemed to me to express anarchism in a clearer and more convincing manner. One time, when I had mentioned the publication to Most, he became enraged. He told me curtly that the people behind the venture were shady characters, that they had been mixed up with " the spy Peukert, who betrayed John Neve, one of our best German comrades, into the hands of the police." It had never occurred to me then to doubt Most and I ceased reading the *Autonomie.*

But nearer acquaintance with the movement and my other experiences showed me Most's partiality. I began to read the *Autonomie* again. Soon I came to the conclusion that, however correct Most might be about the personnel of the paper, its tenets were much closer to what anarchism had come to mean to me than those of the *Freiheit.* The *Autonomie* stressed more the freedom of the individual and the independence of groups. Its entire tone held a powerful appeal for me. My two friends felt the same way. Sasha suggested that we get in touch with the comrades in London.

Before long we learned of the existence of the Group *Autonomie* in New York. Its weekly gatherings were on Saturdays, and we decided to visit the place on Fifth Street. It bore the peculiar name *Zum Groben Michel,* which well corresponded with the rough exterior and gruff manner of its giant owner. The leading spirit of the group was Joseph Peukert.

Having been influenced by Most against Peukert, we long fought the latter's version of the story that held him responsible for the arrest and imprisonment of Neve. But after months of association with Peukert we became convinced that, whatever might have been his share in that terrible affair, he could not have been a deliberate party to treachery.

Joseph Peukert had at one time played a very important rôle in the socialist movement of Austria. But he could in no sense compare with Johann Most. He lacked the vivid personality of the latter, his genius and fascinating spontaneity. Peukert was grave, pedantic, utterly devoid of humour. At first I believed that his sombreness was due to the persecution he had suffered, the accusation of traitor cast against him, which had made him a pariah. But soon I came to understand that his inferiority was conditioned in himself, and that, in fact, it was the dominant force in his hatred of Most. Still our sympathies went out to Peukert. We felt that the feud between the two anarchistic camps — between the followers of Most and those of Peukert — was to a large extent the result of personal vanities. We thought it fair that Peukert be given a hearing before a group of impartial comrades. In this view we were supported by some members of the Pioneers of Liberty, to which both Sasha and Fedya belonged.

At the national conference of the Yiddish anarchist organizations in December 1890 Sasha proposed that the Most-Peukert charges be taken up for a thorough investigation, and that both men be asked to bring their evidence. When Most learned of it, all his personal antagonism and bitterness against Sasha broke out into uncontrolled fury. " That arrogant young Jew," he cried; " that *Grünschnabel* — how dare he doubt Most and the comrades who long ago proved that Peukert was a spy? " Again I felt that Sasha was right in his estimate of Most. Had he not maintained for a long time that Most was a tyrant who wanted to rule with an iron hand under the guise of anarchism? Had he not repeatedly told me that Most was no longer a revolutionist? " You can do what you please," Sasha now said to me, " but I am through with Most and the *Freiheit.*" He would give up his job on the paper at once.

I had been too close to Most, had looked too deeply into his soul, had felt too strongly his charm and fascination, his heights and depths, to give him up so easily. I would go to him and try to smooth his troubled spirit, as I had done so often. I was sure Most loved our beautiful ideal. Had he not given up everything for it? Had he not suffered pain and indignities for its sake? Surely he could be made to see the great harm to the movement which his feud with Peukert had already caused. I would go to him.

Sasha called me a blind worshipper; he had known all along, he said, that Most the man meant more to me than Most the revolutionist. Yet I could not agree with Sasha's rigid distinctions. When I had first heard him emphasize the greater importance of the Cause over life and beauty, something in me had rebelled. But I was never convinced that he was wrong. No one with such singleness of purpose, such selfless devotion, could be wrong. It must be something in myself, I felt, that bound me to the earth, to the human side of those who came into my life. I often thought that I must be weak, that I would never reach Sasha's revolutionary, idealistic heights. But — well, at least I could love him for his zeal. Some day I would show him how great my devotion could be.

I went to the *Freiheit* office to see Most. How changed was his manner to me, what a contrast to my first memorable visit! I felt it even before he said one word. " What do you want with me, now that you are with that dreadful group? " he greeted me. " You have chosen my enemies as your friends." I stepped close to him, remarking that I could not argue in the office. Would he not go out with me that evening — just for old friendship's sake? " Old friendship's sake! " he cried derisively; " it was beautiful while it lasted. Where is it now? You have seen fit to go with my enemies and you have preferred a mere youngster to me! Whoever is not with me is against me! " But while he kept on talking angrily, I thought I detected a change in his tone. It was no longer so harsh. It had been his voice that had originally struck deep into my being; I had learned to love it, to understand its tremulous changeability from the hardness of steel to mellow tenderness. I was always able to distinguish the heights and depths of his emotion by the timbre of his voice. By this I now knew that he was no longer angry.

I took him by the hand. " Please, Hannes, come, won't you? " He pressed me to his heart. " You are a *Hexe;* you are a terrible woman. You will be the undoing of every man. But I love you, I will come."

We went to a café on Sixth Avenue and Forty-second Street. It was a famous gathering-place for theatrical people, gamblers, and prostitutes. He chose the place because comrades never frequented it.

It was a long time since we had been out together, since I had watched the wonderful transformation that Most always underwent after a few glasses of wine. His changed mood would transport me to a different world, a world without discord and strife, without a Cause to bind one, or opinions of comrades to consider. All differences were forgotten. When we separated, I had not spoken to him about the Peukert case.

The next day I received a letter from Most, enclosing data on the Peukert affair. I read the letter first. Again he poured out his heart as on our trip to Boston. His plaint was love, and why it must end; it was not only that he could not continue to share me with another, but that he could no longer support the increasing differences between us. He was sure that I would go on growing, becoming an ever-increasing force in the movement. But this very assurance convinced him that our relations were bound to lack permanence. A home, children, the care and attention ordinary women can give, who have no other interest in life but the man they love and the children they bear him — that was what he needed and felt he had found in Helen. Her attraction for him was not the tempestuous passion I had awakened. Our last embrace was only one more proof of the hold I had on him. It was ecstatic, but it left him in a turmoil, in a conflict, unhappy. The squabbles in the ranks, the precarious condition of the *Freiheit,* and his own impending return to Blackwell's Island, all combined to rob him of peace, to unfit him for work which was, after all, his great task in life. He hoped that I would understand, that I would even help him to find the peace he sought.

I read and reread the letter, locked in my room. I wanted to be alone with all that Most had meant to me, all he had given me. What had I given him? Not so much as even the ordinary woman gives the man she loves. I hated to admit, even to myself, that I lacked what he wanted so much. I knew I could bring him children if I would have the operation. How wonderful it would be to have a child by this unique personality! I sat lost in the thought. But soon something more insistent awakened in my brain — Sasha, the life and work we had together. Would I give it all up? No, no, that was impossible, that should never be! But why Sasha rather than Most? To be sure, Sasha had youth and indomitable zeal. Ah, yes, his zeal — was not that the cement that had bound me to him? But suppose Sasha, too, should want a wife, home, children. What then? Should I be able to give him that? But Sasha would never expect such a thing — he lived only for the Cause and he wanted me also to live only for it.

An agonized night followed that day. I could find no answer and no peace.

ABRAHAM GOLDMAN
EMMA GOLDMAN'S FATHER

CHAPTER VII

A T THE INTERNATIONAL SOCIALIST CONGRESS HELD IN PARIS IN 1889 the decision had been made to turn the first of May into a world-wide holiday of labour. The idea caught the imagination of the progressive workers in every land. The birth of spring was to mark the reawakening of the masses to new efforts for emancipation. In this year, 1891, the decision of the Congress was to find wide application. On the first of May the toilers were to lay down their tools, stop their machines, leave the factories and mines. In festive attire they were to demonstrate with their banners, marching to the inspiring strains of revolutionary music and song. Everywhere meetings were to take place to articulate the aspirations of labour.

The Latin countries had already begun their preparations. The socialist and anarchist publications carried detailed reports of the intense activities scheduled for the great day. In America, too, the call went out to make the first of May an impressive demonstration of the strength and power of the workers. Nightly sessions took place to organize for the event. I was again assigned to canvass the trade unions. The press of the country began a campaign of vituperation, charging the radical elements with plotting revolution. The unions were urged to purge their ranks of the " foreign riff-raff and criminals who came to our country to destroy its democratic institutions." The campaign had its effect. The conservative labour bodies refused to lay down their tools and to participate in the first-of-May demonstration. The others were too small, numerically, and still too terrorized by the attacks on the German unions during the Chicago Haymarket days. Only the most radical among German, Jewish, and Russian organizations held to their original decision. They would demonstrate.

The celebration in New York was arranged by the socialists. They secured Union Square and promised to permit the anarchists to speak from their own platform. But at the last moment the socialist organizers refused to let us erect our platform on the square. Most did not arrive on time, but I was there with a group of young people, including Sasha, Fedya, and several Italian comrades. We were determined to have our say on this great occasion. When it became evident that we could not have our platform, the boys lifted me up on one of the socialist trucks. I began to speak. The chairman left, but in a few minutes he returned with the owner of the wagon. I continued to speak. The man hitched his horse to the truck and started off at a trot. I still continued to speak. The crowd, failing to take in the situation, followed us out of the square for a couple of blocks while I was speaking.

Presently the police appeared and began beating back the crowd. The driver stopped. Our boys quickly lifted me off and hurried me away. The morning papers were filled with a story about a mysterious young woman on a truck who had waved a red flag and urged revolution, "her high-pitched voice putting the horse to flight."

A few weeks later the news arrived that the Supreme Court had decided against John Most's appeal. We knew it meant Blackwell's Island again. Sasha forgot his differences with Most, and I no longer cared that he had cast me out of his heart and life. Nothing mattered now except the cruel fact that Most would be returned to prison, that he would be shaved again, that his deformity, from which he had suffered so much, would again become the butt of ridicule and humiliation.

We were the first in court. Most was brought in, accompanied by his attorneys and his bondsman, our old comrade Julius Hoffmann. Many friends streamed in, Helen Minkin among them. Most seemed indifferent to his doom, holding himself erect and proud. He was again the old warrior, the unflinching rebel.

The proceedings lasted only a few minutes. In the corridor I rushed over to Most, took his hand, and whispered: " Hannes, dear Hannes, I'd give anything to take your place!" "I know you would, my *Blondkopf*. Write to me at the island." Then he was led away.

Sasha accompanied Most to Blackwell's Island. He returned enthusiastic about his splendid bearing: he had never seen him more rebellious, more dignified, more brilliant. Even the newspaper men had been impressed. "We must bury our differences, we must work with Most," Sasha declared,

A mass meeting was decided upon to voice our protest against the decision of the Supreme Court and to raise funds to continue the fight for Most and help make his life in prison as endurable as possible. Sympathy with our imprisoned comrade was general in the radical ranks. Within forty-eight hours we succeeded in filling a large hall, where I was one of the speakers. My speech was not merely about Johann Most, the symbol of universal revolt, the spokesman of anarchism, but also of the man who had been my great inspiration, my teacher and comrade.

During the winter Fedya left for Springfield, Massachusetts, to work for a photographer. After a while he wrote that I could have a job at the same place, taking care of the orders. I was glad of the chance; it would take me away from New York, from the everlasting grind of the sewing-machine. Sasha and I had been supporting ourselves with piece-work on boys' jumpers. Often we worked eighteen hours a day in the one light room of our flat, and I had to do the cooking and the housework besides. Springfield would be a change and a relief.

The work was not hard, and it was soothing to be with Fedya, who was so different from both Most and Sasha. We had many tastes in common outside of the movement: our love for beauty, for flowers, for the theatre. There was very little of the last in Springfield; in fact, the American play and theatre had become abhorrent to me. After Königsberg, St. Petersburg, and the German Irving Place Theatre in New York the ordinary American play seemed flat and tawdry.

Fedya was so successful with his work that it seemed folly to keep on enriching our employer. It occurred to us that we might start out for ourselves and have Sasha with us. Though Sasha had never complained, I could sense in his letters that he was not happy in New York. Fedya suggested that we open our own studio. We decided to go to Worcester, Massachusetts, and to invite Sasha to join us.

We fixed up an office, put out a sign, and waited for customers. But none came, and our little savings were dwindling. We hired a horse and buggy to enable us to visit near-by country places and secure orders from the farmers for crayon enlargements of family photographs. Sasha would drive, and whenever we bumped into trees and sidewalks, he would dilate on the natural cussedness of our horse. Often we travelled for hours before securing any work.

We were struck by the great difference between the New Englanders and the Russian peasant. The latter seldom had enough for himself to eat, yet he would never fail to offer the stranger bread and kvass (cider). The German peasants also, as I remembered from my schooldays, would invite us to their " best room," put milk and butter on the table, and urge us to partake. But here, in free America, where the farmers owned acres of land and much cattle, we were lucky to be admitted at all or be given a glass of water. Sasha used to say that the American farmer lacked sympathy and kindness because he himself had never known want. " He is really a small capitalist," he argued. " It is different with the Russians, or even with the German peasants; they are proletarians. That is why they are warm-hearted and hospitable." I was not convinced. I had worked with proletarians in factories and I did not always find them helpful and generous. But Sasha's faith in the people was infectious and dispelled my doubts.

Frequently we were on the point of giving up. The family we lived with used to advise us to open a lunch-room or ice-cream parlour. The suggestion at first seemed to us absurd; we had neither funds nor aspirations for such a venture. Besides, it was against our principles to engage in business.

Just at that time the radical press was again aroused by new atrocities in Russia. The old yearning took hold of us to return to our native country. But where get enough money for the purpose? The private call sent out by Most had found no adequate response. Then it occurred to us that an ice-cream parlour might prove the means to our end. The more we thought of it, the more convinced we became that it offered the only solution.

Our savings consisted of fifty dollars. Our landlord, who had sug, gested the idea, said he would lend us a hundred and fifty dollars. We secured a store, and within a couple of weeks Sasha's skill with hammer and saw, Fedya's with his paint and brush, and my own good German housekeeping training succeeded in turning the neglected ramshackle place into an attractive lunch-room. It was spring and not yet warm enough for an ice-cream rush, but the coffee I brewed, our sandwiches and dainty dishes, were beginning to be appreciated, and soon we were kept busy till early morning hours. Within a short time we had paid back our landlord's loan and were able to invest in a soda-water fountain and some lovely coloured dishes. We felt we were on the way to the realization of our long-cherished dream.

CHAPTER VIII

IT WAS MAY 1892. NEWS FROM PITTSBURGH ANNOUNCED THAT trouble had broken out between the Carnegie Steel Company and its employees organized in the Amalgamated Association of Iron and Steel Workers. It was one of the biggest and most efficient labour bodies of the country, consisting mostly of Americans, men of decision and grit, who would assert their rights. The Carnegie Company, on the other hand, was a powerful corporation, known as a hard master. It was particularly significant that Andrew Carnegie, its president, had temporarily turned over the entire management to the company's chairman, Henry Clay Frick, a man known for his enmity to labour. Frick was also the owner of extensive coke-fields, where unions were prohibited and the workers were ruled with an iron hand.

The high tariff on imported steel had greatly boomed the American steel industry. The Carnegie Company had practically a monopoly of it and enjoyed unprecedented prosperity. Its largest mills were in Homestead, near Pittsburgh, where thousands of workers were employed, their tasks requiring long training and high skill. Wages were arranged between the company and the union, according to a sliding scale based on the prevailing market price of steel products. The current agreement was about to expire, and the workers presented a new wage schedule, calling for an increase because of the higher market prices and enlarged output of the mills.

The philanthropic Andrew Carnegie conveniently retired to his castle in Scotland, and Frick took full charge of the situation. He declared that henceforth the sliding scale would be abolished. The company would make no more agreements with the Amalgamated Association; it would itself determine the wages to be paid. In fact, he would not recognize the union at all. He would not treat with the employees collectively, as before. He would close the mills, and the men might consider themselves discharged. Thereafter they would have to apply for work individually, and the pay would be arranged with every worker separately. Frick curtly refused the peace advances of the workers' organization, declaring that there was "nothing to arbitrate." Presently the mills were closed. "Not a strike, but a lock-out," Frick announced. It was an open declaration of war.

Feeling ran high in Homestead and vicinity. The sympathy of the entire country was with the men. Even the most conservative part of the press condemned Frick for his arbitrary and drastic methods. They charged him with deliberately provoking a crisis that might assume national proportions, in view of the great numbers of men locked out by Frick's action, and the probable effect upon affiliated unions and on related industries.

Labour throughout the country was aroused. The steel-workers declared that they were ready to take up the challenge of Frick: they would insist on their right to organize and to deal collectively with their employers. Their tone was manly, ringing with the spirit of their rebellious forebears of the Revolutionary War.

Far away from the scene of the impending struggle, in our little ice-cream parlour in the city of Worcester, we eagerly followed developments. To us it sounded the awakening of the American worker, the long-awaited day of his resurrection. The native toiler had risen, he was beginning to feel his mighty strength, he was determined to break the chains that had held him in bondage so long, we thought. Our hearts were fired with admiration for the men of Homestead.

We continued our daily work, waiting on customers, frying pancakes, serving tea and ice-cream; but our thoughts were in Homestead, with the brave steel-workers. We became so absorbed in the news that we would not permit ourselves enough time even for sleep. At daybreak one of the boys would be off to get the first editions of the papers. We saturated ourselves with the events in Homestead to the exclusion of everything else. Entire nights we would sit up discussing the various phases of the situation, almost engulfed by the possibilities of the gigantic struggle.

One afternoon a customer came in for an ice-cream, while I was alone in the store. As I set the dish down before him, I caught the large headlines of his paper: "Latest developments in Home-STEAD — FAMILIES OF STRIKERS EVICTED FROM THE COMPANY HOUSES — WOMAN IN CONFINEMENT CARRIED OUT INTO STREET BY

SHERIFFS." I read over the man's shoulder Frick's dictum to the workers: he would rather see them dead than concede to their demands, and he threatened to import Pinkerton detectives. The brutal bluntness of the account, the inhumanity of Frick towards the evicted mother, inflamed my mind. Indignation swept my whole being. I heard the man at the table ask: "Are you sick, young lady? Can I do anything for you?" "Yes, you can let me have your paper," I blurted out. "You won't have to pay me for the ice-cream. But I must ask you to leave. I must close the store." The man looked at me as if I had gone crazy.

I locked up the store and ran full speed the three blocks to our little flat. It was Homestead, not Russia; I knew it now. We belonged in Homestead. The boys, resting for the evening shift, sat up as I rushed into the room, newspaper clutched in my hand. "What has happened, Emma? You look terrible!" I could not speak. I handed them the paper.

Sasha was the first on his feet. "Homestead!" he exclaimed. "I must go to Homestead!" I flung my arms around him, crying out his name. I, too, would go. "We must go tonight," he said; "the great moment has come at last!" Being internationalists, he added, it mattered not to us where the blow was struck by the workers; we must be with them. We must bring them our great message and help them see that it was not only for the moment that they must strike, but for all time, for a free life, for anarchism. Russia had many heroic men and women, but who was there in America? Yes, we must go to Homestead, tonight!

I had never heard Sasha so eloquent. He seemed to have grown in stature. He looked strong and defiant, an inner light on his face making him beautiful, as he had never appeared to me before.

We immediately went to our landlord and informed him of our decision to leave. He replied that we were mad; we were doing so well, we were on the way to fortune. If we would hold out to the end of the summer, we would be able to clear at least a thousand dollars. But he argued in vain — we were not to be moved. We invented the story that a very dear relative was in a dying condition, and that therefore we must depart. We would turn the store over to him; all we wanted was the evening's receipts. We would remain until closing-hours, leave everything in order, and give him the keys.

That evening we were especially busy. We had never before had so many customers. By one o'clock we had sold out everything. Our receipts were seventy-five dollars. We left on an early morning train.

On the way we discussed our immediate plans. First of all, we would print a manifesto to the steel-workers. We would have to find somebody to translate it into English, as we were still unable to express our thoughts correctly in that tongue. We would have the German and English texts printed in New York and take them with us to Pittsburgh. With the help of the German comrades there, meetings could be organized for me to address. Fedya was to remain in New York till further developments.

From the station we went straight to the flat of Mollock, an Austrian comrade we had met in the *Autonomie* group. He was a baker who worked at night; but Peppie, his wife, with her two children was at home. We were sure she could put us up.

She was surprised to see the three of us march in, bag and baggage, but she made us welcome, fed us, and suggested that we go to bed. But we had other things to do.

Sasha and I went in search of Claus Timmermann, an ardent German anarchist we knew. He had considerable poetic talent and wrote forceful propaganda. In fact, he had been the editor of an anarchist paper in St. Louis before coming to New York. He was a likable fellow and entirely trustworthy, though a considerable drinker. We felt that Claus was the only person we could safely draw into our plan. He caught our spirit at once. The manifesto was written that afternoon. It was a flaming call to the men of Homestead to throw off the yoke of capitalism, to use their present struggle as a stepping-stone to the destruction of the wage system, and to continue towards social revolution and anarchism.

A few days after our return to New York the news was flashed across the country of the slaughter of steel-workers by Pinkertons. Frick had fortified the Homestead mills, built a high fence around them. Then, in the dead of night, a barge packed with strike-breakers, under protection of heavily armed Pinkerton thugs, quietly stole up the Monongahela River. The steel-men had learned of Frick's move. They stationed themselves along the shore, determined to drive back Frick's hirelings. When the barge got within range, the Pinkertons had opened fire, without warning, killing a number of Homestead men on the shore, among them a little boy, and wounding scores of others.

The wanton murders aroused even the daily papers. Several came out in strong editorials, severely criticizing Frick. He had gone too far; he had added fuel to the fire in the labour ranks and would have himself to blame for any desperate acts that might come.

We were stunned. We saw at once that the time for our manifesto had passed. Words had lost their meaning in the face of the innocent blood spilled on the banks of the Monongahela. Intuitively each felt what was surging in the heart of the others. Sasha broke the silence. " Frick is the responsible factor in this crime," he said; " he must be made to stand the consequences." It was the psychological moment for an *Attentat;* the whole country was aroused, everybody was considering Frick the perpetrator of a coldblooded murder. A blow aimed at Frick would re-echo in the poorest hovel, would call the attention of the whole world to the real cause behind the Homestead struggle. It would also strike terror in the enemy's ranks and make them realize that the proletariat of America had its avengers.

Sasha had never made bombs before, but Most's *Science of Revolutionary Warfare* was a good text-book. He would procure dynamite from a comrade he knew on Staten Island. He had waited for this sublime moment to serve the Cause, to give his life for the people. He would go to Pittsburgh.

"We will go with you! " Fedya and I cried together. But Sasha would not listen to it. He insisted that it was unnecessary and criminal to waste three lives on one man.

We sat down, Sasha between us, holding our hands. In a quiet and even tone he began to unfold to us his plan. He would perfect a time regulator for the bomb that would enable him to kill Frick, yet save himself. Not because he wanted to escape. No; he wanted to live long enough to justify his act in court, so that the American people might know that he was not a criminal, but an idealist.

" I will kill Frick," Sasha said, " and of course I shall be condemned to death. I will die proudly in the assurance that I gave my life for the people. But I will die by my own hand, like Lingg. Never will I permit our enemies to kill me."

I hung on his lips. His clarity, his calmness and force, the sacred fire of his ideal, enthralled me, held me spellbound. Turning to me, he continued in his deep voice. I was the born speaker, the propagandist, he said. I could do a great deal for his act. I could articulate its meaning to the workers. I could explain that he had had no personal grievance against Frick, that as a human being Frick was no less to him than anyone else. Frick was the symbol of wealth and power, of the injustice and wrong of the capitalistic class, as well as personally responsible for the shedding of the workers' blood. Sasha's act would be directed against Frick, not as a man, but as the enemy of labour. Surely I must see how important it was that I remain behind to plead the meaning of his deed and its message throughout the country.

Every word he said beat upon my brain like a sledge-hammer. The longer he talked, the more conscious I became of the terrible fact that he had no need of me in his last great hour. The realization swept away everything else — message, Cause, duty, propaganda. What meaning could these things have compared with the force that had made Sasha flesh of my flesh and blood of my blood from the moment that I had heard his voice and felt the grip of his hand at our first meeting? Had our three years together shown him so little of my soul that he could tell me calmly to go on living after he had been blown to pieces or strangled to death? Is not true love — not ordinary love, but the love that longs to share to the uttermost with the beloved — is it not more compelling than aught else? Those Russians had known it, Jessie Helfmann and Sophia Perovskaya; they had gone with their men in life and in death. I could do no less.

" I will go with you, Sasha," I cried; " I must go with you! I know that as a woman I can be of help. I could gain access to Frick easier than you. I could pave the way for your act. Besides, I simply must go with you. Do you understand, Sasha? "

We had a feverish week. Sasha's experiments took place at night when everybody was asleep. While Sasha worked, I kept watch. I lived in dread every moment for Sasha, for our friends in the flat, the children, and the rest of the tenants. What if anything should go wrong — but, then, did not the end justify the means? Our end was the sacred cause of the oppressed and exploited people. It was for them that we were going to give our lives. What if a few should have to perish? — the many would be made free and could live in beauty and in comfort. Yes, the end in this case justified the means.

After we had paid our fare from Worcester to New York, we had about sixty dollars left. Twenty had already been used up since our arrival. The material Sasha bought for the bomb had cost a good deal and we still had another week in New York. Besides, I needed a dress and shoes, which, together with the fare to Pittsburgh, would amount to fifty dollars. I realized with a start that we required a large sum of money. I knew no one who could give us so much; besides, I could never tell him the purpose. After days of canvassing in the scorching July heat I succeeded in collecting twenty-five dollars. Sasha finished his preparatory work and went to Staten Island to test the bomb. When he returned, I could tell by his expression that something terrible had happened. I learned soon enough; the bomb had not gone off.

Sasha said it was due either to the wrong chemical directions or to the dampness of the dynamite. The second bomb, having been made from the same material, would most likely also fail. A week's work and anxiety and forty precious dollars wasted! What now? We had no time for lamentations or regrets; we had to act quickly.

Johann Most, of course. He was the logical person to go to. He had constantly propagated the doctrine of individual acts; every one of his articles and speeches was a direct call to the *Tat*. He would be glad to learn that someone in America had come forward at last to commit a heroic act. Most was certainly aware of the heinous crime of Frick: the *Freiheit* had pointed him out as the responsible person. Most would help.

Sasha resented the suggestion. He said it had been evident from Most's behaviour since his release from Blackwell's Island that he wanted nothing more to do with us. He was too bitter over our affiliation with the Group *Autonomie*. I knew Sasha was right. While Most was in the penitentiary, I had written repeatedly to him, but he never replied. Since he had come out, he had not asked to see me. I knew he was living with Helen, that she was with child; and I had no right to break in on their life. Yes, Sasha was right, the gulf had grown too wide.

I recalled that Peukert and one of his friends had been given charge of a small legacy recently left by a comrade. Among the latter's effects a paper was found authorizing Peukert to use the money and a gun for propaganda purposes. I had known the man and I was sure he would have approved of our plan. And Peukert? He was not, like Most, an outspoken champion of individual revolutionary deeds, but he could not fail to see the significance of an act against Frick. He would surely want to help. It would be a wonderful opportunity for him to silence for ever the current suspicions and doubts about him.

I sought him out the following evening. He refused his aid point-blank. He could not give me the money, much less the gun, he declared, unless he knew for whom and for what. I struggled against the disclosure, but, fearing that all might be lost if I failed to get the money, I finally told him it was for an act on the life of Frick, though I did not mention who was to commit the act. He agreed that such a deed would prove of propagandistic value; but he said that he would have to consult the other members of his group before he could give me what I asked. I could not consent to having so many people know about the plan. They would be sure to spread the news, and it would get to the ears of the press. More than these considerations was the distinct feeling that Peukert did not want to have anything to do with the matter. It bore out my first impression of the man: he was not made of the stuff of heroes or martyrs.

I did not have to tell the boys of my failure. It was written on my face. Sasha said that the act must be carried out, no matter how we got the money. It was now clear that the two of us would not be able to go. I would have to listen to his plea and let him go alone. He reiterated his faith in me and in my strength and assured me of the great joy I had given him when I insisted upon going with him to Pittsburgh. "But," he said, "we are too poor. Poverty is always a deciding factor in our actions. Besides, we are merely dividing our labours, each doing what he is best fitted for." He was not an agitator; that was my field, and it would be my task to interpret his act to the people. I cried out against his arguments, though I felt their force. We had no money. I knew that he would go in any event; nothing would stop him, of that I was certain.

Our whole fortune consisted of fifteen dollars. That would take Sasha to Pittsburgh, buy some necessaries, and still leave him a dollar for the first day's food and lodging. Our Allegheny comrades Nold and Bauer, whom Sasha meant to look up, would give him hospitality for a few days until I could raise more money. Sasha had decided not to confide his mission to them; there was no need for it, he felt, and it was never advisable for too many people to be taken into conspiratorial plans. He would require at least another twenty dollars for a gun and a suit of clothes. He might be able to buy the weapon cheap at some pawnshop. I had no idea where I could get the money, but I knew that I would find it somehow.

Those with whom we were staying were told that Sasha would

leave that evening, but the motive for his departure was not revealed. There was a simple farewell supper, everyone joked and laughed, and I joined in the gaiety. I strove to be jolly to cheer Sasha, but it was laughter that masked suppressed sobs. Later we accompanied Sasha to the Baltimore and Ohio Station. Our friends kept in the distance, while Sasha and I paced the platform, our hearts too full for speech.

The conductor drawled out: " All aboard! " I clung to Sasha. He was on the train, while I stood on the lower step. His face bent low to mine, his hand holding me, he whispered: " My sailor girl," (his pet name for me), " comrade, you will be with me to the last. You will proclaim that I gave what was dearest to me for an ideal, for the great suffering people."

The train moved. Sasha loosened my hold, gently helping me to jump off the step. I ran after the vanishing train, waving and calling to him: " Sasha, Sashenka! " The steaming monster disappeared round the bend and I stood glued, straining after it, my arms outstretched for the precious life that was being snatched away from me.

I woke up with a very clear idea of how I could raise the money for Sasha. I would go on the street. I lay wondering how such a notion could have come to me. I recollected Dostoyevsky's *Crime and Punishment,* which had made a profound impression on me, especially the character of Sonya, Marmeladov's daughter. She had become a prostitute in order to support her little brothers and sisters and to relieve her consumptive stepmother of worry. I visioned Sonya as she lay on her cot, face to the wall, her shoulders twitching. I could almost feel the same way. Sensitive Sonya could sell her body; why not I? My cause was greater than hers. It was Sasha — his great deed — the people. But should I be able to do it, to go with strange men — for money? The thought revolted me. I buried my face in the pillow to shut out the light. " Weakling, coward," an inner voice said. " Sasha is giving his life, and you shrink from giving your body, miserable coward! " It took me several hours to gain control of myself. When I got out of bed my mind was made up.

My main concern now was whether I could make myself attractive enough to men who seek out girls on the street. I stepped over to the mirror to inspect my body. I looked tired, but my complexion was good. I should need no make-up. My curly blond hair showed off well with my blue eyes. Too large in the hips for my age, I thought; I was just twenty-three. Well, I came from Jewish stock. Besides, I would wear a corset and I should look taller in high heels (I had never worn either before).

Corsets, slippers with high heels, dainty underwear — where should I get money for it all? I had a white linen dress, trimmed with Caucasian embroidery. I could get some soft flesh-coloured material and sew the underwear myself. I knew the stores on Grand Street carried cheap goods.

I dressed hurriedly and went in search of the servant in the apartment who had shown a liking for me, and she lent me five dollars without any question. I started off to make my purchases. When I returned, I locked myself in my room. I would see no one. I was busy preparing my outfit and thinking of Sasha. What would he say? Would he approve? Yes, I was sure he would. He had always insisted that the end justified the means, that the true revolutionist will not shrink from anything to serve the Cause.

Saturday evening, July 16, 1892, I walked up and down Fourteenth Street, one of the long procession of girls I had so often seen plying their trade. I felt no nervousness at first, but when I looked at the passing men and saw their vulgar glances and their manner of approaching the women, my heart sank. I wanted to take flight, run back to my room, tear off my cheap finery, and scrub myself clean. But a voice kept on ringing in my ears: "You must hold out; Sasha — his act — everything will be lost if you fail."

I continued my tramp, but something stronger than my reason would compel me to increase my pace the moment a man came near me. One of them was rather insistent, and I fled. By eleven o'clock I was utterly exhausted. My feet hurt from the high heels, my head throbbed. I was close to tears from fatigue and disgust with my inability to carry out what I had come to do.

I made another effort. I stood on the corner of Fourteenth Street and Fourth Avenue, near the bank building. The first man that invited me — I would go with him, I had decided. A tall, distinguished-looking person, well dressed, came close. "Let's have a drink, little girl," he said. His hair was white, he appeared to be about sixty, but his face was ruddy. "All right," I replied. He took my arm and led me to a wine house on Union Square which Most had often frequented with me. "Not here!" I almost screamed; "please, not here." I led him to the back entrance of a saloon on Thirteenth Street and Third Avenue. I had once been there in the afternoon for a glass of beer. It had been clean and quiet then.

That night it was crowded, and with difficulty we secured a table. The man ordered drinks. My throat felt parched and I asked for a large glass of beer. Neither of us spoke. I was conscious of the man's scrutiny of my face and body. I felt myself growing resentful. Presently he asked: "You're a novice in the business, aren't you?" "Yes, this is my first time — but how did you know?" "I watched you as you passed me," he replied. He told me that he had noticed my haunted expression and my increased pace the moment a man came near me. He understood then that I was inexperienced; whatever might have been the reason that brought me to the street, he knew it was not mere looseness or love of excitement. "But thousands of girls are driven by economic necessity," I blurted out. He looked at me in surprise. "Where did you get that stuff?" I wanted to tell him all about the social question, about my ideas, who and what I was, but I checked myself. I must not disclose my identity: it would be too dreadful if he should learn that Emma Goldman, the anarchist, had been found soliciting on Fourteenth Street. What a juicy story it would make for the press!

He said he was not interested in economic problems and did not care what the reason was for my actions. He only wanted to tell me that there was nothing in prostitution unless one had the knack for it. "You haven't got it, that's all there is to it," he assured me. He took out a ten-dollar bill and put it down before me. "Take this and go home," he said. "But why should you give me money if you don't want me to go with you?" I asked. "Well, just to cover the expenses you must have had to rig yourself out like that," he replied; "your dress is awfully nice, even if it does not go with those cheap shoes and stockings." I was too astounded for speech.

I had met two categories of men: vulgarians and idealists. The former would never have let an opportunity pass to possess a woman and they would give her no other thought save sexual desire. The idealists stoutly defended the equality of the sexes, at least in theory, but the only men among them who practised what they preached were the Russian and Jewish radicals. This man, who had picked me up on the street and who was now with me in the back of a saloon, seemed an entirely new type. He interested me. He must be rich. But would a rich man give something for nothing? The manufacturer Garson came to my mind; he would not even give me a small raise in wages.

Perhaps this man was one of those soul-savers I had read about, people who were always cleansing New York City of vice. I asked him. He laughed and said he was not a professional busybody. If he had thought that I really wanted to be on the street, he would not have cared. "Of course, I may be entirely mistaken," he added, " but I don't mind. Just now I am convinced that you are not intended to be a streetwalker, and that even if you do succeed, you will hate it afterwards." If he were not convinced of it, he would take me for his mistress. " For always? " I cried. " There you are ! " he replied; " you are scared by the mere suggestion and yet you hope to succeed on the street. You're an awfully nice kid, but you're silly, inexperienced, childish." " I was twenty-three last month," I protested, resentful of being treated like a child. " You are an old lady," he said with a grin, " but even old folks can be babes in the woods. Look at me; I'm sixty-one and I often do foolish things." " Like believing in my innocence, for instance," I retorted. The simplicity of his manner pleased me. I asked for his name and address so as to be able to return his ten dollars some day. But he refused to give them to me. He loved mysteries, he said. On the street he held my hand for a moment, and then we turned in opposite directions.

That night I tossed about for hours. My sleep was restless; my dreams were of Sasha, Frick, Homestead, Fourteenth Street, and the affable stranger. Long after waking the next morning the dream pictures persisted. Then my eye caught my little purse on the table. I jumped up, opened it with trembling hands — it did contain the ten dollars ! It had actually happened, then !

On Monday a short note arrived from Sasha. He had met Carl Nold and Henry Bauer, he wrote. He had set the following Saturday for his act, provided I could send some money he needed at once. He was sure I would not fail him. I was a little disappointed by the letter. Its tone was cold and perfunctory, and I wondered how the stranger would write to the woman he loved. With a start I shook myself free. It was crazy to have such thoughts when Sasha was preparing to take a life and lose his own in the attempt. How could I think of that stranger and Sasha in the same breath? I must get more money for my boy.

I would wire Helena for fifteen dollars. I had not written my dear sister for many weeks, and I hated to ask her for money, knowing how poor she was. It seemed criminal. Finally I wired her that I had been taken ill and needed fifteen dollars. I knew that nothing would prevent her from getting the money if she thought that I was ill. But a sense of shame oppressed me, as once before, in St. Petersburg, when I had deceived her.

I received the money from Helena by wire. I sent twenty dollars to Sasha and returned the five I had borrowed for my finery.

EMMA GOLDMAN IN 1892

CHAPTER IX

SINCE OUR RETURN TO NEW YORK I HAD NOT BEEN ABLE TO LOOK for work. The tension of the weeks since Sasha's departure, my desperate struggle against letting him go alone, my street adventure, together with the misery I felt for having deceived Helena, completely upset me. My condition was aggravated now by the agonizing wait for Saturday, July 23, the date set by Sasha for his act. I grew restless and aimlessly walked about in the July heat, spending the evenings in *Zum Groben Michel,* the nights at Sachs's café.

In the early afternoon of Saturday, July 23, Fedya rushed into my room with a newspaper. There it was, in large black letters: " YOUNG MAN BY THE NAME OF ALEXANDER BERGMAN SHOOTS FRICK — ASSASSIN OVERPOWERED BY WORKING-MEN AFTER DESPERATE STRUGGLE."

Working-men, working-men overpowering Sasha? The paper was lying! He did the act for the working-men; they would never attack him.

Hurriedly we secured all the afternoon editions. Every one had a different description, but the main fact stood out — our brave Sasha had committed the act! Frick was still alive, but his wounds were considered fatal. He would probably not survive the night. And Sasha — they would kill him. They were going to kill him, I was sure of it. Was I going to let him die alone? Should I go on talking while he was being butchered? I must pay the same price as he — I must stand the consequences — I must share the responsibility!

I had read in the *Freiheit* that Most was to lecture that evening before the German Anarchist Local No. 1. " He will surely speak of Sasha's act," I said to Fedya. " We must go to the meeting."

I had not seen Most for a year. He now looked aged; Blackwell's Island had left its mark. He spoke in his usual manner, but Sasha's act he mentioned only at the end, in a casual way. " The papers report the attempt on the life of Frick by a young man by the name of Bergman," he said. " It is probably the usual newspaper fake. It must be some crank or perhaps Frick's own man, to create sympathy for him. Frick knows that public opinion is against him. He needs something to turn the tide in his favour."

I did not believe my own ears. I sat dumbfounded, fixedly staring at Most. He was drunk, of course, I thought. I looked about me and saw surprise on many faces. Some in the audience seemed impressed by what he had said. I noticed several suspicious-looking men near the exits; detectives, evidently.

When Most finished, I demanded the floor. I spoke scathingly of a lecturer who dared come before the public in a drunken condition. Or was Most sober, I demanded, and merely afraid of the detectives? Why did he invent the ridiculous story about Frick's " own man "? Did he not know who " Bergman " was?

Objections and protests began to be heard and soon the uproar became so great that I had to stop. Most descended from the platform; he would not answer me. Sick at heart, I left with Fedya. We noticed two men following us. For several hours we zigzagged through the streets, finally succeeding in losing them. We walked to Park Row, there to wait for the Sunday morning papers.

In feverish excitement we read the detailed story about the " assassin Alexander Berkman." He had forced his way into Frick's private office on the heels of the Negro porter who had taken in his card. He had immediately opened fire, and Frick had fallen to the ground with three bullets in his body. The first to come to his aid, the paper said, was his assistant Leishman, who was in the office at the time. Working-men, engaged on a carpenter job in the building, rushed in, and one of them felled Berkman to the ground with a hammer. At first they thought Frick dead. Then a cry was heard from him. Berkman had crawled over and got near enough to strike Frick with a dagger in the thigh. After that he was pounded into unconsciousness. He came to in the station-house, but he would answer no questions. One of the detectives grew suspicious about the appearance of Berkman's face and he nearly broke the young man's jaw trying to open his mouth. A peculiar capsule was found hidden there. When asked what it was, Berkman replied with defiant contempt: " Candy." On examination it proved to be a dynamite cartridge. The police were sure of conspiracy. They were now looking for the accomplices, especially for " a certain Bakhmetov, who had registered at one of the Pittsburgh hotels."

I felt that, on the whole, the newspaper accounts were correct. Sasha had taken a poisoned dagger with him. " In case the revolver, like the bomb, fails to work," he had said. Yes, the dagger was poisoned — nothing could save Frick. I was certain that the papers lied when they said that Sasha had fired at Leishman. I remembered how determined he was that no one except Frick should suffer, and I could not believe that working-men would come to the assistance of Frick, their enemy.

In the Group *Autonomie* I found everybody elated over Sasha's act. Peukert reproached me for not having told him for whom I wanted the money and the gun. I waved him aside. He was a weak-kneed revolutionist, I told him; I was convinced that he had been too concerned about himself to respond to my plea. The group decided that the next issue of the *Anarchist,* its weekly paper, should be entirely devoted to our brave comrade, Alexander Berkman, and his heroic deed. I was asked to write an article about Sasha. Except for a small contribution to the *Freiheit* upon one occasion, I had never written for publication before. I was much worried, fearing I should not be able to do justice to the subject. But after a night's struggle and the waste of several pads of paper, I succeeded in writing an impassioned tribute to " Alexander Berkman, the avenger of the murdered Homestead men."

The eulogistic tone of the *Anarchist* seemed to act on Most like a red rag on a bull. He had stored up so much antagonism against Sasha, and his bitterness was so great against us for our participation in the hated Peukert group, that he now began pouring it out in the *Freiheit,* not openly, but in an indirect and insidious way. The following week the *Freiheit* carried a sharp attack on Frick. But the *Attentat* against him was belittled and Sasha made to appear ludicrous. In his article Most hinted that Sasha had " shot off a toy pistol." The arrest of Nold and Bauer in Pittsburgh Most condemned in unmeasured terms, pointing out that they could have had nothing to do with the attempt on Frick, because they had " mistrusted Berkman from the first."

It was true, of course, that the two comrades knew nothing about the planned act. Sasha had decided before he left not to tell them, but I knew that Most had lied when he said that they mistrusted him. Certainly not Carl Nold; Sasha had written me how friendly Carl had been to him. It was only Most's vindictiveness, his desire to discredit Sasha, that had induced him to write as he did.

It was cruelly disillusioning to find the man I had worshipped, loved, and believed in prove himself so unspeakably small. Whatever his personal feelings against Sasha, whom he had always considered his rival, how could Johann Most, the stormy petrel of my fancy, attack Sasha? Great bitterness welled up in my heart against him. I was consumed by the desire to beat back his thrusts, to proclaim aloud the purity and idealism of Sasha, to shout it so passionately that the whole world should hear and know it. Most had declared war — so be it! I would meet his attacks in the *Anarchist*.

Meanwhile the daily press carried on a ferocious campaign against the anarchists. They called for the police to act, to round up " the instigators, Johann Most, Emma Goldman, and their ilk." My name had rarely before been mentioned in the papers, but now it appeared every day in the most sensational stories. The police got busy; a hunt for Emma Goldman began.

My friend Peppie, with whom I was living, had a flat on Fifth Street and First Avenue, round the corner from the police station. I used to pass the latter frequently, going about openly and spending considerable time at the headquarters of the *Autonomie*. Yet the police seemed unable to find me. One evening, while we were away at a meeting, the police, having discovered my whereabouts at last, broke into the flat through the fire-escape and stole everything they could lay their hands on. My fine collection of revolutionary pamphlets and photographs, my entire correspondence, vanished with them. But they did not find what they came to look for. At the first mention of my name in the papers I had disposed of the material left over from Sasha's experiments. Since the police found nothing incriminating, they went after Peppie's servant, but she was too terrorized by the very sight of an officer to give them information. She stoutly denied that she had ever seen any man in the flat who looked like the photograph of Sasha which the detectives had shown her.

Two days after the raid the landlord ordered us out of the flat. This was followed by a more serious blow — Mollock, Peppie's husband, who was working on Long Island, was kidnapped and spirited away to Pittsburgh, charged with complicity in Sasha's act.

Several days after the *Attentat* militia regiments were marched into Homestead. The more conscious of the steel-workers opposed the move, but they were overruled by the conservative labour element, who foolishly saw in the soldiers protection against new attacks by Pinkertons. The troops soon proved whom they came to protect. It was the Carnegie mills, not the Homestead workers.

However, there was one militiaman who was wide awake enough to see in Sasha the avenger of labour's wrongs. This brave boy gave vent to his feelings by calling in the ranks for " three cheers for the man who shot Frick." He was court-martialled and strung up by his thumbs, but he stuck to his cheers. This incident was the one bright moment in the black and harassing days that followed Sasha's departure.

After a long, anxious wait a letter came from Sasha. He had been greatly cheered by the stand of the militiaman, W. L. Iams, he wrote. It showed that even American soldiers were waking up. Could I not get in touch with the boy, send him anarchist literature? He would be a valuable asset to the movement. I was not to worry about himself; he was in fine spirits and already preparing his court speech — not as a defence, he emphasized, but in explanation of his act. Of course, he would have no lawyer; he would represent his own case as true Russian and other European revolutionists did. Prominent Pittsburgh attorneys had offered their services free of charge, but he had declined. It was inconsistent for an anarchist to employ lawyers; I should make his attitude on the matter clear to the comrades. What was that about Hans Wurst (our nickname for Most in order to shield him)? Someone had written him that Most had not approved of his act. Could it possibly be? How stupid of the authorities to arrest Nold and Bauer! They had known nothing whatever about his act. In fact, he had told them he was leaving for St. Louis and bidden them good-bye, thereupon taking a hotel room and registering under the name of Bakhmetov.

I pressed the letter to my heart, covering it with kisses. I knew how intensely my Sasha felt, although he had said not one word about his love and his thoughts of me.

I was considerably alarmed about his decision to represent his own case. I loved his beautiful consistency, but I knew that his English, like my own, was too poor to be effective in court. I feared he would have no chance. But Sasha's wish, now more than ever, was sacred to me, and I consoled myself with the hope that he would have a public trial, that I could have his speech translated, and that we might give the whole proceedings countrywide publicity. I wrote him that I agreed with his decision, and that we were preparing a large meeting where his act would be fully explained and his motives properly presented. I told him of the enthusiasm in the *Autonomie* group and in the ranks of the Jewish comrades; of the fine stand the socialist *Volkszeitung* had taken, and of the encouraging attitude of the Italian revolutionists. I added that we all rejoiced over the courage of the young militiaman, but that he was not the only one who admired Sasha and gloried in his act. I tried to put the derogatory items that had appeared in the *Freiheit* as mildly as possible; I did not wish him disturbed. Still, it was bitterly hard to have to admit that Most had justified Sasha's opinion of him.

We began to prepare for the large meeting on behalf of Sasha. Joseph Barondess was one of the first to offer his help. Since I had seen him a year previously, he had been condemned to prison in connexion with a new cloakmaker strike, but had been pardoned by the Governor of New York State at the request of union labour and in response to his own letter asking for a pardon. Dyer D. Lum, who had been a close friend of Albert Parsons, volunteered to speak; Saverio Merlino, the brilliant Italian anarchist, then in New York, would also address the meeting. My spirits rose: Sasha still had true and devoted comrades.

Our large red posters announcing the mass meeting roused the ire of the press. Were the authorities not going to interfere? The police came out with the threat that our gathering would be stopped, but on the appointed evening the audience was so large and looked so determined that the police did nothing.

I acted as chairman, a new experience for me; but we could get no one else. The meeting was very spirited, every one of the speakers paying the highest tribute to Sasha and his deed. My hatred of conditions which compelled idealists to acts of violence made me cry out in passionate strains the nobility of Sasha, his selflessness, his consecration to the people.

" Possessed by a fury," the papers said of my speech the next morning. " How long will this dangerous woman be permitted to go on? " Ah, if they only knew how I yearned to give up my freedom, to proclaim loudly my share in the deed — if only they knew!

The new landlord notified Peppie that she would have either to ask me to move out or vacate. Poor Peppie! She was being made to suffer for me. When I returned home that night, after a late meeting, I missed the night key in my bag. I was sure I had put it there in the morning. Not wishing to wake the janitor, I sat on the stoop waiting for some tenant to arrive. At last someone came and let me into the house. When I tried to open the door of Peppie's apartment, it refused to yield. I knocked repeatedly, but there was no answer. I grew alarmed, thinking something might have happened. I knocked violently, and finally the servant came out and informed me that her mistress had sent her to say that I must keep away from the flat, because she could no longer endure being pestered by the landlord and the police. Dashing past the woman, I seized hold of Peppie in the kitchen and shook her roughly, berating her as a coward. In the bedroom I gathered up my things, while Peppie broke down in tears. She had locked me out, she whimpered, because of the children, who had been frightened by detectives. I walked out in silence.

I went to the home of my grandmother. She had not seen me for a long time, and she was startled by my looks. She insisted that I was ill and that I must remain with her. Grandmother kept a grocery store on Tenth Street and Avenue B. Her two rooms she shared with the family of her married daughter. The only place for me was the kitchen, where I could go in and out without disturbing the others. Grandmother offered to get me a cot, and both she and her daughter busied themselves to prepare breakfast for me and make me at home.

The papers began reporting that Frick was recovering from his wounds. Comrades visiting me expressed the opinion that Sasha, " had failed." Some even had the effrontery to suggest that Most might have been right in saying that " it was a toy pistol." I was stung to the quick. I knew that Sasha had never had much practice in shooting. Occasionally, at German picnics, he would take part in target-shooting, but was that sufficient? I was sure Sasha's failure to kill Frick was due to the cheap quality of his revolver — he had lacked enough money to buy a good one.

Perhaps Frick was recovering because of the attention he was getting? The greatest surgeons of America had been called to his bedside. Yes, it must be that; after all, three bullets from Sasha's revolver had lodged in his body. It was Frick's wealth that was enabling him to recover. I tried to explain this to the comrades, but most of them remained unconvinced. Some even hinted that Sasha was at liberty. I was frantic — how dared they doubt Sasha? I would write him! I would ask him to send me word that would stop the horrible rumours about him.

Soon a letter arrived from Sasha, written in a curt tone. He was provoked that I could even ask for an explanation. Did I not know that the vital thing was the motive of his act and not its physical success or failure? My poor, tortured boy! I could read between the lines how crushed he was at the realization that Frick remained alive. But he was right: the important thing was his motives, and these no one could doubt.

Weeks passed without any indication of when Sasha's trial would begin. He was still kept on " Murderers' Row " in the Pittsburgh jail, but the fact that Frick was improving had considerably changed Sasha's legal status. He could not be condemned to death. Through comrades in Pennsylvania I learned that the law called for seven years in prison for his attempt. Hope entered my heart. Seven years are a long time, but Sasha was strong, he had iron perseverance, he could hold out. I clung to the new possibility with every fibre of my being.

My own life was full of misery. Grandmother's place was too crowded and I could not prolong my visit with her. I went in search of a room, but my name seemed to frighten the landlords. My friends suggested that I give an assumed name, but I would not deny my identity.

Often I would sit in a café on Second Avenue until three in the morning, or I would ride back and forth to the Bronx in a street-car. The poor old horses seemed as tired as I, their pace was so slow. I wore a blue and white striped dress and a long, grey coat that resembled a nurse's uniform. Soon I found that it gave me considerable protection. Conductors and policemen would often ask me whether I had just come off duty and was taking a breath of air. One young policeman on Tompkins Square was particularly solicitous about me. He frequently entertained me with stories in his luscious Irish brogue, or he would tell me just to snooze off, that he would be near enough to protect me. " You look all in, kid," he would say; " you're working too hard, ain't you? " I had told him that I was on day and night duty, with only a few hours' respite. I could not help laughing inwardly over the humour of my being protected by a policeman! I wondered how my cop would act if he knew who the demure-looking nurse was.

On Fourth Street near Third Avenue I had often passed a house which always had a sign out: " Furnished Room to Rent." One day I went in. No questions were asked about my identity. The room was small, but the rent was high, four dollars a week. The surroundings looked rather peculiar, but I hired the room.

In the evening I discovered that the whole house was tenanted by girls. I paid no attention at first, being busy putting my belongings in order. Weeks had passed since I had unpacked my clothes and books. It was such a comforting sensation to be able to take a scrub, to lie down on a clean bed. I retired early, but was awakened at night by someone knocking on my door. " Who is it ? " I called, still heavy with sleep. " Say, Viola, ain't you goin' to let me in ? I've been knockin' for twenty minutes. What the hell is up ? You said I could come to-night." " You're in the wrong place, mister," I replied; " I'm not Viola."

Similar episodes happened every night for some time. Men called for Annette, for Mildred, or Clothilde. It finally dawned on me that I was living in a brothel.

The girl in the room next to mine was a sympathetic-looking young-ster, and one day I invited her for coffee. I learned from her that the place was not a " regular dump, with a Madam," but that it was a rooming-house where girls were allowed to bring their men. She asked if I was doing good business, as I was so young. When I told her that I was not in the business, that I was only a dressmaker, the girl jeered. It took me some time to convince her that I was not looking for men customers. What better place could I have found than this house full of girls who must need dresses ? I began to consider whether to remain in the house or move out. The thought of living within sight and sound of the life around me made me feel ill. My gracious stranger had been right — I had no knack for such things. There was also the fear that the papers might find out about the nature of the place I was in. Anar-chists were already outrageously misrepresented; it would be grist to the capitalistic mill if they could proclaim that Emma Goldman had been found in a house of prostitution. I saw the necessity of moving out. But I remained. The hardships of the weeks since Sasha had gone, the prospect of again having to join the host of the shelterless, outweighed all other considerations.

Before the week was over, I had become the confidante of most of the girls. They competed with one another in being kind to me, in giving me their sewing to do and helping in little ways. For the first time since my return from Worcester I was able to earn my living. I had my own corner and I had made new friends. But my life was not destined to run smoothly for long.

The feud between Most and our group continued. Hardly a week passed without some slur in the *Freiheit* against Sasha or myself. It was painful enough to be called vile names by the man who had once loved me, but it was beyond endurance to have Sasha slandered and maligned. Then came Most's article " *Attentats-Reflexionen* (Reflections on Propaganda by Deed) " in the *Freiheit* of August 27, which was a complete reversal of everything that Most had till then persistently advocated. Most, whom I had heard scores of times call for acts of violence, who had gone to prison in England for his glorification of tyrannicide — Most, the incarnation of defiance and revolt, now deliberately repudiated the *Tat!* I wondered if he really believed what he wrote. Was his article prompted by his hatred of Sasha, or written to protect himself against the newspaper charge of complicity? He dared even make insinuations against Sasha's motives. The world Most had enriched for me, the life so full of colour and beauty, all lay shattered at my feet. Only the naked fact remained that Most had betrayed his ideal, had betrayed us.

I resolved to challenge him publicly to prove his insinuations, to compel him to explain his sudden reversal of attitude in the face of danger. I replied to his article, in the *Anarchist,* demanding an explanation and branding Most as a traitor and a coward. I waited for two weeks for a reply in the *Freiheit,* but none appeared. There were no proofs, and I knew that he could not justify his base accusations. I bought a horsewhip.

At Most's next lecture I sat in the first row, close to the low platform. My hand was on the whip under my long, grey cloak. When he got up and faced the audience, I rose and declared in a loud voice: " I came to demand proof of your insinuations against Alexander Berkman."

There was instant silence. Most mumbled something about " hysterical woman," but he said nothing else. I then pulled out my whip and leaped towards him. Repeatedly I lashed him across the face and neck, then broke the whip over my knee and threw the pieces at him. It was all done so quickly that no one had time to interfere.

Then I felt myself roughly pulled back. " Throw her out! Beat her up!" people yelled. I was surrounded by an enraged and threatening crowd and might have fared badly had not Fedya, Claus, and other friends come to my rescue. They lifted me up bodily and forced their way out of the hall.

Most's change of position regarding propaganda by deed, his inimical attitude towards Sasha's act, his insinuations against the latter's motive, and his attacks upon me caused widespread dissension in the anarchist ranks. It was no more a feud between Most and Peukert and their adherents. It raised a storm within the entire anarchist movement, splitting it into two inimical camps. Some stood by Most, others defended Sasha and eulogized his act. The strife grew so bitter that I was even refused admission to a Jewish meeting on the East Side, the stronghold of Most's faithful. My public punishment of their adored teacher roused furious antagonism against me and made me a pariah.

Meanwhile we were anxiously waiting for the date of Sasha's trial to be set, but no information was forthcoming. In the second week of September I was invited to speak in Baltimore, my lecture being scheduled for Monday, the 19th. As I was about to ascend the platform, a telegram was handed to me. The trial had taken place that very day and Sasha had been condemned to twenty-two years in prison! Railroaded to a living death! The hall and the audience began to swim before my eyes. Someone took the telegram out of my hands and pushed me into a chair. A glass of water was held to my lips. The meeting must be called off, the comrades said.

I looked wildly about me, gulped down some water, snatched up the telegram, and leaped to the platform. The yellow piece of paper in my hand was a glowing coal, its fire searing my heart and flaming it into passionate expression. It caught the audience and raised it to ferment. Men and women jumped to their feet, calling for vengeance against the ferocious sentence. Their burning fervour in the cause of Sasha and his act resounded like thunder through the great hall.

The police burst in with drawn clubs and drove the audience out of the building. I remained on the platform, the telegram still in my hand. Officers came up and put the chairman and me under arrest. On the street we were pushed into a waiting patrol wagon and driven to the station-house, followed by the incensed crowd.

I had been surrounded by people from the moment the crushing news had come, compelled to suppress the turmoil in my soul and force back

the hot tears that kept swelling in my throat. Now, free from intrusion, the monstrous sentence loomed up before me in all its horror.
Twenty-two years! Sasha was twenty-one, at the most impressionable
and vivid age. The life he had not yet lived was before him, holding
out the charm and beauty his intense nature could extract. And now
he was cut down like a strong young tree, robbed of sun and of light.
And Frick was alive, almost recovered from his wounds and now
recuperating in his palatial summer house. He would go on spilling the
blood of labour. Frick was alive, and Sasha doomed to twenty-two
years in a living tomb. The irony, the bitter irony of the thing, struck
me full in the face.

If only I could shut out the ghastly picture and give vent to tears,
find forgetfulness in everlasting sleep! But there were no tears, there
was no sleep. There was only Sasha — Sasha in convict's clothes, cap-
tive behind stone walls — Sasha with his pale set face pressed to the
iron bars, his steady eyes gazing intently upon me, bidding me go on.

No, no, no, there must be no despair. I would live, I would fight for
Sasha. I would rend the black clouds closing on him, I would rescue
my boy, I would bring him back to life!

CHAPTER X

WHEN I RETURNED TO NEW YORK TWO DAYS LATER, HAVING been discharged by the Baltimore police magistrate with a strong admonition never again to come back to the city, a letter from Sasha was awaiting me. It was written in very small but distinct script and gave the details of the Monday in court. He had repeatedly tried to learn the date of his trial, the letter read, but he could not procure any information about it. On the morning of the 19th he was suddenly ordered to get ready. He had barely time to gather up the sheets of his speech. Strange and antagonistic faces met him in the court-room. In vain he strained his eye for the sight of his friends. He realized that they, too, must have been kept in ignorance of the day of the trial. Yet he hoped against hope for the miracle. But there was not a friendly face anywhere. He was confronted with six indictments, all manufactured from the one act, and among them one charging him with an attempt on the life of John G. A. Leishman, Frick's assistant. Sasha declared that he knew nothing of Leishman; it was Frick whom he had come to kill. He demanded that he be tried on that charge alone, and that the other indictments be quashed, because they were all involved in the major charge. But his objection was overruled.

The jurors were selected in a few minutes, Sasha making no use of his right of challenge. What difference did it make? They were all alike, and he would be convicted anyhow. He declared to the Court that he scorned to defend himself; he wanted only to explain his act. The interpreter assigned to him translated haltingly and wrongly, and after several attempts to correct him Sasha discovered to his horror that the man was blind, as blind as justice in the American courts. He then tried to address the jury in English, but he was impatiently stopped by Judge McClung, who declared that " the prisoner has said enough already." Sasha protested, but in vain. The

District Attorney stepped into the jury-box and held a low conversation with the talesmen, whereupon they brought in a verdict of guilty without even leaving their seats. The Judge was curt and denunciatory. He passed sentence on each count separately, including three indictments for "entering a building with felonious intent," giving the prisoner the maximum on each charge. The total amounted to twenty-one years in the Western Penitentiary of Pennsylvania, at the expiration of which time an additional year was to be served in the Allegheny County Workhouse for "carrying concealed weapons."

Twenty-two years of slow torture and death! He had done his duty, Sasha's letter concluded, and now the end had come. He would depart as he had determined, by his own will and hand. He wanted no effort made in his behalf. It would be of no use and he could not give his consent to an appeal to the enemy. No need of further help for him; whatever campaign could be made must be for his act, and I was to see to that. He was sure that no one else felt and understood his motives so well, no one else could clarify the meaning of his deed with the same conviction. His one deep longing now was for me. If he could only look into my eyes once more and press me to his heart — but as that was denied him, he would keep on thinking of me, his friend and comrade. No power on earth could take that away from him.

I felt Sasha's spirit lifted above everything earthly. Like a brilliant star it illumined my own dark thoughts and brought home to me the realization that there was something greater than personal ties or even love: an all-embracing devotion that understands all and gives all to the last breath.

Sasha's terrible sentence aroused Most to a virulent attack on the courts of Pennsylvania and the judicial criminal who could give a man twenty-two years for an act that legally called for only seven. His article in the *Freiheit* increased my bitterness against him, for had he not helped to weaken the effect of Sasha's deed? I was certain that the enemy would not have dared to railroad Sasha if there had been a concerted radical protest in his behalf. I held Most much more responsible for the inhuman sentence than the Court of the State of Pennsylvania.

Sasha was by no means without friends. They proved their loyalty from the very first. Now two groups came forward to organize the campaign for the commutation of his sentence. The East Side group comprised various social elements, labour men, and leading Jewish socialists. Among them were M. Zametkin, an old Russian revolutionary; Louis Miller, an energetic and influential man in the ghetto; and Isaac Hourwitch, a comparatively recent arrival in America after his exile in Siberia. The last was especially ardent as a spokesman for Sasha. There was also Shevitch, who had from the beginning defended Sasha in the German daily *Volkszeitung*, of which he was editor-in-chief. Our friend Solotaroff, Annie Netter, young Michael Cohn, and others were the most active in the East Side group.

The moving spirit of the American group was Dyer D. Lum, a man of exceptional abilities, a poet and writer on economic and philosophical subjects. With him were John Edelman, the gifted architect and publicist; William C. Owen, an Englishman of literary talents, and Justus Schwab, the well-known German anarchist.

It was most encouraging to see the splendid solidarity in the cause of Sasha. I kept him informed of the efforts in his behalf, painting them in exaggerated colours to cheer him. But nothing seemed to avail; he was in the grip of the twenty-two-year sentence. " It is no earthly use to try to do anything for me," he wrote. " It will take years to accomplish a commutation, and I know that Frick and Carnegie will never consent to it. Without their approval the Pennsylvania Board of Pardons will not act. Besides, I cannot continue for long in this living tomb." His letters were dispiriting, but I held on grimly. I knew his indomitable will and his iron strength of character. I clung tenaciously to the hope that he would arouse himself and not allow himself to be crushed. That hope alone gave me the courage to go on. I joined the newly organized efforts for him. Night after night I was at some meeting voicing the meaning and message of Sasha's act.

Early in November came the first sign of Sasha's reawakened interest in life. His letter informed me that he might have the privilege of a visitor. Prisoners were entitled to one visit a month, but only from a near relative. Could I get his sister from Russia to come to see him? I understood what he meant and wrote him immediately to get the pass.

I had been invited by anarchist groups in Chicago and St. Louis to speak at the approaching anniversary of the 11th of November and I decided to combine the trip with a visit to Sasha. I would go as his married sister, under the name of Niedermann. I was certain that the prison authorities knew nothing about Sasha's sister in Russia. I would impersonate her and they would never suspect my identity. I was hardly known then. The pictures of me in the papers in connexion with

Sasha's act were so unlike me that no one could have recognized me from them. To see my boy again, to press him to my heart, to bring him hope and courage — I lived for nothing else during the weeks and days before the visit.

In a fever I made my preparations. My first stop was to be St. Louis; then Chicago; finally Pittsburgh. A letter from Sasha arrived a few days before my departure. It contained a pass from the Chief Prison Inspector of the Western Penitentiary for Mrs. E. Niedermann, sister of Prisoner A-7, for a visit on the 26th of November. Sasha had asked me to instruct his sister to remain in Pittsburgh two days. In view of the fact that she was coming all the way from Russia to see him, the Inspector had promised him a second visit. I was wild with joy, impatient of every hour that kept me from him. The pass for my visit became my amulet. I would not part with it for a moment.

I arrived in Pittsburgh early on the morning of Thanksgiving Day. I was met by Carl Nold and Max Metzkow, the latter a German comrade who had faithfully stood by Sasha. Nold and Bauer were out on bail awaiting trial " for complicity in the attempt on Frick's life." I had been in correspondence with Carl for some time and I was glad of the opportunity to meet the young comrade who had been kind to Sasha. He was of small stature, frail, with intelligent eyes and a shock of black hair. We greeted each other like old friends.

In the afternoon I went out to Allegheny, accompanied by Metzkow. It was decided that Nold should stay away; he was often followed by detectives and we were afraid that my identity might be discovered before I had a chance to get inside the prison. Not far from the penitentiary Metzkow remained to await my return.

The grey stone building, the high forbidding walls, the armed guards, the oppressive silence in the hall where I was told to wait, and the minutes creeping into endless time settled on my heart with the weight of a nightmare. In vain I tried to shake myself free. At last a harsh voice called: " This way, Mrs. Niedermann." I was taken through several iron doors, along twisting corridors, into a small room. Sasha was there, a tall guard beside him.

My first impulse was to rush up to him and cover him with kisses, but the presence of the guard checked me. Sasha approached me and put his arms around me. As he bent over to kiss me, I felt a small object pass into my mouth.

For weeks I had been looking forward eagerly, anxiously to this visit. A thousand times I had gone over in my mind all I would say to him of my love and undying devotion, of the struggle I was making for his release, but all I could do was to press his hand and look into his eyes.

We began to speak in our beloved Russian, but we were stopped immediately by the cold command of the guard: "Talk English. No foreign languages here." His lynx-like eyes followed our every movement, watched our lips, crept into our very minds. I became tongue-tied, numb in every nerve. Sasha, too, was mute; his fingers kept on playing with my watch-chain and he seemed to hold on to it as a drowning man to a straw. Neither of us could utter a word, but our eyes spoke to each other — of our fears, our hopes, our yearnings.

The visit lasted twenty minutes. Another embrace, another touch of our lips, and our " time was up." I whispered to him to hold on, to hold out, and then I found myself on the prison steps. The iron gate clattered shut behind me.

I wanted to scream, to throw my weight against the door, to pound it with my fists. But the gate stared back at me and mocked. I walked along the front of the prison and into the street. I walked, silently weeping, towards the spot where I had left Metzkow. His presence brought me back to reality and made me conscious of the object Sasha had given me with his kiss. I took it out of my mouth — a small roll tightly wrapped. We went into the back room of a saloon and I unwound the several layers of paper. At last appeared a note with Sasha's diminutive handwriting, each word standing out like a pearl before me. "You must go to Inspector Reed," it read; " he promised me a second pass. Go to his jewellery shop tomorrow. I am counting on you. I'll give you another message of importance — the same way."

I went to Reed's store the next day. I looked shabby in my threadbare coat amid the sparkling jewellery, silver, and gold. I asked to see Mr. Reed. He was a tall, emaciated, thin-lipped creature, with hard and piercing eyes. No sooner had I given my name than he exclaimed: " So this is Berkman's sister! " Yes, he had promised him a second visit, though he did not deserve any kindness. Berkman was a murderer, he had tried to kill a good Christian man. I held on to myself by sheer force; my chance to see Sasha again was at stake. He would call up the prison, Reed continued, to find out at what time I could be admitted. I was to return in an hour.

My heart sank. I had a distinct premonition that there would be no more visits for Sasha. But I came back as directed. As soon as Mr. Reed saw me, his face turned purple and he fairly leaped at me. " You deceiver! " he yelled. " You have already been at the penitentiary! You sneaked in under a false name as his sister. You don't get away with such lies here — you have been recognized by a guard! You are Emma Goldman, that criminal's mistress! There will be no more visits. You might as well make up your mind about it — Berkman will never get out alive! "

He had gone behind the glass counter, which was covered with silverware. In my indignation and rage I swept everything to the floor — plates, coffee-pots and pitchers, jewellery and watches. I seized a heavy tray and was about to throw it at him when I was pulled back by one of the clerks, who shouted to someone to run for the police. Reed, white with fear and frothing at the mouth, signalled to the clerk. " No police," I heard him say; " no scandal. Just kick her out." The clerk advanced towards me, then stopped. " Murderer, coward! " I cried; " if you harm Berkman, I will kill you with my own hands! "

No one moved. I walked out and boarded a street-car. I made sure of not being followed before returning to Metzkow's home. In the evening, when he came back with Nold from work, I told them what had happened. They were alarmed. They regretted that I had lost control of myself, because it would react on Sasha. They agreed that I would have to get out of Pittsburgh at once. The Inspector might put detectives on my trail and have me arrested. The Pennsylvania authorities had been trying to get me ever since Sasha's act.

I was shocked by the thought that Sasha might indeed have to suffer as a result of my outbreak. But the threat of the Inspector that Sasha would never come out of prison alive had been too much for me. I was sure Sasha would understand.

The night was black as I walked with Nold to the station to take the train for New York. The steel-foundries belched huge flames that reflected the Allegheny hills blood-red and filled the air with soot and smoke. We made our way past the sheds where human beings, half man, half beast, were working like the galley-slaves of an era long past. Their naked bodies, covered only with small trunks, shone like copper in the glare of the red-hot chunks of iron they were snatching from the mouths of the flaming monsters. From time to time the steam rising from the water thrown on the hot metal would completely envelop the men; then they would emerge again like shadows. " The children of hell," I said, " damned to the everlasting inferno of heat and noise." Sasha had given his life to bring joy to these slaves, but they had remained blind and continued in the hell of their own forging. "Their souls are dead, dead to the horror and degradation of their lives."

Carl related to me what he knew about Sasha in his Pittsburgh days. It was true that Henry Bauer had suspected Sasha. Henry was a fanatical follower of Most, who had warned him against us as renegades, telling him that we had allied ourselves with "that spy Peukert." When Sasha arrived at the height of the Homestead trouble, Bauer was already prejudiced against him. Henry had confided to Nold that he would examine Sasha's bag while he was asleep and that if he found anything incriminating, he would kill Sasha. With loaded gun Bauer had slept in the same room with Sasha, alert for any suspicious movement and ready to shoot. Nold had been so impressed with Sasha by his open countenance and directness that he could not possibly suspect him. He had agreed with Bauer, trying to convince him that Most was unfair and prejudiced against everyone who disagreed with him. Carl no longer believed so implicitly in Hannes.

Carl's story filled me with horror. What if Sasha had happened to have something in his bag that Bauer might have taken as justifying his suspicions! Enough for the blind Most-worshipper to shoot him! And Most, to what depths his hatred of Sasha had driven him, to what despicable methods! What was there in human passion that forced men to such lengths? My own, for instance, that compelled me to horsewhip Most, to hate him now as he had always hated Sasha, to hate the man I had once loved, the man who had been my ideal. It was all so painfully disturbing, so frightful. I could not grasp it.

Of his own trial Carl spoke lightly. He would even welcome a few years in prison to be near Sasha, to help him bear his heavy ordeal. Faithful Carl! His trust in Sasha and his faith brought me close to him, made him very dear.

Far in the distance, as the train sped on, I could still see the belching flames shoot against the black sky, lighting up the hills of Allegheny. Allegheny, which held what was most precious to me immured perhaps for ever! I had planned the *Attentat* together with him; I had let him go alone; I had approved of his decision to have no lawyer. I strove to shake off the consciousness of guilt, but it would give me no rest until I found forgetfulness in sleep.

CHAPTER XI

OUR WORK FOR THE COMMUTATION OF SASHA'S SENTENCE CON-tinued. At one of our weekly meetings, in the latter part of De-cember, I became conscious of the steady gaze of a man in the audience. He was tall and broad, well built, with soft blond hair and blue eyes. I particularly noticed the peculiar motion of his right leg, swinging back and forth regularly, while his hand kept steadily playing with matches. His monotonous movements were making me drowsy and I repeatedly had to rouse myself with an effort. Finally I walked over to the man and playfully took the matches away from him, remarking: " Children are not allowed to play with fire." " All right, grandmother," he replied in the same spirit, " but you should know that I am a revolutionist. I love fire. Don't you? " He smiled at me, exposing beautiful white teeth. " Yes, in its right place," I retorted, " not here, with so many people about. It makes me nervous. And please stop moving your leg." The man apologized; a bad habit he had acquired in prison, he remarked. A feeling of shame overcame me; I thought of Sasha. I begged the man to go on and not to mind me. Perhaps some day he would tell me about his prison experience. " I have a dear friend there now," I said. Evidently he understood whom I meant. " Berkman is a brave man," he replied. " We know about him in Austria and we admire him tremendously for what he did."

I learned that his name was Edward Brady and that he had just arrived from Austria after completing a term of ten years in prison for the publication of illegal anarchist literature. I found him the most scholarly person I had ever met. His field was not limited, like Most's, to social and political subjects; in fact, he rarely talked about them to me. He introduced me to the great classics of English and French literature. He loved to read Goethe and Shakespeare to me, or translate passages from the French, Jean Jacques Rousseau and Voltaire being his favourites. His English, although with a German accent, was perfect. On one occasion I asked him where he had received his schooling. " In prison," he replied unhesitatingly. He modified it by adding that he had passed through the *Gymnasium* first; but it was in prison that he had done his real studying. His sister used to send him English and French dictionaries, and he made it his practice to memorize so many words every day. In solitary confinement he had always read aloud to himself. It was the only way to survive. Many went crazy, particularly those who had nothing with which to occupy their minds. But for people with ideals prison is the best school, he said. " Then I ought to get to prison as quickly as possible," I remarked, " because I am awfully ignorant." " Don't be in such a hurry," he replied; " we have only just met and you are too young for prison." " Berkman was only twenty-one," I told him. " Yes, that is the pity of it." His voice trembled. " I was thirty when I was imprisoned. I had already lived intensely."

He asked about my childhood and schooldays, evidently trying to change the subject. I had only had three and a half years of *Realschule* in Königsberg, I told him. The régime was harsh, the instructors brutal; I learned scarcely anything. Only my teacher of German had been kind to me. She was a sick woman, slowly dying of consumption, but patient and tender. She would often invite me to her home and give me extra lessons. She was particularly anxious for me to know her favourite writers: Marlitt, Auerbach, Heise, Lindau, and Spielhagen. She loved Marlitt more than the others; so I, too, loved Marlitt. We used to read her novels together and we would both grow tearful over the unhappy heroines. My teacher worshipped the royal house; Frederick the Great and Queen Louise were her idols. " The poor Queen so cruelly treated by that butcher, Napoleon — the gracious, beautiful Queen," she would say with much feeling. She often recited to me the poem, the daily prayer of the good Queen:

Wer nie sein Brot in Tränen ass —
Wer nie die kummervollen Nächte auf seinem Bette weinend sass —
Der kennt euch nicht, Ihr himmlischen Mächte.

The moving stanza completely captured me. I, too, became a devotee of Queen Louise.

Two of my teachers had been altogether terrible. One, a German

Jew, was our instructor in religion; the other taught geography. I hated them both. Occasionally I would avenge myself on the former for his constant beatings, but I was too terrorized by the other even to complain at home.

The great joy of our religious instructor used to be to beat the palms of our hands with a ruler. I used to organize schemes to annoy him: stick pins in his upholstered chair, stealthily tie his long coat-tails to the table, put snails in his pockets — anything I could think of to pay him back for the pain of his ruler. He knew I was the ring-leader and he beat me the more for it. But it was a frank feud that could be met in the open.

Not so with the other man. His methods were less painful, but more dreadful. Every afternoon he would keep one or two of the girls after school-hours. When everybody had left the building, he would send one girl to the next class-room, then force the other on his knee and grasp her breasts or put his hands between her legs. He would promise her good marks if she kept quiet and threaten instant dismissal if she talked. The girls were terrorized into silence. I did not know for a long time about these things, until one day I found myself on his knee. I screamed, reached for his beard, and pulled it violently in my attempt to wriggle out of his hold. He jumped up, and I fell to the floor. He ran to the door to see if anyone was coming in response to my cry; then he hissed into my ear: " If you breathe one word, I'll kick you out of school."

For several days I was too sick with fright to return to school, but I would not say anything. The dread of being dismissed brought back the remembrance of Father's fury whenever I returned with bad marks. I went back to school at last, and for some days the geography lessons passed without incident. Because of my poor eyesight I had to stand close to the map. One day the teacher whispered to me: " You will remain behind." " I will not! " I whispered back. The next moment I felt a stinging pain in my arm. He had stuck his nails into my flesh. My cries broke up the class and brought other instructors to the room. I heard our teacher telling them that I was a dullard, that I never knew my lessons and therefore he had to punish me. I was sent home.

At night my arm hurt a great deal. Mother noticed that it was all swollen and she sent for the doctor, who questioned me. His kindly manner led me to tell him the whole story. " Terrible! " he exclaimed; "the fellow belongs to the madhouse." A week later when I returned to school our geography-teacher was no longer there. He had gone on a journey, we were told.

When the time came for me to join Father in St. Petersburg, I hated to go. I could not part from my sick teacher of German, who had taught me to love everything Teutonic. She had induced one of her friends to give me French and music lessons and had promised to help me through the *Gymnasium*. She wanted me to continue my education in Germany, and I dreamed of studying medicine so that I could be helpful in the world. After much pleading and many tears Mother consented to let me remain with my grandmother in Königsberg, provided I would pass the entrance examination for the *Gymnasium*. I worked day and night and I passed. But to become enrolled I needed a certificate of good character from my religious teacher. I loathed the idea of asking the man for anything; but I felt that my whole future depended on it, and I went to him. In front of the whole class he announced that he would never give me "a good character." I had none, he declared; I was a terrible child and would grow into a worse woman. I had no respect for my elders or for authority, and I would surely end on the gallows as a public menace. I went home heart-broken, but Mother promised to permit me to continue my studies in St. Petersburg. Unfortunately her plans did not materialize. I got only six months of study in Russia. However, the spiritual influences from my association with Russian students were most valuable.

"Those teachers must have been regular beasts," Brady declared; "but you will admit that your religious fellow had a prophetic eye. You are already considered a public menace, and if you go on, you may be given a distinguished death. But console yourself; better people die on the gallows than in palaces."

Gradually a beautiful comradery matured between Brady and me. I now called him Ed. "The other sounds conventional," he had said. At his suggestion we started reading French together, beginning with *Candide*. I read slowly, haltingly, my pronunciation atrocious. But he was a born teacher, and his patience was boundless. On Sundays Ed would play host in the two-room apartment to which I had moved. Fedya and I would be ordered out of the flat until the meal was ready. Ed was a marvellous cook. On rare occasions I would be given the privilege of watching him prepare the meal. He would explain minutely, with evident gusto, every dish and I soon proved a much better pupil in cooking than in French. I learned to prepare many dishes before we were through reading *Candide*.

On Saturdays when I did not have to lecture, we used to visit the saloon of Justus Schwab, the most famous radical centre in New York. Schwab was the traditional Teuton in appearance, over six feet tall, broad-chested, and straight as a tree. On his wide shoulders and strong neck rested a magnificent head, framed in curly red hair and beard. His eyes were full of fire and intensity. But it was his voice, deep and tender, that was his peculiar characteristic. It would have made him famous if he had chosen an operatic career. Justus was too much the rebel and the dreamer, however, to care about such things. The rear room of his little place on First Street was a Mecca for French Communards, Spanish and Italian refugees, Russian politicals, and German socialists and anarchists who had escaped the iron heel of Bismarck. Everyone gathered at Justus's. Justus, as we affectionately called him, was the comrade, adviser, and friend of all. The circle was interspersed with many Americans, among them writers and artists. John Swinton, Ambrose Bierce, James Huneker, Sadakichi Hartmann, and other literati loved to listen to Justus's golden voice, drink his delicious beer and wine, and argue world-problems far into the night. Together with Ed I became a regular frequenter. Ed would dilate on the subtleties of some English, French, or German word, a group of philologists his forum. I would clash swords with Huneker and his friends about anarchism. Justus loved those battles and would urge me on. Then he would pat me on the back and say: " Emmachen, your head is not made for a hat; it is made for the rope. Just look at those soft curves — the rope would easily snuggle into them." At which Ed would wince.

The sweet companionship with Ed did not eliminate Sasha from my mind. Ed was also deeply interested in him and he joined the groups that were carrying on a systematic campaign in Sasha's behalf. Meanwhile Sasha had established an underground mail route. His official notes contained little about himself, but they spoke kindly of the prison chaplain, who had given him books and was showing human interest. His underground letters evidenced how outraged he felt over the sentence of Bauer and Nold. But they also breathed a little hope; he no longer felt so alone, with his two comrades under the same roof. He was trying to establish communication with them, his friends having been placed in a different wing of the prison. For the present, letters from the outside were his only link with life. I must urge our friends to write him often.

The consciousness that my correspondence would be read by the prison censor haunted me. The written words seemed cold and matter-of-fact, yet I wanted Sasha to feel that whatever happened in my life, whoever entered it, he would remain in it always. My letters left me dissatisfied and unhappy. But life went on. I had to work ten, sometimes twelve hours a day at the sewing-machine to earn my living. Almost nightly meetings and the need of improving my neglected education kept me engaged all the time. Somehow Ed made me feel that need more than anyone else had done.

Our friendship gradually ripened into love. Ed became indispensable to me. I had known for a long time that he also cared for me. Of unusual reserve, he had never spoken of his love, but his eyes and his touch were eloquent of it. He had had women in his life before. One of them had given him a daughter, who was living with her mother's parents. He felt grateful to those women, he would often say. They had taught him the mysteries and subtleties of sex. I could not follow Ed when he spoke of these matters, and I was too shy to ask for an explanation. But I used to wonder what he meant. Sex had seemed a simple process to me. My own sex life had always left me dissatisfied, longing for something I did not know. I considered love more important than all else, love which finds supreme joy in selfless giving.

In the arms of Ed I learned for the first time the meaning of the great life-giving force. I understood its full beauty, and I eagerly drank its intoxicating joy and bliss. It was an ecstatic song, profoundly soothing by its music and perfume. My little flat in the building known as the " Bohemian Republic," to which I had moved lately, became a temple of love. Often the thought would come to me that so much peace and beauty could not last; it was too wonderful, too perfect. Then I would cling to Ed with a trembling heart. He would hold me close and his unfailing cheer and humour would dispel my dark thoughts. " You are overworked," he would say. " The machine and your constant anxiety about Sasha are killing you."

In the spring I fell ill, began to lose weight, and grew too weak to walk across the room. Physicians ordered immediate rest and a change of climate. My friends persuaded me to leave New York and I went to Rochester, accompanied by a girl who volunteered as nurse.

My sister Helena thought her place too cramped for a patient and she secured for me a room in a house with a large garden. She spent every spare moment with me, unfailing in her love and care. She took me to a lung-specialist who discovered an early stage of tuberculosis and put me on a special diet. Presently I began to improve, and within two months I had recovered sufficiently to take walks. My doctor was planning to send me for the winter to a sanatorium, when developments in New York gave a different turn to the situation.

The industrial crisis of that year had thrown thousands out of employment, and their condition now reached an appalling state. Worst of all was the situation in New York. Jobless workers were being evicted; suffering was growing and suicides multiplying. Nothing was being done to alleviate their misery.

I could no longer remain in Rochester. My reason told me it was reckless to go back in the middle of my cure. I had grown much stronger and had gained weight. I coughed less and the hæmorrhages had stopped. I knew, however, that I was far from well. But something stronger than reason was drawing me back to New York. I longed for Ed; but more compelling was the call of the unemployed, of the workers of the East Side who had given me my labour baptism. I had been with them in their previous struggles; I could not stay away from them now. I left notes behind for the physician and Helena; I did not have the heart to face them.

I had wired Ed and he met me joyously. But when I told him that I had returned to devote myself to the unemployed, his mood changed. It was insanity, he urged; it would mean the loss of everything I had gained in health through my rest. It might even prove fatal. He would not permit it — I was his now — his, to love and protect and watch over.

It was bliss to know that someone cared so much for me, but I felt it at the same time a handicap. His " to hold and protect "? Did he consider me his property, a dependent or a cripple who had to be taken care of by a man? I had thought he believed in freedom, in my right to do as I wished. It was anxiety about me, fear for my health, he assured me, that prompted his words. But if I was determined to resume my efforts, he would help. He was no speaker, but he could be useful in other ways.

Committee sessions, public meetings, collection of food-stuffs, supervising the feeding of the homeless and their numerous children, and, finally, the organization of a mass meeting on Union Square entirely filled my time.

The meeting at Union Square was preceded by a demonstration, the marching columns counting many thousands. The girls and women were in front, I at their head carrying a red banner. Its crimson waved proudly in the air and could be seen for blocks. My soul, too, vibrated with the intensity of the moment.

I had prepared my speech in writing and it seemed to me inspiring, but when I reached Union Square and saw the huge mass of humanity, my notes appeared cold and meaningless.

The atmosphere in the ranks had become very tense, owing to the events of that week. Labour politicians had appealed to the New York legislature for relief of the great distress, but their pleas met with evasions. Meanwhile the unemployed went on starving. The people were outraged by this callous indifference to the suffering of men, women, and children. As a result the air at Union Square was charged with bitterness and indignation, its spirit quickly communicating itself to me. I was scheduled as the last speaker and I could barely endure the long wait. Finally the apologetic oratory was over and my turn came. I heard my name shouted from a thousand throats as I stepped forward. I saw a dense mass before me, their pale, pinched faces upturned to me. My heart beat, my temples throbbed, and my knees shook.

" Men and women," I began amidst sudden silence, " do you not realize that the State is the worst enemy you have? It is a machine that crushes you in order to sustain the ruling class, your masters. Like naïve children you put your trust in your political leaders. You make it possible for them to creep into your confidence, only to have them betray you to the first bidder. But even where there is no direct betrayal, the labour politicians make common cause with your enemies to keep you in leash, to prevent your direct action. The State is the pillar of capitalism, and it is ridiculous to expect any redress from it. Do you not see the stupidity of asking relief from Albany with immense wealth within a stone's throw from here? Fifth Avenue is laid in gold, every mansion is a citadel of money and power. Yet there you stand, a giant, starved and fettered, shorn of his strength. Cardinal Manning long ago proclaimed that ' necessity knows no law ' and that ' the starving man has a right to a share of his neighbour's bread.' Cardinal Manning was an ecclesiastic steeped in the traditions of the Church, which has always been on the side of the rich against the poor. But he had some humanity, and he knew that hunger is a compelling force. You, too, will have to learn that you have a right to share your neighbour's bread. Your neighbours — they have not only stolen your bread, but they are sapping your blood. They will go on robbing you, your children, and your children's children, unless you wake up, unless you become daring enough to demand your rights. Well, then, demonstrate before the palaces of the rich; demand work. If they do not give you work, demand bread. If they deny you both, take bread. It is your sacred right! "

Uproarious applause, wild and deafening, broke from the stillness like a sudden storm. The sea of hands eagerly stretching out towards me seemed like the wings of white birds fluttering.

The following morning I went to Philadelphia to secure relief and help organize the unemployed there. The afternoon papers carried a garbled account of my speech. I had urged the crowd to revolution, they claimed. " Red Emma has great swaying power; her vitriolic tongue was just what the ignorant mob needed to tear down New York." They also stated that I had been spirited away by some husky friends, but that the police were on my track.

In the evening I attended a group meeting, where I met a number of anarchists I had not known before. Natasha Notkin was the active spirit among them. She was the true type of Russian woman revolutionist, with no other interests in life but the movement. A mass meeting was decided upon for Monday, August 21. On that morning the papers brought the news that my whereabouts had been discovered, that detectives were on their way to Philadelphia with a warrant for my arrest. I felt that the important thing for me was to manage to get into the hall and address the meeting before my arrest could take place. It was my first visit to Philadelphia, where I was unknown to the authorities. The New York detectives would hardly be able to identify me by the pictures that had so far appeared in the press. I decided to go to the hall unaccompanied and slip in unnoticed.

The streets near by were blocked with people. No one recognized me as I walked up the flight of steps leading to the meeting-place. Then one of the anarchists greeted me: " Here's Emma! " I waved him aside, but a heavy hand was immediately on my shoulder, and a voice said: " You're under arrest, Miss Goldman." There was a commotion, people ran towards me, but the officers drew their guns and held back the crowd. A detective gripped my arm and pulled me down the stairs into the street. I was given the choice of riding in the patrol wagon or walking to the police station. I chose to walk. The officers attempted to handcuff me, but I assured them there was no need of it, as I did not intend to escape. On our way a man broke through the crowd and ran up to me. He held out his wallet, in case I needed money. The detectives promptly nabbed him and he was put under arrest. I was taken to police headquarters, in the tower of the City Hall, and locked up for the night.

In the morning I was asked whether I was willing to go back with the detectives to New York. "Not of my own free will," I declared. "Very well, we'll keep you until your extradition has been arranged." I was taken into a room where I was weighed, measured, and photographed. I fought desperately against the photographing, but my head was held pinioned. I closed my eyes, and the photograph must have resembled a sleeping beauty that looked like an escaped felon.

My New York friends were alarmed. They deluged me with telegrams and letters. Ed wrote guardedly, but I sensed his love between the lines. He wanted to come to Philadelphia, bring money, and get a lawyer, but I wired him to await developments. Many comrades visited me in the jail, and from them I learned that the meeting had been allowed to proceed after my arrest. Voltairine de Cleyre had taken my place and had protested vigorously against my suppression.

I had heard about this brilliant American girl and I knew that she had been influenced, like myself, by the judicial murder in Chicago, and that she had since become active in anarchist ranks. I had long wanted to meet her and I had visited her upon my arrival in Philadelphia, but I found her ill in bed. She always suffered a sick spell after a meeting, and she had lectured the previous evening. I thought it splendid of her to have gone to the meeting from a sick-bed and to have spoken in my behalf. I was proud of her comradeship.

The second morning after my arrest I was transferred to Moyamensing Prison to await extradition. I was put into a fairly large cell, its door of solid sheet iron, with a small square in the centre opening from the outside. The window was high and heavily barred. The cell contained a sanitary toilet, running water, a tin cup, a wooden table, a bench, and an iron cot. A small electric lamp hung from the ceiling. From time to time the square in the door would open and a pair of eyes would look in, or a voice would call for the cup and it would be passed back to me filled with tepid water or soup and a slice of bread. Except for such interruptions silence prevailed.

After the second day the stillness became oppressive and the hours crept on endlessly. I grew weary from constant pacing between the window and the door. My nerves were tense with the strain for some human sound. I called for the matron, but no one answered. I banged my tin cup against the door. Finally it brought response. My door was unlocked and a large woman with a hard face came into the cell. It was against the rules to make so much noise, she warned me. If I did it again, she would have to punish me. What did I want? I wanted my mail, I told her. I was sure there was some from my friends, and I also wanted books to read. She would bring a book, but there was no mail, the matron said. I knew she was lying, for I was certain Ed had written, even if no one else. She went out, locking the door after her. Presently she returned with a book. It was the Bible and it recalled to my mind the cruel face of my religious instructor in school. Indignantly I flung the volume at the matron's feet. I had no need of religious lies; I wanted some human book, I told her. For a moment she stood horror-stricken; then she began raging at me. I had desecrated God's word; I would be put in the dungeon; later on I would burn in hell. I replied heatedly that she did not dare punish me, because I was a prisoner of the State of New York, that I had not yet been tried and therefore still had some civil rights. She flung out, slamming the door after her.

In the evening I had a violent headache, caused by the electric light scorching my eyes. I again knocked on the door and demanded to see the doctor. Another woman came, the prison physician. She gave me some medicine and I asked her for some reading-matter, or at least some sewing. Next day I was given towels to hem. Eagerly I stitched by the hour, my thoughts with Sasha and Ed. With crushing clarity I saw what Sasha's life in prison meant. Twenty-two years! I should go mad in a year.

One day the matron came to announce that extradition had been granted and that I was to be taken to New York. I followed her into the office, where I was handed a large package of letters, telegrams, and papers. I was informed that several boxes of fruit and flowers had come for me, but that it was against the rules for prisoners to have such things. Then I was handed over to a heavy-set man. A cab waited outside the prison and we were driven to the station.

We travelled in a Pullman car, and the man introduced himself

as Detective-Sergeant ——. He excused himself, saying he was only doing his duty; he had six children to support. I asked him why he had
not chosen a more honourable occupation and why he had to bring
more spies into the world. If *he* did not do it, someone else would, he
replied. The police force was necessary; it protected society. Would
I have dinner? He would have it brought to the car to save my going
to the diner. I consented. I had not eaten anything decent for a week;
besides, the City of New York was paying for the unsolicited luxury
of my journey.

Over the dinner the detective referred to my youth and the life
" such a brilliant girl, with such abilities " had before her. He went
on to say that I never would earn anything by the work I was doing,
not even my salt. Why shouldn't I be sensible and " look out for number one " first? He felt for me because he was a *Yehude* himself.
He was sorry to see me go to prison. He could tell me how to get
free, even to receive a large sum of money, if I would only be sensible.

" Out with it," I said; " what's on your mind? "

His chief had instructed him to tell me that my case would be
quashed and a substantial sum of money presented to me if I would
give way a little. Nothing much, just a short periodic report of what
was going on in radical circles and among the workers on the East
Side.

A horrible feeling came over me. The food nauseated me. I gulped
down some ice-water from my glass and threw what was left into the
detective's face. " You miserable cur! " I shouted; " not enough that
you act as a Judas, you try even to turn me into one — you and your
rotten chief! I'll take prison for life, but no one will ever buy me! "

" All right, all right," he said soothingly; " have it your own way."

From the Pennsylvania Station I was driven to the Mulberry Street
Police Station, where I was locked up for the night. The cell was
small and ill-smelling, with only a wooden plank to sit or lie down
upon. I heard the clank of cells being locked and unlocked, crying and
hysterical weeping. But it was a relief not to see the bloated face and
not to have to breathe the same air with the loathsome detective.

The next morning I was taken before the Chief. The detective had
told him everything and he was furious. I was a fool, a stupid goose
who did not know what was good for her. He would put me away
for years where I could do no more harm. I let him rave, but before
I left, I told him that the whole country should learn how corrupt the

Chief of Police of New York can be. He raised a chair as if to strike me with it. Then, changing his mind, he called for a detective to take me back to the station-house.

I was overjoyed to find Ed, Justus Schwab, and Dr. Julius Hoffmann waiting for me there. In the afternoon I was brought before a judge and charged with inciting to riot on three counts. My trial was set for the 28th of September; my bail, to the amount of five thousand dollars, was given by Dr. Julius Hoffmann. In triumph my friends took me to Justus's den.

In my accumulated mail I found an underground letter from Sasha. He had read about my arrest. " Now you are indeed my sailor girl," he wrote. He had at last established communication with Nold and Bauer and they were arranging a *sub rosa* prison publication. They had already chosen a name; it was to be called " *Gefängniss-Blüthen* (Prison Blossoms)." I felt a weight lifted off my heart. Sasha had come back, he was beginning to take an interest in life, he would hold out! At most he would have to serve seven years on the first charge. We must work energetically to get his sentence commuted. I was light-hearted and happy in the thought that we might yet succeed in wrenching Sasha from his living grave.

Justus's place was crowded. People I had never before seen now came to express their sympathy. I had suddenly become an important personage, though I could not understand why, since I had done or said nothing that merited distinction. But I was glad to see so much interest in my ideas. I never doubted for a moment that it was the social theories I represented, and not I personally, that was attracting attention. My trial would give me a wonderful chance for propaganda. I must prepare for it. My defence in open court should carry the message of anarchism to the whole country.

I missed Claus Timmermann in the crowd and wondered what could be keeping him away. I turned to Ed and asked what had happened to cause Claus to neglect such an opportunity for free drinks. Ed was at first evasive, but on my insisting he informed me that the police had raided my grandmother's grocery store, expecting to find me there. Later on they arrested Claus. Knowing that he was often under the influence of liquor, the police hoped to learn from him my whereabouts. But Claus refused to talk, whereupon they beat him into unconsciousness and then railroaded him to six months in Blackwell's Island on the charge of resisting arrest.

As my own trial was approaching, Fedya, Ed, Justus, and other friends urged the need of counsel. I knew they were right. Sasha's mock trial had proved that, and now also the fate of Claus. I, too, would have no chance if I went into court without an attorney. But it seemed like a betrayal of Sasha to consent to legal defence. He had refused to compromise, although he knew that a long sentence was awaiting him. How could I do it? I would defend myself.

A week before the trial I received a *sub rosa* letter from Sasha. He had come to realize that as revolutionists we had small chance in an American court in any event, but we were altogether lost without legal defence. He did not regret his own stand; he still held that it was inconsistent for an anarchist to have a legal representative or to spend the workers' money on lawyers; but he felt that my situation was different. As a good speaker I could do much propaganda for our ideals in court, and a lawyer would protect my right to talk. He suggested that some prominent attorney of liberal views, such as Hugh O. Pentecost, might offer his services gratis. I knew it was Sasha's concern for my welfare that induced him to urge me to something he had so bravely denied himself. Or was it that his own experience had taught him our mistake? Sasha's letter and an offer of free counsel from an unexpected quarter changed my mind. The offer came from A. Oakey Hall.

My friends were delighted. A. Oakey Hall was a great jurist, besides being a man of liberal ideas. He had once been mayor of New York, but had proved to be too humane and democratic for the politicians. His affair with a young actress presented the opportunity to make Hall politically impossible. Hall, tall, distinguished-looking, vivacious, gave one the impression of a much younger man than his white hair indicated. I was curious to know why he was willing to take my case free of charge. He explained that it was partly out of sympathy with me and partly because of his antagonism to the police. He knew their corruption, he knew how easily they swear away a man's freedom, and he was anxious to expose their methods. My case would give him the opportunity. The issue of free speech being of national importance, my defence would bring his name before the public again. I liked the man's frankness and agreed to let him plead my case.

My trial began on the 28th of September before Judge Martin, lasting ten days, during which time the court-room was filled with reporters and my friends. The prosecuting attorney presented three indictments against me, but Oakey Hall spoiled his scheme. He pointed out that one could not justly be tried on three separate charges for one offence, and he was sustained by the Judge. Two of the three counts were set aside and I was tried only on the charge of inciting to riot.

At noon on the first day of the trial I went out to lunch with Ed, Justus, and John Henry Mackay, the anarchist poet. But when the court adjourned and my attorney was about to accompany me home, we were stopped. For the remainder of the trial, we were informed, I would be in the custody of the court. I would have to be sent to the Tombs. My counsel protested that I was out on bail, and that only in cases of murder was such procedure permissible. But to no purpose. I had to remain in custody. My friends gave me an ovation, cheering and singing revolutionary songs, the voice of Justus thundering above the rest. I called to them to keep our banner flying and to drink my portion, in addition to their own, to the day when courts and jailers would be no more.

The star witness for the State was Detective Jacobs. He produced notes, taken by him on the Union Square platform, as he claimed, and purporting to represent a verbatim account of my speech. He quoted me as urging " revolution, violence, and bloodshed." Twelve persons who had been at the meeting and had heard me speak came forward to testify in my behalf. Every one of them stated that it would have been a physical impossibility to take notes at my meeting because of the overcrowding on the platform. Jacobs's notes were submitted to a handwriting expert, who declared that the writing was too regular and even to have been written in a standing position in a crowded place. But neither his testimony nor that of the witnesses for the defence availed against the statements of the detective. When I took the stand in my own behalf, District Attorney MacIntyre persisted in questioning me on everything under the sun except my Union Square speech. Religion, free love, morality — what were my opinions on those subjects? I attempted to unmask the hypocrisy of morality, the Church as an instrument for enslavement, the impossibility of love that is forced and not free. Constant interruptions by MacIntyre and orders from the Judge to reply only with yes or no finally compelled me to give up the task.

In his closing speech MacIntyre waxed eloquent over what would happen if " this dangerous woman " were allowed to go free. Property would be destroyed, the children of the rich would be exterminated, the streets of New York would stream with blood. He talked himself into such frenzy that his starched collar and cuffs became flabby and began dripping sweat. It made me more uncomfortable than his oratory.

Oakey Hall delivered a brilliant address ridiculing Jacobs's testimony and castigating the police methods and the stand of the Court. His client was an idealist, he declared; all the great things in our world have been promulgated by idealists. More violent speeches than Emma Goldman had ever made were never prosecuted in court. The moneyed classes of America were seeing red since Governor Altgeld had pardoned the three surviving anarchists of the group hanged in Chicago in 1887. The New York Police sought in the Union Square meeting an opportunity to make Emma Goldman an anarchist target. It was clear that his client was the victim of police persecution. He closed his speech with an eloquent plea for the right of free expression and the acquittal of the prisoner.

The Judge enlarged on law and order, the sanctity of property, and the need of protecting " free American institutions." The jury deliberated for a long time; it was evidently loath to convict. Once the foreman came back for instructions: the jury seemed especially impressed by the testimony of one of my witnesses, a young reporter on the New York *World*. He had been at the meeting and had written a detailed account of it. When he saw his story in the paper the following morning, it was so garbled that he had at once offered to testify to the actual facts. While he was on the witness-stand, Jacobs bent over to MacIntyre, whispered something, and a court attendant was sent out. He soon returned with a copy of the *World* of the morning after the meeting. The reporter could not charge some desk editor in open court with having tampered with his account. He became embarrassed, confused, and obviously very miserable. His report as printed in the *World,* and not as testified to by him on the witness-stand, decided my fate. I was found guilty.

My attorney insisted on an appeal to the higher court, but I refused. The farce of my trial had strengthened my opposition to the State and I would ask no favours from it. I was ordered back to the Tombs until the 18th of October, the day set for sentence.

Before being taken to jail I was allowed a short visit with my friends. I repeated to them what I had already told Oakey Hall: I would not consent to an appeal. They agreed that nothing could be gained except some respite while the case would be pending. A moment's weakness overcame me, the thought of Ed and of our love, so young, so full of happy possibilities. The temptation was great. But — I must go the way many had gone before me. I would get a year or two; what was that compared with Sasha's fate? I would go the way.

In the interval before my sentence the papers carried sensational stories about " anarchists planning to storm the court-room " and " preparations for a forcible rescue of Emma Goldman." The police were getting ready to " cope with the situation," radical quarters were being watched, and the court-house was well guarded. No one except the prisoner, counsel, and press representatives would be allowed in the court building on the day of sentence.

My attorney sent word to my friends of his decision not to be present in court on that date because of my " stubbornness in refusing an appeal to a higher tribunal." But Hugh O. Pentecost would be on hand, not as counsel, but as friend, to protect my legal rights and demand that I be permitted opportunity to speak. Ed informed me that the New York *World* had offered to publish the statement I had prepared for the Court. It would reach a great many more people in that way than my talk in the court-room. I wondered that the *World,* which had carried a falsified report of my Union Square speech, should now offer to publish my statement. Ed said that there was no accounting for the inconsistencies of the capitalist press. At any rate, the *World* had promised to permit him to see the proofs, and thus we should be assured against misrepresentation. My statement would appear in a special edition immediately after sentence had been passed. My friends urged me to let the *World* have the manuscript, and I consented.

On the way from the Tombs to the court New York looked as if it were under martial law. The streets were lined with police, the buildings surrounded by heavily armed cordons, the corridors of the court-house filled with officers. I was called to the bar and asked if I had " anything to say why sentence should not be passed." I had considerable to say; should I be given the chance? No, that was impossible; I could only make a very brief statement. Then I would say only that I had expected no justice from a capitalist court. The Court might do its worst, but it was powerless to change my views, I said.

Judge Martin sentenced me to one year in Blackwell's Island

Penitentiary. On my way to the Tombs I heard the news-boys shout: " Extra! Extra! Emma Goldman's speech in court!" and I felt glad that the *World* had kept its promise. I was at once placed in the Black Maria and taken to the boat that delivers prisoners to Blackwell's Island.

It was a bright October day, the sun playing on the water as the barge sped on. Several newspaper men accompanied me, all pressing me for an interview. " I travel in queenly state," I remarked in light mood; " just look at my satraps." " You can't squelch that kid," a young reporter kept on saying, admiringly. When we reached the island, I bade my escorts good-bye, admonishing them not to write any more lies than they could help. I called out to them gaily that I would see them again within a year and then followed the Deputy Sheriff along the broad, tree-lined gravel walk to the prison entrance. There I turned towards the river, took a last deep breath of the free air, and stepped across the threshold of my new home.

EDWARD BRADY IN 1893

CHAPTER XII

I WAS CALLED BEFORE THE HEAD MATRON, A TALL WOMAN WITH A stolid face. She began taking my pedigree. " What religion? " was her first question. " None, I am an atheist." " Atheism is prohibited here. You will have to go to church." I replied that I would do nothing of the kind. I did not believe in anything the Church stood for and, not being a hypocrite, I would not attend. Besides, I came from Jewish people. Was there a synagogue?

She said curtly that there were services for the Jewish convicts on Saturday afternoon, but as I was the only Jewish female prisoner, she could not permit me to go among so many men.

After a bath and a change into the prison uniform I was sent to my cell and locked in.

I knew from what Most had related to me about Blackwell's Island that the prison was old and damp, the cells small, without light or water. I was therefore prepared for what was awaiting me. But the moment the door was locked on me, I began to experience a feeling of suffocation. In the dark I groped for something to sit on and found a narrow iron cot. Sudden exhaustion overpowered me and I fell asleep.

I became aware of a sharp burning in my eyes, and I jumped up in fright. A lamp was being held close to the bars. " What is it? " I cried, forgetting where I was. The lamp was lowered and I saw a thin, ascetic face gazing at me. A soft voice congratulated me on my sound sleep. It was the evening matron on her regular rounds. She told me to undress and left me.

But there was no more sleep for me that night. The irritating feel of the coarse blanket, the shadows creeping past the bars, kept me awake until the sound of a gong again brought me to my feet. The cells were being unlocked, the doors heavily thrown open. Blue and white striped figures slouched by, automatically forming into a line, myself a part of it. " March! " and the line began to move along the corridor down the steps towards a corner containing wash-stands and towels. Again the command: " Wash! " and everybody began clamouring for a towel, already soiled and wet. Before I had time to splash some water on my hands and face and wipe myself half-dry, the order was given to march back.

Then breakfast: a slice of bread and a tin cup of warm brownish water. Again the line formed, and the striped humanity was broken up in sections and sent to its daily tasks. With a group of other women I was taken to the sewing-room.

The procedure of forming lines — " Forward, march! " — was repeated three times a day, seven days a week. After each meal ten minutes were allowed for talk. A torrent of words would then break forth from the pent-up beings. Each precious second increased the roar of sounds; and then sudden silence.

The sewing-room was large and light, the sun often streaming through the high windows, its rays intensifying the whiteness of the walls and the monotony of the regulation dress. In the sharp light the figures in baggy and ungainly attire appeared more hideous. Still, the shop was a welcome relief from the cell. Mine, on the ground floor, was grey and damp even in the day-time; the cells on the upper floors were somewhat brighter. Close to the barred door one could even read by the help of the light coming from the corridor windows.

The locking of the cells for the night was the worst experience of the day. The convicts were marched along the tiers in the usual line. On reaching her cell each left the line, stepped inside, hands on the iron door, and awaited the command. " Close! " and with a crash the seventy doors shut, each prisoner automatically locking herself in. More harrowing still was the daily degradation of being forced to march in lock-step to the river, carrying the bucket of excrement accumulated during twenty-four hours.

I was put in charge of the sewing-shop. My task consisted in cutting the cloth and preparing work for the two dozen women employed. In addition I had to keep account of the incoming material and the outgoing bundles. I welcomed the work. It helped me to forget the dreary existence within the prison. But the evenings were torturous. The first few weeks I would fall asleep as soon as I touched the pillow. Soon, however, the nights found me restlessly tossing about, seeking sleep in vain. The appalling nights — even if I should get the customary two months' commutation time, I still had nearly two hundred and ninety of them. Two hundred and ninety — and Sasha? I used to lie awake and mentally figure in the dark the number of days and nights before him. Even if he could come out after his first sentence of seven years, he would still have more than twenty-five hundred nights! Dread overcame me that Sasha could not survive them. Nothing was so likely to drive people to madness, I felt, as sleepless nights in prison. Better dead, I thought. Dead? Frick was not dead, and Sasha's glorious youth, his life, the things he might have accomplished — all were being sacrificed — perhaps for nothing. But — was Sasha's *Attentat* in vain? Was my revolutionary faith a mere echo of what others had said or taught me? " No, not in vain! " something within me insisted. " No sacrifice is lost for a great ideal."

One day I was told by the head matron that I would have to get better results from the women. They were not doing so much work, she said, as under the prisoner who had had charge of the sewing-shop before me. I resented the suggestion that I become a slave-driver. It was because I hated slaves as well as their drivers, I informed the matron, that I had been sent to prison. I considered myself one of the inmates, not above them. I was determined not to do anything that would involve a denial of my ideals. I preferred punishment. One of the methods of treating offenders consisted in placing them in a corner facing a blackboard and compelling them to stay for hours in that position, constantly before the matron's vigilant eyes. This seemed to me petty and insulting. I decided that if I was offered such an indignity, I would increase my offence and take the dungeon. But the days passed and I was not punished.

News in prison travels with amazing rapidity. Within twenty-four hours all the women knew that I had refused to act as a slave-driver. They had not been unkind to me, but they had kept aloof. They had been told that I was a terrible " anarchist " and that I didn't believe in God. They had never seen me in church and I did not participate in their ten-minute gush of talk. I was a freak in their eyes. But when they learned that I had refused to play the boss over them, their reserve broke down. Sundays after church the cells would be opened to permit the women an hour's visit with one another. The next Sunday I received visits from every inmate on my tier. They felt I was their friend, they assured me, and they would do anything for me. Girls working in the laundry offered to wash my clothes, others to darn my stockings. Everyone was anxious to do some service. I was deeply moved. These poor creatures so hungered for kindness that the least sign of it loomed high on their limited horizons. After that they would often come to me with their troubles, their hatred of the head matron, their confidences about their infatuations with the male convicts. Their ingenuity in carrying on flirtations under the very eyes of the officials was amazing.

My three weeks in the Tombs had given me ample proof that the revolutionary contention that crime is the result of poverty is based on fact. Most of the defendants who were awaiting trial came from the lowest strata of society, men and women without friends, often even without a home. Unfortunate, ignorant creatures they were, but still with hope in their hearts, because they had not yet been convicted. In the penitentiary despair possessed almost all of the prisoners. It served to unveil the mental darkness, fear, and superstition which held them in bondage. Among the seventy inmates, there were no more than half a dozen who showed any intelligence whatever. The rest were outcasts without the least social consciousness. Their personal misfortunes filled their thoughts; they could not understand that they were victims, links in an endless chain of injustice and inequality. From early childhood they had known nothing but poverty, squalor, and want, and the same conditions were awaiting them on their release. Yet they were capable of sympathy and devotion, of generous impulses. I soon had occasion to convince myself of it when I was taken ill.

The dampness of my cell and the chill of the late December days had brought on an attack of my old complaint, rheumatism. For some days the head matron opposed my being taken to the hospital, but she was finally compelled to submit to the order of the visiting physician.

Blackwell's Island Penitentiary was fortunate in the absence of a " steady " physician. The inmates were receiving medical attendance from the Charity Hospital, which was situated near by. That institution had six weeks' post-graduate courses, which meant frequent changes in the staff. They were under the direct supervision of a visiting physician from New York City, Dr. White, a humane and kindly man. The treatment given the prisoners was as good as patients received in any New York hospital.

The sick-ward was the largest and brightest room in the building. Its spacious windows looked out upon a wide lawn in front of the prison and, farther on, the East River. In fine weather the sun streamed in generously. A month's rest, the kindliness of the physician, and the thoughtful attention of my fellow prisoners relieved me of my pain and enabled me to get about again.

During one of his rounds Dr. White picked up the card hanging at the foot of my bed giving my crime and pedigree. " Inciting to riot," he read. " Piffle! I don't believe you could hurt a fly. A fine inciter you would make! " he chuckled, then asked me if I should not like to remain in the hospital to take care of the sick. " I should, indeed," I replied, " but I know nothing about nursing." He assured me that neither did anyone else in the prison. He had tried for some time to induce the city to put a trained nurse in charge of the ward, but he had not succeeded. For operations and grave cases he had to bring a nurse from the Charity Hospital. I could easily pick up the elementary things about tending the sick. He would teach me to take the pulse and temperature and to perform similar services. He would speak to the Warden and the head matron if I wanted to remain.

Soon I took up my new work. The ward contained sixteen beds, most of them always filled. The various diseases were treated in the same room, from grave operations to tuberculosis, pneumonia, and childbirth. My hours were long and strenuous, the groans of the patients nerve-racking; but I loved my job. It gave me opportunity to come close to the sick women and bring a little cheer into their lives. I was so much richer than they: I had love and friends, received many letters and daily messages from Ed. Some Austrian anarchists, owners of a restaurant, sent me dinners every day, which Ed himself brought to the boat. Fedya supplied fruit and delicacies weekly. I had so much to give; it was a joy to share with my sisters who had neither friends nor attention. There were a few exceptions, of course; but the majority had nothing. They never had had anything before and they would have nothing on their release. They were derelicts on the social dung-heap.

I was gradually given entire charge of the hospital ward, part of my duties being to divide the special rations allowed the sick prisoners. They consisted of a quart of milk, a cup of beef tea, two eggs, two crackers, and two lumps of sugar for each invalid. On several occasions milk and eggs were missing and I reported the matter to a day matron. Later she informed me that a head matron had said that it did not matter and that certain patients were strong enough to do without their extra rations. I had had considerable opportunity to study this head matron, who felt a violent dislike of everyone not Anglo-Saxon. Her special targets were the Irish and the Jews, against whom she discriminated habitually. I was therefore not surprised to get such a message from her.

A few days later I was told by the prisoner who brought the hospital rations that the missing portions had been given by this head matron to two husky Negro prisoners. That also did not surprise me. I knew she had a special fondness for the coloured inmates. She rarely punished them and often gave them unusual privileges. In return her favourites would spy on the other prisoners, even on those of their own colour who were too decent to be bribed. I myself never had any prejudice against coloured people; in fact, I felt deeply for them because they were being treated like slaves in America. But I hated discrimination. The idea that sick people, white or coloured, should be robbed of their rations to feed healthy persons outraged my sense of justice, but I was powerless to do anything in the matter.

After my first clashes with this woman she left me severely alone. Once she became enraged because I refused to translate a Russian letter that had arrived for one of the prisoners. She had called me into her office to read the letter and tell her its contents. When I saw that the letter was not for me, I informed her that I was not employed by the prison as a translator. It was bad enough for the officials to pry into the personal mail of helpless human beings, but I would not do it. She said that it was stupid of me not to take advantage of her goodwill. She could put me back in my cell, deprive me of my commutation time for good behaviour, and make the rest of my stay very hard. She could do as she pleased, I told her, but I would not read the private letters of my unfortunate sisters, much less translate them to her.

Then came the matter of the missing rations. The sick women began to suspect that they were not getting their full share and complained to the doctor. Confronted with a direct question from him, I had to tell the truth. I did not know what he said to the offending matron, but the full rations began to arrive again. Two days later I was called downstairs and locked up in the dungeon.

I had repeatedly seen the effect of a dungeon experience on other women prisoners. One inmate had been kept there for twenty-eight days on bread and water, although the regulations prohibited a longer stay than forty-eight hours. She had to be carried out on a stretcher; her hands and legs were swollen, her body covered with a rash. The descriptions the poor creature and others had given me used to make me ill. But nothing I had heard compared with the reality. The cell was barren; one had to sit or lie down on the cold stone floor. The dampness of the walls made the dungeon a ghastly place. Worse yet was the complete shutting out of light and air, the impenetrable blackness, so thick that one could not see the hand before one's face. It gave me the sensation of sinking into a devouring pit. " The Spanish Inquisition come to life in America " — I thought of Most's description. He had not exaggerated.

After the door shut behind me, I stood still, afraid to sit down or to lean against the wall. Then I groped for the door. Gradually the blackness paled. I caught a faint sound slowly approaching; I heard a key turn in the lock. A matron appeared. I recognized Miss Johnson, the one who had frightened me out of my sleep on my first night in the penitentiary. I had come to know and appreciate her as a beautiful personality. Her kindness to the prisoners was the one ray of light in their dreary existence. She had taken me to her bosom almost from the first, and in many indirect ways she had shown me her affection. Often at night, when all were asleep, and quiet had fallen on the prison, Miss Johnson would enter the hospital ward, put my head in her lap, and tenderly stroke my hair. She would tell me the news in the papers to distract me and try to cheer my depressed mood. I knew I had found a friend in the woman, who herself was a lonely soul, never having known the love of man or child.

She came into the dungeon carrying a camp-chair and a blanket. " You can sit on that," she said, " and wrap yourself up. I'll leave the door open a bit to let in some air. I'll bring you hot coffee later. It will help to pass the night." She told me how painful it was for her to see the prisoners locked up in the dreadful hole, but she could do nothing for them because most of them could not be trusted. It was different with me, she was sure.

At five in the morning my friend had to take back the chair and blanket and lock me in. I no longer was oppressed by the dungeon. The humanity of Miss Johnson had dissolved the blackness.

When I was taken out of the dungeon and sent back to the hospital, I saw that it was almost noon. I resumed my duties. Later I learned that Dr. White had asked for me, and upon being informed that I was in punishment he had categorically demanded my release.

No visitors were allowed in the penitentiary until after one month had been served. Ever since my entry I had been longing for Ed, yet at the same time I dreaded his coming. I remembered my terrible visit with Sasha. But it was not quite so appalling in Blackwell's Island. I met Ed in a room where other prisoners were having their relatives and friends to see them. There was no guard between us. Everyone was so absorbed in his own visitor that no one paid any attention to us. Still we felt constrained. With clasped hands we talked of general things.

My second visit took place in the hospital, Miss Johnson being on duty. She thoughtfully put a screen to shut us out from the view of the other patients, she herself keeping at a distance. Ed took me in his arms. It was bliss to feel again the warmth of his body, to hear his beating heart, to cling hungrily to his lips. But his departure left me in an emotional turmoil, consumed by a passionate need for my lover. During the day I strove to subdue the hot desire surging through my veins, but at night the craving held me in its power. Sleep would come finally, sleep disturbed by dreams and images of intoxicating nights with Ed. The ordeal was too torturing and too exhausting. I was glad when he brought Fedya and other friends along.

Once Ed came accompanied by Voltairine de Cleyre. She had been invited by New York friends to address a meeting arranged in my behalf. When I had visited her in Philadelphia, she had been too ill to speak. I was glad of the opportunity to come closer to her now. We talked about things nearest to our hearts — Sasha, the movement. Voltairine promised to join me, on my release, in a new effort for Sasha. Meanwhile she would write to him, she said. Ed, too, was in touch with him.

My visitors were always sent up to the hospital. I was therefore surprised one day to be called to the Warden's office to see someone. It proved to be John Swinton and his wife. Swinton was a nationally known figure; he had worked with the abolitionists and had fought in the Civil War. As editor-in-chief of the New York *Sun* he had pleaded for the European refugees who came to find asylum in the United States. He was the friend and adviser of young literary aspirants, and he had been one of the first to defend Walt Whitman against the misrepresentations of the purists. Tall, erect, with beautiful features, John Swinton was an impressive figure.

He greeted me warmly, remarking that he had just been saying to Warden Pillsbury that he himself had made more violent speeches during the abolition days than anything I said at Union Square. Yet he had not been arrested. He had told the Warden that he ought to be ashamed of himself to keep " a little girl like that " locked up. " And what do you suppose he said ? He said he had no choice — he was only doing his duty. All weaklings say that, cowards who always put the blame on others." Just then the Warden approached us. He assured Swinton that I was a model prisoner and that I had become an efficient nurse in the short time. In fact, I was doing such good work that he wished I had been given five years. " Generous cuss, aren't you ? " Swinton laughed. " Perhaps you'll give her a paid job when her time is up ? " " I would, indeed," Pillsbury replied. " Well, you'd be a damn fool. Don't you know she doesn't believe in prisons ? Sure as you live, she'd let them all escape, and what would become of you then ? " The poor man was embarrassed, but he joined in the banter. Before my visitor took leave, he turned once more to the Warden, cautioning him to " take good care of his little friend," else he would " take it out of his hide."

The visit of the Swintons completely changed the attitude of the head matron towards me. The Warden had always been quite decent, and she now began showering privileges on me : food from her own table, fruit, coffee, and walks on the island. I refused her favours except the walks; it was my first opportunity in six months to go out in the open and inhale the spring air without iron bars to check me.

In March 1894 we received a large influx of women prisoners. They were nearly all prostitutes rounded up during recent raids. The city had been blessed by a new vice crusade. The Lexow Committee, with the Reverend Dr. Parkhurst at its head, wielded the broom which was to sweep New York clean of the fearful scourge. The men found in the public houses were allowed to go free, but the women were arrested and sentenced to Blackwell's Island.

Most of the unfortunates came in a deplorable condition. They were suddenly cut off from the narcotics which almost all of them had been habitually using. The sight of their suffering was heart-breaking. With the strength of giants the frail creatures would shake the iron bars, curse, and scream for dope and cigarettes. Then they would fall exhausted to the ground, pitifully moaning through the night.

The misery of the poor creatures brought back my own hard struggle to do without the soothing effect of cigarettes. Except for the ten weeks of my illness in Rochester, I had smoked for years, sometimes as many as forty cigarettes a day. When we were very hard pressed for money, and it was a toss-up between bread and cigarettes, we would generally decide to buy the latter. We simply could not go for very long without smoking. Being cut off from the satisfaction of the habit when I came to the penitentiary, I found the torture almost beyond endurance. The nights in the cell became doubly hideous. The only way to get tobacco in prison was by means of bribery. I knew that if any of the inmates were caught bringing me cigarettes, they would be punished. I could not expose them to the risk. Snuff tobacco was allowed, but I could never take to it. There was nothing to be done but to get used to the deprivation. I had resisting power and I could forget my craving in reading.

Not so the new arrivals. When they learned that I was in charge of the medicine chest, they pursued me with offers of money; worse still, with pitiful appeals to my humanity. " Just a whiff of dope, for the love of Christ! " I rebelled against the Christian hypocrisy which allowed the men to go free and sent the poor women to prison for having ministered to the sexual demands of those men. Suddenly cutting off the victims from the narcotics they had used for years seemed ruthless. I would have gladly given the addicts what they craved so terribly. It was not fear of punishment which kept me from bringing them relief; it was Dr. White's faith in me. He had trusted me with the medicines, he had been kind and generous — I could not fail him. The screams of the women would unnerve me for days, but I stuck to my responsibility.

One day a young Irish girl was brought to the hospital for an operation. In view of the seriousness of the case Dr. White called in two trained nurses. The operation lasted until late in the evening, and then the patient was left in my charge. She was very ill from the effect of the ether, vomited violently, and burst the stitches of her wound, which resulted in a severe hæmorrhage. I sent a hurry call to the Charity Hospital. It seemed hours before the doctor and his staff arrived. There were no nurses this time and I had to take their place.

The day had been an unusually hard one and I had had very little sleep. I felt exhausted and had to hold on to the operating-table with my left hand while passing with my right instruments and sponges. Suddenly the operating-table gave way, and my arm was caught. I screamed with pain. Dr. White was so absorbed in his manipulations that for a moment he did not realize what had happened. When he at last had the table raised and my arm was lifted out, it looked as if every bone had been broken. The pain was excruciating and he ordered a shot of morphine. "We'll set her arm later. This has got to come first." "No morphine," I begged. I still remembered the effect of morphine on me when Dr. Julius Hoffmann had given me a dose against insomnia. It had put me to sleep, but during the night I had tried to throw myself out of the window, and it had required all of Sasha's strength to pull me back. The morphine had crazed me, and now I would have none of it.

One of the physicians gave me something that had a soothing effect. After the patient on the operating-table had been returned to her bed, Dr. White examined my arm. "You're nice and chubby," he said; "that has saved your bones. Nothing has been broken — just flattened a bit." My arm was put in a splint. The doctor wanted me to go to bed, but there was no one else to sit up with the patient. It might be her last night: her tissues were so badly infected that they would not hold the stitches, and another hæmorrhage would prove fatal. I decided to remain at her bedside. I knew I could not sleep with the case as serious as it was.

All night I watched her struggle for life. In the morning I sent for the priest. Everyone was surprised at my action, particularly the head matron. How could I, an atheist, do such a thing, she wondered, and choose a priest, at that! I had declined to see the missionaries as well as the rabbi. She had noticed how friendly I had become with the two Catholic sisters who often visited us on Sunday. I had even made coffee for them. Didn't I think that the Catholic Church had always been the enemy of progress and that it had persecuted and tortured the Jews? How could I be so inconsistent? Of course, I thought so, I assured her. I was just as opposed to the Catholic as to the other Churches. I considered them all alike, enemies of the people. They preached submission, and their God was the God of the rich and the mighty. I hated their God and would never make peace with him. But if I could believe in any religion at all, I should prefer the Catholic Church. "It is less hypocritical," I said to her; "it makes allowance for human frailties and it has a sense of beauty." The Catholic sisters and the priest had not tried to preach to me like the missionaries, the minister, and the vulgar rabbi. They left my soul to its own fate; they talked to me about human things, especially the priest, who was a cultured man. My poor patient had reached the end of a life that had been too hard for her. The priest might give her a few moments of peace and kindness; why should I not have sent for him? But the matron was too dull to follow my argument or understand my motives. I remained a " queer one," in her estimation.

Before my patient died, she begged me to lay her out. I had been kinder to her, she said, than her own mother. She wanted to know that it would be my hand that would get her ready for the last journey. I would make her beautiful; she wanted to look beautiful to meet Mother Mary and the Lord Jesus. It required little effort to make her as lovely in death as she had been in life. Her black curls made her alabaster face more delicate than the artificial methods she had used to enhance her looks. Her luminous eyes were closed now; I had closed them with my own hands. But her chiselled eyebrows and long, black lashes were remindful of the radiance that had been hers. How she must have fascinated men! And they destroyed her. Now she was beyond their reach. Death had smoothed her suffering. She looked serene in her marble whiteness now.

During the Jewish Easter holidays I was again called to the Warden's office. I found my grandmother there. She had repeatedly begged Ed to take her to see me, but he had declined in order to spare her the painful experience. The devoted soul could not be stopped. With her broken English she had made her way to the Commissioner of Corrections, procured a pass, and come to the penitentiary. She handed me a large white handkerchief containing matzoth, *gefüllte* fish, and some Easter cake of her own baking. She tried to explain to the Warden what a good Jewish daughter her *Chavele* was; in fact, better than any rabbi's wife, because she gave everything to the poor. She was fearfully wrought up when the moment of departure came, and I tried to soothe her, begging her not to break down before the Warden. She bravely dried her tears and walked out straight and proud, but I knew she would weep bitterly as soon as she got out of sight. No doubt she also prayed to her God for her *Chavele*.

June saw many prisoners discharged from the sick-ward, only a few beds remaining occupied. For the first time since coming to the hospital I had some leisure, enabling me to read more systematically. I had accumulated a large library; John Swinton had sent me many books, as did also other friends; but most of them were from Justus Schwab. He had never come to see me; he had asked Ed to tell me that it was impossible for him to visit me. He hated prison so much that he would not be able to leave me behind. If he should come, he would be tempted to use force to take me back with him, and it would only cause trouble. Instead he sent me stacks of books. Walt Whitman, Emerson, Thoreau, Hawthorne, Spencer, John Stuart Mill, and many other English and American authors I learned to know and love through the friendship of Justus. At the same time other elements also became interested in my salvation — spiritualists and metaphysical redeemers of various kinds. I tried honestly to get at their meaning, but I was no doubt too much of the earth to follow their shadows in the clouds.

Among the books I received was the *Life of Albert Brisbane,* written by his widow. The fly-leaf had an appreciative dedication to me. The book came with a cordial letter from her son, Arthur Brisbane, who expressed his admiration and the hope that on my release I would allow him to arrange an evening for me. The biography of Brisbane brought me in touch with Fourier and other pioneers of socialist thought.

The prison library had some good literature, including the works of George Sand, George Eliot, and Ouida. The librarian in charge was an educated Englishman serving a five-year sentence for forgery. The books he handed out to me soon began to contain love notes framed in most affectionate terms, and presently they flamed with passion. He had already put in four years in prison, one of his notes read, and he was starved for the love of woman and companionship. He begged me at least to give him the companionship. Would I write him occasionally about the books I was reading? I disliked becoming involved in a silly prison flirtation, yet the need for free, uncensored expression was too compelling to resist. We exchanged many notes, often of a very ardent nature.

My admirer was a splendid musician and played the organ in the chapel. I should have loved to attend, to be able to hear him and feel him near, but the sight of the male prisoners in stripes, some of them handcuffed, and still further degraded and insulted by the lip-service of the minister, was too appalling to me. I had seen it once on the fourth of July, when some politician had come over to speak to the inmates about the glories of American liberty. I had to pass through the male wing on an errand to the Warden, and I heard the pompous patriot spouting of freedom and independence to the mental and physical wrecks. One convict had been put in irons because of an attempted escape. I could hear the clanking of his chains with his every movement. I could not bear to go to church.

The chapel was underneath the hospital ward. Twice on Sundays

I could listen on the stairway to my prison flame playing the organ. Sunday was quite a holiday: the head matron was off duty, and we were free from the irritation of her harsh voice. Sometimes the two Catholic sisters would come on that day. I was charmed with the younger one, still in her teens, very lovely and full of life. Once I asked her what had induced her to take the veil. Turning her large eyes upwards, she said: " The priest was young and so beautiful! " The " baby nun," as I called her, would prattle for hours in her cheery young voice, telling me the news and gossip. It was a relief from the prison greyness.

Of the friends I made on Blackwell's Island the priest was the most interesting. At first I felt antagonistic to him. I thought he was like the rest of the religious busybodies, but I soon found that he wanted to talk only about books. He had studied in Cologne and had read much. He knew I had many books and he asked me to exchange some of them with him. I was amazed and wondered what kind of books he would bring me, expecting the New Testament or the Catechism. But he came with works of poetry and music. He had free access to the prison at any time, and often he would come to the ward at nine in the evening and remain till after midnight. We would discuss his favourite composers — Bach, Beethoven, and Brahms — and compare our views on poetry and social ideas. He presented me with an English-Latin dictionary as a gift, inscribed: " With the highest respect, to Emma Goldman."

On one occasion I asked him why he never gave me the Bible. " Because no one can understand or love it if he is forced to read it," he replied. That appealed to me and I asked him for it. Its simplicity of language and legendry fascinated me. There was no make-believe about my young friend. He was devout, entirely consecrated. He observed every fast and he would lose himself in prayer for hours. Once he asked me to help him decorate the chapel. When I came down, I found the frail, emaciated figure in silent prayer, oblivious of his surroundings. My own ideal, my faith, was at the opposite pole from his, but I knew he was as ardently sincere as I. Our fervour was our meeting-ground.

Warden Pillsbury often came to the hospital. He was an unusual man for his surroundings. His grandfather had been a jailer, and both his father and himself had been born in the prison. He understood his wards and the social forces that had created them. Once he remarked to me that he could not bear " stool-pigeons "; he preferred the prisoner who had pride and who would not stoop to mean acts against his fellow convicts in order to gain privileges for himself. If an inmate asseverated that he would reform and never again commit a crime, the Warden felt sure he was lying. He knew that no one could start a new life after years of prison and with the whole world against him unless he had outside friends to help him. He used to say that the State did not even supply a released man with enough money for his first week's meals. How, then, could he be expected to " make good? " He would relate the story of the man who on the morning of his release told him: " Pillsbury, the next watch and chain I steal I'll send to you as a present." " That's my man," the Warden would laugh.

Pillsbury was in a position to do much good for the unfortunates in his charge, but he was constantly hampered. He had to allow prisoners to do cooking, washing, and cleaning for others than themselves. If the table damask was not properly rolled before ironing, the laundress stood in danger of confinement to the dungeon. The whole prison was demoralized by favouritism. Convicts were deprived of food for the slightest infraction, but Pillsbury, who was an old man, was powerless to do much about it. Besides, he was eager to avoid a scandal.

The nearer the day of my liberation approached, the more unbearable life in prison became. The days dragged and I grew restless and irritable with impatience. Even reading became impossible. I would sit for hours lost in reminiscences. I thought of the comrades in the Illinois penitentiary brought back to life by the pardon of Governor Altgeld. Since I had come to prison, I realized how much the release of the three men, Neebe, Fielden, and Schwab, had done for the cause for which their comrades in Chicago had been hanged. The venom of the press against Altgeld for his gesture of justice proved how deeply he had struck the vested interests, particularly by his analysis of the trial and his clear demonstration that the executed anarchists had been judicially killed in spite of their proved innocence of the crime charged against them. Every detail of the momentous days of 1887 stood out in strong relief before me. Then Sasha, our life together, his act, his martyrdom — every moment of the five years since I had first met him I now relived with poignant reality. Why was it, I mused, that Sasha was still so deeply rooted in my being? Was not my love for Ed more ecstatic, more enriching? Perhaps it was his act that had bound me to him with such powerful cords. How insignificant was my own prison experience compared with what Sasha was suffering in the Allegheny purgatory! I now felt ashamed that, even for a moment, I could have found my incarceration hard. Not one friendly face in the court-room to be near Sasha and comfort him — solitary confinement and complete isolation, for no more visits had been allowed him. The Inspector had kept his promise; since my visit in November 1892, Sasha had not again been permitted to see anyone. How he must have craved the sight and touch of a kindred spirit, how he must be yearning for it!

My thoughts rushed on. Fedya, the lover of beauty, so fine and sensitive! And Ed. Ed — he had kissed to life so many mysterious longings, had opened such spiritual sources of wealth to me! I owed my development to Ed, and to the others, too, who had been in my life. And yet, more than all else, it was the prison that had proved the best school. A more painful, but a more vital, school. Here I had been brought close to the depths and complexities of the human soul; here I had found ugliness and beauty, meanness and generosity. Here, too, I had learned to see life through my own eyes and not through those of Sasha, Most, or Ed. The prison had been the crucible that tested my faith. It had helped me to discover strength in my own being, the strength to stand alone, the strength to live my life and fight for my ideals, against the whole world if need be. The State of New York could have rendered me no greater service than by sending me to Blackwell's Island Penitentiary!

CHAPTER XIII

THE DAYS AND WEEKS THAT FOLLOWED MY RELEASE WERE LIKE A nightmare. I needed quiet, peace, and privacy after my prison experience, but I was surrounded by people, and there were meetings nearly every evening. I lived in a daze: everything around me seemed incongruous and unreal. My thoughts continued in captivity; my fellow convicts haunted my waking and sleeping hours, and the prison noises kept ringing in my ears. The command " Close! " followed by the crash of iron doors and the clank-clank of the chains, pursued me when I faced an audience.

The strangest experience I had was at the meeting arranged to welcome me on my release. It took place in the Thalia Theatre and the house was crowded. Many well-known men and women of various social groups in New York had come to celebrate my liberation. I sat listless, in a stupor. I strove to keep contact with reality, to listen to what was going on, to concentrate on what I intended to say, but it was in vain. I kept drifting back to Blackwell's Island. The vast audience imperceptibly changed to the pale, frightened faces of the women prisoners, the voices of the speakers took on the harshness of the head matron. Presently I became conscious of the pressure of a hand on my shoulder. It was Maria Louise, who was presiding at the meeting. She had called me several times and had announced that I was the next to address the gathering. " You seem as if asleep," she said.

I got to my feet, walked to the footlights, saw the audience rise to greet me. Then I tried to speak. My lips moved, but there was no sound. Hideous figures in fantastic stripes emerged from every aisle, slowly moving towards me. I grew faint and helplessly turned to Maria Louise. In a whisper, as if fearing to be overheard, I begged her to explain to the audience that I felt dizzy and that I would speak later. Ed was near and he led me behind the stage into a dressing-

room. I had never before lost control of myself or of my voice, and
the occurrence frightened me. Ed talked reassuringly, telling me that
every sensitive person carried the prison in his heart for a long time.
He urged me to leave the city with him, find a quiet place and greater
peace. Dear Ed, his soft voice and tender way always soothed me.
Now, too, they had the same effect.

Presently the sound of a beautiful voice reached the dressing-room.
Its speech was unfamiliar to me. " Who is speaking now? " I asked.
" That is Maria Rodda, an Italian girl anarchist," Ed replied; " she is
only sixteen years old and has just come to America." The voice electri-
fied me and I was eager to see its owner. I stepped to the door leading
to the platform. Maria Rodda was the most exquisite creature I had
ever seen. She was of medium height, and her well-shaped head, covered with black curls, rested like a lily of the valley on her slender neck.
Her face was pale, her lips coral-red. Particularly striking were her
eyes: large, black coals fired by an inner light. Like myself, very few
in the audience understood Italian, but Maria's strange beauty and
the music of her speech roused the whole assembly to tensest enthusiasm. Maria proved a veritable ray of sunlight to me. My spooks vanished, the prison weights dropped off; I felt free and happy, among
friends.

I spoke after Maria. The audience again rose, to a man, applauding. I sensed that the people were spontaneously responsive to my
prison story, but I was not deceived; I knew intuitively that it was
Maria Rodda's youth and charm that fascinated them and not my
speech. Yet I, too, was still young — only twenty-five. I still had attraction, but compared with that lovely flower, I felt old. The sorrows
of the world had matured me beyond my years; I felt old and sad. I
wondered whether a high ideal, made more fervent by the test of fire,
could stand out against youth and dazzling beauty.

After the meeting the closer comrades gathered at Justus's place.
Maria Rodda was with us and I was anxious to know all about her.
Pedro Esteve, a Spanish anarchist, acted as interpreter. I learned that
Maria had been a schoolmate of Santa Caserio, their teacher having
been Ada Negri, the ardent poetess of revolt. Through Caserio,
Maria, then barely fourteen, had joined an anarchist group. When
Caserio killed Carnot, President of France, their group had been
raided and Maria, with all the other members, was sent to prison. On
her release she came to America, together with her younger sister.
What they learned about Sasha and me convinced them that America,

like Italy, was persecuting idealists. Maria felt that she had work to do among her countrymen in the United States. Would I help her, would I be her teacher, she now begged me. I pressed her close to me as if to ward off the cruel thrusts I knew life would give her. I would be Maria's teacher, friend, comrade. The gnawing voice of envy of an hour ago was silent.

On the way to my room I spoke to Ed about Maria. To my surprise he did not share my enthusiasm. He admitted that she was ravishing, but he thought her beauty would not endure, much less her enthusiasm for our ideals. "Latin women mature young," he said; "they grow old with their first child, old in body and in spirit." "Well, then, Maria should guard against having children if she wants to devote herself to our movement," I remarked. "No woman should do that," Ed replied, emphatically. "Nature has made her for motherhood. All else is nonsense, artificial and unreal."

I had never before heard such sentiments expressed by Ed. His conservatism roused my anger. I demanded to know if he thought me also nonsensical because I preferred to work for an ideal instead of producing children. I expressed contempt for the reactionary attitude of our German comrades on these matters. I had believed that he was different, but I could see that he was like the rest. Perhaps he, too, loved only the woman in me, wanted me only as his wife and the bearer of his children. He was not the first to expect that of me, but he might as well know that I would never be that — never! I had chosen my path; no man should ever take me from it.

I had stopped walking. Ed also stood still. I saw the pained expression on his face, but all he said was: "Please, dearest, come along or we shall soon have a large audience." He took me gently by the arm, but I freed myself and hastened off alone.

My life with Ed had been glorious and complete, without any rift. But now it came; my dream of love and true comradeship suffered a rude awakening. Ed had never stressed his longing, except when he had protested against my joining the movement of the unemployed. I thought then that it was only his concern for my health. How was I to know that it was something else, the interest of the male? Yes, that is what it was, the man's instinct of possession, which brooks no deity except himself. Well, it should not be, even if I had to give him up. All my senses cried out for him. Could I live without Ed, without the joy he gave me?

Weary and miserable, my thoughts dwelt on Ed, on Maria Rodda, and on recollections of Santa Caserio. The latter's image brought to my mind the revolutionary events in France of recent occurrence. A number of *Attentats* had taken place there. There had been also the protests of Émile Henri and Auguste Vaillant against the political corruption, the frenzied speculation with the Panama Canal funds, and the resultant failure of the banks, in which the masses lost their last savings, causing widespread misery and want. Both had been executed. Vaillant's act had had no fatal result; no one had lost his life or even been wounded. Yet he was also condemned to death. Many leading men, among them François Coppée, Émile Zola, and others had pleaded with President Carnot to commute his sentence. He refused, ignoring even the pathetic letter of Vaillant's little child, a girl of nine, who had petitioned for the life of her father. Vaillant was guillotined. Some time later President Carnot, while driving in his carriage, was stabbed to death by a young Italian. On his dagger was found the inscription: " Revenge for Vaillant." The Italian's name was Santa Caserio, and he had tramped on foot from Italy to avenge his comrade, Vaillant.

I had read about his act and other similar occurrences in the anarchist papers Ed used to smuggle into prison. In the light of them my personal grief over my first serious quarrel with Ed now appeared like a mere speck on the social horizon of pain and blood. One by one the heroic names of those who had sacrificed their lives for their ideal or were still being martyred in prison came before me: my own Sasha and the others — all so finely attuned to the injustice of the world, so high-minded, driven by social forces to do the very thing they abhorred most, to destroy human life. Something deep in my consciousness rebelled against such tragic waste, yet I knew there was no escape. I had learned the fearful effects of organized violence: inevitably it begets more violence.

Sasha's spirit, fortunately, however, always hovered over me, helping me to forget everything personal. His letter of welcome on my release was the most beautiful I had so far received from him. It testified not only to his love and his faith in me, but also to his own valour and strength of character. Ed had kept the copies of the *Gefängniss-Blüthen,* the little underground magazine that Sasha, Nold, and Bauer were editing in prison. Sasha's will to life was apparent in every word, in his determination to fight on and not to permit the enemy to crush him. The spirit of the boy of twenty-three was extraordinary. It shamed me for my own faint heart. Yet I knew that the personal would always play a dominant part in my life. I was not hewn of one piece, like Sasha or other heroic figures. I had long realized that I was woven of many skeins, conflicting in shade and texture. To the end of my days I should be torn between the yearning for a personal life and the need of giving all to my ideal.

Ed came early the next day. He was his usual well-poised, outwardly calm self again. But I had looked into the turbulent waters of his soul too often to be misled by his reserve. He suggested that we take a trip. I had been out of prison about a fortnight and we had not yet had one complete day alone. We went to Manhattan Beach. The November air was sharp, the sea stormy; but the sun shone brightly. Ed was never much of a talker, but on this day he spoke a great deal about himself, his interest in the movement, his love for me. His ten years' incarceration had given him much time for reflection. He had come out believing as deeply in the truth and beauty of anarchism as when he had first entered prison. He continued to believe in the ultimate triumph of our ideas, but was now convinced that that time was far off. He no longer looked for great changes in his own lifetime. All he could do was to arrange his own life as nearly true to his vision as possible. In that life he wanted me; he wanted me with all the strength of his being. He admitted that he would be happier if I would give up the platform and devote my time to study, to writing or a profession. That would not keep him in constant anxiety about my life and freedom. "You are so intense, so impetuous," he said, "I fear for your safety." He begged me not to be angry because he believed that woman was primarily a mother. He was sure that the strongest motive in my devotion to the movement was unsatisfied motherhood seeking an outlet. "You are a typical mother, my little Emma, by build, by feeling. Your tenderness is the greatest proof of it."

I was profoundly stirred. When I could find words, poor inadequate words, to convey what I felt, I could only tell him again of my love, of my need of him, of my longing to give him much of what he craved. My starved motherhood — was that the main reason for my idealism? He had roused the old yearning for a child. But I had silenced the voice of the child for the sake of the universal, the all-absorbing passion of my life. Men were consecrated to ideals and yet were fathers of children. But man's physical share in the child is only a moment's; woman's part is for years — years of absorption in one human being to the exclusion of the rest of humanity. I would never give up the one for the other. But I would give him my love and devotion. Surely it must be possible for a man and a woman to have a beautiful love-life and yet be devoted to a great cause. We must try. I proposed that we find a place where we could live together, no longer separated by silly conventions — a home of our own, even if poor. Our love would beautify it, our work would give it meaning. Ed became enthusiastic over the idea and took me in his arms. My strong, big lover, he had always hated the least demonstration of affection in public. Now in his joy he forgot that we were in a restaurant. I teased him on his having renounced his good manners, but he was like a child, gay and frolicsome as I had never seen him before.

Nearly four weeks passed before we could carry out our plans. The papers had turned me into a celebrity, and I soon learned the German truism: "*Man kann nicht ungestraft unter Palmen wandeln.*" I knew of the American craze for celebrities, especially the American women's hunt for anyone in the limelight, be it prize-fighter, baseball-player, matinée idol, wife-killer, or decrepit European aristocrat. Thanks to my imprisonment and the space given to my name in the newspapers, I also became a celebrity. Every day brought stacks of invitations to luncheons and dinners. Everyone seemed eager to " take me up."

Of the many invitations showered on me I welcomed most one from the Swintons. They wrote asking me to come to dinner and to bring Ed and Justus. Their apartment was simply and beautifully furnished and full of curios and gifts. I saw a lovely *samovar* sent them by Russian exiles in recognition of Swinton's tireless work in behalf of Russian freedom, an exquisite set of Sèvres given him by French Communards who had escaped the fury of Thiers and Galliffet after the short-lived Paris Commune of 1871, beautiful peasant embroidery from Hungary, and other gifts of appreciation of the splendid spirit and personality of the great American libertarian.

On our arrival John Swinton, tall and erect, with a silk cap on his white hair, proceeded to scold me for what I had said about the Negroes in prison. He had read in the New York *World* my disclosures of conditions in the penitentiary. He liked the article, but he was grieved to see that Emma Goldman had " the white man's prejudice against the coloured race." I was dumbfounded. I could not understand how anyone, least of all a man like John Swinton, could read race prejudice into my story. I had pointed out the discrimination practised between sick and starved white women and Negro favourites. I should have protested as much had coloured women been robbed of their rations. " To be sure, to be sure," Swinton replied; " still, you should not have emphasized the partiality. We white people have committed so many crimes against the Negro that no amount of extra kindness can atone for them. The matron is no doubt a beast, but I forgive her much for her sympathy with the poor Negro prisoners." " But she was not moved by such considerations! " I protested; " she was kind because she could use them in every despicable way." Swinton was not convinced. He had been closely allied with the most active abolitionists, he had fought and been wounded in the Civil War; it was apparent that his feeling for the coloured race had made him partial. There was no use arguing the matter further; moreover, Mrs. Swinton was calling us to the table.

They were charming hosts. John was especially gracious and full of warmth. He was a man of wide experience in people and affairs and he proved a veritable mint of information to me. I learned for the first time of his share in the campaign to save the Chicago anarchists from the gallows and of other public-spirited Americans who had valiantly defended my comrades. I became acquainted with Swinton's activities against the Russian-American Extradition Treaty, and the part he and his friends had played in the labour movement. The evening with the Swintons showed me a new angle of my adopted country. Until my imprisonment I had believed that except for Albert Parsons, Dyer D. Lum, Voltairine de Cleyre, and a few others America was barren of idealists. Her men and women cared only for material acquisitions, I had thought. Swinton's account of the liberty-loving people who had been and still were in every struggle against oppression changed my superficial judgment. John Swinton made me see that Americans, once aroused, were as capable of idealism and sacrifice as my Russian heroes and heroines. I left the Swintons with a new faith in the possibilities of America. On our way down town I talked with Ed and Justus, telling them that from now on I meant to devote myself to propaganda in English, among the American people. Propaganda in foreign circles was, of course, very necessary, but real social changes could be accomplished only by the natives. Their enlightenment was therefore much more vital, we all agreed.

At last Ed and I had a place of our own. With one hundred and fifty dollars I received from the New York *World* for my article on prisons we furnished a four-room flat on Eleventh Street. Most of our furniture was second-hand, but we had a new bed and couch. The latter, together with a desk and a few chairs, made up my sanctum. Ed was surprised when I stressed the need of a room for myself. It was hard enough to be separated during work hours, he said; in our free hours he wanted me near him. But I held out for my own corner. My childhood and youth had been poisoned by being compelled to share my room with someone else. Ever since I had become a free being, I had insisted on privacy for at least a part of the day and the night.

But for this little cloud our life in our own home started gloriously. Ed was earning only seven dollars a week as an insurance agent, but he seldom returned from work without a flower or some other gift, a lovely china cup or a vase. He knew my love for colour and he never forgot to bring something that would help make our place cheerful and bright. We had many visitors, far too many for Ed's peace of mind. He wanted quiet and to be alone with me. But Fedya and Claus had shared my life in the past, had been part of my struggle. I needed their companionship.

Claus had got along satisfactorily on Blackwell's Island. He had missed his precious beer, of course, but otherwise he had done well. After his release from the island Claus started an anarchist paper, *Der Sturmvogel,* of which he was the main contributor, besides setting up, printing, and even delivering the paper. But, busy as he was, he could not keep out of mischief. Ed had little patience with my friend, whom he nicknamed *Pechvogel.*

Fedya had secured a position on a New York publication soon after my imprisonment. He was doing pen-and-ink sketches and was already being recognized as one of the best in his field. He had begun at fifteen dollars a week, regularly contributing to my needs during my ten months in the penitentiary. Now that he was earning twenty-five, he insisted on my taking at least ten, so as to make any appeal to our comrades unnecessary, which he knew I could not bear. He had remained the same loyal soul, more matured, with growing confidence in himself and his art.

He felt that in order to keep his position he could no longer appear openly in our ranks. But his interest in the movement continued and his anxiety for Sasha did not abate. During my imprisonment he had helped to buy things for Sasha. It was little enough one was permitted in the Western Penitentiary: condensed milk, soap, underwear, and socks. Ed had looked after the matter. Now I was eager to attend to these things myself and I also decided to begin a new campaign for the commutation of Sasha's sentence.

I had been out two months, but I did not forget the unfortunates in prison. I wanted to do something for them. I needed money for this purpose and I also wanted to earn my own living.

Much against Ed's wishes, I began to work as a practical nurse. Dr. Julius Hoffmann sent me his private patients after treating them in St. Mark's Hospital. Dr. White had told me before I left the prison that he would give me work in his office. He could not recommend his patients to me, he had said. " They are mostly stupid, they would be afraid you'd poison them." The dear man kept his word: he employed me for several hours a day, and I also got work in the newly organized Beth-Israel Hospital on East Broadway. I loved my profession and I was able to earn more money than at any time previously. The joy of no longer having to grind at the machine, in or out of a shop, was great; greater still the satisfaction of having more time for reading and for public activity.

Ever since I had come into the anarchist movement I had longed for a friend of my own sex, a kindred spirit with whom I could share the inmost thoughts and feelings I could not express to men, not even to Ed. Instead of friendship from women I had met with much antagonism, petty envy and jealousy because men liked me. Of course, there were exceptions: Annie Netter, always big and generous, Natasha Notkin, Maria Louise, and one or two others. But my bond with these was the movement; there was no close personal, intimate point of contact. The coming into my life of Voltairine de Cleyre held out the hope of a fine friendship.

After her visit to me in prison she had kept on writing wonderful letters of comradeship and affection. In one of them she had suggested that on my release I come straight to her. She would make me rest before her fire-place, she would wait on me, read to me, and try to make me forget my ghastly experience. Shortly after that she wrote another letter saying that she and her friend A. Gordon were coming to New York and were anxious to visit me. I did not want to refuse her — she meant so much to me — but I could not bear to see Gordon. On my first visit to Philadelphia I had met the man at a group circle and he impressed me badly. He was a follower of Most and as such would hate me. At the gathering of the comrades he had denounced

me as a disrupter of the movement, charging me with being in it only
for sensational ends. He would not participate in any meeting where
I was to speak. Not being naïve enough to believe that my imprisonment had added to my importance, I could see no cause for Gordon's
change towards me. I wrote this frankly to Voltairine, explaining that
I preferred not to see Gordon. I was permitted only two visits a
month; I would not give up Ed's visit, the other being taken up by
near friends. Since then I had not heard any more from Voltairine,
but I ascribed her silence to illness.

On my release I had received many letters of congratulation from
friends who shared my ideas as well as from persons unknown to me.
But not one word did I get from Voltairine. When I expressed my
surprise to Ed, he informed me that Voltairine had felt much hurt
because I had refused to permit Gordon to visit me on the island.
I was sorry to learn that such a splendid revolutionist could turn from
me because I did not care to see a friend of hers. Noticing my disappointment, Ed remarked: " Gordon is not only her friend, he is more
than that." But it made no difference; I did not see why a free woman
should expect her friends to accept her lover. I felt that Voltairine
had shown herself too narrow ever again to enable me to be free and
at ease with her. My hope of a close friendship with her was destroyed.

I was somewhat consoled by another woman, young and beautiful,
coming into my life. Her name was Emma Lee. During my imprisonment she had written Ed expressing interest in my case. Her letters
were signed only with her initials; her handwriting being very masculine, Ed had thought her to be a man. " Imagine my surprise," Ed
told me on one of his visits, "when a young and charming woman
walked into my bachelor quarters." But not only was Emma Lee
charming; she also had brains and a fine sense of humour. I was
drawn to her from the first moment when Ed brought her to see me in
prison. After my release Emma Lee and I were much together. At
first she was very reticent about herself, but in the course of time
I learned her story. She had become interested in me because she had
been in prison herself and knew its horrors. She had become a free-
thinker and had emancipated herself from the belief that love is
justified only when sanctioned by law. She had met a man who assured
her that he shared her ideas. He was married and very unhappy. In
her, he said, he had found more than a comrade; he had fallen in love

with her. She loved him in return, but their relationship in the bigoted atmosphere of a small Southern town was soon made impossible. They went to Washington, but there, too, persecution followed. They planned to remove to New York, and Emma Lee returned to her native town to dispose of a piece of property she owned. She had not been there more than a week when her place was set on fire. The house was insured, and presently Emma was arrested on the charge of incendiarism. She was convicted and given five years in prison. During the entire time the man gave no sign of life; he left her to her doom and was keeping under cover in some Eastern city.

Her bitter disillusionment was harder to bear than the imprisonment. The descriptions Emma Lee gave of life in the Southern penitentiary made existence on Blackwell's Island seem like paradise. In that hell-hole Negro convicts, male and female, were flogged for the least infraction of the rules. White women had either to submit to the keepers or starve. The atmosphere was lurid with vile talk and viler acts by keepers and prisoners alike. Emma was forced to be on constant guard against the demands of the Warden and the prison doctor. On one occasion they nearly drove her to murder in self-defence. She would not have come out alive if she had not succeeded in getting a note to a friend in the town, a woman. This friend interested some people who began quietly petitioning the Governor, finally obtaining a pardon for Emma Lee after she had served two years.

Since then she had devoted herself entirely to bringing about fundamental changes in prison conditions. She had already succeeded in getting her former tormentors removed from office, and now she was co-operating with the Society for Prison Reform.

Emma Lee was a rare soul, educated, refined, and free-minded, although she had not read much libertarian literature. Through her own affairs she had also emancipated herself from the anti-Negro prejudice of the Southerner. Most admirable to me was her lack of bitterness towards men. Her own love tragedy had not narrowed her outlook on life. Men were egotistical and thoughtless towards women's needs, she would say; even the freest of them wanted only to possess women. But they were interesting and entertaining. I did not agree with her about the egotism of men, and when I would cite Ed as an exception, she would reply: " There is no doubt he loves you, but — but! " However, they got on famously. They fought about everything, but it was all done in a friendly spirit. I was their common tie. No woman except my own sister Helena loved me as much as Emma did. As for Ed, he showed his affection in so many ways that I could not doubt him. Yet I knew that of the two it was Emma Lee who had looked deeper into my soul.

Emma Lee was employed in the Nurses' Settlement on Henry Street and I often visited her there, sometimes as the guest of the women at the head of the institution. Miss Lillian D. Wald, Lavinia Dock, and Miss MacDowell were among the first American women I met who felt an interest in the economic condition of the masses. They were genuinely concerned with the people of the East Side. My contact with them, as with John Swinton, brought me close to new American types, men and women of ideals, capable of fine, generous deeds. Like some of the Russian revolutionists they, too, had come from wealthy homes and had completely consecrated themselves to what they considered a great cause. Yet their work seemed palliative to me. " Teaching the poor to eat with a fork is all very well," I once said to Emma Lee; " but what good does it do if they have not the food? Let them first become the masters of life; they will then know how to eat and how to live." She agreed with my view that, sincere as the settlement workers were, they were doing more harm than good. They were creating snobbery among the very people they were trying to help. A young girl who had been active in a shirtwaist-makers' strike, for instance, was taken up by them and exhibited as the pet of the settlement. The girl put on airs and constantly talked of the " ignorance of the poor," who lacked understanding for culture and refinement. " The poor are so coarse and vulgar! " she once told Emma. Her wedding was soon to take place at the settlement, and Emma invited me to attend the affair.

It was gaudy, almost vulgar. The bride, dressed in cheap finery, looked utterly out of place in that background. Not that the settlement women were living in luxury; on the contrary, everything was of the simplest, though of the best quality. The very simplicity of the environment exaggerated the shamed poverty of the married couple and the embarrassment of their orthodox parents. It was very painful to behold, most of all the self-importance of the bride. When I congratulated her on choosing such a fine-looking fellow for her husband, she said: " Yes, he's quite nice, but of course he's not of my sphere. You see, I am really marrying below my station."

All winter Ed had been suffering from fallen arches; much walking and climbing of stairs was causing him unbearable pain. In the early spring his condition became so bad that he had to give up his job with the insurance agency. I was earning enough for both of us, but Ed would not accept " support from a woman." My proud sweetheart was compelled to join the ranks of the unemployed looking for work. There was nothing in the great city of New York for a man of his culture and knowledge of languages. " If I were a hod-carrier or a tailor," he would say, " I could get a job. But I'm only a useless intellectual." He worried, lost sleep, grew thin, and became very depressed. His worst misery was that he had to remain at home while I went to work. His male self-respect could not endure such a situation.

It occurred to me that we might try something like our ice-cream parlour in Worcester. It had been successful there; why not in New York? Ed approved of the project and suggested that we proceed at once.

I had saved a little money, and Fedya offered us more. Friends advised Brownsville: it was a growing centre, and a store could be got not far from the race-tracks, where thousands of people were passing daily. So to Brownsville we went, and fixed up a beautiful place. Thousands did pass by there, but they kept on passing. They were in a hurry to get to the race-track, and on their way home they had already visited some ice-cream store nearer the track. Our daily receipts were not enough to cover our expenses. We could not even keep up the weekly payments on the furniture we had bought for the two rooms we had rented in Brownsville. One afternoon a wagon drove up and proceeded to collect beds, tables, chairs, and everything else we had. Ed tried to laugh away our plight, but he was evidently unhappy. We gave up the business and returned to New York. In three months we had lost five hundred dollars, besides the work Ed, Claus, and I had put into the wretched venture.

I had realized at the very beginning of my nursing work that I should have to take up a regular course in a training-school. Practical nurses were paid and treated like servants, and without a diploma I could not hope to get employment as a trained nurse. Dr. Hoffmann urged me to enter St. Mark's Hospital, where he could get me credits for one year because of my experience. It was a great opportunity, but there was also another and a more alluring one. It was Europe.

Ed had always talked with glee of Vienna, of its beauty, charm, and possibilities. He wanted me to go there to study in the Allgemeines

Krankenhaus. I could take up midwifery and other branches of nursing, he advised me. It would give me greater material independence
later on and also enable us to be more together. It would be hard to
endure another year's separation when I had barely been given back
to him; but he was willing to let me go, knowing it was for my good.
It seemed a fantastic idea for people as poor as we, but gradually
Ed's enthusiasm infected me. I agreed to go to Vienna, but I would
combine my trip abroad with a lecture tour in England and Scotland.
Our British comrades had often asked me to come over.

Ed had found a job in the wood work shop of a Hungarian acquaintance. The man offered to lend him money, but Fedya insisted on his
priority as my old friend. He would pay my passage and send me
twenty-five dollars a month during my entire stay in Vienna.

There was a dark shadow, however: the thought of Sasha in prison.
Europe was so far away! Ed and Emma Lee promised to keep in correspondence with him and look after his needs. Sasha himself urged
me to go. Nothing could be done for him now, he wrote, and Europe
would give me the opportunity to meet our great people — Kropotkin,
Malatesta, Louise Michel. I should be able to learn much from them
and be better equipped for my activities in the American movement.
It was just like my consecrated Sasha to think of me always in terms
of the Cause.

On the 15th of August 1895, exactly six years since my new life
in New York had begun, I sailed for England. My departure was quite
different from my arrival in New York in 1889. I was very poor then,
poor in more than merely material things. I was a child, inexperienced
and alone in the whirlpool of the American metropolis. Now I had
experience, a name; I had been through the crucible; I had friends.
Above all, I had the love of a beautiful personality. I was rich, yet
I was sad. The Western Penitentiary lay heavily on my heart, with
the thought of Sasha there.

I again travelled steerage, my means not permitting more than sixteen dollars for the passage. But there were only a few passengers,
some of whom had been no longer in the States than I. They considered themselves Americans and they were treated accordingly, with
more decency than the poor emigrants who had pilgrimed over as I
did to the Promised Land in 1886.

CHAPTER XIV

OUTDOOR MEETINGS IN AMERICA ARE RARE, THEIR ATMOSPHERE always surcharged with impending clashes between the audience and the police. Not so in England. Here the right to assemble constantly in the open is an institution. It has become a British habit, like bacon for breakfast. The most opposing ideas and creeds find expression in the parks and squares of English cities. There is nothing to cause undue excitement and there is no display of armed force. The lone bobby on the outskirts of the crowd is there as a matter of form; it is not his duty to disperse meetings or club the people.

The social centre of the masses is the out-of-door meeting in the park. On Sundays they flock there as they do to music-halls on weekdays. They cost nothing and they are much more entertaining. Crowds, often numbering thousands, drift from platform to platform as they would at a country fair, not so much to listen or learn as to be amused. The main performers at these gatherings are the hecklers, who hugely enjoy bombarding the speakers with questions. Pity him who fails to get the cue from these tormentors or who is not quick enough at repartee. He soon finds himself confused and the helpless butt for boisterous ridicule. All this I learned after I nearly came to grief at my first meeting in Hyde Park.

It was a novel experience to talk out of doors, with only a lone policeman placidly looking on. Alas, the crowd, too, was placid. It felt like climbing a steep mountain to speak against such inertia. I soon grew tired and my throat began to hurt, but I kept on. All at once the audience began to show signs of life. A volley of questions, like bullets, came flying at me from all directions. The unexpected attack, finding me quite unprepared, bewildered and irritated me. I felt my trend of thought slip from me, and my anger rise. Then a man in front called out: " Don't mind it, old girl, go right on. Heckling is a good old British custom." " Good, you call it? " I retorted; " I think it is rotten to interrupt a speaker like that. But all right, fire away, and don't blame me if you get the worst of the bargain." " That's right, old dear," the audience shouted; " go ahead, let's see what you can do."

I had been speaking on the futility of politics and its corrupting influence when the first shot was fired. " How about honest politicians — don't you believe there are such? " " If there are, I never heard of one," I hurled back. " Politicians promise you heaven before election and give you hell after." " 'Ear! 'Ear! " they screamed in approval. I had barely got back to my speech when the next bolt struck me. " I say, old girl, why do you speak of heaven? — Do you believe in such a place? " " Of course not," I replied; " I was only referring to the heaven you stupidly believe in." " Well, if there is no heaven, where else would the poor get their reward? " another heckler demanded. " Nowhere, unless they insist on their right here — take their reward by gaining possession of the earth." I continued that even if there were a heaven, the common people would not be tolerated there. " You see," I explained, " the masses have lived in hell so long they would not know how to behave in heaven. The angel at the gate would kick them out for disorderly conduct." This was followed by another half-hour of fencing, which kept the crowd in spasms. Finally they called for the hecklers to stop, admit defeat, and let me go on.

My fame travelled quickly; the crowds grew in size at every meeting. Our literature sold in large quantities, which delighted my comrades. They wanted me to remain in London because I could do so much good there. But I knew that out-of-door speaking was not for me. My throat would not hold out under the strain and I could not bear the disturbing noises of the street traffic so close at hand. Besides, I realized that people standing up for hours grew too restless and weary to be able to concentrate or to follow a serious talk. My work meant too much to me to turn it into a circus for the amusement of the British public.

More than my exploits in the park I enjoyed meeting people and witnessing the vital spirit which prevailed in the anarchist movement. In the United States activities were being carried on almost exclusively among the foreign element. There were few native anarchists in America, while the movement in England supported several weekly and monthly publications. One of them was *Freedom,* among whose contributors and co-workers were some very brilliant and talented people, including Peter Kropotkin, John Turner, Alfred Marsh, William Wess, and others. *Liberty* was another anarchist publication, issued in London by James Tochatti, a follower of the poet William Morris. The *Torch* was a little paper published by two sisters, Olivia and Helen Rossetti. They were only fourteen and seventeen years old, respectively, but developed in mind and body far beyond their age. They did all the writing for the paper, even setting the type and attending to the press work themselves. The *Torch* office, formerly the nursery of the girls, became a gathering-place for foreign anarchists, particularly those from Italy, where severe persecution was taking place. The refugees naturally flocked to the Rossettis, who were themselves of Italian origin. Their grandfather, the Italian poet and patriot Gabriele Rossetti, had been condemned to death in 1824 by Austria, under whose yoke Italy then was. Gabriele fled to England, settling in London, where he became Professor of Italian at King's College. Olivia and Helen were the daughters of Gabriele Rossetti's second son, William Michael, the famous critic. Evidently the girls had inherited their revolutionary tendencies as well as their literary talents. While in London, I spent much time with them, greatly enjoying their prodigious hospitality and the inspiring atmosphere of their circle.

One of the members of the *Torch* group was William Benham, familiarly known as the " boy anarchist." He attached himself to me, constituting himself my companion at the meetings as well as on trips through the city.

Anarchist activities in London were not limited to the natives. England was the haven for refugees from all lands, who carried on their work without hindrance. By comparison with the United States the political freedom in Great Britain seemed like the millennium come. But economically the country was far behind America.

I had myself experienced want and I knew of the poverty in the large industrial centres of the United States. But never had I seen such abject misery and squalor as I did in London, Leeds, and Glasgow. Its effects impressed me as not being the results of yesterday or even of years. They were century-old, passed on from generation to generation, apparently rooted in the very marrow of the British masses. One of the most appalling sights was that of able-bodied men running ahead of a cab for blocks to be on the spot in time to open the door for a "gentleman." For such services they would receive a penny, or tuppence at most. After a month's stay in England I understood the reason for so much political freedom. It was a safety-valve against the fearful destitution. The British Government no doubt felt that as long as it permitted its subjects to let off steam in unhampered talk, there was no danger of rebellion. I could find no other explanation for the inertia and the indifference of the people to their slavish conditions.

One of my aims in visiting England was to meet the outstanding personalities in the anarchist movement. Unfortunately Kropotkin was out of town, but would be back before I left. Enrico Malatesta was in the city. I found him living behind his little shop, but there was no one to interpret for me, and I could not speak Italian. His kindly smile, however, mirrored a congenial personality and made me feel as if I had known him all my life. Louise Michel I met almost immediately upon my arrival. The French comrades I stayed with had arranged a reception for my first Sunday in London. Ever since I had read about the Paris Commune, its glorious beginning and its terrible end, Louise Michel had stood out sublime in her love for humanity, grand in her zeal and courage. She was angular, gaunt, aged before her years (she was only sixty-two); but there was spirit and youth in her eyes, and a smile so tender that it immediately won my heart. This, then, was the woman who had survived the savagery of the respectable Paris mob. Its fury had drowned the Commune in the blood of the workers and had strewn the streets of Paris with thousands of dead and wounded. Not being appeased, it had also reached out for Louise. Again and again she had courted death; on the barricades of Père Lachaise, the last stand of the Communards, Louise had chosen the most dangerous position for herself. In court she had demanded the same penalty as was meted out to her comrades, scorning clemency on the grounds of sex. She would die for the Cause. Whether out of fear or awe of this heroic figure, the murderous Paris *bourgeoisie* had not dared to kill her. They preferred to doom her to slow death in New Caledonia. But they had reckoned without the fortitude of Louise Michel, her devotion and capacity for consecration to her fellow sufferers. In New Caledonia she became the hope and inspiration of the exiles. In sickness she nursed their bodies; in depression she cheered their spirits. The amnesty for the Communards brought Louise back with the others to France. She found herself the acclaimed idol of the French masses. They adored her as their *Mère Louise, bien aimée.*

Shortly after her return from exile Louise headed a demonstration of unemployed to the Esplanade des Invalides. Thousands were out of work for a long time and hungry. Louise led the procession into the bakery shops, for which she was arrested and condemned to five years' imprisonment. In court she defended the right of the hungry man to bread, even if he has to " steal " it. Not the sentence, but the loss of her dear mother proved the greatest blow to Louise at her trial. She loved her with an absorbing affection and now she declared that she had nothing else to live for except the revolution. In 1886 Louise was pardoned, but she refused to accept any favours from the State. She had to be taken forcibly from prison in order to be set at liberty.

During a large meeting in Havre someone fired two shots at Louise while she was on the platform talking. One went through her hat; the other struck her behind the ear. The operation, although very painful, called forth no complaint from Louise. Instead she lamented her poor animals left alone in her rooms and the inconvenience the delay would cause her woman friend who was waiting for her in the next town. The man who nearly killed her had been influenced by a priest to commit the act, but Louise tried her utmost to have him released. She induced a famous lawyer to defend her assailant and she herself appeared in court to plead with the judge in his behalf. Her sympathies were particularly stirred by the man's young daughter, whom she could not bear to have become fatherless by the man's being sent to prison. Louise's stand did not fail to influence even her fanatical assailant.

Later Louise was to participate in a great strike in Vienne, but she was arrested in the Gare du Lyon as she was about to board the train. The Cabinet member responsible for the massacre of the working-men in Fourmies saw in Louise a formidable force that he had repeatedly tried to crush. Now he demanded her removal from jail to an insane asylum on the ground that she was deranged and dangerous. It was this fiendish plan to dispose of Louise that induced her comrades to persuade her to move to England.

The vulgar French papers continued to paint her as a wild beast, as " *La Vierge Rouge,*" without any feminine qualities or charm.

The more decent wrote of her with bated breath. They feared her, but they also looked up to her as something far above their empty souls and hearts. As I sat near her at our first meeting, I wondered how anyone could fail to find charm in her. It was true that she cared little about her appearance. Indeed, I had never seen a woman so utterly oblivious of anything that concerned herself. Her dress was shabby, her bonnet ancient. Everything she wore was ill-fitting. But her whole being was illumined by an inner light. One quickly succumbed to the spell of her radiant personality, so compelling in its strength, so moving in its childlike simplicity. The afternoon with Louise was an experience unlike anything that had happened till then in my life. Her hand in mine, its tender pressure on my head, her words of endearment and close comradeship, made my soul expand, reach out towards the spheres of beauty where she dwelt.

After my return from Leeds and Glasgow, where I spoke at large meetings and became acquainted with many active and devoted workers, I found a letter from Kropotkin asking me to visit him. At last I was to realize my long-cherished dream, to meet my great teacher.

Peter Kropotkin was a lineal descendant of the Ruriks and in the direct succession to the Russian throne. But he gave up his title and wealth for the cause of humanity. He did more: since becoming an anarchist he had forgone a brilliant scientific career to be better able to devote himself to the development and interpretation of anarchist philosophy. He became the most outstanding exponent of anarchist communism, its clearest thinker and theoretician. He was recognized by friend and foe as one of the greatest minds and most unique personalities of the nineteenth century. On my way to Bromley, where the Kropotkins lived, I felt nervous. I feared I should find Peter difficult of approach, too absorbed in his work for ordinary social intercourse.

But five minutes in his presence put me at my ease. The family was away and Peter himself received me in such a gracious and kindly manner that I felt at home with him at once. He would have tea ready directly, he said. Meanwhile should I like to see his carpenter shop and the articles he had made with his own hands? He took me into his study and pointed with great pride to a table, a bench, and some shelves he had fashioned. They were very simple things, but he gloried in them; they represented labour and he had always stressed the need of combining mental activity with manual effort. Now he could demonstrate how well the two can be blended. No artisan ever looked more lovingly and with greater reverence upon the things created by his hands than did Peter Kropotkin, the scientist and philosopher. His wholesome joy in the products of his toil were symbolic of the burning faith he had in the masses, in their capacity to create and fashion life.

Over the tea which he himself prepared, Kropotkin asked me about conditions in America, about the movement, and about Sasha. He had followed the latter's case and he knew every phase of it, expressing great regard and concern for Sasha. I related to him my impressions of England, the contrasts between its poverty and extreme wealth alongside of political freedom. Was it not a bone thrown to the masses to pacify them, I asked. Peter agreed with my view. He said that England was a nation of shopkeepers engaged in buying and selling instead of producing the necessaries required to keep her people from starvation. " The British *bourgeoisie* has good reason to fear the spread of discontent, and political liberties are the best security against it. English statesmen are shrewd," he continued; " they have always seen to it that the political reins should not be pulled too tightly. The average Britisher loves to think he is free; it helps him to forget his misery. That is the irony and pathos of the English working classes. Yet England could feed every man, woman, and child of her population if she would but release the vast lands now held in monopoly by an old, decaying aristocracy." My visit with Peter Kropotkin convinced me that true greatness is always coupled with simplicity. He was the personification of both. The lucidity and brilliance of his mind combined with his warm-heartedness into the harmonious whole of a fascinating and gracious personality.

I was sorry to leave England; during my short visit I had met many people and made friends and I was enriched by personal contact with my great teachers. The days were indeed glorious. Never had I seen such a luscious green of trees and grass, such a profusion of gardens, parks, and flowers. At the same time I had never seen such dreary and dismal poverty. Nature herself seemed to be discriminating between rich and poor. The clear blue sky in Hampstead looked a dirty grey in the East End, the sunshine a blot of dull yellow. The crass distinctions between the different social layers in England were appalling. They increased my hatred of injustice and my determination to work for my ideal. I begrudged the loss of time which my proposed training as a nurse would involve. But I consoled myself with the hope that I should be better equipped on my return to America. I could not remain in London: my course was to begin on the first of October. I had to leave for Vienna.

Vienna proved even more fascinating than Ed had described it. Ringstrasse, the principal street, with its array of splendid old mansions and gorgeous cafés, the spacious promenades lined with stately trees, and particularly the Prater, more forest than park, made the city one of the most beautiful I had ever seen. The whole was enhanced by the gaiety and light-heartedness of the Viennese people. London seemed a tomb by comparison. There was colour here, life and joy. I longed to become part of it, to throw myself into its generous arms, to sit in the cafés or in the Prater and watch the crowds. But I had come for another purpose; I could not afford to be distracted.

My studies included, besides the subject of midwifery, a course in children's diseases. In my short experience as nurse I had seen how ill-fitted most graduate nurses were to take care of children. They were harsh and domineering and lacked understanding. My own childhood had been made hideous by these things, but it had also filled me with sympathy for children. I had much more patience with them than with grown-ups. Their dependence, aggravated by illness, always moved me deeply. I wanted not merely to give them affection, but to equip myself for their care.

The Allgemeines Krankenhaus, which gave courses on and treated every ill of the human body, offered splendid opportunities to the eager and willing student. I found the place a remarkable institution, a veritable city in itself, with its thousands of patients, nurses, doctors, and care-takers. The men in charge of the departments were world-renowned in their particular spheres. The obstetric courses were fortunate in having at their head a famous gynecologist, Professor Braun. He was not only a splendid teacher, but also a lovable man. His lectures were never dry or tedious. In the very midst of an explanation or even during an operation the Herr Professor would enliven things by a humorous anecdote or by remarks embarrassing to the German lady students. In explaining, for example, the comparatively large birth-rate during the months of November and December, he would say: " It's the carnival, ladies. During that gayest Vienna festival even the most virtuous girls get caught. I do not mean to say that they give way easily to their natural urge. It is only that Nature has made them so fertile. A man has only to look at them, so to speak, and they become pregnant. So we must put it all on Nature and not blame the young things." Again, Professor Braun would outrage some of the more moral students by relating the story of a certain female patient. Several of the male students had been asked to examine her and diagnose the case. One by one they carried out the order, but no one ventured to speak out. They were waiting for the Professor to give his opinion. After his examination the great man said: " Gentlemen, it is a case most of you have already had, or you have it now, or you will have it in the future. Very few can resist the charm of its origin, the pain of its development, or the price of its cure. It happens to be syphilis."

Among those attending the obstetric courses were a number of Jewish girls from Kiev and Odessa. One had even come all the way from Palestine. None of them knew enough German to understand the lectures. The Russians were very poor, compelled to exist on ten roubles a month. It was an inspiration to find such courage and perseverance for the sake of a profession. But when I expressed my admiration, the girls replied that it was quite an ordinary thing: thousands of Russians, both Jewish and Gentile, were doing it. All the students abroad lived on very little; why could not they? " But your lack of German," I asked; " how will you get the lectures or read the text-books? How do you expect to pass your examinations? " They did not know, but they would manage somehow. After all, every Jew understands a little German, they said. Two of the girls were especially sympathetic to me. They were living in a wretched little hole, while I had a large and beautiful room. I asked them to share it with me. I knew that we should have to do night duty in the hospital, but most likely not at the same time. Our living together would reduce their expenses, and I should also be able to help them with their German. Soon our place became a centre for the Russian students of both sexes.

I was known in Vienna as Mrs. E. G. Brady. I had to come abroad under that name, for I should not have been admitted under my own. I had emancipated myself from the notion that one must not assume a fictitious name. I could, of course, have procured a passport on Kershner's citizenship papers, but I had not used his name since I left him. In fact, after that I saw him only once, in 1893, when I was ill in Rochester. I had nothing but painful recollections of that name. Brady was Irish, and I knew it would arouse no suspicion as to my identity. Passports could then be had for the asking.

In Vienna I had to be extremely careful. The Habsburgs were

despotic, the persecution of socialists and anarchists severe. I could therefore not associate openly with my comrades, as I did not wish to be expelled. But it did not prevent me from meeting interesting people active in various social movements.

My studies and frequent night duty in the hospital did not lessen my interest in the cultural events of Vienna, its music and theatres. I met a young anarchist, Stefan Grossmann, who was remarkably well informed about the life of the city. He had many traits I disliked: his efforts to hide his origin in chameleon-like acceptance of every silly Gentile habit irritated me. The very first time I met Grossmann he told me that his fencing-master had admired his *germanische Beine* (Germanic legs). " I don't think that's much of a compliment," I replied; " now, if he had admired your Yiddish nose, that would be something to boast about." However, he came often, and gradually I learned to like him. He was an omnivorous reader and a great admirer of the new literature — Friedrich Nietzsche, Ibsen, Hauptmann, von Hoffmansthal and its other exponents who were hurling their anathemas against old values. I had read some of their works in snatches in the *Arme Teufel,* the weekly published in Detroit by Robert Reitzel, a brilliant writer. It was the one German paper in the States that kept its readers in contact with the new literary spirit in Europe. What I had read in its columns from the works of the great minds that were stirring Europe only whetted my appetite.

In Vienna one could hear interesting lectures on modern German prose and poetry. One could read the works of the young iconoclasts in art and letters, the most daring among them being Nietzsche. The magic of his language, the beauty of his vision, carried me to undreamed-of heights. I longed to devour every line of his writings, but I was too poor to buy them. Fortunately Grossmann had a supply of Nietzsche and other moderns.

I had to do my reading at the expense of much-needed sleep; but what was physical strain in view of my raptures over Nietzsche? The fire of his soul, the rhythm of his song, made life richer, fuller, and more wonderful for me. I wanted to share these treasures with my beloved, and I wrote him long letters depicting the new world I had discovered. His replies were evasive; Ed evidently did not share my fervour for the new art. He was more interested in my studies and in my health, and he urged me not to tax my energies with idle reading. I was disappointed, but I consoled myself that he would appreciate the revolutionary spirit of the new literature when he had a chance to read it for himself. I must get money, I decided, to bring back a supply of books to Ed.

Through one of the students I learned of a lecture course given by an eminent young professor, Sigmund Freud. I found, however, that it would be difficult to attend his series, only physicians and holders of special cards being admitted. My friend suggested that I enroll for the course of Professor Bruhl, who also was discussing sex problems. As one of his students I should have a better chance to secure admission to Freud.

Professor Bruhl was an old man with a feeble voice. The subjects he treated were mystifying to me. He talked of " Urnings," " Lesbians," and other strange topics. His hearers, too, were strange: feminine-looking men with coquettish manners and women distinctly masculine, with deep voices. They were certainly a peculiar assembly. Greater clarity in these matters came to me later on when I heard Sigmund Freud. His simplicity and earnestness and the brilliance of his mind combined to give one the feeling of being led out of a dark cellar into broad daylight. For the first time I grasped the full significance of sex repression and its effect on human thought and action. He helped me to understand myself, my own needs; and I also realized that only people of depraved minds could impugn the motives or find " impure " so great and fine a personality as Freud.

My various interests in Vienna kept me occupied the greater part of the day. Still I managed to attend plays and hear a good deal of music. I heard for the first time the entire *Ring des Nibelungen* and other works of Wagner. His music had always stirred me; the Vienna performances — magnificent voices, splendid orchestra, and masterly leadership — were enthralling. After such an experience it was painful to sit through a Wagner concert conducted by his son. One night Siegfried Wagner conducted his own composition *Der Bärenhäuter*. It was pale enough; but when it came to a work of his illustrious father, he was completely ineffectual. I left the concert in disgust.

Vienna brought me many new experiences. One of the greatest was Eleonora Duse as Magda in Sudermann's *Heimat*. The play itself was a new dramatic event, but what Duse put into it of herself transcended Sudermann's talents and gave to his work its real dramatic depth. Years before, in New Haven, I had seen Sarah Bernhardt in *Fedora*. Her voice, her gestures, her intensity were a revelation. I thought then that no one could rise to greater heights, but Eleonora Duse attained a higher zenith. Hers was a genius too rich and too complete for artifice, her interpretation too real for stage tricks. There were no violent gestures, no unnecessary movements, no studied volume of sound. Her voice, rich and vibrant, held rhythm in every tone, her expressive features reflecting her own wealth of emotion. Eleonora Duse interpreted every nuance of the turbulent nature of Magda blended with her own spirit. It was art reaching towards the heavens, itself a star on the firmament of life.

When examinations drew near, I could no longer indulge in the temptations of the fascinating city on the Danube. Soon I was the proud holder of two diplomas, one for midwifery and one for nursing: I could return home. But I was loath to leave Vienna; it had given me so much. I lingered on for two more weeks. During that time I was a great deal with my comrades and learned much from them about the anarchist movement in Austria. At several small gatherings I lectured on America and our struggle in that country.

Fedya had sent me my return fare, second class, and a hundred dollars to buy myself some clothes. I preferred to invest the money in my beloved books, purchasing a supply of the works of the writers that were making literary history, especially the dramatists. No amount of wardrobe could have given me so much joy as my precious little library. I did not even dare to risk shipping it in my trunk. I took the books with me in a suit-case.

Standing on the deck as the French liner steamed towards the New York dock, I spied Ed long before he saw me. He stood near the gang-plank holding a bunch of roses, but when I came down, he failed to recognize me. It was late afternoon of a rainy day, and I wondered whether it was because of the dusk, my large hat, or the fact that I had grown thin. For a moment I stood watching him scanning the passengers, but when I saw his anxiety growing, I tiptoed up from behind and put my hands over his eyes. He spun round quickly, pressed me tempestuously to his heart, and exclaimed in a trembling voice: " What is the matter with my *Schatz?* Are you ill? " " Nonsense! " I replied, " I have only grown more spiritual. Let's get home and I'll tell you all about it."

Ed had written me that he had changed our quarters for a more comfortable flat, which Fedya had helped to decorate. What I found far excelled my expectations. Our new home was an old-fashioned apartment in the German-inhabited part of Eleventh Street. The windows of the large kitchen overlooked a beautiful garden. The front room was spacious and high-ceilinged, simply but cosily furnished with lovely old mahogany. There were rare prints on the walls, and my books were arranged on shelves. The place had atmosphere and taste.

Ed played the host to me at an elaborate dinner he had prepared, with wine sent by Justus Schwab. He was rich now, he informed me; he was earning fifteen dollars a week! Then he related news of our friends: Fedya, Justus, Claus, and, most of all, Sasha. While I was abroad, I had not been able to keep in direct touch with Sasha, and Ed had acted as our go-between, which meant anxious delays. I was overjoyed to learn that there was mail for me from my brave boy. I thought it wonderful that he should have been able to send out a missive to reach me on the very day of my arrival. Sasha's letter was, as always, permeated with his fine spirit. It contained no complaint about his own life, but showed great interest in activities outside, in my work and impressions of Vienna. Europe was so far away, he wrote; my return to America brought me closer, although he knew that he would never see me again. Perhaps I would come to Pittsburgh on a lecture tour. It would mean something to feel me in the same city.

Before my departure for Europe our friend Isaac Hourwich had proposed that we aid Sasha by an appeal to the Supreme Court on the ground of the illegal proceedings at his trial. After considerable effort and expense we had succeeded in procuring the trial records. It was then discovered that there were no legal reasons on which any procedure for a revision was to be based. Representing his own case, Sasha had omitted to take exceptions to the Judge's rulings, as a result of which no appeal could be made.

During my stay in Vienna several of our American friends had suggested an application to the Board of Pardons. Inwardly I rebelled against such a step on the part of an anarchist. I was certain that Sasha would not approve of it, and therefore I did not even write to him about the proposal. During my absence abroad he had been repeatedly put into the dungeon and kept in solitary confinement until his health gave way. I began to think that consistency, while admirable in oneself, was criminal if allowed to stand in the way of another. It led me to set aside all considerations and to implore Sasha to let us appeal to the Board of Pardons. His reply indicated that he felt indignant and hurt that I should want him to beg for pardon. His act bore its own justification, he wrote; it was a gesture of protest against the injustice of the capitalist system. The courts and the pardon boards were the bulwarks of that system. I must have grown less revolutionary, or perhaps it was only my concern for him that had decided me in favour of such a step. In any case he did not wish me to act against my principles in his behalf.

Ed had sent me that letter to Vienna. It had made me unhappy. It disappointed me, but it did not abate my efforts. Friends in Pennsylvania had informed me that the personal signature of the applicant for a pardon was not necessary in that State. I again wrote to Sasha, emphasizing that I considered his life and freedom too valuable to the movement to refuse to make an appeal. Some of the greatest revolutionists had, when serving long terms, appealed in order to gain their freedom. But if he still felt it inconsistent to take the step for his own sake, would he not permit our friends to do so for mine? I could no longer bear, I explained, the consciousness of his being in prison for an act in which I had been almost as much involved as he. My plea seemed to make some impression on Sasha. In his reply he reiterated that he had no faith whatever in the Board of Pardons; but his friends on the outside were in a better position to judge the step they intended to take and therefore he would offer no further objections. He added that there were certain other matters he would like to talk over; could not Emma Lee try to get a permit?

Emma had moved to Pittsburgh, where she secured a position in a hotel as supervisor of its linen department. She had begun a correspondence with the prison chaplain, whom she gradually interested in an attempt to have Sasha's right to visits restored. After months of waiting the chaplain succeeded in having a permit sent to Emma Lee. But when she called at the penitentiary, the Warden refused to let her see Sasha. " I, and not the chaplain, am the sole authority here," he told Emma; " as long as I am in charge, no one will be allowed to see Prisoner A-7."

Emma Lee felt that a violent protest on her part would only hurt Sasha's chances with the Board of Pardons. She showed greater control than I had on that fatal day at Inspector Reed's store. We continued to cling to the hope that our efforts would tear Sasha from the clutches of the enemy.

I communicated with Voltairine de Cleyre, reminding her of her promise to help in our efforts for Sasha. She replied promptly by composing a public call in his behalf, but she sent it to Ed instead of to me. For a moment I felt angry at what I considered a slight, but when I read the document, my wrath melted away. It was a prose poem full of moving power and beauty. I wrote her my thanks without reference to our misunderstanding. She did not reply.

The campaign for the appeal was launched, the entire radical element supporting our efforts. A prominent Pittsburgh lawyer had become interested and consented to take the case to the Pennsylvania Board of Pardons.

We worked energetically, driven on by great expectations. Sasha's hopes, too, were reviving; life, pulsating life, now seemed to open before him. But our joy was short-lived. The Board refused to act on the appeal. Berkman would have to complete his first seven years' sentence before the " actual wrong " of his other sentences could be considered, the Board held. It was evident that nothing displeasing to Carnegie and Frick would be done.

The shock to me was crushing, and I dreaded its effect on Sasha. How should I write to him, what should I say to help him over the cruel blow? Ed's reassuring words that Sasha was brave enough to hold out until 1897 did not help me. I lost hope that a commutation would ever be granted him. The threat of Inspector Reed that Sasha would not be allowed out alive was ringing in my ears. Before I could bring myself to write him, a letter arrived from Sasha. He had not banked much on a favourable outcome, his letter read, and he was not much disappointed. The action of the Board merely proved once more the close alignment of the American Government and the plutocracy. It was what we anarchists had always claimed. The promise of the Board to reconsider the appeal in 1897 was merely a trick to hoodwink public opinion and to tire out the friends who had been working for him. He was sure the flunkeys of the steel interests would never act in his behalf. But it did not matter. He had survived the first four years and he meant to keep on fighting. " Our enemies shall never have the chance to say that they have broken me," he wrote. He knew he could always count on my support and on that of the new friends he had gained. I must not despair or relax in my zeal for our Cause. My Sasha, my wonderful Sasha — he was not only brave, as Ed had said; he was a tower of strength. As so often since that day when the steam monster at the Baltimore and Ohio Station had snatched him away from me, he stood out like a shining meteor on the dark horizon of petty interests, personal worries, and the enervating routine of everyday existence. He was like a white light that purged one's soul, inspiring even awe at his detachment from human frailties.

CHAPTER XV

A RENAISSANCE WAS NOW TAKING PLACE IN ANARCHIST RANKS; greater activity was being manifested than at any time since 1887, especially among American adherents. *Solidarity,* an English publication started in 1892 by S. Merlino and suspended later on, reappeared in '94, gathering about itself a number of very able Americans. Among them were John Edelman, William C. Owen, Charles B. Cooper, Miss Van Etton, an energetic trade-unionist, and a number of others. A social science club was organized, with weekly lectures. The work attracted considerable attention among the intelligent native element, not failing, of course, also to call forth virulent attacks in the press. New York was not the only city where anarchism was being expounded. In Portland, Oregon, the *Firebrand,* another English weekly, was being published by a group of gifted men and women, including Henry Addis and the Isaak family. In Boston Harry M. Kelly, a young and ardent comrade, had organized a co-operative printing shop which was publishing the *Rebel.* In Philadelphia activities were carried on by Voltairine de Cleyre, H. Brown, Perle McLeod, and other courageous advocates of our ideas. In fact, all over the United States the spirit of the Chicago martyrs had been resurrected. The voice of Spies and his comrades was finding expression in the native tongue as well as in every foreign language of the peoples in America.

Our work had received considerable incentive through the arrival of two British anarchists, Charles W. Mowbray and John Turner. The former had come in 1894, shortly after my release from prison, and was now active in Boston. John Turner, who was the more cultivated and better informed of the two, had been invited to the States by Harry Kelly. For some reason his lectures were at first poorly attended and it became necessary for us in New York to look after the arrangements. I had met John and his sister Lizzie during my stay in London. Both of them had strongly appealed to me by reason of their warmth, geniality, and friendliness. I loved especially to talk to John; he was familiar with the social movements in England and was himself closely allied with the trade-union and co-operative elements, as well as with the *Commonweal,* founded by William Morris. But his best efforts were devoted to the propaganda of anarchism. John Turner's coming to America gave me an opportunity to test my ability to speak in English, as I often had to preside at his meetings.

The free-silver campaign was at its height. The proposition for the free coinage of silver at the ratio with gold of sixteen to one had become a national issue almost overnight. It gained in strength by the sudden ascendancy of William Jennings Bryan who had stampeded the Democratic Convention by an eloquent speech and the catch phrase: "You shall not press down upon the brow of labour the crown of thorns, you shall not crucify mankind upon the cross of gold." Bryan was running for the presidency: the "silver-tongued" orator had caught the fancy of the man in the street. The American liberals, who so easily fall for every new political scheme, went over to Bryan on free silver almost to a man. Even some anarchists were carried away by his slogans. One day a well-known Chicago comrade, George Schilling, arrived in New York to enlist the co-operation of the Eastern radicals. George was an ardent follower of Benjamin Tucker, the leader of the individualist school of anarchism, and a contributor to his paper, *Liberty.* But, unlike Tucker, he was closer to the labour movement and also more revolutionary than his teacher. The wish for a popular awakening in the United States was father to George's belief that the free-silver issue would become a force to undermine both monopoly and the State. The vicious attacks on Bryan in the press helped his cause by leading George and many others to regard him as a martyr. The papers spoke of Bryan as a "tool in the blood-stained hands of Altgeld, the anarchist, and Eugene Debs, the revolutionist."

I could not share the enthusiasm for Bryan, partly because I did not believe in the political machine as a means of bringing about fundamental changes, and also because there was something weak and superficial about Bryan. I had a feeling that his main aim was to get into the White House rather than "strike off the chains" from the people. I resolved to steer clear of him. I sensed his lack of sincerity and I did not trust him. For this attitude I was assailed from two different sides on the same day. First it was Schilling who urged me to join the free-

silver campaign. " What are you Easterners going to do," he asked
when I met him, " when the West marches in revolutionary ranks
towards the East? Are you going to continue talking, or will you join
forces with us? " He assured me that my name had travelled to the
West and that I could be a valuable factor in the popular movement
to free the masses from their despoilers. George was very optimistic
in his ardour, but he failed to convince me. We parted as friends,
George shaking his head over my lack of judgment about the impending revolution.

In the evening we had a visitor, the former Burgess of Homestead,
a man named John McLuckie. I remembered his determined stand during the steel strike against the importation of blacklegs and I appreciated his solidarity with the workers. I was glad to meet the large,
jovial fellow, a true type of the old Jeffersonian democrat. He told me
that he had been asked by Voltairine to see me about Sasha. He had
gone to her to inform her that Berkman was no longer in the Western
Penitentiary. He, as well as many other people in Homestead, believed that Berkman had never intended to kill Frick; he had committed the act only to arouse sympathy for the latter. The excessive
sentence he had been given was merely a ruse on the part of the Pennsylvania courts to deceive the public. The Homestead workers felt
sure that Alexander Berkman had been let out of prison long ago. Voltairine had given McLuckie material which proved how ridiculous his
story was and had sent him to me for more proofs.

I listened to the man, unable to conceive that anyone in his senses
could believe such a thing about Sasha. He had sacrificed his youth,
he had already spent five years in the penitentiary, had suffered the
dungeon, solitary confinement, and brutal physical attacks. Persecution by the prison authorities had even driven him to attempt suicide.
Yet he was being suspected by the very people for whom he was willing to lay down his life. It was preposterous, cruel. I stepped into my
room, took Sasha's letters, and handed them to McLuckie. " Read,"
I said, " and then tell me if you still believe the impossible stories you
have just told me."

He took up one of the letters from the pile, read it carefully, then
scanned several others. Presently he held out his hand. " My dear,
brave girl," he said, " I am sorry, I am awfully sorry, to have doubted
your friend." He assured me that he now realized how wrong he and
his people had been. " You can count on me to help," he added, feel-

ingly, " in any effort you may make to get Berkman out of prison."
Then he referred to Bryan, dwelling on the exceptional opportunity to
assist Sasha if I would join the free-silver campaign. My activities
would bring me in close contact with the prominent politicians of the
Democratic Party, and they could afterwards be approached to secure a pardon. He himself would undertake to see the leaders and he
was certain of success if he could assure them of my services. He
pointed out that I would have no responsibilities about the business
end. He would travel with me and arrange everything. Of course, I
would be paid a generous salary.

McLuckie was frank and decent, though evidently childishly ignorant of my ideas. Perhaps it was also his suggestion that I might help
Sasha that made him sympathetic to me. Still, I could have nothing
to do with Bryan, feeling he would use the workers merely as a
stepping-stone to power.

My visitor took no offence. He left with regrets that I was so lacking in practical sense, but he promised faithfully to enlighten his people in Homestead in regard to Berkman.

Together with Ed and several other close friends I discussed the
possible origin of the dreadful rumours about Sasha. I was sure that
they had been created by the attitude of Most. I remembered that
the press had widely commented on Most's statement that Sasha had
used a " toy pistol to shoot Frick up a bit." Johann Most — my life
was so full I had nearly forgotten him. The bitterness his betrayal of
Sasha had aroused had given way to a dull feeling of disappointment
in the man who had once meant so much to me. The wound he had
struck had partly healed, yet leaving behind a sensitive scar. Mc-
Luckie's visit had torn the wound open again.

My encounters with Schilling and McLuckie made me aware of a
large new field for activity. What I had done so far was only the first
step of usefulness in our movement. I would go on a tour now, study
the country and its people, come close to the pulse of American life.
I would bring to the masses the message of a new social ideal. I was
eager to start at once, but I determined first to become more pro-
ficient in English and to earn some money. I did not want to be dependent on the comrades or take pay for my lectures. Meanwhile I
could continue my work in New York.

I was full of enthusiasm for the future, but in proportion as my
spirits rose, Ed's interest in my aims waned. I had known for a long

time that he begrudged every moment which took me away from him. I was also aware of our decided differences as far as the woman question was concerned. But outside of that, Ed had moved along with me, had always been helpful and ready to aid in my efforts. Now he became disgruntled, critical of everything I was doing. As the days passed, he grew more morose. Often on my return from a late meeting I would find him with a set face, frigidly silent, nervously swinging his leg. I yearned to come close to him, to share my thoughts and plans with him; but his reproachful look would numb me. In my room I would wait expectantly, but he would remain away and then I would hear him wearily drag himself to bed. It hurt me to the quick, for I loved him deeply. Outside of my interest in the movement and Sasha, my great passion for Ed had displaced everything else.

I still had a very tender feeling for my erstwhile artist lover, the more so because I thought he needed me. On my return from Europe I had found him very much changed. He had risen in his profession and was earning considerable money. He remained as generous to me as in our days of poverty, having aided me financially all through my stay in Vienna and later furnishing my new apartment. Indeed, there was no change in his attitude towards me. But it did not take me long to discover that the movement had lost its former meaning for Fedya. He now lived in a different circle, and his interests were different. Art auctions absorbed him, and all his leisure he spent at sales. He had craved beauty so long that, now that he had some means, he wanted to gorge himself with it. Studios became his great passion. Every few months he would furnish one with the most exquisite things, only to discard it shortly for another, which he would decorate with new hangings, vases, canvases, carpets, and what not. All the beautiful things in our flat had come from his *ateliers*. I could not bear the thought of Fedya's wandering so far away from our past interests that he would not offer any more financial help to the movement. But as he had never had much sense of material values, I was not surprised to find him so extravagant. I was even concerned more about his choice of new friends, nearly all of them men who worked on newspapers. A dissipated, cynical lot they were, their main objects in life being drink and women. Unhappily they had succeeded in imbuing Fedya with the same spirit; I was grieved to see my idealistic friend going the way of so many empty in head and heart. Sasha had always felt that the social struggle would prove a mere passing phase in Fedya's life, but I had hoped that when Fedya should be drawn into other channels, they would be those of art. His drift towards meaningless and trivial pleasures, for which he was entirely too fine, was most painful. Fortunately he still felt close to us. He had great regard for Ed, and his affection for me, while no longer the same as in the past, was yet warm enough to counteract, at least partly, the disintegrating influence of his new surroundings.

He came often to our house. On one occasion he asked me to pose, this time for a pen-and-ink sketch he had promised Ed. During the sittings I thought of our common past, of our affection that had been so tender, perhaps too tender to survive the sway Ed's personality exercised over me; probably also because Fedya's love was too yielding for my turbulent nature, which could find expression only in the clashing of wills, in resistance and the surmounting of obstacles. Fedya still attracted me, but it was Ed who consumed me with intense longing, Ed who turned my blood to fire, Ed whose touch intoxicated and exalted me. The sudden change from his usual self to a discontented and hypercritical attitude was too galling to endure. But my pride would not let me make the first step to break his silence. Fedya told me that Ed had greatly admired his sketch of me and had praised it as a splendid piece of work, expressive of much of my being. In my presence, however, Ed would not say a word about it.

But one evening Ed's reserve broke down. " You are drifting away from me! " he cried excitedly. " I can see that my hopes of a beautiful life with you must be given up. You have wasted a year in Vienna, you have acquired a profession only to throw it over for those stupid meetings. You have no concern about anything else; your love has no thought of me or my needs. Your interest in the movement, for which you are willing to break up our life, is nothing but vanity, nothing but your craving for applause and glory and the limelight. You are simply incapable of a deep feeling. You have never understood or appreciated the love I have given you. I have waited and waited for a change, but I see it is useless. I will not share you with anybody or anything. You will have to choose! " He paced the room like a caged lion, turning from time to time to fasten his eyes on me. All that had been accumulating in him for weeks now streamed out in accusation and reproaches.

I sat in consternation. The familiar old demand that I " choose " kept droning in my ears. Ed, who had been my ideal, was like the others. He would have me forswear my interests and the movement, sacrifice everything for love of him. Most had repeatedly given me the same ultimatum. I stared at him unable to speak or move, while he continued stalking about the room in uncontrolled anger. Finally he picked up his coat and hat and left.

For hours I sat as if paralysed; then a violent ring brought me to my feet. It was a call to a confinement case. I took the bag which I had been keeping ready for weeks and walked out with the man who had come for me.

In a two-room flat on Houston Street, on the sixth floor of a tenement-house, I found three children asleep and the woman writhing in labour pains. There was no gas-jet, only a kerosene lamp, over which I had to heat the water. The man looked blank when I asked him for a sheet. It was Friday. His wife had washed Monday, he told me, and all the bed-linen had got dirty since. But I might use the table-cloth; it had been put on that very evening for the Sabbath. " Diapers or anything else ready for the baby? " I asked. The man did not know. The woman pointed to a bundle which consisted of a few torn shirts, a bandage, and some rags. Incredible poverty oozed from every corner.

With the use of the table-cloth and an extra apron I had brought I prepared to receive the expected comer. It was my first private case, and the shock over Ed's outburst helped to increase my nervousness. But I steeled myself and worked on desperately. Late in the morning I helped to bring the new life into the world. A part of my own life had died the evening before.

For a week my grief over Ed's absence was dulled by work. The care of several patients and Dr. White's operations, at which I assisted, left me little time for repining. The evenings were occupied with meetings in Newark, Paterson, and other near-by towns. But at night, alone in the flat, the scene with Ed haunted and tortured me. I knew he cared for me, but that he could leave as he did, stay away so long, and give no sign of his whereabouts made me resentful. It was impossible to reconcile myself to a love that denied the beloved the right to herself, a love that throve only at the expense of the loved one. I felt I could not submit to such a sapping emotion, but the next moment I would find myself in Ed's room, my burning face on his pillow, my heart contracting with yearning for him. At the end of two weeks my longing mastered all my resolutions; I wrote him at his place of work and begged him to return.

He came at once. Folding me to his heart, between tears and laughter, he cried: " You are stronger than I; I have wanted you every moment, ever since I closed that door. Every day I meant to come back, but I was too cowardly. Nights I have been walking round the house like a shadow. I wanted to come in and beg you to forgive and forget. I even went to the station when I knew you had to go to Newark and Paterson. I could not bear to think of your going home alone late at night. But I was afraid of your scorn, afraid you would send me away. Yes, you are braver and stronger than I. You are more natural. Women always are. Man is such a silly, civilized creature! Woman has retained her primitive impulses and she is more real."

We took up our common life again, but I spent less time on my public interests. Partly it was due to the numerous calls on my professional services, but more to my determination to devote myself to Ed. As the weeks passed, however, the still small voice kept on whispering that the final rupture would only temporarily be deferred. I clung desperately to Ed and his love to ward off the impending end.

My profession of midwife was not very lucrative, only the poorest of the foreign element resorting to such services. Those who had risen in the scale of material Americanism lost their native diffidence together with many other original traits. Like the American women they, too, would be confined only by doctors. Midwifery offered a very limited scope; in emergencies one was compelled to call for the aid of a physician. Ten dollars was the highest fee; the majority of the women could not pay even that. But while my work held out no hope of worldly riches, it furnished an excellent field for experience. It put me into intimate contact with the very people my ideal strove to help and emancipate. It brought me face to face with the living conditions of the workers, about which, until then, I had talked and written mostly from theory. Their squalid surroundings, the dull and inert submission to their lot, made me realize the colossal work yet to be done to bring about the change our movement was struggling to achieve.

Still more impressed was I by the fierce, blind struggle of the women of the poor against frequent pregnancies. Most of them lived in continual dread of conception; the great mass of the married women submitted helplessly, and when they found themselves pregnant, their alarm and worry would result in the determination to get rid of their expected offspring. It was incredible what fantastic methods despair could invent: jumping off tables, rolling on the floor, massaging the stomach, drinking nauseating concoctions, and using blunt instruments. These and similar methods were being tried, generally with great injury. It was harrowing, but it was understandable. Having a large brood of children, often many more than the weekly wage of the father could provide for, each additional child was a curse, " a curse of God," as orthodox Jewish women and Irish Catholics repeatedly told me. The men were generally more resigned, but the women cried out against Heaven for inflicting such cruelty upon them. During their labour pains some women would hurl anathema on God and man, especially on their husbands. " Take him away," one of my patients cried, " don't let the brute come near me — I'll kill him ! " The tortured creature already had had eight children, four of whom had died in infancy. The remaining were sickly and undernourished, like most of the ill-born, ill-kept, and unwanted children who trailed at my feet when I was helping another poor creature into the world.

After such confinements I would return home sick and distressed, hating the men responsible for the frightful condition of their wives and children, hating myself most of all because I did not know how to help them. I could, of course, induce an abortion. Many women called me for that purpose, even going down on their knees and begging me to help them, " for the sake of the poor little ones already here." They knew that some doctors and midwives did such things, but the price was beyond their means. I was so sympathetic; wouldn't I do something for them ? They would pay in weekly instalments. I tried to explain to them that it was not monetary considerations that held me back; it was concern for their life and health. I would relate the case of a woman killed by such an operation, and her children left motherless. But they preferred to die, they avowed; the city was then sure to take care of their orphans, and they would be better off.

I could not prevail upon myself to perform the much-coveted operation. I lacked faith in my skill and I remembered my Vienna professor who had often demonstrated to us the terrible results of abortion. He held that even when such practices prove successful, they undermine the health of the patient. I would not undertake the task. It was not any moral consideration for the sanctity of life; a life unwanted and forced into abject poverty did not seem sacred to me. But my interests embraced the entire social problem, not merely a single aspect of it, and I would not jeopardize my freedom for that one part of the human struggle. I refused to perform abortions and I knew no methods to prevent conception.

I spoke to some physicians about the matter. Dr. White, a conservative, said: "The poor have only themselves to blame; they indulge their appetites too much." Dr. Julius Hoffmann thought that children were the only joy the poor had. Dr. Solotaroff held out the hope of great changes in the near future when woman would become more intelligent and independent. "When she uses her brains more," he would tell me, "her procreative organs will function less." It seemed more convincing than the arguments of the other medicos, though no more comforting; nor was it of any practical help. Now that I had learned that women and children carried the heaviest burden of our ruthless economic system, I saw that it was mockery to expect them to wait until the social revolution arrives in order to right injustice. I sought some immediate solution for their purgatory, but I could find nothing of any use.

My home life was anything but harmonious, though externally all seemed smooth. Ed was apparently calm and contented again, but I felt cramped and nervous. If I attended a meeting and was detained later than expected, it would make me uneasy and I would hasten home in perturbation. Often I refused invitations to lecture because I sensed Ed's disapproval. Where I could not decline, I worked for weeks over my subject, my thoughts dwelling on Ed rather than on the matter in hand. I would wonder how this point or that argument might appeal to him and whether he would approve. Yet I never could get myself to read him my notes, and if he attended my meetings, his presence made me self-conscious, for I knew that he had no faith in my work. It served to weaken my faith in myself. I developed strange nervous attacks. Without preliminary warning I would fall to the ground as if knocked down by a heavy blow. I did not lose consciousness, being able to see and understand what was going on around me, but I was not able to utter a word. My chest felt convulsed, my throat compressed; I had an agonizing pain in my legs as if the muscles were being pulled asunder. This condition would last from ten minutes to an hour and leave me utterly exhausted. Solotaroff, failing to diagnose the trouble, took me to a specialist, who proved no wiser. Dr. White's examination also gave no results. Some physicians said it was hysteria, others an inverted womb. I knew the latter was the real cause, but I would not consent to an operation. More and more I had become convinced that my life would never know harmony in love for very long, that strife and not peace would be my lot. In such a life there was no room for a child.

From various parts of the country came requests for a series of lectures. I was very eager to go, but I lacked the courage to broach the matter to Ed. I knew he would not consent, and his refusal would most likely bring us nearer to a violent separation. My physicians had strongly advised a rest and change of scene, and now Ed surprised me by insisting that I ought to go away. " Your health is more important than any other consideration," he said, " but first you must drop the silly notion that you have to earn your own living." He was making enough for both now, and it would make him happy if I would give up my nursing and stop making myself ill by helping hapless brats into the world. He welcomed the opportunity to take care of me, to afford me leisure and recuperation. Later on, he said, I should be in condition to go on a tour. He realized how much I wanted it and he knew what an effort it was to me to play the devoted wife. He enjoyed the home I had made so beautiful for him, he went on, but he could see that I was not contented. He was sure a change would do me good, give me back my old spirit, and bring me back to him.

The weeks that followed were happy and peaceful. We were much together, making frequent trips to the country, attending concerts and operas. We took up reading together again, and Ed helped me to understand Racine, Corneille, Molière. He cared only for the classics; Zola and his contemporaries were repellent to him. But when alone during the day I indulged in the more modern literature, besides planning a number of lectures for my forthcoming tour.

In the midst of my preparations came the news of tortures in the Spanish prison of Montjuich. Three hundred men and women, mostly trade-unionists, with a sprinkling of anarchists, had been arrested in 1896 as a result of a bomb explosion in Barcelona during a religious procession. The entire world was appalled by the resurrection of the Inquisition, by prisoners being kept for days without food or water, flogged, and burned with hot irons. One even had had his tongue cut out. The fiendish methods were used to extort confessions from the unfortunates. Several went mad and in their delirium implicated their innocent comrades, who were immediately condemned to death. The person responsible for these horrors was the Prime Minister of Spain, Canovas del Castillo. Liberal-minded papers in Europe, like the *Frankfurter Zeitung* and the Paris *Intransigeant,* were arousing public sentiment against the nineteenth-century Inquisition. Advanced members of the House of Commons, the Reichstag, and the Chamber of Deputies were calling for action to stay the hand of Canovas. Only America remained dumb. Excepting the radical publications, the press maintained a conspiracy of silence. Together with my friends I strongly felt the necessity of breaking through that wall. In conference with Ed, Justus, John Edelman, and Harry Kelly, who had come from Boston, and with the co-operation of Italian and Spanish anarchists, we decided to start our campaign with a large mass meeting. A demonstration in front of the Spanish Consulate in New York was to follow. As soon as our efforts became public, the reactionary papers began to urge the authorities to stop " Red Emma," that term having stuck to me since the Union Square meeting. On the night of our gathering the police appeared in full force, crowding even the platform so that the speakers could hardly make a gesture without touching an officer. When my turn came to speak, I gave a detailed account of the methods that were being used in Montjuich, and called for a protest against the Spanish horrors.

The pent-up emotions of the audience, aroused to a high pitch, broke into thunderous applause. Before it fully subsided, a voice from the gallery called out: " Miss Goldman, don't you think someone of the Spanish Embassy in Washington or the Legation in New York ought to be killed in revenge for the conditions you have just described? " I felt intuitively that my questioner must be a detective, attempting to trap me. There was a movement among the police near me as if preparing to lay hands on me. The audience was hushed in tense expectation. For a moment I paused; then I replied calmly and deliberately: " No, I do not think any one of the Spanish representatives in America is important enough to be killed, but if I were in Spain now, I should kill Canovas del Castillo."

Several weeks later came the news that Canovas del Castillo had been shot dead by an anarchist whose name was Angiolillo. At once the New York papers started a veritable hunt for the leading anarchists to secure their opinions of the man and his deed. Reporters pestered me day and night for interviews. Did I know the man? Had I been in correspondence with him? Had I suggested to him that Canovas be killed? I had to disappoint them. I did not know Angiolillo and had never corresponded with him. All I knew was that he had acted while the rest of us had only talked about the fearful outrages.

We learned that Angiolillo had lived in London and that he was known among our friends as a sensitive young man, an ardent student, a lover of music and books, poetry being his passion. The Montjuich tortures had haunted him and he decided to kill Canovas. He went to Spain, expecting to find the Prime Minister in Parliament, but he learned that Canovas was recuperating from his " labours of State " at Santa Agueda, a fashionable summer resort. Angiolillo journeyed there. He met Canovas almost immediately, but the man was accompanied by his wife and two children. " I could have killed him then," Angiolillo said in court, " but I would not risk the lives of the innocent woman and children. It was Canovas I wanted; he alone was responsible for the crimes of Montjuich." He then visited the Castillo villa, introducing himself as the representative of a conservative Italian paper. When he was face to face with the Prime Minister, he shot him dead. Mme Canovas ran in at that moment and hit Angiolillo full in the face. " I did not mean to kill your husband," Angiolillo apologized to her, " I aimed only at the official responsible for the Montjuich tortures."

The *Attentat* of Angiolillo and his frightful death vividly recalled to me the period of July 1892. Sasha's Calvary had now lasted five years. How close I had come to sharing a similar fate! — the lack of a paltry fifty dollars had prevented my accompanying Sasha to Pittsburgh — but can one estimate the spiritual travail and suffering the experience involved? Yet the price was worth the lesson I had gained from Sasha's deed. Since then I had ceased to regard political acts, as some other revolutionists did, from a merely utilitarian standpoint or from the view of their propagandistic value. The inner forces that compel an idealist to acts of violence, often involving the destruction of his own life, had come to mean much more to me. I felt certain now that behind every political deed of that nature was an impressionable, highly sensitized personality and a gentle spirit. Such beings cannot go on living complacently in the sight of great human misery and wrong. Their reactions to the cruelty and injustice of the world must inevitably express themselves in some violent act, in supreme rending of their tortured soul.

I had spoken in Providence a number of times without the least trouble. Rhode Island was still one of the few States to maintain the old tradition of unabridged freedom of speech. Two of our open-air gatherings, attended by thousands, went off well. But the police had evidently decided to suppress our last meeting. Arriving with several friends at the square where the assembly was to take place, we found a member of the Socialist Labor Party talking, and, not wishing to interfere with him, we set up our box farther away. My good comrade John H. Cook, a very active worker, opened the meeting, and I began to speak. Just then a policeman came running towards us, shouting: " Stop your jabbering! Stop it this minute or I'll pull you off the box! " I went on talking. Someone called out: " Don't mind the bully — go right on! " The policeman came up, puffing heavily. When he got his breath he snarled, " Say, you, are you deaf? Didn't I tell you to stop? What d'you mean not obeying the law? " " Are you the law? " I retorted; " I thought it is your duty to maintain the law, not to break it. Don't you know the law in this State gives me the right of free speech? " " The hell it does," he replied, " I'm the law." The audience began hooting and jeering. The officer started to pull me off the improvised platform. The crowd looked threatening and began closing in on him. He blew his whistle. A patrol wagon dashed up to the square, and several policemen broke through the crowd with their clubs swinging. The officer, still holding on to me, shouted: " Drive those damn anarchists back so I can get this woman. She's under arrest." I was led to the patrol wagon and literally thrown into it.

At the police station I demanded to know by what right I had been interfered with. " Because you're Emma Goldman," the sergeant at the desk replied. " Anarchists have no rights in this community, see? " He ordered me locked up for the night.

It was the first time since 1893 that I had been arrested, but, constantly expecting to fall into the clutches of the law, I had made it a practice to carry a book with me when going to meetings. I wrapped my skirts around me, climbed up on the board placed for a bed in my cell, pressed close to the barred door, through which shimmered a light, and started to read. Presently I became aware of someone moaning in the adjoining cell. " What is it? " I called in a whisper; " are you ill? " A woman's voice replied between sobs: " My children, my motherless children! Who is going to take care of them now? My sick husband, what'll become of him? " Her weeping became louder. " Say, you drunken lout, stop that squealing! " a matron shouted from somewhere. The crying was checked, and I heard the woman walking up and down her cell like a caged animal. When she quieted down a little I asked her to tell me her troubles; perhaps I could be of help. I learned that she was the mother of six children, the eldest fourteen, the baby only a year old. Her husband had been ill for ten months, unable to work, and in her despair she had helped herself to a loaf of bread and a can of milk from the grocery store in which she had once worked. She was caught in the act and turned over to the police. She begged to be let off for the night in order not to frighten her family, but the officer insisted on her going with him, not even giving her a chance to send a message to her home. She was brought to the station-house after the evening meal. The matron told her she could order some food if she had the price. The woman had not eaten all day; she was faint with hunger and ill with anxiety; but she had no money.

I rapped for the matron and asked her to send out for supper for me. In less than fifteen minutes she returned with a tray of ham and eggs, hot potatoes, bread, butter, and a large pot of coffee. I had given her a two-dollar bill, and she handed back fifteen cents. " You have fancy prices here," I said. " Sure thing, kid, did you think this was a charity joint? " Seeing that she was in a good humour, I requested her to pass part of the meal to my neighbour. She did, but not without commenting: " You're a regular fool to waste such a feed on a common sneak-thief."

The next morning I was taken, together with my neighbour and other unfortunates, before a magistrate. I was held over under bond, and as the amount could not be raised immediately I was returned to the station-house. At one o'clock in the afternoon I was again called for, this time to see the Mayor. That individual, no less bulky and bloated than the policeman, informed me that if I would promise under oath never to return to Providence he would let me go. " That's nice of you, Mayor," I replied; " but inasmuch as you have no case against me, your offer isn't quite so generous as it appears, is it? " I told him that I would make no promises whatever, but that if it would relieve his mind, I could tell him that I was about to start on a lecture tour to California. " It may take three months or more, I don't know. But I do know that you and your city cannot do without me much longer than that, so I am determined to come back." The Mayor and his flunkies roared, and I was released.

On my arrival in Boston I was shocked by a report in the local papers of the shooting at Hazleton, Pennsylvania, of twenty-one strikers. The men were miners on their way to Latimer, in the same State, to induce the workers there to join the strike. The Sheriff had met them on the public road and would not allow them to go on. He commanded them to return to Hazleton, and when they refused, he and his posse opened fire.

The papers stated that the Sheriff had acted in self-defence; the mob had been threatening. Yet there was not one casualty among the posse, while twenty-one working-men had been mowed down and a number of others wounded. It was evident from the report that the men had gone out with empty hands, without any intention of offering resistance. Everywhere workers were slain, everywhere the same butchery! Montjuich, Chicago, Pittsburgh, Hazleton — the few for ever outraging and crushing the many. The masses were the millions, yet how weak! To awaken them from their stupor, to make them conscious of their power — that is the great need. Soon, I told myself, I should be able to reach them throughout America. With a tongue of fire I would rouse them to a realization of their dependence and indignity! Glowingly I visioned my first great tour and the opportunities it would offer me to plead our Cause. But presently my reverie was disturbed by the thought of Ed. Our common life — what would become of it? Why could it not go hand in hand with my work? My giving to humanity would only increase my own need, would make me love and want Ed more. He would, he must, understand; he had himself suggested my going away for a time. The image of Ed filled me with warmth, but my heart fluttered with apprehension.

I had been away from Ed only two weeks, but my longing for him was more intense than it had been on my return from Europe. I could hardly contain myself until the train came to a stop in the Grand Central Station, where he met me. At home everything seemed new, more beautiful and enticing. Ed's endearing words sounded like music in my ears. Sheltered and protected from the strife and conflict outside, I clung to him and basked in the sunshine of our home. My eagerness to go on a long tour paled under the fascination of my lover. A month of joy and abandon followed, but my dream was soon to suffer a painful awakening.

It was caused by Nietzsche. Ever since my return from Vienna I had been hoping that Ed would read my books. I had asked him to do so and he promised he would when he had more time. It made me very sad to find Ed so indifferent to the new literary forces in the world. One evening we were gathered at Justus's place at a farewell party. James Huneker was present and a young friend of ours, P. Yelineck, a talented painter. They began discussing Nietzche. I took part, expressing my enthusiasm over the great poet-philosopher and dwelling on the impression of his works on me. Huneker was surprised. " I did not know you were interested in anything outside of propaganda," he remarked. "That is because you don't know anything about anarchism," I replied, "else you would understand that it embraces every phase of life and effort and that it undermines the old, outlived values." Yelineck asserted that he was an anarchist because he was an artist; all creative people must be anarchists, he held, because they need scope and freedom for their expression. Huneker insisted that art has nothing to do with any ism. "Nietzsche himself is the proof of it," he argued; "he is an aristocrat, his ideal is the superman because he has no sympathy with or faith in the common herd." I pointed out that Nietzsche was not a social theorist but a poet, a rebel and innovator. His aristocracy was neither of birth nor of purse; it was of the spirit. In that respect Nietzsche was an anarchist, and all true anarchists were aristocrats, I said.

Then Ed spoke. His voice sounded cold and constrained, and I sensed the tempest behind it. "Nietzsche is a fool," he said, "a man with a diseased mind. He was doomed from birth to the idiocy which finally overtook him. He will be forgotten in less than a decade, and so will all those other pseudo-moderns. They are contortionists in comparison with the truly great of the past."

"But you haven't read Nietzsche!" I objected heatedly; "how can you talk about him?" "Oh, yes, I have," he retorted, "I read long ago all the silly books you brought from abroad." I was dumbfounded. Huneker and Yelineck turned on Ed, but my hurt was too great to continue the discussion.

He had known how I had wanted him to share my books, how I had hoped and waited for him to recognize their value and significance. How could he have kept me in suspense, how could he have remained silent after he had read them? Of course, he had a right to his opinion; that I believed implicitly. It was not his differing from me that had stabbed me to the quick; it was his scorn and ridicule of what had come to mean so much to me. Huneker, Yelineck, strangers in a measure, welcomed my appreciation of the new spirit, while my own lover made me appear silly, childish, incapable of judgment. I wanted to run away from Justus's place, to be alone; but I checked myself. I could not bear an open conflict with Ed.

Late at night, when we returned home, he said to me: "Let's not spoil our beautiful three months; Nietzsche is not worth it." I felt wounded to the heart. "It isn't Nietzsche, it is you — you," I cried excitedly. "Under the pretext of a great love you have done your utmost to chain me to you, to rob me of all that is more precious to me than life. You are not content with binding my body, you want also to bind my spirit! First the movement and my friends — now it's the books I love. You want to tear me away from them. You're rooted in the old. Very well, remain there! But don't imagine you will hold me to it. You are not going to clip my wings, you shan't stop my flight. I'll free myself even if it means tearing you out of my heart."

He stood leaning against the door of his room, his eyes closed, giving no sign of having heard a word I said. But I no longer cared. I stepped into my own room, my heart cold and empty.

The last few days were outwardly calm, even friendly, Ed helping me to prepare for my departure. At the station he embraced me. I knew he wanted to say something, but he remained silent. I, too, could not speak.

When the train pulled out and Ed's form receded, I realized that our life would never be the same any more. My love had received too violent a shock. It was now like a cracked bell; never again would it ring the same clear, joyous song.

CHAPTER XVI

Y FIRST STOP WAS PHILADELPHIA. I HAD VISITED THE CITY MANY times since my arrest in 1893, always addressing Jewish audiences. On this occasion I was invited to lecture in English before several American organizations. While in the City of Brotherly Love I stayed at the house of Miss Perle McLeod, the president of the Ladies' Liberal League. I should have preferred the warmer hospitality of my old friend Natasha Notkin, with whom I felt at home, in the congenial atmosphere of my Russian comrades, but it had been suggested that the apartment of Miss McLeod was more accessible to the Americans who would want to meet me.

The meetings were not badly attended, but, still aching from the distressing scene with Ed, I did not feel fully equal to the situation, and my lectures lacked inspiration. Yet my visit was not altogether useless. I gained a footing and made a number of friends, among them a most interesting woman, Susan Patten. I knew through Sasha that she was one of his constant American correspondents. I liked her on account of that and for her fine spirit.

In Washington I spoke before a German free-thought society. After the lecture I met a group of *Reitzel Freunde,* as the readers of the *Armer Teufel* called themselves. Most of them looked more like butchers than idealists. One man, who boasted of being an employee of the United States Government, talked much of beauty in art and letters — not for the ignorant mob, of course, but for the choice few. He had no patience with anarchism, because " it wanted to make all alike." " How could a hod-carrier, for instance, claim the same rights as I, an educated man ? " he asked me. He didn't think that I seriously believed in such equality, or that any other leading anarchist did. He was sure we were merely using it as a bait. He did not blame us at all; " the rabble should be made to pay."

" How long have you been reading the *Armer Teufel*? " I inquired.
" Since its first issue," he proudly replied. " And that is all you got
from it? Well, all I can say is that my friend Robert has been casting
his pearls before a swine." The man jumped to his feet and angrily
left the room amidst the boisterous laughter of the rest of the
company.

Another Reitzel " friend " introduced himself as a brewer from Cincinnati. He moved closer to me and began to talk of sex. He had heard
that I was the " great champion of free love " in the United States. He
was delighted to see that I was not only clever, as I had just proved, but
also young and charming, not at all like the rigid blue-stocking he had
imagined me to be. He, too, believed in free love, though he didn't
think most men and women were ripe for it, especially women who
always try to hold on to the man. But " Emma Goldman, that's another
matter." His lewd and smirking manner nauseated me. I turned my
back upon him and went to my room. Very tired, I fell asleep almost
immediately. I was awakened by a persistent tap-tap on my door.
" Who is it? " I called. " A friend," came in reply; " won't you open? "
It was the voice of the brewer from Cincinnati. Jumping out of bed,
I shouted as loud as I could: " If you don't leave instantly, I shall wake
the whole house! " " Please, please! " he pleaded through the door,
" don't make any scene. I'm a married man, with grown children. I
thought you believed in free love." Then I heard him hurrying off.

Of what avail are lofty ideals, I wondered. The government clerk
who dares put himself above the hod-carrier; the respectable pillar of
society, to whom free love is only a means for clandestine affairs —
both readers of Reitzel, the brilliant rebel and idealist! Their heads
and hearts have remained as sterile as the Sahara. The world must be
full of such people, the world I have set out to awaken. A sense of futility came over me and of dismal isolation.

On the way from Washington to Pittsburgh it poured incessantly.
I was chilled to the bone and oppressed by the memory of Homestead
and of Sasha. Always on my visits to the Steel City a heavy weight
would settle on my heart. The sight of the belching fires from the huge
furnaces scorched my soul.

The presence at the station of Carl Nold and Henry Bauer somewhat cheered my dejection. My two comrades had been liberated from
the Western Penitentiary in May of that year (1897). I had never
met Bauer before, but Carl brought back the days of our first

meeting, in November 1892. The friendship begun then had become strengthened through our correspondence while Carl was in prison. Our meeting now was to cement further the bond between us. It was good to see the dear, vivacious face again. Prison had made him more thoughtful, yet it had not dampened his joy in life. Bauer, large and jovial, towered over us like a giant. "The elephant and his family," he remarked, walking between us, while Carl and I vainly tried to keep pace with his huge steps.

On my former visits in Pittsburgh I had always stopped with my good friend Harry Gordon and his family. Harry was one of our best workers, a faithful and enthusiastic friend. Mrs. Gordon, a simple and tender-hearted woman, was very much attached to me. She always went out of her way to make my stay in her home as pleasant and comfortable as her husband's small wages would permit. I loved being with the Gordons, and I asked my companions to take me to them. They, however, were bent on celebrating my arrival first.

There were to be no lectures in Pittsburgh. Carl and Henry had begun a new move for Sasha's release, an appeal to the Board of Pardons to be backed exclusively by labour elements. I had no faith left in such steps, but I did not want to communicate my pessimism to my friends. Both of them were in a jovial mood. They had arranged a little dinner in a near-by restaurant, in a room all by ourselves where we would be undisturbed. We drank our first glass standing, in silence. It was to Sasha. His spirit hovered over us and brought us closer to each other in our common aims and work. Then Carl and Henry recounted to me their prison experience and the years they had spent under the same roof with Sasha. They had brought out a message for me which they feared to trust to the mails: Sasha was planning an escape.

His scheme was a masterly one; it fairly took my breath away. But even if he should succeed in getting out of prison, I reflected, where would he go? In America he would have to keep under cover for the rest of his life. He would be a haunted man, to be captured in the end. It would be different in Russia. Similar escapes had been repeatedly carried out there. But Russia had a revolutionary spirit and the political was a persecuted unfortunate in the eyes of the workers and the peasant; he could count on their sympathy and assistance. In the United States, on the other hand, nine-tenths of the workers themselves would immediately join in the hunt for Sasha. Nold and Bauer agreed with me, but they asked me not to communicate my fears to Sasha. He had reached the limit of endurance; his eyes were failing, his health was breaking down, and he had again been brooding on suicide. The hope of escape and the elaboration of his plan energized his fighting spirit. We must not discourage him, but perhaps we would induce him to wait until every legal means for his release had been tried.

So deeply engrossed had we become in our talk that we had lost all sense of time. In surprise we discovered that it was long after midnight. My companions thought it too late to go to the Gordons' and suggested taking me to a little hotel kept by a reader of the *Armer Teufel*. On the way I related to them my experience with the Washington *Reitzel Freunde,* but Bauer assured me that the Pittsburgh hotel man was of a different type. He really turned out to be very friendly. " Indeed, there is surely room for Emma Goldman in my place," he said genially. We were about to mount the stairs when the hysterical voice of a woman burst upon our ears. " A room for Emma Goldman ! " she screamed. " This is a respectable family hotel, no place for that shameless creature, the free lover of a convict ! " " Let's get out of this," I urged my friends. Before we had a chance to move, the hen-pecked husband banged his fist on the counter, demanding to know who was boss. "Tell me that, you Xantippe ! " he yelled. " Am I, or am I not, master in this house ? " With a devastating look in my direction the woman slunk out of the room. The master became calm and kindly again. He couldn't let me go out in the awful weather, he protested; I must stay at least for the night. But I had had enough, and we left.

" Why not come to my den ? " Carl suggested. Together with his wife and little boy he occupied one room and a kitchen, and they would be glad to share them with me. Dear, generous Carl did not know the dread I had of going into people's houses uninvited. But I was very tired and weary and I did not wish to hurt Carl. " I will go anywhere you take me, Carolus, even to hell," I said; " only let's get there quickly."

At last we reached Nold's place, in Allegheny, Bauer having gone home. The door opened on a dimly lit room. A buxom young woman, somewhat dishevelled, met us, and Carl introduced her to me. I had the impression that she resented my intrusion. The place was small, containing only one bed, in which the child lay sleeping. I looked questioningly at Carl. " It's all right, Emma," he said; " Nellie and I will sleep on the floor, and you will share the bed with the kid." I hesitated, inclined to leave, but the rain was coming down in torrents. I turned to the woman to apologize for the discomfort I was causing, but she would not listen; in silence she walked into the kitchen, closing the door. Half dressed, I lay down on the bed alongside of the little boy and immediately fell asleep. I was awakened by someone shouting: " He's killing me! Help! Police! " The room was pitch-dark. I jumped up in terror, not realizing at first what was happening. Groping, I found a table and matches. When I had struck a light, I saw two bodies rolling on the floor, fighting. The woman held Carl pressed down with her knees and was trying to get at his throat, at the same time yelling for the police. Carl was beating back her hands and making frantic efforts to extricate himself. I had never seen a more disgusting sight. I pulled the woman off Carl, snatched up my things, and was out on the street before either of them had come to his senses. My mind in a turmoil, I ran in the beating rain to Henry's place, rousing him out of bed and telling him what had happened. He accompanied me immediately on my search for a hotel. Carl had dashed out after me, and the three of us walked in the downpour to Pittsburgh, the hotels in Allegheny being closed at that late hour. We canvassed a number of hostelries, but were refused everywhere, no doubt because I looked so wet and disreputable, without any suitcase, for that had been left at Carl's. It was nearly morning when at last we found a little hotel that would receive me.

With shaking knees and chattering teeth I crawled into bed, drawing the blankets over my face to shut out the hideousness of life. But in vain I sought forgetfulness in sleep. Dark shadows seemed to envelop me on every side. The sinister walls of the penitentiary that held Sasha, his years of suffering, my own prison days, the ghastly experience of an hour ago, all blended into a grinning, fantastic mockery of darkness and despair. Yet somewhere in the distance there quivered a faint shimmer of light. I knew it; I recognized it; it emanated from Ed. The thought of our love, our home, pierced the gloom for an instant. I stretched out trembling hands, but they encountered only empty space, empty and cold as my own heart.

Three days later I arrived in Detroit. The lure of that city had always been to me Robert Reitzel. His wit and peerless pen had fascinated me from the time I began to read his paper. His courageous

defence of the Chicago martyrs and his bold effort to save their lives
had impressed him on my mind as an unflinching rebel and fighter.
The vision I had of him had become strengthened by his stand in behalf of Sasha. While Most, knowing Sasha and his revolutionary
ardour, had calumniated him and disparaged his act, Reitzel had
gloried in the man and his *Attentat*. His article "*Im Hochsummer
fiel ein Schuss*" was an exalted and moving tribute to our brave boy.
It brought Reitzel very close to me and made me long to know him
personally.

Almost five years had passed since I had first met the editor of
the *Armer Teufel,* while he was visiting New York. The recollection
of that experience now stood out vividly before me. It was late one
evening, while still at my sewing-machine, that I heard violent knocking on the shutters of my window. "Let in the errant knights!"
boomed the bass of Justus. Beside him I saw a man almost as tall and
broad-shouldered as himself, whom I at once recognized as Robert
Reitzel. Before I could greet him, he began to upbraid me playfully.
"A fine anarchist you are!" he thundered. "You preach the need of
leisure, and work longer than a galley-slave. We have come to break
your chains, and we are going to take you with us if we have to use
force. March! Little girl, get ready! Come on out here, since you
don't seem too anxious to invite us into your virgin chamber." My
unexpected visitors were standing in full view of the street-lamp.
Reitzel wore no hat. A shock of blond hair, already considerably
greyed, fell in confusion over his high forehead. He looked big and
strong, more youthful and vital than Justus. He was holding on to the
windowsill with both hands, his eyes inquisitively scrutinizing my face.
"What's the verdict?" he exclaimed; "am I acceptable?" "Am
I?" I questioned in return. "You have passed long ago," he replied,
"and I have come to give you the prize, to offer myself as your
knight."

Soon I was walking between the two men in the direction of Justus's
place. There we were met by hilarious hurrahs and "*Hoch soll er
leben,*" and calls for more wine. Justus, with his usual graciousness,
rolled up his sleeves, got behind the counter, and insisted on playing
host. Robert gallantly offered his arm to lead me to the head of the
table. As we walked up the aisle Justus intoned the wedding-march
from *Lohengrin.* The strains were taken up by the whole group of
men, who had splendid voices.

Robert was the spirit of the gathering. His humour was more sparkling than the wine freely partaken of by all present. The amount he consumed transcended even Most's ability in that regard; and the more he imbibed, the more eloquent he grew. His stories, very colourful and amusing, came gushing like water from a brook. He was inexhaustible. Long after most of the others had caved in, my knight kept on singing and talking of life and love.

It was almost daybreak when, accompanied by Robert, I stepped into the street, clinging to his arm. A great longing possessed me to embrace the fascinating man at my side, so fine and beautiful in body and mind. I felt sure he was also strongly attracted to me; he had shown it all through the evening in his every glance and touch. As we walked along I could feel his agitation of passionate desire. Where could we go? The thought flitted through my mind, as in increasing excitement I walked close to him, waiting and madly hoping that he would make some suggestion.

" And Sasha? " he suddenly asked. " Do you hear often from our wonderful boy? " The spell was broken. I felt thrust back into the world of misery and strife. During the rest of the walk we talked of Sasha and his act, of Most's attitude and its dire effects. It was another Robert now; it was the rebel and fighter against injustice.

At my door he took me in his arms, with hot breath whispering: " I want you! Let's forget the ugliness of life." Gently I freed myself from his embrace. " Too late, my dear," I replied; " the mysterious voices of the night are silent, the dissonances of the day have begun." He understood. Gazing affectionately into my eyes, he said: " This is only the beginning of our friendship, my brave Emma. We will meet again soon in Detroit." I threw my window wide open and watched the rhythmic swing of his well-knit body until he disappeared round the corner. Then I went back to my life and to my machine.

A year later came the news of Reitzel's illness. He was suffering from spinal tuberculosis, which resulted in the paralysis of his lower extremities. He was bedridden, like Heine, whom he so greatly admired and whom in a certain measure he resembled in spirit and feeling. But even in his mattress-grave Robert could not be daunted. Every line he wrote was a clarion call to freedom and battle. From his sick-bed he had prevailed on the Central Labor Union of his city to invite me as speaker to that year's eleventh of November commemoration. " Come a few days earlier," he had written me, " so that we can resume our friendship of the days when I was still young."

I arrived in Detroit late in the afternoon on the day of the scheduled meeting and was met by Martin Drescher, whose stirring poems had often appeared in the *Armer Teufel*. To my amusement and the astonishment of the crowd at the station, Drescher, tall and awkward, kneeled before me, holding out a bunch of red roses, and delivering himself of the following: " From your knight, my Queen, with his undying love." " And who may be the knight? " I queried. " Robert, of course! Who else would dare send his love to the Queen of the Anarchists? " The crowd laughed, but the man on his knees before me was not disturbed. To save him from catching a bad cold (there was snow on the ground) I held out my hand, saying: " Now, vassal, take me to my castle." Drescher got up, bowed low, gave me his arm, and solemnly led me to a cab. " To the Randolph Hotel," he commanded. On our arrival there, we found half a score of Robert's friends awaiting us. The owner himself was one of the *Armer Teufel* admirers. " My best room and wines are at your disposal," he announced. I knew it was Robert's thoughtfulness and friendship that had paved the way and secured for me the affection and hospitality of his circle.

Turner Hall was filled to the limit, the audience in tune with the spirit of the evening. The event was made more festive by the singing of a chorus of children and the masterly reading of a fine revolutionary poem by Martin Drescher. I was scheduled to speak in German. The impression on me of the Chicago tragedy had not paled with the passing years. That night it seemed more poignant, perhaps because of the nearness of Robert Reitzel, who had known, loved, and fought for our Chicago martyrs and who was himself now slowly dying. The memory of 1887 took living form, personifying their Calvary and inspiring me to heights of exaltation, of hope and life springing from heroic death.

At the conclusion of the meeting I was called back to the platform to receive from the hands of a golden-haired maiden of five a huge bouquet of red carnations, too large for her wee body. I pressed the child to my heart and carried her off, bouquet and all.

Later in the evening I met Joe Labadie, a prominent individualist anarchist of picturesque appearance, who introduced to me the

Reverend Dr. H. S. McCowan. Both expressed regret that I had not spoken in English. "I came especially to hear you," Dr. McCowan informed me, whereupon Joe, as everyone affectionately called Labadie, remarked: "Well, why don't you offer Miss Goldman your pulpit? Then you could hear our 'Red Emma' in English." "That's an idea!" the minister replied; "but Miss Goldman is opposed to churches; would you speak in one?" "In hell if need be," I said, "provided the Devil won't pull at my skirts." "All right," he exclaimed, "you shall speak in my church, and no one shall pull at your skirts or curtail a word of what you want to say." We agreed that my lecture should be on anarchism, it being a subject most people knew almost nothing about.

With the flowers my "knight" had sent me came also a note asking me to visit him any time after the meeting, since he would be awake. It seemed strange for a sick person to keep such late hours, but Drescher assured me that Robert felt best after sundown. His house was the last on the street, overlooking a large open space. "Luginsland," Robert had named it; it was all his eye had looked upon for the past three and a half years. His inner vision, though, keen and penetrating, wandered to distant lands and climes, bringing to him all the cultural wealth they contained. The bright light streaming through his bay window could be seen from afar; it reminded me of a lighthouse, with Robert Reitzel its keeper. Song and laughter sounded from the house. On entering Reitzel's room I found it filled with people; the smoke was so thick that it obscured Robert from view and blurred the faces of those present. His voice called out jovially: "Welcome to our sanctum! Welcome to the den of your adoring knight!" Robert, in a white shirt open wide at the neck, sat in bed propped up against a mountain of pillows. Except for the ashy colour of his face, the increased greyness of his hair, and his thin, transparent hands, there was no indication of his illness. His eyes alone spoke of the martyrdom he was suffering. Their care-free light was gone. With aching heart I put my arms around him, pressing his beautiful head to me. "So motherly?" he objected. "Aren't you going to kiss your knight?" "Of course," I stammered.

I had almost forgotten the others in the room, to whom Robert now began introducing me as the "Vestal of the Social Revolution." "Look at her!" he cried, "look at her; does she resemble the monster pictured by the press, the fury of a hetæra? Behold her black dress and white collar, prim and proper, almost like a nun." He was making me embarrassed and self-conscious. " You are praising me as if I were a horse you wanted to sell," I finally objected. It did not dismay him in the least. " Didn't I say you are prim and proper ? " he declared triumphantly; " you don't live up to your reputation. *Wein her,*" he called; " let's drink to our Vestal ! " The men surrounded Robert's bed, glasses in hand. He emptied his to the dregs and then flung it against the wall. " Emma is now one of us. Our pact is sealed; we will be true to her to our last breath ! "

An account of the meeting and of my speech had preceded me to Reitzel, the manager of his paper having brought back a glowing report. When I mentioned McCowan's invitation, Robert was delighted. He knew the Reverend Doctor, whom he considered a rare exception in the " outfit of soul-savers." I told Robert about my friend in Blackwell's Island, the young priest, relating how fine and understanding he was. " A pity you met him in prison," Robert teased me, " else you might have found in him an ardent lover." I was sure I could not love a priest. " That's nonsense, my dear — love has no concern with ideas," he replied; " I have loved girls in every town and village and they were not remotely so interesting as your priest seems to be. Love has nothing to do with any ism, and you'll find it out when you grow older." In vain I insisted that I knew all about it. I was no child, being nearly twenty-nine. I was confident I should never fall in love with anyone who did not share my ideas.

The next morning I was awakened in my hotel by the announcement that a dozen reporters were waiting to interview me. They were eager for a story on my proposed speech in Dr. McCowan's church. They showed me the morning papers with the glaring headlines: " EMMA SHOWS MOTHER INSTINCT — FREE LOVER IN A DETROIT PULPIT — RED EMMA CAPTURES HEART OF MCCOWAN — CONGREGATIONAL CHURCH TO BE TURNED INTO HOTBED OF ANARCHY AND FREE LOVE."

For several succeeding days the front page of every paper in Detroit was filled with the impending desecration of the church and the portending ruin of the congregation by " Red Emma." Reports about members' threatening to leave and committees' besieging poor Dr. McCowan followed one another. " It will mean his neck," I said to Reitzel when I saw him the day before the meeting, " and I'd hate to be the cause of it." But Robert held that the man knew what he was doing; it was only right for him to stick to his guns, if only to test his independence in the church. " At any rate, I must offer to withdraw," I suggested, " to give McCowan a chance to recall his invitation if he feels like it." A friend was dispatched to the minister, but he sent word that he would go through with his plan no matter what happened. " A church that refuses the right of expression to the most unpopular person or creed is no place for me," he said. " You must not mind the consequences to me."

In the Tabernacle the Reverend Dr. McCowan presided. In a short speech, which he read from a prepared text, he set forth his own position. He was not an anarchist, he declared; he had never given much thought to it and he really knew very little about it. It was for that reason that he had visited Turner Hall on the night of November 11. Unfortunately Emma Goldman had spoken in German, and when it was suggested that he might hear her in English in his own pulpit, he had accepted the idea at once. He felt that the members of his church would be glad to hear the woman who had for years been persecuted as a " social menace "; as good Christians, he thought, they would be charitable to her. He then turned over the pulpit to me.

I had decided to stick strictly to the economic side of anarchism and to avoid as far as possible matters of religion and sexual problems. I felt I owed it to the man who was making such a courageous stand. At least his congregation should have no cause to say that I had used the Tabernacle to attack their God or to undermine the sacred institution of marriage. I succeeded better than I had expected. My lecture, lasting an hour, was listened to without any interruption and was much applauded at the end. " We won ! " Dr. McCowan whispered to me when I sat down.

He rejoiced too soon. The applause had barely died away when an elderly woman rose belligerently. " Mr. Chairman," she demanded, " does Miss Goldman believe in God or does she not ? " She was followed by another. " Does the speaker favour killing off all rulers ? " Then a small, emaciated man jumped to his feet and in a thin voice cried : " Miss Goldman ! You're a believer in free love, aren't you ? Now, wouldn't your system result in houses of prostitution at every lamp-post ? "

" I shall have to answer these people straight from the shoulder," I remarked to the minister. " So be it," he replied.

" Ladies and gentlemen," I began, " I came here to avoid as much as possible treading on your corns. I had intended to deal only with the basic issue of economics that dictates our lives from the cradle to the grave, regardless of our religion or moral beliefs. I see now that it was a mistake. If one enters a battle, he cannot be squeamish about a few corns. Here, then, are my answers: I do not believe in God, because I believe in man. Whatever his mistakes, man has for thousands of years past been working to undo the botched job your God has made." The house went frantic. " Blasphemy! Heretic! Sinner! " the women screamed. " Stop her! Throw her out! "

When order was restored, I continued: " As to killing rulers, it depends entirely on the position of the ruler. If it is the Russian Tsar, I most certainly believe in dispatching him to where he belongs. If the ruler is as ineffectual as an American president, it is hardly worth the effort. There are, however, some potentates I would kill by any and all means at my disposal. They are Ignorance, Superstition, and Bigotry — the most sinister and tyrannical rulers on earth. As for the gentleman who asked if free love would not build more houses of prostitution, my answer is: they will all be empty if the men of the future look like him."

There was instant pandemonium. In vain the chairman pounded for order. People jumped up on benches, waved their hats, shouted, and would not leave the church until the lights were turned out.

The next morning most of the papers reported the Tabernacle meeting as a disgraceful spectacle. There was general condemnation of the action of Dr. McCowan in permitting me to speak in the Tabernacle. Even the famous agnostic Robert Ingersoll joined the chorus. " I think that all the anarchists are insane, Emma Goldman among the rest," he stated; " I also think that the Reverend Dr. McCowan is a generous man — not afraid. However, it is not commendable for a crazy man or woman to be invited to talk before any public assemblage." Dr. McCowan resigned from the church. " I'm going to a mining town," he told me; " I am sure the miners will appreciate my work much better." I was sure they would.

My correspondence with Ed after I left New York was of a friendly nature, though constrained. When I reached Detroit, I found a long letter from him in the old loving spirit. He made no reference to our last scene. He was anxiously waiting for me to return, he wrote, and he hoped to have me back for the holidays. " When one's sweetheart is married to public life, one must learn to be *genügsam* [content with little]," his letter read. I could not imagine Ed being *genügsam,* but I understood that he was trying to meet my needs. I loved Ed and I wanted him, but I was determined to go on with my work. I greatly missed him, however, and his charm, which had not ceased to attract me. I wired him that I was on my way to visit sister Helena and that I should be home within a week.

Outside of a brief visit after my release from prison, I had not been in Rochester since 1894. It seemed ages, so much had happened in my life. Changes had also taken place in the fortunes of my beloved sister Helena. The Hochsteins now occupied more comfortable quarters in a little house with a touch of green in the back. Their steamship agency, though yielding small returns, had nevertheless improved their condition. Helena continued to shoulder the main burden; her children needed her even more than before, and so did the business. Most of their customers were Lithuanian and Lettish peasants, who performed the hardest labour in the United States. Their wages were small, yet they managed to send money to their families and bring them over to America. Poverty and drudgery had made them dull and suspicious, and this required tact and patience in dealing with them. My brother-in-law, Jacob, usually extremely reserved and quiet, would often lose his temper when confronted with such stupidity. But for Helena most of the customers would have turned to some better business man than Jacob Hochstein, the scholar. She knew how to smooth the troubled waters. Her sympathies were with these wage-slaves and she understood their psychology. She did more than merely sell them tickets and forward their money; she entered into their barren lives. She wrote their letters home for them and helped them over many difficulties. Nor were they the only ones to come to Helena to be comforted and aided. Almost the entire neighbourhood brought their troubles to her. While my precious sister would lend an attentive ear to everybody's tale of woe, she herself never complained, never lamented her own unfulfilled hopes, the dreams and aspirations of her youth. I realized keenly what a force was lost in the rare creature; hers was a large nature compressed in too limited a space.

The day of my arrival offered no chance for communion with Helena. In the evening, when the children were asleep and the office closed, we could talk. She would not pry into my life; what I told her she accepted with understanding and affection. She herself spoke mostly about the children, hers and Lena's, and of the hard life of our parents. I knew well enough her reasons for constantly dwelling on the difficulties of our father. She strove to bring me closer to him and to help to a better understanding. She had suffered greatly because of our mutual antagonism, which in me had developed into hatred. She had been horrified at the message I had sent her three years previously when she had notified me that Father was near Death's door. He had undergone a dangerous operation on his throat, and Helena had called me to his bedside. " He should have died long ago," I had wired back. Since then she had tried repeatedly to change my attitude towards the man whose harshness had marred the childhood of all of us.

The memory of our sad past had made Helena more kind and generous. It was her beautiful spirit and my own development that gradually healed me of the bitterness I bore my father. I came to understand that it is ignorance rather than cruelty that makes parents do so many dreadful things to their helpless children. During my short stay in Rochester in 1894, I had seen my father for the first time in five years. I still felt estranged, but no longer so hostile. On that visit I found Father physically broken, a mere shadow of his former strong and energetic self. His condition was constantly growing worse. Ten hours' work in the shop on dry food were destructive to his weakened and nervous state of health, aggravated by the taunts and indignities he had to endure. He was the only Jew, a man of nearly fifty, a foreigner not familiar with the language of the country. Most of the youngsters who worked with him were of foreign parents, but they had acquired the worst American traits without any of the fine qualities. They were crude, coarse, and heartless. They throve on the pranks and tricks they played on the " sheeny." Repeatedly they had so molested and harassed him as to cause him to faint. He would be brought home, only to compel himself to go back the next day. He could not afford to lose the job that paid him ten dollars a week.

The sight of Father so ill and worn softened the last vestige of my animosity towards him. I began to regard him as one of the mass of the exploited and enslaved for whom I was living and working.

In our talks Helena had always argued that Father's violence in his youth had been due to his exceptional energy, which found no adequate outlet in such a small place as Popelan. He had been ambitious for himself and his family, dreaming of the large city and the big things he could do there. The peasants eked out a poor existence on their land; but most of the Jews, with practically every profession closed to them, lived upon the peasants. Father was too honest for such methods, and his pride smarted under daily indignities from the officials he had to deal with. The failure of his life, the lack of opportunity to put his abilities to good use, had embittered him and made him ill-natured and hard towards his own.

My years of contact with the lives of the masses, the social victims in and out of prison, and my wide reading had shown me the dehumanizing effect of misplaced energy. In numerous instances I had watched people who had started life with ambition and hope being thwarted by a hostile environment. Only too often they had grown vindictive and ruthless. The understanding I gained through my own struggle had come to my sister through her highly sensitive nature and her unusual intuitiveness. She was wise without having known much of life.

I saw a great deal of my sister Lena and her family on this visit. She already had four children, and a fifth was on the way. She was worn by too frequent child-bearing and the struggle to make ends meet. The only joy Lena had was her children. The most radiant of the four was little Stella, who had always been my sunbeam in grey Rochester. She was ten now, very intelligent, high-strung, and full of exaggerated fancies about her *Tante Emma*, as she called me. Since my previous visit Stella had begun to correspond with me, in quaint and extravagant outpourings of the yearnings of her young soul. The severity of her father and his preference for her younger sister were great and real tragedies to the sensitive child. Having to share the same bed with her caused Stella great misery. Her people had no patience with " such whims "; besides, they were too poor to afford extra space. But I understood Stella only too well: her tragedy was a repetition of what I myself had suffered at her age. I was happy in the thought that the little one had Helena near, to whom she could take her troubles, and that she felt the need of confiding in me. " I hate the people who are mean to my *Tante Emma*," Stella wrote when she was barely seven. " When I grow up, I will fight for her."

There was also my brother Yegor. Until the age of fourteen he was, like most American boys, crude and wild. He loved Helena because she had been so devoted to him. I had evidently not so impressed myself on his mind. I was just a sister, like Lena — nothing to be excited about. But on my visit in 1894 I seemed to awaken a deeper feeling in him. Since then he had become, like Stella, closely attached

to me, perhaps because I had prevailed upon Father not to compel
the boy to continue at school. Yegor had shown himself clever at his
studies, and this led the old man to hope that his youngest son would
realize his own bankrupt ambitions to be a man of learning. His
eldest boy, Herman, had proved a disappointment in this regard. He
could do wonders with his hands, but he hated school, and Father
finally lost hope of ever seeing his Herman become a " man of the professions." He sent him to a machine shop, where the boy soon proved
that he was much more at home with the most intricate machine than
with the simplest book lesson. He became a new being, serious and concentrated. Father could not get over the disappointment; yet hope
springs eternal. With Yegor doing well at school, Father again began
to vision college diplomas. But again his plans were frustrated. My
visit saved the situation. My arguments in behalf of " our baby " had
a better effect than the pleas I had once urged in my own behalf.
Yegor went to work in the same shop with Herman. Subsequently
the boy underwent a radical change: he became enamoured of study.
The life of a working-man and the lunch-basket he had so greatly admired lost their glamour. The shop, with its noises and coarseness,
revolted him. To read and learn was now his ambition. Contact with
the misery of the workers' lot brought Yegor closer to me. " You
have become my heroine," he wrote me; " you have been in prison,
you are with the people and in touch with the aims of youth." I would
understand his awakening, he added; his hopes were centred on me,
for only I could induce our father to permit him to go to New York.
He wanted to study. But, strange to say, instead of being glad, Father
objected. He had lost faith in the fickle boy, he declared. Besides, the
wages Yegor was earning were needed in the house now that his own
health was failing and he could not continue much longer at work. It
required days of pleading and my offer to take Yegor to my home in
New York before Father yielded. Yegor had his wish and now saw
his dream about to be fulfilled, and thus I won his lasting devotion.

My stay in Rochester this time proved to be my first unclouded
visit with my family. It was a novel experience to be accepted with
warmth and affection by those who had always been strangers to me.
My dear sister Helena and the two young lives that needed me helped
me to closer communion with my parents.

On my way to New York I thought much about my frequent talks
with Ed in regard to my taking up a course of medicine. It had been

my aspiration when I was still in Königsberg, and my studies in Vienna had again awakened that desire. Ed had seized upon the idea with enthusiasm, assuring me he would soon be able to pay my way through college. My arrangements to have Yegor in New York with us and to assist him would, however, postpone the realization of my hope of becoming a doctor. I also feared Ed might resent the new obstacle and dislike having my brother in the house. I would certainly not force him on Ed.

I found Ed in splendid condition and fine spirits. Our little apartment looked festive, as my sweetheart always made it on my homecomings. Far from objecting to my plans about Yegor, Ed immediately consented to have him: with my brother in the house, he said, he would not feel so lonely during my absences. Did Yegor talk much, he inquired anxiously. He himself could sit for hours without uttering a word, and he was greatly relieved when I told him that Yegor was a studious and reticent boy. As to my proposed study of medicine, Ed was confident that we should be able to carry out the idea before long. He was " on the way to riches," he assured me with a serious face; his partner had perfected an invention, a novelty in albums, which would certainly prove a great success. " We want you as our third partner," he announced jubilantly; " you might take the contraption on the road with you on your next tour." Again, as in the early stages of our life, he began to indulge in fancies of the things he would do for me when we became rich.

Yegor arrived after New Year's Day. Ed liked him from the first, and before long my brother was completely charmed by my beloved. I was soon to go on a new tour, and it was a great comfort to know that my two " children " would keep each other company in my absence.

CHAPTER XVII

EQUIPPED WITH A DOZEN CAREFULLY PREPARED LECTURES AND supplied with a sample of the invention, I started out full of hope to win converts to our Cause and orders for the new album. My percentage on the sales would help to pay my travelling expenses, relieving me of the unpleasant necessity of the comrades supporting my tours.

Charles Shilling, a Philadelphia anarchist, whom I had met on my previous visits in that city, had undertaken all arrangements for my lectures and had also invited me to stay with his family. Both he and Mrs. Shilling were charming hosts, and Charles a most effective organizer. In six large meetings I spoke on the New Woman, the Absurdity of Non-Resistance to Evil, the Basis of Morality, Freedom, Charity, and Patriotism. Lecturing in English was still rather difficult, but I felt at home when the questions began. The more opposition I encountered, the more I was in my element and the more caustic I became with my opponents. After ten days of intensive activities and warm *camaraderie* with the Shillings and other new friends, I left for Pittsburgh.

Carl, Henry, Harry Gordon, and Emma Lee had arranged fourteen lectures in the Steel City and adjoining towns, except in the place I wanted most to go to, Homestead. No hall could be had there. My first pilgrimage was, as always, to the Western Penitentiary. I went out with Emma Lee. We walked close to the wall, and she noticed that now and then I ran my hand along the rough surface. If only thoughts and feelings could be transferred, the intensity of mine would penetrate the grey pile and reach through to Sasha. Almost five years had passed since his imprisonment. The Warden and the keepers had tried their utmost to break his spirit, but they had reckoned without Sasha's power of resistance. He remained undaunted, clinging with every fibre to the determination to come back to life and freedom. In that he was sustained by many friends, none more devoted than Harry Kelly, the Gordons, Nold, and Bauer. They had been working for months on the new appeal for pardon. Their efforts, begun in November 1897, found support among various elements. Through the help of Harry Kelly, who was canvassing the workers' organizations in Sasha's behalf, strong resolutions favouring his release had been passed by the United Labor League of Western Pennsylvania. The American Federation of Labor, at its convention in Cincinnati, the Bakers' International Union, the Boston Central Union, and many other labour bodies throughout the United States had taken favourable action. Two of the best Pittsburgh lawyers had been engaged, and the necessary funds raised. There was tremendous interest in Sasha and his case, and our friends were certain of results. I felt rather sceptical, but as I walked along the prison wall that separated me from our brave boy, I hoped against hope that I might be proved wrong.

Continuous lecturing and meeting many people were a strenuous job. It brought on several nervous attacks, which left me weak and spent. Yet I could not rest. I begrudged every minute that took me away from my work, especially because popular interest in our ideas seemed so great. Some of the newspapers, contrary to their usual custom, gave fair reports of my meetings; the Pittsburgh *Leader* even published a whole-page story, actually saying kind things about me. " Miss Goldman does not look at all the vicious being she is pictured," it wrote among other things. " You would not judge from her personal appearance that she carried bombs about in her clothes or that she was capable of the incendiary utterances which have marked her platform career. On the contrary, she is rather prepossessing than otherwise. As she converses, her face lights up with intelligent ardour. Indeed, the chances are ninety-nine in a hundred that a stranger asked to guess what and who she was would tell you she was a school-teacher or a woman whose mind runs in progressive channels."

The writer surely believed he was bestowing a compliment when he said I looked like a school-teacher. He meant it for the best, no doubt, but my vanity was hurt, nevertheless. Did I really look so inane, I wondered.

In Cleveland I delivered three lectures. The reports in the papers were very amusing. One simply stated that " Emma Goldman is crazy " and " her doctrines demoniacal ravings." Another enlarged upon my " fine manners, more like a lady than a bomb-thrower."

To Detroit I returned as to a dear old friend, and I went to Robert Reitzel straight from the train. His condition had been steadily grow-ing worse, but his will to live would not be extinguished. I found my knight paler and more emaciated than before. The suffering he had been through since my last visit lined his face, but he had not lost his characteristic wit and humour. It was both joy and agony to see him. Yet he would not have me sad. He launched into stories that were convulsing by virtue of his great gift for comical recital. Particularly funny were his experiences as pastor of a German Reformed congre-gation, a position he held when he first came to America. Once he was requested to preach in Baltimore. The evening before he had spent in the circle of gay friends, with whom he worshipped at the shrine of wine and song till early dawn. Spring was in the air; the trees were alive with birds singing lustily to their mates. All of nature was vibrant with naked voluptuousness. The spirit of adventure was upon Robert when he walked out into the breaking day. Hours later he was found riding astride a beer-barrel, stripped to the skin, and stentoriously serenading the lady of his heart. Alas, she happened to be the fair daughter of a prominent member of the congregation that had invited the young pastor. There was no German sermon in Baltimore that day.

Unforgettable were the hours I spent with my knight. The sunshine of his spirit drew me into its orbit and made me reluctant to tear my-self away. I wished I could pour sustenance into the sick body from the youth and strength that were mine.

Cincinnati was dull and disappointing after Detroit. A complaining letter from Ed made it doubly so. He could not bear my long absence, he wrote; better a thousand times to make a radical break, to live with-out me, than to have me only in snatches. I replied, assuring Ed of my love and of my desire for a home with him; but I reiterated that I would not be bound and kept in a cage. In such a case I should have to give up our common life altogether. What I prized most was freedom, freedom to do my work, to give myself spontaneously and not out of duty or by command. I could not submit to such demands; rather would I choose the path of a homeless wanderer; yes, even go without love.

St. Louis was not less dreary, but on the last day the police came to the rescue. They broke up the meeting in the middle of my speech and hustled everybody out. There was some consolation in the thought that the extensive quotations from my speech in the papers would reach a greater audience than the hall could hold. Moreover, the action of the authorities gained me many friends among Americans who still believed in freedom of expression.

Chicago, city of our Black Friday, cause of my rebirth! Next to Pittsburgh it was the most ominous and depressing to me. But I no longer felt as friendless there as on previous occasions when the fury of 1887 was still active and the opposition from the followers of Most was blind and bitter against me. My imprisonment and succeeding activities had won me friends and turned the tide in my favour. I now had the support of various labour unions which the efforts of Peukert had secured for me. Since 1893 he had been living in Chicago and spreading propaganda there. I found sweet hospitality with Comrade Appel, a prominent local anarchist, who, together with his vivacious wife and children, made their home a pleasant place to visit. The *Free Society* group was doing splendid work in Chicago, and a series of fifteen lectures had been arranged by them for me.

The gatherings themselves were of the usual character, with no special incidents occurring. But several events lent significance to my stay in the city, proving a lasting factor in my life. Among them were my meeting Moses Harman and Eugene V. Debs, and my rediscovery of Max Baginski, a young comrade from Germany.

In the exciting August days of 1893, in Philadelphia, when the police were hunting for me, two young men had called to see me. One was my old friend John Kassel; the other was Max Baginski. I was particularly glad to meet Max, who was one of the young rebels who had played such an important part in the revolutionary movement in Germany. He was of medium height, spiritual-looking, and frail, as if he had just been through a long illness. His blond hair stood up in defiance of the persuasions of a comb, his intelligent eyes appearing small through the thick glasses he wore. His pronounced features were an unusually high forehead and a face contour that looked as Slavic as his name sounded. I tried to engage him in conversation, but he seemed depressed and indisposed to talk. I wondered whether the large scar on his neck was the cause of his self-consciousness. In the years following I did not see Max again until my release from prison, and then only casually. Subsequently I heard that he had gone to Chicago to take charge of the *Arbeiter Zeitung,* the publication formerly edited by August Spies.

On my previous visits to Chicago I had refrained from going to the office of the paper to seek out Baginski. I had heard that he was a staunch adherent of Most, and I had suffered too much persecution from the latter's followers to care to meet any more of them. The appearance of a friendly notice in the *Arbeiter Zeitung* about my lectures, and an unaccountable urge to see Max again, induced me to look him up on my arrival in the city.

The office of the *Arbeiter Zeitung,* made famous by the Chicago events, was on Clark Street. The medium-sized room was divided by a grating, behind which I saw a man writing. By the scar on his neck I recognized Max Baginski. At the sound of my voice he rose quickly, opened the wire door, and with a buoyant: " Well, dear Emma, are you here at last? " he embraced me. The greeting was so unexpectedly warm that it immediately quieted my apprehensions of him as a blind follower of Most. He asked me to wait a moment to enable him to finish the last paragraph of the article he was writing. " Done! " he exclaimed cheerily after a short time; " let's get out of this prison. We'll go to lunch at the Blue Ribbon Restaurant."

It was past noon when we reached the place; five o'clock found us still there. The silent, depressed young man of my brief encounter in Philadelphia was very much alive and an interesting conversationalist, now intensely serious, again light-hearted as a boy. We discussed the movement, Most and Sasha. Far from being fanatical and narrow, Max showed greater breadth, sympathy, and understanding than I had found among even the best of the German anarchists. He greatly admired Most, he said, for the heroic struggle he had made and the persecutions he had endured. Yet Most's attitude towards Sasha had produced a very painful impression on Max and his co-workers in the " *Jungen* " group in Germany. They had all sided with Sasha, and still did, Max assured me; but since his coming to America he had begun better to appreciate Most's tragedy in the alien land in which he could never take root. In the United States Most was out of his sphere, without the inspiration and impetus that come from the life and struggle of the masses. Most, of course, had considerable German support in the country, but it is only the native element in a country that can bring about fundamental changes. It must have been the helplessness of his position in America and the absence of a native anarchist movement that had caused Most to turn against propaganda by deed and, with it, against Sasha.

I could not accept Max's explanation of Most's betrayal of what he had propagated for years. But his generous attempt objectively to analyse the causes that had brought about the change in Most gave me an insight into the character of Max. There was nothing petty about him, no trace of rancour or desire to censor, no vestige of a partisan spirit. He impressed me as a big personality; to be with him was like breathing the pure air of green fields.

My joy in Max was heightened by the discovery that he shared my admiration for Nietzsche, Ibsen, and Hauptmann, and that he knew many more whose names I had not even heard. He had known Gerhart Hauptmann personally and had accompanied him on his rounds through the districts where the weavers live in Silesia. Max was then editor of a labour paper, *Der Proletarier aus dem Eulengebirge*, published in the locality which had furnished the dramatist with the material for his two powerful social canvases, *Die Weber* and *Hannele*. The ghastly poverty and wretchedness had embittered the weavers and had made them suspicious. They were loath to talk to the young man with the ascetic face resembling a priest who had come to question them about their lives. But they knew Max. He was of the people and with them, and they trusted him.

Max related to me some of his experiences on his tramps with Gerhart Hauptmann. Everywhere they found appalling misery. Once they came upon an old weaver in a barren hut. On a bench lay a woman with a little baby, covered with rags. The child's emaciated body was a mass of sores. There was no food and no wood in the house. Utter destitution grinned from every corner. In another place there lived a widow with her grand-daughter of thirteen, a girl of extraordinary beauty. They shared the room with a weaver and his wife. All during his talk with them Hauptmann had kept stroking the child's head. "It was no doubt she who gave him the inspiration for his Hannele," Max commented; "I know how he was impressed by that tender flower in its dreadful environment." For a long time afterwards Hauptmann continued sending gifts to the little girl. He could sympathize with those disinherited because he knew from personal experience what poverty was; he had often gone hungry while a student in Zürich.

I felt I had found a kindred spirit in Max, one with understanding and appreciation of what had come to mean so much to me. The wealth of his mind and his sensitive personality held irresistible appeal. Our intellectual kinship was spontaneous and complete, finding also its emotonal expression. We became inseparable, each day revealing to me new beauty and depth in his being. He was matured mentally far beyond his years, while psychically he was of the world of romance, of rare gentleness and refinement.

Another great event during my stay in Chicago was meeting Moses Harman, the courageous champion of free motherhood and woman's economic and sexual emancipation. His name had first become familiar to me through reading *Lucifer,* the weekly paper he was publishing. I knew of the persecution he had endured and of his imprisonment by the moral eunuchs of America, with Anthony Comstock at their head. Accompanied by Max, I visited Harman at the office of *Lucifer,* which was also the home that he shared with his daughter Lillian.

One's mental picture of great personalities usually proves false upon nearer contact. With Harman it was the contrary; I had not sufficiently visualized the charm of the man. His erect carriage (in spite of a lame leg, the result of a Civil War bullet), his striking head, with its flowing white hair and beard, together with his youthful eyes, combined to make the man a most impressive figure. There was nothing austere or forbidding about him; in fact, he was all kindliness. That characteristic explained his supreme faith in the country that had struck him so many blows. I was no stranger to him, he assured me. He had been outraged by the treatment I had received at the hands of the police, and he had protested against it. "We are comrades in more than one respect," he commented, with a pleasant smile. We spent the evening discussing problems affecting woman and her emancipation. During the talk I expressed doubt as to whether the approach to sex, so coarse and vulgar in America, was likely to change in the near future and Puritanism be banished from the land. Harman was sure it would. "I have seen such great changes since I began my work," he said, "that I am convinced we are not far now from a real revolution in the economic and sexual status of woman in the United States. A pure and ennobling feeling about sex and its vital rôle in human life is bound to develop." I called his attention to the growing power of Comstockism. "Where are the great men and women who can check that stifling force?" I asked; "outside of yourself and a handful of others the Americans are the most puritanical people in the world." "Not quite," he replied; "don't forget England, which has only recently suppressed Havelock Ellis's great work on sex." He had faith in America and in the men and women that had been fighting for years, even suffering calumny and imprisonment for the idea of free mother-hood.

During my stay in Chicago I attended a Labour convention in session in the city. I met a number of people there prominent in trade-union and revolutionary ranks, among them Mrs. Lucy Parsons, widow of our martyred Albert Parsons, who took an active part in the proceedings. The most striking figure at the convention was Eugene V. Debs. Very tall and lean, he stood out above his comrades in more than a physical sense; but what struck me most about him was his naïve unawareness of the intrigues going on around him. Some of the delegates, non-political socialists, had asked me to speak and had the chairman put me on the list. By obvious trickery the Social Democratic politicians succeeded in preventing my getting the floor. At the conclusion of the session Debs came over to me to explain that there had been an unfortunate misunderstanding, but that he and his comrades would have me address the delegates in the evening.

In the evening neither Debs nor the committee was present. The audience consisted of the delegates that had extended the invitation to me and of our own comrades. Debs arrived, all out of breath, almost at the close. He had tried to get away from the various sessions in order to hear me, he said, but he had been detained. Would I forgive him and take lunch with him the next day? I had the feeling that possibly he had been a party to the petty conspiracy to suppress me. At the same time I could not reconcile his frank and open demeanour with mean actions. I consented. After spending some time with him I was convinced that Debs was in no way to blame. Whatever the politicians in his party might be doing, I was sure that he was decent and high-minded. His belief in the people was very genuine, and his vision of socialism quite unlike the State machine pictured in Marx's communist manifesto. Hearing his views, I could not help exclaiming: " Why, Mr. Debs, you're an anarchist! " " Not Mister, but Comrade," he corrected me; " won't you call me that? " Clasping my hand warmly, he assured me that he felt very close to the anarchists, that anarchism was the goal to strive for, and that all socialists should also be anarchists. Socialism to him was only a stepping-stone to the ultimate ideal, which was anarchism. " I know and love Kropotkin and his work," he said; " I admire him and I revere our murdered comrades who lie in Waldheim, as I do also all the other splendid fighters in your movement. You see, then, I am your comrade. I am with you in your struggle." I pointed out that we could not hope to achieve freedom by increasing the power of the State, which the socialists were aiming at. I stressed the fact that political action is the death-knell of the economic struggle. Debs did not dispute me, agreeing that the revolutionary spirit must be kept alive notwithstanding any political objects, but he thought the latter a necessary and practical means of reaching the masses.

We parted good friends. Debs was so genial and charming as a human being that one did not mind the lack of political clarity which made him reach out at one and the same time for opposite poles.

The following day I visited Michael Schwab, one of the Chicago martyrs whom Governor Altgeld had pardoned. Six years in the Joliet Penitentiary had undermined his health, and I found him in the hospital with tuberculosis. It was amazing to witness with what endurance and fortitude an ideal can imbue one. Schwab's wasted body, the hectic flush on his cheeks, his eyes shining with the fatal fever in his blood, convincingly spoke of the tortures he had endured during the harrowing trial, through the months of waiting for reprieve, followed by the execution of his comrades, and his own long years in prison. Yet Michael said hardly a word about himself, nor did he permit a complaint to escape him. His ideal was uppermost in his mind, and everything bearing upon it was still his sole interest. I felt with a feeling of awe for the man whose staunch and proud spirit the cruel powers had failed to break.

My presence in Chicago gave me the opportunity to fulfil a wish of long standing: to do honour to our precious dead by placing a wreath upon their grave in Waldheim Cemetery. Before the monument erected to their memory we stood in silence, Max and I, our hands clasped. The inspired vision of the artist had transformed stone into a living presence. The figure of the woman on a high pedestal, and the fallen hero reclining at her feet, were expressive of defiance and revolt, mingled with pity and love. Her face, beautiful in its great humanity, was turned upon a world of pain and woe, one hand pointing to the dying rebel, the other held protectingly over his brow. There was intense feeling in her gesture, and infinite tenderness. The tablet on the back of the base was engraved with a significant passage from Governor Altgeld's reasons for pardoning the three surviving anarchists.

It was nearly dark when we made our way out of the cemetery. My thoughts wandered back to the time when I had opposed the erection of the monument. I had argued that our dead comrades needed no stone to immortalize them. I realized now how narrow and bigoted I had been, and how little I had understood the power of art. The monument served as the embodiment of the ideals for which the men had died, a visible symbol of their words and their deeds.

Before I left Chicago, the news reached me of Robert Reitzel's death. While his friends knew that the end was only a question of weeks, yet we were stunned. My own loss was the more poignant because of my closeness to my dear "knight." His rebellious ardour and artistic soul stood so vividly before me that I could not think of him as dead. It was particularly on my last visit to him that I came fully to appreciate his true greatness, the heights to which he could rise. A thinker and poet, he was not content merely to fashion beautiful words; he wanted them to be living realities, to help in awakening the masses to the possibilities of an earth freed from the shackles the privileged few had forged. His dream was of things radiant, of love and freedom, of life and joy. He had lived and fought for that dream with all the passion of his soul.

Now Robert was dead, his ashes strewn over the lake. His great heart beat no more; his turbulent spirit was at rest. Life continued on its course, made more desolate without my knight, robbed of the force and beauty of his pen, the poetic splendour of his song. Life continued, and with it grew stronger the determination for greater effort.

Denver was a centre of our work, with a number of men and women of the individualist as well as of the communist school of anarchism active there. They were nearly all native born; some of them could trace their ancestry to the pioneers of colonial days. Lizzie and William Holmes, co-workers of Albert Parsons and his close friends, and their circle were persons of keen and clear minds, grounded in the economic aspects of the social struggle and well-informed otherwise also. Lizzie and William had been in the thick of the eight-hour struggle in Chicago and were contributors as well to the *Alarm* and other radical publications. The death of Albert Parsons had been an even greater blow to them than to most comrades because of their year-long friendship. Now living in Denver in poor quarters and barely earning enough to sustain life, they were still as devoted to the Cause as in the days when their faith was young and their hopes high. We spent much time discussing the movement and particularly the period of 1887. Their picture of Albert Parsons, the rebel and the man, was most vivid: To Parsons, anarchism had not been a mere theory of the future. He had made it a living force in his everyday existence, in his home life and relations with his fellows. Descended from an old Southern family that prided itself on caste, Albert Parsons felt kinship with the most degraded of humanity. He had grown up in an atmosphere that tenaciously clung to the idea of slavery as a divine right, and State honours as the only thing worth while in the world. He not only repudiated both, but married a young mulatto. There was no room for colour distinctions in Albert's ideal of human brotherhood, and love was more powerful than man-made barriers. The same generous quality had impelled him to leave his place of safety and deliberately walk into the clutches of the Illinois authorities. The urge of sharing the fate of his comrades was more important than anything else. And yet Albert passionately loved life. His fine spirit manifested itself even in his last moments. Far from giving way to rancour or lamentations, Parsons intoned his favourite song, *Annie Laurie,* its strains ringing in his prison cell on the very day of execution.

My journey from Denver to San Francisco through the Rocky Mountains was replete with new experience and sensations. I had looked at the Swiss mountains when I had stopped for a few days in Switzerland on my way from Vienna. But the sight of the Rockies, austere and forbidding, was overwhelming. I could not free myself from the thought of the puerility of all man's efforts. The whole human race, myself included, appeared like a mere blade of grass, so insignificant, so pathetically helpless, in the face of those crushing mountains. They terrified me, yet held me by their beauty and grandeur. But when we reached the Royal Gorge, and our train slowly picked its way along the winding arteries hewn by the hand of Labour, relief came and renewed faith in my own strength. The forces that had penetrated those colossi of stone were everywhere at work bearing witness to the creative genius and inexhaustible resources of man.

To see California for the first time in early spring, after twenty-four hours through drab Nevada, was like beholding a fairyland after a nightmare. Never before had I seen nature so lavish and resplendent. I was still under its spell when the scene changed to one of less exuberance, and the train pulled into Oakland.

My stay in San Francisco was most interesting and delightful. It enabled me to do the best work I had accomplished till then, and it brought me in contact with many free and rare spirits. The headquarters of anarchist activity on the Coast was *Free Society,* edited and published by the Isaak family. They were unusual people, Abe Isaak, Mary, his wife, and their three children. They had been Mennonites, a liberal religious sect in Russia, of German origin. In America the Isaaks had first settled in Portland, Oregon, where they came under the influence of anarchist ideas. Together with some native comrades, among whom were Henry Addis and H. J. Pope, the Isaaks founded an anarchist weekly called the *Firebrand.* Because of the appearance in the latter of Walt Whitman's poem, " A Woman Waits for Me," their paper was suppressed, its publishers arrested, and H. J. Pope imprisoned for obscenity. The Isaak family then started *Free Society,* later moving to San Francisco. Even the children co-operated in the undertaking, often working eighteen hours a day, writing, setting up type, and addressing wrappers. At the same time they did not neglect other propagandist activities.

The particular attraction of the Isaaks for me was the consistency of their lives, the harmony between the ideas they professed and their application. The comradeship between the parents and the complete freedom of every member of the household were novel things to me. In no other anarchist family had I seen children enjoy such liberty or so independently express themselves without the slightest hindrance from their elders. It was amusing to hear Abe and Pete, boys of sixteen and eighteen respectively, hold their father to account for some alleged infraction of principle, or criticize the propaganda value of his articles. Isaak would listen with patience and respect, even if the manner of the criticism were adolescently harsh and arrogant. Never once did I see the parents resort to the authority of superior age or wisdom. Their children were their equals; their right to disagree, to live their own lives and learn, was unquestioned.

" If you can't establish freedom in your own home," Isaak often said, " how can you expect to help the world to it? " To him and to Mary that was just what freedom meant: equality of the sexes in all their needs, physical, intellectual, and emotional.

The Isaaks maintained this attitude in the *Firebrand,* and now again in *Free Society.* For their insistence on sex equality they were severely censored by many anarchists in the East and abroad. I had welcomed the discussion of these problems in their paper, for I knew from my own experience that sex expression is as vital a factor in human life as food and air. Therefore it was not mere theory that had led me at an early stage of my development to discuss sex as frankly as I did other topics and to live my life without fear of the opinion of others. Among American radicals in the East I had met many men and women who shared my view on this subject and had the courage to practise their ideas in their sex life. But in my own immediate ranks I was very much alone. It was therefore a revelation to find that the Isaaks felt and lived as I did. It helped to establish a strong personal bond between us besides our common anarchist ideal.

Notwithstanding nightly lectures in San Francisco and adjoining towns, a mass meeting to celebrate the first of May, and a debate with a socialist, we still found time for frequent social gatherings jovial enough to be disapproved by the purists. But we did not mind it. Youth and freedom laughed at rules and strictures, and our circle consisted of people young in years and in spirit. In the company of the Isaak boys and the other young chaps I felt like a grandmother — I was twenty-nine — but in spirit I was the gayest, as my young admirers often assured me. We had the joy of life in us, and the California wines were cheap and stimulating. The propagandist of an unpopular cause needs, even more than other people, occasional light-hearted irresponsibility. How else could he survive the hardships and travail of existence? My San Francisco comrades could work strenuously; they took their tasks very seriously; but they could also love, drink, and play.

CHAPTER XVIII

MERICA HAD DECLARED WAR WITH SPAIN. THE NEWS WAS NOT
unexpected. For several months preceding, press and pulpit were
filled with the call to arms in defence of the victims of Spanish atrocities in Cuba. I was profoundly in sympathy with the Cuban and
Philippine rebels who were striving to throw off the Spanish yoke.
In fact, I had worked with some of the members of the Junta engaged
in underground activities to secure freedom for the Philippine Islands.
But I had no faith whatever in the patriotic protestations of America
as a disinterested and noble agency to help the Cubans. It did not require much political wisdom to see that America's concern was a matter of sugar and had nothing to do with humanitarian feelings. Of
course there were plenty of credulous people, not only in the country at
large, but even in liberal ranks, who believed in America's claim. I
could not join them. I was sure that no one, be it individual or government, engaged in enslaving and exploiting at home, could have
the integrity or the desire to free people in other lands. Thenceforth
my most important lecture, and the best-attended, was on Patriotism
and War.

In San Francisco it went over without interference, but in the
smaller California towns we had to fight our way inch by inch. The
police, never loath to break up anarchist meetings, stood complacently by and thus encouraged the patriotic disturbers who sometimes made speaking impossible. The determination of our San Francisco group and my own presence of mind saved more than one
critical situation. In San Jose the audience looked so threatening that I
thought it best to dispense with a chairman and carry the meeting myself. As soon as I began to speak, bedlam broke loose. I turned to the
trouble-makers with the request that they choose someone of their
own crowd to conduct the meeting. " Go on ! " they shouted; " you're

only bluffing. You know you wouldn't let us run your show!'" "Why not?" I called back. "What we want is to hear both sides, isn't that so?" "Betcher life!" someone yelled. "We must secure order for that, mustn't we?" I continued; "I seem unable to do so. Supposing one of you boys comes up here and shows me how to keep the rest quiet until I have stated my side of the story. After that you can state yours. Now be good American sports."

Boisterous cries, shouts of "Hurrah," calls of "Smart kid, let's give her a chance!" kept the house in confusion for a few minutes. Finally an elderly man stepped up on the platform, banged his cane on the table, and in a voice that would have crumbled the walls of Jericho, bellowed: "Silence! Let's hear what the lady has to say!" There was no further disturbance during my speech of an hour, and when I finished, there was almost an ovation.

Among the most interesting people I met in San Francisco were two girls, the Strunsky sisters. Anna, the elder, had attended my lecture on Political Action. She had been indignant, I afterwards learned, because of my "unfairness to the socialists." The next day she came to visit me "for a little while," as she said. She remained all afternoon, and then invited me to her home. There I met a group of students, among them Jack London, and the younger Strunsky girl, Rose, who was ill. Anna and I became great friends. She had been suspended from Leland Stanford University because she had received a male visitor in her room instead of in the parlour. I told Anna of my life in Vienna and of the men students with whom we used to drink tea, smoke, and discuss all through the night. Anna thought that the American woman would establish her right to liberty and privacy, once she secured the vote. I did not agree with her. I argued that the Russian woman had long ago established, even without the vote, her social and moral independence. Out of it had developed a beautiful *camaraderie,* which makes the relations of the sexes so fine and wholesome among advanced Russians.

I wanted to go to Los Angeles, but I knew no one there capable of organizing my meetings. The few German anarchists I had corresponded with in that city advised me not to come. Certain of my lectures, especially the one on the sex question, they wrote, would militate against their work. I had almost abandoned the idea of Los Angeles when encouragement came from an unexpected quarter. A young man whom I knew as Mr. V., from New Mexico, offered to act as my manager. He was to be in Los Angeles on business, he informed me, and he would be glad to help me arrange one meeting. Mr. V., who was a fine Jewish type, at first attracted my attention at my lectures; he attended every evening and always asked intelligent questions. He was also a frequent visitor at the house of the Isaaks and was evidently interested in our ideas. He was a likable person and I agreed to have him organize one lecture.

In due time my "manager" wired me that all was ready. When I arrived, he met me at the station with a bunch of roses and took me to a hotel. It was one of the best in Los Angeles and I felt it inconsistent for me to put up at such a fashionable place; but Mr. V. argued that it was mere prejudice, a thing he had not expected from Emma Goldman. "Don't you want the meeting to be a success?" he asked. "Of course," I replied, "but what has it to do with staying in expensive hotels?" "Very much," he assured me; "it will help advertise the lecture." "Such matters are not considered from that viewpoint in anarchist ranks," I protested. "The worse for your ranks," he retorted; "that's why you reach so few people. Wait till the meeting; then we will talk." I consented to remain.

The luxurious room he had reserved for me, filled with flowers, was another surprise. Then I discovered a black velvet dress prepared for me. "Is this going to be a lecture or a wedding?" I demanded of Mr. V. "Both," he replied promptly, "though the lecture is to come first."

He had rented one of the best theatres in the town, and surely, my manager expostulated, I must understand that I could not appear in the shabby dress I had worn in San Francisco. Moreover, if I did not like the gown he had chosen, I could change it. It was necessary that I make the best possible showing on my first visit to Los Angeles. "But what interest have you in doing all this?" I persisted. "You told me you are not an anarchist." "I'm on the road to being one," he replied. "Now be sensible. You agreed to have me as your manager, so let me manage this affair in my own way." "Are all managers so solicitous?" I inquired. "Yes, if they know their business and like their artists a little," he said.

The following days the papers were full of Emma Goldman, "under the management of a wealthy man from New Mexico." To avoid the reporters Mr. V. took me out for long walks and rides in the Mexican quarter of the town, to restaurants and cafés. One day he induced me to accompany him to a Russian friend of his, who turned out to be the most fashionable tailor in town and who talked me into letting him take my measurements for a suit. On the afternoon of the lecture I found a simple but beautiful black chiffon dress in my room. Things appeared mysteriously, as in the fairy-tales my German nurse used to tell me. Almost every day brought new surprises, happening in a strange but unostentatious manner.

The meeting was large and rather tumultuous, with patriots present in great numbers. They repeatedly attempted to create confusion, but the clever chairmanship of the " rich man from New Mexico " steered the evening to a peaceful conclusion. Then many people came up to introduce themselves as radicals and to urge me to remain in Los Angeles, offering to arrange more lectures for me. From the obscurity of a complete stranger I had become almost a celebrity, thanks to the efforts of my manager.

Late that evening, in a little Spanish restaurant, away from the crowds, Mr. V. asked me to marry him. Under ordinary circumstances I should have considered such an offer an insult, but everything the man had done was in such good taste that I could not be angry with him. " I and marriage! " I exclaimed. " You didn't ask whether I love you. Besides, have you so little faith in love that you must put a lock and key on it? " " Well," he replied, " I don't believe in your free-love stuff. I should want you to continue your lectures; I'd be happy to help you and secure you so that you will be able to do more and better work. But I couldn't share you with anyone else."

The old refrain! How often had I heard it since I had become a free human being. Radical or conservative, every male wants to bind the woman to himself. I told him flatly: " No! "

He refused to take my answer as final. I might change my mind, he said. I assured him there was no chance of my marrying him: I did not propose to forge chains for myself. I had done it once before; it should not happen again. I wanted only " that free-love stuff "; no other " stuff " had any meaning to me. But Mr. V. was not in the least perturbed. His love was not of the moment only, he felt confident. He would wait.

I bade him good-bye, left the fashionable hotel, and went to stay with some Jewish comrades I had met. For another week I lectured at well-attended meetings, later organizing a group of sympathizers to continue the work. Then I returned to San Francisco.

As a sequel to my activities in Los Angeles an article appeared in the *Freiheit* denouncing me for having stayed in an expensive hotel and having allowed a rich man to arrange my meeting. My behaviour had " queered anarchism with the workers," the writer claimed. Considering that anarchism had never before had a hearing in Los Angeles in English, and that as a result of my meeting systematic propaganda was now about to be carried on among Americans, the charges seemed to me ridiculous. It was another of the many silly accusations that often appeared against me in Most's weekly. I ignored it, but *Free Society* published a reply by a German comrade who called attention to the good results accomplished by my visit to Los Angeles.

In New York Ed and my brother Yegor met me at the station. Yegor was overjoyed to have me back; Ed, always reserved in public, now appeared unusually so. I thought it was due to my brother's presence, but when he continued to keep aloof even when we were alone, I realized that some change had taken place in him. He was as attentive and considerate as usual, and our home as sweet as ever; but he had become different.

For my part, I was not conscious of any emotional change towards Ed — I knew it even before my return. Now, in his presence, I felt sure that, whatever our intellectual differences, I still loved and wanted him. But his frigid behaviour held me in check.

Although very busy during my tour, I had not neglected the commission Ed had given me for his firm. I had solicited orders for the " invention " and had succeeded in closing several substantial contracts with large stationery stores in Western cities. Ed was delighted and praised my efforts. But about my tour and my work, he asked no questions and showed not the slightest interest. This served to add resentment to my dissatisfaction with the condition of things at home. The haven that had given me so much joy and peace now became stifling.

Fortunately there was no time for brooding. The textile strike in Summit, New Jersey, was demanding my services. It presented the usual situation; meetings were either prohibited or broken up by police clubs. It required skilful manœuvring to meet in the woods outside of Summit. I was kept very much engaged, with hardly any time to see Ed. On the rare occasions when we were together, he would remain silent. Only his eyes spoke and they were full of reproach.

When the strike was over I decided to have it out with Ed. I could

bear the situation no longer. I did not get to it for several weeks, however, owing to the international hunt for anarchists that resulted from
the shooting of the Empress of Austria by Luccheni. Though I had
never before heard the name of the man, I was nevertheless shadowed
by the police and pilloried by the press as if I were the one who had
killed the unfortunate woman. I refused to raise the cry of " Crucify! "
against Luccheni, especially because I had learned through the Italian
anarchist press that he had been a child of the street, forced into
military service in his youth. He had witnessed the savagery of war
on the African front, had been brutally treated in the Army, and had
led a life of wretchedness ever since. It was sheer desperation that had
driven the man to his deed of misplaced protest. Everywhere in our
social scheme life was cheap, wasted, and degraded. Why should this
boy, then, be expected to have any reverence for it? I declared my
sympathy with the woman who had long been *persona non grata* at
the Austrian court and who therefore could not have been responsible
for the crimes committed by the Crown. I saw no propagandistic value
in Luccheni's act. He was a victim no less than the Empress; I refused
to join in the savage condemnation of the one or in the sickening sentimentality expressed for the other.

My attitude again called forth the anathema of the press and the
police. Naturally I was not alone; nearly every leading anarchist
throughout the world had to endure similar attacks. But in the States,
and particularly in New York City, I was the black sheep.

Luccheni's act had evidently struck terror into the hearts of the
crowned and even the elected rulers, between whom the bonds of
sympathy were evident. The secret conclaves of the powers resulted
in the decision to hold an international anti-anarchist congress in Rome.
The revolutionary and liberty-loving elements in the United States
and Europe realized the impending danger to freedom of thought and
expression and immediately set to work to stem the tide. Everywhere
meetings were held to protest against the international conspiracy of
authority. In New York no hall could be found where my appearance
would be tolerated.

In the midst of this work came an urgent request from the Alexander Berkman Defense Association in Pittsburgh for greater activity
in behalf of his pardon. The case, which was to be heard in September,
was now set for December 21. The attorneys advised that the decision of the Board of Pardons would largely depend on the stand of

Andrew Carnegie in the matter and therefore they urged seeing the steel-magnate. It was an inane suggestion, which would certainly not be approved by Sasha; such a step was sure to put us all in a ridiculous position. I knew no one likely to consent to approach Carnegie, and I was positive he would not act in the case, anyway. Some of our well-wishers insisted, nevertheless, that he was humane and interested in advanced ideas. As proof of it they adduced the fact that, some time previously, Carnegie had invited Peter Kropotkin to be his guest. I knew that Peter had refused the doubtful honour, replying in effect that he could not accept the hospitality of a man whose interests had imposed an inhumanly excessive sentence on his comrade Alexander Berkman and continued to keep him buried in the Western Penitentiary. Carnegie's eagerness to have Kropotkin visit him was an indication that he would listen favourably to a plea for the liberation of Sasha, some of our friends held. I opposed the idea, but finally succumbed to the arguments of Justus and Ed, who pointed out that we should not allow our own feelings to stand in the way of Sasha's freedom. Justus suggested that we write to Benjamin R. Tucker, requesting him to see Carnegie in the matter.

I knew Tucker only through his writings in *Liberty*, the individualist-anarchist publication, of which he was founder and editor. He wielded a forceful pen and he had done much to introduce his readers to some of the best works in German and French literature. But his attitude towards communist-anarchists was very narrow and charged with insulting rancour. "Tucker doesn't impress me as a large nature," I said to Justus, who insisted that I was wrong and that we must at least give the man a chance. A short letter, signed by Justus Schwab, Ed Brady and me, was sent to Benjamin R. Tucker, stating our case and asking whether he would consent to see Carnegie, who was expected shortly from Scotland.

Tucker's reply was a lengthy epistle setting forth the conditions on which he would approach Carnegie. He would, he wrote, say to him: " In determining your attitude you surely will take it for granted, as I take it for granted, that they approach you as penitent sinners asking forgiveness and seeking remission of penalty. Their very appearance before you in person or by proxy on such an errand must be taken to indicate that what they once regarded as a wise act of heroism they now regard as a foolish act of barbarism . . . that the six years of Mr. Berkman's imprisonment have convinced them of the error of their ways. . . . Any other explanation of the prayer of these petitioners is inconsistent with their lofty character; certainly it is not to be supposed for a moment that men and women of their courage and dignity after shooting a man down deliberately and in cold blood would then descend to the basely humiliating course of begging their victims to grant them the freedom to assault them again. . . . I myself do not appear here today before you as a penitent sinner. In my record in this matter there is nothing for which I have occasion to apologize. I reserve all my rights. . . . I have refused to commit, counsel, or sanction violence, but since circumstances may arise when a policy of violence might seem advisable, I decline to surrender my liberty of choice. . . ."

The letter contained not a word about Sasha's sentence, which, even from a legal view-point, was barbarous; not a word about the torture he had already endured; not a single expression of ordinary humanity from Mr. Tucker, the exponent of a great social ideal. Nothing but cold calculation how to belittle Sasha and his friends while at the same time advancing his own lofty position. He was incapable of seeing that one might feel a wrong done to others more intensely than one done to oneself. He could not grasp the psychology of a man whom the brutality of Frick during the Homestead lock-out had caused to express his protest by an act of violence. Nor was he apparently willing to comprehend that Sasha's friends could endeavour to secure his liberation without necessarily having become convinced of " the error of their ways."

We now turned to Ernest Crosby, a leading single-taxer and Tolstoyan, who was also a gifted poet and writer. He was a man of a very different calibre, understanding and sympathetic even where he did not entirely agree. He visited us in the company of a younger man, whom I knew to be Leonard D. Abbott. When we placed our case before Mr. Crosby, he agreed at once to see Carnegie. There was only one thing that troubled him, he explained. If Carnegie should demand a guarantee that Alexander Berkman, when free, would not again commit an act of violence, what answer was he to give? He himself would never ask such a thing, aware that no one could say what he might do under pressure. But as the intermediary he felt it necessary to be informed by us on the matter. Of course, it was impossible for us to give such a guarantee, and I knew that Sasha would never make any pledges of " reform " or allow them to be made for him.

The matter finally ended with our decision not to apply to Carnegie at all. Sasha's case was not even brought before the Board of Pardons at the time intended. Its members were found to be too prejudiced against him, and it was hoped that the new Board, which was to take office in the following year, might prove more impartial.

After long efforts to procure a hall for our protest meeting against the anti-anarchist congress we succeeded in obtaining Cooper Union. It still adhered to the principle established by its founder to give every political opinion a hearing. My friends feared that I should be arrested, but I was determined to see the thing through. I felt desperate at the attempt to crush the last vestiges of free speech, and sick at heart over my personal life at home. In fact, I was really hoping for an arrest as an escape from everybody and everything.

On the eve of the meeting Ed unexpectedly broke his silence. " I can't bear to have you face this danger," he said, " without trying once more to reach you. While you were on tour, I had definitely decided to stifle my love and try to meet you on terms of comradeship. But I realized the absurdity of such a decision the moment I saw you at the station. Since then I have gone through a severe struggle, deciding even to leave you altogether. But I cannot do it. I would let things drift till you go on tour again, but now that you are in danger of arrest, I have to speak out, to try to bridge the gap between us."

" But there is no gap," I exclaimed excitedly, "unless you persist in making one! Of course, I have outgrown many of the conceptions still so dear to you. I can't help it; but I love you, don't you understand? I love you, no matter what or who comes into my life. I need you, and I need our home. Why will you not be free and big and take what I can give? "

Ed promised to try again, to do anything not to lose me. Our reunion brought back memories of our young love in my little flat in the Bohemian Republic.

The meeting at Cooper Union passed without trouble. Johann Most, who had promised to address the audience, failed to appear. He would not speak on the same platform with me; he still preserved all his bitterness.

Three weeks later Ed fell ill with pneumonia. All my care and love were pitted against the great dread I felt at the possibility of losing the precious life. The big strong man, who used to make light of illness and who had often hinted " that such things were inherent only in the female species," now clung to me like an infant and would not have me out of sight even for a moment. His impatience and irascibility transcended those of ten sick women. But he was so ill that I did not mind his constant demands upon my care and attention.

Fedya and Claus came to offer their help as soon as they learned of Ed's condition. One of them would relieve me at night to permit me a few hours' rest. During the crisis my anxiety was too intense for sleep. Ed was in a high fever, tossing about and even trying to jump out of bed. His vacant look gave no indication of recognition, yet he would grow more restless at the touch of either of the boys. At one moment when he had got quite frenzied, Fedya and Claus were about to try to hold him down by force. " Let me manage him myself," I said, bending over my darling, trying to pour my very soul into his wild eyes and pressing him to my anxious heart. Ed struggled for a while, then his rigid body relaxed, and with a sigh he fell back on his pillow, all covered with sweat.

At last the crisis was over. In the morning Ed opened his eyes. His hand groped for mine, and in a faint voice he asked: " Dear nurse, must I kick the bucket? " " Not this time," I comforted him, " but you must be very quiet." His face lit up with his old beautiful smile, and he dozed off again.

When Ed was already on his feet, though still very weak, I had to leave for a meeting I had promised to address long before his illness. Fedya remained with him. When I returned, late at night, Fedya was gone and Ed fast asleep. There was a note from Fedya saying that Ed was feeling fine and had urged him to go home.

In the morning Ed was still asleep. I took his pulse and noticed that he was breathing heavily. I became alarmed and sent for Doctor Hoffmann. The latter expressed concern over Ed's unusually protracted sleep. He asked to see the box of morphine he had left for Ed to take. Four powders were missing! I had given Ed one before going away, and I had impressed upon Fedya that he was not to get any more. Ed had taken four times the ordinary dose — no doubt in an attempt to end his life! He wanted to die — now — after I had barely rescued him from the grave! Why? Why?

" We must get him on his feet and walk the floor with him," the doctor ordered; " he is alive, he is breathing; we must keep him alive." We supported his drooping body up and down the room, from time to time applying ice to his hands and face. Gradually his face began to lose its deathly pallor, and his lids responded to pressure.

" Who would ever have thought that a reserved and quiet person like Ed would be capable of such a thing? " the doctor remarked. " He'll sleep on for many more hours, but no need to worry. He'll live."

I was shocked by Ed's attempted suicide and tried to fathom what particular cause had induced his action. On several occasions I was on the point of asking him for an explanation, but he was in such cheerful humour and recuperating so well that I was afraid to dig up the ghastly affair. He himself never referred to it.

Then one day he surprised me by mentioning that he had not intended to take his life at all. My leaving him to go to the meeting when he was still so ill had enraged him. He knew from past experience that he could stand a large dose of morphine, and he swallowed several powders, " just to scare you a little and cure you of your mania for meetings, which stops at nothing, not even at the illness of the man you pretend to love."

His words staggered me. I felt that the seven years of our life together had failed to make Ed grasp the pain and travail of my inner growth. A " mania for meetings " — that was all that it meant to him.

There followed days of conflict between my love for Ed and the realization that life had lost its content and meaning. At the end of my bitter struggle I knew that I must leave him. I told Ed that I should have to go, for good.

" Your desperate act to tear me from my work," I said, " has convinced me that you have no faith in me or my aims. Whatever little of it you had in former years is no more. Without your faith and your co-operation our relationship has no value to me." " I love you more now than I did in the early days! " he interrupted me excitedly. " It is no use, dear Ed, to deceive ourselves or each other," I continued. " You want me only as your wife. Well, that is not enough for me. I need understanding, harmony, the exaltation that results from unity of ideas and purpose. Why go on until our love is poisoned by bitterness and made ugly with recrimination? Now we can still part as friends. I'm going on tour anyway; it will be less painful that way."

His frenzied pacing of the room came to a stop. He looked at me in silence, as if trying to penetrate my innermost being. " You're all wrong, you're terribly wrong," he cried desperately; then he turned and left the room.

I began preparations for my tour. The day of departure was approaching, and Ed pleaded with me to permit him to see me off. I declined; I was afraid I might give way at the last moment. That day Ed came home at noon to have lunch with me. Both of us pretended to be cheerful. But at parting his face darkened for a moment. Before leaving he embraced me, saying: " This isn't the end, dearest — it cannot be! This is your home, now and for ever! " I could not speak; my heart was too full of grief. When the door had closed on Ed, I was unable to restrain my sobs. Every object about me assumed a strange fascination, speaking to me in many tongues. I realized that to linger meant to weaken my determination to leave Ed. With palpitating heart I walked out of the house I had loved and cherished as my home.

CHAPTER XIX

THE FIRST STOP ON MY TOUR WAS IN BARRE, VERMONT. THE ACTIVE group there consisted of Italians employed mostly in the stone-quarries, which furnished the principal industry of the city. Very little time was left me for introspection into my personal life; there were numerous meetings, debates, private gatherings, and discussions. I found generous hospitality with my host, Palavicini, a comrade who had worked together with me in the textile strike in Summit. He was a cultivated man, well-informed not only on the international labour movement, but also on the new tendencies in Italian art and letters. At the same time I met also Luigi Galleani, the intellectual leader of the Italian activities in the New England States.

Vermont was under the blessings of Prohibition, and I was interested in learning its effects. In company with my host I made the rounds of some private homes. To my astonishment I found that almost all of them had been turned into saloons. In one such place we came upon a dozen men visibly under the influence of liquor. Most of them were city officials, my companion informed me. The stuffy kitchen, with the children of the family inhaling the foul air of whisky and tobacco, constituted the drinking-den. Many such places were thriving under the protection of the police, to whom part of the income was regularly paid. " That is not the worst evil of Prohibition," my comrade remarked; " its most damnable side is the destruction of hospitality and good-fellowship. Formerly you could offer a drink to callers or have one offered to you. Now, with most people turned into saloon-keepers, your friends expect you to buy booze or to buy it from you."

Another result of Prohibition was the increase of prostitution. We visited several houses on the outskirts of the town, all doing a flourishing business. Most of the " guests " were travelling salesmen, with a sprinkling of farmers. By the closing of the saloons the brothel became the only place where the men coming into town could find some distraction.

After two weeks' activity in Barre the police suddenly decided to prevent my last meeting. The official reason for it was supposed to be my lecture on war. According to the authorities, I had said: " God bless the hand that blew up the Maine." It was of course obviously ridiculous to credit me with such an utterance. The unofficial version was more plausible. " You caught the Mayor and the Chief of Police in Mrs. Colletti's kitchen, dead drunk," my Italian friend explained, " and you have looked into their stakes in the brothels. No wonder they consider you dangerous now and want to get you out."

It was not until I reached Chicago that I began to make my efforts count. As on my preceding tour, I was invited to speak by many labour organizations, including the conservative Woodworkers' Union, which had never before allowed an anarchist within its sacred portals. A number of lectures were also arranged for me by American anarchists. It was strenuous work and I should probably not have been able to carry it through but for the exhilarating companionship of Max Baginski.

As on previous occasions, my headquarters were again with the Appels. At the same time Max and I rented a little place near Lincoln Park, our *Zauberschloss* (fairy-castle), as he christened it, to which we might escape in our free hours. There we would often feast on the basketfuls of delicacies, fruit, and wine the extravagantly big-natured Max would bring. Then we would read *Romeo und Juliet auf dem Lande,* the beautiful story by Gottfried Keller, and the works of our favourites: Strindberg, Wedekind, Gabriele Reuter, Knut Hamsun, and, best of all, Nietzsche. Max knew and understood Nietzsche and deeply loved him. It was only by the aid of his remarkable appreciation that I became aware of the full significance of the great poet-philosopher. After readings came long walks in the park and talks about interesting people in the German movement, about art and literature. The month in Chicago was filled with interesting work, the fine comradeship of new friends, and exquisite hours of joy and harmony with Max.

The Paris Exposition, which was being planned for 1900, suggested the idea to our European comrades of holding an anarchist congress at about the same time. There would be reduced fares, and many of our friends would be able to come from different countries.

I had received an invitation; I spoke to Max about it and asked him to come with me. A trip to Europe together — the very thought of it transported us with ecstasy. My tour would last till August; then we could carry out our new plan. We might journey to England first; I was sure the comrades would want me to lecture there. Then to Paris. "Think of it, dearest — Paris!" "Wonderful, glorious!" he cried. "But the fare — have you thought of that, my romantic Emma?" "That's nothing. I will rob a church or a synagogue — I'll get the money somehow! We must go anyhow. We must go in quest of the moon!" "Two babes in the woods," Max commented; "two sane romantics in a crazy world!"

On my way to Denver I made a side trip to Caplinger Mills, an agricultural district in south-western Missouri. My only previous contact with farm life in the United States had been years before when I had canvassed Massachusetts farmers for orders to enlarge the pictures of their worthy ancestors. I had found them so dull, so rooted in old social traditions, that I did not even care to tell them what I stood for. I was sure they would think me possessed of the devil. It very much surprised me, therefore, to receive an invitation from Caplinger Mills to lecture there. The comrade who wrote that she had arranged my meetings was Kate Austen, whose articles I had read in *Free Society* and other radical publications. Her writings showed her to be a logical thinker, well-informed, and of revolutionary fibre, while her letters to me indicated an affectionate, sensitive being.

At the station I was met by Sam Austen, Kate's husband, who announced that Caplinger Mills was twenty-two miles distant from the railroad. "The roads are very bad," he said; "I'm afraid I'll have to tie you to the seat of my wagon, else you may be shaken out." I soon found he had not been exaggerating. We had hardly covered half the way when there came a violent jolt and the cracking of wheels. Sam landed in a ditch, and when I attempted to get up, I felt sore all over. He lifted me out of the wagon and set me down by the wayside. Waiting and rubbing my aching joints, I tried to smile to encourage Sam.

While he was tinkering the broken wheel, my thoughts went back to Popelan and our long rides in the big sleigh drawn by a fiery *troika*. My blood tingled with the mystery of the night, the starry heavens above me, the white-clad expanse, the music of the merry bells, and the peasant songs of Petrushka at my side. The danger from the

wolves, whose howling could be heard in the distance, made the outings more adventurous and romantic. On our return home there would
be a feast of hot potato pancakes baked in delicious goose grease,
steaming tea with *varenya* (jam) Mother had made, and vodka for
the servants. Petrushka always let me taste a little from his glass.
"You're a regular drunkard," he would tease me. That was indeed
my reputation since the day when they had found me in a stupor in
our cellar underneath a beer-barrel. Father would never permit us
to taste liquor, but one day — I was about three years old then —
I had trotted down to the cellar, put my mouth to a faucet, and drank
the queer-tasting stuff. I woke up in my bed, deathly sick, and would
no doubt have been given a sound thrashing had not our dear old
nurse kept me hidden away from Father. . . .

At last we arrived in Caplinger Mills at the Austen farm. "Put
her to bed right away and give her a hot drink," Sam directed, "else
she'll hate us for the rest of her life for having taken her over that
road." After a hot bath and a good massage I felt much refreshed,
though still aching in every joint.

My week with the Austens showed me new angles of the small
American farmer's life. It made me see that we had been wrong to
regard the farmer in the States as belonging to the *bourgeoisie*. Kate
said it was true only of the very rich landowner who raised everything on a large scale; the vast mass of farmers in America were even
more dependent than the city workers. They were at the mercy of the
bankers and the railroads, not to speak of their natural enemies,
storm and drought. To combat the latter and nourish the leeches who
sap the farmer he must slave endless hours in every kind of weather
and live almost on the edge of penury. It is his toilsome lot that makes
him hard and close-fisted, Kate thought. She lamented especially the
drab existence of the farmer's wife. "The womenfolk have nothing
but cares, drudgery, and frequent child-bearing."

Kate had come to Caplinger only after her marriage. Before that
she had lived in small towns and villages. Left in charge of eight
brothers and sisters at her mother's death, when she herself was
only eleven years old, she had had no time for much study. Two years
in a district school was all the learning her father had been able to
afford for her. I wondered how she had managed to gain so much
knowledge as her numerous articles implied. "From reading," she
informed me. Her father had been a constant reader, at first of

Ingersoll's works, later of *Lucifer* and other radical publications. The events in Chicago in 1887 had exerted upon her, as also upon me, the greatest influence. Since then she had closely followed the social struggle and had studied everything she could get hold of. The range of her reading, judging by the books I found in the Austen household, was very wide. Works on philosophy, on social and economic questions, and on sex were side by side with the best in poetry and fiction. They had been her school. She was thoroughly informed, besides possessing an enthusiasm extraordinary in a woman who had hardly come in contact with life.

" How can a woman of your brains and abilities go on living in such a dull and limited sphere? " I inquired.

" Well, there is Sam," she replied, " who shares everything with me and whom I love, and the children. And there are my neighbours who need me. One can do much even here."

The attendance at my three meetings testified to Kate's influence. From a radius of many miles the farmers came, on foot, in wagons, and on horseback. Two lectures I gave in the little country schoolhouse, the third in a large grove. It was a most picturesque gathering, with the faces of my listeners lit up by lanterns they had brought with them. From the questions some of the men asked, which centred mainly on the right to the land under anarchism, I could see that at least some of them had not come out of mere curiosity, and that Kate had awakened them to the realization that their own difficulties were part of the larger problems of society.

The whole Austen family dedicated itself to me during my stay. Sam took me over the fields on horseback, having given me a sober old mare to ride. The children fulfilled my wishes almost before I had a chance to express them, and Kate was all affectionate devotion. We were much alone together, which gave her a chance to tell me about herself and her surroundings. The greatest objection some of her neighbours had to her was her stand on the sex question. " What would you do if your husband fell in love with another woman? " a farmer's wife had once asked her. " Wouldn't you leave him? " " Not if he still loved me," Kate had promptly replied. " And shouldn't you hate the woman? " " Not if she were a fine person and really loved Sam." Her neighbour had said that if she didn't know Kate so well, she would consider her immoral or crazy; even as it was, she was sure Kate could not possibly love her husband or she would never consent to share him with anybody else. "The joke of it is," Kate added, "that the husband of this neighbour is known to be after every skirt, and she is not aware of it. You have no idea what the sexual practices of these farmers are. But it is the result mostly of their dreary existence," she hastened to add; "no other outlet, no distraction, no colour of any sort in their lives. It is different in the city; even the poorest working-man there can sometimes go to a show or a lecture, or find some interest in his union. The farmer has nothing but long and arduous toil in the summer, and empty days in the winter. Sex is all they have. How should these people understand sex in its finer expressions, or love that cannot be sold or bound? It's an uphill fight, but we must strive on," my dear comrade concluded.

Time passed only too quickly. Presently I had to leave in order to keep my engagements in the West. Sam offered to take me to the station by a shorter route, which was "only fourteen miles." Kate and the rest of the family accompanied us.

CHAPTER XX

AT THE HEIGHT OF MY CALIFORNIA ACTIVITIES A LETTER CAME that shattered my visions of harmonious love: Max wrote me that he and his comrade " Puck " were about to go abroad together, financed by a friend. I laughed aloud at the folly of my hopes. After the failure with Ed how could I have dreamed of love and understanding with anyone else? Love and happiness — empty, meaningless words, vain reaching out for the unattainable. I felt robbed by life, defeated in my yearning for a beautiful relationship. I still had my ideal to live for, as I consoled myself, and the work I had set myself to do. Why expect more from life? But where get strength and inspiration to keep up the struggle? Men had been able to do the world's work without the sustaining power of love; why should not also women? Or is it that woman needs love more than man? A stupid, romantic notion, conceived to keep her for ever dependent on the male. Well, I would not have it; I would live and work without love. There is no permanency anywhere in nature or in life. I must drain the moment and then let the goblet fall to the ground. It is the sole protection against taking root, only to be painfully pulled up again. My young friends in San Francisco had been calling. The vision of life with Max had stood in the way. Now I could respond; I must respond in order to forget.

After visiting Portland and Seattle I went to Tacoma, Washington. Everything had been prepared for a meeting there, but when I arrived, I found that the owner of the hall had backed out, and no other place could be secured. At the last moment, when all hopes had been given up, the spiritualists came to the rescue. I delivered several lectures before them, but at the subject of Free Love even they balked. Evidently the spirits continued in heaven the moral standards they had set during their embodiment.

Spring Valley, Illinois, a large mining section, had a strong anarchist group, consisting mostly of Belgians and Italians. They had invited me for a series of lectures, culminating in a demonstration on Labour Day. Their efforts were crowned with great success. Although it was broiling hot, the miners turned out with their wives and children, dressed in their finest. I headed the procession, carrying a large red flag. In the garden hired for the speeches the platform had no awning. I spoke with the hot sun beating down on my head, which had already begun to ache during the long march. In the afternoon, at our picnic, the comrades brought nineteen babies to be baptized by me in " true anarchist fashion," as they said. I got on an empty beer-barrel, no other stand being available, and addressed the audience. I felt that the ones who needed baptism were really the parents, baptism in the new ideas of the rights of the child.

The local papers the following day carried two leading stories: one that Emma Goldman " drank like a trooper "; the other that she " had baptized anarchist children in a barrel of beer."

During my previous visit in Detroit with Max I had met one of Robert Reitzel's staunchest friends, Herman Miller, and another devotee of the *Armer Teufel,* Carl Stone. Miller was president of the Cleveland Brewing Company and a man of considerable means. How he ever came to his position was a puzzle to all who knew him. He was a dreamer and visionary, a lover of freedom and beauty, and a very generous spirit. For years he had been the main support of the *Armer Teufel.* His finest trait was his art of giving. Even when he tipped a waiter, it was done in a delicate and almost apologetic way. As for his friends, Herman fairly showered gifts on them, in a manner as though they were bestowing a favour on him. On this occasion my host outdid himself in thoughtfulness and generosity. The days spent with him and Stone, in the company of the Ruedebusches, Emma Clausen, and other friends, were a round of good fellowship and comradeship.

Both Miller and Stone showed great interest in my struggle and plans for the future. Asked about the latter, I informed them that I had none, except to work for my ideal. Didn't I wish to secure myself materially, by having some profession, for instance, Herman suggested. I had always wanted to study medicine, I told him, but had never had the means for it. I was completely taken off my feet by Herman's unexpectedly offering to finance my studies. Stone also wanted to share the expense, but the two friends thought it impracticable to turn the entire amount over to me. " I understand you always have a string of people needing help; you will be sure to give the money away," Herman said. They agreed to secure me for five years with an income of forty dollars a month. The same day Herman, accompanied by Julia Ruedebusch, took me to the best store in Detroit, " to help rig Emma out for her trip." A beautiful blue Scotch cloth cape was among the numerous things I cherished from my shopping tour. Carl Stone presented me with a gold watch; it was clam-shaped, and I wondered why he had chosen such a peculiar form. " In token of a gift you have, so rare in your sex: the ability to keep mum," he said. " That is indeed a compliment from a male ! " I retorted, to the amusement of the rest.

Before I took leave of my dear friends in Detroit, Herman shyly and unobtrusively put an envelope in my hand. " A love-letter," he said, " to be read on the train." The " love-letter " contained five hundred dollars, with a note : " For your passage, dear Emma, and to keep you from care until we meet in Paris."

The last hope of legal redress for Sasha was gone when the new Board of Pardons refused to hear our appeal. There was nothing left except the desperate venture Sasha had been planning for a considerable time — an escape. His friends used every means to dissuade him from the idea during the campaign made in his behalf by Carl, Henry, Gordon, and Harry Kelly. With the possibility of release gone, I could do nothing but submit to Sasha's wishes, though with an anxious heart.

His letters, after I informed him that we would go ahead with his scheme, showed him to have undergone a wonderful transformation. He was buoyant again, full of hope and vigour. Soon he would send a friend to us, he wrote, a most trustworthy person, a fellow prisoner whom he called " Tony." The man would be released within a few weeks, and he would then bring us the necessary details of the plan. " It will not fail if my instructions are faithfully carried out," he wrote. He explained that two things would be required: dependable comrades of grit and endurance, and some money. He was sure I would find both.

Before long " Tony " was released, but certain preparatory work in Sasha's behalf kept him in Pittsburgh, and we could not get in personal touch with him. I learned, however, that Sasha's plan involved the digging of a tunnel from the outside into the prison, and that Sasha had entrusted " Tony " with all the necessary diagrams and measurements to enable us to do the work. The scheme seemed fantastic, the desperate design of one driven to stake everything, even his life, upon the throw of a card. Yet I was carried away by the project, so cleverly conceived, and worked out with utmost care. I reflected a long time upon whom to approach in regard to the undertaking. There were plenty of comrades who would be willing to risk their lives to rescue Sasha, but few who had the requisites for such a difficult and hazardous task. I finally decided upon our Norwegian friend Eric B. Morton, whom we had nicknamed " Ibsen." He was a veritable viking, in spirit and physique, a man of intelligence, daring, and will-power.

The plan appealed to him at once. Without hesitation he promised to do anything that would be required, and he was ready to start there and then. I explained that there would be an unavoidable delay; we had to wait for "Tony." Something was apparently detaining him much longer than he had expected. I was loath to leave for Europe without being sure that Sasha's plan was being carried out and I confessed to Eric that I felt uneasy about going at all. " It will be maddening to be three thousand miles away while Sasha's fate is hanging in the balance," I said. Eric understood my feelings in the matter, but he thought that as far as the proposed tunnel was concerned, I could do nothing. " In fact, your absence may prove of greater value," he argued, "than your presence in America. It will serve to ward off suspicion that something is being done for Sasha." He agreed with me that the question of Sasha's safety after the escape was of paramount importance. He feared, as I did, that Sasha could not remain very long in the country without being apprehended. " We'll have to get him away as quickly as possible to Canada or Mexico, and thence to Europe," he suggested. " The tunnel will require months of work, and that will give you time to prepare a place for him abroad. There he will be recognized as a political refugee, and as such he will not be extradited."

I knew Eric was a very level-headed man, entirely reliable. Still I hated to go away without seeing " Tony," learning the details of the plan, and finding out all he could tell us about Sasha. Eric quieted my apprehensions by promising to take charge of the entire matter and to begin operations as soon as " Tony " arrived. He was a man of convincing manner and strong personality, and I had the fullest faith in his courage and ability to carry out successfully Sasha's directions. He was, moreover, splendid company, full of cheer, and with a fine sense of humour. At parting he jubilantly assured me that together with Sasha we should soon all meet in Paris to celebrate his escape.

Still " Tony " failed to appear and his absence filled me with misgivings. Involuntarily I thought of the unreliability of prisoners' promises. I remembered the great things several of the women in Blackwell's Island were going to do for me upon their release. They were all soon drawn into the whirlpool of life and personal interests, their best prison intentions slipping away from them. It is rare indeed that a released prisoner is willing and able to carry out the promises made to his fellow sufferers remaining behind the bars. " Tony " was probably like the majority, I thought. Still, I had several weeks yet before sailing — perhaps " Tony " would turn up in the meantime.

Since leaving New York on my last tour I had not corresponded with Ed, but on my return I had received a letter from him begging me to come to the apartment and occupy it until I left for Europe. He could not endure the idea that I should be with strangers when I had a home of my own. " There is no reason for your not staying here," he wrote; " we are still friends, and the flat, with everything in it, is yours." At first I was inclined to refuse; I dreaded a revival of our former relationship and the old struggle. But Ed was so persistent in his letters that I finally returned to the place that had been my home for so many years. Ed was charming, full of tact, considerately non-invasive. Our flat had separate entrances; we came and went our different ways. It was the busy season for Ed's firm, and my time was fully occupied by raising money for Sasha's project and getting ready for my trip abroad. On my occasional free evenings or Saturday afternoons Ed would invite me to dinner or to the theatre, afterwards going to Justus's place. He never once referred to our old life. Instead we discussed my plans for Europe and he seemed greatly interested in them. He was pleased to hear that Herman Miller and Carl Stone were to finance my study of medicine, and he promised to pay me a visit in Europe, as he was planning to go abroad the following year. His mother had been ailing of late; she was growing old and he was anxious to see her as soon as possible.

Justus's place continued to be the most interesting in New York, but its former gaiety was dampened by the alarming condition of its host. I had not been informed, while touring the country, of his illness, and on my return I was appalled to find him wasted and weak. His friends had urged him to go for a rest; Mrs. Schwab and their son could manage the place in his absence. But Justus would not consent. He laughed and joked as usual, but his glorious voice had lost its old ring. It was heart-rending to see our " giant oak " beginning to break.

Funds to carry out Sasha's undertaking had to be raised under cover of a supposed new legal move. Only very few comrades could be told about the real object for which the money was needed. The man who could help most was S. Yanofsky, editor of the *Freie Arbeiter Stimme,* the Yiddish anarchist weekly. He had only recently come from England, where he had edited the *Arbeiter Freund;* he was clever and wielded an incisive pen. I knew him as a worshipper of Most, which was no doubt the reason for his antagonistic attitude towards me at our first meeting. His sarcastic manner had made a disagreeable impression on me, and I disliked having to approach him. But it was for Sasha's sake, and I went to see him.

To my surprise I found Yanofsky very much interested and willing to help. He expressed doubts about the chances of the plan's success, but when I informed him that Sasha was desperate at the thought of continuing eleven more years in his grave, Yanofsky promised to do his utmost to raise the necessary money. With " Ibsen " and several other reliable friends in Pittsburgh to look after the undertaking, and with Yanofsky to assist with the financial end, my anxiety was considerably allayed.

Harry Kelly was then in England. I had written him about my coming to Europe and he immediately invited me to stay in the house where he was living with his wife and child. The London comrades, Harry wrote, were planning a large eleventh-of-November meeting and would be glad to have me as one of the speakers. At the same time a letter arrived from the anarchists in Glasgow, inviting me for lectures. Besides, there was much to be done for our congress. I had received credentials as a delegate from several groups. Some of the American comrades, among them Lizzie and William Holmes, Abe Isaak, and Susan Patten, asked me to present their papers on various topics. I had a great deal of work before me and it was time to start on my journey. But to my distress there was still no word from " Tony."

One evening I went to Justus's place, where I had promised to meet

Ed. I found him in the circle of his philologic cronies, discussing, as usual, the etymology of words. An old literary friend, whom I had not seen for a long time, was there, and while I waited for Ed, I conversed with him. It grew late, but Ed showed no disposition to leave. I told him I was going home, and I left, accompanied by the writer, who lived in the same neighbourhood. At my door I bade him goodbye and immediately went to bed.

I awoke from a ghastly dream that terrified me by lightning and rumbling. But the thunder and crashing of things seemed to continue, and presently I became aware that it was real, happening next door, in Ed's room. He must be crazed by drink, I thought. Yet I had never seen Ed intoxicated to the extent of losing control of himself. What had happened to make Ed so violent as to come home and smash up things in the middle of the night? I wanted to call, to cry out to him, but I was somehow restrained by the continued clatter of objects falling and breaking. After a while it subsided and I heard Ed throw himself heavily on the couch. Then all was quiet.

I kept awake, my eyes burning, my heart beating tumultuously. At daybreak I dressed hastily and opened the door separating my room from Ed's. The sight was appalling: the floor was littered with broken furniture and china; the sketch Fedya had made of me, which Ed had cherished as his greatest treasure, lay torn and trampled upon, its frame smashed. Table and chairs were overturned and broken. In the midst of the confusion lay Ed, half-dressed and fast asleep. In anger and disgust I ran back to my room, slamming the door behind me.

I saw Ed once more, the next day, before I sailed. His haggard look of misery sealed my lips. What was there to say or explain? The debris of our things were the symbol of our wrecked love, of the life that had been so full of colour and promise.

Many friends came to the steamer to say adieu to me and to Mary Isaak, who was sailing with me. Ed was not among them, and I was grateful for it. It would have been even more difficult to control my tears in his presence. It was most painful to say good-bye to Justus, whom we all knew to be dying of tuberculosis. He looked very ill, and I felt saddened by the thought that I might never see him alive again. It was hard also to part from my brother. I was glad to be able to leave him some money, and I would contribute to his needs from the monthly allowance my Detroit friends were to send me. I could manage on less; I had done it in Vienna. The boy had taken deep hold on my heart; he was so tender and considerate that his affection had become something very precious in my life. As the big liner steamed out, I remained on deck to watch the receding silhouettes of New York.

Our crossing was uneventful, except for a raging storm. We arrived in London two days too late for the eleventh-of-November meeting and at the height of the Boer War. In the house where Harry Kelly and his family were living there was only one room vacant, and that was in the basement. Even in clear weather it had but little daylight, while on foggy days the gas-jet had to be kept going all the time. The fire-place warmed only one's side or back, never the entire body, and I constantly had to keep changing my position to balance, to some extent, the atmospheric difference between the fire and the cold room.

Having been in London during its best season, in late August and September, I used to think that people exaggerated when they spoke of the horrors of the London fogs, the dampness and greyness of its winter. But I realized this time that they had hardly done justice to the reality. The fog was like a monster, stealthily creeping up and enveloping the victim in its chilly embrace. Mornings I would awaken with a leaden feeling, my mouth parched. In vain the hope of enjoying a ray of light by opening the blinds; the blackness from the outside would soon creep into the room. Poor Mary Isaak, coming from sunny California, was depressed by the London weather even worse than I. She had planned to stay a month, but after one week she was anxious to leave.

CHAPTER XXI

THE WAR MADNESS IN ENGLAND WAS SO GREAT, SOME OF THE comrades informed me, that it would be almost impossible to deliver my lectures as had been planned. Harry Kelly was of the same opinion. " Why not hold anti-war mass meetings? " I suggested. I referred to the splendid gatherings we had in America during the Spanish War. Now and then there had been attempts at interference, and several lectures had to be given up, but on the whole we had been able to carry through our campaign. Harry thought, however, that it would be impossible in England. His description of violent attacks on speakers (the jingo spirit being at its height) and of meetings being broken up by patriotic mobs sounded discouraging. He was sure it would be even more dangerous for me, a foreigner, to speak on the war. I was in favour of trying it, anyhow. I simply could not be in England and keep silent on the matter. Did not Great Britain believe in free speech? " Mind you," he warned me, " it is not the authorities who interfere with meetings, as in America; it is the mob itself, both rich and poor." I insisted, nevertheless, on making an attempt. Harry promised to consult the other comrades about it.

At the invitation of the Kropotkins I went out with Mary Isaak to Bromley. This time Mrs. Kropotkin and her little daughter, Sasha, were at home. Both Peter and Sophia Grigorevna received us with affectionate cordiality. We discussed America, our movement there, and conditions in England. Peter had visited the States in 1898, but I was at the time on the Coast and unable to attend his lectures. I knew, however, that his tour had been very successful and that he had left a most gratifying impression. The proceeds of his meetings had helped to revive *Solidarity* and inject new life into our movement. Peter was particularly interested in my tours through the Middle West and California. " It must be a splendid field," he remarked, " if you can cover the same ground three times in succession." I assured him that it was, and that much of the credit for my success in California had been due to *Free Society*. "The paper is doing splendid work," he warmly agreed, "but it would do more if it would not waste so much space discussing sex." I disagreed, and we became involved in a heated argument about the place of the sex problem in anarchist propaganda. Peter's view was that woman's equality with man had nothing to do with sex; it was a matter of brains. "When she is his equal intellectually and shares in his social ideals," he said, "she will be as free as he." We both got somewhat excited, and our voices must have sounded as if we were quarrelling. Sophia, quietly sewing a dress for her daughter, tried several times to direct our talk into less vociferous channels, but in vain. Peter and I paced the room in growing agitation, each strenuously upholding his side of the question. At last I paused with the remark: "All right, dear comrade, when I have reached your age, the sex question may no longer be of importance to me. But it is *now*, and it is a tremendous factor for thousands, millions even, of young people." Peter stopped short, an amused smile lighting up his kindly face. "Fancy, I didn't think of that," he replied. "Perhaps you are right, after all." He beamed affectionately upon me, with a humorous twinkle in his eye.

During dinner I broached the plan for the anti-war meetings. Peter was even more emphatic than Harry had been. It was out of the question, he thought; it would endanger my life; moreover, because I was a Russian, my stand on the war would unfavourably affect the status of the Russian refugees. "I'm not here as a Russian, but as an American," I protested. "Moreover, what do these considerations matter when such a vital issue as war is involved?" Peter pointed out that it mattered very much to people who had death or Siberia staring them in the face. He insisted, nevertheless, that England was still the only asylum in Europe for political refugees and that its hospitality should not be forfeited by meetings.

My first public appearance in London, in the Athenæum Hall, was a dismal failure. I had caught a severe cold that affected my throat so that my speaking was painful not only to myself but to the audience as well. I could hardly be heard. No less distressing was my nervousness when I learned that the most distinguished Russian refugees and some noted Englishmen had come to hear me. The names of those Russians had always symbolized to me all that was heroic in the struggle against the tsars. The thought of their presence filled me with awe. What could I say to such men, and how say it?

Harry Kelly acted as chairman, straightway proceeding to tell the audience that his comrade Emma Goldman, who had faced squadrons of police in America, had just confided to him that she was panicky before this assembly. The latter thought it a good joke and laughed heartily. Inwardly I raged at Harry, but the good humour of the audience and its evident desire to put me at my ease somewhat relieved my nervous tension. I plodded through my lecture, aware all the time that I was delivering a rotten speech. The questions that followed, however, gave me back my self-possession. I felt more in my element, and I did not care any more who was present. I regained my ordinary determined and aggressive manner.

My meetings in the East End offered no difficulties. There I was among my people; I knew their lives, hard and barren everywhere, but more so in London. I was able to find the right words to reach them; I was my own self in their midst. My nearer comrades were a warm and genial lot. The moving spirit of the work in the East End was Rudolph Rocker, a young German, who presented the peculiar phenomenon of a Gentile editor of a Yiddish paper. He had not associated much with Jews until he came to England. In order to fit himself the better for his activities in the ghetto, he had lived among the Jews and mastered their language. As editor of the *Arbeiter Freund* and by his brilliant lectures Rudolph Rocker was doing more for the education and revolutionizing of the Jews in England than the ablest members of their own race.

The same good-fellowship which prevailed among my Jewish comrades was evident also in the English anarchist circles, especially in the group that published *Freedom*. That monthly had gathered about it a coterie of able contributors and workers who co-operated most harmoniously. It was a joy to find things going so well, to meet the dear old friends and make so many new ones.

At a social evening at the Kropotkins', I met a number of illustrious people, among them Nikolai Tchaikovsky. He had been the genius of the revolutionary movement of the Russian youth in the seventies that crystallized in the famous circles bearing his name. It was a great event to meet the man who was to me the personification of everything that was inspiring in the emancipation movement of Russia. He was of magnificent physique and idealistic appearance, a personality that

could easily appeal to young and eager souls. Tchaikovsky was surrounded by friends, but after a while he came over to the corner where
I was sitting and engaged me in conversation. Peter had told him that
I intended to study medicine. How did I propose to do it and go on
with my activities at the same time, he wondered. I explained that
I planned to come to England for lectures, during the summer, perhaps even go to America; in any case I did not think of giving up the
movement altogether. " Unless you do that," he said, " you'll be a
bad doctor; and if you are in earnest about your profession, you'll
become a bad propagandist. You can't do both." He advised me to
think it over before undertaking something that was sure to destroy
my usefulness in the movement. His words disturbed me. I was confident that I could do both things if I was determined enough and
continued with my social interests. But somehow he had succeeded in
putting doubt into my mind. I began to question myself; did I really
want to take five years out of my life to gain a doctor's degree?

Before long, Harry Kelly came to inform me that some of the comrades had agreed to arrange an anti-war meeting and that steps would
be taken to ensure security. Their plan was to bring a score of men
from Canning Town, a suburb known for the fighting spirit and
strength of its men. They would protect the platform and prevent a
possible rush of the jingoes. Tom Mann, the labour man who had
played a leading part in the recent dockers' strike, would be asked to
preside. I should have to be smuggled into the hall before the patriots
could have a chance to do anything, Harry explained. Tchaikovsky
was to attend to that.

On the appointed day, accompanied by my escort, I reached South
Place Institute a few hours before the crowd began to gather. Very
soon the hall was filled. When Tom Mann stepped on to the platform,
there was loud booing, which drowned the applause of our friends.
For a time the situation looked hopeless, but Tom was an experienced
speaker, skilled in the handling of crowds. The audience soon subsided. When I made my appearance, however, the patriots got out of
leash again. Several tried to get on the platform, but the Canning
Town men held them back. I stood silent for some moments, not
knowing just how to approach the infuriated Britishers. I was certain
I could achieve nothing by the direct and blunt manner that had invariably succeeded with my American audiences. Something different
was needed, something that would touch their pride. My visit in 1895

and my experiences this time had taught me to know the pride of Englishmen in their traditions. " Men and women of England! " I shouted above the din, " I have come here in the firm belief that a people whose history is surcharged with the spirit of rebellion and whose genius in every field is a shining star upon the firmament of the world can be naught but liberty- and justive-loving. Nay, more, the immortal works of Shakespeare, Milton, Byron, Shelley, and Keats, to mention only the greatest in the galaxy of poets and dreamers of your country, must needs have enlarged your vision and quickened your appreciation of what is the most precious heritage of a truly cultivated people; I mean the grace of hospitality and a generous attitude towards the stranger in your midst."

Complete silence in the hall.

" Your behaviour tonight hardly sustains my belief in the superior culture and breeding of your country," I went on; " or is it that the fury of war has so easily destroyed what it has taken centuries to build up? If that is so, it should be enough to repudiate war. Who is there who would supinely sit by when what is best and highest in a people is being throttled before his very eyes? Certainly not your Shelley, whose song was of liberty and revolt. Certainly not your Byron, whose soul could find no peace when the greatness of Greece was endangered. Not they, not they! And you, are you so forgetful of your past, is there no echo in your soul of your poets' songs, your dreamers' dreams, your rebels' calls? "

Silence continued, my hearers apparently bewildered by the unexpected turn of my speech, dumbfounded by the high-sounding words and compelling gestures. The audience became absorbed in my talk, carried to a pitch of enthusiasm which finally broke forth in loud applause. After that it was easy sailing. I delivered my lecture on War and Patriotism as I had given it all through the United States, merely changing the parts that had dealt with the causes of the Spanish-American hostilities to those behind the Anglo-Boer War. I concluded with the gist of Carlyle's idea of war as a quarrel between two thieves, themselves too cowardly to fight, compelling boys of one village and another into uniforms with guns in their hands and then letting them loose like ferocious beasts against each other.

The house went wild. Men and women waved their hats and shouted themselves hoarse in approval. Our resolution, a powerful protest against the war, was read by the Chair and adopted with only one dissenting voice. I bowed in the direction of the objector and said:

" There is what I call a brave man who deserves our admiration. It requires great courage to stand alone, even if one is mistaken. Let us all join in hearty applause for our daring opponent."

Even our guard from Canning Town could no longer hold back the surging crowd. But there was no danger any more. The audience had turned from fierce antagonism to equally burning devotion, ready to protect me to the last drop of its blood. In the committee room Tchaikovsky, who had joined in enthusiastic demonstration, waving his hat like an excited youngster, embraced me, praising my mastery of the situation. " I am afraid I was somewhat of a hypocrite," I remarked. " All diplomats are," he replied, " but diplomacy is necessary at times."

My first mail from America contained letters from Yegor, Ed, and Eric Morton. My brother wrote that Ed had sought him out the day after my departure and had begged him to come back to the house, as he could not bear the loneliness. " You know, my dear *Chavele,* I always liked Ed," his letter read; " I simply couldn't refuse, and so I went back. Two weeks later Ed brought some woman into the apartment and she has been there ever since. It made me sick to see her among your things, in the atmosphere you had created. That's why I moved out again." Ed had asked Yegor to take the furniture, books, and other things that belonged to me, but he could not do it: he felt too unhappy over the whole matter. Ed had consoled himself quickly, I reflected. Well, why not? I wondered who the woman was.

Ed's letter contained no mention of the new relationship in his life. He merely inquired what he should do with my things. He was planning to move up-town, he wrote, and he did not want to take what he had always considered mine. I cabled him that I wanted nothing but my books and asked him to pack them in a box and store it with Justus.

Eric wrote in his usual jovial way. All was well with our plans. A house had been rented, and he was going to move into it with his friend K. They were expecting a strenuous ordeal, because K " was preparing for her forthcoming concert." They had already hired a piano so she could practise, and he would be busy with his invention. The money I had left him would cover the trip of himself and K to Pittsburgh and keep them going for a time. " As to our engineer, T, he seems to suffer from self-importance, but he will do. Everything else when we meet in Paris to celebrate my invention."

I was amused at the manner in which Eric had worded his letter, with a view to safety, of course. But even I was puzzled by some of its contents. K was no doubt Kinsella, his friend, whom I had met in Chicago. But what on earth did he mean by a concert and a piano? I knew the woman had a good voice and was also a trained pianist, but what would she do with these talents in the house from which the tunnel was to be dug? The " engineer " was apparently " Tony." Evidently he had shown up at last, but it was obvious that Eric did not like him. I hoped that they could get along until the project was completed. I must write dear Eric, I decided, to be very, very patient.

During my London stay I also spoke at a German meeting arranged by comrades of the *Autonomie* Club. In the discussion I was attacked by a young German. "What does Emma Goldman know about the life of the workers, anyway? " my opponent demanded; " she never worked in a factory and she's just like the other agitators, having a good time, travelling round and enjoying herself. We, the proletarians, we of the blue blouse, are the only ones who have a right to talk about the suffering of the masses." It was obvious that the boy knew nothing about me, nor did I find it necessary to enlighten him on my work in factories and my knowledge of the lives of the people. But I was intrigued by his reference to the blue blouse. What could that signify, I wondered.

After the meeting two men of about my own age came up to see me. They begged me not to hold all the comrades responsible for the stupid attack of the youth. They knew him well; he was doing nothing in the movement except boast of his proletarian trade mark, the blue blouse. In the early period of the movement, the men explained, the German intelligentsia began to wear the blue blouse of the workers, partly in protest against conventional and formal attire, but more especially to be able to approach the masses more easily. Since then some charlatans in the social movement had used that mode of dressing as a sign of their adherence to strict revolutionary principles. " And also because they haven't a white shirt," the dark-looking man put in, " or because they don't have to wash their necks so often." I laughed heartily and asked him why he was so vindictive. " Because I can't bear sham! " the man replied almost gruffly. The two introduced themselves as Hippolyte Havel and X, the former a Czech, the latter a German. X soon excused himself, and Havel asked me to take dinner with him.

My escort was of small stature, very dark, with large eyes gleaming in his pale face. He was dressed fastidiously, even to the point of gloves, which no men in our ranks wore. It struck me as dandyish, especially in a revolutionist. In the restaurant I noticed that Havel took off only one glove, keeping the other on all through the meal. I was on the point of asking him the reason, but he seemed so self-conscious that I did not wish to embarrass him. After a few glasses of wine he became more animated, talking in nervous staccato sentences. He had come to London from Zürich, he told me, and though not long in the city, he knew it well and would be happy to take me about. It would have to be Sunday afternoon, or late in the evening, his only free time.

Hippolyte Havel proved to be a veritable encyclopædia. He knew everybody and everything in the movement of the various European countries. I detected bitterness in his tone when he spoke of certain comrades in the *Autonomie* Club. It affected me unpleasantly, but on the whole he was exceedingly entertaining. It was already too late to catch a bus, and Havel hailed a cab to take me home. When I offered to pay the driver, he became incensed. " Just like an American, flaunting your money! I'm working, and I can afford to pay!" he protested. I ventured to suggest that for an anarchist he was strangely conventional to object to a woman's right to pay. Havel smiled for the first time during the whole evening, and I could not help noticing that he had beautiful white teeth. When I shook his hand, still encased in the glove, he gave a suppressed groan. " What is it? " I asked. " Oh, nothing," he replied, " but for a little lady you do have a strong grip."

There was something strange and exotic about the man. He was evidently very nervous and ungenerous in his estimate of people. Still, he was fascinating, even disturbing.

My Czech comrade came frequently, sometimes with his friend, but usually alone. He was far from gay company; in fact, he rather depressed me. Unless he had drunk a little, it was difficult to get him to converse; at other times he seemed tongue-tied. Gradually I learned that he had come into the movement when only eighteen and that he had been in prison several times, once for a term of eighteen months. On the last occasion he had been sent to the psychopathic ward, where he might have remained had he not aroused the interest of Professor Krafft-Ebing, who declared him sane and helped him back to freedom. He had been active in Vienna and expelled from there, after which he had tramped through Germany, lecturing and writing for anarchist publications. He had visited Paris, but was not allowed to remain there long, being expelled. Finally he had gone to Zürich and thence to London. As he had no trade, he was compelled to accept any kind of job. At the time, he was working in an English boarding-house as an all-round man. His duties began at five in the morning and consisted in lighting the fires, cleaning the boots of the guests, washing dishes, and doing other kinds of "degrading and humiliating work." "But why degrading? Labour is never degrading," I protested. "Labour, as it is now, is always degrading!" he insisted vehemently; "in an English boarding-house it is even worse; it is an outrage on all human sensibilities, besides the drudgery it involves. Look at my hands!" With a nervous jerk he tore off his glove and the bandage underneath. His hand, red and swollen, was a mass of blisters. "How did it happen, and how can you keep on working?" I asked. "I got it from cleaning filthy boots in the early morning chill and carrying coals and wood to keep the fires going. What else can I do without a trade in a foreign country? I might starve, sink into the gutter, or end in the Thames," he added. "But I'm not just ready for it. Besides, I'm only one of the many thousands; why fuss about it? Let's talk about more cheerful things." He continued conversing, but I hardly heard what he said. I took his poor blistered hand, conscious of an irresistible desire to put it to my lips, in infinite sympathy and tenderness.

We went about together a good deal, visiting the poor quarters, Whitechapel and similar districts. On week-days the streets were littered with foul rubbish, and the smell of fried fish was nauseating. On Saturday nights the spectacle was even more harrowing. I had seen drunken women on the Bowery, old social dregs, their scraggy hair loose, their incongruous hats tilted to one side and skirts sweeping the sidewalk. "Bummerkes," the Jewish children called them. It used to make me furious to see the thoughtless youngsters taunt and chase those poor derelicts. But nothing compared in brutality and degradation with the sights I witnessed in the East End of London: drunken women lurching out of the public houses, using the vilest language and fighting until they would literally tear the clothes off one another. Small boys and girls hanging round the drinking-places in sleet and cold, infants in dilapidated carriages in a stupor from the whisky-soaked "suckers," the elder children keeping watch and greedily drinking the ale their parents would bring out to them from time to time. Too often I saw such pictures, more terrible than any conceived by Dante. Every time, filled with rage, disgust, and shame, I would promise myself never to go back to the East End, yet I would invariably return. When I broached the situation to some of my comrades, they thought me overwrought. Such conditions existed in every large city, they claimed; it was capitalism with its resultant sordidness. Why should I feel more disturbed in London than anywhere else?

Gradually I began to realize that the pleasure I found in Havel's company was due to more than ordinary comradeship. Love was making its claims again, daily more insistent. I was afraid of it, afraid of the new pain, the new disappointments in store. Yet my need of it in the dismal surroundings was stronger than my apprehensions. Havel, too, cared for me. He had grown more timid, more restless and fidgety. He had been in the habit of coming to see me alone, but one evening he visited me with his friend, who remained for hours and showed no intention of leaving. I suspected that Havel had brought him because he did not trust himself to be alone with me, and that only increased my yearning. Finally, long after midnight, his friend left. No sooner was he gone than we found ourselves, hardly conscious how, in each other's embrace. London receded, the cry of the East End was far away. Only the call of love sounded in our hearts, and we listened and yielded to it.

I felt reborn with the new joy in my life. We would go together to Paris and later to Switzerland, we decided. Hippolyte also wanted to study and we planned to live very frugally on thirty dollars a month, ten out of my forty going to my brother. Hippolyte thought he could earn a little with articles, but we would not mind if we should have to forgo some comforts. We had each other and our love. But it was first necessary to induce my sweetheart to give up his dreadful job. I wanted him to have a month's rest from his boarding-house grind. It took considerable argument to persuade him, but two weeks away from cleaning filthy boots raised his spirits so much that he seemed a different being.

One afternoon we called on the Kropotkins. Hippolyte was a great admirer of the *Genossenschafts-Bewegung,* a co-operative movement more advanced, as he believed, than the British. He soon got into heated discussion with Peter, who did not see any particular merit in the German experiment. I had noticed on previous occasions that

Hippolyte could not hold his own in an argument. He would grow irritable and frequently become personal. He tried to avoid it with Peter, but, the discussion presently getting beyond his control, he broke off suddenly and became oppressively silent. Kropotkin was unpleasantly impressed, and, on the pretext of having work to do, I made haste to leave. On the street he began to abuse Peter, denouncing him as the " pope of the anarchist movement," who could not tolerate a dissenting opinion. I felt outraged and we exchanged hot words. By the time we reached my room we realized how childish it was to allow our tempers to becloud our young love.

Accompanied by Hippolyte, I attended the Russian New Year *vetcherinka,* which proved a great event for me. There I met some of the outstanding personalities of the Russian colony, among them I. Goldenberg, with whom I had worked in New York in the campaign against the Russian-American Extradition Treaty; E. Serebriakov, well known for his revolutionary activities; V. Tcherkesoff, a prominent theoretician of anarchism, as well as Tchaikovsky and Kropotkin. Almost everyone present had a record of heroic effort, of years of prison and exile. Among those present was also Michael Hambourg, with his sons Mark, Boris, and Jan, already promising musicians.

The affair was more sedate than similar gatherings in New York. Serious problems were discussed, only the younger people caring to dance. Later in the evening Peter entertained us at the piano, while Tcherkesoff swung twelve-year-old Sasha Kropotkin round the floor, their example followed by some of the others. Tchaikovsky, towering high above me, bowed comically when he asked me to dance. It was a memorable evening.

In Glasgow, the first stop on my Scottish tour, the meetings had been arranged by our good comrade Blair Smith, who was also my host. Everybody was very kind and friendly to me, but the city itself proved a nightmare, in some respects even worse than London. On a Saturday night, returning home on the tramway, I counted seven children on the street, dirty and undernourished, staggering along with their mothers, all under the influence of drink.

Edinburgh was a treat after Glasgow, spacious, clean, and attractive, with poverty not so obvious. It was there I first met Tom Bell, of whose propagandistic zeal and daring we had heard much in America. Among his exploits was a free-speech experiment he had made while in Paris. He had urged the French anarchists to make a stand for open-air meetings, on the English plan, but the Paris comrades considered such an attempt impossible. Tom decided to demonstrate that it was feasible to speak in the open regardless of the police.

He distributed handbills announcing that on the following Sunday afternoon he would, on his own responsibility, hold an open-air meeting at the Place de la République, one of the busy centres of Paris. When he reached the square at the appointed time, there was a great crowd waiting. As he made his way to the centre of the Place, several police agents approached him. Not sure whether he was the announced speaker, they hesitated a moment. Tom had picked out his lamp-post, one with a big ornamental base half-way up and a cross-piece at the top. Just as the police stepped up to him, he sprang up the post. His feet were firm on the base, and in a second his wrist was chained to the cross-piece. He had secured by a padlock a strong steel chain round his wrist, and now he quickly whipped the two ends round the cross-piece and fastened them by another padlock that locked automatically. The police got after him at once, but they could do nothing; the man was securely chained. They sent for a file. Meanwhile the crowd kept increasing and Tom went on nonchalantly talking to them. The officers raged, but he continued his speech till his voice gave out. Then he produced the key, opened the padlock and coolly came down. The police threatened him with terrible things " for insults to the Army and the law," but all Paris laughed at them and held them up to ridicule. The authorities thought it best to hush up the matter, and Tom was not prosecuted. After a fortnight in jail he was expelled as " too dangerous a man to be allowed loose in France."

Another of Tom Bell's exploits took place on the occasion of the visit of Tsar Nicholas II to England. The Queen was at Balmoral at the time. The royal schedule was to have the Tsar land at Leith, where he would be met by the Prince of Wales (later King Edward VII); subsequently he was to come to Windsor and London.

Tom Bell agreed with his friend McCabe to help in the reception of the Tsar. McCabe had a shrivelled hand and arm, but he was as game as Tom. Together they laid their plans. They were in Edinburgh at the time, and when they reached Leith, they found an enormous number of police at the dock, including British, Russian, and French secret-service men. The streets were barricaded and lined all the way by soldiers and bobbies, with detectives swarming everywhere. Behind the barricade was a row of Highlanders; behind them territorials, these again supported by infantry. The situation looked hopeless — no chance for any action. Tom Bell and McCabe decided to separate; "each knew that the other would do his damnedest," as Tom afterwards said. He heard a faint cheer from the school-children as the pretty uniforms went by. Then came the carriages. The Tsar's was easily distinguished. Tom made out the Russian autocrat sitting in the back seat, the Prince of Wales facing him. It seemed impossible to do anything, up to the last moment, and it was possible only at that moment and at no other. The guards had been alert and vigilant till — just as the Tsar's carriage came level with them. In an instant Tom dived right through them, under the barricade and to the side of the carriage, shouting into the Tsar's face: " Down with the Russian tyrant! To hell with all the empires! " Just at that moment he became conscious of his friend Mac, who had also got through, also shouting close by.

The British authorities did not dare bring Bell and McCabe before a Scottish jury. Most probably they feared that prosecution would mean more publicity. Not one word appeared in the papers about the incident. " The Tsar appeared pale," they wrote. No doubt. He cut his visit short, going home again, not through Leith or any other Scottish seaport, but from an obscure fishing-village, whence he was taken to his yacht by boat.

I was naturally eager to meet the adventurous comrade. I found him living with John Turner's sister Lizzie, the lovely girl I had met in London in 1895. Tom was a very sick man, suffering from asthma, but he was picturesque — tall, with red hair and beard, just the type capable of unusual performances.

I departed from England for Paris, together with Hippolyte, arriving in that city on a drizzling January morning and stopping in a hotel on Boulevard Saint-Michel. Four years previously, in 1896, I had visited the city on my way from Vienna. That experience had been a great disappointment. The people I then stopped with, German anarchists, lived in a suburb, worked hard during the day, and were too tired to go out at night, and my French was not sufficient to enable me to go about alone. On the only free Sunday, friends had taken me to the Bois de Boulogne. Outside of that I had seen practically nothing of Paris, which I had longed so much to know, but I had promised myself that some day I would return to enjoy the delights of the wonderful city.

Now the opportunity was at hand at last, made more wonderful by the rebirth of love in my life. Hippolyte had been in Paris before and knew its charms; he made a perfect companion. For a month we were completely engrossed in the wonders of the city and in each other. Every street, every stone almost, had its revolutionary story, every district its heroic legend. The beauty of Paris, her reckless youth, her thirst for joy and ever-changing moods, held us in their sway. The Mur des Fédérés at Père Lachaise revived the memory of the high hopes and the black despair of the last days of the Commune. It was there that the rebels had made their last heroic stand, finally to be slain by order of Thiers and Galliffet. Place de la Bastille, once the dreaded tomb of the living dead, razed to the ground by the accumulated wrath of the people of Paris, brought back to us the unspeakable pain and suffering that glowed into regenerating hope in the days of the great revolution, whose history had so much influenced our own lives.

Our cares and worries were forgotten in the world of beauty, in the treasures of architecture and art, created by the genius of man. The days were passing like a dream from which one feared to awaken. But I had come to Paris also for another purpose. It was time to begin the preparatory work for our congress.

France had been the cradle of anarchism, fathered for a long time by some of her most brilliant sons, of whom Proudhon was the greatest. The battle for their ideal had been strenuous, involving persecution, imprisonment, and often even the sacrifice of life. But it had not been in vain. Thanks to them anarchism and its exponents had come to be regarded in France as a social factor to be reckoned with. No doubt the French *bourgeoisie* continued to dread anarchism and to persecute it through the machinery of the State. I had occasion to witness the brutal manner in which the French police handled radical crowds, as well as proceedings in the French courts when dealing with social offenders. Still, there was a vast difference in the approach and methods used by the French in dealing with anarchists from the American way. It was the difference between a people seasoned in revolutionary traditions and one which had merely skimmed the surface of a struggle for independence. That difference was everywhere apparent, strikingly so in the anarchist movement itself. In the various groups I did not meet a single comrade who used the high-sounding term " philosophic " to mask his anarchism, as many did in America, because they thought it more respectable.

We were soon carried into the tide of the varied activities that went on in the anarchist ranks. The revolutionary-syndicalist movement, given new impetus by the fertile mind of Pelloutier, was permeated with anarchist tendencies. Nearly all the leading men of the organization were outspoken anarchists. The new educational efforts, known as the *Université Populaire,* were backed almost exclusively by anarchists. They had succeeded in enlisting the support and co-operation of university men in every field of learning, giving popular lectures on various branches of science before large classes of workers. Neither were the arts neglected. The volumes of Zola, Richepin, Mirbeau, and Brieux and the splendid plays produced in the Théâtre Antoine were a part of anarchist literature similar to the writings of Kropotkin, while the works of Meunier, Rodin, Steinlen, and Grandjouan were discussed and appreciated in revolutionary ranks to a greater extent than by the *bourgeois* elements that lay claim to being the sponsors of art. It was inspiring to visit the anarchist groups, watch their efforts, and observe the growth of our ideas on French soil.

My studies of the movement, however, did not allay my personal interest in people, always stronger with me than theories. Hippolyte was quite the reverse; he disliked meeting people and he was diffident in their presence. After a short while I knew nearly every one of the leading personalities in our movement in France, as well as those connected with other social work in Paris. Among the latter was the circle of *L'Humanité Nouvelle,* which published a magazine of the same name. Its able editor, Auguste Hamon, author of *La Psychologie du Militaire,* as also its contributors, belonged to a group of young artists and writers keenly alive to their time and its needs.

Of the people I met I was most impressed by Victor Dave. He was an old comrade who during forty years had participated in anarchist activities in various European countries. He had been a member of the first International, a co-worker of Michael Bakunin, and the teacher of Johann Most. He had begun a brilliant career as a student of history and philosophy, but later he chose to dedicate himself to his social ideal. I had learned much of Dave's history from Johann Most, who greatly admired him. I also knew the part he had played in the events that led to the accusations against Peukert in connexion with the arrest and conviction of John Neve. Dave was still certain of Peukert's guilt, yet there was no trace of personal animosity in him. He was kindly and jovial. Though sixty, he was as alert in mind and spirit as in his student days. Eking out a meagre existence as contributor to anarchist and other publications, he yet retained the buoyancy and humour of youth. I spent much time with him and his lifelong companion, Marie, an invalid for many years, but still interested in public affairs. Victor was a great linguist and as such invaluable in helping me to arrange the material I had brought for the congress and in making translations into different languages.

The most fascinating thing about Victor Dave was his innate feeling for life and ready enjoyment of fun. He was the freest and gayest among the many comrades I met in Paris, a companion after my own heart. But our good humour was often marred by Hippolyte's fits of extreme depression. From the very first he had taken a strong dislike to Victor. He would refuse to join us on our outings, yet peevishly resent having been left behind. Ordinarily his feeling would express itself in mute reproach, but the least quantity of liquor would incite him to abuse Victor. At first I took his outbreaks lightly, but gradually they began to affect me, making me uneasy when I was away from him. I loved the boy; I knew his unhappy past had left wounds in his soul that made him morbidly self-conscious and suspicious. I wanted to help him to a better understanding of himself and a broader approach to others. I hoped that my affection would soften his virulence. When sober, he regretted his attacks on Victor, and at such moments he would be all tenderness, clinging to our love. It led me to hope that he might outgrow his acrimonious moods. But the scenes kept recurring, and my apprehension increased.

In the course of time I realized that Hippolyte's resentment was directed not only against Victor, but against every man of my acquaintance. Two Italians I had worked with in behalf of Cuban freedom, as well as during the Summit strike, arrived in Paris to attend the Exposition. They came to see me and invited me out to dinner. On my return I found Hippolyte in a ferment of wrathful indignation. Some time later my good friend Palavicini came over with his wife and child. Hippolyte immediately began to concoct impossible stories about the man. Life with Hippolyte was growing more distressing, yet I could not think of parting.

CHAPTER XXII

A LETTER FROM CARL STONE UNEXPECTEDLY CHANGED MY PLANS regarding the study of medicine. " I thought it was understood when you left for Europe," he wrote, " that you were to go to Switzerland to study medicine. It was solely for that purpose that Herman and I offered to give you an allowance. I now learn that you are at your old propaganda and with a new lover. Surely you do not expect us to support you with either. I am interested only in E. G. the woman — her ideas have no meaning whatever to me. Please choose." I wrote back at once: " E. G. the woman and her ideas are inseparable. She does not exist for the amusement of upstarts, nor will she permit anybody to dictate to her. Keep your money."

I could not believe that Herman Miller had had anything to do with the miserable letter. I was sure that I should hear from him in due time. Of the amount he had given me I still had enough money left for several months. The two hundred dollars from Stone I had turned over to Eric to be used in connexion with the tunnel. I experienced a sense of relief that the matter was closed. When the allowance stopped and no word reached me from Herman, I concluded that he also had changed his mind. It was rather disappointing, but I was happy that I should no longer be dependent on moneyed people. Tchaikovsky was right, after all; one could not devote himself to an ideal and to a profession at the same time. I would return to America to take up my work.

One evening as I was about to go with Hippolyte to an important committee session, the hotel maid handed me a visiting-card. I was overjoyed to see on it the name of Oscar Panizza, whose brilliant writings in the *Armer Teufel* had delighted me for years. Presently a tall, dark man entered, introducing himself as Panizza. He had learned through Dr. Eugene Schmidt of my presence in Paris and was anxious to " meet Cassandra, our dear Robert's friend." He asked me to spend the evening with him and Dr. Schmidt. " We are going up to see Oscar Wilde first," he said, " and we want you to come with us. Afterwards we will have dinner."

What a marvellous event to meet Panizza and Wilde the same evening! In a flurry of anticipation I knocked at Hippolyte's door to tell him about it. I found him pacing his room, waiting for me in great irritation. " You don't mean you are not going to the session! " he cried angrily. " You have promised, you are expected, you have undertaken work to do! You can meet Oscar Wilde some other time, and Panizza too. Why must it be tonight? " In my excitement I had forgotten all about the session. Of course, I could not go back on it. With heavy heart I went downstairs to tell Panizza that I was not able to come that evening. Could we not meet tomorrow or the next day? We agreed on the following Saturday, at luncheon. He would invite Dr. Schmidt again, but he could not promise as to Oscar Wilde. The latter was in poor health and not always able to be about; but he would try his best to arrange a meeting.

On Friday Dr. Schmidt called to say that Panizza had left unexpectedly, but he was to return to Paris before long, and he would see me then. The doctor must have read disappointment on my face. " It is lovely outside," he remarked, " come for a walk." I was grateful, sick with regret for having given up the rare opportunity of meeting Oscar Wilde and of spending an evening with Panizza.

During our walk in the Luxembourg I told the doctor of the indignation I had felt at the conviction of Oscar Wilde. I had pleaded his case against the miserable hypocrites who had sent him to his doom. " You! " the doctor exclaimed in astonishment, " why, you must have been a mere youngster then. How did you dare come out in public for Oscar Wilde in puritan America? " " Nonsense! " I replied; " no daring is required to protest against a great injustice." The doctor smiled dubiously. " Injustice? " he repeated; " it wasn't exactly that from the legal point of view, though it may have been from the psychological." The rest of the afternoon we were engaged in a battle royal about inversion, perversion, and the question of sex variation. He had given much thought to the matter, but he was not free in his approach, and I suspected that he was somewhat scandalized that I, a young woman, should speak without reservations on such tabooed subjects.

On my return to the hotel I found Hippolyte in a state of sulky depression. Somehow it irritated me more than on any previous occasion. Without a word I left for my room. On my table lay a pile of letters, among them one that sent my pulse beating faster. It was from Max. He and Puck were in Paris, he wrote. They had arrived the previous night and were anxious to see me. I ran to Hippolyte, waving the letter and crying: "Max is in town! Think of it — Max!" He stared at me as if I had lost my wits. "Max — what Max?" he asked darkly. "Why, Max Baginski! What other Max could mean so much to me?" No sooner had I spoken than I realized my tactlessness. But to my surprise Hippolyte exclaimed: "Max Baginski! Why, I know all about him and I wanted to meet him long ago. I am glad he is here." Never before had I heard my "bitter Putzi," as I called him, express such a warm interest in a member of his own sex. Throwing my arms around his neck, I cried: "Let's go to Max right away!" He pressed me to him and looked intently into my eyes. "What is it?" I asked. "Oh, just to reassure myself of your love," he replied. "If only I could be certain of it, I should want nothing else in the world." "Silly boy," I said, "of course you can be sure of it." He declined to accompany me to see Max and Puck; he wanted me to see them first. Later he would meet us.

On my way the precious moments I had lived through with Max sprang vividly to life. It did not seem possible that a year had passed since. Even the shock of his going to Europe without me became resurrected in its old poignancy. Much had happened during the year to help me over the blow, but now it came back with renewed force. Why see Max — why start it all over again, I asked myself bitterly. He could not have cared if he was able to give me up so easily. I would not go through the same agony again. I would write him a note to tell him that it would be best for us not to meet any more. I stepped into a café, got paper and pen, and began to write. I started several times, but could not formulate my thought. I was in the throes of ever-increasing agitation. At last I paid the waiter and almost ran in the direction of the hotel where Max was stopping.

At the sight of his dear face, at the sound of his gay greeting, "Well, my little one, do we actually meet in Paris!" a change instantly came over me. The sweet tenderness of his voice dissolved my resentment and soothed the storm within me. Puck also welcomed me with the greatest warmth. She looked better and more vivacious than in Chicago. Soon the three of us were on our way to my hotel to get

Hippolyte. Our evening together, which lasted until three o'clock in the morning, was a merry celebration, worthy of the spirit of Paris. I was particularly happy to see the effect Max exerted on Hippolyte. The latter ceased to be moody; he became more sociable and less resentful towards other men.

Some of the documents I had received to be read at the congress treated of the importance of the discussion of sex problems in the anarchist press and lectures. Kate Austen's paper was particularly strong, giving the history of the American movement for freedom in love. Kate was no mincer of words; frankly and directly she set forth her views of sex as a vital factor in life. Victor assured me that certain French comrades would not consent to have Kate's paper read at the congress; surely not to discuss it. I could hardly believe it. The French, of all people! Victor explained that not being puritanical does not always mean being free. " The French have not the same serious attitude towards sex as the idealists in America," he said. " They are cynical about it and cannot see more than the mere physical side. Our older French comrades have always loathed such an attitude, and in protest against it they have outdone the Puritans. They now fear that any discussion of sex would serve only to increase the misconceptions of anarchism." I was not convinced, but a week later Victor informed me that one group had definitely decided not to have the American reports dealing with sex read at the congress. They might be taken up at private gatherings, but not at public meetings with the press representatives present.

I protested, and declared that I would immediately get in touch with the comrades in the United States and ask them to relieve me of the credentials and the instructions they had given me. While realizing that the matter in question was only one of the numerous issues involved in anarchism, yet I could not co-operate with a congress that attempted to silence opinion or suppress views that failed to meet the approval of certain elements.

One day, while in a café with Max and Victor, I read in the afternoon papers about the killing of King Humbert by an anarchist. The name of the *Attentäter* was Gaetano Bresci.

I remembered the name as that of an active comrade of the anarchist group in Paterson, New Jersey. Strange that he should have committed such an act, I thought; he had impressed me so differently from most of the other Italians I knew. He was not at all of an excitable temperament and not easily aroused. What could have induced him to take the life of the King of Italy, I wondered. Victor ascribed the protracted hunger riots in Milan, in 1898, as the probable cause of Bresci's deed. Many workers' lives had been lost on that occasion through the attack of the soldiery upon the starving and unarmed people. They had marched towards the palace to demonstrate their misery, the women carrying their children in their arms. They had found the palace surrounded by a strong military force under command of General Bava Beccaris. The people ignored the order to disperse, whereupon the General gave the signal that resulted in a massacre of the demonstrants. King Humbert complimented Beccaris upon his " brave defence of the royal house," decorating him for his murderous work.

Max and Victor agreed with me that those tragic events must have induced Bresci to come all the way from America to carry out his act. Max thought I was lucky not to be in the States, else I would surely be held responsible in some way for the death of Humbert, as had invariably been the case in the past whenever any political act of violence took place anywhere in the world. I was less concerned about such an eventuality than over the fate that awaited Bresci. I knew what tortures would be his lot in prison and I recalled the fearful treatment of Luccheni, a similar victim of the ruthless social struggle.

We remained for some time in the café, discussing the incredible waste of human life involved in the terrible war of the classes in every country. I confided to my friends the doubts that had been assailing me since Sasha's act, though I fully realized the inevitability of such deeds resulting from existing conditions.

Shortly afterwards I learned through Victor that the Neo-Malthusian Congress was soon to meet in Paris. Its sessions would have to be secret because the French Government proscribed any organized attempt to limit offspring. Dr. Drysdale, the pioneer of birth limitation, and his sister were already in Paris, and other delegates were arriving from various countries. In France it was largely Paul Robin and Madeleine Verné, who were backing the Neo-Malthusian movement, Victor explained.

I knew Madeleine Verné, but who was Paul Robin? My friend informed me that he was one of the great libertarians in the field of education. Out of his own means he had bought a large tract of land on which he established a school for destitute children. Sempuis, the place was called. Robin had taken homeless waifs from the street or from orphan asylums, the poorest and the so-called bad children. " You should see them now! " Victor said; " Robin's school is a living example of what can be done in education by an attitude of understanding and love for the child." He promised to afford me an opportunity to attend the Neo-Malthusian Congress and to visit Sempuis.

The Neo-Malthusian conference, having to meet under cover, every session in a different place, had a very small attendance, of not more than a dozen delegates. But what it lacked in numbers it made up in vital interest. Dr. Drysdale, the venerable advocate of family limitation, was full of enthusiasm for the cause. Miss Drysdale, his sister, Paul Robin, and their co-workers were admirable in the simplicity and earnestness with which they presented the subject, and very brave in the demonstration of preventive methods. I marvelled at their ability to discuss such a delicate matter so frankly and in such an inoffensive manner. I thought of my former patients on the East Side and the blessing it would have meant to them if they could have procured the contraceptives described at these sessions. The delegates were amused when I told them of my vain efforts, as midwife, to find some way of helping the poor women in the States. They thought that, with Anthony Comstock supervising American morals, it would take many years before methods to prevent conception could be discussed openly in that country. I pointed out to them, however, that even in France they had to meet in secret and I assured them that I knew many people in America brave enough to do good, even if prohibited, work. At any rate, I decided to take the matter up on my return to New York. I was complimented on my attitude by the delegates and supplied with literature and contraceptives for my future work.

My money was dwindling fast, but still we could not forgo the pleasure of visiting theatres and museums and hearing music. The concerts at the Trocadero were particularly interesting, among them those by the Finnish orchestra, including folk-songs by magnificent artists, with Mme Aïno Ackté, the prima donna of the Paris Opéra, as the soloist. The Russian Balalaika Orchestra, Wagner performances, and a recital by Ysaye, the magician of the violin, were rare treats. A favourite place was the Théâtre Libre, managed by Antoine; it was the only dramatic venture in Paris worth seeing. With the exception of

Sarah Bernhardt, the Coquelins, and Mme. Réjane, the Paris stage impressed me as declamatory. Compared with Eleonora Duse even "Divine Sarah" appeared theatrical. The one play in which she was her great self was *Cyrano de Bergerac,* with Coquelin playing Cyrano to her Roxane. The group under Antoine had abolished the star system; their ensemble acting was of the highest order.

During my stay in Europe I could not correspond with Sasha directly. Our letters passed through a friend, entailing long delays. Sasha was permitted to write only one letter a month; on rare occasions, thanks to the friendship of the prison chaplain, he was allowed an extra letter. In order to keep in touch with as many correspondents as possible, Sasha had devised a scheme of dividing his writing-paper into four, five, or even six separate parts, each filled on both sides with diminutive writing, clear as an etching. The recipient of his letter on the outside would cut the sheet according to the indicated divisions and then mail the various parts as directed. His last note to me had been cheerful, even jocular. He had asked for souvenirs of the Exposition and detailed accounts of things happening in Paris. But that was over two months ago, nothing having reached me since. Eric also wrote seldom, only a line or two about the "invention," which was apparently progressing slowly. I was beginning to grow anxious. Max and Hippolyte tried to explain away my fears and forebodings, but it was evident that they were also very uneasy.

One morning I was awakened at an early hour by Hippolyte violently knocking on my door. He entered excitedly, a French newspaper in his hand. He started to say something; his lips moved, but he could not utter a word. "What is it?" I cried in instinctive apprehension. "Why don't you speak?" "The tunnel, the tunnel!" he whispered hoarsely; "it has been discovered. It is in the paper."

With fainting heart I thought of Sasha, his terrible disappointment at the failure of the project, the disastrous consequences, his desperate position. Sasha again thrust back into the black hopelessness of eleven more years in his inferno. What now? What now? I must go back to America at once. I should have never gone away! I had failed Sasha, I felt; I had left him when he needed me most. Yes, I must go back to America as quickly as possible.

But that very afternoon a cable from Eric B. Morton prevented my putting the plan into immediate action. "Sudden illness. Work suspended. Sailing for France," the message read. I should have to await his arrival.

The nervous tension of the days that followed would have been beyond my endurance were it not for the intensive work I had to do. Within a fortnight Eric appeared. I hardly recognized him; the change he had undergone since I saw him in Pittsburgh was appalling. The big, strong viking had grown very thin, his face ashen and covered with blisters full of pus.

As soon as Tony finally got in touch with him, Eric related, he went to Pittsburgh to attend to the preliminary arrangements. His first impression of Tony was not very favourable. Tony seemed obsessed by his self-importance over his part in Sasha's projects. Sasha had devised a special cipher for underground communications, and Tony, being the only person able to read it, exploited the situation by arbitrary behaviour and directions. Not a mechanic, Tony had little idea of the difficulties involved in the construction of the tunnel, and the danger attending the digging of it. The house they had rented on Sterling Street was almost directly opposite the main gate of the prison and about two hundred feet distant from it. From the cellar of the house the tunnel had to be dug in a slightly circular line in the direction of the southern gate, then underneath it and into the prison yard towards an outhouse indicated by Sasha on his diagram. Sasha was to manage somehow to leave the cell-block, reach the outhouse unobserved, tear up its wooden flooring, and, opening the tunnel, crawl through into the cellar of the house. There he would find citizen's clothes, money, and cipher directions where to meet his friends. But work on the tunnel was taking more time and money than had been expected. Eric and the other comrades working on the tunnel came upon unexpected difficulties in the rocky formation of the soil in the neighbourhood of the prison wall. It was found necessary to dig underneath its foundations, and there Eric and his co-workers were nearly asphyxiated by poisonous fumes leaking into the tunnel from some unknown source. This unforeseen trouble resulted in much delay and involved the installation of machinery to supply fresh air to the men toiling prostrate in the narrow passage deep in the bowels of the earth. The sounds of digging might attract the attention of the alert look-outs on the prison wall, and Eric hit upon the idea of hiring a piano and inviting a woman friend of his, Kinsella, a splendid musician, to come to his aid. Her singing and playing masked the noises from below, and the guards on the wall greatly enjoyed the fine performances of Kinsella.

The " invention " was a most ingenious undertaking, but also very dangerous, requiring great engineering skill and the utmost care in avoiding the least suspicion on the part of the prison guards and the passers-by on the street. At the first sign of danger the pianist would press an electric button near at hand to warn the diggers underground to cease operations immediately. Then all would remain quiet till she would again burst out into song. The staccato piano chords would be the signal that all was well. " Digging under such conditions was no snap," Eric continued. " To save time and expense we had decided to make the tunnel very narrow, just wide enough for a person to crawl through. Our work therefore could not be carried on even by kneeling. We had to lie flat on the stomach and do the drilling with one hand. It was so exhausting it was impossible to keep at it more than half an hour at a time. Naturally progress was slow. But what was more exasperating was that Tony constantly shifted from one idea to another. We wanted to keep strictly to Sasha's plans. The latter insisted on it all the time and we felt that he, being on the inside, knew best. But Tony was bent on carrying out his own notions. Sasha evidently considered it too dangerous to give us directions even in his underground letters; he did so only in his cipher, which no one except Tony could read. Therefore we were compelled to take our instructions from Tony. Well, at last the tunnel was finished."

" And then — and then? " I cried unable to contain myself any longer.

" Why, didn't anyone write you? " Eric asked in surprise. " When Sasha tried to make his escape through the hole in the prison yard where the tunnel terminated, according to Tony's directions, he found it covered with a pile of bricks and stone. They were putting up a new building in the penitentiary and they had emptied a wagon-load of rock just over the spot that Tony had selected as the terminal of the tunnel. You can imagine how Sasha must have felt about it, and the danger to which he had exposed himself by escaping from the cell-house only to have to return again. The most dreadful thing about it was that, as we learned later, Sasha had repeatedly warned Tony against ending the tunnel in the middle of the prison yard, as Tony had proposed to him. Sasha was absolutely against it, knowing that it was bound to prove a failure. His original plan called for the tunnel to terminate in a deserted outhouse, about twenty feet from that hole. Believing that we had dug the tunnel to the point desired by Sasha, and that our work was completed, we departed for New York, only Tony remaining in Pittsburgh. Sasha was desperate at Tony's arbitrary change from his instructions. He insisted that the digging be continued farther and up to the outhouse, according to his diagram. Tony finally realized the fatal results of his mad obstinacy. He notified Sasha that his wishes would be carried out and he immediately left for New York to see us with a view to raising more money to complete the tunnel. Our house opposite the prison was left vacant. During Tony's absence children playing in the street somehow got into the cellar, discovered the secret passage, and notified their parents, among whom was the agent of the house. Strange to say, he proved also to be a guard in the Western Penitentiary."

I sat silent, crushed by the thought of what Sasha must have gone through during the weeks and months of suspense and anxious waiting for the completion of the tunnel, only to have all his hopes blighted almost in sight of liberty.

"The most amazing thing is," Eric continued, "that to this day the prison officials have been unable to find out for whom the tunnel was intended. The police departments of Pittsburgh and Allegheny, as well as the State authorities, agreed that the tunnel was one of the cleverest pieces of engineering they had ever seen. The Warden and the Board of Prison Inspectors suspect Sasha, but they can find no proof to support their charges, while the police claim the tunnel was intended for a certain Boyd, a prominent forger serving a long term. No clues have been discovered; but at any rate they put Sasha in solitary."

"In solitary!" I screamed. "No wonder I haven't heard from him for so long!" "Yes, he's under very severe punishment," Eric admitted. The purgatory Sasha had already endured, the ghastly years still ahead of him, flitted through my mind. "They will kill him!" I groaned. I knew they were killing him inch by inch, and here I was away in Paris and unable to help him, to do anything, anything! "Better a thousand times for me to have been in prison than to sit by and helplessly see them murdering Sasha!" I cried. "That wouldn't do Sasha any good," Eric retorted; "in fact, it would make it harder for him, harder to bear his lot. You must realize that, so why eat your heart out?"

Why, why? Could I explain what those years had been to me, ever since that black day in July 1892. Life is inexorable; it does not let you pause at any point. My own life had been crowded with events, following each in quick succession. There had been little time to indulge in retrospection of the past, but it had eaten into my consciousness, and nothing could ever still its gnawing. Yet life kept on its course. There was no cessation.

Eric was hardly able to keep on his feet. He was completely exhausted by what he had endured working in the tunnel; its poisonous fumes had infected his blood and produced a serious skin-disease. His condition became so bad that he had to be put to bed and I nursed him for weeks. But the dear man, true viking that he was, kept laughing and joking, with never a word of complaint or regret over the perilous hardships he had endured in the luckless venture to aid Sasha's escape.

Our scheduled congress did not take place. At the last moment the authorities prohibited the public gathering of foreign anarchists. We held some sessions, nevertheless, in private homes, in the environs of Paris. Under the circumstances and in view of the necessary secrecy of our proceedings, we had time to discuss only the most urgent problems.

The presence of Eric involved additional expenditure, and I found it imperative to earn some money. He had worked his way across and he did not have a cent left. A number of friends were living in the same hotel with me and I conceived the idea of preparing breakfast and luncheon for them. It was a big job to cook for twelve and even more persons on a single alcohol burner. Hippolyte was very helpful, being much better at marketing than I, as well as a first-class chef. Our " boarders " were nearly all foreign comrades, easily satisfied with the meals we served. It enabled us to earn a little money, though far from enough. Hippolyte and I contrived to take small parties to the Exposition. I did pretty well, though it was boring to guide dull Americans about. One chap, on seeing Voltaire's statue, demanded to know who " that guy " was and what had been his business. Several school-teachers, who had been recommended to me by a friend, almost fell into a faint when they saw the nude statues in the Luxembourg. I would return home thoroughly disgusted with the rôle of cicerone.

One afternoon I came back to my hotel determined never again to serve as guide to sightseers unless it be to a certain very hot place. In my room I found a huge bouquet of flowers and a note beside it. The handwriting was unfamiliar, the contents puzzling: " An admirer of long standing would like you to join him for a pleasant evening. Will you meet him tonight at the Café du Chatelet? You may bring a friend along." I wondered who the man could be.

The " admirer of long standing " turned out to be none other than Eric. With him were three other comrades from America. " What's up? " both Hippolyte and I asked simultaneously. " Have you discovered a gold-mine? " " Not exactly," Eric replied; " my grandmother, who died a few months ago, left me a legacy of seven hundred francs, which I received today. We're going to blow it all in tonight." " Don't you want to get back to the United States? " I inquired. " Of course I do." " Then let me have half of your legacy for your return fare," I suggested; " the rest I am perfectly willing to help you blow in." Laughingly he turned three hundred and fifty francs over to me for safe-keeping.

We dined, wined, and made merry. Everyone was gay and still firm on his feet when at two o'clock in the morning we landed at the Rat Mort, a famous Montmartre cabaret, where Eric ordered champagne. Across from us sat a very attractive French girl, and Eric asked if he might invite her to our table. " Sure," I said, " the only woman in the company of five men, I can afford to be generous." The girl joined us, drank, and danced with the boys. Our viking, remarkably lithe despite his two hundred pounds, danced like a nymph. After an exciting waltz the boys lifted their glasses in a toast to E. G., and I drank mine down without a stop. Suddenly all went black before me.

I woke up in my room with a splitting headache, deathly ill. The French girl of the cabaret was sitting near my bed. " What has happened? " I demanded. " *Rien du tout, chérie;* you felt a bit sick last night," she replied. I asked her to call my friends, and in a short time Eric and Hippolyte entered. " I feel as if I had been poisoned," I told them. " Not quite," Eric retorted; " but one of the boys poured a glass of cognac into your champagne." " And then? " " Then we had to carry you downstairs. We hailed a cab, but we could not make you get into it. You sat down on the sidewalk and shouted that you were Emma Goldman, the anarchist, protesting that you would not be forced. It took the five of us to get you into the cab." I was dumbfounded; I could not remember a thing about it.

" We were none of us any too steady on our feet," Eric went on. " But we sobered up quick enough when we saw in what condition you were." " And the girl — how does she happen to be here? " I asked. " She simply would not let us take you without her accompanying you. She must have thought we were bandits intending to rob you. She insisted on coming with us." " But the poor girl lost her earnings for the night," I protested.

Hippolyte put twenty francs in an envelope and sent the girl home in a cab. In the late afternoon she returned to me. " What do you mean by insulting me? " she cried, almost weeping; " do you think a girl who makes her living on the street has no feelings? That she would take money for helping a friend in distress? No, indeed, nursing isn't my profession, and I won't be paid for it." I held out my hand to her and drew her down to me. I was affected almost to tears by the beauty of that child-woman and her fine, tender spirit.

The inspiring atmosphere of our movement in Paris and my other delightful experiences in the city made me wish to prolong my stay. But it was time to leave. Our money was almost entirely exhausted. Besides, detectives had already been at the hotel looking for information about Mme Brady. It was a wonder the police had not yet ordered me out of the country. Victor Dave suggested that it was because of the Exposition; the authorities wanted to avoid unpleasant publicity about foreigners. On an early morning, dark and drizzling, Eric, Hippolyte, and I drove to the railroad station. We were followed by several secret-service men in a cab and one on a bicycle. They waved good-bye to us as the train pulled out, but one of them we found in the compartment next to our coupé. He followed us to Boulogne, leaving only when we boarded the boat.

Only thanks to the gift sent me by my dear friend Anna Stirling were we able to pay our hotel bills and fares, and still have about fifteen dollars left. It would be enough for tips and other expenses during our journey. I knew I could borrow some money in New York, and Eric said he would wire to Chicago for funds, when necessary.

When the steamer was a few hours out, Hippolyte became seasick, getting worse with the increasing motion. On the third day he was so ill that the doctor ordered iced champagne. He looked so yellow and thin that I was afraid he would not last to the end of the trip. Meanwhile Eric had developed a ravenous appetite. Three times each day he would begin at the top of the menu and end at the bottom. " Don't make the waiter work so hard! " I pleaded with him; " we haven't enough money for tips." But he kept on feeding. He was a born sailor, he loved the sea, and he grew jollier and more hungry every day. At the end of the crossing I had just two dollars and fifteen cents left, which

I divided among the stewards and stewardesses that had served Hippolyte and me. Our viking was left to face the music. The brave fellow, who had for months lived in constant danger of a cave-in in the tunnel, now quailed before the employees of the ship. He actually kept in hiding. The dining-room steward was inexorable and he pursued Eric. But when the latter stood before him shamefaced, like a schoolboy, with his pockets turned inside out, the cruel steward took pity and let him go.

My precious " baby " brother, tall and handsome, was at the dock to greet me. He was considerably surprised to see me return with a bodyguard of two. We went immediately to a pawnshop to hock my clamshell watch, for which I received ten whole dollars, enough to pay for a week's rent in a Clinton Street room and treat the company to dinner.

CHAPTER XXIII

D IRECTLY I WAS SETTLED IN MY NEW ROOM, I WENT TO SEE JUSTUS Schwab. I found him in bed, a mere shadow of his former self. A lump rose in my throat at the sight of our giant so wasted. I knew that Mrs. Schwab worked very hard taking care of the saloon and I begged her to let me nurse Justus. She promised, though she was sure that the sick man would have no one attend him but herself. We were all aware of the tender relationship that existed between Justus and his family. His wife had been his companion all through the years. She had always been the picture of health, but Justus's illness, worry, and overwork were visibly telling on her; she had lost her bloom and looked wan.

While I was talking to Mrs. Schwab, Ed came in. He became embarrassed on seeing me; I also was confused. He quickly regained control of himself and approached us. Mrs. Schwab excused herself by saying she had to look after her patient, and we were left alone. It was a painful moment, to which neither of us could for some time find the right approach.

I had not been in touch with Ed during my stay abroad, but I knew of his life through our common friends, who had written me about the birth of Ed's child. I asked him how it felt to be a father. He became animated at once, launching into a pæan over his little daughter and enlarging upon her charm and remarkable intelligence. I was amused to see that baby-hater waxing so enthusiastic. I remembered that he had always refused to move into a house where there were children. " I see you don't believe me," he remarked presently; " you are astonished that I am so excited about it. Well, it isn't because *I* happen to be the father, but because my little girl is really an exceptional child." It was amazing to hear it from the man who used to say that " most human beings are foolish, but parents are both foolish and blind: they imagine their children to be prodigies and expect the whole world to be of the same opinion."

I assured him that I did not doubt him, but in order that I might make quite certain he had better let me see the wonder-child. "You really want to see her? You really want me to bring her to you?" he cried. "Why, yes, of course," I replied; "you know I have always been fond of children — why should I not be of yours?" He was silent for a while. Then he said: "Our love has not been much of a success, has it?" "Is love ever?" I responded; "ours lasted seven years, which most people would consider a long time." "You have grown wise during the past year, dear Emma," he answered. "No, only older, dear Ed." We parted with the promise of meeting again soon.

At the Russian New Year's *vetcherinka* Ed was present in the company of a woman — his wife, I was sure. She was large, and she talked in a rather loud voice. Ed had always abhorred this trait in women; how did he stand it now? Friends besieged me, and comrades from the East Side came to question me about the movement in England and in France. I did not see Ed again that evening.

The most urgent necessity on my arrival in America was to secure employment. I had left my visiting-card with several of my medical friends, but weeks passed and not a single call came. Hippolyte tried to get something to do on the Czech anarchist weekly. There was plenty of work there, but no payment; it was considered unethical to accept money for writing for an anarchist paper. All the foreign-language publications, with the exception of the *Freiheit* and the *Freie Arbeiter Stimme,* were got out by the voluntary labour of men who earned their living at some trade, giving their evenings and Sundays gratis to the needs of the movement. Hippolyte, not having a profession, was even more helpless in New York than he had been in London. Boarding-houses in America rarely employed men.

At last on Christmas Eve Dr. Hoffmann sent for me. "The patient is a morphine addict," he informed me, "a very difficult and trying case. The night nurse had to be given a week off; she could not stand the strain. You have been called to substitute for a week." The prospect was not enticing, but I needed work.

It was almost midnight when I arrived with the doctor at the patient's house. In a large room on the second floor a woman was lying half dressed on the bed, in a stupor. Her face, framed in a mass of black hair, was white and she was breathing heavily. Looking about,

I noticed on the wall the portrait of a heavy man peering at me out of small, hard eyes. I recognized the likeness as that of a person I had seen before, but I could not recollect where or under what circumstances. Dr. Hoffmann began giving me directions. The patient's name was Mrs. Spenser, he said. He had been treating her for some time, trying to cure her of the drug habit. She had been making good progress, but recently she had suffered a relapse and taken to morphine again. Nothing could be done for her until she came out of her stupor. I should watch her pulse and keep her warm. Mrs. Spenser hardly stirred during the night. I tried to while away the time by reading, but I could not concentrate. The picture of the man on the wall haunted me. When the day nurse arrived, the patient was still asleep, though breathing more normally.

Soon my week was nearly over. During the entire time Mrs. Spenser had shown no interest in her surroundings. She would open her eyes, stare vacantly, and doze off to sleep again. When I came on duty on the sixth night, I found her fully conscious. Her hair looked neglected and I asked her whether she would like me to comb and braid it. She consented gladly. While I was doing it, she inquired what my name was. " Goldman," I said. " Are you related to Emma Goldman, the anarchist? " " Very much so," I replied, " I am the guilty party." To my surprise she appeared much pleased to have such a " famous person " for her nurse. She asked me to take full charge of her case, saying that she liked me better than her other nurses. It was flattering to my professional vanity, but I did not feel it right to have the other nurses discharged on my account. Besides, the strain of twenty-four hours' straight duty would make it impossible for me to give her the care she needed. She begged me to stay, promising that I should have every afternoon off and a rest during the night.

Some time later Mrs. Spenser inquired whether I knew the original of the portrait. I told her he looked familiar, but that I could not place him. She did not discuss the matter further.

The house, the furniture, the large library of good books, all bespoke the intelligence and good taste of their owner. There was a curious, mystifying air about the apartment, heightened by the daily visits of a woman, coarse-looking and gaudily attired. The moment she arrived my patient would send me on an errand. I welcomed the opportunity for a walk in the fresh air, wondering at the same time who the person might be with whom Mrs. Spenser had always to be alone. At first I suspected that the strange visitor might be supplying her with drugs, but as there were no evil consequences to my patient, I dismissed the matter as not being my concern.

At the end of the third week Mrs. Spenser was able to go downstairs to her parlour. In the process of putting the sick-room in order I came across peculiar slips of paper marked: " Jeannette, 20 times; Marion, 16; Henriette, 12." There were about forty names of women, each checked off by a number. What a strange record! I thought. When about to join my patient in the sitting-room, I was arrested by a voice that I recognized as that of Mrs. Spenser's visitor. " MacIntyre was at the house again last night," I heard her say, " but none of the girls wanted him. Jeannette said she preferred twenty others to that filthy creature." Mrs. Spenser must have heard my step, for the conversation suddenly broke off, and she called through the door, " Is that you, Miss Goldman? Please come in." As I entered, the tea-tray I carried crashed to the ground, and I stood staring at a man sitting next to my patient on the sofa. It was the original of the portrait and I immediately recognized him as the detective-sergeant who had been instrumental in sending me to the penitentiary in 1893.

The slips of paper, the report I had just overheard — I understood it all in a flash. Spenser was the keeper of a " house," and the detective her paramour. I fled to the second storey, filled with the one idea of getting out and away from the house. Hastening downstairs with my suit-case, I saw Mrs. Spenser at the bottom of the stairs, hardly able to stand, her hands nervously gripping the banister. I realized that I could not leave her in that state; I was responsible to Dr. Hoffmann, for whom I must wait. I led Mrs. Spenser to her room and put her to bed.

She burst into hysterical sobbing, begging me not to go away and assuring me that I should never have to see the man again; she would even have his portrait removed. She admitted being the keeper of a house. " I dreaded to have you find it out," she said, " but I did think that Emma Goldman, the anarchist, would not condemn me for being a cog in a machine I did not create." Prostitution was not of her making, she argued; and since it existed, it did not matter who was " in charge." If not she, it would be someone else. She did not think keeping girls was any worse than underpaying them in factories; at least she had always been kind to them. I could inquire of them myself if I wished. She talked incessantly, weeping herself into exhaustion. I remained.

Mrs. Spenser's " reasons " did not influence me. I knew that

everyone offered the same excuse for vile deeds, the policeman as well
as the judge, the soldier as well as the highest war-lord; everybody
who lives off the labour and degradation of others. I felt, however,
that in my capacity as nurse I could not concern myself with the particular trade or occupation of my patients. I had to minister to their
physical needs. Besides, I was not only a nurse, I was also an anarchist
who knew the social factors behind human action. As such, even more
than as a nurse I could not refuse her my services.

My four months with Mrs. Spenser gave me considerable experience
in psychology. She was an unusual person, intelligent, observant, and
understanding. She knew life and men, all sorts of men, in every
social stratum. The house she kept was " high-class "; among its
patrons were some of the strongest pillars of society: doctors, lawyers,
judges, and preachers. The man whom the girls " hated like the pest "
was none other, I found out, than a New York lawyer prominent in
the nineties — the very same who had assured the jury that Emma
Goldman, if free, would endanger the lives of the children of the
rich and cover the streets of New York with blood.

Indeed, Mrs. Spenser knew men, and, knowing them, she felt nothing but contempt and hatred for them. Over and again she would say
that not one of her girls was so depraved as the men who bought them,
or so barren of common humanity. Her sympathies were always on
the side of the girls when a " guest " complained. That she had intense feeling for suffering she often demonstrated, and not only in her
dealings with the girls, many of whom I met and talked with;
she was kind to every beggar on the street. She loved children passionately. When she would come upon some urchin, no matter how ragged
or filthy, she would pet him and give him money. Repeatedly I heard
her lament: " If I only had a child! A child of my own! "

Her story was a veritable novel. As a girl of sixteen, very beautiful,
she fell in love with a dashing army officer in Ruthenia, her native
country. By promises of marriage he made her his mistress. When she
became pregnant, he took her to Vienna, where an operation almost
killed her. After she had recuperated, the man went with her to Cra-
cow, where he left her in a house of prostitution. She had no money,
did not know a soul in the city, and found herself a slave in the house.
Later one of the patrons bought her free and took her on a long
voyage. For five years she travelled over Europe with her keeper, and
then she again was stranded, without friends, the street her only

refuge. Several years passed. She had grown wise; she had saved some money and she decided to go to America. Here she drifted into acquaintance with a wealthy politician. When he left her, she had enough money to open up a house.

The remarkable trait about Mrs. Spenser was that she had not become affected by the life through which she had passed. There was not a coarse grain in her and she remained touchingly sensitive, a lover of music and of good literature.

Dr. Hoffmann's treatment gradually weaned her from the use of drugs, but it left her physically weak and subject to attacks of dizziness. She could not go out alone and I became her companion as well as nurse. I read to her, accompanied her to concerts, the opera, and the theatre, occasionally even to lectures in which she was interested.

While nursing Mrs. Spenser I became engaged in work preparatory to the projected visit of Peter Kropotkin. He had notified us that he was coming to America to deliver a series of lectures at the Lowell Institute on Ideals in Russian Literature, and that he would also be able to talk on anarchism if we wished it. We were enthusiastic over the prospect. I had missed the lectures of our dear comrade on his previous tour. In England I had had no opportunity to hear him. We all felt that Peter's lectures and gracious personality would be of inestimable value to our movement in the United States. When Mrs. Spenser heard of my activity, she immediately offered to relieve me evenings, so that I might have more leisure to devote to the work.

From all parts of the city people came streaming in to Grand Central Palace to hear Peter Kropotkin on the first Sunday afternoon in May. For once even the papers were decent: they could not gainsay the man's charm, the power of his intellect, the simplicity and logic of his delivery and argumentation. In the audience was also Mrs. Spenser, completely carried away by the speaker.

A social evening was being prepared for Kropotkin, an unofficial affair, to enable him to meet the comrades and others in sympathy with our ideas. Mrs. Spenser inquired whether she would be admitted. " What if your friends find out who I am ? " she asked anxiously. I assured her that my friends were in no way akin to Anthony Comstock and that no one would by word or deed make her feel out of place. She looked wonderingly at me out of her luminous eyes.

The evening before the social gathering several of the more intimate comrades dined with our beloved teacher. I related the story of

Mrs. Spenser. Peter was much interested; she was a real human document, he thought. Indeed, he would meet my patient, and autograph a copy of his *Memoirs* for her, as she had requested. Before I left, Peter embraced me. "You are giving a convincing example of the beauty and humanity of our ideals," he remarked. I knew that he, so rich in compassion, understood why I had remained to care for the social pariah.

At last my patient was far enough advanced in her cure to dispense with me. I was eager to go on tour. The comrades in a number of cities had been urging me to come for lectures. There were also other reasons. One of them was Pittsburgh. I had no hopes of being able to see Sasha; he had been deprived of visits entirely after my dreadful encounter with Prison Inspector Reed. Since the failure of the tunnel my tortured boy had been in solitary, with all his privileges taken away. The rare *sub rosa* notes he was able to send out gave no indication of what he was enduring. They only helped to increase my feeling of the hopelessness of his situation. I kept on writing to him, but it was like sending letters into the void. I had no way of knowing whether they reached him. The prison authorities would never let me see Sasha again, but they could not prevent me from going to Pittsburgh, where I could feel nearer to him.

Hippolyte had left for Chicago to work on the *Arbeiter Zeitung*. The offer of employment had come at a period when life had become insupportable to him, and he in turn had added much to my unhappiness. The thought that he would now have the soothing companionship of Max, as well as work he was fitted to do, gave me much consolation. I was planning to meet him in Chicago.

Ed came often to visit me or to invite me to dinner. He was charming and there was no sign of the storm that had tossed us about for seven years. It had given way to a calm friendship. He did not bring his little daughter and I suspected that the mother must have objected to my seeing the child. Whether she also resented our companionship I had no way of knowing. Ed never mentioned her. When he learned that I was about to begin a lecture tour, he asked me again to act as the representative of his firm.

Before leaving for the West I kept a previous engagement in Paterson, New Jersey, where the local Italian group had arranged a meeting for me. Our Italian comrades were always most hospitable, and on this occasion they prepared an informal social to follow my lecture. I was glad of the opportunity to find out more about Bresci and his life. What I learned from his closest comrades convinced me once more how difficult it is to gain a real insight into the human heart and how likely we all are to judge men by superficial indications.

Gaetano Bresci was one of the founders of *La Questione Sociale,* the Italian anarchist paper published in Paterson. He was a skilful weaver, considered by his employers a sober, hard-working man, but his pay averaged only fifteen dollars a week. He had a wife and child to support; yet he managed to donate weekly contributions to the paper. He had even saved a hundred and fifty dollars, which he lent to the group at a critical period of *La Questione Sociale.* His free evenings and Sundays he used to spend in helping with the office work and in propaganda. He was beloved and respected for his devotion by all the members of his group.

Then one day Bresci had unexpectedly asked that his loan to the paper be returned. He was informed that it was impossible; the paper had no funds and had, in fact, a deficit. But Bresci insisted and even refused to offer any explanation for his demand. Finally the group succeeded in securing enough money to pay back the debt to Bresci. But the Italian comrades bitterly resented Bresci's behaviour, branding him as a miser, who loved money above his ideal. Most of his friends even ostracized him.

A few weeks later came the news that Gaetano Bresci had killed King Humbert. His act brought home to the Paterson group the realization of how cruelly they had wronged the man. He had insisted on the return of his money in order to secure the fare to Italy! No doubt the consciousness of the injustice done Bresci rested heavier on the Italian comrades than his resentment against them. To make amends, in a sense, the Paterson group charged itself with the support of their martyred comrade's child, a beautiful little girl. His widow, on the other hand, gave no indication that she either understood the spirit of her child's father or was in sympathy with his great sacrifice.

The subject of my lecture in Cleveland, early in May of that year, was Anarchism, delivered before the Franklin Liberal Club, a radical organization. During the intermission before the discussion I noticed a man looking over the titles of the pamphlets and books on sale near the platform. Presently he came over to me with the question: " Will you suggest something for me to read? " He was working in Akron, he explained, and he would have to leave before the close of the meeting.

He was very young, a mere youth, of medium height, well built, and carrying himself very erect. But it was his face that held me, a most sensitive face, with a delicate pink complexion; a handsome face, made doubly so by his curly golden hair. Strength showed in his large blue eyes. I made a selection of some books for him, remarking that I hoped he would find in them what he was seeking. I returned to the platform to open the discussion and I did not see the young man again that evening, but his striking face remained in my memory.

The Isaaks had moved *Free Society* to Chicago, where they occupied a large house, which was the centre of the anarchist activities in that city. On my arrival there, I went to their home and immediately plunged into intense work that lasted eleven weeks. The summer heat became so oppressive that the rest of my tour had to be postponed until September. I was completely exhausted and badly in need of rest. Sister Helena had repeatedly asked me to come to her for a month, but I had not been able to spare the time before. Now was my opportunity. I would have a few weeks with Helena, the children of my two sisters, and Yegor, who was spending his vacation in Rochester. He had two college chums with him, he had written me; to make the circle of young people complete I invited Mary, the fourteen-year-old daughter of the Isaaks, to come with me for a holiday. I had earned some money on orders for Ed's firm and I could afford to play Lady Bountiful to the young people and grow younger with them.

On the day of our departure the Isaaks gave me a farewell luncheon. Afterwards, while I was busy packing my things, someone rang the bell. Mary Isaak came in to tell me that a young man, who gave his name as Nieman, was urgently asking to see me. I knew nobody by that name and I was in a hurry, about to leave for the station. Rather impatiently I requested Mary to inform the caller that I had no time at the moment, but that he could talk to me on my way to the station. As I left the house, I saw the visitor, recognizing him as the handsome chap of the golden hair who had asked me to recommend him reading-matter at the Cleveland meeting.

Hanging on to the straps on the elevated train, Nieman told me that he had belonged to a Socialist local in Cleveland, that he had found its members dull, lacking in vision and enthusiasm. He could not bear to be with them and he had left Cleveland and was now working in Chicago and eager to get in touch with anarchists.

At the station I found my friends awaiting me, among them Max.

I wanted to spend a few minutes with him and I begged Hippolyte to take care of Nieman and introduce him to the comrades.

The Rochester youngsters took me to their hearts. My two sisters' children, my brother Yegor and his chums, and young Mary, all combined to fill the days with the loveliness only young ardent souls can give. It was a new and exhilarating experience, to which I completely abandoned myself. The roof of Helena's house became our garden and the gathering-place where my youthful friends confided to me their dreams and aspirations.

Our picnics with the young folks were especially delightful. Harry, sister Lena's eldest child, was a Republican at ten, a regular campaign spellbinder. It was fun to hear him defend McKinley, his hero, and argue against *Tante* Emma. He shared the family admiration for me, regretting, however, that I did not belong to his camp. Saxe, Harry's brother, was of an entirely different type. In character he resembled Helena much more than his own mother, having a good deal of the former's shyness and timidity, and giving the same impression of sadness. He also shared Helena's boundless capacity for love. His ideal was David, Helena's youngest son, whose word was sacred to Saxe. This was not surprising, because David was a splendid specimen of a boy. Of fine physique and pleasing appearance, his unusual musical talents and his love of fun won him the heart of everyone. I loved all these children, but next to Stella it was Saxe who came nearest my heart, perhaps mainly because I was aware that he lacked the coarser equipment necessary for the struggle of life.

My holiday in Rochester was somewhat marred by a notice in *Free Society* containing a warning against Nieman. It was written by A. Isaak, editor of the paper, and it stated that news had been received from Cleveland that the man had been asking questions that aroused suspicion, and that he was trying to get into the anarchist circles. The comrades in Cleveland had concluded that he must be a spy.

I was very angry. To make such a charge, on such flimsy grounds! I wrote Isaak at once, demanding more convincing proofs. He replied that, while he had no other evidence, he still felt that Nieman was untrustworthy because he constantly talked about acts of violence. I wrote another protest. The next issue of *Free Society* contained a retraction.

The Pan-American Exposition, held at Buffalo, interested me and I had long wanted also to see the Niagara Falls. But I could not leave my precious youngsters behind and I did not have enough money to take them with me. Dr. Kaplan, a Buffalo friend, who knew that I was holidaying with my family, solved our difficulties. He had asked me before to pay him a visit and bring my friends along. When I wrote him that my means would not allow such a luxury, he called me up on the long-distance telephone and offered to contribute forty dollars towards expenses and be our host for a week. In merry anticipation of the adventure, I took the older children to Buffalo. We were treated to a round of festivities, " did " the Falls, saw the Exposition, and enjoyed music and parties, as well as gatherings with comrades, at which the young generation participated in the discussions on a footing of equality.

On our return to Rochester I found two letters from Sasha. The first, *sub rosa,* dated July 10, had evidently been delayed in transmission. Its contents threw me into despair. It read:

> From the hospital. Just out of the strait jacket, after eight days.
> For over a year I was in the strictest solitary; for a long time mail and reading-matter were denied me. . . . I have passed through a great crisis. Two of my best friends died in a frightful manner. The death of Russell, especially, affected me. He was very young, and my dearest and most devoted friend, and he died a terrible death. The doctor charged the boy with shamming, but now he says it was spinal meningitis. I cannot tell you the awful truth—it was nothing short of murder, and my poor friend rotted away by inches. When he died, they found his back one mass of bedsores. If you could read the pitiful letters he wrote, begging to see me and to be nursed by me! But the Warden wouldn't permit it. In some manner his agony seemed to communicate itself to me, and I began to experience the pains and symptoms that Russell described in his notes. I knew it was my sick fancy; I strove against it, but presently my legs showed signs of paralysis, and I suffered excruciating pain in the spinal column, just like Russell. I was afraid that I would be done to death like my poor friend. . . . I was on the verge of suicide. I demanded to be relieved from the cell, and the Warden ordered me punished. I was put in the strait jacket. They bound my body in canvas, strapped my arms to the bed, and chained my feet to the posts. I was kept that way eight days, unable to move, rotting in my own excrement. Released prisoners called the attention of our new Inspector to my case. He refused to believe that such things were being done in the penitentiary. Reports spread that I was going blind and insane. Then the Inspector visited the hospital and had me released from the jacket.

I am in pretty bad shape, but they have put me in the general ward now, and I am glad of the chance to send you this note.

The fiends! It would have been a convenient way to send Sasha into the madhouse or to make him take his own life. I was sick with the thought that I had been living in a world of dreams, youthful fancies and gaiety, while Sasha was undergoing hellish tortures. My heart cried out: " It isn't fair that he alone should go on paying the price — it isn't fair! " My young friends clustered around me in compassion. Stella's large eyes were filled with tears. Yegor held out the other letter, saying: " This is of a later date. It may have better news." I was almost afraid to open it. I had barely read the first paragraph when I cried in joy: " Children — Stella — Yegor! Sasha's term has been commuted! Only five years more and he will be free! Think of it, only five more years! " Breathlessly I went on reading. " I can visit him again! " I exclaimed. " The new Warden has restored his privileges — he can see his friends! " I ran about the room laughing and crying.

Helena rushed up the stairs, followed by Jacob. " What is it? What has happened? " I could only cry: " Sasha! My Sasha! " Gently my sister drew me down on the sofa, took the letter from my hand, and read it aloud in a trembling voice:

> *Direct to Box A 7.*
> *Allegheny City, Pa.*
> *July 25, 1901.*

DEAR FRIEND,—

I cannot tell you how happy I am to be allowed to write to you again. My privileges have been restored by our new Inspector, a very kindly man. He has relieved me from the cell, and now I am again on the range. The Inspector requested me to deny to my friends the reports which have recently appeared in the papers concerning my condition. I have not been well of late, but now I hope to improve. My eyes are very poor. The Inspector has given me permission to have a specialist examine them. Please arrange for it through our local comrades.

There is another piece of very good news, dear friend. A new commutation law has been passed, which reduces my sentence by $2\frac{1}{2}$ years. It still leaves me a long time, of course; almost four years here, and another year in the workhouse. However, it is a considerable gain, and if I should not get into solitary again, I may—I am

almost afraid to utter the thought—I may live to come out. I feel
as if I am being resurrected.

The new law benefits the short-timers proportionately much more
than the men with longer sentences. Only the poor lifers do not
share in it. We were very anxious for a while, as there were many
rumours that the law would be declared unconstitutional. Fortunately, the attempt to nullify its benefits proved ineffectual. Think
of men who will see something unconstitutional in allowing the prisoners a little more good time than the commutation statute of 40 years
ago. As if a little kindness to the unfortunates—really justice—is
incompatible with the spirit of Jefferson! We were greatly worried
over the fate of this statute, but at last the first batch has been released, and there is much rejoicing over it.

There is a peculiar history about this new law, which may interest you; it sheds a significant side-light. It was especially designed
for the benefit of a high Federal officer who was recently convicted
of aiding two wealthy Philadelphia tobacco-manufacturers to de-
fraud the Government of a few millions, by using counterfeit tax
stamps. Their influence secured the introduction of the commutation bill and its hasty passage. The law would have cut their sentences almost in two, but certain newspapers seem to have taken
offence at having been kept in ignorance of the "deal," and protests
began to be voiced. The matter finally came up before the Attorney
General of the United States, who decided that the men in whose
special interest the law was engineered could not benefit by it, because a State law does not affect U.S. prisoners, the latter being
subject to the Federal Commutation Act. Imagine the discomfiture
of the politicians! An attempt was even made to suspend the operation of the statute. Fortunately it failed, and now the "common"
State prisoners, who were not at all meant to profit, are being released. The legislature has unwittingly given some unfortunates
here much happiness.

I was interrupted in this writing by being called out for a visit.
I could hardly credit it: the first comrade I have been allowed to
see in nine years! It was Harry Gordon, and I was so overcome by
the sight of the dear friend, I could barely speak. He must have prevailed upon the new Inspector to issue a permit. The latter is now
Acting Warden, owing to the serious illness of Captain Wright. Perhaps he will allow me to see my sister. Will you kindly communicate
with her at once? Meantime I shall try to secure a pass. With renewed hope, and always with green memory of you,

ALEX

" At last, at last the miracle ! " Helena exclaimed amid tears. She had always admired Sasha. Since his imprisonment she had taken a keen interest in his condition and in every bit of news that had come out of his living grave. She had shared my grief, and now she rejoiced with me over the wonderful news.

Once more I stood within the prison walls of the Western Penitentiary, with fast-beating heart straining to catch the sound of Sasha's step. Nine years had passed since that November day in 1892 when for a fleeting moment I had been brought face to face with him, only again to be wrenched away — nine years replete with the torment of endless time.

" Sasha ! " I rushed forward with outstretched arms. I saw the guard, beside him a man in a grey suit, the same greyness in his face. Could it really be Sasha, so changed, so thin and wan ? He sat mute at my side, fumbling with the fob of my watch-chain. I waited tensely, listening for a word. Sasha made no sound. Only his eyes stared at me, sinking into my very soul. They were Sasha's eyes, startled, tortured eyes. They made me want to weep. I, too, was mute.

" Time's up ! " The sound almost froze my blood. With heavy steps I turned to the corridor, out of the enclosure, through the iron gate into the street.

The same day I left Allegheny City for St. Louis, where I was met by Carl Nold, whom I had not seen for three years. He was the same kind Carl, eager for news of Sasha. He had already learned of the unexpected change in his status and he was highly elated over it. " So you have seen him ! " he cried. " Tell me quickly all about him."

I told him what I could of the ghastly visit. When I had finished he said : " I am afraid your visit to the prison came too soon after his year in solitary. A whole year of enforced isolation, never a chance to exchange a word with another human being, or to hear a kindly voice. You grow numb and incapable of giving expression to your longing for human contact." I understood Sasha's fearful silence.

The following day, September 6, I canvassed every important stationery and novelty store in St. Louis for orders for Ed's firm, but I failed to interest anyone in my samples. Only in one store was I told to call the next day to see the boss. As I stood at a street-corner wearily waiting for a car, I heard a newsboy cry : " Extra ! Extra ! President McKinley shot ! " I bought a paper, but the car was so jammed that it was impossible to read. Around me people were talking about the shooting of the President.

Carl had arrived at the house before me. He had already read the account. The President had been shot at the Exposition grounds in Buffalo by a young man by the name of Leon Czolgosz. " I never heard the name," Carl said; " have you? " " No, never," I replied. " It is fortunate that you are here and not in Buffalo," he continued. " As usual, the papers will connect you with this act." " Nonsense! " I said, " the American press is fantastic enough, but it would hardly concoct such a crazy story."

The next morning I went to the stationery store to see the owner. After considerable persuasion I succeeded in getting an order amounting to a thousand dollars, the largest I had ever secured. Naturally I was very happy over it. While I was waiting for the man to fill out his order, I caught the headline of the newspaper lying on his desk: " ASSASSIN OF PRESIDENT MCKINLEY AN ANARCHIST. CONFESSES TO HAVING BEEN INCITED BY EMMA GOLDMAN. WOMAN ANARCHIST WANTED."

By great effort I strove to preserve my composure, completed the business, and walked out of the store. At the next corner I bought several papers and went to a restaurant to read them. They were filled with the details of the tragedy, reporting also the police raid of the Isaak house in Chicago and the arrest of everyone found there. The authorities were going to hold the prisoners until Emma Goldman was found, the papers stated. Already two hundred detectives had been sent out throughout the country to track down Emma Goldman.

On the inside page of one of the papers was a picture of McKinley's slayer. " Why, that's Nieman! " I gasped.

When I was through with the papers, it became clear to me that I must immediately go to Chicago. The Isaak family, Hippolyte, our old comrade Jay Fox, a most active man in the labour movement, and a number of others were being held without bail until I should be found. It was plainly my duty to surrender myself. I knew there was neither reason nor the least proof to connect me with the shooting. I would go to Chicago.

Stepping into the street, I bumped into " V.," the " rich man from New Mexico " who had managed my lecture in Los Angeles some years before. The moment he saw me he turned white with fear. " For God's sake, Emma, what are you doing here? " he cried in a quavering voice; " don't you know the police of the whole country are looking for you? " While he was speaking, his eyes roved uneasily over the street. It was evident he was panicky. I had to make sure that he would not disclose my presence in the city. Familiarly I took his arm and whispered: " Let's go to some quiet place."

Sitting in a corner, away from the other guests, I said to him: " Once you assured me of your undying love. You even made me an offer of marriage. It was only four years ago. Is anything left of that affection? If so, will you give me your word of honour that you will not breathe to anybody that you have seen me here? I do not want to be arrested in St. Louis — I intend to give Chicago that honour. Tell me quickly if I can depend on you to keep silent." He promised solemnly.

When we reached the street, he walked away in great haste. I was sure he would keep his word, but I knew that my former devotee was no hero.

When I told Carl I was going to Chicago, he said that I must be out of my senses. He pleaded with me to give up the idea, but I remained adamant. He left me to gather up a few trusted friends, whose opinion he knew I valued, hoping they would be able to persuade me not to surrender myself. They argued with me for hours, but they failed to change my decision. I told them jokingly that they had better give me a good send-off, as we probably should never again have an opportunity for a jolly evening together. They engaged a private dining-room at a restaurant, where we were treated to a Lucullan meal, and then they accompanied me to the Wabash Station, Carl having secured a sleeper for me.

In the morning the car was agog with the Buffalo tragedy, Czolgosz and Emma Goldman. " A beast, a bloodthirsty monster! " I heard someone say; " she should have been locked up long ago." " Locked up nothing! " another retorted; " she should be strung up to the first lamp-post."

I listened to the good Christians while resting in my berth. I chuckled to myself at the thought of how they would look if I were to step out and announce: " Here, ladies and gentlemen, true followers of the gentle Jesus, here is Emma Goldman! " But I did not have the heart to cause them such a shock and I remained behind my curtain.

Half an hour before the train pulled into the station I got dressed. I wore a small sailor hat with a bright blue veil, much in style then. I left my glasses off and pulled the veil over my face. The platform was jammed with people, among them several men who looked like detectives. I asked a fellow-passenger to be kind enough to keep an eye on my two suit-cases while I went in search of a porter. I finally got one, walking the whole length of the platform to my luggage, then back again with the porter to the check-room. Securing my receipt, I left the station.

The only person who knew of my coming was Max, to whom I had sent a cautious wire. I caught sight of him before he saw me. Passing him slowly, I whispered: " Walk towards the next street. I'll do the same." No one seemed to follow me. After some zigzagging with Max and changing half a dozen street-cars we reached the apartment where he and Millie (" Puck ") lived. Both of them expressed the greatest anxiety about my safety, Max insisting that it was insanity to have come to Chicago. The situation, he said, was a repetition of 1887; the press and the police were thirsty for blood. " It's *your* blood they want," he repeated, while he and Millie implored me to leave the country.

I was determined to remain in Chicago. I realized that I could not stay at their home, nor with any other foreign comrades. I had, however, American friends who were not known as anarchists. Max notified Mr. and Mrs. N., who I knew were very fond of me, of my presence and they came at once. They also were worried about me, but they thought I would be safe with them. It was to be only for two days, as I was planning to give myself up to the police as quickly as possible.

Mr. N., the son of a wealthy preacher, lived in a fashionable neighbourhood. " Imagine anybody believing I would shelter Emma Goldman," he said when we had arrived in his house. Late in the afternoon, on Monday, when Mr. N. returned from his office, he informed me that there was a chance to get five thousand dollars from the Chicago *Tribune* for a scoop on an interview. " Fine ! " I replied; "we shall need money to fight my case." We agreed that Mr. N. should bring the newspaper representative to his apartment the next morning, and then the three of us would ride down to police headquarters together. In the evening Max and Millie arrived. I had never before seen my friends in such a state of nervous excitement. Max reiterated that I must get away, else I was putting my head in the noose. " If you go to the police, you will never come out alive," he warned me. " It will be the same as with Albert Parsons. You must let us get you over to Canada."

Millie took me aside. " Since Friday," she said, " Max has not slept or taken food. He walks the floor all night and keeps on saying: ' Emma is lost; they will kill her.' " She begged me to soothe Max by promising him that I would escape to Canada, even if I did not intend doing so. I consented and asked Max to make the necessary arrangements to get me away. Overjoyed, he clasped me in his arms. We arranged for Max and Millie to come the next morning with an outfit of clothes to disguise me.

I spent the greater part of the night tearing up letters and papers and destroying what was likely to involve my friends. All preparations completed, I went to sleep. In the morning Mrs. N. left for her office, while her husband went to the Chicago *Tribune*. We agreed that if anyone called, I was to pretend to be the maid.

About nine o'clock, while taking a bath, I heard a sound as if someone was scratching on the window-sill. I paid no attention to it at first. I finished my bath leisurely and began to dress. Then came a crash of glass. I threw my kimono over me and went into the dining-room to investigate. A man was clutching the window-sill with one hand while holding a gun in the other. We were on the third floor and there was no fire-escape. I called out: " Look out, you'll break your neck! " " Why the hell don't you open the door? Are you deaf? " He swung through the window and was in the room. I walked over to the entrance and unlocked it. Twelve men, led by a giant, crowded into the apartment. The leader grabbed me by the arm, bellowing: " Who are you? " " I not speak English — Swedish servant-girl." He released his hold and ordered his men to search the place. Turning to me, he yelled: " Stand back! We're looking for Emma Goldman." Then he held up a photo to me. " See this? We want this woman. Where is she? " I pointed my finger at the picture and said: " This woman I not see here. This woman big — you look in those small boxes will not find her — she too big." " Oh, shut up! " he bawled; " you can't tell what them anarchists will do."

After they had searched the house, turning everything upside down, the giant walked over to the book-shelves. " Hell, this is a reg'lar preacher's house," he remarked: " look at them books. I don't think Emma Goldman would be here." They were about to leave when one of the detectives suddenly called: " Here, Captain Schuettler, what about this? " It was my fountain-pen, a gift from a friend, with my name on it. I had overlooked it. " By golly, that's a find! " cried the

Captain. " She must have been here and she may come back." He ordered two of his men to remain behind.

I saw that the game was up. There was no sign of Mr. N. or the *Tribune* man, and it could serve no purpose to keep the farce up longer. " I am Emma Goldman," I announced.

For a moment Schuettler and his men stood there as if petrified. Then the Captain roared: " Well, I'll be damned! You're the shrewdest crook I ever met! Take her, quick! "

When I stepped into the cab waiting at the curb, I saw N. approaching in the company of the *Tribune* man. It was too late for the scoop, and I did not want my host recognized. I pretended not to see them.

I had often heard of the third degree used by the police in various American cities to extort confessions, but I myself had never been subjected to it. I had been arrested a number of times since 1893; no violence, however, had ever been practised on me. On the day of my arrest, which was September 10, I was kept at police headquarters in a stifling room and grilled to exhaustion from 10.30 a.m. till 7 p.m. At least fifty detectives passed me, each shaking his fist in my face and threatening me with the direst things. One yelled: " You was with Czolgosz in Buffalo! I saw you myself, right in front of Convention Hall. Better confess, d'you hear? " Another: " Look here, Goldman, I seen you with that son of a bitch at the fair! Don't you lie now — I seen you, I tell you! " Again: " You've faked enough — you keep this up and sure's you're born you'll get the chair. Your lover has confessed. He said it was your speech made him shoot the President." I knew they were lying; I knew I had not been with Czolgosz except for a few minutes in Cleveland on May 5, and for half an hour in Chicago on July 12. Schuettler was most ferocious. His massive bulk towered above me, bellowing: " If you don't confess, you'll go the way of those bastard Haymarket anarchists."

I reiterated the story I had told them when first brought to police headquarters, explaining where I had been and with whom. But they would not believe me and kept on bullying and abusing me. My head throbbed, my throat and lips felt parched. A large pitcher of water stood on the table before me, but every time I stretched out my hand for it, a detective would say: " You can drink all you want, but first answer me. Where were you with Czolgosz the day he shot the President? " The torture continued for hours. Finally I was taken to the

Harrison Street Police Station and locked in a barred enclosure, exposed to view from every side.

Presently the matron came to inquire if I wanted supper. "No, but water," I said, "and something for my head." She returned with a tin pitcher of tepid water, which I gulped down. She could give me nothing for my head except a cold compress. It proved very soothing, and I soon fell asleep.

I woke up with a burning sensation. A plain-clothes man held a reflector in front of me, close to my eyes. I leaped up and pushed him away with all my strength, crying: "You're burning my eyes!" "We'll burn more before we get through with you!" he retorted. With short intermissions this was repeated during three nights. On the third night several detectives entered my cell. "We've got the right dope on you now," they announced; "it was you who financed Czolgosz and you got the money from Dr. Kaplan in Buffalo. We have him all right, and he's confessed everything. Now what you got to say?" "Nothing more than I have already said," I repeated; "I know nothing about the act."

Since my arrest I had had no word from my friends, nor had anyone come to see me. I realized that I was being kept *incommunicado*. I did get letters, however, most of them unsigned. "You damn bitch of an anarchist," one of them read, "I wish I could get at you. I would tear your heart out and feed it to my dog." "Murderous Emma Goldman," another wrote, "you will burn in hell-fire for your treachery to our country." A third cheerfully promised: "We will cut your tongue out, soak your carcass in oil, and burn you alive." The description by some of the anonymous writers of what they would do to me sexually offered studies in perversion that would have astounded authorities on the subject. The authors of the letters nevertheless seemed to me less contemptible than the police officials. Daily I was handed stacks of letters that had been opened and read by the guardians of American decency and morality. At the same time messages from my friends were withheld from me. It was evident that my spirit was to be broken by such methods. I decided to put a stop to it. The next time I was given one of the opened envelopes, I tore it up and threw the pieces into the detective's face.

On the fifth day after my arrest I received a wire. It was from Ed, promising the backing of his firm. "Do not hesitate to use our name. We stand by you to the last." I was glad of the assurance, because it relieved me of the need of keeping silent about my movements on business for Ed's house.

The same evening Chief of Police O'Neill of Chicago came to my cell. He informed me that he would like to have a quiet talk with me. " I have no wish to bully or coerce you," he said; " perhaps I can help you." " It would indeed be a strange experience to have help from a chief of police," I replied; " but I am quite willing to answer your questions." He asked me to give him a detailed account of my movements from May 5, when I had first met Czolgosz, until the day of my arrest in Chicago. I gave him the requested information, but without mentioning my visit to Sasha or the names of the comrades who had been my hosts. As there was no longer any need of shielding Dr. Kaplan, the Isaaks, or Hippolyte, I was in a position to give practically a complete account. When I concluded — what I said being taken down in shorthand — Chief O'Neill remarked: " Unless you're a very clever actress, you are certainly innocent. I think you are innocent, and I am going to do my part to help you out." I was too amazed to thank him; I had never before heard such a tone from a police officer. At the same time I was sceptical of the success of his efforts, even if he should try to do something for me.

Immediately following my conference with the Chief I became aware of a decided change in my treatment. My cell door was left unlocked day and night, and I was told by the matron that I could stay in the large room, use the rocking-chair and the table there, order my own food and papers, receive and send out mail. I began at once to lead the life of a society lady, receiving callers all day long, mostly newspaper people who came not so much for interviews as to talk, smoke, and relate funny stories. Others, again, came out of curiosity. Some women reporters brought gifts of books and toilet articles. Most attentive was Katherine Leckie, of the Hearst papers. She possessed a better intellect than Nelly Bly, who used to visit me in the Tombs in 1893, and had a much finer social feeling. A strong and ardent feminist, she was at the same time devoted to the cause of labour. Katherine Leckie was the first to take my story of the third degree. She became so outraged at hearing it that she undertook to canvass the various women's organizations in order to induce them to take the matter up.

One day a representative of the *Arbeiter Zeitung* was announced. With joy I saw Max, who whispered to me that he could secure admission only in that capacity. He informed me that he had received a letter from Ed with the news that Hearst had sent his representative to Justus Schwab with an offer of twenty thousand dollars if I would come to New York and give him an exclusive interview. The money would be deposited in a bank acceptable to Justus and Ed. Both of them were convinced, Max said, that Hearst would spend any amount to railroad me. " He needs it to whitewash himself of the charge of having incited Czolgosz to shoot McKinley," he explained. The Republican papers of the country had been carrying front-page stories connecting Hearst with Czolgosz, because all through the McKinley administration the Hearst press had violently attacked the President. One of the newspapers had cartooned the publisher standing behind Czolgosz, handing him a match to light the fuse of a bomb. Now Hearst was among the loudest of those demanding the extermination of the anarchists.

Justus and Ed, as well as Max, were unconditionally opposed to my return to New York, but they had felt it their duty to inform me of Hearst's offer. " Twenty thousand dollars! " I exclaimed; " what a pity Ed's letter arrived too late! I certainly would have accepted the proposal. Think of the fight we could have made and the propaganda! " " It is well you still keep your sense of humour," Max remarked, " but I am happy the letter came too late. Your situation is serious enough without Mr. Hearst to make it worse."

Another visitor was a lawyer from Clarence Darrow's office. He had come to warn me that I was hurting my case by my persistent defence of Czolgosz; the man was crazy and I should admit it. " No prominent attorney will accept your defence if you ally yourself with the assassin of the President," he assured me; " in fact, you stand in imminent danger of being held as an accessory to the crime." I demanded to know why Mr. Darrow himself did not come if he was so concerned, but his representative was evasive. He continued to paint my case in sinister colours. My chances of escape were few at best, it seemed, too few for me to allow any sentimentality to aggravate it. Czolgosz was insane, the man insisted; everybody could see it, and, besides, he was a bad sort to have involved me, a coward hiding behind a woman's skirts.

His talk was repugnant to me. I informed him that I was not willing to swear away the reason, character, or life of a defenceless human being and that I wanted no assistance from his chief. I had never met

Darrow, but I had long known of him as a brilliant lawyer, a man of broad social views, an able writer and lecturer. According to the papers he had interested himself in the anarchists arrested in the raid, especially the Isaaks. It seemed strange that he should send me such reprehensible advice, that he should expect me to join the mad chorus howling for the life of Czolgosz.

The country was in a panic. Judging by the press, I was sure that it was the people of the United States and not Czolgosz that had gone mad. Not since 1887 had there been evidenced such lust for blood, such savagery of vengeance. "Anarchists must be exterminated!" the papers raved; "they should be dumped into the sea; there is no place for the vultures under our flag. Emma Goldman has been allowed to ply her trade of murder too long. She should be forced to share the fate of her dupes."

It was a repetition of the dark Chicago days. Fourteen years, years of painful growth, yet fascinating and fruitful years. And now the end! The end? I was only thirty-two and there was yet so much, so very much, undone. And the boy in Buffalo — his life had scarce begun. What was his life, I wondered; what the forces that drove him to this doom? "I did it for the working people," he was reported to have said. The people! Sasha also had done something for the people; and our brave Chicago martyrs, and the others in every land and time. But the people are asleep; they remain indifferent. They forge their own chains and do the bidding of their masters to crucify their Christs.

CHAPTER XXIV

BUFFALO WAS PRESSING FOR MY EXTRADITION, BUT CHICAGO asked for authentic data on the case. I had already been given several hearings in court, and on each occasion the District Attorney from Buffalo had presented much circumstantial evidence to induce the State of Illinois to surrender me. But Illinois demanded direct proofs. There was a hitch somewhere that helped to cause more delays. I thought it likely that Chief of Police O'Neill was behind the matter.

The Chief's attitude towards me had changed the behaviour of every officer in the Harrison Street Police Station. The matron and the two policemen assigned to watch my cell began to lavish attentions on me. The officer on night duty now often appeared with his arms full of parcels, containing fruit, candy, and drinks stronger than grape-juice. " From a friend who keeps a saloon round the corner," he would say, " an admirer of yours." The matron presented me with flowers from the same unknown. One day she brought me the message that he was going to send a grand supper for the coming Sunday. " Who is the man and why should he admire me? " I inquired. " Well, we're all Democrats, and McKinley is a Republican," she replied. " You don't mean you're glad McKinley was shot? " I exclaimed. " Not glad exactly, but not sorry, neither," she said; " we have to pretend, you know, but we're none of us excited about it." " I didn't want McKinley killed," I told her. " We know that," she smiled, " but you're standing up for the boy." I wondered how many more people in America were pretending the same kind of sympathy with the stricken President as my guardians in the station-house.

Even some of the reporters did not seem to be losing sleep over the case. One of them was quite amazed when I assured him that in my professional capacity I would take care of McKinley if I were called upon to nurse him, though my sympathies were with Czolgosz. "You're a puzzle, Emma Goldman," he said, " I can't understand you. You sympathize with Czolgosz, yet you would nurse the man he tried to kill." " As a reporter you aren't expected to understand human complexities," I informed him. " Now listen and see if you can get it. The boy in Buffalo is a creature at bay. Millions of people are ready to spring on him and tear him limb from limb. He committed the act for no personal reasons or gain. He did it for what is his ideal: the good of the people. That is why my sympathies are with him. On the other hand," I continued, " William McKinley, suffering and probably near death, is merely a human being to me now. That is why I would nurse him."

" I don't get you, you're beyond me," he reiterated. The next day there appeared these headlines in one of the papers: " EMMA GOLD- MAN WANTS TO NURSE PRESIDENT; SYMPATHIES ARE WITH SLAYER."

Buffalo failed to produce evidence to justify my extradition. Chicago was getting weary of the game of hide-and-seek. The authorities would not turn me over to Buffalo, yet at the same time they did not feel like letting me go entirely free. By way of compromise I was put under twenty-thousand-dollar bail. The Isaak group had been put under fifteen-thousand-dollar bail. I knew that it would be almost impossible for our people to raise a total of thirty-five thousand dollars within a few days. I insisted on the others being bailed out first. Thereupon I was transferred to the Cook County Jail.

The night before my transfer was Sunday. My saloon-keeper admirer kept his word; he sent over a huge tray filled with numerous goodies: a big turkey, with all the trimmings, including wine and flowers. A note came with it informing me that he was willing to put up five thousand dollars towards my bail. " A strange saloon-keeper! " I remarked to the matron. " Not at all," she replied; " he's the ward heeler and he hates the Republicans worse than the devil." I invited her, my two policemen, and several other officers present to join me in the celebration. They assured me that nothing like it had ever before happened to them — a prisoner playing host to her keepers. " You mean a dangerous anarchist having as guests the guardians of law and order," I corrected. When everybody had left, I noticed that my day watchman lingered behind. I inquired whether he had been changed to night duty. " No," he replied, " I just wanted to tell you that you are not the first anarchist I've been assigned to watch. I was on duty when Parsons and his comrades were in here."

Peculiar and inexplicable the ways of life, intricate the chain of events! Here I was, the spiritual child of those men, imprisoned in the city that had taken their lives, in the same jail, even under the guardianship of the very man who had kept watch in their silent hours. Tomorrow I should be taken to Cook County Jail, within whose walls Parsons, Spies, Engel, and Fischer had been hanged. Strange, indeed, the complex forces that had bound me to those martyrs through all my socially conscious years! And now events were bringing me nearer and nearer — perhaps to a similar end?

The newspapers had published rumours about mobs ready to attack the Harrison Street Station and planning violence to Emma Goldman before she could be taken to the Cook County Jail. Monday morning, flanked by a heavily armed guard, I was led out of the station-house. There were not a dozen people in sight, mostly curiosity-seekers. As usual, the press had deliberately tried to incite a riot.

Ahead of me were two handcuffed prisoners roughly hustled about by the officers. When we reached the patrol wagon, surrounded by more police, their guns ready for action, I found myself close to the two men. Their features could not be distinguished: their heads were bound up in bandages, leaving only their eyes free. As they stepped to the patrol wagon, a policeman hit one of them on the head with his club, at the same time pushing the other prisoner violently into the wagon. They fell over each other, one of them shrieking with pain. I got in next, then turned to the officer. "You brute," I said, "how dare you beat that helpless fellow?" The next thing I knew, I was sent reeling to the floor. He had landed his fist on my jaw, knocking out a tooth and covering my face with blood. Then he pulled me up, shoved me into the seat, and yelled: "Another word from you, you damned anarchist, and I'll break every bone in your body!"

I arrived at the office of the county jail with my waist and skirt covered with blood, my face aching fearfully. No one showed the slightest interest or bothered to ask how I came to be in such a battered condition. They did not even give me water to wash up. For two hours I was kept in a room in the middle of which stood a long table. Finally a woman arrived who informed me that I would have to be searched. "All right, go ahead," I said. "Strip and get on the table," she ordered. I had been repeatedly searched, but I had never before been offered such an insult. "You'll have to kill me first, or get your keepers to put me on the table by force," I declared; "you'll never get me to do it otherwise." She hurried out, and I remained alone. After a long wait another woman came in and led me upstairs, where the matron of the tier took charge of me. She was the first to inquire what was the matter with me. After assigning me to a cell she brought a hot-water bottle and suggested that I lie down and get some rest.

The following afternoon Katherine Leckie visited me. I was taken into a room provided with a double wire screen. It was semi-dark, but as soon as Katherine saw me, she cried: " What on God's earth has happened to you? Your face is all twisted!" No mirror, not even of the smallest size, being allowed in the jail, I was not aware how I looked, though my eyes and lips felt queer to the touch. I told Katherine of my encounter with the policeman's fist. She left swearing vengeance and promising to return after seeing Chief O'Neill. Towards evening she came back to let me know that the Chief had assured her the officer would be punished if I would identify him among the guards of the transport. I refused. I had hardly looked at the man's face and I was not sure I could recognize him. Moreover, I told Katherine, much to her disappointment, that the dismissal of the officer would not restore my tooth; neither would it do away with police brutality. " It is the system I am fighting, my dear Katherine, not the particular offender," I said. But she was not convinced; she wanted something done to arouse popular indignation against such savagery. " Dismissing wouldn't be enough," she persisted; " he should be tried for assault."

Poor Katherine was not aware that I knew she could do nothing. She was not even in a position to speak through her own paper: her story about the third degree had been suppressed. She promptly replied by resigning; she would no longer be connected with such a cowardly journal, she had told the editor. Yet not a word had she breathed to me of her trouble. I learned the story from a reporter of another Chicago daily.

One evening, while engrossed in a book, I was surprised by several detectives and reporters. " The President has just died," they announced. " How do you feel about it? Aren't you sorry?" " Is it possible," I asked, " that in the entire United States only the President passed away on this day? Surely many others have also died at the same time, perhaps in poverty and destitution, leaving helpless dependents behind. Why do you expect me to feel more regret over the death of McKinley than of the rest?"

The pencils went flying. " My compassion has always been with the living," I continued; " the dead no longer need it. No doubt that is the reason why you all feel so sympathetic to the dead. You know that you'll never be called upon to make good your protestations." " Damned good copy," a young reporter exclaimed, " but I think you're crazy."

I was glad when they left. My thoughts were with the boy in Buffalo, whose fate was now sealed. What tortures of mind and body were still to be his before he would be allowed to breathe his last! How would he meet the supreme moment? There was something strong and determined about his eyes, emphasized by his very sensitive face. I had been struck by his eyes on first seeing him at my lecture in Cleveland. Was the idea of his act already with him then or had some particular thing happened since that compelled his deed? What could it have been? " I did it for the people," he had said. I paced my cell trying to analyse the probable motives that had decided the youth in his purpose.

Suddenly a thought flitted through my mind — that notice by Isaak in *Free Society*! — the charge of " spy " against Nieman because he had " asked suspicious questions and tried to get into the anarchist ranks." I had written Isaak at the time, demanding proofs for the outrageous accusation. As a result of my protest *Free Society* had contained a retraction to the effect that a mistake had been made. It had relieved me and I had given the matter no further thought. Now the whole situation appeared in a new light, clear and terrible. Czolgosz must have read the charge; it must have hurt him to the quick to be so cruelly misjudged by the very people to whom he had come for inspiration. I recalled his eagerness to secure the right kind of books. It was apparent that he had sought in anarchism a solution of the wrongs he saw everywhere about him. No doubt it was that which had induced him to call on me and later on the Isaaks. Instead of finding help the poor youth saw himself attacked. Was it that experience, fearfully wounding his spirit, that had led to his act? There must also have been other causes, but perhaps his great urge had been to prove that he was sincere, that he felt with the oppressed, that he was no spy.

But why had he chosen the President rather than some more direct representative of the system of economic oppression and misery? Was it because he saw in McKinley the willing tool of Wall Street and of the new American imperialism that flowered under his administration? One of its first steps had been the annexation of the Philippines, an act of treachery to the people whom America had pledged to set free during the Spanish War. McKinley also typified a hostile and reactionary attitude to labour: he had repeatedly sided with the masters by sending troops into strike regions. All these circumstances, I felt, must have exerted a decisive influence upon the impressionable Leon, finally crystallizing in his act of violence.

Throughout the night thoughts of the unfortunate boy kept crowding in my mind. In vain I sought to divest myself of the harassing reflections by reading. The dawning day still found me pacing my cell, Leon's beautiful face, pale and haunted, before me.

Again I was taken to court for a hearing and again the Buffalo authorities failed to produce evidence to connect me with Czolgosz's act. The Buffalo representative and the Chicago judge sitting on the case kept up a verbal fight for two hours, at the end of which Buffalo was robbed of its prey. I was set free.

Ever since my arrest the press of the country had been continually denouncing me as the instigator of Czolgosz's act, but after my discharge the newspapers published only a few lines in an inconspicuous corner to the effect that " after a month's detention Emma Goldman was found not to have been in complicity with the assassin of President McKinley."

Upon my release I was met by Max, Hippolyte, and other friends, with whom I went to the Isaak home. The charges against the comrades arrested in the Chicago raids had also been dismissed. Everyone was in high spirits over my escape from what they had all believed to be a fatal situation. " We can be grateful to whatever gods watch over you, Emma," said Isaak, " that you were arrested here and not in New York." " The gods in this case must have been Chief of Police O'Neill," I said laughingly. " Chief O'Neill! " my friends exclaimed; " what did he have to do with it? " I told them about my interview with him and his promise of help. Jonathan Crane, a journalist friend of ours present, broke out into uproarious laughter. " You are more naïve than I should have expected, Emma Goldman," he said; " it wasn't you O'Neill cared a damn about! it was his own schemes. Being on the *Tribune,* I happen to know the inside story of the feud in the police department." Crane then related the efforts of Chief O'Neill to put several captains in the penitentiary for perjury and bribery. " Nothing could have come more opportunely for those blackguards than the cry of anarchy," he explained; " they seized upon it as the police did in 1887; it was their chance to pose as saviours of the country and incidentally to whitewash themselves. But it wasn't to O'Neill's interest to let those birds pose as heroes and get back into the department. That's why he worked for you. He's a shrewd Irishman. Just the same, we may be glad that the quarrel brought us back our Emma."

I asked my friends their opinion as to how the idea of connecting my name with Czolgosz had originated. " I refuse to believe that the boy made any kind of a confession or involved me in any way," I stated; " I cannot think that he was capable of inventing something which he must have known might mean my death. I'm convinced that no one with such a frank face could be so craven. It must have come from some other source."

"It did!" Hippolyte declared emphatically. " The whole dastardly story was started by a *Daily News* reporter who used to hang round here pretending to sympathize with our ideas. Late in the afternoon of September 6 he came to the house. He wanted to know all about a certain Czolgosz or Nieman. Had we associated with him? Was he an anarchist? And so forth. Well, you know what I think of reporters — I wouldn't give him any information. But unfortunately Isaak did."

" What was there to hide? " Isaak interrupted. " Everybody about here knew that we had met the man through Emma, and that he used to visit us. Besides, how was I to know that the reporter was going to fabricate such a lying story? "

I urged the Chicago comrades to consider what could be done for the boy in the Buffalo jail. We could not save his life, but we could at least try to explain his act to the world and we should attempt to communicate with him, so that he might feel that he was not forsaken by us. Max doubted the possibility of reaching Czolgosz. He had received a note from a comrade in Buffalo informing him that no one was permitted to see Leon. I suggested that we secure an attorney. Without legal aid Czolgosz would be gagged and railroaded, as Sasha had been. Isaak advised that a lawyer be engaged in the State of New York, and I decided to leave immediately for the East. My friends argued that it would be folly to do so; I should surely be arrested the moment I reached the city, and turned over to Buffalo, my fate sealed. But it was unthinkable to me to leave Czolgosz to his doom without making an effort in his behalf. No considerations of personal safety should influence us in the matter, I told my friends, adding that I would remain in Chicago for the public meeting that must be organized to explain our attitude to Czolgosz and his *Attentat*.

On the evening of the meeting one could not get within a block of Brand's Hall, where it was to be held. Strong detachments of police were dispersing the people by force. We tried to hire another hall, but the police had terrorized the hall-keepers. Our efforts to hold a meeting being frustrated, I resolved to state my position in *Free Society*.

" Leon Czolgosz and other men of his type," I wrote in my article, entitled: " The Tragedy of Buffalo," " far from being depraved creatures of low instincts are in reality supersensitive beings unable to bear up under too great social stress. They are driven to some violent expression, even at the sacrifice of their own lives, because they cannot supinely witness the misery and suffering of their fellows. The blame for such acts must be laid at the door of those who are responsible for the injustice and inhumanity which dominate the world." After pointing out the social causes for such acts as that of Czolgosz, I concluded: " As I write, my thoughts wander to the young man with the girlish face about to be put to death, pacing his cell, followed by cruel eyes:

> Who watch him when he tries to weep
> And when he tries to pray,
> Who watch him lest himself should rob
> The prison of its prey.

My heart goes out to him in deep sympathy, as it goes out to all the victims of oppression and misery, to the martyrs past and future that die, the forerunners of a better and nobler life." I turned the article over to Isaak, who promised to have it set up at once.

The police and the press were continuing their hunt for anarchists throughout the country. Meetings were broken up and innocent people arrested. In various places persons suspected of being anarchists were subjected to violence. In Pittsburgh our good friend Harry Gordon was dragged out into the street and nearly lynched. A rope already around his neck, he was saved at the last moment by some bystanders who were touched by the pleading of Mrs. Gordon and her two children. In New York the office of the *Freie Arbeiter Stimme* was attacked by a mob, the furniture demolished, and the type destroyed. In no case did the police interfere with the doings of the patriotic ruffians. Johann Most was arrested for an article in the *Freiheit* reproducing an essay on political violence by Karl Heinzen, the famous '48 revolutionist, then dead many years. Most was out on bail awaiting his trial. The German comrades in Chicago arranged an affair to raise funds for his defence and invited me to speak. Our feud of 1892 was a matter of the past to me. Most was again in the clutches of the police, in danger of being sent to Blackwell's Island, and I gladly consented to do all I could for him.

Returning to the Isaak home after the meeting, I found the proofs of my article. Looking them over, I was surprised by a paragraph that changed the entire meaning of my statement. It was, I was sure, no other than Isaak, the editor, who was responsible for the change. I confronted him, demanding an explanation. He readily admitted that he had written the little paragraph, " to tone down the article," he explained, " in order to save *Free Society.*" " And incidentally your skin! " I retorted hotly. " For years you've been denouncing people as cowards who could not meet a dangerous situation. Now that you yourself are face to face with one, you draw in your horns. At least you should have asked my permission to make the change."

It required a long discussion to alter Isaak's attitude. He saw that my view was sustained by the rest of the group — his son Abe, Hippolyte, and several others — whereupon he declared that he renounced all responsibility in the matter. My article finally appeared in its original form. Nothing happened to *Free Society.* But my faith in Isaak was shaken.

On my way back to New York I stopped off in Rochester. Arriving in the evening, I walked to Helena's place in order to avoid recognition. A policeman was stationed at the house, but he did not know me. Everyone gasped when I made my appearance. " How did you get by? " Helena cried; " didn't you see the officer at the door? " " Indeed I saw him, but he evidently didn't see me," I laughed. " Don't you folks worry about any policeman; better give me a bath," I cried lightly. My nonchalance dispelled the family's nervous tension. Everybody laughed and Helena clung to me in unchanged love.

All through my incarceration my family had been very devoted to me. They had sent me telegrams and letters, offering money for my defence and any other help I might need. Not a word had they written about the persecution they had been subjected to on my account. They had been pestered to distraction by reporters and kept under surveillance by the authorities. My father had been ostracized by his neighbours and had lost many customers at his little furniture store. At the same time he had also been excommunicated from the synagogue. My sister Lena, though in poor health, had also been given no peace. She had been terrorized by the police ordering Stella to appear at headquarters, where they had kept the child the whole day, plying her with questions about her aunt Emma Goldman. Stella had bravely refused to answer, defiantly proclaiming her pride and faith in her *Tante* Emma. Her courage, combined with her youth and beauty, had won general admiration, Helena said.

Even more cruel had been the teachers and pupils of the public school. " Your aunt Emma Goldman is a murderess," they had taunted our children. School was turned into a hideous nightmare for them. My nephews Saxe and Harry had suffered most. Harry's grief over the violent death of his hero was more real than with most of the adults in the country. He deeply felt the disgrace that his own mother's sister should be charged with responsibility for it. Worse yet, his schoolmates denounced him as an anarchist and criminal. The persecution aggravated his misery and completely alienated him from me. Saxe's unhappiness, on the other hand, resulted from his strong feeling of loyalty to me. His mother and Aunt Helena loved Emma and they had told him she was innocent. They must know better than his schoolmates. Their boisterous aggressiveness had always repelled him; now more than ever he avoided them. My unexpected appearance and outwitting the officer on guard must have quickened Saxe's imagination and increased his admiration for me. His flushed face and shining eyes were eloquent of his emotion. His hovering near me all evening said more than his quivering lips could tell.

It was balm to my bruised spirit to find such a haven of love and peace in the circle of my family. Even my sister Lena, who had often in the past disapproved of my life, now showed warmest affection. Brother Herman and his gentle wife lavished attentions upon me. The imminent danger I had faced, which still threatened me, had served to establish a bond between my family and me stronger than we had ever felt before. I wanted to prolong my happy stay in Rochester to recuperate from the ordeal of Chicago. But the thought of Czolgosz tormented me. I knew that in New York I could make some effort in his behalf.

At the Grand Central Station I was met by Yegor and the two chums who had spent that wonderful month with us in Rochester. Yegor looked distressed; he had tried hard to find a place for me, but had failed. No one would rent even a furnished room to Emma Goldman. Our friends who happened to have a vacant room would not run the risk of my staying with them for fear of being evicted. One of the boys offered to let me have his room for a few nights. " No need to worry," I comforted Yegor; " I am taken care of for the present, and in the meantime I will find an apartment."

After a long search for a flat I realized that my brother had not been exaggerating. No one would have me. I went to see a young prostitute I had once nursed. " Sure, kid, stay right here! " she welcomed me. " I'm tickled to death to have you. I'll bunk with a girl friend for a while."

The encouraging telegram I had received in Chicago from Ed had been followed by a number of letters assuring me that I could count on him for whatever I might need: money, help and advice, and, above all, his friendship. It was good to know that Ed remained so staunch. When we met upon my return to New York, he offered me the use of his apartment while he and his family would be staying with friends. " You won't find much changed in my place," he remarked; " all your things are intact in the room that is my sanctum, where I often dream of our life together." I thanked him, but I could not accept his generous proposal. He was too tactful to press the matter, except to inform me that his firm owed me several hundred dollars in commissions.

" I need the money badly," I confided to Ed, " to send somebody to Buffalo to see Czolgosz. Possibly something can be done for him. We also ought to organize a mass meeting at once." He stared at me in bewilderment. " My dear," he said, shaking his head, " you are evidently not aware of the panic in the city. No hall in New York can be had and no one except yourself would be willing to speak for Czolgosz." " But no one is expected to eulogize his act! " I argued; " surely there must be a few people in the radical ranks who are capable of sympathy for a doomed human being." " Capable perhaps," he said doubtfully, " but not brave enough to voice it at this time." " You may be right," I admitted, " but I intend to make sure of it."

A trusted person was dispatched to Buffalo, but he soon returned without having been able to visit Czolgosz. He reported that no one was permitted to see him. A sympathetic guard had disclosed to our messenger that Leon had repeatedly been beaten into unconsciousness. His physical appearance was such that no outsider was admitted, and for the same reason he could not be taken to court. My friend further reported that, notwithstanding all the torture, Czolgosz had made no confession whatever and had involved no one in his act. A note had been sent in to Leon through the friendly guard.

I learned that an effort had been made in Buffalo to secure an attorney for Czolgosz, but no one would accept his defence. That made me even more determined to raise my voice in behalf of the poor unfortunate, denied and forsaken by everyone. Before long, however, I became convinced that Ed had been right. No one among the English-speaking radical groups could be induced to participate in a meeting to discuss the act of Leon Czolgosz. Many were willing to protest against my arrest, to condemn the third degree and the treatment I had received. But they would have nothing to do with the Buffalo case. Czolgosz was not an anarchist, his deed had done the movement an irreparable injury, our American comrades insisted. Most of the Jewish anarchists, even, expressed similar views. Yanofsky, editor of the *Freie Arbeiter Stimme,* went still further. He kept up a campaign against Czolgosz, also denouncing me as an irresponsible person and declaring that he would never again speak from the same platform with me. The only ones who had not lost their heads were of the Latin groups, the Italian, Spanish, and French anarchists. Their publications had reprinted my article on Czolgosz that had appeared in *Free Society.* They wrote sympathetically of Leon, interpreting his act as a direct result of the increasing imperialism and reaction in this country. The Latin comrades were anxious to help with anything I might suggest, and it was a great comfort to know that at least some anarchists had preserved their judgment and courage in the madhouse of fury and cowardice. Unfortunately the foreign groups could not reach the American public.

In desperation I clung to the hope that by perseverance and appeals I should be able to rally some public-spirited Americans to express ordinary human sympathy for Leon Czolgosz, even if they felt that they must repudiate his act. Every day brought more disappointment and heart-ache. I was compelled to face the fact that I had been fighting against an epidemic of abject fear that could not be overcome.

The tragedy in Buffalo was nearing its end. Leon Czolgosz, still ill from the maltreatment he had endured, his face disfigured and head bandaged, was supported in court by two policemen. In its all-embracing justice and mercy the Buffalo court had assigned two lawyers to his defence. What if they did declare publicly that they were sorry to have to plead the case of such a depraved criminal as the assassin of " our beloved " President! They would do their duty just the same! They would see to it that the rights of the defendant were protected in court.

The last act was staged in Auburn Prison. It was early dawn, October 29, 1901. The condemned man sat strapped to the electric chair. The executioner stood with his hand on the switch, awaiting the signal. A warden, impelled by Christian mercy, makes a last effort to save the sinner's soul, to induce him to confess. Tenderly he says: " Leon, my boy, why do you shield that bad woman, Emma Goldman? She is not your friend. She has denounced you as a loafer, too lazy to work. She said you had always begged money from her. Emma Goldman has betrayed you, Leon. Why should you shield her? "

Breathless silence, seconds of endless time. It fills the death chamber, creeps into the hearts of the spectators. At last a muffled sound, an almost inaudible voice from under the black mask.

" It doesn't matter what Emma Goldman has said about me. She had nothing to do with my act. I did it alone. I did it for the American people."

A silence more terrible than the first. A sizzling sound — the smell of burnt flesh — a final agonized twitch of life.

CHAPTER XXV

I T WAS BITTER HARD TO FACE LIFE ANEW. IN THE STRESS OF THE past weeks I had forgotten that I should again have to take up the struggle for existence. It was doubly imperative; I needed forgetfulness. Our movement had lost its appeal for me; many of its adherents filled me with loathing. They had been flaunting anarchism like a red cloth before a bull, but they ran to cover at his first charge. I could no longer work with them. Still more harrowing was the gnawing doubt of the values I had so fervently believed in. No, I could not continue in the movement. I must first take stock of my own self. Intensive work in my profession, I felt, was the only refuge. It would fill the void and make me forget.

I had lost my identity; I had assumed a fictitious name, for no landlord was willing to lodge me, and most of my erstwhile comrades and friends proved equally brave. The situation revived memories of 1892, of the nights spent in Tompkins Square, or riding in horsecars to Harlem and back to the Battery, and later among the girls in the house on Fourth Street. I had endured that life rather than make the concession of changing my name. It was weak and inconsistent, I had then thought, to give in to popular prejudices. Some of those who now denied Czolgosz had praised me for joining the homeless brigade rather than compromise. All this had no meaning for me any longer. The struggle and disappointment of the past twelve years had taught me that consistency is only skin-deep in most people. As if it mattered what name you took, as long as you kept your integrity. Indeed, I would take another name, the most common and inoffensive I could think of. I became Miss E. G. Smith.

I met with no further objections from landlords. I rented a flat on First Street; Yegor and his chum Dan moved in with me, our furniture purchased on the instalment plan. Thereupon I went out to call on my physicians, to apprise them of the fact that henceforth they could recommend me as E. G. Smith.

By the end of the day's tramp I gained one more proof that I had become a pariah. Several doctors I visited, men who had known me for years and who had always been entirely satisfied with my work as a nurse, were indignant that I had dared to call on them. Did I want to get their names in the papers or cause them trouble with the police? I was being shadowed by the authorities; how could I expect them to recommend me? Dr. White was more humane. He had never credited the stories connecting me with Czolgosz, he assured me; he was certain that I was incapable of murder. Still he could not employ me in his office. "Smith is an ordinary enough name," he said, "but how long do you suppose it will be before you are discovered? I cannot take the chance; it would mean my ruin." He was anxious, however, to help me in some other manner, perhaps with money. I thanked him and went my way.

I visited Dr. Julius Hoffmann and Dr. Solotaroff. They at least had not changed towards me and they were eager to recommend cases. Unfortunately my good friend Solotaroff had fallen ill with an affection of the heart and was compelled to give up his outside practice. His office patients rarely needed nurses, but he promised to speak to other East Side doctors. Dear, faithful comrade, since I had climbed those six flights of stairs to his flat on my first arrival in New York twelve years previously, he had never failed me once.

It was evident my prospects were not very bright. I knew it involved a desperate struggle to win new ground, but I was determined to start all over again. I would not submit passively to the forces that were trying to crush me. "I must, I will, go on, for the sake of Sasha and of my brother, who need me," I told myself.

Sasha! I had not heard from him for nearly two months, and I also had been unable to write him. While under arrest, I could not express myself freely, and the last month had been too dreary and depressing. I was sure that of all people my dear Sasha would understand the social meaning of the Buffalo shot, and that he would appreciate the boy's integrity. Dear Sasha! Since the unexpected commutation of his prison term his spirit had grown buoyant. "Only five years more," he had written in his last letter; "just think, dear friend, only five years more!" To see him free at last, resurrected; what were all my hardships compared with that moment? In that hope I plodded on

Occasionally I was called to a case; at other times I had orders for dresses.

I seldom went out. We could not afford music or theatres, and I dreaded to appear at public meetings. The last one, shortly after my return from Chicago, had nearly ended in a riot. I had gone to hear my old friend Ernest Crosby speak at the Manhattan Liberal Club. I had attended its weekly meetings since 1894, often participated in the discussions, and was known by everybody. The moment I entered the hall this time, I sensed an atmosphere of antagonism. Except for Crosby and several others, the audience seemed to resent my presence. At the close of the lecture, as the people were filing out of the hall, a man called out: " Emma Goldman, you are a murderess, and fifty million people know it! " In a moment I found myself surrounded by an excited crowd, crying: " You're a murderess! " Some voices were raised in my defence, but they were drowned in the general clamour. A clash was imminent. I got up on a chair and shouted: " You say fifty million people know that Emma Goldman is a murderess. The population of the United States being considerably more than that, there must be a great number willing to inform themselves before making irresponsible accusations. It is a tragedy to have a fool in the family, but to have fifty million maniacs in a nation is a calamity indeed. As good Americans you should refuse to swell their number."

Someone laughed, others followed, and soon the audience was in good humour again. But I left sick with disgust, determined to stay away from meetings, even from people. I saw only the few friends that came to our house, and occasionally I visited Justus.

Justus had been opposed to my coming to New York. Even now he feared for my safety; I was in danger of being kidnapped and taken to Buffalo, he thought, and he strongly urged a body-guard for me. It was good to see him so concerned, and I sought to humour him. His old friends, among them Ed and Claus, often gathered in his place to cheer him. We all knew that Death was daily creeping nearer and that before long he would claim his toll.

Early one morning Ed called to tell me that the end had come. I was asked to be one of the speakers at the funeral of Justus, but I felt compelled to refuse. I knew I could not express in words what he had meant in my life. Champion of freedom, sponsor of labour's cause, pleader for joy in life, Justus had a surpassing capacity for friendship, a veritable genius for responding generously and beautifully. He had always been reticent about his own great life and work. For me to sing his praises in the market-place would have been a breach of faith. The vast throng of people from every rank that followed the remains to the crematorium testified to the deep affection and high regard Justus had inspired in those who knew him.

The loss of Justus increased the dullness of my life. The small circle of friends who used to meet at his place was now scattered; more and more I withdrew into my own four walls. The struggle for the necessities of existence became more severe. Solotaroff, ill again, could not help me with employment; Dr. Hoffmann was out of the city. I was again compelled to take piece-work from the factory. I had advanced in the trade; I was sewing gaudy silk morning gowns now. The many ruffles, ribbons, and laces required painstaking effort, affecting my lacerated nerves until I felt like screaming. The one bright spot in the drabness that was now my life was my dear brother and his chum Dan.

Yegor had brought him to me when I was still living in my little room on Clinton Street. He had attracted me from the first, and I knew that he was also strongly drawn to me. I was thirty-two, while he only nineteen, naïve and unspoiled. He had laughed at my misgivings over the difference in our ages; he did not care for young girls, he said; they were generally stupid and could give him nothing. I was younger than they, he thought, and much wiser. He wanted me more than anyone else.

His pleading voice had been like music to me; yet I had struggled against it. One of my reasons for going on tour in May had been the hope of escaping my growing affection for the boy. In July, when we all met in Rochester, the storm I had repressed so long swept over me and engulfed us both. Then came the Buffalo tragedy and the horrors in its wake. They stifled the mainsprings of my being. Love seemed a farce in a world of hate. Since we had moved into our little flat, we were thrown together a great deal, and love again raised its insistent voice. I responded. It made me forget the other calls — of my ideal, my faith, my work. The thought of a lecture or meeting had become repugnant to me. Even concerts and theatres had lost their attraction because of my fear, grown almost to an obsession, of meeting people or being recognized. Dejection was upon me, the feeling that my existence had lost its meaning and was bereft of content.

Life dragged on with its daily cares and worries. By far the greatest of them was Sasha's reported condition. Friends in Pittsburgh had written that he was again being persecuted by the prison authorities, and that his health was breaking down. At last, on December 31, a letter arrived from him. No greater New Year's gift could have come to me. Yegor knew that I liked to be alone on such occasions, and he thoughtfully tiptoed out of the room.

I pressed my lips to the precious envelope, opening it with trembling fingers. It was a long *sub rosa* letter, dated December 20 and written on several slips of paper in the very small script Sasha had acquired, each word standing out clear and distinct.

"I know how your visit and my strange behaviour must have affected you," he wrote. "The sight of your face after all these years completely unnerved me. I could not think, I could not speak. It was as if all my dreams of freedom, the whole world of the living, were concentrated in the shiny little trinket that was dangling from your watch-chain. I couldn't take my eyes off it, I couldn't keep my hand from playing with it. It absorbed my whole being. And all the time I felt how nervous you were at my silence, and I couldn't utter a word."

The frightful months since my visit to Sasha had obscured the poignancy of my disappointment at that time. His lines again revived it. But his letter showed how closely he had followed the events. "If the press mirrored the sentiments of the people," he continued, "the nation must have suddenly relapsed into cannibalism. There were moments when I was in mortal dread for your very life, and for the safety of the other arrested comrades. . . . Your attitude of proud self-respect and your admirable self-control contributed much to the fortunate outcome. I was especially moved by your remark that you would faithfully nurse the wounded man, if he required your services, but that the poor boy, condemned and deserted by all, needed and deserved your sympathy and aid more than the President. More strikingly than your letters, that remark discovered to me the great change wrought in us by the ripening years. Yes, in us, in both, for my heart echoed your beautiful sentiment. How impossible such a thought would have been to us in the days of a decade ago! We should have considered it treason to the spirit of revolution; it would have outraged all our traditions even to admit the humanity of an official representative of capitalism. Is it not significant that we two — you living in the very heart of anarchist thought and activity, and I in the atmosphere of absolute suppression and isolation — should have arrived at the same evolutionary point after ten years of divergent paths?"

The dear, faithful pal — how big and brave it was of him so frankly to admit the change! As I read on I grew even more astounded at the amount of knowledge Sasha had acquired since his imprisonment. Works of science, philosophy, economics, even metaphysics — he had evidently read a great many of them, critically studied and digested them. His letter stirred a hundred memories of the past, of our common life, our love, our work. I was lost in recollections; time and space disappeared; the intervening years became blotted out, and I relived the past. My hands caressed the letter, my eyes dreamily wandering over the lines. Then the word " Leon " fastened my gaze, and I continued to read:

" I have read of the beautiful personality of the youth, of his inability to adapt himself to brutal conditions, and of the rebellion of his soul. It throws a significant light upon the causes of the *Attentat*. Indeed, it is at once the greatest tragedy of martyrdom and the most terrible indictment of society that it forces the noblest men and women to shed human blood, though their souls shrink from it. The more imperative it is that drastic methods of this character be resorted to only as a last extremity. To prove of value they must be motived by social rather than individual necessity and be aimed against a direct and immediate enemy of the people. The significance of such a deed is understood by the popular mind, and in that alone lies the propagandistic, educational import of an *Attentat,* except if it is exclusively an act of terrorism."

The letter dropped from my hand. What could Sasha mean? Did he imply that McKinley was not " an immediate enemy of the people "? Not a subject for an *Attentat* of " propagandistic, educational import "? I was bewildered. Had I read right? There was still another passage: " I do not believe that Leon's deed was terroristic, and I doubt whether it was educational, because the social necessity for its performance was not manifest. That you may not misunderstand, I repeat: as an expression of personal revolt it was inevitable, and in itself an indictment of existing conditions. But the background of social necessity was lacking, and therefore the value of the act was to a great extent nullified."

The letter fell to the floor, leaving me in a daze. A strange, dry voice screamed out: " Yegor! Yegor! "

My brother ran in. " What has happened, dear? You're all trembling. What's the matter? " he cried in alarm. " The letter! " I whispered hoarsely. " Read it; tell me if I've gone mad."

" A beautiful letter," I heard him say, " a human document, though Sasha does not see social necessity in Czolgosz's act."

" But how can Sasha," I cried in desperation, " he of all people in the world — himself misunderstood and repudiated by the very workers he had wanted to help — how can *he* misunderstand so ? "

Yegor tried to soothe me, to explain what Sasha had meant by " the necessary social background." Picking up another slip of the letter, he began reading to me :

" The scheme of political subjection is subtle in America. Though McKinley was the chief representative of our modern slavery, he could not be considered in the light of a direct and immediate enemy of the people. In an absolutism the autocrat is visible and tangible. The real despotism of republican institutions is far deeper, more insidious, because it rests on the popular delusion of self-government and independence. That is the source of democratic tyranny, and as such it cannot be reached with a bullet. In modern capitalism economic exploitation rather than political oppression is the real enemy of the people. Politics is but its handmaid. Hence the battle is to be waged in the economic rather than the political field. It is therefore that I regard my own act as far more significant and educational than Leon's. It was directed against a tangible, real oppressor, visualized as such by the people."

Suddenly a thought struck me. Why, Sasha is using the same arguments against Leon that Johann Most had urged against Sasha. Most had proclaimed the futility of individual acts of violence in a country devoid of proletarian consciousness and he had pointed out that the American worker did not understand the motives of such deeds. No less than I had Sasha then considered Most a traitor to our cause as well as towards himself. I had fought Most bitterly for it — Most, who had been my teacher, my great inspiration. And now Sasha, still believing in acts of violence, was denying " social necessity " to Leon's deed.

The farce of it — the cruel, senseless farce! I felt as if I had lost Sasha — I broke down in uncontrollable sobbing.

In the evening Ed came for me. We had agreed several days previously to celebrate the New Year together, but I felt too crushed to go. Yegor pleaded with me, saying it would help to distract me. But I was shaken to the roots. When the New Year came, I lay ill in bed.

Dr. Hoffmann was again treating Mrs. Spenser and I was called to nurse her. The work compelled me to take life up once more. I followed my daily routine almost unconsciously, out of habit, my mind brooding on Sasha. It was peculiar self-deception on his part, I kept on saying to myself, to believe that his act had been more valuable than Leon's. Had the years of solitary confinement and suffering led him to think his act had been better understood by the people than Czolgosz's was? Perhaps it had served him as a prop to lean on during his terrible prison years. It was that, no doubt, that had kept him alive. Yet it seemed incredible that a man of his clarity and judgment should be so blind to the value of Leon's political act.

I wrote Sasha several times pointing out that anarchism does not direct its forces against economic injustices only, but that it includes the political as well. His replies only emphasized the wide difference in our view-points. They increased my misery and made me realize the futility of continuing the discussion. In despair I stopped writing.

After the death of McKinley the campaign against anarchism and its adherents continued with increased venom. The press, the pulpit, and other public mouthpieces were frantically vying with each other in their fury against the common enemy. Most ferocious was Theodore Roosevelt, the new-fledged President of the United States. As Vice-President he succeeded McKinley to the presidential throne. The irony of fate had, by the hand of Czolgosz, paved the way to power for the hero of San Juan. In gratitude for that involuntary service Roosevelt turned savage. His message to Congress, intended largely to strike at anarchism, was in reality a death-blow to social and political freedom in the United States.

Anti-anarchist bills followed each other in quick succession, their congressional sponsors busy inventing new methods for the extermination of anarchists. Senator Hawley evidently did not consider his professional wisdom sufficient to slay the anarchist dragon. He declared publicly that he would give a thousand dollars to get a shot at an anarchist. It was a cheap offer considering the price Czolgosz had paid for his shot.

In my bitterness I felt that the American radicals who had shown the white feather when courage and daring were so needed were mainly responsible for the developments. No wonder the reactionaries so brazenly clamoured for despotic measures. They saw themselves complete masters of the situation in the country, with hardly any organized opposition. The Criminal Anarchy law, rushed through the New York legislature, and a similar statute in New Jersey, helped to strengthen my conviction that our movement in the United States was paying dearly for its inconsistencies.

Signs of an awakening in our ranks gradually began to manifest themselves; voices were being raised against the impending danger to American liberties. But I had the feeling that the psychological moment had been neglected; nothing could be done to stem the tide of reaction. At the same time I could not reconcile myself to the fearful situation. My indignation was roused by the mad pack howling for our lives. Yet I remained benumbed and inert, unable to do anything except torment myself with everlasting whys and wherefors.

In the midst of the harassing situation we were ordered out of our flat, the landlord having somehow learned my identity. With great difficulty we found quarters in the very heart of the ghetto, on Market Street, on the fifth floor of a congested tenement. East Side landlords were used to having every kind of radical as their tenants. Moreover, the new place was cheaper and had the advantage of light rooms. It was fatiguing to climb so many flights of stairs a score of times a day, but it was preferable to having heavy-footed tenants over our heads. Orthodox Jews take Jehovah literally, especially his command to multiply. There was not a family in the house with fewer than five children, and some had eight or ten. Notwithstanding my love for children, I could not have remained long in the flat with the constant tramp of little feet over my head.

My good friend Solotaroff succeeded in inducing several East Side doctors to give me employment. Their patients, Jews and Italians, were mostly from the poorest families, their living-quarters consisting generally of two or three rooms for six or more people. Their incomes averaged about fifteen dollars a week, and the trained nurse was paid four dollars a day. For them nurses were luxuries indulged in only in very serious illness. Nursing under such conditions was not only difficult, but extremely painful. I was pledged to keep up the standard of pay in my profession. I could not give my services for a lower price, and therefore had to find other ways of helping those poor people than by merely taking care of their sick.

I was mostly on night duty because few nurses were willing to take night cases, while I preferred them. The presence of relatives and their constant interference, much talking and weeping, and, above all, their horror of fresh air made day work most trying for me. " You wicked one ! " an old lady once berated me for opening a window in the sick-room; "do you want to kill my child ? " At night I had a free hand to give my patients the attention they needed. With the help of a book and a large pot of coffee, brewed by myself, the night hours passed quickly.

While I never refused any case, whatever the nature of the disease, I preferred to nurse children; they are so pathetically helpless when ill; they respond so gratefully to patience and kindness.

Working under an assumed name brought me many amusing experiences. Once a young socialist I knew called me to nurse his mother. She had double pneumonia, he informed me; she was a large woman and very hard to handle. About to accompany the man, I noticed that he was fidgety, as if he wanted to say something, but did not know how. " What is it? " I asked. His mother had been violently antagonistic to me during the McKinley panic, he confided to me; she had repeatedly said: " If I had that woman, I would soak her in kerosene and burn her alive." He wanted me to know it before taking the case. " It was generous of your mother," I said, " but in her present condition she will hardly be able to carry out her threat." My young socialist was very much impressed.

After three weeks of struggle our patient succeeded in cheating the black-hooded gentleman. She had sufficiently recovered to do without a night nurse, and I was preparing to leave. To my surprise the young socialist announced that his mother wanted the day nurse discharged and me in her place. "Miss Smith is a wonderful nurse," she had told her son. " Do you know who she really is ? " he asked: " it's the terrible Emma Goldman ! " " My God," his mother cried, " I hope you have not told her what I said about her." The boy admitted that he had. " And she nursed me so fine? Oi, a wonderful nurse ! "

With the advent of warm weather the number of my patients decreased. I did not regret it; I was very tired and needed a rest. I wanted more time for reading and leisure to be with Dan, Yegor, and Ed. A sweet and harmonious *camaraderie* with the latter had replaced our turbulent emotions of the past. Our separation had had a profound effect on Ed, made him more tolerant and mellow, more understanding. In his little girl and in much reading he found solace. Our intellectual companionship had never before been so stimulating and enjoyable.

I had everything a human being could wish, yet there was chaos in my mind, an ever-growing craving in my heart. I longed to take up the old struggle, to make my life count for more than a mere round of personal interests. But how get back — where begin again? It seemed to me that I had burned the bridges behind me, that I could never again span the gap that had grown so wide since the dreadful Buffalo days.

One morning the young English anarchist William McQueen called on me. I had met him on my first tour through England in 1895; he had arranged my meetings in Leeds and had been my host. I had also met him several times since his arrival in America. He now came to invite me to speak in Paterson in behalf of the striking silk-weavers. McQueen and the Austrian anarchist Rudolph Grossmann were going to address a mass meeting, and the strikers had asked me to come.

It was the first time since the Czolgosz tragedy that I had been approached by workers, or even by my own comrades. I seized upon the chance as a desert wanderer falls upon a well.

The night before the meeting I had a nightmare, waking up with screams that brought Yegor to my bed. In a cold sweat and shaking in every nerve I related to my brother all I could remember of my oppressive dream.

I dreamed I was in Paterson. The large hall was crowded, myself on the platform. I stepped to the edge and began to speak. I seemed to be carried along on the human sea at my feet. The waves rose and fell in tune with the inflections of my voice. Then they rushed away from me, faster and faster, carrying the people with them. I remained on the platform, all alone, my voice hushed in the silence around me. Alone, yet not quite. Something was stirring, taking form, growing before my eyes. I stood tense, breathlessly waiting. The form was advancing, coming to the very edge of the platform, carrying itself erect, head thrown back, its large eyes gleaming into mine. My voice struggled in my throat, and with a great effort I cried out: " Czolgosz! Leon Czolgosz! "

Fear possessed me that I should not be able to speak at the Paterson meeting. In vain I sought to rid myself of the feeling that when I stepped upon the platform, the face of Czolgosz would emerge from the crowd. I wired McQueen that I could not come.

The next day the papers carried the news of the arrest of McQueen and Grossmann. It horrified me to think that I had allowed a dream to keep me from responding to the call of the strikers. I had permitted myself to be influenced by a spook and had stayed safe at home while my young comrades were in danger. " Will the Czolgosz tragedy haunt me to the end of my days? " I kept asking myself. The answer came sooner than I anticipated.

" BLOODY RIOTS — WORKERS AND PEASANTS KILLED — STUDENTS WHIPPED BY COSSACKS. . . ." The press was filled with the events that were happening in Russia. Once more the struggle against tsarist autocracy was being brought to the attention of the world. The appalling brutality on one side, the glorious courage and heroism on the other, tore me out of the lethargy that had paralysed my will since the Buffalo days. With accusing clarity I realized that I had left the movement at its most critical moment, had turned my back on our work when I was most needed, that I had even begun to doubt my life's faith and ideal. And all because of a handful that had proved to be base and cowardly.

I tried to excuse my faint-heartedness by the deep concern I felt in the forsaken boy. My indignation against the weaklings had sprung, I argued with myself, from my sympathy with Czolgosz. No doubt that had been the impelling motive for my stand — so impelling, indeed, that it had even turned me against Sasha because he had failed to see in Czolgosz's act what had been so clear to me. My bitterness had extended to that dear friend and had made me forget that he was in prison and still needed me.

Now, however, another thought hammered in my brain, the thought that there might have been other motives, motives not quite so selfless as I had made myself and others believe. My own inability to face the first great issue in my life now made me see that the self-assurance with which I had always proclaimed that I could stand alone had deserted me the moment I was called upon to make good. I had not been able to bear being repudiated and shunned; I could not brave defeat. But, instead of admitting it to myself at least, I had kept on beating my wings in blind fury. I had become embittered and had drawn back within myself.

The qualities I had most admired in the heroes of the past, and also in Czolgosz, the strength to stand and die alone, had been lacking in me. Perhaps one needs more courage to live than to die. Dying is of a moment, but the claims of life are endless — a thousand small and petty things which tax one's strength and leave one too spent to meet the testing hour.

I emerged from my tortuous introspection as from a long illness, not yet in possession of my former vigour, but with a determination to try once more to steel my will to meet the exigencies of life, whatever they might be.

My first faltering step after the months of spiritual death was a letter to Sasha.

The news from Russia stirred the East Side radicals into intense activity. Trade-unionists, socialists, and anarchists set aside their political differences, the better to be able to help the victims of the Russian régime. Large meetings were held and funds raised for the sufferers in prison and exile. I took up the work with new-born strength. I stopped nursing in order to devote myself entirely to the needs of Russia. At the same time there was also enough happening in America to tax our utmost energies.

The coal-miners were on strike. Conditions in the coal districts were appalling and aid was urgently needed. The politicians in the labour movement were busy talking for the press and doing little for the strikers. Whatever backbone they had shown in the beginning of the strike caved in when the man with the Big Stick appeared on the scene. President Roosevelt suddenly evinced an interest in the miners. He would help the strikers, he announced, if their representatives would be reasonable and give him a chance to go after the mine-owners. That was manna for the politicians in the unions. They immediately transferred the burden of responsibility to the presidential shoulders of Teddy. No need to worry any more; his official wisdom would find the right solution of vexing problems. Meanwhile the miners and their families were starving and the police browbeating those who came to the coal region to encourage the strikers.

The radical elements refused to be duped by the President's interest, nor did they have greater faith in the sudden change of heart of the employers. They worked steadily to raise funds and keep up the spirit of the men. The heat had grown too oppressive for public meetings, which meant a lull in our efforts. Still we were able to canvass unions, hold picnics, and arrange other affairs to raise money. My return to public activity rejuvenated me and gave me a new interest in life.

I was asked to undertake a lecture tour for the purpose of raising funds for the miners and the victims in Russia. We had reckoned, however, without the authorities in the strike districts. Our people there could secure no halls; on the rare occasions when a landlord was brave enough to rent us his place, the police broke up our gatherings. In several towns, among them Wilkesbarre and McKeesport, I was met by the guardians of the law at the station and turned back. It was finally decided that I should concentrate my efforts in the larger cities of the strike regions. In these I met with no difficulties until I reached Chicago.

My first lecture there dealt with Russia and took place in a crowded West Side hall. As usual the police were present, but they did not interfere. " We believe in freedom of speech," one of the officials told our committee, " so long as Emma Goldman talks on Russia." Fortunately my work for the miners was almost exclusively in the unions, and the police could do nothing there.

My last lecture was to be given at the Chicago Philosophical Society, an organization with a free platform. Their weekly gatherings had always been held in Handel Hall, on which the society had a long lease. The owners of the place had never before objected to either the speakers or their subjects, but on the Sunday scheduled for my talk Handel Hall was barred to the people. The janitor, pale and trembling, declared that detectives had been " to see " him. They had informed him about the Criminal Anarchy Law, which would make him liable to arrest, imprisonment, and a fine if he allowed Emma Goldman to speak. It happened that no such law had been passed in Illinois, but what did that matter? I delivered the proscribed lecture, nevertheless. Another hall-keeper, better versed in his legal rights and not so easily frightened, consented to let me speak on the dangerous subject of the Philosophic Aspects of Anarchism.

My tour was trying and strenuous, made more so by the necessity of speaking surrounded by watch-dogs ready to spring on me at any moment, as well as by being compelled to change halls at a moment's notice. But I welcomed the difficulties. They helped to rekindle my fighting spirit and to convince me that those in power never learn to what extent persecution is the leaven of revolutionary zeal.

I had barely returned home when news came of Kate Austen's death. Kate, the most daring, courageous voice among the women of America! Risen from the depths, she had reached intellectual heights many educated people could not touch. She loved life, and her soul was aflame for the oppressed, the suffering, and the poor. How splendid she had been all through the Buffalo tragedy! Only a month ago she had written, within the shadow of her own death, a glowing tribute to Czolgosz. And now she was gone, and with her one of the truly great personalities in our ranks. Her death was the loss not merely of a comrade, but also of a precious friend. Excepting Emma Lee she was the only woman who had come close to me and who understood the complexities of my being better than I did myself. Her sensitive response had helped me through many hard moments. Now she was dead, and my heart was heavy.

In a hectic life like mine sorrows and joys follow each other so rapidly that they leave no time to dwell too long on either. My grief over Kate's loss was still acute when another shock came. Voltairine de Cleyre was shot and severely wounded by a former pupil of hers. A telegram from Philadelphia informed me that she was in the hospital in a critical condition and suggested that I raise money for her care.

I had seen little of Voltairine since our unfortunate misunderstanding in 1894. I had heard that she was not well and that she had gone to Europe to regain her health. On my last visit in Philadelphia I had been told that she was having a severe struggle to make a living by teaching English to Jewish immigrants and giving music lessons, while at the same time keeping up her activities in the movement. I admired her energy and industry, but I was hurt and repelled by what seemed to me her unreasonable and small attitude toward me. I could not seek her out, nor had she communicated with me in all these years. Her fearless stand during the McKinley hysteria had helped much to increase my respect for her, and her letter in *Free Society* to Senator Hawley, who had said he would give a thousand dollars to have a shot at an anarchist, had made a lasting impression on me. She had sent her address to the senatorial patriot and had written him that she was ready to give him the pleasure to shoot an anarchist free of charge, on the sole condition that he permit her to explain to him the principles of anarchism before he fired.

" We must begin to raise money for Voltairine at once," I said to Ed. I knew she would resent a public appeal in her behalf, and Ed agreed that it was necessary to approach our friends privately on the matter. Solotaroff, first to be advised by us, responded beautifully, even though he was in poor health and his office practice was yielding very little. He suggested that Gordon, Voltairine's former lover, should be seen; he had become a successful physician and he was financially well able to help Voltairine, who had done so much for him. Solotaroff volunteered to speak to Gordon.

The result of our canvass was very encouraging, though we also met with some disagreeable experiences. An East Side friend of Voltairine's declared that he did not believe in " private charity," and there were also others whose sympathies had become blunted by material success. But generous souls made up for the rest, and soon we collected five hundred dollars. Ed went to Philadelphia with the money. Upon his return he reported that two of the bullets had been extracted. The third could not be touched because it was embedded too close to the heart. Voltairine's main concern, Ed told us, was about the boy who had attempted her life and she had already declared that she would not prosecute him.

Max and Millie were visiting New York for Christmas, and the occasion proved an unexpected and joyful treat. Ed had been urging me for some time to permit him to realize his long-cherished dream of dressing me up in " decent clothes." The time had come to carry out his promise, he insisted; I must go with him to the best shops and give my fancy free rein.

I realized as soon as we were in the fashionable emporium that an untrammelled fancy is an expensive thing, and I did not want to bankrupt Ed. "Let's run away quickly," I whispered; "this is no place for us." " Run away? Emma Goldman run away?" Ed teased; "you'll stay long enough to have your measurements taken and leave the rest to me."

On Christmas Eve boxes began to arrive at my apartment: a wonderful coat with a real astrakhan collar, muff, and turban to match. There were also a dress, silk underwear, stockings, and gloves. I felt like Cinderella. Ed beamed when he called and found me all rigged out. " That's the way I have always wanted you to look," he exclaimed; " some day everybody may be able to have beautiful things like these."

At the Hofbrau Haus we found Max and Millie already waiting for us. Millie was also dressed for the occasion, and Max was in fine mettle. He asked whether I had married a Rockefeller or struck a gold-mine. I was entirely too swell for a proletarian like himself, he laughed. " Such duds deserve at least three bottles of *Trabacher*," he cried, forthwith ordering them. We were the merriest party in the place.

Millie preceded Max to Chicago. He lingered on for a few days and we spent the time in long walks, visiting galleries and concerts. On the evening of his departure I accompanied Max to the station. While we stood on the platform, chatting, we were approached by two men who turned out to be detectives. They put us under arrest and took us to the police station, where we were cross-examined and then discharged. "On what grounds were we arrested?" I demanded. "Just on general principles," the desk sergeant answered pleasantly. "Your principles are rotten!" I retorted heatedly. "Go on, now," he roared, "you're Red Emma, ain't you? That's enough."

A letter from Solotaroff informed me that Gordon had refused to aid Voltairine. The latter had drudged for years to help him through college, and now that she was ill, he had not even a kind word for her. My intuition about him had been correct. We agreed that she should not be told of the cruel indifference of the man who had meant so much to her.

Voltairine not only refused to prosecute the youth who had shot her, but even appealed to our press to aid his defence. "He is sick, poor, and friendless," she wrote; "he is in need of kindness, not prison." In a letter to the authorities she pointed out that the boy had been jobless for a long time and that as a result of worry he suffered from delusions. But the law had to have its pound of flesh: the youth was found guilty and given a sentence of six years and nine months.

The effect of the verdict on Voltairine caused a very serious relapse that kept us in anxious suspense for weeks. Finally she was declared out of danger and able to leave the hospital.

The Philadelphia papers furnished an amusing side to the tragic incident. Like the rest of the American press they had for years been filled with invectives against anarchism and anarchists. "Fiends incarnate — champions of murder and destruction — cowards" were among the most delicate epithets applied to us. But when Voltairine refused to prosecute her assailant and pleaded in his behalf, the same editors wrote that "anarchism is really the doctrine of the Nazarene, the gospel of forgiveness."

CHAPTER XXVI

THE ANTI-ANARCHIST IMMIGRATION LAW WAS AT LAST SMUGGLED through Congress, and thereafter no person disbelieving in organized government was to be permitted to enter the United States. Under its provisions men like Tolstoy, Kropotkin, Spencer, or Edward Carpenter could be excluded from the hospitable shores of America. Too late did the lukewarm liberals realize the peril of this law to advanced thought. Had they opposed in a concerted manner the activities of the reactionary element, the statute might not have been passed. The immediate result of this new assault on American liberties, however, was a very decided change of attitude towards anarchists. I myself now ceased to be considered anathema; on the contrary, the very people who had been hostile to me began to seek me out. Various lecture forums, like the Manhattan Liberal Club, the Brooklyn Philosophical Society, and other American organizations invited me to speak. I accepted gladly because of the opportunity I had been wanting for years to reach the native intelligentsia, to enlighten it as to what anarchism really means. At these gatherings I made new friends and met old ones, among them Ernest Crosby, Leonard D. Abbott, and Theodore Schroeder.

At the Sunrise Club I came to know many persons of advanced ideas. Among the most interesting were Elizabeth and Alexis Ferm, John and Abby Coryell. The Ferms were the first Americans I met whose ideas on education were akin to mine; but while I merely advocated the need of a new approach to the child, the Ferms translated their ideas into practice. In the Playhouse, as their school was called, the children of the neighbourhood were bound by neither rules nor text-books. They were free to go or come and to learn from observation and experience. I knew no one else who so well understood child psychology as Elizabeth and who was so capable of bringing out the best in the young. She and Alexis considered themselves single-taxers, but in reality they were anarchists in their views and lives. It was a great treat to visit their home, which was also the school, and to witness the beautiful relationship that existed between them and the children.

The Coryells had much of the same quality, John possessing exceptional depth of mind. He impressed me as being more European than American, and indeed he had seen much of the world. As a young man he had been United States consul at Canton, China. Later he had lived in Japan, had travelled extensively, and had associated with people of various countries and races. It had served to give him a wider outlook on life and a deeper understanding of human beings. John had considerable talent as a writer; he was the author of the original Nick Carter stories, and he had earned a name and money under the pseudonym of Bertha M. Clay. He was also a frequent contributor to the *Physical Culture* magazine, because of his interest in health matters and because it gave him his first chance to express himself freely on the subjects he had at heart. He was one of the most generous persons I had ever met. His writings had brought him a fortune, of which he had kept almost nothing, having given lavishly to those in need. His greatest charm lay in his rich sense of humour, no less incisive because of his polished manner. The Coryells and the Ferms became my dearest American friends.

I also saw a great deal of Hugh O. Pentecost. He had undergone many changes since I had first met him during my trial in 1893. He did not impress me as a strong character, but he was among the most brilliant speakers in New York. He lectured Sunday mornings on social topics, his eloquence attracting large audiences. Pentecost was a frequent visitor at my apartment, where he used to " feel natural," as he often said. His wife, a handsome, middle-class woman, keenly disliked her husband's poor friends, and her eyes were upon the influential subscribers to his lectures.

Once I had arranged a little party in my flat, with Pentecost as one of my guests. Shortly before the party I met Mrs. Pentecost and asked her if she would like to come. " Thank you so much," she said, " I shall be delighted; I love slumming." " Isn't it fortunate? " I remarked. " Otherwise you would never meet interesting people." She did not attend the party.

My public life grew colourful. Nursing became less strenuous when several of my " charges " moved out of my apartment and thus reduced my expenses. I could afford to take longer rests between cases. It gave me the opportunity to do much reading that had been neglected for some time. I enjoyed my new experience of living alone. I could go and come without considering others and I did not always find a crowd at home upon my return from a lecture. I knew myself well enough to realize that I was not easy to live with. The dreadful months following the Buffalo tragedy had driven me desperate with the struggle to find my way back to life and work. The timid radicalism of the people on the East Side had made me impatient and intolerant with the striplings who talked about the future, yet did nothing in the present. I enjoyed the boon of retirement and the companionship of a few chosen friends, the dearest among them Ed — no longer jealously watching, possessively demanding every thought and every breath, but giving and receiving free and spontaneous joy.

Often he would visit me weary and depressed. I knew it was the growing friction in his home; not that he had ever spoken about it, but now and then a chance remark disclosed to me that he was not happy. Once, in the course of a conversation, he remarked : " In prison I used to take solitary confinement rather than share my cell with anybody. The constant jabber of a cell-mate used to drive me frantic. Now I have to listen to incessant talk, and there is no solitary for me to get away to." On another occasion he gave vent to irony regarding the girls and women that pretend to hold advanced ideas until they have safely captured their man and then fiercely turn against those ideas for fear of losing their provider. To cheer him I would turn the talk into other channels, or ask about his daughter. At once his face would light up and his depression lift. One day he brought me a picture of the little one. I had never seen such a striking resemblance. I was so moved by the beautiful face of the child that unthinkingly I cried out : " Why don't you ever bring her to see me ? " " Why ? " he replied, vehemently ; " the mother ! The mother ! If you only knew the mother ! " " Please, please ! " I remonstrated ; " don't say anything more ; I don't want to know about her ! " He began excitedly to pace the floor, breaking out into a torrent of words. " You must ; you must let me speak ! " he cried. " You must let me tell you all I have suppressed so long." I tried to stop him, but he paid no attention.

" Rage and bitterness against you drove me to that woman," he continued, tempestuously; " yes, and to drink. For weeks after our last break-up I kept drinking. Then I met the woman. I had seen her at radical affairs before, but she had never meant anything to me. Now she excited me; I was maddened by the loss of you and by drink. So I took her home. I quit working and gave myself up to a wild debauch, hoping to blot out the resentment I felt against you for going away." With a sharp pain in my heart I seized his hand, crying: " Oh, Ed, not resentment? " " Yes, yes! Resentment! " he repeated; " even hate! I felt it then because you had so easily given up our love and our life. But don't interrupt me; I must get it out of my system."

We sat down. Putting his hand over mine, he continued somewhat more calmly: " The drunken debauch went on for weeks. I wasn't aware of time, I didn't go anywhere or see anybody. I stayed at home in a stupor of drink and sex. One day I woke up with my mind terribly clear. I was sick of myself and of the woman. I told her brutally that she would have to go; that I had never intended our affair to be a permanent thing. She did what women usually do; she said I was a cruel and unscrupulous seducer. When she saw that it did not impress me, she began weeping and begging and finally she declared that she was pregnant. I was staggered; I felt it was impossible, yet I didn't believe she would deliberately invent such a thing. I had no money and I could not let her shift for herself. I was trapped and I had to go through with it. A few months under the same roof made me realize that we didn't have a single thought in common. Everything about her repelled me; her shrill voice all over the house, her constant chatter and gossip. They grated on my nerves and often drove me out of the house, but the thought that she was carrying my child always brought me back. Two months before it was born, she taunted me, during one of our bickering wrangles, with having tricked me. She had not been pregnant at all when she had first told me. I decided then and there to leave her as soon as the child was born. You'll laugh, but the birth of the little one woke strange chords in my soul. It made me forget all that was lacking in my life. I stayed."

" Why torture yourself, dear Ed? " I tried to soothe him; " why rake up the past? " He brushed me gently aside. " You must listen," he insisted; " you had everything to do with the beginning; it's only fair you should listen to the very end."

" When you returned from Europe," he went on, " the contrast between our past life and my present existence appeared more glaring. I wanted to take my child and come to you to plead once more for our love. But you were wrapped up in other people and in your public activities. You seemed to be completely cured of what you had once felt for me."

"You were wrong!" I cried, "I still loved you even when we had drifted apart." "I see it now, my dear, but at the time you appeared indifferent and aloof," he replied. "I could not turn to you. I sought what relief I could in my child. I read, and I found — yes, I found — some forgetfulness in the works we used to argue about; I could understand them better. But my nerves had become blunted; I no longer winced at the sound of the shrill voice. Her recriminations had made me hard and cynical. Besides, I had discovered a way to stop the stream," he added with a chuckle. "What was it?" I asked, glad of his lighter tone; "perhaps I could also use it on some people." "Well, you see," he explained, "I take out my watch, hold it up to the lady's face, and tell her I'll give her five minutes to get through. If by that time she still keeps it up, I leave the house." "And it works?" I inquired. "Like magic. She dashes into the kitchen, and I go into my room and lock the door." I laughed, though I really wanted to cry at the thought of Ed, who had always loved refinement and peace, forced into degrading, vulgar scenes.

"The break has come, though, at last," he went on. "It had to, anyway, even if you and I had not become good friends again. It was bound to come as soon as I began to realize the effect those quarrels were having on the child." He added that for a long time he had wanted to go to Europe to see his mother again, but he had lacked the means. Now he was in a position to do so. He would take his child to Vienna with him, and he asked me to accompany him.

"How do you mean, take the child?" I cried. "The mother, what about her? It's her child, too, isn't it? It must mean everything to her. How can you rob her of it?" Ed got on his feet and raised me up also. His face close to mine, he said: "Love! Love! Haven't you always insisted that the love of the average mother either smothers the child with kisses or kills it with blows? Why this sudden sentimentality for the poor mother?" "I know, I know, my dear," I answered; "I haven't changed my views. Just the same, the woman endures the agony of birth and she nourishes the infant with her own substance. The man does almost nothing, and yet he claims the child. Can't you see how unjust it is, Ed? Go to Europe with you? I'd do it at once. But I cannot have a mother robbed of her child on my account." He charged me with not being free; I was like all feminists who rail against man for the wrongs he supposedly does to woman, without seeing the injustices that the man suffers, and also the child. He would go anyway and take his little girl along. Never would he allow his child to grow up in an atmosphere of strife.

Ed left me in a turmoil of conflicting emotions. I had to admit to myself that it had indeed been I who had driven him into that woman's arms. I knew, as I had known when I had gone away from him, that I could not have acted otherwise. All the same, I had been the cause. I recalled vividly Ed's violent outburst on that terrible night; it was evidence enough of his agony of spirit. There was no blinking my part in his misery; why, then, did I refuse him now when he needed me even more? Why did I deny him the help he asked for his child? The woman certainly meant nothing to me; why should I have scruples about her loss? I had always held that the mere physical process of motherhood does not make a woman a real mother; yet I had talked to Ed against robbing her!

After much thought I concluded that my feeling in regard to the mother of Ed's child was deeply embedded in my sentiments for motherhood in general, that blind, dumb force that brings forth life in travail, wasting woman's youth and strength, and leaving her in old age a burden to herself and to those to whom she has given birth. It was this helplessness of motherhood that had made me recoil from adding to its pain.

The next time Ed came I tried to explain this to him, but he could not follow me. He said he had always credited me with being able to reason like a man, objectively; now he felt I was arguing subjectively, like all women. I replied that the reasoning faculties of most men had not impressed me to the point of wishing to imitate them, and that I preferred to do my own thinking as a woman. I repeated what I had already told him: that I should be supremely happy to go with him if he went alone, or to visit him in Europe some time later, but that I could not run off with another woman's child.

I was afraid that my stand would throw a shadow on my new friendship with Ed, but he proved to be big and fine about it. His visits became beautiful events. He was planning to leave for Europe in June, together with his child.

Early in April he told me he would be very busy for a week. His firm had to buy a large stock of lumber, and the transaction was to keep him out of town for a few days. But he would remain in touch with me and wire the moment he got back. During his absence I was called on a night case in Brooklyn, to nurse a consumptive boy. It was a long and tedious journey to and fro; I would return home very tired, barely able to take my bath, and fall asleep as soon as I struck the pillow. One morning, very early, I was roused out of bed by persistent and violent ringing. It was Timmermann, whom I had not seen for more than a year. "Claus!" I cried; "what brings you at such an hour?"

His manner was unusually quiet and he looked strangely at me. "Sit down," he said at last in a solemn voice; "I have something to tell you." I wondered what had happened to him. "It's about Ed," he began. "Ed!" I cried, suddenly alarmed; "is anything the matter with him? Is he ill? Have you a message for me?"

"Ed — Ed — " he stammered — "Ed has no more messages." I held out my hand as if to ward off a blow. "Ed died last night," I heard Claus say in a shaken voice. I stood staring at him. "You're drunk!" I cried; "it can't be!" Claus took my hand and gently pulled me down beside him. "I'm a messenger of evil; of all your friends I had to be the one to bring you this news. Poor, poor girl!" He stroked my hair furtively. We sat in silence.

Finally Claus spoke. He had gone to Ed's house to meet him for supper; he had waited until nine o'clock, but Ed did not return, so he decided to leave. At that moment a cab drove up to the house. The driver inquired for Brady's apartment, saying that Mr. Brady was in the cab, sick. Would someone help to carry him up? Neighbours came out and surrounded the cab. Ed was inside, sunk back in the seat, unconscious and breathing heavily. People carried him upstairs, while Claus ran for a doctor. When he came back the cabman was gone. All he had been able to tell was that he had been called to a saloon near the Long Island station, where he had found the gentleman hunched up in a chair, bleeding from a cut on his face. He was conscious, but able only to give his address. The saloon-keeper explained that the gentleman had asked for a drink and had taken it standing at the bar. Then he had paid and started towards the toilet. On the way he had suddenly fallen down in a heap, striking his forehead against the bar. That was all any of them knew.

The doctor had worked frantically to revive Ed; but it was in vain. He died without regaining consciousness.

Claus's voice was droning in my ears, but I barely heard what he was saying. Nothing mattered but that Ed had been stricken among strangers, stuffed into a cab, alone at the moment of his greatest need. Oh, Ed, my splendid friend, robbed of life when so close to the fullness of it! The cruelty of it, the senseless cruelty! My heart cried out in protest, my throat choked with tears that would not come to my eyes to relieve my poignant grief.

Claus got to his feet remarking that he must notify other friends and help with the funeral arrangements. "I will go with you!" I declared. "I will see Ed again." "Impossible!" Claus objected. "Mrs. Brady has already stated that she will not let you in. She said you had robbed her of Ed when he was alive and she will keep you away now that he is dead. You would only have to go through with an ugly scene."

I remained alone with memories of my life with Ed. In the late afternoon Yegor came, shaken by the news. He had loved Ed and was profoundly overcome now. His sweet concern melted my frozen heart. With his arms about me I found the tears that would not come before. We sat close together, talking of Ed, his life, his dreams, and premature end. It grew late and I remembered the sick boy in Brooklyn waiting for me. I might not be near my precious dead, but I could at least go to the aid of my young patient struggling for life.

Funerals had always been abhorrent to me; I felt that they expressed grief turned inside out. My loss was too deep for it. I went to the crematory and found the ceremony over, the coffin already closed. The friends who knew of my bond with Ed lifted the cover again for me. I approached to look at the dear face, so beautifully serene in sleep. The silence about me made death less gruesome.

Suddenly a shriek echoed through the place, followed by another and another. A female voice, hysterically crying: "My husband! My husband! He is mine!" The shrieking woman, her black widow's veil resembling a crow's wings, threw herself between me and the coffin, pushing me back and falling over the dead. A little blonde girl with frightened eyes, suffocating with sobs, was clutching at the woman's dress.

For a moment I stood petrified with horror. Then I slowly moved towards the exit, out into the open, away from the revolting scene. My mind was full of the child, the replica of its father, its life now to be so different from what he had intended.

CHAPTER XXVII

MEMORIES OF MY FORMER LIFE WITH ED FILLED ME WITH LONG-
ing for what had again been just within my reach, only to be
snatched away. Recollections of the past compelled me to look into
the most hidden crevices of my being; their strange contradictions tore
me between my hunger for love and my inability to have it for long.
It was not only the finality of death, as in the case of Ed, nor the
circumstances that had robbed me of Sasha in the springtime of our
lives, that always came between. There were other forces at work to
deny me permanency in love. Were they part of some passionate
yearning in me that no man could completely fulfil or were they inherent in those who for ever reach out for the heights, for some
ideal or exalted aim that excludes aught else? Was not the price they
exacted conditioned in the very nature of the thing I wished to achieve?
The stars could not be climbed by one rooted in a clod of earth.
If one soared high, could he hope to dwell for long in the absorbing
depths of passion and love? Like all who had paid for their faith,
I too would have to face the inevitable. Occasional snatches of love;
nothing permanent in my life except my ideal.

Yegor remained in my flat, while I accompanied my patient and
his mother to Liberty, New York. I had never nursed consumptives
before and had not witnessed their indomitable will to live and the
consuming fires of their withering flesh. At the moment when everything seemed at an end, my patient would take a new leap, followed
by days of rekindled hope for a future of work that would tax the
vitality of the strongest. Here was the boy of eighteen, a mere bundle
of bone and skin, with burning eyes and hectic cheeks, talking of the
life he might never have.

With his reawakened will invariably came the urge of the body, the
craving for sex. It was not until I had spent four months with him

that I realized what the youth had been desperately trying to suppress. I was far from the thought that it was my presence that was adding fuel to the smouldering fires within him. A few things had aroused my suspicion, but I had put them aside as signs of my patient's feverish state. Once, as I was taking his pulse, he suddenly seized my hand and pressed it excitedly in his own. At another time, when I bent over to straighten his covers, I felt his hot breath very close to the back of my neck. Often I noticed his large burning eyes following me about.

The boy slept in the open, on the screened veranda. To be within reach, at night I stayed in the room adjoining the porch. His mother was always with him part of the day to give me some time to rest. Her bedroom was behind the dining-room, farthest away from the veranda. The care of my tubercular case was more exacting than any I had nursed before, but years of experience had made me alert to the least stirring of a patient. It was hardly ever necessary for the boy to use the little bell on his table; I could hear him the moment he began to move.

One night I had gone in to my patient several times to find him peacefully slumbering; very tired, I also fell asleep. I was awakened by a feeling of something pressing on my chest. I discovered my patient sitting on my bed, his hot lips pressed to my breast, his burning hands caressing my body. Anger made me forget his precarious condition. I pushed him away and leaped to the floor. "You madman!" I cried; "get to your bed at once or I will call your mother!" He held out his hands in silent entreaty and started to walk towards the porch. Halfway over, he fell down, shaken by a paroxysm of coughing. Frightened out of my resentment, I was for a moment at a loss what to do. I dared not call his mother; his presence in my room would make her think I had failed her son when he had called me. Nor could I leave him where he was. He weighed little, and desperation increases one's strength. I raised him up and carried him to his bed. His excitement brought on a new hæmorrhage, and my anger gave way to pity for the poor boy, so near death, yet so tenaciously reaching out for life.

All through his attack he clung to my hand, between fits of coughing begging me to spare his mother and forgive him for what he had done. I kept on turning over in my mind how I could resign. It was clear I should have to leave. What excuse could I give? I could not tell his mother the truth; she would not believe it of her son, and even if she did, she would be too shocked and hurt to understand the urge that had impelled the boy. I should have to say that I was tired out by constant nursing and needed rest; and of course I would give her time to find another nurse. But weeks passed before I could carry out my resolve. My patient was very ill and his mother herself almost a physical wreck from anxiety. When at last the patient had once more escaped his doom and was better again, I begged to be allowed to go.

On my return to New York I found that I should have to look for a new abode again: once more my neighbours had objected to having Emma Goldman in the house. I moved into a larger place, my brother Yegor and our young comrade Albert Zibelin sharing the apartment with me. Various elements were combined in Albert's make-up; his father, an active anarchist, was French; his mother an American Quaker of sweet and gentle disposition. He was born in Mexico, where as a child he had roamed freely in the hills. Later he lived with Elisée Reclus, the celebrated French scientist and exponent of anarchism. His fine heritage and the beneficial influences in his early life had produced splendid results in Albert; he was beautiful in body and spirit. He grew into an ardent lover of freedom and became a tender and thoughtful friend, altogether a rare character among the young American boys of my acquaintance.

This time our co-operative venture began more promisingly. Each member talked less of equal responsibility and did more to relieve the burden of the others. It was doubly fortunate for me because of the many calls of the movement upon my energies. With Albert as chef, and the help of Yegor and Dan, when the latter visited us, I was able to devote myself more to my public interests, which were shared also by the boys.

Since I had begun writing to Sasha again, we had been drawing closer together. He had not quite three years more to endure, and he was full of new hope, planning what he would do after his release. For several years past he had been much interested in one of his prison mates, a consumptive boy by the name of Harry. In every letter Sasha referred to his friend, especially while I was nursing my tubercular patient. I had to keep him informed of the methods and treatment I applied. His interest in Harry had even suggested to him the study of medicine when he should leave prison. Meanwhile he was eager for what I could send him: medical books, journals, and everything else bearing on the white plague.

Sasha's letters breathed a zest in life that carried me along and filled me with increased admiration for him. I, too, began to dream and plan for the great moment when my heroic boy would be free again and united with me in life and work. Only thirty-three months more and his martyrdom would be at an end!

Meanwhile John Turner had announced his coming to the States. He had been in America in 1896 and had lectured extensively during seven months. He was planning a new tour and wished especially to study the conditions of the men and women employed as clerks and sales-people in the United States. He had been very successful in England with the Shop Assistants' Union, which he had developed into a powerful organization. Under his leadership the status of those employees had been improved to a very considerable degree. While the conditions of that class of workers in America were not quite so bad as in England prior to the efforts of Turner and his union colleagues, we were sure that the men needed awakening. There was no one so capable of accomplishing it as John Turner.

For that reason, as well as because of the contribution Turner would make to the more general spread of our ideas, we hailed his proposed visit and immediately began to arrange a series of lectures for our brilliant English comrade. His first meeting we organized for October 22 at Murray Hill Lyceum.

Like so many others, John Turner had become an anarchist as a result of the Haymarket tragedy of 1887. His attitude to the State and to political action had induced him to refuse the candidacy for Parliament offered him by his union. "My place is among the rank and file," Turner had stated at the time; "my work is not in so-called 'public affairs,' which are part of the organized exploitation of labour. Even the small palliatives possible through Parliament would be gained by organized Labour much quicker by pressure from outside than by the representatives inside the House of Commons." His stand showed his grasp of social forces and his devotion to his ideal. While he had never ceased to work for anarchism, he considered activity in the unions his most vital purpose. He maintained that anarchism without the masses is bound to remain a mere dream, lacking living force. He felt that to reach the toilers one must take part in their daily economic struggle.

His opening address was on "Trade Unionism and the General Strike." Murray Hill Lyceum was filled to the doors with people from every walk of life. The police were present in large numbers. I in-

troduced our British comrade to the audience and then went to the
rear of the hall to look after our literature. When John had finished
speaking, I noticed several plain-clothes men approach the platform.
Sensing trouble, I hastened over to John. The strangers proved immigration officials who declared Turner was under arrest. Before the
audience had time to realize what was happening, he was rushed out
of the hall.

Turner was given the honour of being the first to fall under the
ban of the Federal Anti-Anarchist Law passed by Congress on March
3, 1903. Its main section reads: "No person who disbelieves in or
who is opposed to all organized governments, or who is a member
of or affiliated with any organization entertaining or teaching such
disbelief in or opposition to all governments . . . shall be permitted
to enter the United States." John Turner, well known in his own
country, respected by thinking people and having access to every
European land, was now to be victimized by a statute conceived in
panic and sponsored by the darkest elements in the United States.
When I announced to the audience that John Turner had been arrested and would be deported, the meeting unanimously resolved that
if our friend had to go, it should not be without a fight.

The Ellis Island authorities thought they were going to have it all
their own way. For several days no one, not even his lawyer, was
allowed to see Turner. Hugh O. Pentecost, whom we engaged to
represent the prisoner, immediately started habeas corpus proceedings.
That stayed the deportation and checked the arbitrary methods of
the Ellis Island Commissioner. At the first hearing the judge sustained,
of course, the immigration authorities by ordering Turner deported.
But we still had an appeal to the Federal Supreme Court in reserve.
Most of our comrades opposed such a step as inconsistent with our
ideas, a waste of money that could achieve no results. While I had no
illusions about what the Supreme Court was likely to do, I felt that
the fight for Turner would be splendid propaganda by bringing the
absurd law to the attention of the intelligent public. Last but not
least it would serve to awaken many Americans to the fact that the
liberties guaranteed in the United States, among which the right of
asylum was the most important, had become nothing but empty
phrases to be used as fire-crackers on the Fourth of July. The main
point, however, was whether Turner would be willing to continue
a prisoner on Ellis Island, perhaps for many months, until the Supreme

Court should decide his case. I wrote to ask him about it, receiving an immediate reply to the effect that he was "enjoying the hospitality of Ellis Island," and that he was entirely at our disposal to help make the fight.

While there had been a decided change in public opinion towards me since 1901, I was still very much taboo to the majority. I realized that if I wished to help Turner and participate in the activities against the deportation law, I had better remain in the background. My assumed name of Smith secured for me a willing ear with people who were sure to see red on meeting Emma Goldman. Still, a goodly number of American radicals knew me and were advanced enough not to be frightened by my ideas. With their help I succeeded in organizing a permanent Free Speech League, its members coming from various liberal elements. Among them were Peter E. Burroughs, Benjamin R. Tucker, H. Gaylord Wilshire, Dr. E. B. Foote, Jr., Theodore Schroeder, Charles B. Spahr, and many others well known in progressive circles. At its first meeting the league decided to have Clarence Darrow represent Turner before the Supreme Court.

The next step taken by the league was to arrange a meeting in Cooper Union. The Free Speech Leaguers were mostly professional men and very busy. It was left to me to do the suggesting and directing and to pester people until they promised their support. I had to visit numerous unions, as a result of which I collected sixteen hundred dollars. What was more difficult, I succeeded in persuading Yanofsky, editor of the *Freie Arbeiter Stimme,* who was at first opposed to the appeal, to open his columns to our publicity. Gradually I got other persons interested, the most active being Bolton Hall and his secretary, A. C. Pleydell, both untiring in their work on the case.

Bolton Hall, whom I had met several years before, was one of the most charming and gracious personalities it has been my good fortune to know. An unconditional libertarian and single-taxer, he had entirely emancipated himself from his highly respectable background except for his conventional dress. His frock-coat, high silk hat, gloves, and cane made him a conspicuous figure in our ranks, particularly so when he visited trade unions in behalf of Turner, or when he appeared before the American Longshoremen's Union, whose organizer and treasurer he was. But Bolton knew what he was about. He claimed that nothing impressed working-men so much as his fashionable attire. To my remonstrances he would reply: "Don't you see it is my silk hat that gives my speech importance?"

The Cooper Union meeting met with tremendous success, the speakers representing all shades of political opinion. Some were apologetic for having come to plead in behalf of an anarchist; as congressmen and college professors they could not afford to be as outspoken as they felt. Others, more daring, however, set the real tone of the meeting. Among them were Bolton Hall, Ernest Crosby, and Alexander Jonas. Letters and telegrams were read from William Lloyd Garrison, Edward M. Shepard, Horace White, Carl Schurz, and the Rev. Dr. Thomas Hall. They were unconditional in their condemnation of the outrageous law and of the attempts of Washington to destroy the fundamental principles guaranteed by the Declaration of Independence and the Constitution of the United States.

I sat in the audience, very much gratified with the results of our efforts, amused to think that most of those good people on the platform were unaware that it was Emma Goldman and her anarchist comrades who had arranged and managed the meeting. No doubt some of the respectable liberals, those who always offered profuse apologies for every bold step they contemplated making, would have been shocked out of their wits had they known that "wild-eyed anarchists" had had anything to do with the affair. But I was a hardened sinner; I did not feel the least scruple for having gone into a conspiracy to induce the timid gentlemen to express themselves on such a vital issue.

Amidst the excitement of the campaign I was called by Dr. E. B. Foote to a case. I had tried several times previously to get work with him, but although he was a prominent free-thinker, he had yet fought shy of employing the dangerous Emma Goldman. Since the Turner appeal we had come in contact a good deal, and that was probably what had changed his mind. At any rate he sent for me to take charge of one of his patients, and New Year's Eve 1904 found me at the bedside of the man entrusted to my care. The midnight merry-making on the street awakened memories of the great day, a year past, spent with Max, Millie, and Ed.

Being compelled to move to new quarters every now and then had become a habit with me, and I no longer minded it. I now rented part of a flat at 210 East Thirteenth Street, the rest of the apartment being occupied by Mr. and Mrs. Alexander Horr, friends of mine. I was preparing to go on tour. Yegor had work outside the city, and Albert was leaving for France, so I was glad when the Horrs offered to share their flat. Little did I dream that I was going to remain ten years in the place.

The Free Speech League had asked me to visit a number of cities in behalf of the John Turner fight, and I had also received two other invitations: one from the garment-workers in Rochester, and the other from miners in Pennsylvania. The Rochester tailors had had trouble with some clothing firms, among them that of Garson and Meyer. It was strangely significant that I should be called to speak to the wage-slaves of the man who had once exploited my labour for two dollars and fifty cents a week. I welcomed the opportunity, which would also enable me to see my family.

Within the last few years I had felt more drawn to my people, Helena remaining nearest to me. I always stayed with her on my visits to Rochester, and my folks had learned to take it as a matter of course. My arrival this time was the occasion for a general family reunion. It gave me a chance to get in closer touch with my brother Herman and his charming young wife, Rachel. I learned that the boy who could not memorize his lessons at school had become a great mechanical expert, his specific line the construction of intricate machinery. When it grew late and the other members of the family retired, I remained with my dear Helena. We always had much to say to each other, and it was nearly morning when we separated. Sister consoled me by saying I could sleep late.

I had hardly dozed off when I was awakened by a messenger bringing a letter. Glancing at the signature first, in a half-drowsy state, I saw with surprise that it was signed " Garson." I read it several times to make sure that I was not dreaming. He felt proud that a daughter of his race and city had achieved nation-wide fame, he wrote; he was glad of her presence in Rochester and he would consider it an honour to welcome me at his office soon.

I handed the letter to Helena. " Read it," I said, " and see how important your little sister has become." When she got through, she asked: " Well, what are you going to do?" I wrote on the back of the letter: " Mr. Garson, when I needed you, I came to you. Now that you seem to need me, you will have to come to me." My anxious sister was worried about the outcome. What could he want and what would

I say or do? I assured her that it was not difficult to guess what Mr. Garson wanted, but I intended, nevertheless, to have him tell it to me in person and in her presence. I would receive him in her store and treat him "as a lady should."

In the afternoon Mr. Garson drove up in his carriage. I had not seen my former employer for eighteen years, and during that time I had hardly given him a thought. Yet the moment he entered, every detail of the dreadful months in his shop stood out as clearly as if it had happened but yesterday. I saw the shop again and his luxurious office, American Beauties on the table, the blue smoke of his cigar swelling in fantastic curves, and myself standing trembling, waiting until Mr. Garson would deign to notice me. I visioned it all again and I heard him saying harshly: "What can I do for you?" Everything to the minutest detail I recalled as I looked at the old man standing before me, silk hat in hand. The thought of the injustice and humiliation his workers were suffering, their driven and drained existence, agitated me. I could barely suppress the impulse to show him the door. If my life depended on it, I could not have asked Mr. Garson to sit down. It was Helena who offered him a chair — more than he had done for me eighteen years before.

He sat down and looked at me, evidently expecting me to speak first. "Well, Mr. Garson, what can I do for you?" I finally asked. The expression must have recalled something to his mind; it seemed to confuse him. "Why, nothing at all, dear Miss Goldman," he presently replied; "I just wanted to have a pleasant talk with you." "Very well," I said, and waited. He had worked hard all his life, he related, "just like your father, Miss Goldman." He had saved penny by penny and in that way had accumulated a little money. "You may not know how difficult it is to save," he went on, "but ask your father. He works hard, he is an honest man, and he is known in the whole city as such. There isn't another man in Rochester more respected and who has so much credit as your father."

"Just a moment, Mr. Garson," I interrupted; "you forgot something. You forgot to mention that you had saved by the assistance of others. You were able to put aside penny by penny because you had men and women working for you."

"Yes, of course," he said apologetically, "we had 'hands' in our factory, but they all made good livings."

"And were they all able to open factories from their savings of penny by penny?"

He admitted that they were not, but it was because they were ignorant and spendthrift. "You mean they were honest working-men like my father, don't you?" I continued. "You've spoken in such high terms of my father, you certainly will not accuse him of being a spendthrift. But though he has worked like a galley-slave all his life, he has accumulated nothing and he has not been able to start a factory. Why do you suppose my father and others remained poor, while you succeeded? It is because they lacked the forethought to add to their shears the shears of ten others, or of a hundred or several hundred, as you have done. It isn't the saving of pennies that makes people rich; it is the labour of your 'hands' and their ruthless exploitation that has created your wealth. Eighteen years ago there was an excuse for my ignorance of it, when I stood like a beggar before you, asking for a rise of a dollar and a half in pay. There is no excuse for you, Mr. Garson—not now, when the truth of the relation between labour and capital is being cried from the house-tops."

He sat looking at me. "Who would have thought that the little girl in my shop would become such a grand speaker?" he said at last. "Certainly not you!" I replied, "nor could she have if you had had your way. But let's come down to your request that I visit your office. What is it you want?"

He began talking about labour's having its rights; he had acknowledged the union and its demands (whenever reasonable) and had introduced many improvements in his shop for the benefit of his workers. But times were hard and he had sustained heavy losses. If only the grumblers among his employees would listen to reason, be patient awhile, and meet him half-way, everything could be amicably adjusted. "Couldn't you put this before the men in your speech," he suggested, "and make them see my side a little? Your father and I are great friends, Miss Goldman; I would do anything for him if he should be in trouble — lend him money or help in any way. As to his brilliant daughter, I have already written you how proud I am that you come from my race. I should like to prove it by some little gift. Now, Miss Goldman, you are a woman, you must love beautiful things. Tell me what you'd like best."

His words did not rouse my anger. Perhaps it was because I had expected some such offer from his letter. My poor sister was regarding me with her sad, anxious eyes. I rose quietly from my chair; Garson did the same and we stood facing each other, a senile smile on his withered face.

"You've come to the wrong person, Mr. Garson," I said; "you cannot buy Emma Goldman."

"Who speaks of buying?" he exclaimed. "You're wrong; let me explain."

"No need of it," I interrupted him. "Whatever explanation is necessary I will make tonight before your workers who have invited me to speak. I have nothing more to say to you. Please go."

He edged out of the room, silk hat in hand, followed by Helena, who saw him to the door.

After careful consideration I decided to say nothing at the meeting about his offer. I felt it might obscure the main issue, the wage dispute, and possibly affect the chances of a settlement in favour of the employees. Moreover, I did not want the Rochester papers to get hold of the story; it would have been too much grist for their scandal-mongering mills. But I did relate to the workers that evening the venture of Garson into political economy, repeating the explanation he had given as to how he had acquired his wealth. My audience was greatly amused, which was the only result of Garson's visit.

During my brief stay in Rochester I had another caller, much more interesting than Mr. Garson: a newspaper woman who introduced herself as Miss T. She came to interview me, but she stayed to tell a remarkable story. It was about Leon Czolgosz.

She had been on the staff of one of the Buffalo dailies in 1901, she related, assigned to the Exposition grounds during the President's visit. She had stood very near McKinley and had watched the people filing by to shake his hand. In the procession she noticed a young man pass along with the rest, a white handkerchief wrapped around his hand. Reaching the President, he raised a revolver and fired. A panic followed, the crowd scattering in all directions. Bystanders picked up the wounded McKinley and carried him into Convention Hall; others pounced upon the assailant and beat him as he lay prostrate. Suddenly there was a fearful scream. It came from the boy on the ground. A burly Negro was over him, digging his nails into the youth's eyes. The ghastly scene made her sick with horror. She hastened to her paper's office to write her account.

When the editor had read her story, he informed her that the stuff about the Negro gouging Czolgosz's eyes would have to come out. "Not that the anarchist dog didn't deserve it," he remarked; "I'd have done it myself. But we need the sympathy of our readers for the President, not for his murderer."

Miss T. was not an anarchist; in fact, she knew nothing of our ideas, and she was against the man who had attacked McKinley. But the scene she had witnessed and the brutality of the editor softened her towards Czolgosz. She tried repeatedly to get an assignment to interview him in jail, but without success. She learned from other reporters that Czolgosz had been so badly beaten and tortured that he could not be seen. He was ill and it was feared he might not live to be taken to court. Some time later she was ordered to cover the trial.

The court-room was guarded by a heavily armed force and filled with curiosity-seekers, mostly well-dressed women. The atmosphere was tense with excitement, all eyes on the door from which the prisoner was to enter. Suddenly there was a stirring in the crowd. The door was flung open, and a young man, supported by policemen, was half-carried into the room. He looked pale and emaciated; his head was bandaged, his face swollen. It was a repulsive sight until one caught his eyes — large, wistful eyes, that kept roving over the court-room, searching with terrible intensity, apparently for some familiar face. Then they lost their intentness, turning brilliant as if illumined by some inner vision. "Dreamers and prophets have such eyes," Miss T. continued; "I was filled with shame to think that I did not have the courage to cry out to him that he was not alone, that I was his friend. For days afterwards those eyes haunted me. During two years I couldn't go near a newspaper office; even now I am only doing free-lance work. The moment I think of a steady job that might bring me another such experience, I see those eyes. I have always wanted to meet you," she added, "to tell you about it."

I pressed her hand in silence, too overcome to speak. When I had mastered my emotion, I told her I wished I could believe that Leon Czolgosz had been conscious that there was at least one friendly spirit near him in that court-room full of hungry wolves. What Miss T. told me bore out all that I had guessed and what I had learned about Leon in 1902 when I visited Cleveland. I had hunted up his parents; they were dark people, the father hardened by toil, the stepmother with a dull, vacant look. His own mother had died when he was a baby;

at the age of six he had been forced into the street to shine shoes and sell papers; if he did not bring enough money home, he was punished and deprived of meals. His wretched childhood had made him timid and shy. At the age of twelve he began his factory life. He grew into a silent youth, absorbed in books and aloof. At home he was called "daft"; in the shop he was looked upon as queer and "stuck-up." The only one to be kind to him was his sister, a timid, hard-working drudge. When I saw her, she told me that she had been once to Buffalo to see Leon in jail, but he had asked her not to come again. "He knew I was poor," she said; "our family was pestered by the neighbours, and father was fired from his job. So I didn't go again," she repeated, weeping.

Perhaps it was just as well, for what could the poor creature give to the boy who had read queer books, had dreamed queer dreams, had committed a queer act, and had even been queer in the face of death. People out of the ordinary, those with a vision, have ever been considered queer; yet they have often been the sanest in a crazy world.

In Pennsylvania I found the condition of the miners since the "settlement" of the strike worse than in 1897 when I had gone through the region. The men were more subdued and helpless. Only our own comrades were alert, and even more determined since the shameful defeat of the strike, brought about by the treachery of the union leaders. They were working part time, barely earning enough to live on, yet somehow they managed to contribute to the propaganda. It was inspiring to see such consecration to our cause.

Two experiences stood out on my trip. One happened down in a mine, the other in the home of a worker. As on my previous visits, I was taken to the pit to talk to the men in one of the shafts during lunch-hour. The foreman was away, and the miners eager to hear me. I sat surrounded by a group of black faces. During my talk I caught sight of two figures huddled together — a man withered with age and a child. I inquired who they were. "That's Grandpa Jones," I was told; "he's ninety and he has worked in the mines for seventy years. The kid is his great-grandchild. He says he's fourteen, but we know he's only eight." My comrade spoke in a matter-of-fact manner. A man of ninety and a child of eight working ten hours a day in a black pit!

After the first meeting I was invited by a miner to his home for the night. The small room assigned me had already three occupants: two children on a narrow cot, and a young girl in a folding bed. I was to share the bed with her. The parents and their infant girl slept in the next room. My throat felt parched; the stifling air in the room made me cough. The woman offered me a glass of hot milk. I was tired and sleepy; the night was heavy with the breathing of the man, the pitiful wailing of the infant, and the monotonous tramp of the mother trying to quiet her baby.

In the morning I asked about the child. Was it ill or hungry that it cried so much? Her milk was too poor and not enough, the mother said; the baby was bottle-fed. A horrible suspicion assailed me. "You gave me the baby's milk!" I cried. The woman attempted to deny it, but I could see in her eyes that I had guessed correctly. "How could you do such a thing?" I upbraided her. "Baby had one bottle in the evening, and you looked tired and you coughed; what else could I do?" she said. I was hot with shame and overcome with wonder at the great heart beneath that poverty and those rags.

Back in New York from my short tour, I found a message from Dr. Hoffmann calling me again to nurse Mrs. Spenser, I could undertake only day duty, my evenings being taken up with the Turner campaign. The patient consented to the arrangement, but after a few weeks she urged me to take care of her during the night. She had become more to me than merely a professional case, but her present surroundings were repugnant. It was one thing to know that she lived from the proceeds of a brothel, quite different to have to work in such a house. To be sure, my patient's business now went by the respectable name of a Raines hotel. Like all legislation for the elimination of vice, the Raines Law only multiplied the very thing it claimed to abolish. It relieved the keepers of responsibility towards the inmates and increased their revenue from prostitution. The customers no longer had to come to Mrs. Spenser. The girls were now compelled to solicit on the street. In rain or cold, well or ill, the unfortunates had to hustle for business, glad to take anyone who consented to come, no matter how decrepit or hideous he might be. They had, furthermore, to endure persecution from the police and pay graft to the department for the right to "work" in certain localities. Each district had its price, according to the amount the girls were able to get from the men. Broadway, for instance, paid more in graft than the Bowery. The policeman on the beat took care that there should be no unauthorized competition. Any girl who dared trespass on another's beat was arrested and often sent to the workhouse. Naturally the girls clung to their territory and fought the intrusion of any colleague who did not "belong" there.

The new law also resulted in certain arrangements between the Raines-hotel-keepers and the street girl: the latter received a percentage from the liquor she could induce her guests to consume. That became her main source of income since brothels had been abolished and she was thrown out on the street. She was forced to accept what she could from the man, especially because he had also to pay for the hotel room. To meet the many claims on her she had to imbibe heavily in order to induce her customers to drink more. To see those poor slaves and their males going in and out of Mrs. Spenser's hotel all through the night, tired, harassed, and generally drunk, to be compelled to overhear what went on, was more than I could bear. Moreover, Dr. Hoffmann had told me that there was no hope of permanent cure for our patient. Her persistent use of drugs had broken her will and weakened her power of resistance. No matter how well we should succeed in weaning her, she would always go back to them. I informed my patient that I must resign. She flew into a rage, berating me bitterly and concluding by saying that if she could not have me when she wanted me, she preferred that I leave altogether.

I needed all my strength for public work, of which the John Turner campaign was the most important. While his appeal was pending, the attorneys succeeded in getting our comrade out on five-thousand-dollar bail. He immediately started on tour, visiting a number of cities and delivering lectures to crowded houses. Had he not been arrested and threatened with deportation, he would have reached only very limited audiences, whereas now the press dealt at length with the Anti-Anarchist Law and with John Turner, and large crowds had the opportunity of hearing anarchism expounded in a logical and convincing manner.

John had come to America on a leave of absence from his union. It was nearing expiration and he resolved to return to England without waiting for the verdict of the Supreme Court. When the decision was finally handed down, it proved to be just what we had expected. It upheld the constitutionality of the Anti-Anarchist Law and sustained the order for Turner's deportation. However, the ridiculous statute would hereafter defeat its own ends: European comrades wishing to come to the United States would no longer feel bound to confide their ideas to the busybodies of the Immigration Department.

Henceforth I gave more time to English propaganda, not only because I wanted to bring anarchist thought to the American public, but also to call attention to certain great issues in Europe. Of these the struggle for freedom in Russia was among the least understood.

CHAPTER XXVIII

For a number of years the Friends of Russian Freedom, an American group, had been doing admirable work in enlightening the country about the nature of Russian absolutism. Now that society was inactive and the splendid efforts of the radical Yiddish press were confined entirely to the East Side. The sinister propaganda carried on in America by the representatives of the Tsar through the Russian Church, the Consulate, and the New York *Herald,* under the ownership of James Gordon Bennett, was widespread. These forces combined to picture the autocrat as a kind-hearted dreamer not responsible for the evils in his land, while the Russian revolutionists were denounced as the worst of criminals. Now that I had greater access to the American mind, I determined to use whatever ability I possessed to plead the heroic cause of revolutionary Russia.

My efforts, together with the other activities in behalf of Russia, received very considerable support by the arrival in New York of two Russians, members of the Socialist-Revolutionary Party, Rosenbaum and Nikolaev. They came unannounced and unheralded, but the work they accomplished was of far-reaching consequences and paved the way for the visits of a number of distinguished leaders of the Russian libertarian struggle. Within a few weeks after his arrival Rosenbaum succeeded in welding together the militant elements of the East Side into a section of the S. R. Although aware that this party did not agree with our ideas of a non-governmental society, I became a member of the group. It was their work in Russia that attracted me and compelled me to help in the labours of the newly formed society. Our spirits were greatly raised by the news of the approaching visit of Catherine Breshkovskaya, affectionately called Babushka, the Grandmother of the Russian Revolution.

Those familiar with Russia knew of Breshkovskaya as one of the most heroic figures in that country. Her visit would therefore be an event of exceptional interest. We had no anxiety about her success with the Yiddish population — her fame guaranteed it. But the American audiences knew nothing about her, and it might be difficult to get them interested. Nikolaev, who was very close to Babushka, informed us that she was coming to the States not only to raise funds, but also to arouse public sentiment. He visited me frequently to discuss methods of co-operating with the Friends of Russian Freedom. George Kennan was perhaps the only American who knew Babushka and who had written about her; Lyman Abbott, of the *Outlook,* was also interested. Nikolaev suggested that I see them. I laughed at his naïveté in believing that Emma Goldman could approach those ultra-respectable people. "If I go under my own name," I told him, "I should queer Breshkovskaya's chances, while under the obscure name of Smith I'd get no recognition at all." Alice Stone Blackwell came to my mind.

In 1902 I had come across some translations of Russian poetry by Miss Blackwell, and later I had read her sympathetic articles about the Russian struggle. I had written her expressing my appreciation, and in her reply she had asked me to recommend someone who could translate Jewish poetry into English prose. I did so, and thereafter we continued in correspondence. I now wrote to Miss Blackwell about our efforts to get in touch with Americans in behalf of Russia, mentioning Nikolaev, who could give her detailed information about present conditions in his country. Miss Blackwell responded at once. She was soon to be in New York, she wrote; she would visit me and also bring with her the Honourable William Dudley Foulke, president of the recently reorganized Society of the Friends of Russian Freedom.

Foulke was an ardent devotee of Roosevelt. "The poor man is sure to have a stroke when he finds out who Miss Smith is," I remarked to Nikolaev. I had no worry about Miss Blackwell; she was of old New England stock and an energetic champion of liberty. She knew my identity. But Roosevelt's man — what would happen when he came? Nikolaev lightly dismissed my apprehensions, saying that in Russia the greatest revolutionists had worked under fictitious names.

Before long, Alice Stone Blackwell arrived, and while we were having tea, there came a knock at the door. I opened it to a short, stout man all out of breath after his climb of the five flights. "Are you Miss Smith?" he panted. "Yes," I replied brazenly; "you are Mr. Foulke, aren't you? Please come in." The good Rooseveltian Republican in Emma Goldman's flat at 210 East Thirteenth Street, sipping tea and discussing ways and means to undermine the Russian autocracy, would certainly have made a delicious story for the press. I took great care to keep the newspapers out of it, however, and the conspiratory session went off without a hitch. Both Miss Blackwell and the Honourable William D. Foulke were much impressed by Nikolaev's account of the horrors in Russia.

Several weeks later Miss Blackwell informed me that a New York branch of the Friends of Russian Freedom had been organized, with the Reverend Minot J. Savage as president, and Professor Robert Erskine Ely as secretary, the body planning to do everything in its power to bring Mme Breshkovskaya before the American public. It was a quick and gratifying result of our little gathering. But Ely! I had met him during Peter Kropotkin's visit in 1901; an extremely timid man, he seemed, for ever in fear that his connexion with anarchists might ruin his standing with the backers of the League for Political Economy, of which he was head. To be sure, Kropotkin was an anarchist, but he was also a prince and a scientist, and he had lectured before the Lowell Institute. I felt that to Ely the *prince* was the important feature about Kropotkin. The British have royalty and love it, but some Americans love it because they would like to have it. It did not matter to them that Kropotkin had discarded his title in joining the revolutionary ranks. Dear Peter had been not a little shocked to discover it. I remembered the anecdote he had told us about his stay in Chicago, when his comrades had arranged for him to go to Waldheim to visit the graves of Parsons, Spies, and the other Haymarket martyrs. The same morning a group of society women, led by Mrs. Potter Palmer, invited him to a luncheon. "You will come, Prince, will you not?" they pleaded. "I am sorry, ladies, but I have a previous engagement with my comrades," he excused himself. "Oh, no, Prince; you *must* come with us!" Mrs. Palmer insisted. "Madam," Peter replied, "you may have the Prince, and I will go to my comrades."

My impression of Professor Ely made me feel that it would be better for his peace of mind, as well as for the work for Babushka, if he were not enlightened about E. G. Smith's identity. I was again obliged to act through an intermediary, as in the Turner case, remaining in the background. If timorous souls were deceived, it was not of my choosing; it was their narrow-mindedness that made it necessary.

When Catherine Breshkovskaya arrived, she was immediately surrounded by scores of people, many of them moved more by curiosity than by genuine interest in Russia. I did not wish to swell the number, and so I waited. Nikolaev had told her about me and she asked to see me.

The women in the Russian revolutionary struggle, Vera Zassulitch, Sophia Perovskaya, Jessie Helfman, Vera Figner, and Catherine Breshkovskaya, had been my inspiration ever since I had first read of their lives, but I had never met one of them face to face. I was greatly excited and awed when I reached the house where Breshkovskaya was staying. I found her in a barren flat, badly lighted and inadequately heated. Dressed in black, she was wrapped in a thick shawl, a black kerchief over her head, leaving the ends of her waving grey hair exposed. She gave the impression of a Russian peasant woman, except for her large grey eyes, expressive of wisdom and understanding, eyes remarkably youthful for a woman of sixty-two. Ten minutes in her presence made me feel as if I had known her all my life; her simplicity, the tenderness of her voice, and her gestures, all affected me like the balm of a spring day.

Her first appearance in New York was at Cooper Union and proved the most inspiring manifestation I had seen for years. Babushka, who had never before had a chance to face such a vast gathering, was somewhat nervous at first. But when she got her bearings, she delivered a speech that swept her audience off its feet. The next day the papers were practically unanimous in their tributes to the grand old lady. They could afford to be generous to one whose attack was levelled against far-off Russia instead of their own country. But we welcomed the attitude of the press because we knew that publicity would arouse interest in the cause Babushka had come to plead. Subsequently she spoke in French at the Sunrise Club before the largest assembly in the history of that body. I acted as interpreter, as I did also at most of the private gatherings arranged for her. One of these took place at 210 East Thirteenth Street and was attended by a crowd far too big for my small apartment. Ernest Crosby, Bolton Hall, the Coryells, Gilbert E. Roe, and many members of the University Settlement were present, among them Phelps Stokes, Kellogg Durland, Arthur Bullard, and William English Walling, as well as women prominent in radical ranks. Lillian D. Wald, of the Nurses' Settlement, responded warmly; she arranged receptions for Babushka and succeeded in interesting scores of people in the Russian cause.

Often after the late gatherings Babushka would come with me to my flat to spend the night. It was amazing to see her run up the five flights with an energy and vivacity that put me to shame. "Dear Babushka," I once said to her, "how have you been able to keep your youth after so many years of prison and exile?" "And how did you manage to retain yours, living in this soul-destroying, materialistic country?" she returned. Her long exile had never been stagnant; it was always rejuvenated by the stream of politicals passing through. "I had much to inspire and sustain me," she said; "but what have you in a country where idealism is considered a crime, a rebel an outcast, and money the only god?" I had no answer except that it was the example of those who had gone before, herself included, and the ideal we had chosen that gave us courage to persevere. The hours with Babushka were among the richest and most precious experiences of my propaganda life.

Our strenuous work for Russia at this time received additional significance by the news of the appalling tragedy of January 22 in St. Petersburg. Thousands of people, led by Father Gapon, assembled before the Winter Palace to appeal to the Tsar for relief, had been brutally mowed down, massacred in cold blood by the autocrat's henchmen. Many advanced Americans had held aloof from Babushka's work. They were willing enough to pay homage to her personality, her courage and fortitude; they were sceptical, however, about her description of conditions in Russia. Things could not be quite so harrowing, they claimed. The butchery on "Bloody Sunday" gave tragic significance and incontestable proof to the picture Babushka had painted. Even the lukewarm liberals could no longer close their eyes to the situation in Russia.

At the Russian New Year's ball we greeted the advent of 1905 standing in a circle, Babushka dancing the *kazatchok* with one of the boys. It was a feast for the eyes to see the woman of sixty-two, her spirit young, cheeks ruddy, and eyes flashing, whirling about in the popular Russian dance.

In January Babushka went on a lecture tour, and I could turn to other interests and activities. My dear Stella had come from Rochester in the late fall to live with me. It had been her great dream to do so since early childhood. My narrow escape during the McKinley hysteria had changed the attitude of my sister Lena, Stella's mother, making her more kindly and affectionate towards me. She no longer begrudged me Stella's love, having learned to understand how deep was my concern for her child. Stella's parents realized that their daughter would have better opportunity for development in New York, and that she would be safe with me. I was happy in the anticipation of having with me my little niece, whose birth had brightened my dark youth. Yet when the long-awaited moment arrived, I was too busy with Babushka to give much time to Stella. The old revolutionist was captivated by my niece, and she in turn completely fell under Babushka's charm. Still we both longed to have more of each other, and now, with the departure of the revolutionary "Grandmother," we could at last come closer together.

Stella soon found a position as secretary to a judge, who would no doubt have died of horror had he known that she was the niece of Emma Goldman. I took up nursing again, but before long, Babushka returned from her Western tour and once more I had to devote my time to her and her mission. She had confided to me that she required a dependable person to be entrusted with the task of smuggling ammunition into Russia. I thought at once of Eric and I told her of the courage and endurance he had shown while digging the tunnel for Sasha. She was particularly impressed by the fact that Eric was an excellent sailor and capable of running a launch. " That would facilitate the transport through Finland and it would arouse less suspicion than if attempted by land," she had said. I put Babushka in touch with Eric. He made a most favourable impression on her. " Just the person needed for the job," she said, " cool-headed, brave, and a man of action." When she returned to New York, Eric accompanied her, arrangements for his sailing having already been made. It was good to see our jolly viking again before he left on his perilous journey.

Before the grand old lady's departure I gave her a farewell party at 210 East Thirteenth Street, attended by her old friends and the many new ones the dear woman had made. She lent atmosphere to the evening, infecting everybody with her big and free spirit. There was no cloud on "Grandmother's" brow, although she knew, as we all did, what dangers she would face in returning to the lair of Russian autocracy.

Not until Babushka left the country did I realize how strenuous the month had been. I was utterly exhausted and unable to face the ordeal of nursing. I had realized for some time past that I could not keep up much longer the hard work, responsibility, and anxiety my profession involved while continuing my platform activities. I had tried taking cases of body massage, but I found them even more of a strain than nursing. I had spoken of my predicament to one of my American friends, a woman manicurist who was making a comfortable living by working only five hours a day in her own office. She suggested that I could do the same with facial and scalp massage. Many professional women needed it for the restfulness it gave them, and she would recommend her clients to me. It seemed absurd for me to engage in such a thing, but when I spoke to Solotaroff about it, he urged that it was the best thing I could do to earn my living and still have time left for the movement. My good friend Bolton Hall was of the same opinion; he at once offered to lend me money to fix up a place and also promised to be my first patient. "Even if your skill won't bring back hair on my head," he remarked, "I will have you pinned down for an hour to listen to my arguments on single tax." Some of my Russian friends saw the undertaking in a different light; a massage parlour would well serve, they thought, as a cover for the Russian work we were to go on with. Stella greatly favoured the idea because it would relieve me of the long hours of nursing. The result of it all was that I went in search of an office, which I found without much difficulty on the top floor of a building on Broadway at Seventeenth Street. It was a small place, but it had a view over the East River and plenty of air and sunlight. With the borrowed capital of three hundred dollars and a few lovely draperies lent me by women friends, I established myself in a very attractive parlour.

Before long, patients began to arrive. By the end of June I had earned enough to cover expenses and pay back part of my debt. It was hard work, but most of those who came for treatment were interesting people; they knew me and there was no need of hiding my identity. Still more important, I did not have to work in noisy, congested quarters, and I was relieved from the anxiety I used to feel over the probable outcome of my nursing cases. Every rise in the temperature of my charges used to alarm me, and a death would upset me for weeks. In all my years of nursing I had never learned detachment or indifference to suffering.

During the hot summer months many of my patients left for the country. Stella and I decided that we also needed a vacation. In our search for a suitable place we came upon Hunter Island, in Pelham Bay, near New York, as ideal a spot as we could wish for. But it belonged to the city and we had not the least notion how to secure the necessary permission to pitch a tent. Stella had an inspiration; she would ask her judge. A few days later she came triumphantly waving a piece of paper. "Now, darling," she cried, "will you still insist that judges are useless? Here is the permit to pitch a tent on Hunter Island!"

A friend of mine, Clara Felberg, together with her sister and brother, joined us. We were just beginning to settle down on our island and enjoy its peace and beauty when Clara brought back from New York the announcement that the Paul Orleneff troupe was stranded in the city. Its members had been thrown out of their apartment for failure to pay the rent, and they were without means of livelihood.

Pavel Nikolayevitch Orleneff and Mme Nazimova had come to America in the early part of 1905, taking the East Side by storm with their wonderful production of Tchirikov's *The Chosen People*. It was said that Orleneff had been prevailed upon by a group of writers and dramatists in Russia to take the play abroad as a protest against the wave of pogroms then sweeping Russia. The Orleneff troupe arrived at the very height of our activities for Babushka, which had prevented my getting in touch with the Russian players. But I had attended every performance. With the exception of Joseph Kainz, I knew no one to compare with Paul Orleneff, and even Kainz had created nothing so overwhelming as Orleneff's Raskolnikov in *Crime and Punishment,* or his Mitka Karamazov. His art was, like that of Eleonora Duse, the very living of every nuance of human emotion. Alla Nazimova was very fine as Leah in *The Chosen People,* as she was in all her rôles. As to the rest of the cast, nothing like its ensemble acting had ever been seen on the American stage before. It was therefore a shock to learn that Orleneff's troupe, who had given us so much, should find themselves stranded, without friends or funds. We might pitch a tent for Orleneff on our island, I thought, but how help his ten men? Clara promised to borrow some money, and within a week the entire troupe was on the island with us. It was a motley crowd and a motley life, and our hopes for a restful summer soon went by the board. During the day, when Stella and I had to return to the heat of the city, we regretted that Hunter Island had ceased to be a secluded spot. But at night, sitting around our huge bonfire, with Orleneff in the centre, guitar in hand, softly strumming an accompaniment to his own singing, the whole troupe joining in on the chorus, the strains echoing far over the bay as the large *samovar* buzzed, our regrets of the day were forgotten. Russia filled our souls with the plaint of her woe.

The spiritual proximity of Russia brought Sasha poignantly near. I knew how profoundly he would enjoy our inspiring nights; how he would be stirred and soothed by the songs of the native land he had always passionately loved. It was the month of July 1905. Just thirteen years before, he had left me to stake his life for our cause. His Calvary was soon to end, but only to continue in another place; he still had to serve another year in the workhouse. The judge who had added the extra year to the inhuman sentence of twenty-one now appeared more barbarous than on that trial day in September 1892. But for that, Sasha would be free now, out of the power of his jailers.

It somewhat lessened my misery to think that Sasha would have to spend only seven months in the workhouse, the Pennsylvania law granting five months' commutation on his final year. But even that consolation was soon destroyed. A letter from Sasha informed me that, though he was legally entitled to a five months' reduction, he had learned that the workhouse authorities had decided to regard him as a "new" prisoner and to allow him only two months' time off, provided his behaviour was "good." Sasha was to be forced to drain the bitter cup to the last drop.

Several months previously Sasha had sent to me a friend whom he called "Chum." His name was John Martin, I learned, and he was socialistically inclined. He was a civilian instructor in the prison weaving-shops; he had accepted the job less out of necessity than because he was planning to aid the prisoners. He had learned about Sasha shortly after he had come to work in the Western Penitentiary. Since then he had got in close touch with him and had been able to help him a little. I knew from Sasha's letters that the man used to take great risks in order to do kind things for him and others.

John Martin broached a new appeal to the Pardon Board, to get the year in the workhouse set aside. He could not bear to think that Alex, as he called Sasha, after so many years in one hell should have to go to another. I was deeply touched by Martin's beautiful spirit, but we had failed in our previous attempts to rescue Sasha and I was sure that we could expect no better success now. Moreover, I knew that he himself would not want it tried. He had endured thirteen

years and I was certain he would prefer to stand the additional ten
months rather than have to go begging again. My attitude was justified by a letter from Sasha. He wanted nothing from the enemy, he
wrote.

The sickening anxiety of the days preceding his transfer was finally
over. Two days later I received his last note from the penitentiary.
It read:

> DEAREST GIRL:
> It's Wednesday morning, the 19th, at last!
>
> > *Geh stiller, meines Herzens Schlag*
> > *Und schliesst euch alle meine alten Wunden,*
> > *Denn dieses ist mein letzter Tag,*
> > *Und dies sind seine letzten Stunden!*[1]
>
> My last thoughts within these walls are of you, dear friend, the
> Immutable.
>
> > > > SASHA

Only ten months more to the 18th of May, the glorious day of
liberation—the day of your triumph, Sasha, and mine!

When I returned to our camp that afternoon, Orleneff was the
first to notice my feverish excitement. "You look inspired, Miss
Emma," he cried: "what wonderful thing has happened to you?" I
told him about Sasha, of his youth in Russia, his life in America, his
Attentat and long years in prison. "A character for a great tragedy!"
Orleneff exclaimed enthusiastically; "to interpret him, to visualize
him to the people—I'd love to play the part!" It was balm to see
the great artist so carried away by the force and beauty of Sasha's
spirit.

Orleneff urged me to help him get in touch with my American
friends, to be his interpreter and manager. Like the genius he was, he
lived only in his art; he knew and cared for nothing else. It was
enough to watch Orleneff saturate himself with the part he was to
play, to realize how truly great an artist he was. Every nuance and
shade of the character he was to interpret was created by him be-
forehand inch by inch, agonized over for weeks, until it assumed a
complete and living form. In his efforts for perfection he was re-

---

[1] " Go slower, beating heart of mine — and close, ye bleeding wounds — this is my final
day — and these its waning hours."

lentless with himself and equally so with his troupe. More than once in the middle of the night the obsessed creature would tear me out of my sleep by shouting and yelling outside my tent: " I have it! I have it! " Drowsy with sleep, I would inquire what the great find was, and it would prove to be a new inflection in Raskolnikov's monologue or some significant gesture in Mitka Karamazov's drunkenness. Orleneff was literally afire with inspiration. It gradually communicated itself to me, causing me to scheme how to make the world see his art as it was unfolded to me in the unforgettable weeks on Hunter Island.

For some time I could do little except take care of Pavel Nikolayevitch and his numerous guests. Several dependable newspapermen whom I knew interviewed Orleneff about his plans, and meanwhile work began on the Third Street hall that was being remodelled into a theatre. Orleneff insisted on going to town every day to direct this work, which necessitated disputes with the owner over every detail. Paul could not speak anything except Russian, and there was no one but myself to interpret for him. I had to divide my time between my office and the future theatre. In the late afternoon we would return to our island, half-dead with heat and fatigue, Orleneff a nervous wreck from the thousand petty irritations with which he was entirely unfitted to cope.

The superabundance of poison ivy on Hunter Island and the legions of mosquitoes finally drove us into the city. Only the troupe of sturdy peasant actors remained, compelled to defy both pests because they had no other place to go. After Labour Day the number of my patients increased and the preliminary work for the Russian performances began, involving a large correspondence and a personal canvass of my American friends. James Huneker, whom I had not seen for several years, promised to write about Orleneff, and other critics also pledged support. Our efforts were aided by a number of wealthy Jews, among them the banker Seligman.

The members of the East Side Committee on their return from the country set to work in earnest to fulfil their promise to Orleneff. There were readings of plays in some of their homes, especially at Solotaroff's and at Dr. Braslau's, the latter now the host of Pavel Nikolayevitch. Themselves the parents of an artist daughter, Sophie, who had already begun to train for an operatic career, Doctor and Mrs. Braslau could well understand the psychology and moods of their guest.

They had much feeling for him and patience, while some of the East Siders talked about him in terms of dollars and cents. The Braslaus were charming people, genuine, hospitable Russian souls; the evenings in their home always gave me a feeling of freedom and release.

The radical Jewish press actively aided the work of publicity. Abe Cahan, of the socialist daily *Forward,* often attended the readings of plays and wrote a great deal of the significance of Orleneff's art. Considerable publicity was also given him by the *Freie Arbeiter Stimme* and other East Side Yiddish papers.

The various activities, including my office work and lectures, filled my time. Nor did I neglect the friends who were wont to gather at my apartment. Among my many visitors were M. Katz and Chaim Zhitlovsky. Katz held a special place in my affections: he and Solotaroff had been my most faithful friends during my ostracism following the feud with Most and later again at the time of the McKinley hysteria. In fact, I had been thrown together with dear Katz much more than with Solotaroff, both in our work and in more intimate social gatherings.

Zhitlovsky had come to America with Babushka. A Socialist Revolutionist, he was also an ardent Judaist. He never tired urging upon me that as a Jewish daughter I should devote myself to the cause of the Jews. I would say to him that I had been told the same thing before. A young scientist I had met in Chicago, a friend of Max Baginski, had pleaded with me to take up the Jewish cause. I repeated to Zhitlovsky what I had related to the other: that at the age of eight I used to dream of becoming a Judith and visioned myself in the act of cutting off Holofernes' head to avenge the wrongs of my people. But since I had become aware that social injustice is not confined to my own race, I had decided that there were too many heads for one Judith to cut off.

Our circle at 210 East Thirteenth Street was increased by the arrival from Chicago of Max, Millie, and their six-months-old baby girl. The State and Church champions of the sanctity of motherhood had shown their true colours as soon as they discovered that Millie had dared to become a mother without the permission of established authority. She was forced to give up her position as a teacher in the Chicago schools, which she had held for a number of years. It happened at a very unfortunate time, after Max had left the editorial staff of the *Arbeiter Zeitung.* The paper, founded by August Spies, had been gradually deserting its non-political policy. Max had for years fought the Socialist politicians who were trying to turn the *Arbeiter Zeitung* into a vote-catching medium. No longer able to endure the atmosphere of strife and intrigue, he had resigned.

Max hated the dehumanizing spirit of the city and its crushing grind. He longed for nature and the soil. Thanks to the generosity of my friend Bolton Hall, I found myself in a position to offer Max and his little family a small place in the country, three and a half miles out of Ossining, which Bolton had given me when I was being pestered by the landlords. "No one will be able to drive you out of it," he had said; "you can have it to use for the rest of your life, or you can pay for it when you strike a gold-mine." The house was old and shaky, and there was no water on the premises. But its rugged beauty and seclusion, and the gorgeous view from the hill, made up for what was lacking in comfort. With Hall's permission, Max, Millie, and their baby settled on the farm.

The number of my patients had increased considerably, among them being women representing fourteen different professions, besides men from every walk of life. Most of the women claimed to be emancipated and independent, as indeed they were in the sense that they were earning their own living. But they paid for it by the suppression of the mainsprings of their natures; fear of public opinion robbed them of love and intimate comradeship. It was pathetic to see how lonely they were, how starved for male affection, and how they craved children. Lacking the courage to tell the world to mind its own business, the emancipation of the women was frequently more of a tragedy than traditional marriage would have been. They had attained a certain amount of independence in order to gain their livelihood, but they had not become independent in spirit or free in their personal lives.

CHAPTER XXIX

THE NEWS OF THE RUSSIAN REVOLUTION OF OCTOBER 1905 WAS electrifying and carried us to ecstatic heights. The many tremendous events that had happened since the massacre in front of the Winter Palace had kept us in far-away America in constant tension. Kalayev and Balmashov, members of the Fighting Organization of the Social Revolutionary Party, had taken the lives of Grand Duke Sergius and Shipiaghin in retaliation for the butchery of January 22. Those acts had been followed by a general strike throughout the length and breadth of Russia, participated in by large sections from every stratum in society. Even the most insulted and degraded human beings, the prostitutes, had made common cause with the masses and had joined the general strike. The ferment in the Tsar-ridden land had finally come to a head; the subdued social forces and the pent-up suffering of the people had broken and had at last found expression in the revolutionary tide that swept our beloved *Matushka Rossiya*. The radical East Side lived in a delirium, spending almost all of its time at monster meetings and discussing these matters in cafés, forgetting political differences and brought into close comradeship by the glorious events happening in the fatherland.

It was at the very height of those events that Orleneff and his troupe made their first appearance in the little theatre on Third Street. Who cared if the place was ugly, the acoustics unspeakably bad, the stage too small to move about on, the scenery atrociously painted, the incongruous properties borrowed from a dozen different friends? We were too full of new-born Russia, too inspired by the thought of the great artists that were to depict for us the dreams of life. When the curtain rose for the first time, triumphant joy rolled like thunder from the audience to the people on the stage. It raised them to heights of artistic expression that surpassed anything they had done before.

The little theatre became an oasis in New York dramatic art. Hundreds of Americans attended the performances, and even though they did not understand the language, they were carried away by the magic of the Orleneff troupe. Sunday evenings were professional nights, the theatre filled to overflowing with theatre-managers and men and women of the stage. Ethel Barrymore and her brother John, Grace George, Minnie Maddern Fiske and Harrison Grey Fiske, her husband, Ben Greet, Margaret Anglin, Henry Miller, and scores of others, besides every writer and critic in town, were frequent guests. " Miss Smith," as Orleneff's manager, received them, took them backstage to see the idol, and interpreted their compliments to him, taking care, however, not always to render his replies.

On one occasion, at an after-theatre party given for Orleneff and Mme Nazimova by a certain very prominent theatre-manager, the host began asking Orleneff some rather peculiar questions: " Why do you hold your head in such a queer way in the part of Oswald, when you first appear on the stage? . . . Don't you think it would be more effective if you could cut the talk of that guy in *Crime and Punishment?* . . . Couldn't you make more money if you gave plays with happy endings? " I transmitted the questions all at once. " Tell the man he's a fool! " Orleneff cried, his brows drawn angrily together; " tell him he should be a chimney-sweep and not a theatre-manager. Tell him to go to hell! " He let loose a deluge of Russian oaths too spicy for the respectable Anglo-Saxon ear. Nazimova sat tense, talking French and pretending not to hear, yet watching me stealthily out of large and anxious eyes. My interpretation of Orleneff's outburst was somewhat " diplomatic."

The Russian Revolution had barely begun to flower when it was thrust back into the depths and stifled in the blood of the heroic people. Cossack terror stalked through the land, torture, prison, and the gallows doing their deadly work. Our bright hopes turned to blackest despair. The whole East Side profoundly felt the tragedy of the crushed masses.

The renewed massacres of Jews in Russia brought tears and sorrow to numerous Jewish homes in America. In their disappointment and bitterness, even advanced Russians and Jews turned against everything Russian, and as a result the audience at the little theatre began to dwindle. And then, out of the darkness of some slimy corner, came hideous whispers that Orleneff had members of the Black Hundred, the organized Russian Jew-baiters, in his troupe. A veritable boycott followed. No Jewish store, restaurant, or café would accept posters or advertisements of the Russian plays. The radical press protested vehemently against these utterly unfounded rumours, but without effect. Orleneff was heart-broken over the malicious charges. He had put his very soul into Nachman, the hero of *The Chosen People,* and had pleaded for the Russian cause. Ruin was staring him in the face, with creditors pressing on every side, and the performances barely paying for rent.

Orleneff had once told me of a testimonial performance that had been arranged for him and Mme Nazimova in London by Beerbohm Tree. It had been a brilliant affair, attended by the most distinguished men and women of the British stage. It occurred to me that we might try a similar plan in New York. It would help raise the desperately needed money and perhaps also calm the troubled waters of the East Side, for I knew from years of experience the effect of American opinion upon the immigrant members of my race. I accompanied Orleneff to Arthur Hornblow, editor of the *Theatre Magazine,* who had repeatedly expressed his admiration for the Russian troupe. Mr. Hornblow also knew the person behind Miss Smith and had always been very charming to that dangerous individual.

Mr. Hornblow gave us a royal welcome. He liked the idea of the testimonial and he suggested that the three of us call on Harrison Grey Fiske, lessee of the Manhattan Theatre and successful manager of Mrs. Fiske. Mr. Fiske was interested immediately; he would give us all the help we needed and he also would induce his wife to participate. But he could not offer us the theatre; it had been condemned by the building-department and was soon to be torn down. The interview over, Mr. Hornblow asked us to wait in the hall, as he had something private to say to Mr. Fiske. Soon the latter came out of his office and, placing both hands on my shoulders, cried: "Emma Goldman, aren't you ashamed of yourself to come to me under an assumed name? Don't you know that Mrs. Fiske and I have always been denounced as rebels and trouble-makers because we introduce modern plays and refuse to bow to the theatre trust? Miss Smith, indeed! Who the hell is Miss Smith? Emma Goldman — that's the girl! Now shake, and don't ever doubt me again."

More help and encouragement came from other quarters. Four matinées in the Criterion Theatre and two out-of-town engagements — Boston for a week, and Chicago for a fortnight — put new life into the Russian troupe. The matinées were made possible by a group of American women, admirers of Orleneff, the most active among them being Ethel Barrymore and two society women, cousins of President Roosevelt.

The Boston and Chicago engagements took considerable correspondence to materialize. When everything was ready, Orleneff insisted that I accompany the troupe. In Boston it was the Twentieth Century Club that did the most to aid Orleneff and Nazimova. At the various receptions given in their honour by the club I met Professor Leo Wiener and other Harvard men, Mrs. Ole Bull, who was very active for the success of the troupe, Mr. Nathan Haskell Dole, the translator of Russian works, Dr. Konikov, and scores of other leading Bostonians.

Chicago proved to be much more satisfactory. The social groups of the city backing the venture, including the Jewish and Russian radicals, combined to fill the Studebaker Theatre night after night. Notwithstanding the numerous social affairs, I repeatedly managed to steal away to deliver lectures arranged by my comrades. My " double " life would have shocked many a Puritan, but I led it quite bravely. I had got used to shedding the skin of Miss Smith and wearing my own, but on several occasions the process failed to work.

The first time was when Orleneff and his leading lady were invited to the home of Baron von Schlippenbach, the Russian consul. I told Orleneff that not even for his sake could Emma Goldman be comfortable, in any guise, under the roof of a person that represented the Russian imperial butcher. Another occasion was in connexion with the Hull House. I had met Jane Addams as E. G. Smith at the office of the Studebaker Theatre when she had come to order seats. It had been a business transaction, on neutral ground, calling for no enlightenment as to my identity. But to come to her sanctum under an assumed name, when she herself was supposed to stand for advanced social ideas, seemed an unfair advantage and was distasteful to me. I therefore called up Miss Addams to tell her that Miss Smith could not attend her Orleneff party, but that Emma Goldman would, if welcome. I could hear by the catch in her breath that the disclosure had been made somewhat too suddenly.

When I related the incident to Orleneff, he got very angry. He knew that Jane Addams had made a great fuss over Kropotkin during his visit in Chicago, that she had hung her place with Russian peasant work, and that she and her helpers had worn Russian peasant costumes. How could she, then, object to me, he wondered. I explained that Peter, who hated display of any kind, certainly had had nothing to do with the Russianization of Hull House; furthermore, I did not happen to be known to Miss Addams as a princess.

There were other receptions for my Russians, one at the University, the other at the home of Mrs. L. C. Counley-Ward. I attended both of them under my safe passport. Mrs. Ward lived on the lake front in a palatial home. There was a large crowd at the party, more curious than interested. The hostess herself was very unpretentious and most charming. It was, however, her mother, a woman of eighty, a sweet and distinguished-looking lady, who won my heart. In simple manner she entertained us with an account of her exploits in the abolition movement and in the pioneer work for woman's emancipation. Her flushed face and bright eyes evidenced that she still preserved the rebellious spirit of her youth, and I felt uncomfortable to have stolen into her gracious presence under a false name. The next day I wrote her and her daughter asking forgiveness for my deception and explaining the reason that compelled me to live and work under a pseudonym. I received beautiful letters from both of them, saying that they had understood it was Emma Goldman who had honoured their home. For a number of years thereafter we kept in touch with each other.

Upon our return to New York, Orleneff informed me that he would like to remain in America for several seasons if a guarantee fund could be raised. I submitted the idea to some of the people interested in the Russian troupe. At the end of several conferences sixteen thousand dollars was raised and more pledged. Someone suggested that Orleneff go under the management of Charles Frohman. Orleneff felt outraged; he had never submitted to such a yoke in Russia, he declared; much less would he do it in America. There was only one manager he would recognize, and that was "Miss Emma." He knew that I would never attempt to interfere, as the ordinary manager usually does, with what he was to play or how.

The disappointment over the committee's determination to change his management, and the decision of Mme Nazimova to remain in America and prepare herself for the English stage, had a very depressing effect on Orleneff. He was so set on leaving the country that he would no longer continue with the testimonial we had planned.

During my connexion with his work Orleneff had often urged me to accept a salary. At no time had there been enough money in his treasury for such an extra expense, and he always insisted that the company be paid first, even when he and Nazimova had to go short. The little they did get was due entirely to her resourcefulness. Out of almost nothing at all and with the help of only her Russian maid Alla Nazimova managed to create all the costumes, not alone for herself, but for the whole troupe; thus also were all the court dresses for *Tsar Feodor,* rich and colourful as they were, made by her. But small as the returns were, Orleneff wanted me to have a share in them. I had refused because I had been earning my living, and I could not bear to be an additional burden. Orleneff had once asked me what I would like to do most if I had money, and I had replied that I should want to publish a magazine that would combine my social ideas with the young strivings in the various art forms in America. Max and I had often discussed such a venture, greatly needed. It had been our cherished dream for a long time, though apparently hopeless. Now Orleneff broached the matter again, and I submitted my plan to him. He offered to give a special performance for the purpose and promised to see Nazimova about playing Strindberg's *Countess Julia,* a drama she had always wanted to present with him. He did not care particularly for the part of Jean, he said, but "You have done so much for me," he added, "I will stage the piece."

Before long, Orleneff had set a definite date for the performance. We rented the Berkeley Theatre, printed announcements and tickets, and, with the help of Stella and a few young comrades, set to work to fill the house. At the same time we arranged a gathering at 210 East Thirteenth Street, to which we invited a number of people we knew would be interested in the magazine venture we had in mind: Edwin Björkman, the translator of Strindberg, Ami Mali Hicks, Sadakichi Hartmann, John R. Coryell, and some of our comrades. When our friends left that night, the expected child had a name, *The Open Road,* as well as foster-parents and a host of others anxious to help in its care.

I walked on air. At last my preparatory work of years was about to take complete form! The spoken word, fleeting at best, was no longer to be my only medium of expression, the platform not the only place where I could feel at home. There would be the printed thought, more lasting in its effect, and a place of expression for the young idealists in art and letters. In *The Open Road* they should speak without fear of the censor. Everybody who longed to escape rigid moulds, political and social prejudices, and petty moral demands should have a chance to travel with us in *The Open Road.*

Amidst the rehearsals of *Countess Julia* a swarm of creditors descended upon Orleneff. They had him arrested and the theatre closed, and I had to drop my work to find bondsmen and someone to pay his rent. When things were arranged and Orleneff released, he was too distressed by his experience to continue the rehearsals. There were only two weeks left before the opening night, and I knew he would not go on the stage unless he was sure of his part. To relieve his misery I suggested that he give some other play in which he had already appeared. We agreed on *Ghosts,* the character of Oswald being among Orleneff's greatest creations. Unfortunately, theatre audiences do not care to see the same play many times; when the change of program was announced, a number of people demanded their money back. They wanted to see *Countess Julia* and nothing else. We should have had a substantial turn-out, anyhow, had the gods not chosen the night of the performance for sending down a torrent of rain. The thousand dollars or more we had hoped to realize dwindled down to two hundred and fifty, a sorry capital with which to launch a magazine. Our disappointment was great, but we refused to let it affect our zeal.

We had enough for the first number, which we decided to issue in the historic revolutionary month of March. What other free-lance publication had ever started with more? Meanwhile we sent out a general appeal to our friends. Among the responses we received one from Colorado bearing the heading: *The Open Road.* It threatened to set the law on us for infringement of copyright! Poor Walt Whitman would have surely turned in his grave if he knew that someone had dared to legalize the title of his great poem. But there was nothing for us to do except to christen the child differently. Friends sent in new names, but we did not find one expressing our meaning.

While visiting the little farm one Sunday, Max and I went for a buggy ride. It was early in February, but already the air was perfumed by the balm of spring. The soil was beginning to break free from the grip of winter, a few specks of green already showing and indicating life germinating in the womb of Mother Earth. "Mother Earth," I thought; "why, that's the name of our child! The nourisher of man, man freed and unhindered in his access to the free earth!" The title

rang in my ears like an old forgotten strain. The next day we returned to New York and prepared the copy for the initial number of
the magazine. It appeared on the first of March 1906, in sixty-four
pages. It's name was *Mother Earth*.

Paul Orleneff sailed back to Russia soon afterwards, leaving a
large part of himself in the hearts of all of us who had exulted in his
genius. The American theatre and what passed as drama in the country seemed, thereafter, commonplace and vulgar to me. But I had new
work to do, fascinating and absorbing.

With *Mother Earth* off the press and mailed to our subscribers, I
left a substitute in my office and, together with Max, started on tour.
We had large audiences in Toronto, Cleveland, and Buffalo. It was
my first visit to the last-named city since 1901. The police were still
haunted by the shades of Czolgosz; they were in force and commanded that no language but English be spoken. That prevented Max
from delivering his address, but I did not permit the opportunity to
pass without paying my respects to the police. The second meeting, the
next evening, was stopped before we could get into the hall.

While still in Buffalo, we received the news of the death of Johann
Most. He had been on a lecture tour and had died in Cincinnati, fighting for his ideal to the very last. Max had loved Most devotedly
and he was quite unnerved by the blow. And I — all my early feeling
for Hannes now perturbed me as if there had never been the bitter
clash that separated us. Everything he had given me in the years when
he had inspired and taught me stood before me now and made me
realize the senselessness of that feud. My own long struggle to find
my bearings, the disillusionments and disappointments I had experienced, had made me less dogmatic in my demands on people than I
had been. They had helped me to understand the hard and lonely
life of the rebel who had fought for an unpopular cause. Whatever
bitterness I had felt against my old teacher had given way to deep
sympathy long before his death.

I had tried on several occasions to let him feel the change in me,
but his unyielding attitude convinced me that there had been no cor-
responding change in him. The first time I had approached him, after
many years, had been in 1903, at a reception given upon his release
after his third term at Blackwell's Island. His hair had grown white,
yet his face was still ruddy and his blue eyes shone with the old fire.
We collided near the steps of the platform, he coming down as I was

going up to speak. Without the least sign of recognition, without a word, he stepped coldly aside to let me pass. Later in the day I saw him surrounded by a lot of hangers-on. I longed to go over and take him by the hand, as in the old days, but his cold stare was still upon me and made me turn away.

In 1904 Most gave a performance of Hauptmann's *Weavers* at the Thalia Theatre. His interpretation of Baumert was a superb piece of acting that brought back to memory all he had told me of his passionate yearning for the theatre. How different his life might have been had he been able to satisfy that craving! Recognition and glory instead of hatred, persecution, and prison.

Again the old feeling for Most welled up in my heart, and I went behind the stage to tell him how splendidly he had played. He accepted my praise in the same manner as he did that of the scores of others who flocked about him. It apparently meant nothing more to him.

The last time I saw Most was at the great memorial meeting for Louise Michel. She had died while lecturing in Marseilles, in February 1905. Her death had united all the revolutionary sections of New York in a demonstration in honour of the wonderful woman. Together with Catherine Breshkovskaya and Alexander Jonas, Most represented the old guard that came to pay homage to the dead rebel and fighter. I was listed to speak after Most. We stood on the platform side by side for a moment. It was the first time in years that we had been seen together in public, and the audience evidenced great enthusiasm. Most turned away from me, without even a greeting, and left without another look in my direction.

And now the old warrior was dead! Sadness overcame me at the thought of the suffering that had made him so inexorable and harsh.

When Max and I returned to New York, we learned that a memorial meeting was being arranged for Most, to take place in the Grand Central Palace. We were both asked to speak. I was informed that the invitation to me had been protested against by some of Most's supporters, especially his wife, who considered it " sacrilegious " for Emma Goldman to pay tribute to Johann Most. I had no desire to intrude, but the younger comrades in the German ranks, as well as many of the Yiddish anarchists, insisted on my speaking.

On the appointed afternoon the place was crowded, every German and Yiddish labour organization being represented at the gathering.

There were also great numbers from our own ranks, from every foreign-language anarchist group. It was an impressive affair and proved the great appreciation of the genius and spirit of Johann Most. I spoke only a short time, but I was told afterwards that my tribute to my old teacher had affected even my enemies in the *Freiheit* group.

JOHANN MOST IN 1890

My office lease was about to expire, and from some remarks of the janitor I gathered that it would not be renewed. I was not disturbed, as I had decided to discontinue massaging. I could not attend to all the work myself and I did not care to exploit help. Moreover, *Mother Earth* was requiring all my time. The friends who had enabled me to open the beauty parlour were indignant at my giving it up when it was beginning to show success. I had paid my debts and I even had a little surplus on hand. The experience I had gained and the people I had met were worth much more than material returns. Now I would be free, free from disguise and subterfuge. There was also something else from which I had to free myself. It was my life with Dan.

Too great differences in age, in conception and attitude, had gradually loosened our ties. Dan was a college boy of the average American level. Neither in our ideas nor in our views of social values had we much in common. Our life lacked the inspiration of mutuality in aim and purpose. As time passed, the certainty kept growing that our relationship could not continue. The end came abruptly one night, when I was bruised with endless misunderstanding. When I returned to my apartment in the afternoon of the following day, Dan had departed, and thus one more fond hope had been buried with the past.

I was free to devote myself entirely to *Mother Earth*. But even more important was the approaching event I had longed for and dreamed about during fourteen years — Sasha's release.

May 1906 came at last. Only two more weeks remained till Sasha's resurrection. I had become restless, assailed by perturbing thoughts. What would it be like to stand face to face with Sasha again, his hand in mine, with no guard between us? Fourteen years are a long time, and our lives had flowed in different channels. What if they had moved too far apart to enable them to converge again into the life and comradeship that had been ours when we had parted? The thought of such a possibility sickened me with fear. I busied myself to still my fluttering heart: *Mother Earth,* arrangements for a short tour, preparations for lectures. I had planned to be the first at the prison gate when Sasha would step out into freedom, but a letter from him requested that we meet in Detroit. He could not bear to see me in the presence of detectives, reporters, and a curious mob, he wrote. It was a bitter disappointment to have to wait longer than I had planned, but I knew his objection was justified.

Carl Nold now lived with a woman friend in Detroit. They occupied a small house, surrounded by a garden, away from the noise and confusion of the city. Sasha could rest quietly there. Carl had shared Sasha's lot under the same prison roof and had remained one of his staunchest friends. It was only fair that he should participate in the great moment with me.

Buffalo, Toronto, Montreal, meetings, crowds — I went through them in a daze, conscious only of one thought — *the 18th of May,* the date of Sasha's release. I reached Detroit on the early morning of that day, with the vision of Sasha impatiently pacing his cell before his final liberation. Carl met me at the station. He had arranged a public reception for Sasha and a meeting, he informed me. I listened confused, constantly watching the clock striking off the last prison minutes of my boy. At noon a telegram arrived from friends in Pittsburgh: "Free and on the way to Detroit." Carl snatched up the wire, waved it frantically, and shouted: "He is free! Free!" I could not share his joy; I was oppressed by doubts. If only the evening would come and I could see Sasha with my own eyes!

Tense I stood at the railroad station, leaning against a post. Carl and his friend were near, talking. Their voices sounded afar, their bodies were blurred and faint. Out of my depths suddenly rose the past. It was July 10, 1892, and I saw myself at the Baltimore and Ohio Station in New York, standing on the steps of a moving train, clinging to Sasha. The train began moving faster; I jumped off and ran after it, with outstretched hands, crying frantically: "Sasha! Sasha!"

Someone was tugging at my sleeve, voices were calling: "Emma! Emma! The train is in. Quick — to the gate!" Carl and his girl ran ahead, and I too wanted to run, but my legs felt numb. I remained riveted to the ground, clutching at the post, my heart throbbing violently.

My friends returned, a stranger walking between them, with swaying step. "Here is Sasha!" Carl cried. That strange-looking man—was that Sasha, I wondered. His face deathly white, eyes covered with large, ungainly glasses; his hat too big for him, too deep over his head—he looked pathetic, forlorn. I felt his gaze upon me and saw his outstretched hand. I was seized by terror and pity, an irresistible desire upon me to strain him to my heart. I put the roses I had brought into his hand, threw my arms around him, and pressed my lips to his. Words of love and longing burned in my brain and remained unsaid. I clung to his arm as we walked in silence.

On reaching the restaurant Carl ordered food and wine. We drank to Sasha. He sat with his hat on, silent, a haunted look in his eyes. Once or twice he smiled, a painful, joyless grin. I took off his hat. He shrank back embarrassed, looked about furtively, and silently put his hat on again. His head was shaved! Tears welled up into my eyes; they had added a last insult to the years of cruelty; they had shaved his head and dressed him in hideous clothes to make him smart at the gaping of the outside world. I choked back my tears and forced a merry tone, pressing his pale, transparent hand.

At last Sasha and I were alone in the one spare room of Carl's home. We looked at each other like children left in the dark. We sat close, our hands clasped, and I talked of unessential things, unable to pour out what was overflowing in my heart. Utterly exhausted, I wearily dragged myself to bed. Sasha, shrinking into himself, lay down on the couch. The room was dark, only the gleam of Sasha's cigarette now and then piercing the blackness. I felt stifled and chilled at the same time. Then I heard Sasha groping about, come closer, touch me with trembling hands.

We lay pressed together, yet separated by our thoughts, our hearts beating in the silence of the night. He tried to say something, checked himself, breathed heavily, and finally broke out in fierce sobs that he vainly tried to suppress. I left him alone, hoping that his tortured spirit might find relief in the storm that was shaking him to the roots. Gradually he grew calm and said he wanted to go out for a walk, the walls were crushing him. I heard him close the door, and I was alone in my grief. I knew with a terrible certainty that the struggle for Sasha's liberation had only begun.

I woke up with the feeling that Sasha needed to go away some-where, alone, to a quiet place. But meetings and receptions had been arranged in Detroit, Chicago, Milwaukee, and New York; the com-rades wanted to meet him, to see him again. The young people especially were clamouring to behold the man who had been kept buried alive for fourteen years for his *Attentat*. I was beset with anxiety about him, but there would be no escape for him, I felt, until all the scheduled affairs were over. He would then be able to go to the little farm and perhaps find his way slowly back to life.

The Detroit papers were full of our visit with Carl, and before we left the city, they even had me married to Alexander Berkman and on our honeymoon. In Chicago the reporters were constantly on our trail, the meetings under heavy police guard. The reception in Grand Central Palace, New York, because of its size and the intense enthu-siasm of the audience, depressed Sasha even more than the others. But now the misery was at an end and we went out to the little Ossining farm. Sasha was pleased with it; he loved its wildness, seclusion, and quiet. And I was filled with new hope for him and for his release from the grip of the prison shadows.

Having been starved for so many years, he now ate ravenously. It was extraordinary what an amount of food he could absorb, especially of his favourite Jewish dishes, of which he had been de-prived so long. It was nothing at all for him to follow up a substantial meal with a dozen *blintzes* (a kind of Yiddish pancake containing cheese or meat) or a huge apple pie. I cooked and baked, happy in his enjoyment of the food. Most of my friends were in the habit of paying court to my culinary art, but no one ever did so much justice to it as my poor, famished Sasha.

Our country idyll was short-lived. The black phantoms of the past were again pursuing their victim, driving him out of the house and robbing him of peace. Sasha roamed the woods or lay for hours stretched on the ground, silent and listless.

The quiet of the country increased his inner turmoil, he told me. He could not endure it; he must go back to town. He must find work to occupy his mind or he would go mad. And he must make a living; he would not be supported by public collections. He had already de-clined to accept the five hundred dollars the comrades had raised for him, and had distributed the money among several anarchist publi-cations. There was another thing that tormented him: the thought of his unfortunate comrades of so many years. How could he enjoy peace and comfort, knowing that they were deprived of both? He had pledged himself to voice their cause and to cry out against the horrors within prison walls. Yet he was doing nothing but eating, sleeping, and drifting. He could not go on that way, he said.

I understood his suffering, and my heart bled for my dear one, so bound by the past. We returned to 210 East Thirteenth Street, and there the struggle grew more intense, the struggle for adjustment to living. In his depleted physical condition Sasha could find no work to do, and the atmosphere surrounding me appeared strange and alien to him. With the passing weeks and months his misery increased. When we were alone in the flat, or in the company of Max, he breathed a little freer, and he was not unhappy with Becky Edelson, a young comrade who often came to visit us. All my other friends irritated and disturbed him; he could not bear their presence and he always looked for some excuse to leave. Generally it was dawn before he returned. I would hear his weary steps as he went to his room, hear him fling himself dressed upon his bed and fall into restless sleep, always disturbed by frightful nightmares of his prison life. Repeatedly he would awaken with fearful shrieks that chilled my blood with terror. Entire nights I would pace the floor in anguish of heart, racking my brain for some means to help Sasha find his way back to life.

It occurred to me that a lecture tour might prove a wedge to it. It would enable him to unburden himself of what lay so heavily on his mind — prison and its brutality — and it would help him perhaps to readjust himself to life away from the work he considered mine. It might bring back his old faith in himself. I prevailed upon Sasha to get in touch with our people in a few cities. Soon he had numerous applications for lectures. Almost immediately it brought about a change; he became less restless and depressed, somewhat more communicative with the friends who came to see me, and he even showed an interest in the preparations for the October issue of *Mother Earth*.

That number was to contain articles on Leon Czolgosz, in memory of the fifth anniversary of his death. Sasha and Max strongly favoured the idea of a memorial issue, but other comrades fought against it on the ground that anything about Czolgosz would hurt the cause as well as the magazine. They even threatened to withdraw their material support. I had promised myself when I started *Mother Earth* never to permit anyone, whether group or individual, to dictate its policy; opposition now made me the more determined to go through with my plan of dedicating the October number to Czolgosz.

As soon as the magazine was off the press, Sasha began his tour. His first stops were Albany, Syracuse, and Pittsburgh. I hated the idea of his going back to the dreadful city so soon, particularly because I knew that according to the provisions of the Pennsylvania commutation law Sasha remained at the mercy of the authorities of that State for eight years, during which period they had the legal right to arrest him at any time for the slightest offence and send him back to the penitentiary to complete his full term of twenty-two years. Sasha was set, however, on lecturing in Pittsburgh, and I clung to the faint hope that speaking in that city might free him from his prison nightmare. I felt relieved when a telegram came from him saying that the Pittsburgh gathering had been a success, and that all was well.

His next stop was Cleveland. On the day after his first meeting in that city I received a wire informing me that Sasha had left the house of the comrade with whom he had spent the night and had not yet returned. It did not disturb me very much, knowing how the poor boy dreaded contact with people. He had probably decided to go to a hotel, I thought, to be by himself, and he would undoubtedly appear for the lecture in the evening. But at midnight another wire notified me that he had not attended the meeting, and that the comrades were worried. I, too, became alarmed and telegraphed Carl in Detroit, the next city Sasha was expected in. There could be no answer the same day, and the night, full of black forebodings, seemed to stand still. The morning newspapers carried large headlines about the "disappearance of Alexander Berkman, the recently freed anarchist."

The shock completely unnerved me. I was too paralysed at first to form any idea of what might have happened to him. Finally two possibilities presented themselves: that he had been kidnapped by the authorities in Pittsburgh, or — more likely and terrible — that he might have ended his life. I was frantic that I had failed to plead with him not to go to Pittsburgh. Yet, though fearful of his danger, the more dreadful thought persisted in my brain, the thought of suicide. Sasha had been in the throes of such depression that he had said repeatedly he did not care to live, that prison had unfitted him for life. My heart rebelled in passionate protest against the cruel forces that could drive him to leave me just when he had come back. I was tormented by bitter regrets that I had suggested the idea of the lecture tour.

For three days and three nights we in New York and our people in every city searched police stations, hospitals, and morgues for Sasha, but without result. Cables came from Kropotkin and other European anarchists inquiring about him, and streams of people besieged my flat. I was nearly mad with uncertainty, yet dreaded to make up my mind that Sasha had taken the fatal step.

I had to go to Elizabeth, New Jersey, to address a meeting. Long public life had taught me not to expose joy or sorrow to the idle gaze of the market-place. But how hide what now was obsessing my every thought? I had promised weeks previously, and I was compelled to go. Max accompanied me. He had already bought our tickets and we were almost at the railroad gate. Suddenly I was seized by a feeling of some impending calamity. I stopped short. "Max! Max!" I cried, "I can't go! Something is pulling me back to the flat!" He understood and urged me to return. It would be all right, he assured me; he would explain my absence and speak in my stead. Hastily pressing his hand, I dashed off to catch the first ferry-boat back to New York.

On Thirteenth Street near Third Avenue I saw Becky running towards me, excitedly waving a yellow slip of paper. "I've been looking for you everywhere!" she cried. "Sasha is alive! He is waiting for you at the telegraph office on Fourteenth Street!" My heart leaped to my throat. I snatched the paper from her. It read: "Come. I am waiting for you here." I ran full speed towards Fourteenth Street. When I got to the office, I came face to face with Sasha. He was leaning against the wall, a small hand-bag at his side.

"Sasha!" I cried; "oh, my dear — at last!" At the sound of my voice he pulled himself together, as if out of a harrowing dream. His lips moved, but he remained silent. His eyes alone told of his suffering and despair. I took his arm and steadied him, his body shaking as in a chill. We had almost reached 210 East Thirteenth Street when he suddenly cried: "Not here! Not here! I can't see anybody in your flat!" For a moment I did not know what to do; then I hailed a cab and told the driver to go to the Park Avenue Hotel.

It was dinner-hour, and the lobby filled with guests. Everybody was in evening dress; conversation and laughter blended with the strains of music from the dining-hall. When we were alone in a room,

Sasha grew dizzy and had to be helped to the couch, where he fell down in a heap. I ran to the telephone and ordered whisky and hot broth. He drank eagerly, indicating that it refreshed him. He had not eaten in three days, nor taken off his clothes. I prepared a bath for him, and while helping him to undress, my hand suddenly came in contact with a steel object. It was a revolver he was trying to hide in his hip pocket.

After the bath and another hot drink Sasha spoke to me. He had hated the idea of the tour the moment he got out of New York, he said. The approach of each lecture would throw him into a panic and fill him with an irresistible desire to escape. The meetings had been badly attended and lacked spirit. The homes of the comrades he had stopped with were congested, with no separate corner for him. More terrible even had been the constant stream of people, the incessant questions. Still he had kept on. Pittsburgh had somewhat relieved his depression; the presence of a horde of police, detectives, and prison officials had roused his fighting spirit and had lifted him out of himself. But Cleveland was a ghastly experience from the moment he arrived. There was no one to meet him at the station, and he spent the day in an exhausting search to locate comrades. The audience in the evening was small and inert; after the lecture came an endless ride to the farm of the comrade whose guest he was to be. Worn and sick unto death, he fell into a heavy sleep. He awoke in the middle of the night and was horrified to find a strange man snoring at his side. His years of solitude in prison had made close human proximity a torture to him. He rushed out of the house, into the country road, to look for some hiding-place where he could be alone. But peace would not come, nor relief from the feeling that he was unfit for life. He determined to end it.

In the morning he walked to the city and bought a revolver. He decided to go to Buffalo. No one knew him there, no one would discover him in life or claim him in death. He roamed through the city all day and night, but New York drew him with irresistible force. Finally he went there and spent two days and nights circling around 210 East Thirteenth Street. He was in constant terror of meeting anyone, yet he could not keep away. Each time on returning to his squalid little room on the Bowery he would take up the revolver for the final gesture. He went to the park nearby, determined to make an end. The sight of little children playing turned his mind to the past and the "sailor girl." "And then I knew that I could not die without seeing you again," he concluded.

His story held me breathless, unable and afraid to break its thread. Sasha's inner conflict was so overwhelming that my own excruciating uncertainty during those three days seemed nothing in comparison. Infinite tenderness filled me for the man who had already died a thousand deaths and who was again attempting to escape life. I became possessed of a burning craving to defeat the ominous forces that were pursuing my unfortunate friend.

I held out my hand to him and begged him to come home with me. "Only Stella is there, my dearest," I pleaded, "and I will see that no one intrudes upon you." At the flat I found Stella, Max, and Becky waiting anxiously for our return. I took Sasha through the corridor into my room and put him to bed. He went off to sleep like a weary child.

Sasha remained in bed for several days, asleep most of the time and only half-aware of his surroundings during his waking hours. Max, Stella, and Becky relieved me in taking care of him; no one else was allowed to disturb the quiet in my apartment.

A group of young anarchists had arranged a gathering to discuss Leon Czolgosz and his act. At the meeting three of the boys were arrested. I knew nothing about the matter until I was awakened early one morning by violent ringing of the bell and informed of the arrest. We immediately called a meeting to protest against the suppression of free speech, the announced speakers being Bolton Hall, Harry Kelly, John Coryell, Max Baginski, and I. On the appointed evening Sasha, who was beginning to feel a little better, wanted to go. Fearing he might be upset again, I persuaded him to attend the theatre with Stella instead.

When I arrived with Max and the Coryells in the hall, we found a small audience, but the walls were lined with policemen. Young Julius Edelson, brother of Becky, who had been arrested at the previous meeting, but had been bailed out by Bolton Hall, had just ascended the rostrum. He had spoken about ten minutes when there came a commotion; several officers dashed forward and pulled Julius off the platform, while other policemen charged the crowd, drawing the chairs from under the people, dragging the girls out by the hair, and clubbing the men. Crying and cursing, the audience rushed for the exits. When I got to the stairs with Max, a policeman gave him a violent kick that nearly sent him down to the bottom, while another struck me in the back and told me I was under arrest. " You're just the one we want ! " he roared; "we'll teach you how to protest ! " In the patrol wagon I found myself in the company of eleven " dangerous criminals," all of them young boys and girls, members of the offending group. Bolton Hall and Harry Kelly and the Coryells had somehow escaped the brutality of the police. Pending our indictment we were admitted to bail.

Our arrest produced one beneficial result; it immediately roused Sasha's fighting spirit. " My resurrection has come ! " he cried, when he heard of what had happened at the meeting; "there is work for me to do now ! " My joy over Sasha's awakening, and the realization of the danger the arrested youngsters were facing, increased my strength and energy. Soon we organized for the fight, with Hugh O. Pentecost and Meyer London as our legal advisers and with considerable material support from our American and foreign friends. Already at the police-court hearing it became evident that there was no case against us, but the District Attorney was out for glory. What better way of getting it than by saving the city from anarchy? It was an easy job now, with the Criminal Anarchy Law on the statute-book. The judge seemed willing enough to oblige the District Attorney, but most of the criminal anarchists before him looked so young and inoffensive that His Honour was dubious about any jury's convicting them. To save his face he held us over for "further examination."

While I always preferred certainty in such matters, I should have welcomed the delay had I been able to continue my lecture work. But the police kept up a systematic raid upon all English anarchist activities; not in the open manner in which they had suppressed the meeting, but in a more insidious way. They terrorized the hall-keepers, thereby making it practically impossible for me to get a hearing in any public place in New York. Even so harmless an affair as a *Mother Earth* masked ball, arranged to raise funds for our publication, was broken up. Fifty officers had come down to the hall and ordered the people to get out, tearing off their masks. When that failed to provoke trouble, they forced the owner to close the hall. It meant a great financial loss.

We organized a *Mother Earth* Club, giving weekly lectures on various topics and occasionally also musicales. The police were furious; they had been hounding us for nine weeks, and still we would not be put down. Something more drastic and intimidating had to be done to save the sacred institutions of law and order. The next move of the authorities took place at a meeting that was to be addressed by Alexander Berkman, John R. Coryell, and Emma Goldman. They arrested all the speakers. A criminal anarchist, fifteen years of age, who happened to be at the door was also taken along to complete the quartet. I had intended to speak on the " Misconceptions of Anarchism," a lecture I had delivered only two weeks previously before the Brooklyn Philosophical Society. Detectives from the newly created Anarchist Squad had been present, yet no arrest had taken place. It was obvious that they had not dared to interfere with a non-anarchist society, even though the speaker was Emma Goldman. It might have taught the Brooklyn philosophers that it was not anarchism but the Police Department that was destroying the little liberty that still existed in the United States. On the way to the police station the inspector in charge of the Anarchist Squad asked me whether I did not intend to cease my agitation. When I assured him that I was more determined than ever to go on, he informed me that thereafter I would be arrested every time I attempted to speak in public.

For a while it seemed as if Sasha had really found himself again and would be able to continue with me in our common life and work. He had been eager for activity since the day of our arrest, but after two months his interest gave way again to the gloom which had pursued him since he got out of prison. He thought that the main reason for his depression was his material dependence on me, which was galling to him. To free him from it I induced a good comrade to lend Sasha some money to set up a small printing shop. It helped to revive Sasha's spirits and he began to work assiduously to advance the venture. Presently he was installed in a complete printing outfit of his own that enabled him to do small jobs. But the happiness was not to last; new difficulties besieged him. He could not get a union label because as a compositor he was not permitted to do pressman's work, while to employ a pressman would be exploitation. He found himself in the same position I had been in with my massage establishment, and, rather than live off the labour of others or do non-union jobs, he gave up his shop. The old misery was upon him again.

Gradually I came to see that it was not so much the question of earning a living that harassed Sasha as something deeper and more bitter to face: the contrast between his dream-world of 1892 and my reality of 1906. The world of ideals he had taken with him to prison at twenty-one had defied the passage of time. Perhaps it was fortunate that it was so; it had been his spiritual support through all the terrible fourteen years, a star to illumine the blackness of his prison existence. It had even coloured his mind's-eye view of the outside world — of the movement, his friends, and especially myself. During that time life had kicked me about, forced me into the current of events, to sink or to swim — I had ceased to be the little "sailor girl" whose image had remained with Sasha from former days. I was a woman of thirty-seven who had undergone profound changes. I no longer fitted into the old mould, as he had expected me to. Sasha saw and felt it almost immediately upon his release. He had tried to understand the mature personality which had burst forth from the shell of the inexperienced girl, and, failing, he became resentful, critical, and often condemnatory of my life, my views, and my friends. He charged me with intellectual aloofness and revolutionary inconsistency. Every thrust from him cut me to the quick and made me cry out my grief. Often I wanted to run away, never to see him again, but I was held by something greater than the pain: the memory of his act, for which he alone had paid the price. More and more I realized that to my last breath it would remain the strongest link in the chain that bound me to him. The memory of our youth and of our love might fade, but his fourteen years' Calvary would never be eradicated from my heart.

A way out of the distressing situation suggested itself in the imperative need of my going on tour for *Mother Earth*. Sasha could remain in charge as editor of the magazine; it would help to release him from his cramped feeling and enable him to find freer expression. He liked Max, and there were able contributors to assist him: Voltairine de Cleyre, Theodore Schroeder, Bolton Hall, Hippolyte Havel, and others. Sasha readily accepted the plan, and I was relieved that he did not suspect how hard it was for me to go away so soon after he had come back to me. His release — I had waited for it with such intensity, and now I should not even be with him on the first anniversary of the day so long and anxiously looked forward to.

The death of Hugh O. Pentecost came as a shock to all of us who knew and appreciated the man and his work. The news reached us through the press, as we were not informed by his widow. Pentecost had been a firm believer in cremation as the more beautiful way of disposing of a person's remains. Naturally everybody expected him to be cremated and many of his friends planned to attend and send floral tributes. Great was our astonishment when we learned that Hugh O. Pentecost had been buried instead, and that he had been given a funeral in accordance with religious rites. It was sheerest irony, considering that the one thing which Hugh O. had held high throughout his entire life was free-thought. His political changes had been many: single-taxer, socialist, and anarchist — he had been all of them at one time or another. It was different with his attitude to religion and the Church. Irrevocably he had turned from them to convinced atheism. The presence of a minister at his grave was therefore the worst outrage to his memory, and an insult to his free-thought friends. It seemed like the fulfilment of a subconscious fear Pentecost had often voiced to me: "It is very hard to live decently, but still harder to die decently." Another of his frequent expressions was that love is more difficult to escape than hate. He meant the kind of love that binds one with soft arms and tender words stronger than chains. His inability to tear himself away from those "soft arms" had been behind the repeated changes of his social ideas. It had even led him to play false to the memory of the Chicago anarchists, among whose staunchest defenders he had been until ambition made him seek the post of Assistant District Attorney of New York. "I may have been mistaken," he had declared, "in saying that the Haymarket trial was a miscarriage of justice." Neither in life nor in death had Hugh O. Pentecost been permitted to remain true to himself.

Our work for Russia received considerable zest by the arrival of Grigory Gershuni. He had escaped from Siberia in a cabbage-barrel and had come to the States via California. Gershuni had been a schoolteacher, believing that only by the education of the masses could Russia be redeemed from the yoke of the Romanoffs. For many years he had been an ardent Tolstoyan, opposed to every form of active resistance. But incessant opposition and violence by the despotism had gradually taught Gershuni the inevitability of the methods pursued by the militant revolutionists in his country. He had joined the Fighting Organization of the Socialist-Revolutionist Party and had become one of its dominant figures. He had been condemned to death, but ultimately his sentence was commuted to lifelong imprisonment in Siberia.

Grigory Gershuni, like all the great Russians I had met, was of touching simplicity, extremely reticent about his own heroic life and fired to the exclusion of any personal interest by the vision of the liberation of the Russian masses. Moreover, he possessed what many Russian rebels lacked: a keen, practical sense, exactitude, and responsibility for tasks undertaken.

I saw much of this exceptional man during his stay in New York. I learned that his extraordinary escape had been aided by two young anarchists. Working in the carpenter shop of the prison, they had skilfully drilled undetectable air-holes in the barrel to be used by Gershuni, later nailing him up within. Gershuni never tired of praising the devotion and daring of those two boys, mere children in years, yet so courageous and dependable in their revolutionary zeal.

About this time we began to prepare for the celebration of *Mother Earth's* first birthday. It seemed incredible that the magazine should have survived the hardships and difficulties of the past twelve months. The failure of some of the New York literati to live up to their promises to write for it had been only one of the ill winds which had pursued my child. They were enthusiastic at first, until they realized that *Mother Earth* pleaded for freedom and abundance in life as the basis of art. To most of them art meant an escape from reality; how, then, could they be expected to support anything that boldly courted life? They left the new-born one to shift for itself. Their places were soon filled, however, by braver and freer spirits, among them Leonard Abbott, Sadakichi Hartmann, Alvin Sanborn, all of whom regarded life and art as the twin flames of revolt.

This difficulty overcome, another arose: condemnation from my own ranks. *Mother Earth* was not revolutionary enough, they claimed, the reason no doubt being that it treated anarchism less as a dogma than as a liberating ideal. Fortunately many of my comrades stood by me, giving generously to the support of the magazine. And my own personal friends, even those who were not anarchists, were faithfully devoted to the publication and to every fight I made against continued police persecution. Altogether it was a rich and fruitful year, full of promise for the future of *Mother Earth*.

CHAPTER XXXI

OUR HEARINGS ON THE CHARGE OF CRIMINAL ANARCHY WERE repeatedly postponed and finally dropped altogether. That set me free to start on my projected tour to the Coast, the first since 1897. Before I had gone very far, my meetings were stopped by the police in three cities — Columbus, Toledo, and Detroit.

The action of the authorities in Toledo was especially reprehensible because the Mayor, Brand Whitlock, was supposed to be a man of advanced ideas, known as a Tolstoyan and "philosophical" anarchist. I had met a number of American individualists who called themselves philosophical anarchists. On closer acquaintance they invariably proved neither philosophers nor anarchists, and their belief in free speech always had a "but" to it.

Mayor Whitlock, however, was also a single-taxer, a member of a group of Americans who stood out as the most valiant champions of free speech and press. In fact, the single-taxers had always been the first to support me in my fights against police interference. I was therefore greatly surprised to find a single-tax mayor guilty of the same arbitrary attitude as any ordinary city official. I asked some of his admirers how they could explain such behaviour on the part of a man like Whitlock. Much to my astonishment, they informed me that he was under the impression that I had come to Toledo for the express purpose of fomenting trouble among the automobile-workers then on strike. He was trying to bring about a settlement between the bosses and their employees, and he thought it best not to permit me to speak.

"Evidently your Mayor knows that his settlement is likely to benefit the owners and not the strikers," I remarked, "else he would not fear what I might say."

I informed them that until I arrived in Toledo, I had not even known about the strike. I had come to lecture on the "Misconceptions of Anarchism." I cheerfully admitted, however, that if the strikers asked me to speak, I should tell them to steer clear of politicians, who are the worst meddlers and who help to break the backbone of every economic struggle. This was reported to a group of American liberals, who at once set to work to arrange a special meeting for me.

The most spirited among them was a venerable old woman, Mrs. Kate B. Sherwood. In abolition times she had helped many a fugitive slave to safety, and she did not change with the years. She was a fervent feminist, a great libertarian in economic and educational fields, as well as a lovable personality. The dear lady must have read the Riot Act to the Mayor, because there was no further interference in Toledo with my lectures.

In Minneapolis I had an amusing experience. I was invited to address an organization of professional men known as the Spook Club. I was told that no woman had ever before been admitted into the holy presence of the Spookers, but that I had been made an exception. Not believing in special privileges, I wrote to the club that in my capacity as nurse I had never known nervousness when I had to lay out the dead. But to face living corpses alone would prove disconcerting to me. I would brave the task of preparing the Spookers for burial if I could have a few husky members of my own sex to assist me. The poor Spook Club was flabbergasted. To consent to my request involved the danger of a female invasion. To refuse was to expose themselves to public ridicule. Male conceit conquered its lily-white purity. "Bring your regiment along, Emma Goldman," the Spookers replied, "and take the consequences." My women friends and I created almost a revolution in the club. Alas, not in the heads, but only in the hearts of the Spookers. We made them conscious that there is nothing duller in all the world than exclusive gatherings of men or of women, who are yet never able to eliminate each other from their minds. On this occasion everybody felt relief from sex obsession, natural and at ease. The evening was very interesting. Indeed, I was assured that it was considered the most stimulating intellectual treat in the club's history, and the most hilarious besides.

The liberal attitude of the Spookers towards me was only part of the general change which had taken place in the past six years in regard to anarchism. The tone of the press was no longer so vindictive. The papers in Toledo, Cincinnati, Toronto, Minneapolis, and

Winnipeg were extraordinarily decent in their reports of my meetings. In a long editorial one Winnipeg paper said:

> Emma Goldman has been accused of abusing freedom of speech in Winnipeg, and Anarchism has been denounced as a system that advocates murder. As a matter of fact, Emma Goldman indulged, while in Winnipeg, in no dangerous rant and made no statement that deserved more than moderate criticism of its wisdom or logic. Also, as a matter of fact, the man who claims that Anarchism teaches bomb-throwing and violence doesn't know what he is talking about. Anarchism is an ideal doctrine that is now, and always will be, utterly impracticable. Some of the gentlest and most gifted men of the world believe in it. The fact alone that Tolstoi is an Anarchist is conclusive proof that it teaches no violence.
>
> We all have a right to laugh at Anarchy as a wild dream. We all have a right to agree or disagree with the teachings of Emma Goldman. But we should not make ourselves ridiculous by criticizing a lecturer for the things that she did not say, nor by denouncing as violent and bloody a doctrine that preaches the opposite of violence.

After my coast-to-coast lecture tour I returned to New York at the end of June with a net result of a considerable number of subscribers to *Mother Earth* and a substantial surplus from the sale of literature to sustain the magazine during the inactive summer months.

In the early spring our European comrades had issued a call for an anarchist congress to be held in Amsterdam, Holland, in August. Some of the groups in the cities I had visited had requested me to attend the gathering as their delegate. It was gratifying to have the confidence of my comrades, and Europe always had its lure for me. But there was Sasha, only one year out of prison, and I had already been away from him for months. I longed to see him again and to try to bridge the gap which his imprisonment had created between us.

Sasha had done splendidly on *Mother Earth* while I was away. He had surprised everybody by the vigour of his style and the clarity of his thoughts. It was an amazing achievement for a man who had gone into prison ignorant of the English language and who had never written for publication before. His letters to me during my four months on tour were free from depression, and he showed much interest in the magazine and my work. I was proud of Sasha and his efforts, and I was full of hope that we might yet dispel the clouds that had been hanging in our sky since he had re-entered the outside world. These considerations made me hesitate to go to Amsterdam. I would decide when I reached New York, I told my comrades.

On my return I found Sasha as I had left him — in the same mental turmoil, in torturing conflict between the vision that had inspired his deed and the reality that confronted him now. He continued to dwell in the past, in the mirage he had created for himself during his living death. Everything in the present was alien to him, made him wince and avoid it. It was bitter irony that I, of all Sasha's friends, should cause him the deepest disappointment and pain — I who had never had him out of my mind in all the cruel years, or out of my heart, no matter who else had been there, not even Ed, whom I had loved more deeply and intensely than anyone else. Yet it was I who most roused Sasha's impatience and resentment; not in a personal sense, but because of the changes I had undergone in my attitude to life, to people, and to our movement. We did not seem to have a single thought in common. Yet I felt bound to Sasha, bound for ever by the tears and blood of fourteen years.

Often, when I could no longer bear up under his censure and condemnation, I would fight back with harsh and bitter words, then run to my room and cry out in pain against the differences that were tearing us apart. Yet I would always come back to Sasha, feeling that whatever he had said or done was nothing in the light of what he had endured. I knew *that* would ever weigh heaviest in the balance with me and bring me to his side at every moment of his need. Just now it seemed that I was of little help. Sasha appeared to feel more at ease when I was away.

I decided to comply with the request of my Western comrades to represent them at the anarchist congress. Sasha said he would continue on the magazine until my return, but that his heart was not in *Mother Earth*. He wanted a weekly propaganda paper that would reach the workers. He had already discussed the project with Voltairine de Cleyre, Harry Kelly, and other friends. They had agreed with him that such a paper was needed and had promised to sign an appeal for the necessary funds. They had been worried, however, that I might misunderstand, that I might consider the new publication a competitor of *Mother Earth*. "What a ridiculous notion," I protested; "I claim no monopoly of the movement. By all means try to get out a weekly paper. I will add my name to the call." Sasha was quite moved, embraced me tenderly, and sat down to write the appeal. My poor boy! If only I could have had the assurance that his project would bring him peace, help him back to life and to the work his mastery of language and his pen should enable him to do!

More and more I was beginning to see that there was an inner resentment in Sasha, perhaps not even conscious, against being part of the activities I had created for myself. He longed for something of his own making, something that would express his own self. I hoped fervently that the weekly paper would prove the means of his release and that it might succeed.

I was getting ready for my trip abroad; Max was going, too, representing some German groups at the Amsterdam congress. We both needed to get away from our environment for a while. The farm had not turned out the roseate reality he had hoped for. A farm never does for city people who come to the land with romantic notions about nature and with no ability to cope with her hardships. Our place in Ossining had proved too primitive and the winter too harsh for Max's little daughter. Another reason was the isolation of Millie, which she was unable to bear. My friends had moved to the city and were trying desperately to make ends meet, Max by occasional articles for German papers and contributions to *Mother Earth,* Millie by sewing. The stress she had endured since the birth of her child had made her nervous and irritable, and Max shrank into his shell at the least disharmony. Like myself he longed to get away from conditions that were agonizing, yet of no one's making.

Sasha was much more alive now, thanks to his plan for a weekly paper. There was also another factor that helped to raise his spirits. He had gained many friends among our young comrades, and he was especially attracted by young Becky Edelson. I felt considerably relieved about him. *Mother Earth* also did not worry me; I left it secure until my return and I was certain of its quality, with Sasha as its editor, and John Coryell, Hippolyte Havel, and others as collaborators.

Hippolyte and I had long ago drifted apart in our old relation, but our friendship had remained as strong as before, as had also our common interest in the social struggle. His great historical knowledge and his feeling for events made him most valuable to our magazine.

In the middle of August 1907 Max and I waved our friends goodbye from the Holland-America pier. Besides our mission at the congress, we both looked upon our trip as a quest for something to fill our inner void. The calm sea and the ever-soothing companionship of Max helped me to relax from the tension of the months preceding and following Sasha's liberation. By the time we reached Amsterdam, I was again in full control of myself, eager with anticipation of the people I should meet, our congress, and the work to be done.

I had heard a great deal about the extreme cleanliness of the Dutch, but until I went for a walk in Amsterdam on the morning after our arrival, I did not know how uncomfortable Hollanders could make it for the passers-by. I had gone out with Max to take a look at the quaint old town. We found every balcony adorned with buxom servants in colourful dress, arms and legs bare, furiously beating carpets and rugs. A pleasant picture indeed, but the whirlwind of dust and dirt they were lustily shaking on to our defenceless heads filled our throats and covered our clothes. Still we could have stood it if we had not been at the same time treated to a shower of cold water meant for the plants. The unexpected bath was more than the Dutch cleanliness we had bargained for.

The congress was my third attempt to attend an international anarchist gathering. In 1893 such a conclave had been planned, and it was to take place during that year's exposition in Chicago. I had been chosen to represent several New York groups, but my trial and imprisonment had prevented my attendance. At the eleventh hour the Chicago police had prohibited the congress, but it was held just the same — in the most unlikely place imaginable. A comrade, employed as clerk in one of the city departments, had smuggled a dozen delegates into a room in the City Hall.

The second time had been in Paris, in 1900, where I was closely connected with the preparatory work of our congress. The French police, too, had made open conferences impossible. The sessions held under cover, while exciting enough, had made constructive work impossible.

It was certainly a commentary on democratic America and republican France that an international anarchist congress, prohibited in both countries, should have the right to meet quite openly in monarchical Holland. Eighty men and women, most of them hounded and persecuted in their own countries, were here able to address large meetings, gather in daily session, and discuss openly such vital problems as revolution, syndicalism, mass insurrection, and individual acts of violence, without any interference from the authorities. We went about the city singly or in groups, had social gatherings in restaurants or cafés, talked, and sang revolutionary songs until early morning hours, yet we were not shadowed, spied upon, or in any way molested.

More remarkable still was the attitude of the Amsterdam press. Even the most conservative newspapers treated us, not as criminals or lunatics, but as a group of serious people who had come together for a serious purpose. Those papers were opposed to anarchism, yet they did not misrepresent us or distort anything said at our sessions.

One of the vital subjects discussed at length by the congress was the problem of organization. Some delegates deprecated Ibsen's idea, as presented by Dr. Stockmann in *An Enemy of the People,* to the effect that the strongest is he who stands alone. They preferred Peter Kropotkin's view, so brilliantly elucidated in all his books, that it is mutual aid and co-operation that secure the best results. Max and I, however, stressed the need of both. We held that anarchism does not involve a choice between Kropotkin and Ibsen; it embraces both. While Kropotkin had thoroughly analysed the social conditions that lead to revolution, Ibsen had portrayed the psychologic struggle that culminates in the revolution of the human soul, the revolt of individuality. Nothing would prove more disastrous to our ideas, we contended, than to neglect the effect of the internal upon the external, of the psychologic motives and needs upon existing institutions.

There is a mistaken notion in some quarters, we argued, that organization does not foster individual freedom; that, on the contrary, it means the decay of individuality. In reality, however, the true function of organization is to aid the development and growth of personality. Just as the animal cells, by mutual co-operation, express their latent powers in the formation of the complete organism, so does the individuality, by co-operative effort with other individualities, attain its highest form of development. An organization, in the true sense, cannot result from the combination of mere nonentities. It must be composed of self-conscious, intelligent individualities. Indeed, the total of the possibilities and activities of an organization is represented in the expression of individual energies. Anarchism asserts the possibility of an organization without discipline, fear, or punishment and without the pressure of poverty: a new social organism, which will make an end to the struggle for the means of existence — the savage struggle which undermines the finest qualities in man and ever widens the social abyss. In short, anarchism strives towards a social organization which will establish well-being for all.

There were many interesting and vital personalities in the group of delegates, among them Dr. Friedberg, once member of the Social Democratic Party and Alderman of Berlin, who had become a brilliant exponent of the general strike and anti-militarism. Notwithstanding an indictment for high treason hanging over him, he took a most active part in the proceedings of the congress, oblivious of the danger awaiting him on his return home. There were also Luigi Fabbri, one of the ablest contributors to the educational Italian magazine *Università Populare;* Rudolph Rocker, who was doing splendid work among the Jewish population of London as lecturer and editor of the Yiddish *Arbeiter Freind;* Christian Cornelissen, one of the keenest intellects in our movement in Holland; Rudolph Grossmann, publisher of an anarchist paper in Austria; Alexander Schapiro, active among revolutionary trade unions in England; Thomas H. Keell, one of our most devoted workers on the London *Freedom;* and other capable and energetic comrades.

The French, Swiss, Belgian, Austrian, Bohemian, Russian, Serbian, Bulgarian, and Dutch delegates were all men of spirit and ability, but the most outstanding personality among them was Enrico Malatesta. Of fine and sensitive nature, Malatesta had already in his youth embraced revolutionary ideals. Later he met Bakunin, in whose circle he was the youngest, affectionately called "Benjamin." He wrote a number of popular pamphlets that found wide distribution, particularly in Italy and Spain, and he was editor of various anarchist publications. But his literary activities did not prevent him from participating also in the actual daily struggles of the workers. He had played an important rôle, together with the celebrated Carlo Cafiero and the famous Russian revolutionist Sergius "Stepniak" (Kravtchinsky), in the uprising in Benevento, Italy, in 1877. His interest in popular rebellion runs like a red thread throughout his life. Whether he happened to be in Switzerland, France, England, or the Argentine, an uprising in his native country always brought him to the aid of the people. In 1897 he had again taken an active part in the rebellion in southern Italy. His entire life was one of storm and stress, his energies and exceptional abilities devoted to the service of the anarchist cause. But whatever his work in the movement, he always insisted on remaining materially independent of it, earning his living by manual labour, which was a principle of his life. The considerable inheritance from his father, consisting of land and houses in Italy, he had deeded without any remuneration to the workers who occupied them, himself continuing to exist most frugally on the earnings of his own hands. His name was one of the best-known and best-beloved in Latin countries.

I had met this grand old anarchist fighter in London in 1895, for a few brief moments. On my second visit, in 1899, I discovered that Enrico Malatesta had gone to the States to lecture and edit the Italian anarchist paper *La Questione Sociale*. While there, he was shot by a deluded Italian patriot, but Enrico, true anarchist that he was, refused to prosecute his assailant. In Amsterdam I had the first real chance to come into daily contact with him. Max and I quickly fell under the spell of Malatesta. We loved his capacity to throw off the weight of the world and give himself to play in his leisure. Every moment spent with him was a joy, whether he exulted over the sight of the sea or frolicked in a public garden.

The most important constructive result of our congress was the formation of an International Bureau. Its secretariate consisted of Malatesta, Rocker, and Schapiro. The purpose of the bureau, the headquarters of which were in London, was to bring into closer contact the anarchist groups and organizations of the various countries, to make a thorough and painstaking study of the labour struggle in every land, and to supply data and material concerning it to the anarchist press. The bureau was also to begin immediate preparations for another congress, to be held in the near future in London.

Upon the closing of our sessions we attended the anti-militarist congress, arranged by the Dutch pacifist anarchists, among whom Domela Nieuwenhuis was the most prominent. Domela's origin had certainly not forecast his becoming an enemy of authority. His ancestors were nearly all ministers of the Church. He himself had been a preacher of the Lutheran faith, but his progressive spirit lifted him out of the narrow path of theology. Domela joined the Social Democratic Party, became its foremost representative in Holland, and was elected the first Socialist member of Parliament. But he did not remain there very long. Like Johann Most and the great French anarchist Pierre Proudhon, Nieuwenhuis soon realized that nothing vital could come for liberty from parliamentary activities. He resigned his post, declaring himself an anarchist.

Since then he had devoted all his time and large private fortune to our movement, especially to the propaganda of anti-militarism. Domela was of striking and winning appearance — tall and straight, with expressive features, large blue eyes, flowing white hair and beard. He radiated kindness and sympathy and was the embodiment of the ideal he fought for. One of his characteristic traits was a broad tolerance. He was for years a vegetarian and teetotaller, yet meat and wine never left his table. "Why should my family or guests be deprived of anything that I do not care for?" he once said as he poured out the wine for us at dinner.

Before we left for France, I had occasion to address a gathering of Dutch transport workers. Once more I saw the difference between the independence of the Dutch workers, in spite of their monarchy, and democratic United States, where most of the people know precious little of independence. Several detectives had sneaked into the meeting. They were discovered by the committee, however, and were unceremoniously put out. I could not help comparing this show of spirit to the lack of it in American trade unions, so infested with the Pinkerton detective pest.

At last we were back in Paris, her lure again upon me, her reckless youth in my veins. I grew younger and more eager for all that my beloved city on the Seine could give. There was much more to learn and to absorb than in previous years.

There was also my own Stella, whom I had not seen for many months. She and dear old Victor Dave awaited us at the station and carried us off to a café. Stella was already quite Parisienne, proud of her French and her familiarity with restaurants where the cuisine was good and prices reasonable. Victor, his hair whiter, still preserved his youthful gait and his former capacity for fun. We joked and laughed more during our first dinner in Paris than I had laughed in months. The particular cause for our merriment was Stella's unsuspecting boss, no less a personage than the American Consul, whose secretary she was. Emma Goldman's devoted niece, and still the Consulate had not been blown up!

While we were yet in Holland, news had come that Peter Kropotkin had at last been readmitted to France. Peter loved the country and its people. To him France signified the cradle of liberty, the French Revolution the symbol of all that the world had of social idealism. To be sure, France was very short of the glory my great teacher had invested her with; his own eighteen months' incarceration in a French prison and subsequent expulsion had demonstrated it. Yet by some peculiar partiality Peter hailed France as the banner-bearer of freedom and the most cultured country in the world. We knew that nothing he had personally suffered had changed his feeling about the French people, and we rejoiced that he was now able to satisfy his longing to return.

Peter was already in Paris when we arrived, living but a few doors from my hotel, on Boulevard Saint-Michel. I found him in higher spirits than I had ever seen him before; he looked more vigorous and vivacious. Pretending not to know the reason, I inquired what had brought about the happy change. " Paris, Paris, my dear! " he cried. " Is there any other city in the world that gets into one's blood like Paris? " We discussed the movement in France and the work of the local groups. His favourite child was *Temps Nouveaux,* the paper he had helped to establish, yet his sense of the rights of other groups, even if they disagreed with him, was too great and his love of justice too strong to discourage the opposing elements. There was something large and beautiful about him. No one could be in his presence very long without feeling inspired by him.

Though he was busy with many things, especially the revision of his manuscript of *The Great French Revolution,* Peter would not let me go until I had told him everything about our congress. He was particularly pleased with our stand on organization and our insistence on the right of individual as well as collective revolt.

With the help of Monatte I was able to make a study of syndicalism in action at the Confédération du Travail. The leaders were nearly all anarchists, men of a much sturdier and more interesting type than one usually meets in Paris. Not only were Pouget, Pataud, Delasalle, Grueffulhieus, and Monatte brilliant exponents of new labour theories; they also had practical knowledge and experience in the daily struggle of the workers. Together with their colleagues they had converted the Bourse du Travail into a beehive of activity. Every union had its office there; many published their papers in the common printing shop, *La Voix du Peuple,* the weekly organ of the C. G. T., being perhaps the most instructive and ably edited labour paper in the world. There were night classes where the workers were taught every aspect of the intricate industrial system. Lectures were given on scientific and economic subjects, and a well-equipped dispensary and *crèche* were maintained by the workers themselves. The institution represented a practical effort to teach the masses how to make the coming revolution and how to help the new social life to birth.

Observation and study at the very source of syndicalism convinced me that it represented the economic arena where Labour could match its strength against the organized forces of its capitalist foe.

To these experiences were added others, no less enlightening, with the group of modern artists who by pen and brush were voicing the social protest, with Steinlen and Grandjuan doing the most forceful work. I did not find Steinlen, but Grandjuan proved to be a simple, kindly soul, a born rebel, the artist and idealist in the truest sense. He was at work on a set of drawings depicting phases of proletarian life. His idea was to portray Labour, pathetic in dumb helplessness, slowly awakening to the consciousness of germinating strength. He expressed his belief that the mission of art is to inspire the vision of a new dawn. "In this respect all our artists are revolutionaries," Grandjuan assured me. "Steinlen and the others are doing for art what Zola, Mirbeau, Richepin, and Rictus have done for letters. They are bringing art in rapport with the currents of life, the great human struggle for the right to know and live life."

I spoke to Grandjuan about *Mother Earth* and what it had been trying to do in America. He at once offered to make a cover-design for it, and before I left Paris, he sent it to me. It was significant in conception and expressive in its design.

The trial of nine anti-militarists and a splendid educational experiment at Rambouillet, near Paris, by Sébastien Faure, were among my other important experiences during this visit to France. The group involved in the trial consisted of one girl and eight boys, the oldest not more than twenty-three years of age. They had distributed a manifesto among soldiers urging them to use their arms against their superiors instead of against their brother working-men — certainly a very grave offence from the standpoint of military interests. In an American court those youths would have been browbeaten, terrorized, and railroaded to prison for a long term. In Paris they became the accusers, thundering anathema against the State, patriotism, militarism, and war. Far from being interfered with, the defiant denunciation of the young prisoners was listened to with attention and respect. The bold *plaidoirie* of the counsel for the defence, the distinguished persons who came to testify to the idealism of the accused, and the entire atmosphere of the court combined to make the anti-militarist trial one of the most dramatic events I had witnessed.

True, the prisoners were found guilty and sentenced to small terms, the longest being three years. Since it was France, the girl was set free altogether. In my adopted country their punishment would have been incomparably more severe and they would have undoubtedly been held also for contempt of court because of their frank avowal of their opinions and acts and the ridicule they heaped on the judge and the prosecuting attorney.

It struck me that behind the difference between American and French legal procedure was a fundamental difference in attitude to social revolt. Frenchmen had gained from their Revolution the understanding that institutions are neither sacred nor unalterable, and that social conditions are subject to change. Rebels are therefore considered in France the precursors of coming upheavals.

In America the ideals of the Revolution are dead — mummies that must not be touched. Hence the hatred and condemnation which meet the social and political rebel in the United States.

Long before I came to Paris, I had read in our French press of a unique educational experiment by the anarchist Sébastien Faure. I had heard him speak in 1900 and was carried away by his truly great eloquence. Moreover, Sébastien Faure's unusual personal history made me feel that the modern school organized by him must be of more than ordinary interest.

Beginning life as a priest, Faure had broken the shackles of Catholicism and become its formidable foe. In 1897, during the Dreyfus affair, he had joined the campaign led by Emile Zola, Anatole France, Bernard Lazare, and Octave Mirbeau against the reactionary forces in France. Faure became a fervent spokesman of Dreyfus, lecturing throughout the country, exposing the military clique that had railroaded an innocent man to Devil's Island to cover its own corruption. After that, Faure completely emancipated himself from belief in authority, whether in heaven or upon earth. Anarchism became his goal, the work for its achievement his passionate endeavour.

"La Ruche" (the Beehive), as Faure's school was called, was situated on the outskirts of Rambouillet, an ancient French village. With only a few people to help him, Faure had turned a wild, uncultivated stretch of land into a flourishing farm growing fruit and vegetables. He had taken twenty-four orphan children and those of parents too poor to pay and was housing, feeding, and clothing them at his own expense. He had created an atmosphere at La Ruche that released the life of the child from discipline and coercion of any sort. He had discarded the old methods of education and in their place he established understanding for the needs of the child, confidence and trust in its possibilities, and respect for its personality.

Not even at Cempuis, the school of the venerable libertarian Paul Robin, which I had visited in 1900, was the spirit of comradeship and co-operation between pupils and teachers so complete as at La Ruche. Robin, too, felt the need of a new approach to the child, but he still remained somewhat tied to the old text-books on education. La Ruche had freed itself also from them. The hand-painted wall-paper in the dormitory and class-rooms, picturing the life of plants, flowers, birds, and animals, had a more quickening effect on the imagination of the children than any "regular" lessons. The free grouping of the children around their teachers, listening to some story or seeking explanation for puzzling thoughts, amply made up for lack of old-fashioned instruction. In discussing problems of the education of the young, Faure showed an exceptional grasp of child psychology. The results accomplished by his school within two years were highly gratifying. "It is surprising how frank, kind, and affectionate the children are to each other," he said. "The harmony between themselves and the adults at La Ruche is highly encouraging. We should feel at fault were the children to fear or honour us merely because we are their elders. We leave nothing undone to gain their confidence and love; that accomplished, understanding will replace duty; confidence, fear; and affection, sternness." No one has yet fully realized the wealth of sympathy, kindness, and generosity hidden in the soul of the child. The effort of every true educator should be to unlock that treasure — to stimulate the child's impulses and call forth the best and noblest tendencies. What greater reward can there be for one whose life-work is to watch over the growth of the human plant than to see it unfold its petals and to observe it develop into a true individuality?

My visit to La Ruche was a valuable experience that made me realize how much could be done, even under the present system, in the way of libertarian education. To build the man and woman of the future, to unshackle the soul of the child — what grander task for those who, like Sébastien Faure, are pedagogues, not by the mere grace of a college degree, but innately, born with the gift to create, as the poet or the artist is?

Paris, always enriching one with new impressions, made it difficult for me to leave. Many friends had also endeared themselves to me, among them Max Nettlau, whom I had first met in London in 1900 and who had introduced me there to the museums and other British art treasures. In Paris I saw much of Nettlau. He was one of the most intellectual men of our movement, a scientist and historian. At the time he was collecting additional material for his monumental work on Michael Bakunin.

A few days before we left Paris, there arrived Jo Davidson, the young American sculptor. I had known him in New York and was interested in his work. He had found a studio, he told us, but there was not much in it. I had quite an outfit in my *ménage* — dishes, pots, kettles, a coffee-percolator, and an alcohol lamp on which I had often prepared feasts for a dozen visitors. In triumphal procession we carried the swag through the streets, Jo with a large bundle on his back, Max on one side of him, frying-pan and kettle slung over his shoulders, I on the other with the coffee-pot. When everything had been safely deposited in Jo's studio, we retired to a café to celebrate the inauguration of a budding artist in real Bohemian life.

Amid brilliant sunshine Max and I left Paris. It was bleak and penetrating when we reached London, with no change in the weather during our stay of two weeks. The first thing to greet us on our arrival were press dispatches from America reporting that the Federal authorities were planning to keep me out of the country under the provisions of the Anti-Anarchist Law. I paid no attention to the matter at first, believing it to be a newspaper fabrication. I was a citizen by my marriage to Kershner. Before long, letters from several attorney friends in the United States confirmed the rumours. They informed me that Washington was determined to refuse me readmission, and they urged me to sail back as quickly and quietly as possible.

Meetings for me had already been arranged in Scotland and I felt I ought not to disappoint my comrades. I decided to go on with my work, but soon I was made to realize that I should not be able to leave England without the United States Government's being apprised of my movements.

It was after a lecture in Holborn Town Hall in London that I became aware that I was being watched by Scotland Yard. A score of detectives dogged my heels from the moment I left the meeting-place. Rudolph Rocker, Milly, his wife, Max, and several other friends were with me at the time. We zigzagged London for hours, now and then stopping at restaurants and saloons, but our "shadows" kept close by and would not relinquish their prey. Finally the Rockers suggested that we go to their flat in the East End; we must lead the detectives to believe that we were going to spend the night at their home, which would be our only chance to get away unobserved early in the morning. The lights in the house were turned out and we sat in the dark, conspiring how to delude Scotland Yard. At dawn Milly went down to reconnoitre. No one was in sight. Friends in another part of the city were awaiting us. We were taken to a suburb, to the house of our horticulturist comrade Bernard Kampfmayer. He and his wife were not active in the movement at the time and therefore not under surveillance by the authorities. I hated to disappoint our Scottish comrades, but I could not afford to risk being held up on my arrival in America and forced into a legal fight. I therefore resolved to return home. After three days with our hosts, Max and I left for Liverpool, sailing from there to New York via Montreal.

The Canadian immigration authorities proved less inquisitive than the American and we experienced no trouble whatever getting into Canada. On the way from Montreal to New York the Pullman porter took our tickets, together with a generous tip, and he did not show up again until we were safely in New York. It was two weeks later, at my first public appearance, that the newspapers learned of my being back in the States. They tried frantically to find out how I had managed to get in and I suggested that they inquire of the immigration authorities.

On my return I found *Mother Earth* in a deplorable condition financially. Very little had come in during my absence, and the monthly expenses had far exceeded the amount I had left for the maintenance of the magazine. Something had to be done at once, and, being the only one who could raise funds, I lost no time in arranging various affairs to secure aid for the publication and also decided upon an immediate tour.

Sasha's critical attitude to me had not changed; if anything, it had become more pronounced. At the same time his interest in young Becky had grown. I became aware that they were very close to each other, and it hurt me that Sasha did not feel the need of confiding in me. I knew that he was not communicative by nature, yet something within me felt both offended and injured at his apparent lack of trust. I had realized even before I left for Europe that my physical

attraction for Sasha had died with his prison years. I had clung to
the hope that when he learned to understand my life, to know that
my having loved others had not changed my love for him, his old
passion would flame up again. It was painful to see that the new love
that had come to Sasha completely excluded me. My heart rebelled
against the cruel thing, but I knew that I had no right to complain.
While I had experienced life in all its heights and depths, Sasha had
been denied it. For fourteen years he had been starved for what youth
and love could give. Now it had come to him from Becky, ardent and
worshipful as only an eager girl of fifteen can be. Sasha was two
years younger than I, thirty-six, but he had not lived for fourteen
years, and in regard to women he had remained as young and naïve
as he had been at twenty-one. It was natural that he should be attracted to Becky rather than to a woman of thirty-eight who had
lived more intensely and variedly than other women double her age.
I saw it all clearly enough, yet at the same time I felt sad that he should
seek in a child what maturity and experience could give a hundredfold.

Barely five weeks after my return from Europe I was again on a
tramp through Massachusetts, Connecticut, and the State of New
York. Then came Philadelphia, Baltimore, Washington, D. C., and
Pittsburgh. The Chief of Police in Washington at first announced that
he would not let me speak. When some prominent liberals called his
attention to the fact that he had no business to interfere with the right
of free speech, he told my committee that they could go ahead with
my meetings. At the same time he revoked the licence of the hall-
keeper. When the owner threatened a legal fight, the Chief issued
a temporary licence permitting entertainments and meetings "not
objectionable to the district authorities." My meetings did not take
place.

Pittsburgh brought back many memories — Sasha's martyrdom and
the pilgrimages I used to make to the prison, the hopes I had cherished
and that had not been fulfilled. Yet gladness was in my soul: Sasha
had escaped his prison grave and I had had a large share in bringing
it about. No one could take that consolation away from me.

CHAPTER XXXII

ALL THROUGH THE WINTER OF 1907 AND 1908 THE COUNTRY WAS in the grip of financial depression. Thousands of workers in every large city were idle, in poverty and misery. The authorities, instead of devising ways and means to feed the starving, aggravated the appalling conditions by interfering with every attempt to discuss the causes of the crisis.

The Italian and Jewish anarchists in Philadelphia had called a meeting for the purpose. Voltairine de Cleyre and Harry Weinberg, an eloquent Yiddish agitator, addressed the gathering. Someone in the audience urged a demonstration in front of the City Hall to demand work. The speakers advised against it, but the crowd surged out into the street. Half-way to the City Hall the workers were attacked by the police and beaten. The next day Voltairine and Weinberg were arrested and held under fifteen-hundred-dollar bail each, charged with inciting to riot.

In Chicago the police had dispersed a large demonstration of the unemployed, using the same methods upon the defenceless men and women. Similar outrages had happened throughout the country. Touring under such conditions was a great strain and yielded barely enough to pay expenses; my situation was aggravated by a very severe cold I had caught, which racked me with a fearful cough. But I kept on in the hope of a favourable change by the time I should reach Chicago. I planned to stay with my dear friends Annie and Jake Livshis. The fourteen meetings organized for me would be successful, I thought, for I had become well known in Chicago and had many friends willing to help.

Two days before my arrival a Russian youth who had been clubbed by the police during the unemployment demonstration called at the house of the Chief of Police, with the intention of taking his life, as the papers reported. I did not know the boy, yet my meetings were immediately suppressed and my name was connected with the matter. Upon my arrival in Chicago I was not met by the friends who had invited me to be their guest, but by two other comrades, one of them a stranger to me. Hurriedly they led me away from the crowd and informed me that the Livshis' house was surrounded by detectives, and that I would be taken instead to the home of the comrade I had now met for the first time. Both men advised me to leave the city at once, since the police were determined not to permit me to speak. I refused to be stampeded. "I will stay in Chicago and do what I have done in similar situations: fight for our right to be heard," I declared.

At the home of my host I became aware that his wife was terrorized lest the police find out that I was with them. All through the night she kept going to the window to see whether they had not already arrived. In the morning she began quarrelling with her husband over my having been brought into the house. I was sure to get them into trouble, she said, and they would be ostracized by their neighbours.

I should have gone to a hotel, but it was certain that I would not be admitted. Fortunately, two Russian-American girls came to invite me. One of them, Dr. Becky Yampolsky, I knew through correspondence. Her apartment consisted of an office and a living-room, she informed me, but she would be glad to share the latter with me. I accepted eagerly. At Yampolsky's I met William Nathanson, a young student active in the Yiddish anarchist movement. He offered to help in anything I might decide to undertake. His comradely spirit and Becky's hospitable concern soon made me forget the madhouse I had escaped.

My first question was about the unfortunate boy, whose name was Lazarus Overbuch. Who was he and why had he gone to the Chief of Police? I was informed that very little was known about him. He had not been in our ranks, nor had he belonged to any anarchist group. It had been learned through his sister that he had not been long in America. In Russia he and his family had been among the victims of the terrible Kishinev massacre. During the march of the unemployed in Chicago he had witnessed similar brutalities practised upon workers for daring to demonstrate their poverty and need. In a free country, as he believed America to be, he saw the same inhumanity and cruelty. No one knew the exact reason for his visit to the Chief of Police. The boy had been killed by the Chief's son almost directly after he had been admitted into the house.

At the inquest Chief Shippey stated that Overbuch, after handing him a letter, had tried to shoot his son, one bullet having lodged in his body. On examination it was found that young Shippey had not been wounded at all. Overbuch was killed by a thirty-eight-calibre gun, while according to the Chief's statement, the revolver found on the boy was of thirty-two calibre. That did not prevent the police, however, from starting raids on everyone known to be an anarchist, as well as closing up the headquarters of our comrades and confiscating their library.

The old trick of the police of terrorizing landlords made it impossible to get any hall for me. Every step I made was watched. Detectives were on my trail from the moment it became known that I was staying at the house of my young medical friend. Meanwhile the papers continued to print fantastic stories about anarchism and Emma Goldman, and how we were conspiring to defeat the police. Washington got busy. Commissioner of Immigration Sargent declared he did not know how Emma Goldman had managed to return to America after her trip to Amsterdam. He admitted that he had directed an inquiry to discover the official who had neglected his instructions not to permit me to re-enter. It was tragicomic to see a powerful country moving heaven and hell to gag one little woman. It was fortunate that my bump of vanity was only mildly developed.

When I had almost given up hope of being able to speak in Chicago, Becky Yampolsky brought word that Dr. Ben L. Reitman had offered us a vacant store he was using for gatherings of unemployed and hobos. We could hold our meetings there, he had said, and he had also asked to see me to discuss the matter. In the press accounts of the unemployed parade in Chicago, Reitman had been mentioned as the man who had led the march and who had been among those beaten by the police. I was curious to meet him.

He arrived in the afternoon, an exotic, picturesque figure with a large black cowboy hat, flowing silk tie, and huge cane. " So this is the little lady, Emma Goldman," he greeted me; "I have always wanted to know you." His voice was deep, soft, and ingratiating. I replied that I also wanted to meet the curiosity who believed enough in free speech to help Emma Goldman.

My visitor was a tall man with a finely shaped head, covered with a mass of black curly hair, which evidently had not been washed for some time. His eyes were brown, large, and dreamy. His lips, disclosing beautiful teeth when he smiled, were full and passionate. He looked a handsome brute. His hands, narrow and white, exerted a peculiar fascination. His finger-nails, like his hair, seemed to be on strike against soap and brush. I could not take my eyes off his hands. A strange charm seemed to emanate from them, caressing and stirring.

We discussed the meeting. Dr. Reitman said that the authorities had assured him that they did not object to my speaking in Chicago. "It is up to her to find a place," they had told him. He was glad to help me put them to a test. His place could seat over two hundred people; it was filthy, but his hobos would help him clean it up. Once I had carried through the venture in his hall, it would be easy to get any place I wanted. With much enthusiasm and energy my visitor elaborated on the plan to defeat the police by our gathering at the headquarters of the Brotherhood Welfare Association, as he called his place. He stayed several hours, and when he went away, I remained restless and disturbed, under the spell of the man's hands.

With the help of his hobos Reitman cleaned his store, built a platform, and arranged benches to seat two hundred and fifty people. Our girls prepared little curtains to make the place attractive and to shut out the curious gaze. All was ready for the event, the press carrying sensational stories about Reitman and Emma Goldman, who were conspiring against police orders. On the afternoon of the scheduled gathering the store was visited by officials from the building and fire departments. They questioned the doctor as to how many he expected to seat. Sensing trouble, he said fifty. "Nine," decided the building-department. "The place is not safe for more," echoed the fire department. With one stroke our meeting was condemned, and the police scored another victory.

This new outrage aroused even some of the newspapers. The *Inter-Ocean* opened its columns to me, and for several days my articles appeared on its pages, reaching many thousands of readers with each issue. I was thus enabled to place before a large public the tragic Overbuch case, the part played by the Chief and his son, and the conspiracy to suppress free speech, and finally also to present my ideas, in complete freedom from censorship. The editor, of course, reserved the right to put glaring headlines over my article and to denounce anarchism in his editorials; but as I wrote over my own signature, what I had to say was not in the least affected by anything else that appeared in the paper.

The *Inter-Ocean* was anxious to stage a *coup* over the police. They offered me an automobile from which to address crowds in the city; they would supply reporters, photographers, flash-lights, and other paraphernalia "to make the venture hum." I would not consent to such a circus performance; it could not establish my right of free speech and it would give only a vulgar atmosphere to what was sacred to me.

Meeting-places being closed, I suggested to the comrades that we arrange a social and concert at the Workmen's Hall, my name not to appear in the public announcements. I would try to elude the watch-dogs and get into the hall at the appointed time. Only a few members of our group were apprised of the plan, the others being left under the impression that the sole purpose of the social was to raise funds for our fight.

One outsider was drawn into our secret, and that was Ben Reitman. Some comrades objected on the ground that the doctor was a new-comer and as such not to be trusted. I argued that the man had shown a large spirit in offering his place, and that he had been of great help in securing publicity for our efforts. There could be no doubt about his interest. I did not convince the objectors, but the other comrades agreed that Reitman should be told.

That night I could not sleep. I tossed about in a disturbed state of mind, questioning myself why I had pleaded so warmly for a person I really knew almost nothing about. I had always opposed ready confidence in strangers. What was there in this man that had made me trust him? I had to admit to myself that it was his intense attraction to me. From the moment he had first entered Yampolsky's office, I had been profoundly stirred by him. Our being much together since had strengthened his physical appeal for me. I was aware that he also had been aroused; he had shown it in every look, and one day he had suddenly seized me in an effort to embrace me. I had resented his presumption, though his touch had thrilled me. In the quiet of the night, alone with my thoughts, I became aware of a growing passion for the wild-looking handsome creature, whose hands exerted such fascination.

On the evening of our social gathering, March 17, I succeeded in slipping away through the back entrance of Yampolsky's house while the detectives were waiting for me out in front. I got safely through the police lines near the hall. The audience was large and many officers were inside, stationed against the walls. The concert had begun and someone was playing a violin solo. In the half-light I walked to the front of the platform. When the music was over, Ben Reitman ascended the platform to announce that a friend they all knew would address the gathering. I quickly got up and began to speak. The first tones of my voice and the ovation by the crowd brought the police to the platform. The Captain in charge pulled me off by force, almost ripping open my dress. At once confusion broke out. Fearing that some of our young people might be moved to a rash act, I called out: "The police are here to cause another Haymarket riot. Don't give them a chance. Walk out quietly and you will help our cause a thousand times more." The audience applauded and intoned a revolutionary song, filing out in perfect order. The Captain, infuriated because he had failed to gag me altogether, pushed me towards the exit, cursing and swearing. When we got to the stairs, I refused to budge until my coat and hat, which remained in the hall, were brought to me. I was standing with my back against the wall, waiting for my wraps, when I saw Ben Reitman dragged out by two officers, pushed down the stairs and into the street. He passed me without a look or a word. It affected me disagreeably, but I thought that he had pretended not to know me in order to dupe the officers. He would surely come to Yampolsky's when he had shaken off the police, I reassured myself. I was led out, followed by policemen, detectives, newspaper men, and a large crowd to the door of Becky Yampolsky's home.

I found our comrades already in her office, discussing in what manner the authorities and reporters had learned that I would be present at the gathering. I sensed that they were suspecting Reitman. I felt indignant, but said nothing; I expected he would soon come and speak for himself. But the night wore on and the doctor failed to appear. The suspicion of my comrades grew stronger and communicated itself to me. "He must have been detained by the police," I tried to explain. Faithful Becky and Nathanson agreed that that must be the reason, but the others doubted it. I spent a wretched night, clinging to my faith in the man, yet fearing that he might be at fault.

Reitman called early next morning. He had not been arrested, he said, but for certain important reasons he could not come to Becky's after the meeting. He had no idea who had notified the press and the authorities. I looked searchingly at him, trying to fathom his soul. Whatever doubts I had had the night before melted like ice at the first rays of the sun. It seemed impossible that anyone with such a frank face could be capable of treachery or deliberate lies.

The action of the police resulted in most of the newspapers, which had formerly incited the authorities to "stamp out anarchy," in editorial protests against my having been brutally treated. Some stated that it had not been the police but Emma Goldman's coolness and courage that had prevented bloodshed. One paper wrote: "Captain Mahoney acted contrary to orders in ejecting Emma Goldman from Workmen's Hall, where she was to have lectured. By preventing her from speaking, they played into her hands and gave point to the passionate assertions of her followers that there is no such thing as a constitutional right of free speech."

For days following, the Chicago press published articles and letters of protest by well-known men and women. One was from William Dudley Foulke, voicing his indignation against the suppression of Emma Goldman and free speech. Another was signed by Dr. Kuh, a prominent Chicago physician. The most gratifying result was the stand of Rabbi Hirsch in regard to the action of the police at our social. The next Sunday his sermon was devoted to an objective exposition of anarchism. Among other things he pointed out the stupidity of the authorities in attempting by violent methods to stamp out an ideal that had as its spokesmen some of the noblest spirits of the world. An additional contribution to the change of attitude was made by Dr. Kuh when he invited me to his house to meet his brother and other friends interested in the fight for free speech. The formation of a Free Speech League resulted, with some of the most prominent radicals in Chicago as members.

The league urged me to remain in the city until it could establish my right to speak. Unfortunately compliance with their wishes was excluded on account of the lecture dates already arranged in Milwaukee and other Western towns. It was agreed that I should return later.

The suppression of my meetings in Chicago advertised me through the length and breadth of the country as I had not been since the Buffalo tragedy. I had repeatedly visited Milwaukee before, but I had not been able to attract much attention. Now the attendance was far beyond the capacity of our halls, and great numbers had to be turned away. Even the socialists came in force, among them Victor Berger, their leader. I had met him once before and had found him as intolerant of the ideas I represented as only a Marxian socialist can be. Now he even praised me for the fight I had been making. The demand for anarchist literature increased to a most gratifying degree.

I had every reason to be satisfied with the Milwaukee response and to be happy in the circle of my good comrades, yet I was restless and discontented. A great longing possessed me, an irresistible craving for the touch of the man who had so attracted me in Chicago. I wired for him to come, but once he was there, I fought desperately against an inner barrier I could neither explain nor overcome. After my scheduled meetings I returned with Reitman to Chicago. The police were no longer on my trail, and for the first time in weeks I was able to enjoy some privacy, to move about freely, and to talk with friends without fear of being under surveillance. To celebrate my release from the everlasting presence of detectives the doctor took me out to dinner. He spoke of himself and his youth, telling me of his wealthy father, who had divorced his mother and left her in poverty to shift for herself and her two children. The boy's *Wanderlust* had asserted itself at the age of five, always luring him to the railroad tracks. He ran away at the age of eleven, tramped over the United States and Europe, always close to the depths of human existence, to vice and crime. He had worked as janitor in the Chicago Polytechnic, where the professors took an interest in him. He had married at the age of twenty-three and was divorced soon after a child had come from the short union. He spoke of his passion for his mother, the influence of a Baptist preacher on him, and of many adventures, some colourful and some bleak, all of which had gone into the making of his life.

I was enthralled by this living embodiment of the types I had only known through books, the types portrayed by Dostoyevsky and Gorki. The misery of my personal life, the hardships I had endured through the weeks in Chicago, seemed to vanish. I was care-free and young again. I craved life and love, I yearned to be in the arms of the man who came from a world so unlike mine.

That night at Yampolsky's I was caught in the torrent of an elemental passion I had never dreamed any man could rouse in me. I responded shamelessly to its primitive call, its naked beauty, its ecstatic joy.

The day brought me back to earth and to the work for my ideal, which brooked no other god. On the eve of my departure from Minneapolis for Winnipeg some friends invited me to a restaurant for dinner. Ben was to meet us there later. We were a gay party, making merry in the last hours of my strenuous Chicago stay. Soon Ben arrived, and with him came a heightened mood.

Not far from us sat a group of men, one of whom I recognized as Captain Schuettler, whose presence seemed to me to pollute the very air. Suddenly I saw him motion towards our table. To my amazement, Ben rose and walked over to Schuettler. The latter greeted him with a jovial: "Hello, Ben," familiarly pulling him down to his side. The others, evidently police officials, all seemed to know Ben and be on friendly terms with him. Anger, disgust, and horror all mingled together, beat against my temples, and made me feel ill. My friends sat staring at each other and at me, which increased my misery. .

Ben Reitman, whose embrace had filled me with mad delight, chumming with detectives! The hands that had burned my flesh were now close to the brute who had almost strangled Louis Lingg, near the man who had threatened and bullied me in 1901. Ben Reitman, the champion of freedom, hob-nobbing with the very sort of people who had suppressed free speech, who had clubbed the unemployed, who had killed poor Overbuch. How could he have anything to do with them? The terrible thought struck me that he might be a detective himself. For some moments I was utterly dazed. I tried to eliminate the dreadful idea, but it kept growing more insistent. I recalled our social on March 17 and the treachery that had brought the police and the reporters to that gathering. Was it Reitman who had informed them? Was it possible? And I had given myself to that man! I, who had been fighting the enemies of freedom and justice for nineteen years, had exulted in the arms of a man who was one of them.

I strove to control myself and suggested to my friends that we leave. The comrades who accompanied me to the train were kind and understanding. They talked of the good work I had done and their plans for my return. I was grateful for their tact, but I longed for the train to take me away. At last it pulled out and I was alone, alone with my thoughts and the storm in my heart.

The night was endless. I tossed about between nerve-racking doubts and shame that I could still reach out for Ben. In Milwaukee I found a wire from him asking why I had rushed away. I did not reply. Another telegram in the afternoon said: "I love you, I want you.

Please let me come." I replied: "Do not want love from Schuettler's friends." In Winnipeg a letter awaited me, a mad outpouring of passion, and a piteous pleading to let him explain.

My days were busy with work for the meetings, which made it less difficult to be brave and resist my desire for Ben. But the nights were a raging conflict. My reason repudiated the man, but my heart cried out for him. I fought frantically against his lure, trying to stifle my craving by throwing myself completely into my lectures.

On the way back from Canada I was held up at the American border, taken off the train by the immigration inspector, and plied with questions as to my right to enter the United States. The satrap of Washington had evidently studied the anti-anarchist statutes. He puffed and sweated for his promotion rather than for the glory of Uncle Sam. I informed him I had lived in the country twenty-three years, while the Anti-Anarchist Law applied only to persons who had been in the country less than three years. Moreover, I was an American citizen by marriage. The immigration officer almost collapsed. He had seen medals dangling in the air and he hated to let them escape.

Returning to Minneapolis, I again found letters from Ben beseeching me to let him come. I struggled against it for a time, but in the end a strange dream decided the issue. I dreamed that Ben was bending over me, his face close to mine, his hands on my chest. Flames were shooting from his finger-tips and slowly enveloping my body. I made no attempt to escape them. I strained towards them, craving to be consumed by their fire. When I awoke, my heart kept whispering to my rebellious brain that a great passion often inspired high thoughts and fine deeds. Why should I not be able to inspire Ben, to carry him with me to the world of my social ideals?

I wired: "Come," and spent twelve hours between sickening doubt and mad desire to believe in the man. It could not be that my instinct should be so misleading, I reiterated to myself — that anyone worthless could so irresistibly appeal to me.

Ben's explanation of the Schuettler scene swept my doubts away. It was not friendship for the man or connexion with the police department that had made him known to them, he said. It was his work among tramps, hobos, and prostitutes, which often brought him in contact with the authorities. The outcasts always came to him when in trouble. They knew and trusted him and he understood them much better than the so-called respectable people. He had been part of the underworld himself, and his sympathies were with the derelicts of society. They had made him their spokesman, and as such he frequently called on the police to plead in their behalf. "It never was anything else," Ben pleaded; "please believe me and let me prove it to you." Whatever might have been at stake, I had to believe in him with an all-embracing faith.

CHAPTER XXXIII

WHILE MY MEETINGS WERE BEING SUPPRESSED IN CHICAGO, Sasha was subjected to similar persecution in the East. His lectures were stopped in a number of cities in Massachusetts, and the Union Square demonstrations of the unemployed at which he presided were forcibly dispersed by the police. I was worried about Sasha and wired him to let me know whether it was necessary for me to return to New York. The next morning I read in the newspapers that a bomb had exploded at Union Square, and that Alexander Berkman was arrested in connexion with it. I forgot our disagreements. Sasha was in trouble, and I not at his side to help and comfort him! I resolved to leave for New York immediately, but before I could carry out my decision, a telegram came from Sasha, telling me that the authorities had tried to implicate him in the Union Square affair; failing in that, they had charged him with "inciting to riot." That charge also had to be dropped for lack of proof. A letter explained that there was no need for me to worry and that the only victim of the tragic affair at Union Square was a young comrade, Selig Silverstein, a gentle fellow who had been badly clubbed. He had been mangled by the explosion and had later been tortured at police headquarters. Physical suffering and mental anguish had brought about his end. Sasha's description of the police brutality, and of the comrade so brave and stoical to the last, increased my hatred of the machinery of government and its organized violence. It made me more determined to go on with my work until the last breath.

Before I started out for California, Ben asked to let him come with me on the tour. He had enough money to pay his own way, he assured me. He would help with the work, arrange meetings, sell literature, or do anything else to be near me. The suggestion made me happy with anticipation. It would be wonderful to have someone with me on the long and weary tramps through the country, someone who was lover, companion, and manager. Yet I hesitated. My lectures, deducting my own expenses, left only small margins for *Mother Earth*. They could hardly bring enough to cover an additional burden, and I was not willing to accept Ben's co-operation without his sharing in the results. There was also another consideration — my comrades. They had helped faithfully, if not always efficiently; they were sure to see in Ben an interloper. He was from another world; moreover, he was impetuous and not always tactful. Clashes would surely follow, and I already had had to face far too many. I found it difficult to decide, but my need of Ben, of what his primitive nature could yield, was compelling. I resolved to have him; let the rest take care of itself.

Sitting beside Ben in the rushing train, his hot breath almost touching my cheek, I listened to him reciting one of his favourite Kipling stanzas:

> I sits and looks across the sea
> Until it seems that no one's left but you and me.

"You and me, my blue-eyed Mommy," he whispered.

Was this to be the beginning of a new chapter in my life, I wondered. What was it going to bring? My whole being was suffused with a feeling of comfort and security. Blissfully I closed my eyes and nestled closer to my lover. This was a new and great force, which I knew had come to stay.

The meetings in San Francisco were being looked after by my friend Alexander Horr; not expecting any trouble where I had never been interfered with before, I felt at ease.

I had reckoned, however, without the ambitious Chief of Police of San Francisco. Envious, perhaps, of the laurels carried off by his colleagues in the East, Chief Biggey seemed anxious to gain similar glory. He was at the station himself, accompanied by a retinue of officers and equipped with a large automobile. They all piled in and dashed after the taxi that was taking Ben, Horr, and me to the St. Francis Hotel. There he stationed four detectives to watch over my welfare.

The pomp of my entry into the hotel aroused the misgivings of the management and the curiosity of the guests. Unable to account for the unexpected homage, I turned to Horr for an explanation.

"Don't you know," he said with a perfectly sober face, "rumours have gone abroad that you are coming to San Francisco to blow up

the American fleet now in the harbor." "Stop your ridiculous invention," I replied; "you do not expect me really to believe that." He
insisted that he was in earnest, that Biggey had boasted that he
would protect the fleet against "the whole bunch of Emma Goldman
and her gang." My friend had purposely reserved a room for me at the
highly respectable St. Francis; one living in such a place would not
be suspected of association with bombs. "Never mind what people will
think," I retorted; "this place is loud and gaudy, and I can't endure
having to run the gauntlet of the rich and vulgar people here." Poor
Horr looked crest-fallen and went to find other quarters.

Meanwhile I was not left in peace. I was besieged by reporters
with cameras, photographed against my will, and asked endless questions, the main one being whether I had really come to blow up the
fleet.

"Why waste a bomb?" I replied. "What I should like to do with
the fleet, with the entire Navy, and the Army too, would be to dump
them in the bay. But as I have not the power to do it, I have come
to San Francisco to point out to the people the uselessness and waste
of military institutions, whether they operate on land or on sea."

At midnight my friend returned. He had found a place, although
it was very far from town. It was the cottage of Joe Edelsohn, in
which there was room enough for Ben and me. I knew Joe as a splendid
comrade, and I was glad to be able to get out of the St. Francis Hotel,
however far I'd have to walk. The three of us, together with all our
baggage, loaded into a taxi and, followed by four detectives in another
car, arrived at Joe's house. The plain-clothes men remained on watch,
in the morning replaced by mounted police. This was kept up all
through my stay in the city.

One day Ben took me to the Presidio, the military encampment at
San Francisco. He knew the chief physician of its hospital; he had
worked with him during the earthquake and had assisted in taking
care of patients. We were followed to the very door of the hospital,
but we had the satisfaction of seeing the detectives kept out, while
Emma Goldman, the foe of militarism, was entertained by the physician in charge and shown through the wards.

My meetings were veritable battle encampments. For blocks the
streets were lined with police in autos, on horseback, and on foot.
Inside the hall were heavy police guards, the platform surrounded
by officers. Naturally this array of uniformed men advertised our

meetings far beyond our expectations. Our hall had a seating capacity of five thousand, and it proved too small for the crowds that clamoured for admittance. Lines formed hours before the time set for the opening of my lectures. Never in all the years since I had first gone on tour, with the exception of the Union Square demonstration in 1893, had I seen masses so eager and enthusiastic. It was all due to the stupendous farce staged by the authorities at huge expense to San Francisco taxpayers.

The most interesting meeting took place one Sunday afternoon when I spoke on "Patriotism." The crowds struggling to get in were so large that the doors of the hall had to be closed very early to prevent a panic. The atmosphere was charged with indignation against the police, who were flaunting themselves importantly before the assembled people. My own endurance had almost reached breaking-point because of the annoyances caused by the authorities, and I went to the meeting determined to vent in no uncertain terms my protest. When I looked into the faces of the excited audience, I sensed at once that very little encouragement from me would be needed to arouse them to violent action. Even the dull mind of Biggey responded to the temper of the situation. He came over to beg that I try to pacify the people. I promised on condition that he would reduce the number of his men in the hall. He consented and gave orders to the officers to file out. Out they marched, like guilty schoolboys, accompanied by the jeering and hooting of the crowd.

The subject I had selected for the meeting was particularly timely because of the patriotic stuff which had been filling the San Francisco papers for days past. The presence of so vast an audience testified that I had chosen well. The people were certainly eager to hear some other version of the nationalist myth. "Men and women," I began, "what is patriotism? Is it love of one's birthplace, the place of childhood's recollections and hopes, dreams and aspirations? Is it the place where, in childlike naïveté, we used to watch the passing clouds and wonder why we, too, could not float so swiftly? The place where we used to count the milliard glittering stars, terror-stricken lest each one an eye should be, piercing the very depths of our little souls? Is it the place where we would listen to the music of the birds and long to have wings to fly, even as they, to distant lands? Or the place where we would sit at Mother's knee, enraptured by tales of great deeds and conquests? In short, is it love for the spot, every inch representing dear and precious recollections of a happy, joyous, and playful child-hood?

"If that were patriotism, few American men of today could be called upon to be patriotic, since the place of play has been turned into factory, mill, or mine, while deafening sounds of machinery have replaced the music of the birds. Nor can we hear any longer the tales of great deeds, for the stories our mothers tell today are but those of sorrow, tears, and grief.

"What, then, is patriotism? ' Patriotism, sir, is the last resort of scoundrels,' said Dr. Johnson. Leo Tolstoy, the greatest anti-patriot of our times, defined patriotism as the principle that justifies the train-ing of wholesale murderers; a trade that requires better equipment for the exercise of man-killing than the making of such necessities as shoes, clothing, and houses; a trade that guarantees better returns and greater glory than that of the honest workingman."

The uproarious applause that interrupted me showed that the five thousand people were in sympathy with my ideas. I proceeded with an analysis of the origin, nature, and meaning of patriotism, and its terrific cost to every country. At the close of my speech of an hour, delivered amid tense silence, a storm rolled over me and I felt myself surrounded by men and women clamouring to shake my hand. I was dizzy from the excitement and oblivious of what was being said to me. Suddenly I became aware of a tall figure in the uniform of a soldier holding out his hand to me. Before I had time to think, I took it. When the audience saw that, pandemonium broke loose. People threw their hats in the air, stamped their feet, and yelled in uncontrolled joy over the sight of Emma Goldman clasping hands with a soldier. It all happened so quickly that I had no time to ask the man's name. All he said was: "Thank you, Miss Goldman," and then he slipped away as unobserved as he appeared. It was a dramatic ending to a highly dramatic situation.

The next morning I read in the papers that a soldier leaving Emma Goldman's meeting had been followed by plain-clothes men to the Presidio, and that they had reported him to the military authorities. Later the press stated that the soldier's name was William Buwalda, that he had been placed under military arrest and would be "court-martialled for attending Emma Goldman's meeting and for shaking hands with her." It seemed preposterous; nevertheless we set to work immediately to organize a committee for his defence and to raise money for his fight. After that Ben and I left for Los Angeles.

The most interesting events in that city, outside of large and lively meetings, were a debate with Mr. Claude Riddle, a socialist, and a visit with George A. Pettibone. I had debated with a number of socialists before, but my opponent this time proved the most fair-minded of them all. That was a crime in the eyes of his party and he was at once suspended from membership. It was a coincidence no less interesting than significant that a United States soldier and a socialist should fall under the ban at the same time for daring to have anything to do with Emma Goldman.

George A. Pettibone, with Charles H. Moyer and William D. Haywood, had been the victim of a conspiracy to crush the Western Miners' Federation. For years the mine-owners of Colorado had waged relentless war against the workers' organization without success. When they discovered that the spirit of the union could not be broken and the leaders neither bullied nor bought, they sought other means to destroy them. In February 1906 the three had been arrested in Denver on the charge of having killed Ex-Governor Steunenberg. So complete was the autocracy of money and power that the prisoners were rushed to Boise City without a semblance of legality, the train and extradition papers having been prepared even before the arrest. The only evidence against the labour defendants had been furnished by a Pinkerton spy, Harry Orchard.

For a year their lives had hung in the balance. The press in general had been inciting the Idaho authorities to send them to the gallows. The tone in this man-hunt had been set by President Roosevelt, who had branded Moyer, Haywood, and Pettibone as "undesirable citizens."

The immediate and concerted campaign of labour and radical bodies throughout the country had succeeded in frustrating the mine-owners. In this agitation the anarchists had played a large part, devoting their energy and means to save the indicted men. I had lectured about the case all through the country, while *Mother Earth* had proclaimed their innocence and urged the workers to declare a general strike, if need be, to rescue their comrades from the noose. On the day of their acquittal the *Mother Earth* group had wired Roosevelt: "Undesirable citizens victorious. Rejoice." It was an expression of our contempt for the man who, though President of the United States, had joined the pack of hounds.

I had had no opportunity of meeting any of the three men before or since the trial. In Los Angeles I learned that Pettibone was living in the city in the strictest retirement, his health shattered by his jail experience. When he heard of my arrival, he sent a friend to tell me that he had wanted for many years to meet me.

I found him with the stamp of death on his face, but with enthusiasm for labour's cause still shining in his eyes. He talked of many things, among them of the judicial murder in Chicago, in 1887, which had proved a great factor in awakening his rebellious spirit, as it had mine. He dwelt on the events that had been meant to furnish a second eleventh of November, but instead had turned into a red-letter day for the labour forces. He related many incidents of his conflicts with the Pinkertons and told how he used to make game of their cowardice and stupidity. He spoke of the authorities having attempted to induce him to turn against his comrades. "Just think of it!" he said; "they appealed to my interests as a business man and the chances I'd have to get free and become prosperous. How were those soul-and-mind-impoverished creatures to know that I would have preferred death a thousand times rather than hurt one hair of the other boys."

In Portland, Oregon, we learned the cheerful news that the two halls rented for my lectures, the Arion, belonging to a German society, and the Y.M.C.A., had been refused at the last moment. Fortunately the city had a number of people to whom the right of free speech was not merely a theory. Foremost among them was ex-Senator Charles Erskine Scott Wood, distinguished lawyer, writer, and painter and a man of considerable cultural influence in the town. He was a fine-looking man of gracious personality, and a libertarian in the truest sense. He had been instrumental in securing the two halls, and he was very much distressed that the owners should have backed out. He tried to console me with the assurance that the Arion Society could be held legally responsible, because they had signed a contract for the rental of their hall. When I told him that I never invoked the law against anyone, although the law had often been invoked against me, Mr. Wood exclaimed: "So that's the kind of dangerous anarchist you are! Now that I have found you out, I shall have to take others into my confidence. I shall have to ask them to meet the real Emma Goldman." Within a few days he not only introduced various persons to me, but he also inspired Mr. Chapman, one of the editors of the *Oregonian,* to write about my lectures, and the Reverend Doctor Elliot, a Unitarian minister, to offer me his church. He induced a considerable number of prominent men and women of the city to declare themselves publicly in favour of my right to be heard.

After this it was easy sailing. A hall was secured, and the meetings were attended by large and representative audiences. Mr. Wood presided at my first lecture and delivered a brilliant introductory speech. With such a backing I should have captured my hearers even if I had been less aroused on this occasion. I was at a high emotional pitch over the news in the morning papers of the treatment accorded William Buwalda. He had been court-martialled, dismissed from the Army, degraded, and sentenced to the military prison on Alcatraz Island for five years. This, notwithstanding the admission of his superior officers that he had been an exemplary soldier in the United States Army for fifteen years. That was the punishment meted out to the man whose crime, as General Funston had stated, had consisted in "attending Emma Goldman's meeting in uniform, applauding her speech, and shaking hands with that dangerous anarchist woman."

My subject was "Anarchism." What better argument did I need than the outrage by the State on William Buwalda, by the State and its military machine, from which there is no redress or escape? My speech was fiery, igniting everyone present, even those who had come out of curiosity. At the close of my lecture I made an appeal for an immediate campaign to arouse public opinion against the sentence of Buwalda. The assembly generously responded with money and pledges to organize the work for his speedy release. Mr. Wood was chosen treasurer, and a considerable sum was contributed on the spot.

The audiences at my meetings kept increasing, the crowds representing every social stratum; lawyers, judges, doctors, men of letters, society women, and factory girls came to learn the truth about the ideas they had been taught to fear and to hate.

We had started for Butte, Montana, after successful meetings in Seattle and Spokane. The trip gave me opportunity to observe the Western farmer and the Indians on the reservations. The Montana farmer differed very little from his New England brother. I found him just as inhospitable and close-fisted as the farmers Sasha and I had canvassed for crayon portraits in 1891. Montana is among the most beautiful States, its soil rich and fertile far beyond the unyielding

New England sod. Yet those farmers were unkind, greedy, and suspicious of the stranger. The Indian reservation revealed to me the blessings of the white man's rule. The true natives of America, once masters of the length and breadth of the land, a simple and sturdy race possessing its own art and conception of life, had dwindled to mere shadows of what they had once been. They were infected with venereal disease; their lungs were eaten by the white plague. In return for their lost vigour they had received the gift of the Bible. The kindly and helpful spirit of the Indians was very cheering after the forbidding attitude of their white neighbours.

My tour, more eventful than any previous one, was at an end, and I was on my way to New York. Ben remained in Chicago for a visit with his mother and would join me in the autumn. It was a painful wrench to separate after the intimacy of four months. Only four months since that strange being had come so unexpectedly into my life, and already I felt him in every pore, consumed by longing for his presence!

I had tried all through the months to explain to myself the appeal Ben had for me. With all my absorption in him, I was not deceived about the difference that existed between us. I knew from the first that we had intellectually very little in common, that our outlook on life, our habits, our tastes, were far apart. In spite of his degree of M.D. and his work for the outcast, I had felt Ben to be intellectually crude and socially naïve. He had profound sympathy for society's derelicts, he understood them, and he was their generous friend, but he had no real social consciousness or grasp of the great human struggle. Like many liberal Americans, he was a reformer of surface evils, without any idea of the sources from which they spring. That alone should have been enough to keep us apart, and there were still other and graver differentiations.

Ben was typically American in his love of publicity and of show. The very things I most disliked were inherent in the man I now loved with a fierce passion. Our first serious disagreement had been over a newspaper photographer Ben had "wished" on me without my knowledge or consent. It was during our trip from Chicago to Salt Lake City. The man was on the train and Ben must needs tell him that Emma Goldman was among the passengers. At the next stop, as I was walking along the platform, I suddenly found myself confronting a camera ready to "shoot." I had been often annoyed by invasive American methods and I always ran from them. But there was no place to run to this time. Instinctively I held up a paper before my face. To Ben it was merely a caprice. He could not understand my deep-seated repulsion to the habitual imposition of the newspaper men. He could not comprehend that one who had been so long before the public could still shrink from the vulgarity of being made a public show.

Through all my travels I had managed to keep to myself while *en route* from one city to another. On this tour our fellow-passengers, the train crew, and even the station-masters knew the glad tidings that Emma Goldman was in their midst. Our car became a magnet that drew all the curiosity-mongers who were about. It was manna to Ben, but torture to me.

Moreover, Ben had the American swagger, which he would display with particular gusto at our meetings and in the homes of comrades. The antagonism his manner aroused caused me great distress and I lived in constant fear of what he might do next. Indeed, there were many elements in my lover to jar my nerves, outrage my taste, and sometimes even make me suspicious of him. Yet it all did not weigh in the scale against the magic that bound me to him and filled my soul with new warmth and colour.

I could find but two explanations of the riddle: First, Ben's child-like nature, unspoiled, untrained, and utterly lacking in artifice. Whatever he said or did came spontaneously, dictated by his intensely emotional nature. It was a rare and refreshing trait, though not always pleasant in its effects. The second was my great hunger for someone who would love the woman in me and yet who would also be able to share my work. I had never had anyone who could do both.

Sasha had been but a short time in my life, and. he had been too obsessed by the Cause to see much of the woman who craved expression. Hannes and Ed, who had loved me profoundly, had wanted merely the woman in me; all the others had been attracted by the public personality only. Fedya belonged to the past. He had married, had a child, and disappeared from my ken. My friendship with Max, still as fragrant as it had always been, was less of the senses than of the understanding. Ben had come when I had greatest need of him; our four months together had proved that in him were combined the emotions I had yearned for so long.

Already he had greatly enriched my life. As helpmate in my work he had shown his interest and his worth. With complete absorption and abundance of energy Ben had achieved wonders in the size of our meetings and the increased sales of literature. As travelling companion he had made my trip a new, delightful experience. He was touchingly tender and solicitous, most comforting in releasing me from the petty annoyances and details involved in travelling. As lover ·he had unleashed elements in me that made all differences between us disappear as so much chaff in a storm. Nothing mattered now except the realization that Ben had become an essential part of myself. I would have him in my life and in my work, whatever the cost.

That the cost would not be small I already knew by the opposition to him which was growing in our ranks. Some of my comrades sensed Ben's possibilities and his value to the movement. Others, however, were antagonistic to him. Of course, Ben did not feel at ease under those circumstances. He could not understand why people standing for freedom should object to anyone's behaving naturally. He was particularly nervous about my New York friends. How would they act towards him and our love? Sasha — what would he say? My account of Sasha's act, his imprisonment and suffering, had stirred Ben profoundly. "I can see Berkman is your greatest obsession," he had once said to me; "no one will ever have a chance alongside of him." "Not an obsession, but a fact," I had told him; "Sasha has been in my life so long that I feel we have grown together like the Siamese twins. But you need fear no rivalry from him. Sasha loves me with his head, not with his heart."

He was not convinced and I could see he was worried. I myself was apprehensive because of the difference in their personalities. Yet I hoped that Sasha, who had touched the depths of life, would understand Ben better than the rest. As for Max, I knew that, whatever his reaction to Ben, he was too considerate to cast any shadow on my love.

More and more the upkeep of *Mother Earth* was draining my energies. The support from our comrades and from my American friends, considerable as it was, proved insufficient. My tours had become the main source of revenue for the magazine, for the publication of our literature and the other expenses involved. The last tour had left us an unusually large margin, yet by August we were again without funds. My new lecture course could not begin until October. Fortunately help came from an unexpected quarter.

My friend Grace Potter, one of the contributors to *Mother Earth,* was working on the New York *World*. She induced her editor to accept an article from me on "What I Believe." I would be paid two hundred and fifty dollars for it, Grace informed me, and I could write with full freedom. I accepted, glad of the opportunity to reach a large audience and at the same time also to earn some money. After the article appeared, exactly as I had written it, I was given the right to publish it in brochure form. "What I Believe" became the best-seller of years. Now we could pay the printer for the current issue and have enough money left for Ben's trip to New York.

I waited for his arrival like a schoolgirl in love for the first time. He came with his old eagerness, ready to throw himself into the work of our magazine. He was his own self when we were alone, but he became a changed creature in the presence of my friends. With them he would grow nervous, inarticulate, and dull, or he would ask silly questions that made them suspicious of him. I was sick with disappointment. I knew that it was only panic that made Ben so awkward and I believed that he would feel more at home on the farm. There life was simpler — Ben would find himself; and Sasha, who was with Becky and other friends on the farm, would be patient and help him along.

My hopes proved vain. Not that Sasha or the other friends were unkind to Ben, but the atmosphere was strained, and no one seemed to find the right word. The situation acted on Ben as on a child expected to be on its good behaviour. He began to show off and brag, boast of his exploits, and talk nonsense, which made matters worse. I felt ashamed of Ben, bitterly resentful of my friends, and angry with myself for having brought him into their midst.

My deepest grief was Sasha. He said nothing to Ben, but he said plenty of cutting things to me. He scoffed at the idea that I could love such a man. It was nothing but a temporary infatuation, he felt sure. Ben lacked social feeling, he had no rebel spirit, and he did not belong in our movement, he insisted. Moreover, he was too ignorant to have passed through college or to have earned a degree. He would write to the university to find out. This, coming from Sasha, completely unnerved me. "You are a zealot," I cried; "you judge human quality by your criterion of one's value to the Cause, as the Christians do from the standpoint of the Church. That has been your attitude towards me since your release. The years of struggle and travail I suffered for my growth mean nothing to you, because you are

bound in the confines of your creed. With all your talk of the movement, you thrust back the outstretched hand of a man who comes to
learn about your ideals. You and the other intellectuals prate about
human nature, yet when someone out of the ordinary appears, you
don't even try to understand him. But all that can have no bearing on
my feeling for Ben. I love him, and I will fight for him to the death!"

I left the farm with Ben. I was sick from the scene with Sasha, the
harsh words I had hurled in his face; and I was tortured by my own
doubts. I had to admit to myself that much that Sasha had said about
Ben was true. I could see his defects much better than anyone else and
I knew how lacking he was. But I could not help loving him.

It had been my plan to devote the winter to New York. I was tired
out from trains, strange places, and other people's "atmosphere."
Here I had my home, limited and crowded though it was. *Mother
Earth* also needed my presence. I was certain that if I lectured through
the winter, I should attract large Yiddish and English audiences. I
had talked it over with Ben and he had decided to move to New York
and devote himself to my task.

But now Ben hated the city and hated 210 East Thirteenth Street.
He could never do any good there, he felt. With me on the road he
would be able to put his energies into the work and he would grow,
develop, and become a force. I, too, wanted to get away from the
disharmony and the censure of the people nearest to me. I was anxious
to give Ben a better chance, to help him to an understanding of himself, to bring out what was finest in him.

The previous year I had received an invitation from Australia.
J. W. Fleming, our most active comrade there, had even raised enough
money for my fare. At that time I could not decide to go away so far
and make the long journey alone. With Ben at my side the voyage
would be turned into a joy and give me a much needed rest, free from
strife. Ben was wild with the idea of Australia; he could talk of nothing
else and was eager to start at once. But there were many arrangements
to make before I could go on a two years' tour. We decided to leave in
October for California, lecturing on the way. By February we would
cover the ground, raise enough money to secure the New York end
for a time, then sail to the new land, where there were new friends to
win, fresh minds and hearts to awaken.

My one anxiety was *Mother Earth*. Would Sasha consent to continue in charge? On my return from the last tour I had found him

better adjusted to life, much surer of himself and more devoted to our magazine than he had been. He had, besides, created many activities of his own while I was away. He had organized the Anarchist Federation, with groups all over the country, and had gained many admirers and friends. When I submitted my Australian plan to Sasha, he expressed surprise that I should have made such a sudden decision, but he assured me that I could be at ease about our work in New York. He would look after everything, and with Max and Hippolyte to help him the magazine and the office would be secure. I was sad that Sasha should show no regret whatever about my going away for so long, but I was too absorbed in my new venture to allow his lack of interest to affect me.

We shipped fifteen hundred pounds of literature to Victoria, Australia. We got in touch with our friends all along the route to California, and within a few weeks our arrangements were made. Ben was all eagerness to discover new ground. "All the world shall know what my Mommy can do," he proclaimed.

On Labour Day a meeting of the unemployed was to take place in Cooper Union. Ben was helping to arrange it and he was also asked to speak. I wanted him to make a good impression and urged him to prepare his notes. He tried industriously, but nothing came of his efforts. It was not of any particular importance what he might say, he told me; he wanted the audience to hear Emma Goldman, and as I had not been invited, I must write out what I would want to say at such a gathering. The suggestion was as fantastic as most of Ben's ideas, but rather than have him make a rambling talk, I prepared a short paper on the meaning of Labour Day.

Cooper Union was crowded. The "anarchist police squad" was present in force, as were also Sasha, Becky, Hippolyte, and I. All went well, Ben holding the audience better than I had expected while he was reading his paper. At the end he announced that what he had just read had been prepared by that "much maligned woman the anarchist Emma Goldman." The house applauded thunderously, but the committee in charge of the meeting became panicky. The chairman offered a profuse apology for the "unfortunate occurrence" and sailed into a violent attack on Ben. The latter had already left the platform and could therefore not reply. Sasha rose to protest. Before he had a chance to be properly heard by the crowd, the police pulled him out of the hall and placed him under arrest. Becky, who had followed Sasha, was also arrested and both were rushed to the station-house. They were confronted by a burly desk sergeant, who received them with the remark: "You should have been brought here on a stretcher." When Hippolyte called at the police station to find out about our friends, he was refused information. "We have that son of a b— anarchist Berkman at last," he was told; "we'll fix him this time."

The New York police department had tried repeatedly to get Sasha into their clutches. The previous year, after the Union Square bomb explosion, they had almost succeeded in involving him. I was naturally worried and at once got in touch with Meyer London, the socialist attorney, and other friends, to help us rescue Sasha.

For hours London and Hippolyte waited at the police station to see Sasha and Becky before they would be taken to the night court. Finally they were informed that the case would not come up until morning. No sooner had they left than the two prisoners were hustled into court, tried, and convicted without a chance to say a word in their defence. Sasha was sentenced to the workhouse for five days on the charge of disorderly conduct, while Becky was fined ten dollars for "vagrancy."

Not wanting to involve me, Becky had refused to say where her home was. As a matter of fact, she had been living with us for more than two years. She had been arrested at one of our meetings, which caused her expulsion from high school. Her home conditions were desperately poor and cramped and I had invited her to our flat. Her fine was paid by our dear friend Bolton Hall.

The papers the next day were filled with lurid stories of a "riot prevented by the prompt action of the police," and as usual I was pestered by reporters for days. I did not mind the annoyance, too happy in the thought that Sasha had been given a short sentence. What were five days to a man who had served fourteen years? I went to Blackwell's Island to see him. Memories of my own sojourn on the island and of my two visits to the Western Penitentiary came to my mind. How different the situation had been then — how hopeless and bleak Sasha's chances to come out alive! Now we both joked over the five days. "I can do them on one toe," Sasha laughed. I left him with the old certainty that whatever our disagreements, our friendship was of an eternal quality. I still felt the hurt caused by his attitude towards Ben, yet I knew that nothing could ever come beween us.

Everything was ready for my departure. Ben was to precede me to do advance work. A few days before leaving he sent me a letter thirty pages long, a rambling, incoherent account of things he had done since we first met. He had been reading *The Power of a Lie,* by the Norwegian author Boyer, he wrote; it had struck deep into him, and he felt impelled to confess to me the falsehoods he had told and the mean things he had done while on tour with me. It was giving him no rest. He could keep silent no longer.

He had lied when he had told me that it was not he who had disclosed the plan of my speaking at the social in Chicago last March. He had not informed the police, but he had confided it to a reporter, who had promised to keep it to himself. He had lied when he had given "important matters" as the reason for not calling on me that evening to explain about the presence of the police. He had gone straight from the hall to a girl he cared about. He had lied when he had assured me that he had money to pay his way on the trip with me. He had borrowed the money, gradually paying it back from the sales of our literature. He had also taken money from the receipts to send to his mother. He loved her passionately, and he had always looked after her. He had not dared to tell me that his mother depended on him, because he feared I would send him away. Every time I had expressed surprise that money was apparently missing from our accounts, he had lied. The excuses he had given for so often vanishing after my meetings or for staying away during the day were all false. He had gone with other women, women he had met at the lectures or somewhere else. In nearly every city he had gone with women. He did not love them, but they attracted him physically to the point of obsession. He had always had such obsessions and probably always would have. These women had never meant anything more than a moment's distraction. He always forgot them afterwards; often he did not even know their names. Yes, he had gone with other women during the four months; yet he loved only me. He had loved me from the first, and each day his passion for me had increased. I was the greatest force in his life, my work his deepest concern. He would prove it if I only would not send him away, if I would forgive him his lies and his betrayal, if only I would again have confidence in him. But even if I should send him away after I had read the letter, he would still feel relieved that he had confessed to me. He realized now how disintegrating and crushing is the power of a lie.

I had the feeling of sinking into a swamp. In desperation I clutched the table in front of me and tried to cry out, but no sound came from my throat. I sat numb, the terrible letter seeming to creep over me, word by word, and drawing me into its slime.

I was brought back to myself by Sasha's arrival. Sasha — at this moment — of all people! How he would feel justified by this letter in all he had said about Ben! I broke out in uncontrollable laughter.

"Emma, your laugh is terrible. It cuts like a knife. What is it?"

"Nothing, nothing, only I must get out on the street or I shall choke."

I snatched up my coat and hat and ran down the five flights. I walked for hours, the letter burning in my head.

This was the man whom I had taken into my heart, my life, my work! Fool, lovesick fool that I was, blinded by passion not to see what everyone else saw. I, Emma Goldman, to be carried away like any ordinary woman of forty by a mad attraction for a young man, a stranger picked up at a chance meeting, an alien to my every thought and feeling, the reverse of the ideal of man I had always cherished. No, no! It was impossible! The letter could not be true; it was all an invention, imaginary; it could not be real. Ben was impressionable, susceptible to every influence, always seeing his own reflection in the books he read. He loved to dramatize himself and his life. The tragedy of the peasant in Boyer's novel who thoughtlessly, even need-lessly, tells a lie and is forced to lie for the rest of his life to sustain his first falsehood is vividly depicted. Ben must have read himself into that character. That was all. That *must* be all. All this I thought as I walked for hours, torn between my intense desire to believe in him, and my feeling that I had given myself to a man lacking all integrity, a creature I could never trust again.

Days of anguish followed, tortured by attempts to explain and ex-cuse Ben's acts, attempts irritating and vain. Over and again I re-peated to myself: "Ben comes from a world where lies prevail in all human relations. He does not know that free spirits in their love and tasks honestly and frankly share everything life brings; that among people with ideals no one need cheat, steal, or lie. He is of another world. What right have I to condemn, I who claim to teach new values of life?" "But his obsessions? His going with every woman?" My heart cried out in protest. "Women he does not love, does not even respect. Can you justify that, too? No, no!" came from the depths of my woman's soul. "Yes," replied my brain, "if it is his nature, his dominant need, how can I object? I have propagated freedom in sex. I have had many men myself. But I loved them; I have never been able to go indiscriminately with men. It will be painful, lacerating, to feel myself one of many in Ben's life. It will be a fearful price to pay for my love. But nothing worth while is gained except at heavy cost. I've paid dearly for the right to myself, for my social ideal, for everything I have achieved. Is my love for Ben so weak that I shall not be able to pay the price his freedom of action demands?" There was no answer. In vain did I strive to harmonize the conflicting elements that were warring in my soul.

Dazed and hardly aware of my surroundings, I jumped out of bed. It was still dark. Like a sleep-walker I got into my clothes, felt my way to Sasha's room, and shook him out of sleep.

"I must go to Ben," I said. "Will you take me to him?"

Sasha was startled. He switched on the light and searchingly looked at me. But he asked no questions and said nothing. He hurriedly dressed and accompanied me.

We walked in silence. My head swam, my feet were unsteady. Sasha put my arm in his. In my purse was a key to the house where Ben was rooming. I let myself in, then turned to Sasha for a moment. Without a word I closed the door and ran up the two flights, bursting into Ben's room.

He jumped up with a cry. "Mommy, you've come at last! You have forgiven, you have understood." We clung to each other, everything else wiped out.

CHAPTER XXXIV

IN PLANNING OUR TOUR TO TAKE PLACE DURING THE PRESIDEN-
tial campaign we had overlooked the interest of the American
masses in the political circus. The result was failure of the initial part
of our trip. In Indianapolis, the first city to bring out a large attendance, my lecture was suppressed in the usual manner. The Mayor
expressed regret that the police had overstepped their powers, but of
course he could not act against the department. The Chief said that
stopping the meeting might have been bad law, but that it was good
common sense.

We were more fortunate in St. Louis, where we experienced no
interference. There I met William Marion Reedy, the editor of the
St. Louis *Mirror*. He and his paper were an oasis in the desert of
American intellectuality. Reedy, a man of ability, broad culture, and
rich humour, also possessed a courageous spirit. His fellowship made
our stay in St. Louis a pleasant event and brought me large and varied
audiences. After my departure he published in his weekly an article
that he called "The Daughter of the Dream." No finer appreciation
of my ideas and no greater tribute to me had ever been written by a
non-anarchist before.

In Seattle Ben and I were arrested. His offence consisted in putting
his weight too heavily against the door of the hall, which he had
found barred; mine was in protesting against his arrest. At the
station-house it developed that the price of my manager's offence was
a dollar and a half, representing the amount the landlord demanded
for his broken lock. After we paid for this injury to the sanctity of
property, we were both released. Of course, there were no further
meetings in Seattle and no redress for the loss we had sustained.

In Everett no hall was open to us. In Bellingham our train was met
by detectives. They followed us to the hotel, and when we went out to

find a restaurant, they put us under arrest. "Would you please wait until we have dined?" Ben asked with an engaging smile. "Sure," said our protectors, "we will wait." It was bright and warm in the restaurant, drizzling and chilly outside, but we took no pity on our watch-dogs. We lingered long over our meal, well aware that we should have the whole night before us in a place neither warm nor bright. In the station-house we were presented with the warrant. It was a document worthy of immortality. "Emma Goldman and Dr. Ben L. Reitman," it read, "anarchists and outlaws, having conspired to hold an unlawful assembly," and so forth in the same spirit. We were given the choice between leaving Bellingham at once or going to the city jail. It being the first hospitality offered us in the State of Washington, we decided in favour of the jail. At midnight the offer to get out of town was repeated, but having already made myself at home in the cell, I refused to leave. Ben did likewise.

In the morning we were taken before a magistrate, who placed us under five-thousand-dollar bail. It was only too apparent that the judge knew that the police had undertaken more than they would be able to carry through. We could not be tried for merely "attempting" to hold a meeting, but we were at their mercy, just the same. We knew no one in town likely to bail us out, and we had no means of getting in touch with a lawyer. I was interested, however, to find out how far legalized stupidity could go.

In the afternoon two strangers arrived. They introduced themselves as Mr. Schamel, attorney, and Mr. Lynch. The former volunteered his services gratis; the latter offered to be our bondsman.

"But you don't know us," I said in astonishment. "How can you risk so much money?"

"Oh, yes," said Mr. Schamel, "we do know you. We are not anarchists, but we feel that anyone who will stand up for an ideal as you have done is worthy of trust."

If I had not been afraid of shocking them, I should have embraced them in open court. The old fossil on the bench, who had blustered when we appeared friendless before him in the morning, was personified politeness now. We were quickly bailed out, entertained at a restaurant by our new friends, and accompanied to the train.

When we reached Blaine, on the Canadian border, a man came into our car, walked straight up to me, and inquired: "You are Emma Goldman, are you not?" — "And who are you?" — "I am a Canadian immigration inspector. I have orders to invite you to leave the train." What could one do but comply with such a gentlemanly request? At the office the inspector in charge seemed very much surprised that I looked like a lady and had no bombs about me. He assured us that he had gathered from the stories in the American press that I was a very dangerous person. He had therefore decided to hold up my entry into Canada until he could receive instructions from Ottawa. Meanwhile he asked me, as his guest, to make myself at home in his hut. I could have anything I wanted in the way of food and drink. In case of delay we would be given the best rooms in the local hotel. He spoke in a polite manner, his tone more friendly than I had ever heard from an American official. While the result was the same, I did not feel quite so indignant over the new interference.

The next morning our jovial inspector informed us that Ottawa had wired to let Emma Goldman proceed. There was no law in monarchical Canada to forbid my entry into the country. American democracy, with its anti-anarchist laws, was made to appear rather ludicrous.

San Francisco held a special attraction. The ex-soldier William Buwalda, as a result of our agitation in his behalf, had been pardoned by President Roosevelt. He was released after ten months' imprisonment, two weeks before our arrival in the city.

Owing to a terrific rain-storm my first meeting, in the Victory Theatre, was poorly attended. We were not discouraged, however, because of the wide publicity given my series of eight lectures and two debates. The following afternoon William Buwalda called on me, a very different man in his civilian clothes from the soldier whose hand I had clasped for a fleeting moment that memorable afternoon on the platform of Walton's Pavilion. His fine, open face, intelligent eyes, and firm mouth were indicative of an independent character. I wondered how he had stood fifteen years of military service without becoming warped. Buwalda related that he had joined the Army mainly because of tradition. American-born, he was of Dutch stock and nearly all the men of his family had done military service in Holland. He had believed in American freedom and he had considered its army forces a necessary protection. On several occasions he had come across my name in the papers. He had thought Emma Goldman a crank and had paid little attention to articles about me. " That is not very flattering," I interrupted: " how could you be so rude to a lady? "

"It is true, though," he replied with a smile. Military people live in a world of their own, he explained, and he had been particularly occupied for several years past. He had taken up a course of veterinary surgery because he was passionately fond of horses, and he had also studied shorthand. Added to his duties in the barracks, it had kept him too busy for other interests.

He had come upon my meeting accidentally, while out for a walk. He had seen the large crowd and the police before the Walton Pavilion. It had made him curious and he thought it a good opportunity to practise his stenography by taking down the speech. "Then you appeared," he continued, "a little, unassuming figure in black, and you started to talk. I began to feel disturbed. I thought at first it was the heat in the hall and the tense atmosphere. I did not forget the purpose that had brought me. For a while I was able to follow you; then I became distracted by your voice. I felt myself carried along by your sledge-hammer arraignment of all I held high. I was filled with resentment. I wanted to raise my voice in protest, to challenge your statements before the whole assembly. But the more I resisted your influence, the more I fell under its sway. Your eloquence held me breathless to the end of your speech. I felt confused and eager to escape. Instead I was caught by the crowd and found myself standing on the platform holding out my hand to you."

"And then?" I asked. "Did you see the detectives following you? Did you realize that they would cause you trouble?"

"I don't remember how I got out of the hall, and I did not feel that I had done anything wrong. I was upset by what I had heard and in the grip of the turmoil you had caused in me. All the way to the Presidio I kept thinking: 'She's wrong, she's entirely wrong! Patriotism is not the last resort of scoundrels. Militarism isn't only murder and destruction!' After the plain-clothes men had reported me to my superior officer, I was put under arrest. I thought it was all a mistake, that I had been taken for someone else and that I should be freed in the morning. To think otherwise would have meant that you were right, and my whole being rebelled against that. For several days I clung to the belief that you had misrepresented the Government which I had served for fifteen years; that my country was too fair and too just to be guilty of your unreasonable charges. But when I was brought before the military tribunal, I began to see that you had spoken the truth. I was asked what you had done for me that I should mix with

such a dangerous person, and I replied: 'She has made me think.'
Yes, you had made me think, Emma Goldman, for the first time in all
my forty years."

I held out my hand to him and said: " Now that you are free from
your military shackles, we can shake hands without fear. Let us be
friends."

He took my hand eagerly. "Friends for life and comrades as well,
dear, big, little Emma."

I was so carried away by his story that I had forgotten it was time
to prepare for my meeting. Never being able to eat before a lecture,
I did not mind going without dinner. But for my guest I had proved
a poor hostess. My new comrade gallantly assured me that he did
not care for food.

When we came within a block of the hall, we saw the streets filled
with people. I thought it was our announcements that had brought
out the vast crowd, but when we reached the Victory Theatre, I was
received with open arms by detectives and put under arrest. Buwalda
protested and was also arrested. We were hustled into the patrol
wagon to find that Ben, too, had met with the same fate. As the wagon
rattled through the streets, he hurriedly related that the police had
ordered everyone out of the theatre, freely using their clubs. He had
objected to their methods, of course, and was put under arrest. He
had sent someone with a warning to me, but evidently the comrade
had found me gone.

At police headquarters William Buwalda was discharged with a
severe reprimand for associating with "dangerous criminals." Ben
and I were charged with " conspiracy, making unlawful threats, using
force and violence, and disturbing the public peace." In the morning
we were taken before a judge, who held us for trial under sixteen-
thousand-dollar bail each. The same day Alexander Horr was arrested
for distributing a handbill protesting against the action of the authorities. The task of raising our bond and arranging for counsel and publicity fell to Cassius V. Cook, a man I had met only casually a few
years before. But he proved to be a tower of strength.

Within a few days Sasha and other New York friends telegraphed
that five thousand dollars would be sent towards our bail and that
money was being raised for our defence. From all over the country
protests and contributions began pouring in. Charles T. Sprading, of
Los Angeles, whom I had first met in Denver on my maiden tour to

the Coast in 1897, our buoyant Charlie, of ready wit and merry pranks, wired two thousand dollars as bail. The Forresters, and other friends, helped in a similar way. What did our trouble matter with such good comradeship to aid us?

Our lawyers, Messrs. Kirk and King, intelligent and brave men, exerted themselves in our behalf, and within a few days Mr. Kirk succeeded in having our bail released. We were to be liberated and placed in his custody. But unexpectedly another indictment came, charging us with "unlawful assemblage, denouncing as unnecessary all organized government," and—horror of horrors—with "preaching anarchist doctrines." Bail was set at two thousand dollars each. I was to be tried first, Ben to follow.

Among the sensational reports in the San Francisco press regarding the raid of our meeting and our arrest was one enlarging upon "Emma Goldman's lack of sentiment and feeling." While in jail, she had been given a telegram announcing her father's death, the paper stated, which she received without the least sign of emotion. As a matter of fact, my father's end, though not unexpected, had affected me deeply and had recalled to me the details of his wasted life. An invalid for over thirty years, he had of late been more frequently ill than usually. When I had seen him on my last visit to Rochester, in October, I had been shocked to find him so near death. The giant he had once been was now shattered by the storms of life.

With the passing years had come to me better understanding of Father, and mutual sympathy had drawn us gradually closer. My beloved Helena had had much to do with my change towards him. It was helped also by my awakening to the complexities of sex as a force dominating our feelings. I had learned to understand better my own turbulent nature, and my experiences had made me see what had been obscure to me so long in the character of my father. His violence and hardness had only been symptoms of an intensely sexual nature that had failed to find adequate expression.

My parents had been brought together in the traditional Jewish orthodox fashion, without love. They were mismated from the first. Mother had been left a widow at twenty-three, with two children, a little store her only earthly possession. Whatever love she had had died with the young man to whom she had been married at the age of fifteen. Father had brought into the match a fire of passionate youth. His wife was only one year his senior and radiantly beautiful. The impelling need of his nature drove him to her and made him more insistent in proportion as Mother fought back his insatiable hunger. My coming had marked her fourth childbirth, each one nearly bringing her to the grave. I recalled some remarks I had heard her make when I was too young to understand their meaning. They illuminated much that had been dark to me and caused me to realize what a purgatory my parents' intimacy must have been for them both. No doubt they would have been shocked had anyone called to their attention the true source of the struggle between them and of Father's uncontrollable temper. With the decline of health came also a lessening of his erotic vitality and a resultant psychic change. Father grew more mellow, patient, and kindly. The affection he had rarely shown his own children he now lavished on those of my two sisters. When I once referred to the harsh methods he had used towards us, he assured me that it could not be true. The tenderness that had come into his nature blotted out even the remembrance of past severity. The best in him, formerly hidden by emotional stress, by the struggle for existence and years of physical suffering, came into its own at last. He now felt and gave us a newly born affection, which in its turn awakened our love for him.

The court farce in San Francisco, ending in our acquittal, did more for anarchism than months of our propaganda might have accomplished. But the most significant event was William Buwalda's letter to the military authorities and his entry into our ranks. The historic document, published in the May 1909 issue of *Mother Earth,* read as follows:

Hudsonville, Michigan
April 6, 1909

Hon. Joseph M. Dickinson,
Secretary of War,
Washington, D. C.

Sir: —

After thinking the matter over for some time I have decided to send back this trinket[1] to your Department, having no further use for such baubles, and enable you to give it to some one who will appreciate it more than I do.

It speaks to me of faithful service, of duty well done, of friendships inseparable, friendships cemented by dangers and hardships

[1] The medal awarded William Buwalda for faithful service in the Philippines.

and sufferings shared in common in camp and in the field. But, sir, it also speaks to me of bloodshed—possibly some of it unavoidably innocent—in defence of loved ones, of homes; homes in many cases but huts of grass, yet cherished none the less.

It speaks of raids and burnings, of many prisoners taken and, like vile beasts, thrown in the foulest of prisons. And for what? For fighting for their homes and loved ones.

It speaks to me of G. O. 100, with all its attendant horrors and cruelties and sufferings; of a country laid waste with fire and sword; of animals useful to man wantonly killed; of men, women, and children hunted like wild beasts, and all this in the name of Liberty, Humanity, and Civilization.

In short, it speaks to me of War—legalized murder, if you will— upon a weak and defenceless people. We have not even the excuse of self-defence.

Yours sincerely,
WM. BUWALDA
R. R. No. 3
Hudsonville, Michigan

Our departure for Australia had been set for January. The arrest and subsequent free-speech fight in San Francisco forced us to postpone it until April. At last we were ready, our trunks packed, a grand farewell party arranged for us. We were about to secure passage when a telegram from Rochester demolished our plans. "Washington revoked Kershner's citizenship papers," it read; "dangerous to leave country."

My sister had written me months before that two suspicious-looking individuals had been snooping about to secure data on Kershner. He had left the city years previously and nothing had been heard from him since then. Not finding Kershner, the men had pestered his parents and tried to get information from them. I had dismissed the matter from my mind at the time as of no consequence. But now the blow came. I was deprived of my citizenship without even an opportunity to contest the action of the Federal authorities. I knew that if I should leave the country, I should not be permitted to re-enter it. My Australian tour had to be abandoned at a great financial loss, not to mention the expenditures invested by our Australian friends in preparing for my activities there. It was a bitter disappointment, much mitigated, fortunately, by the undaunted optimism of my hobo manager. His zeal merely increased with the obstacles we encountered. His energy was dynamic and tireless.

Australia eliminated from our itinerary, we went to Texas instead. El Paso, San Antonio, and Houston were new ground. I was cautioned to avoid the Negro question, but though I made no concessions to the prejudices of the South, I was in no way molested, nor was there any police interference. I even walked with Ben from El Paso to Mexico and back again before the United States immigration inspector had time to realize the chance he had missed to save his Government from the Emma Goldman menace.

CHAPTER XXXV

I NEEDED A REST BADLY, BUT, OUR TOUR THIS TIME HAVING brought us more glory than cash, I could not afford to take it. In fact, we were so short of funds that we were compelled to reduce the size of *Mother Earth* from sixty-four to thirty-two pages. Our financial condition made it necessary for me to start lecturing again. Ben joined me in New York in the latter part of March, and by the 15th of April he had succeeded in organizing for me a series of lectures on the drama. All went well at first, but May proved to be a record-breaker. During that month I was stopped by the police in eleven different places.

I had had similar experiences before, but the Chief of Police of New Haven outdid his colleagues by a novel way of interference. He allowed Ben and me to enter the hall we had hired, and then placed a detachment of officers at the doors to keep everybody else out. Great numbers, among them many students who had come to hear me, found themselves barred. The Chief soon learned, however, that "originality" is a costly thing. The local papers, which had never before protested against the infringement of Emma Goldman's rights, now pilloried the police for " interfering with a peaceable assembly."

The authorities of New York had always been stupid in their methods of persecuting anarchists; but never had their folly been quite so great as when they swept down on Lexington Hall on the third Sunday of my lecture course. The seditious subject on that occasion was "Henrik Ibsen as the Pioneer of Modern Drama." Before the opening of the meeting several detectives had called on the hall-keeper and threatened him and his family with arrest if he allowed me to speak. The poor man was frightened, but the rent had already been paid and Ben held the receipt. The landlord could do nothing and the plain-clothes men left, taking him along to the station-house.

Just as I started to speak, the Anarchist Squad arrived, spreading themselves out in the hall. The moment I uttered the name "Henrik Ibsen," the sergeant in charge jumped to the platform and bellowed: "You're not sticking to your subject. If you do it again, we'll stop the meeting."

"That is exactly what I am doing," I replied quietly, and continued with my lecture.

The officer kept interfering, repeatedly ordering me to "stick to my subject." Somewhat impatiently I said: "I am sticking to my subject. Ibsen is my subject."

"Nothing of the kind!" he yelled. "Your subject is the drama and you're talking about Ibsen."

The merriment of the audience added to the indignation of my scholarly interruptor. Before I could proceed, he commanded his men to clear the hall, which they did by pulling the chairs from under the people and using their sticks freely.

It happened that these Sunday morning lectures were attended almost exclusively by Americans, some of whom traced their ancestry to the Pilgrim Fathers. Among them was Mr. Alden Freeman of East Orange, the son of a prominent Standard Oil Company shareholder. It was his first experience with the police and he was naturally indignant at their behaviour, as were also the other blue-blooded Americans.

To us, for years targets of persecution, the breaking up of my lecture was no unusual happening. Not only my meetings, but gatherings of workers had been frequently suppressed without the least cause. In the twenty years of my public activity I had always been in uncertainty to the very last minute as to whether I should be permitted to speak or not, and whether I should sleep in my own bed or on a board in a police station.

When the *Mayflower* descendants had read about such police tactics, they had undoubtedly thought I had given cause; that I had perhaps urged the use of violence or bombs. They had never objected, nor had the press. This time, however, the affront was offered to "real" Americans, among them even the son of a millionaire, the partner and bosom-friend of Rockefeller. Such a thing could not be tolerated. Even the New York *Times* waxed indignant, and the other dailies followed suit. Letters of protest began to fill the papers. My good friend William Marion Reedy, of the St. Louis *Mirror,* and Mr. Louis F. Post, of the *Public,* branded the persecution of Emma Goldman as a deliberate conspiracy of the police of the country to Russianize the American Constitution. As a result of the situation there was formed a Free Speech Society, and a manifesto was issued signed by American men and women in every walk of life. Writers, painters, sculptors, lawyers, doctors, and people of every shade of opinion came forward to fight the New York police methods.

Mr. Alden Freeman had throughout his life believed that free speech was a fact and not a mere pretence. He was genuinely shocked to come face to face with reality and he at once identified himself with the campaign of the newly created committee to establish free speech. Mr. Freeman was confident that I would be permitted to speak in East Orange, his home town, and generously offered to arrange a meeting for me there. He also invited me to be his guest at the luncheon of the Mayflower Society, of which he was a member. "Once people see that you are not as you have been described in the papers, they will be glad to come and hear you," he said.

The Mayflowerites proved to be uninteresting, the speeches dull. Towards the end of the luncheon my presence became known. A bomb hurled into the unsuspecting gathering could have produced no more disastrous effect. There was dead silence for a moment. Then some of the guests scrambled to their feet and haughtily marched out. The women present seemed too paralysed to move and fumbled for their smelling-bottles. Some of them looked daggers at Mr. Freeman. Only a few reckless ones ventured to face the dragon. It was amusing to me, but painfully disappointing to my host, the second blow within a short time to his cherished ideas of American freedom and traditions.

The third came soon after the luncheon. The Mayflower Society discussed his expulsion or forced resignation because he had dared to bring Emma Goldman into their presence. But it did not dismay Mr. Freeman. Bravely he proceeded to arrange a meeting for me in his home town.

On the appointed evening we found the hall barred by the police, who announced that there would be no lecture. Mr. Freeman then invited the assembled audience to his home; the meeting would take place on his lawn, he declared. Triumphantly we marched through the streets of aristocratic East Orange, past palatial dwellings, followed by a vast crowd, including police and reporters. It was a demonstration such as the quiet town had never seen before.

Mr. Freeman's house was a fine mansion, surrounded by a beautiful garden. It was private ground, and the police knew that their authority stopped where property rights began. They did not dare to trespass and remained outside the gate. The garage where our gathering took place was more comfortable than some workmen's homes. The coloured lights trembled like shadows in the night, throwing fantastic silhouettes. It was a picture suggesting the legendary birthplace of the Christ-child, the hallelujahs changed into a song of freedom and revolt.

As a result of the East Orange episode people I had never heard of before came to offer their help, subscribe to *Mother Earth,* and secure our literature. By the grace of the police club they had been made to realize that Emma Goldman was neither assassin, witch, nor crank, but a woman with a social ideal the authorities were trying to suppress.

The Free Speech Society began its campaign with a large meeting in Cooper Union. Although it was the end of June and scorchingly hot, the old historic hall was crowded with people of the most diversified social and political tendencies. The speakers also differed on almost every issue, but all were held together by a common bond: the imperative need to put a stop to the growing despotism of the police department. Mr. Alden Freeman presided and gave a humorous account of how he, the son of a Standard Oil man, had been "driven into the arms of anarchism." He continued in a serious tone to describe the purpose of the gathering. "If Emma Goldman sat on this platform with a gag between her teeth, and a policeman on each side of her," he declared, "the picture would simply and plainly express the reason for our being here tonight and would also explain why it is that letters and telegrams of protest and sympathy are pouring in upon the Free Speech Committee from the Atlantic to the Pacific, and from the Gulf to the Great Lakes."

The speakers that followed expressed themselves in a similar vein, the most brilliant talk being made by Voltairine de Cleyre, who contended that "free speech means nothing if it does not mean the freedom to say what others don't like to hear."

Almost an immediate effect of the meeting and of the energetic campaign of the committee was the dismissal by Mayor McClellan of Police Commissioner General Bingham, whose military régime had been responsible for the suppressive methods.

While busy with these activities, I received a letter from a man on the editorial staff of the Boston *Globe,* informing me that a contest for a new Declaration of Independence was being planned by the paper. Several radicals had already promised to participate; would not I also like to send in a contribution? The writer further stated that the best essay would be published in the *Globe* and would be paid for. I replied that though in these days few Americans cared for independence, I would participate for the fun of it. My article, which I kept almost entirely in the form of the Declaration of Independence, giving it new phrasing and meaning, was forwarded to the *Globe,* and in the course of time I received an envelope containing a check and the galley proofs of my Declaration. The accompanying letter from my newspaper friend explained that the owner had chanced upon the proofs on the editor's desk. "Send that woman a check and return her damned anarchist declaration," he had ordered; "I don't want her in the *Globe.*"

The current issue of *Mother Earth* was about to go to press, and we just had time to insert my article by leaving out a less important one. On the 4th of July the new Declaration of Independence was read by thousands, as we sold many copies and distributed a great number free of charge.

In September I went with Ben on a short tour through Massachusetts and Vermont. We were stopped, stopped, and stopped, either by direct police interference or by the intimidation of the hall-owners. In Worcester, Massachusetts, I spoke out of doors, thanks to the aid of the Reverend Dr. Eliot White and his wife, Mrs. Mabel A. White. They followed the example of our friend Alden Freeman and extended to us the hospitality of their spacious lawn. Anarchism was heard there not under the Stars and Stripes, but under a more appropriate canopy — the limitless sky and the myriads of glittering stars, while the large trees shaded us from the curious who had come to stare.

The most important event of our Worcester visit was an address given by Sigmund Freud on the twentieth anniversary of Clark University. I was deeply impressed by the lucidity of his mind and the simplicity of his delivery. Among the array of professors, looking stiff and important in their university caps and gowns, Sigmund Freud, in ordinary attire, unassuming, almost shrinking, stood out like a giant among pygmies. He had aged somewhat since I had heard him in

Vienna in 1896. He had been reviled then as a Jew and irresponsible innovator; now he was a world figure; but neither obloquy nor fame had influenced the great man.

On my return to New York new struggles absorbed me. There was the shirtwaist-makers' strike, involving fifteen thousand employees, and that of the steel-workers at McKeesport, Pennsylvania. Money had to be raised for both fights. The anarchists always being among the first to respond to every need, I had to address numerous meetings and visit labour bodies to plead the cause of their fellow unionists.

Then came the uprising in Spain. In protest against the slaughter in Morocco the Spanish workers had declared a general strike. As usual the American press misrepresented the situation. It necessitated an immediate campaign on our part to present the events in their true light and significance. Our Spanish comrades in America called for my help and I gave it gladly.

Before long we received the news of the arrest in Barcelona of Francisco Ferrer, anarchist and libertarian educationist, who was charged with responsibility for the general strike. We realized the imminent danger facing our comrade and the necessity of arousing intelligent American public opinion in his behalf.

In Europe many noted men and women of advanced thought had already begun an intensive campaign in favour of Francisco Ferrer. In America there were too few to make a similar effort, and the situation therefore required the greater activity on our part. Meetings, conferences, *Mother Earth,* and a constant stream of people kept us busy from early morning until late hours of night.

I had an engagement in Philadelphia, where Ben had preceded me by several days. On his arrival he was informed by comrades that all radical gatherings had of late been suppressed in the City of Brotherly Love. Ben, still imbued with American trust in police officials, went to see the Director of Public Safety, who was the tsar of Philadelphia. That potentate not only received him gruffly, but declared that he would never permit Emma Goldman to speak in "his" city. The local single-taxers passed resolutions denouncing the despotic decision and sent a committee to the City Hall to demand that I be given the right to speak. Seeing that I had friends among Americans, the dictator in the police department drew in his horns. "Emma Goldman can speak," he declared, "if she will submit to a small formality: to let me read her lecture notes."

I would, of course, do nothing of the kind, since I did not believe in censorship. Thereupon the director decided that I could not speak. "The meeting can proceed," he announced, "but Emma Goldman will not be allowed in the Odd Fellows' Temple, if I have to call out the whole police department to prevent her."

He kept his promise. He placed six plain-clothes men at my unsolicited disposal, who were stationed at the entrance of the little hotel where I was stopping. In the evening, when I started for Odd Fellows' Hall, accompanied by the attorney of the Philadelphia Free Speech League, the detectives followed at our heels. For blocks the hall was lined with police on foot, on horseback, and in automobiles. Not only was I barred from entering, but I was forced to return to the hotel along the route dictated by the officers, who would not let me out of sight until I was back in my room. The meeting took place and was addressed by anarchists, socialists, and single-taxers, but not by Emma Goldman, and thus Philadelphia was saved.

The single-taxers and the members of the Free Speech League insisted that the case should be tested in the courts. I had no faith in legal procedure, but my friends argued that if I refused, the police would undoubtedly continue their tactics, whereas a legal fight would focus public attention on their Russian methods of trying to gag me. Voltairine de Cleyre also was in favour of having a test made, and I consented.

Meanwhile the papers carried sensational stories about the situation, and the detectives remained at the hotel. The owner, somewhat of a liberal, was exceedingly decent to me, but the undesirable publicity was injuring his business. We therefore moved to one of the larger hostelries. I was just beginning to unpack my things in the new place when I was informed by telephone that there had been a mistake: the rooms assigned to us had been reserved before and there were no others vacant in the house. The same thing happened in several other hotels. There were no objections to Ben, but they would not have me.

I finally found shelter with some American friends. During three weeks their place was under constant watch and I was shadowed from the moment I left the house until I returned. Moreover, the police tried to bribe my host's servant to watch my room and report what was happening. But the dear soul refused. She helped me instead to escape for one whole day from the vigilance of the detectives.

My presence was urgently needed in New York. On Sunday morning, October 13, this servant took Ben and me through the back entrance, across several yards, and out into an alley. Without having been observed we reached the railroad station and were soon speeding east.

Our mission in New York was a mass meeting to commemorate Francisco Ferrer, the victim of popery and militarism in Spain.

The Romish Church had for eight years waged a relentless war against Francisco Ferrer. He had dared to strike her in her most vulnerable spot. Between 1901 and 1909 he had founded 109 modern schools and his example and influence had led the liberal elements to organize three hundred non-sectarian educational institutions. Catholic Spain had never before witnessed such daring, but it was mainly Ferrer's Modern School that gave the Church fathers no peace. They were wroth at the attempt to free the child from superstition and bigotry, from the darkness of dogma and authority. Church and State saw the danger to their dominion of centuries and they tried to crush Ferrer. They had almost succeeded in 1906. At that time they had caused his arrest in connexion with Morral's attempt on the life of the Spanish King.

Mateo Morral, a young anarchist, had devoted his private fortune to the library of the Modern Schools and had worked with Ferrer in the capacity of librarian. After the failure of his act he had ended his own life. It was then that the Spanish authorities discovered the connexion of Mateo Morral with the Modern School. Francisco Ferrer was arrested. It was known throughout Spain that Ferrer was opposed to acts of political violence, that he firmly believed in and preached modern education as against force. It did not save him, however, from the powers that be. World-wide protests had rescued him in 1906, but now Church and State insisted on their pound of flesh.

While Francisco Ferrer was being sought by the authorities he was living with a comrade ten miles from Barcelona. He was in perfect safety there and he could have escaped the fury of the Church and military cliques which demanded his death. Then he read the official proclamation that anyone harbouring him would be shot. He decided to give himself up. The anarchist friends at whose house he was staying were a poor family with five children; they knew their danger, yet they pleaded with Ferrer to remain with them. To quiet their fears for his safety, he promised. But at night, while everyone was asleep,

Ferrer left through the window of his room and walked to Barcelona. He was recognized a short distance from the city and arrested.

After a mock trial Francisco Ferrer was condemned to death and shot within the walls of Montjuich prison. He died as he had lived, proclaiming with his last breath: " Long live the Modern School!"

After the Francisco Ferrer commemoration meeting in New York I returned to Philadelphia to continue our free-speech fight. While awaiting the court's decision in the test case, a social gathering was arranged in my room for the committee backing our campaign. We were quietly discussing things over our coffee when there came violent knocking. Several officers rushed into the room.

" You're holding a secret meeting," their leader declared, and ordered the people out.

" How dare you intrude upon my birthday party?" I replied. " These are my guests who have come to celebrate my birthday. Is that a crime in Philadelphia?"

" Birthday, eh?" the officer sneered; " I didn't know anarchists celebrated birthdays. We'll wait outside to see how late you'll celebrate."

Some of the single-taxers who were present were very indignant; not, however, because the police had forcibly disturbed our friendly circle, but on account of their violation of the sacredness of private property. My visitors soon dispersed and I was left wondering whether the greater difficulty confronting us anarchists was the hold upon man of the sanctity of property or his belief in the State.

Our campaign closed with a large meeting under the auspices of the Free Speech League. Leonard D. Abbott presided, while among the speakers were ex-Congressman Robert Baker, Frank Stephens, Theodore Schroeder, George Brown (the " shoemaker philosopher "), Voltairine de Cleyre, and Ben Reitman. Letters protesting against my gagging were read from Horace Traubel, Charles Edward Russell, Rose Pastor Stokes, Alden Freeman, William Marion Reedy, and others.

Some time later the Director of Public Safety in Philadelphia was dismissed from office on charges of graft and bribery.

CHAPTER XXXVI

I N THE LATTER PART OF 1909 NEW YORK AGAIN EXPERIENCED A
vice crusade. The reformers had discovered the white-slave traffic!
They got busy, though they were without the slightest notion regarding the sources of the evil they were trying to eradicate.

I had had considerable opportunity to come in contact with prostitution; first in the house in which I was once compelled to live, then during the two years when I nursed Mrs. Spenser, and finally at Blackwell's Island. I had also read and gathered much material on the subject. I therefore felt much better equipped to discuss the problem than the moral busybodies who were now attracting so much attention. I prepared a lecture on the white-slave traffic, dealing with its causes, effects, and possible elimination. It became the strongest drawing card in my new course and also aroused the most heated criticism and discussion. The lecture was published in the January issue of *Mother Earth* and subsequently in pamphlet form.

Shortly afterwards Ben and I went on our annual tour. Everywhere we met with complaints from our subscribers that they had not received the January number of the magazine. I wired Sasha about it and he went after the postal authorities. He was informed that some copies had been held up on the complaint of Anthony Comstock. While we felt flattered that we were at last given a place among other victims of Comstockery, we nevertheless demanded to know the reason for the unexpected honour.

After several calls Sasha succeeded in getting into the august presence of the keeper of American morals. Comstock admitted that *Mother Earth* had been held up, but denied that it had been done on his complaint.

"The matter is now in my hands," he told Sasha; "the reason for it is Miss Goldman's article on the white-slave traffic." At Comstock's request Sasha accompanied him to the office of the District Attorney, where St. Anthony held a secret conference lasting two hours. After that came a prolonged consultation with the Chief Post Office Inspector. Finally the censor declared that nothing objectionable had been found in the article.

The next day the New York *Times* contained an interview with Comstock in which he entirely denied the whole matter. It was "a scheme of Emma Goldman to attract attention to her publication," he stated. He had made no complaint against the magazine, he said, nor had it been held up by the Post Office. It required another week of energetic work by Sasha, canvassing various postal departments and repeatedly wiring to Washington, before the January issue was finally released.

If Comstock had been decent enough at least to inform us of his intention in advance, we should have printed fifty thousand copies of the proscribed number. Even as it was, his interference helped to advertise our publication. The demand for *Mother Earth* greatly increased, but unfortunately we had only our usual edition on hand.

For the first time since the free-speech fight in Chicago in 1908 I could go back to that city. The police, perhaps mindful of the publicity they had given anarchism at that time by their treatment of me, actually assured Ben that I should not be molested any more. The promise made my manager enthusiastic with anticipation of the work awaiting us in his native town. He wired for dates and subjects and then threw himself with all his elemental strength into the arrangements for a series of lectures.

Chicago had been significant in my life. I owed my spiritual birth to the martyrs of 1887. Ten years later I found Max there, whose understanding and tender companionship had not ceased to inspire and sustain me through the years. It was also in Chicago, in 1901, that I had been brought close to death because of my attitude towards Leon Czolgosz, and was it not Chicago that had given me Ben? Ben, with all his faults, irresponsibility, and obsessions — the man who had already caused me greater agony of spirit than anyone else in my life, and who had brought me deeper devotion and a complete consecration to my work. Only two years we had been together, and during that period he had tested my soul a hundred times, my brain always in rebellion against the strange boy whose nearness was yet a vital need to me.

I had been lecturing in the city on Lake Michigan since 1892, but it was only on this visit that I realized its possibilities. Within ten days I addressed six English and three Yiddish meetings, attended by large crowds that were sufficiently interested to pay admission and to purchase large quantities of our literature. It was certainly a notable achievement, and it was brought about almost entirely through the efforts of Ben. My satisfaction in having gained ground in Chicago was mingled with pride in him, pride because his most antagonistic opponents in our ranks had come to see and admire his sincerity and his talent for organizing. In this city at least Ben had conquered the hearts of many comrades and had won their co-operation and support.

In my travels through the United States I had always found university towns the most indifferent to the social struggle. American student bodies were ignorant of the great issues in their native land and lacked sympathy with the masses. I was therefore not enthusiastic when Ben suggested our invading Madison, Wisconsin.

Great was my surprise when I discovered an entirely new note in the University of Wisconsin. I found the professors and pupils vitally interested in social ideas, and a library containing the best selection of books, papers, and magazines. Professors Ross, Commons, and Jastrow and several others proved to be exceptions to the average American educator. They were progressive, alive to the problems of the world, and modern in the interpretation of their subjects.

A group of students invited us to lecture in the Y.M.C.A. hall on the campus. Ben spoke on the relation between education and agitation, and I discussed the difference between Russian and American college men. It was news to our hearers to learn that the Russian intelligentsia saw in education, not a mere means to a career, but something to enable them to understand life and the people, so that they could teach and help them. American students, on the other hand, were interested mostly in their diplomas. As to the social struggle, American university men knew little about it and cared still less. Our talks on this occasion were followed by spirited discussions and proved to us that our audiences had become very much aware of their relation to the masses and of their debt to the workers who produced all wealth.

The trustees of the Y.M.C.A. building could think of nothing wiser than to refuse the hall for our further gatherings. It was, of course, the best advertising for our meetings. It brought scores of students to the hall we had secured in town and made them more eager than ever to hear us speak. Subsequently I learned from the librarian that there had been a greater demand for books on anarchism since I had come to the city than during the entire previous existence of the library.

The excitement my presence in Madison created and the large attendance at our meetings were too much for the conservative townsfolk. Their spokesman, the *Democrat,* sounded the alarm against " the spirit of anarchy and the revolution rampant in college." The editor chose as his special target Professor Ross, who had been my host and who had also advised the students to go to my lectures and had even attended them himself. The newspaper almost caused the dismissal of the professor. Fortunately he had left on a long-planned trip to China shortly after my visit. The ravings of the *Democrat* soon died out, and when Dr. Ross returned from the Orient, he was able to take up his work without further molestation.

As manager of the Orleneff troupe I had often attended social functions, but as propagandist I had always managed to keep away from idle entertainments. The man who now steered me through the shoals of society luncheons and would-be Bohemian dinners was William Marion Reedy, the brilliant editor of the St. Louis *Mirror.* His suave manner could smuggle the most dangerous contraband into the enemy's camp. There were many questions hurled at me at my first luncheon with the "nice" people of St. Louis, where plenty of water was served and little spirit. The one enlivening element at the affair was Bill Reedy, who was like sparkling wine at a prayer-meeting.

My second appearance was at the Artists' Guild, a society composed of "respectable" Bohemians. Their bohemianism made me think of Jack London's exploits in the East End of London as portrayed in his *Children of the Abyss,* when he had stood in the bread-line, waited hours to be given a chance to shovel coal, and had himself locked up in the workhouse, in the comforting consciousness that at any time he could go back to his lodgings, take a bath, change his linen, and eat a hearty dinner.

The majority of the Guilders impressed me as people to whom "bohemianism" was a sort of narcotic to help them endure the boredom of their lives. Of course there were others, those who knew the struggle that is the lot of every sincere and free person, whether he aspires to an ideal in life or in art. To them I addressed my talk on "Art in Life," pointing out, among other things, that life in all its variety and fullness is art, the highest art. The man who is not part of the stream of life is not an artist, no matter how well he paints sunsets or composes nocturnes. It certainly does not mean that the artist must hold a definite creed, join an anarchist group or a socialist local. It does signify, however, that he must be able to feel the tragedy of the millions condemned to a lack of joy and beauty. The inspiration of the true artist has never been the drawing-room. Great art has always gone to the masses, to their hopes and dreams, for the spark that kindled their souls. The rest, "the many, all too many," as Nietzsche called mediocrity, have been mere commodities that can be bought with money, cheap glory, or social position.

My lecture on the drama was particularly apropos because of the efforts which were being made at the time by ministers and virtuous ladies to purify the stage. It was, however, my talk on Francisco Ferrer that brought the largest audience and aroused the deepest interest.

More satisfactory than "breaking into society" were the hours spent at Faust's with Billy Reedy and the sweet companionship of Ben and Ida Capes. In theory Bill and I were five thousand years apart. He had said as much in his pen portrait of me, "The Daughter of the Dream." But in reality the editor of the St. Louis *Mirror* was very much of an anarchist. His breadth of vision, tolerance, and generous support of every social rebel brought him very near to me. We had many literary tastes in common, and his rich Irish humour and ready wit enlivened the hours we passed together.

I told him about another evening I had spent at Faust's, in 1901, with Carl Nold and the other friends, before I had gone to Chicago to give myself up to the police. "You sat here enjoying food and drink while two hundred detectives were searching for you up and down the land!" he exclaimed. "Oh, my God, my God, what a woman!" He broke into spasms, his eyes bulging in wonder, his fat belly shaking with laughter. After receiving several slaps on the back and a few gulps of water, Billy regained his breath, but he continued to cry all through the evening: "Oh, my God, what a woman!"

The Capeses were near to me in a deeper sense than Bill because of the bond of our ideal and our struggle for it. Long before I had met them, I had heard of their zeal in our cause and their ever-ready response to its needs. Much later I learned how Ben had become awakèned to social consciousness. " It was at one of your meetings in St. Louis," he told me; " I had come with a bunch of kids to rotten-egg you because you were an enemy of God and man. Your talk that evening moved me profoundly and changed the entire course of my life. I had come to scoff, and I remained to pray to the new vision you had created for me." Since then he had never faltered in his devotion to this vision, nor to our friendship, which became stronger and more beautiful through the years.

Michigan State University is only ten hours removed from the University of Wisconsin, but in spirit it was fifty years behind. Instead of broad-minded professors and keen students, I was confronted with five hundred university rowdies in our hall, whistling, howling, and acting like lunatics. I had addressed difficult crowds in my day — longshoremen, sailors, steel-workers, miners, men aroused by war hysteria. They resembled boarding-school girls compared with the tough gang that had come this time, evidently intent upon breaking up the meeting. Before I reached the hall, these believers in the sanctity of private property had torn up all our literature. This done, they were amusing themselves by throwing pieces of coal at the cut-glass vase on the platform. The place was packed with men, only one other woman besides myself being present, Dr. Maud Thompson. She, poor soul, was jammed in at the door and could not reach the platform. In any event she would have done no good, as I had no intention of appealing to the " chivalry " of these adolescents.

Several students who had entertained us at a fraternity dinner grew anxious about my safety and offered to call the police. I felt that such a step would only aggravate the situation and perhaps cause a riot. I informed them that I would face the music myself and take the consequences.

My appearance on the platform was greeted with shouts, bells, stamping of feet, and cries of " Here she is, the anarchist bomb-thrower; here's the free lover! You can't speak in our town, Emma! Get out — you'd better get out!"

I saw clearly that if the situation was to be met, I must not show nervousness or lose patience. I folded my arms and stood there facing the young savages while the deafening noises continued. During a slight lull I said: " Gentlemen, I can see you are in a sporting mood, you want a contest. Very well, you shall have it. Just go on with the noise. I will wait until you are through."

There was an amazed silence for a moment, and then they again broke loose. I continued to stand, my arms folded, all my will-power concentrated in my stare. Gradually the yelling subsided and then someone cried: "All right, Emma, let's hear about your anarchism!" The cry was taken up by others, and after a while comparative quiet prevailed. Then I began to speak.

I talked for an hour amid repeated interruptions, but before long, silence settled over the assembly. Their behaviour, I told them, was the best proof of the effects of authority and of its system of education. "You are the result of it," I said; "how can you know the meaning of freedom of thought and speech? How can you feel respect for others or be kind and hospitable to a stranger in your midst? Authority at home, in the school, and in the body politic destroys those qualities. It turns the individual into a parrot repeating time-worn slogans, until he becomes incapable of thinking for himself or of feeling social wrongs. But I believe in the possibilities of youth," I continued, "and you are young, gentlemen, very, very young. That is fortunate, because you are still uncorrupted and impressionable. The energy you have so ably demonstrated this afternoon could be put to better use. It could be applied for the benefit of your fellows. But you have wasted your efforts in smashing a beautiful vase and in destroying the literary labours of men and women who live, work, and often die for their vision of a better future."

As soon as I had finished, they broke out with the college yell. It was the highest tribute, I was told later, that I could receive. Towards the evening a committee of students came to my hotel to offer apologies for the behaviour of their comrades and to pay the damage for the literature and vase. "You won, Emma Goldman," they said, "you have made us ashamed. Next time you visit our city, we will give you a different welcome."

This was not the only interesting event that happened to us in Ann Arbor. There was also the meeting with Dr. William Boehm, instructor at the university, and with his wife, Dr. Maud Thompson, a very fine woman of tender nature. On the day of my lecture Ben and I had been their guests at luncheon. We spent the hour in a heated argument with Boehm, an adherent of "scientific socialism." At the meeting afterwards he forgot our theoretic differences; comradely sympathy and concern spoke louder than his cold science, and he was ready to fight for me.

In Buffalo we found an unusual personality in the secretary of the

Mayor. Only America could produce such a contradiction: he was a radical and a non-believer, yet he was at the same time bound by his New England conscience. He was a dreamer of great dreams, wasting his energies in small deeds; a politician and an opportunist, afraid of public opinion, yet recklessly ignoring it. He had nothing to gain and considerable to lose in urging the Mayor to let me speak. But he championed my rights with a Puritan doggedness.

The Chief of Police attempted to stop my meeting. The Mayor, urged on by his secretary, refused to acquiesce. It was a contest in which superior intelligence scored over official narrow-mindedness.

The ways of the gods are strange; for some reason there was no further interference on this tour. We went on our way quietly, ploughing old fields, breaking new ground, and meeting interesting people who added zest and colour to our work.

Fair newspaper treatment of an anarchist was by no means an everyday occurrence. In Denver, much to my surprise, three papers devoted their columns to verbatim accounts of my lectures. The dramatic critic of the local *Times* even made a discovery. "Emma Goldman," he wrote, "is being treated as an enemy of society because, like Dr. Stockmann in Ibsen's *Enemy of the People,* she is pointing out our ills and defects."

As the divorce-mill of the country, Reno attracts a certain class of women. They flock there to buy their freedom from one owner in order to sell themselves more profitably, as often is the case, to another. Respectability has it easy. No heart-aches, no soul-struggle of the free woman, who suffers a thousand torments in the readjustment from an old to a new emotional experience. Just a piece of paper, easily obtainable when one has money to appease public opinion and one's own conscience. Yet the divorcees in the hotel where we had registered were scandalized.

"What, Emma Goldman under the same roof with us! Emma Goldman, the champion of free love! Such a person cannot be tolerated," they declared. What could the poor owner do? The divorcees, like the poor, are always there and are profitable guests. I had to leave the hotel. The humour of the situation was that the very women who had objected to my staying in the same place with them helped to crowd my lectures on "The Failure of Marriage" and "The Meaning of Love."

It was in Reno that I was inaugurated into the art of gambling.

I had never before seen gambling-houses wide open, with people besieging the roulette tables. It was interesting to watch the expression and behaviour of the men and women obsessed by the passion. I, too, tried my "luck," but after losing fifty cents I gave up the attempt to coax fortune.

In San Francisco I learned that Jack London lived in the neighbourhood. I had met him with other young socialist students at the Strunskys' on my first visit to California, in 1897. I had since read most of his works and I was naturally eager to renew our acquaintance. There was also another reason: the Modern School the Ferrer Association was planning to establish in New York. We had been fortunate in securing the active help of some very vital persons in its educational work, among them Lola Ridge, Manuel Komroff, Rose and Mary Yuster. I wanted to interest Jack London in our project. I wrote requesting him to attend my lecture on Francisco Ferrer.

His reply was characteristic. " Dear Emma Goldman," it read, " I have your note. I would not go to a meeting even if God Almighty were to speak there. The only time I attend lectures is when I am to do the talking. But we want you *here*. Will you not come to Glen Ellen and bring whomever you have with you? "

Who could resist such an amiable invitation? I had only two friends with me, Ben and my erstwhile attorney, E. E. Kirk, but even if I had brought a whole caravan, Jack and Charmian London would have welcomed them, so warm and genuine was the hospitality of those two dear people.

How different was the real Jack London from the mechanical, bell-button socialist of the *Kempton-Wace Letters!* Here was youth, exuberance, throbbing life. Here was the good comrade, all concern and affection. He exerted himself to make our visit a glorious holiday. We argued about our political differences, of course, but there was in Jack nothing of the rancour I had so often found in the socialists I had debated with. But, then, Jack London was the artist first, the creative spirit to whom freedom is the breath of life. As the artist he did not fail to see the beauties of anarchism, even if he did insist that society would have to pass through socialism before reaching the higher stage of anarchism. In any case it was not Jack London's politics that mattered to me. It was his humanity, his understanding of and his feeling with the complexities of the human heart. How else could he have created his splendid *Martin Eden*, if he did not have in himself the elements that had contributed to the soul-struggle and undoing of his hero? It was this Jack London, and not the devotee of a mechanistic creed, who lent meaning and joy to my visit to Glen Ellen.

Charmian, Jack's wife, was a gracious hostess, gentle and loving in her expectant motherhood. She was as active and spirited as if she were not so near to the birth of her child — too strenuous, I feared, in her daily occupations. During our three days' stay Charmian hardly rested, except after dinner, when she would sew on the outfit for the baby while we argued, joked, and drank into the wee hours of the morning.

For fifteen years before this my lectures had been made possible by my comrades, who had always given me their best assistance. But they had never been able to reach a large American public. Some of them had been too centred in their own language-group activities to trouble about interesting the native element. The results during those years were scant and unsatisfactory. Now with Ben as my manager my work was lifted out of its former narrow confines. On this tour I visited thirty-seven cities in twenty-five States, among them many places where anarchism had never been discussed before. I lectured one hundred and twenty times to vast audiences, of which twenty-five thousand paid admission, besides the great number of poor students or unemployed admitted without charge. The most gratifying part of the enlarged scope of my work was that ten thousand pieces of literature were sold and five thousand distributed free. Not least important were the various free-speech fights, with the entire expense for them raised at our own gatherings. Nor had other activities been neglected. Our appeals for the newly organized Francisco Ferrer Association and for many strikes had brought considerable material response.

Nevertheless I was roundly condemned by some of the comrades. They considered it really treason that I, an anarchist, should travel with a manager, and an ex-tramp at that, a man of unsettled habits, who was not even a comrade. I was not disturbed, however, though it was painful to find such sectarianism in our ranks. I took heart in the certainty that during the past two years I had done better work and that I had made anarchism more widely known than in the previous years. And it had been the skill and devotion of Ben that had brought it about.

CHAPTER XXXVII

MAY 18, THE DAY OF SASHA'S RESURRECTION, REMAINED GRAVEN on my heart, although my yearly tours had always prevented my being with him on the anniversary of his release. In a spiritual sense, however, neither space nor time could separate me from Sasha or make me forget the day I had longed and worked for throughout the years of his imprisonment. On May 18 this year a telegram from him found me in Los Angeles. It filled me with great joy, for it brought the news that he had determined to begin his prison memoirs. I had often urged him to write them, believing that if he could re-create his prison life on paper, it might help him to get rid of the phantoms that were making his readjustment to life so difficult. Now he had decided it at last, on Our Day, the day that represented the most significant moment in both our lives. I immediately notified him that I would soon return to relieve him in the *Mother Earth* office, and that I would devote myself for the rest of the summer to his needs.

I was also to do some writing, to revise my lectures for publication. Ben had put that bee in my bonnet and had talked of it all through our tour. I thought that I could not find time for it; moreover, no publisher would accept a book by me. But Ben already visioned my essays as a best-seller at our meetings; his optimism and persistence were too infectious to withstand for long.

Formerly upon the completion of our tours Ben had always remained in Chicago with his mother, to whom he was fondly attached. This time I wanted to have him in New York to give me more leisure to be with Sasha and also for my own writing. But the *Wanderlust* was in Ben's blood, as compelling as in his old tramp days. Not to burden *Mother Earth*, he would work his way across to Europe, he said. Since we had always been separated during a part of the summer, it would make no difference, he argued, whether he was in Chicago or in London.

Shortly after Ben's departure, Sasha and I went out to the little farm. We loved the beauty and restfulness of the place. He pitched a tent on one of the highest hills, which gave him a gorgeous view over the Hudson. I was occupied in setting the house in order. Meanwhile Sasha began to write.

Notwithstanding the many police raids I had suffered since Sasha had gone to Pittsburgh in 1892, I had managed to rescue some copies of "The Prison Blossoms," which he had published *sub rosa* in the penitentiary. Carl Nold, Henry Bauer and several other friends also had kept copies. They were helpful to Sasha, but they were insignificant in comparison with the memory of what he had lived through in that house of the living dead. All the horrors he had known, the agony of body and soul, the suffering of his fellow-prisoners, all this he had now to dig out from the depths of his being and re-create. The black spectre of fourteen years again began to haunt his waking and sleeping hours.

Day after day he would sit at his desk staring into vacancy, or he would write as if driven by furies. What he had written he often wanted to destroy, and I would wrestle with him to save it, as I had fought through all the years to save him from his grave. Then would come days when Sasha would vanish into the woods to escape human contact, to escape me, and above all to escape himself and the ghosts that had come to life since he had begun to write. I would torment myself to find the right way and the right word with which to soothe his harassed spirit. It was not only because of my affection for him that I took up this struggle each day; it was also because I perceived in the very first chapter of his writing that Sasha was in the birth-throes of a great work. No price on my part seemed too high to help it to life.

While on the farm, one evening I fell and hurt myself. A friend, a young medical man who was visiting us, diagnosed my injury as a broken knee-cap, but I would not give up the writing I had planned to do that night. With a cold compress over my knee, my leg suspended, I worked until six in the morning. After a few hours' sleep I felt no pain, and, having to be in New York that day, I busied myself with preparing supplies. I baked, made my special brand of " Boston " beans and compote, and then walked three and a half miles to the railroad station. When I tried to get on the train, I knew there was something very wrong with my knee. That night was excruciating, and in the morning I had to send for a physician. He supported the previous diagnosis of a broken knee-cap and advised an operation. Two other medical friends agreed with him and suggested the St. Francis Hospital.

"Dr. Stewart, the famous surgeon, is there," one of my friends said; "he would do a fine job."

"Dr. Stewart!" I exclaimed; "not the man who was called to treat McKinley?"

"The very one," he replied.

"What a strange coincidence!" I remarked. "Do you think he will consent when he learns who I am?"

"Of course," my friend assured me; "besides, you can register as Kershner."

After an X-ray had been taken, Dr. Stewart came to tell me that my knee-bone was broken on the side. "But how did you manage to tear your ligaments?" he asked. When I told him I had been on my feet all day, he threw up his hands. But he did not intend to operate, he informed me. "Knees never work the same after an operation," he said; "I will give you the slow treatment, the conservative method. It takes more time and patience, but it is better in the end," he remarked with a twinkle in his eye.

"Found out," I thought; "this about the conservative method is for my special benefit."

It was an unpleasant pill for an anarchist to swallow, but female vanity decided against a stiff knee, and I consented to the "conservative method." I was taken back to my flat and laid up for weeks in a plaster cast and splints. Meanwhile Sasha's writing had been interrupted and my own book postponed, which was harder to bear than the pain in my knee. Learning of my accident, Ben cut short his stay abroad and returned to New York. It was soothing and comforting to have him, and I was almost glad I had been laid up.

In another week I was back on the farm, hopping about on crutches, acting as light domestic for five persons, spending the evenings with Sasha, and the nights on my book, which I completed in two months. As I had foreseen, no publisher would accept my manuscript. Ben urged that we get the book out ourselves. Our printer was willing to give us credit, but where get the other necessary funds? "Borrow," my optimistic manager advised; "we'll sell enough on our next tour to pay back the entire cost."

Ben was attending to the office of *Mother Earth* and to the publication of my book, and I returned again to our Ossining farm, where Sasha was still working on his memoirs. Our intention was to remain there as long as the weather would permit, but unexpected events soon changed our plans. News came of the explosion in the Los Angeles *Times* building and of the impending danger to a group of anarchists in Japan. Both matters necessitated immediate and concentrated effort on our part, and we hastened back to New York early in October.

The Merchants' and Manufacturers' Association of Los Angeles, with Harrison Grey Otis, the owner of the Los Angeles *Times* at their head, had for years carried on a relentless war on the Pacific Coast against organized labour. Their determined opposition had frustrated every attempt to organize the workers in Los Angeles and thus enable them to improve their condition. In consequence Otis and his paper were bitterly hated by the labour elements in California.

On the night of October 1 an explosion blew up the *Times* building, involving the sacrifice of twenty-two employees. Otis raised the cry of "Anarchy!" The press, the State, and the Church combined in an attack on everybody known to sympathize with labour, many preachers being the most rabid in their thirst for vengeance. Even before the cause of the *Times* explosion had been ascertained, the anarchists were being held responsible. We took up the challenge of the enemy and warned the toilers that it was not only anarchism that was in danger but also organized labour. We felt this work to be of paramount importance at the moment, to which all other efforts had to be subordinated. Sasha had no more chance to continue his memoirs.

At the same time news reached us from Japan about the arrest of a number of anarchists for an alleged plot on the life of the Mikado. The outstanding figure of the group was Denjiro Kotoku. He knew his country better than European writers like Lafcadio Hearn, Pierre Loti, or Mme Gauthier, who had painted Japan in roseate colours. Kotoku had personally experienced the miserable conditions under which the workers slaved, and the barbarism of the political régime. For years he had devoted himself to awaking the intelligentsia and the masses of Japan to the needs of the situation. He was a man of brilliant mind, an able writer, and the translator of some of the works of Karl Marx, Leo Tolstoy, and Peter Kropotkin. In cooperation with Lien Sun Soh and Mme Ho Chin he had propagated anarchism in the University of Tokio among Japanese and Chinese students. The Government had repeatedly imprisoned him for his activities, without dampening our comrade's ardour. The authorities finally decided to " eliminate " him by involving him in the plot against the Emperor.

On November 10 the Associated Press announced that " the special tribunal appointed to try the plotters against the life of the Mikado found twenty-six persons guilty, including the ringleaders, Kotoku and his wife, Sugano Kano. The Court recommended the severest penalty under clause 73, which provides capital punishment for conspirators against the Imperial family."

There was no time to lose if anything was to be done to stay the hand of the executioner in Japan. With the help of our friend Leonard D. Abbott, president of the Free Speech League, we initiated a protest that soon assumed national proportions. Letters and telegrams were forwarded to the Japanese Ambassador in Washington, the Consul-General in New York, and the American newspapers. A committee of persons prominent in public life interviewed the Japanese representatives in the United States. The great American protest was evidently not to the liking of the satraps of the Mikado. They strove their utmost to blacken the character of the condemned men and exerted their persuasive powers to prevail upon our committee to give up their efforts. In response we intensified our work, holding private and public meetings, bombarding the press, and otherwise working strenuously to arouse public opinion over the judicial crime about to be committed in Japan.

Among the many friends who participated in this campaign was Sadakichi Hartmann, poet, writer, painter, and a marvellous reader of the poems and stories of Whitman and Poe. I had first met him in 1894; subsequently he had become a steady contributor to our magazine. Partly Japanese himself, Sadakichi was familiar with conditions in Japan and the case of Kotoku. At our request he wrote a powerful manifesto that was widely distributed in behalf of the condemned comrades.

In January 1911 Ben and I again started on our annual tour. Before we left, my selected lectures, *Anarchism and Other Essays,* came off the press. The book also contained a biographic sketch of the author by Hippolyte Havel, comprising the most significant events of my public career. Some of the lectures in the volume had been repeatedly suppressed by the police. Even when I had been able to deliver them, it had never been without anxiety and travail. They represented a mental and spiritual struggle of twenty years, the conclusions arrived at after much reflection and growth. I owed the inspiration to write the book to Ben, but the main assistance, including the revision and the reading of proofs, was due to Sasha. It was hard to say which of us was the happier at seeing my first literary effort in print.

Before going on tour I was able to participate in the inauguration of the Francisco Ferrer Centre at St. Mark's Place, New York, which was organized by the efforts of Leonard D. Abbott, Harry Kelly, Sasha, and other friends. There the Ferrer Association began Sunday and evening classes, preparatory to the Modern School, which we hoped would emerge from our humble beginnings. My great satisfaction at the event was due not only to the funds I had helped to raise, but also to having secured Bayard Boyesen as instructor and secretary of our school.

Mr. Boyesen had been a member of the Department of English and Comparative Literature at Columbia University. Profoundly stirred by the martyrdom of Francisco Ferrer, he had presided at our second memorial meeting. Being censured for it by the president of Columbia, Boyesen resigned his post at the university. He was induced to join the Ferrer Association and to assume the secretaryship of the Modern School. In this capacity he could expect neither salary nor glory, but his interest in the proposed educational venture outweighed all other considerations.

Nothing of particular moment happened on our tour till we reached Columbus, Ohio. There we were gagged and had to begin a fight for free speech. It happened that the United Mine Workers were having their convention in the city at the time. The militant elements were incensed over the action of the police. They staged a demonstration in our hall in protest against the interference and also against their own leaders because the latter had voted down a motion to have me address the convention. The result was an " invitation " to me from the latter. The curious document read:

DEAR MADAM:
   Pursuant to the action of our Convention you are hereby cordially invited to address the delegates of the United Mine Workers

of America at one P.M. tomorrow, January 19th, in session at Memorial Hall.

Subsequent to this action of our Convention, notice was served on us by the custodian that before addressing the delegation it will be necessary to get permission from the County Commissioners; otherwise you would not be allowed. I would suggest that you have Mr. Reitman take this matter up with the Commissioners and avoid any complications or unpleasantness which might ensue if you undertook to deliver an address without permission of the Commissioners.

However, I assure you that as far as our Convention is concerned there would be no objection.

Very truly yours,
EDWIN PERRY
Secretary-Treasurer, U. M. W. of A.

P. S. Have just been advised by the Custodian that the Commissioners refuse to allow you to speak under any circumstances tomorrow morning at the Memorial Hall.

When our miner friends of the rank and file were informed of the ruse to prevent my speaking, they decided unanimously to march to the meeting-place that we had secured; but first they would go to Memorial Hall, where the convention was holding its sessions. And then the unexpected happened. The custodians of Memorial Hall shut their doors, not only to me, but to all the delegates. Even those who had opposed my speaking now felt outraged, and joined the procession to our hall.

I was introduced by Delegate E. S. McCullough, an eloquent man, and received by the audience with enthusiasm. The most gratifying aspect of the situation was the genuine response of the delegates to the necessity of the general strike as the most effective weapon at labour's command.

In Detroit we received the appalling news of the execution of our comrades in Japan. Denjiro Kotoku and his wife, Sugano Kano, Dr. S. Oishi, a physician educated in the United States, A. Morichiki, agricultural engineer, and their co-workers had been judicially assassinated. Their crime had been, as with our Chicago martyrs, love of their fellows and consecration to an ideal.

"Long live anarchy!" Denjiro Kotoku had cried with his last breath.

"Banjoi! (For ever)," had replied his companions in death. "I have lived for liberty and I die for liberty, for liberty is my life," had exclaimed Sugano Kano. The East had met the West, united by the same tie of blood.

William Marion Reedy's efforts in my behalf this year brought even greater results than on the previous occasions in St. Louis. Thanks to him and his friend Alice Martin, who was at the head of a dancing-school, I was enabled to speak in the Odeon Recital Hall. My subjects "Kotoku" and "Victims of Morality" attracted great numbers of people who had never before ventured near an anarchist meeting. The lectures at the Women's Wednesday Club on "Tolstoy" and "Galsworthy's *Justice*" proved rather strong food for the delicate palates of the St. Louis society ladies.

On this visit I made the acquaintance of Roger Baldwin, Robert Minor, and Zoe Akins. Baldwin was helpful in arranging a luncheon at one of the large hotels, where I met a group of social workers and reformers. He had also been instrumental in securing the Women's Wednesday Club for the two drama lectures. He was a very pleasant person, though not very vital, rather a social lion surrounded by society girls, whose interest in the attractive young man was apparently greater than in his uplift work.

Robert Minor, a talented cartoonist, impressed me as more effective and interesting, both as an artist and as a socialist.

Zoe Akins, exotic and vivacious, proved to be a strange American product. Of an ultra-conservative family, her early influences reactionary to the last degree, she yet was trying to break her bonds and find untrammelled expression for her life. A frequent visitor at my hotel, she entertained me with the amusing recital of her exploits in dodging her respectable relatives in order to spend time with her Bohemian friends.

On my return to Madison, Wisconsin, I found Professor Ross and the other instructors less "reckless" than on my previous visit. The cause of it was no doubt the university appropriation bill, pending before the legislature. However they may dislike the idea, professors are also proletarians; intellectual proletarians, to be sure, but even more dependent upon their employer than ordinary mechanics. State universities cannot function without appropriations; hence the need of caution on the part of the faculty. But the students were not deterred. They came in much larger numbers than in the previous year.

The State of Kansas, like Massachusetts, lives on past glory. Had it not given John Brown to the cause of the slaves? Had not the rebel voice of Moses Harman sounded there? Had it not been the stronghold of free thought? Whatever its historic claim to progress, Kansas now gave no sign of it. The Church and Prohibition had evidently performed the last rites at the interment of liberalism. Lack of interest in ideas, smugness, and self-complacency characterized most cities of the State of Kansas.

The exception was Lawrence, the university seat. Here it was largely a group of advanced students who put life into an otherwise sleepy town. The most active among them was Harry Kemp. He prevailed upon the Good Government Club, a body of law-students, to invite the dangerous anarchist to address them on "Why Laws Fail." My interpretation proved a novel experience to them. Some argued and fought against my view-point with youthful arrogance. Others admitted that I had helped them to see the flaws in the scheme which they had heretofore considered perfect.

Our own meetings were attended by members of the faculty and students. My talk on "Victims of Morality" ended in a hilarious manner. In the course of the lecture I pointed out that men, no matter how loose in their own sexual habits, always insist that the women they marry must be "pure" and virtuous. During the discussion a man in the audience arose to protest. "I am forty," he announced, "and I have remained pure." He was sickly looking, quite evidently emotionally starved. "I would advise a medical examination," I replied. In an instant, the house was in an uproar. The cause of the hilarity I learned only after the meeting. Harry Kemp informed me that my virtuous opponent was a professor of botany, who was always very frank in his lectures on plant life, but extremely rigid on the subject of sex among human beings. I wished I had known that the poor man was on the faculty. I might not have been so drastic in my reply. I hated smugness, yet I was sorry to have made the Puritan professor a target for adolescent mischief.

I found California seething with discontent. The Mexican revolution and the arrest of the two McNamara brothers had aroused labour on the Pacific Coast to a high pitch. The despotic régime of Diaz and the ruthless exploitation of the Mexican people by native and American interests had been unmasked by Ricardo Flores Magón and his brother Enrique, the representatives of the Junta of the Mexican Liberal Party. Their contentions were fully supported by

Carlo de Fornaro in his book *Diaz, Tsar of Mexico*. For his disclosures Mr. Fornaro, a well-known New York artist, was arrested
for criminal libel and sentenced to prison for a year, the United States
Government thus acting as lackey for the American oil interests in
Mexico. Another volume, *Barbarous Mexico,* by John Kenneth Turner, had also severely arraigned the legalized robbery of the helpless
peons and castigated the despicable rôle America was playing in their
enslavement.

The revolution in Mexico was the expression of a people awakened
to the great economic and political wrongs in their land. The struggle
inspired large numbers of militant workers in America, among them
many anarchists and I.W.W.'s (Industrial Workers of the World),
to help their Mexican brothers across the border. Thoughtful persons on the Coast, intellectuals as well as proletarians, were imbued
with the spirit behind the Mexican revolution.

Another factor to intensify the atmosphere was the new attempt
to crush labour. Since the explosion of the *Times* building in the previous year (October 1910) a veritable man-hunt had been carried on
by the private detective agency of William J. Burns in the interests of
California employers. John J. McNamara, secretary-treasurer of
the International Association of Bridge and Structural Iron Workers,
was kidnapped and taken back to California. He was charged with
having caused the Los Angeles *Times* explosion and other acts of
dynamiting. At the same time his brother J. B. McNamara and a man
known as Ortie McManigal were also arrested.

Though denounced by the press as anarchists, the McNamara
brothers were, as a matter of fact, good Roman Catholics and members of the conservative American Federation of Labor. Perhaps they
would have been the first to resent the charge of anarchy, since they
knew nothing of our ideas and were unaware of their relation to the
struggle of the workers. Simple trade-unionists, the McNamaras did
not realize that the conflict between capital and labour is a social issue
embracing all life, and that its solution is not a mere matter of higher
wages or shorter hours; they did not know that the problem involved
the abolition of the wage system, of all monopoly and special privileges. But while the McNamaras were not anarchists, they were of the
exploited class, and therefore we were with them. We saw in their
persecution another attempt of the plutocracy to crush organized
labour. To us their case was a repetition of the conspiracy in Chicago

in 1887 and in Idaho in 1906. It was the identical policy of wealth and power everywhere — in Spain, Italy, Russia, Japan, and the United States. The McNamaras were our brothers, their cause ours. From this view-point the anarchists of the entire United States rallied to the support of the men awaiting their doom in the Los Angeles County Jail.

The intense feeling created by these events partially found an outlet on the Coast at my meetings, which were attended by great numbers. I delivered eleven lectures in Los Angeles, two in San Diego, two in Fresno, and eight in San Francisco, as well as participating in a debate. Puget Sound was equally responsive. Portland, Seattle, and Spokane gave us large audiences.

Since the Haywood, Moyer, and Pettibone trial in Boise City I had wanted to go there, but we had had no opportunity to make the trip. On this tour we were within four hundred miles, by no means a small jump. But what were four hundred miles to an old tramp like Ben and a wandering Jew like me? Nor were we deterred by the fact that we knew no one in the city who could help with meetings. My efficient manager had broken virgin soil before; he would attempt it again. When I reached Boise, twenty-four hours after Ben, I found all arrangements made for two Sunday lectures. There was a police ordinance against paid admission on the Sabbath, but the Boise people knew how to evade the law. "You simply give everyone a piece of literature equivalent to your admission charge, see?" the hall landlady had instructed Ben.

The following day we drove out to the Idaho penitentiary where Haywood, Moyer, and Pettibone had been incarcerated. Since then another star was there, the spy Harry Orchard. It seemed just retribution that he, the detectives' tool who had helped to prepare the trap for his comrades, should have been caught in it himself. He was a self-confessed desperado of eighteen murders. The State had used his testimony in its effort to hang the labour leaders and in gratitude had spared his life. It would no doubt have let him go free altogether if it had dared to face the widespread indignation. I could not help thinking of the significant similarity in the new crime the State of California was preparing by using the spy Ortie McManigal to destroy the brothers McNamara.

Harry Orchard, a stocky individual with a bull's neck, sallow complexion, and shifting eyes, was a "model" prisoner, we were told, "religious and devout." He knew what was good for him, the Judas of his class. I felt as if something loathsome were crawling near me; I could not remain in the prison to breathe the same air with him. To me the worst of human monstrosities had always been the informer and the spy.

The most interesting aspect of our tour was the absence of police interference. It was the first time in my public career that I had been left free to carry my message. I enjoyed the novel experience. and made good use of it, knowing that I should not be left in peace for long.

When I returned to New York, I found myself viciously attacked, this time not by the authorities, but by a socialist publication. I was charged with being in the employ of the Russian Tsar! This astounding revelation appeared in the London *Justice,* May 13, 1911, the official organ of the Social Democratic Party of England.

> The notorious Emma Goldman has been attacking the socialists of Milwaukee lately. She says they are cheap politicians without any revolutionary purposes—pretty much what our "impossibilists" say of us! Emma Goldman has had a remarkably free run in the United States for a good many years, and some people have wondered how it is that this female fire-brand should carry on her propaganda of violence so long and with such impunity. But it is not generally known that Emma Goldman is in the pay of the police, though the fact has leaked out recently. At one time she was employed by Mr. A. E. Olarovsky, of the Russian Secret Police in San Francisco, as an agent and a spy. It is the same, we may be sure, in nine cases out of ten, with those "prominent" anarchists who only kill people with their mouths, who are never on hand when an outrage occurs, and who manage to escape so mysteriously when their associates are arrested.

I was at first sick about this crazy charge. But then I remembered that denunciation equally scurrilous had been cast against a greater person than I, Michael Bakunin, the father of anarchism. The men who had hounded Bakunin were Friedrich Engels and Karl Marx. Since that time, when the founders of socialism had split the First International by their demagogic methods, socialists everywhere had used similar tactics. I felt flattered that I should meet with the same fate as my illustrious comrade and I considered it beneath my self-respect to reply to such calumny. Just the same, I would have given much to trace the origin of the damnable story.

It seemed preposterous for any sane person to believe me capable of such treachery. My friends in England and the United States protested vigorously. Members of labour organizations did so through their unions in the form of resolutions. In England proofs were demanded of the editor of *Justice,* but no proofs were forthcoming. At the anniversary dinner of the Francisco Ferrer Center in New York, Moses Oppenheim, an old socialist, and my friends Harry Kelly and Leonard D. Abbott paid their respects to the man responsible for the base invention. This was followed by a letter signed by a large number of men and women prominent in the world of labour, art, and letters.

> Editor of *Justice*
> London, England
>
> We note in your issue of May 13th, in an article entitled "Anarchist Agents," the statement:
>
> "It is not generally known that Emma Goldman is in the pay of the police, though the fact has leaked out recently. At one time she was employed by Mr. A. E. Olarovsky, of the Russian Secret Police in San Francisco, as an agent and a spy."
>
> We write to protest in the most emphatic manner against this outrageous slander. It passes our comprehension why you should soil your columns by printing such an absolutely unsupported charge against one of the most devoted and beloved representatives of the radical movement in America. Emma Goldman has given the best years of her life to the anarchist cause. Her integrity is above suspicion. There is not an iota of truth in the charge.

The protest was widely circulated in socialist and liberal papers, but there was no retraction from the editor of *Justice.*

My friend Rose Strunsky, who was then in England, undertook to see the man, but somehow he could nowhere be found. She submitted the matter to Mr. H. H. Hyndman, the head of the British Social Democratic Party. He was requested to compel the editor, Mr. Harry Quelch, to give proof of his accusation. Mr. Hyndman promised, but he never did so.

As a law-abiding British subject Mr. Quelch knew the libel laws of his country. It would have been an easy thing for me to sue him for malicious slander. He would have been forced to produce proof or pay damages and perhaps also go to prison. But I adhere to my anarchist views and to my refusal to invoke the law against anybody, no matter how great his villainy. Evidently Quelch had speculated on that, and I had no other way to compel him to retract. However, the protest in my behalf had one effect. It silenced him. Neither in his paper nor on the platform did he ever again mention my name.

Shortly afterwards another charge was made against me, this time by detective William J. Burns. In a newspaper interview he declared that "Emma Goldman was urging working-men to contribute to the defence of the murderers McNamara." I stated in the press that I not only urged the workers to contribute, but that I also called on them to deliver a mortal blow to "justice" that was supported by spies and a government maintained by and for detectives. It was a commentary on the London followers of Marx that an American detective should be better informed about Emma Goldman than they.

During the summer Sasha and I again went out to our retreat on the Hudson and he resumed work on his book. Fortunately, I had no writing to do and I was not handicapped by crutches any more. I could devote my time to Sasha and look after his comfort. I sought to encourage him in his work: with him I had lived through the agony of his prison years, and now the turmoil of his spirit re-echoed in my heart.

The end of the summer saw his *Prison Memoirs* completed. It was a document profoundly moving, a brilliant study of criminal psychology. I was filled with wonder to see Sasha emerge from his Calvary an artist with a rare gift of music in his words.

"Now for New York and the publishers!" I cried; "surely there will be many who will appreciate the dramatic appeal of your work, the understanding and sympathy for those you have left behind."

We hastened back to the city and I began to canvass the publishers. The more conservative houses refused even to read the manuscript the moment they learned the author's name. "Alexander Berkman, the man who shot Frick!" the representative of a large firm exclaimed; "no, we can't have him on our shelves." "It is a vital literary work," I urged; "aren't you interested in that and in his interpretation of prisons and crime?" They were looking for such a book, he said, but they could not afford to risk the name of the author.

Some publishers asked whether Alexander Berkman would be

willing to use a pseudonym. I resented the suggestion and pointed out that *Prison Memoirs* was a personal story, the product of years of suffering and pain. Could the writer be expected to hide his identity concerning something that was flesh of his flesh and blood of his blood?

I turned to some of the " advanced " publishers and they promised to read the manuscript. I waited anxiously for weeks, and when they at last requested me to come, I found them enthusiastic. " It is a remarkable work," one said, "but would Mr. Berkman leave out the anarchist part?" Another insisted on eliminating the chapters relating to homosexuality in prison. A third suggested other changes. Thus it went on for months. I clung to the hope that someone of literary and human judgment would accept the manuscript. I still believed that we could discover in America what Dostoyevsky had found in tsarist Russia — a publisher courageous enough to issue the first great American study of a " House of the Dead." In vain.

Finally we decided to publish the book ourselves. In our predicament I turned to my friend Gilbert E. Roe, a lawyer by profession, an anarchist by feeling, and one of the kindest of men it has been my good fortune to know.

Through all the years since we had first met, Gilbert and Mrs. Roe remained among my staunchest friends and most generous contributors to our work. From the initial issue of *Mother Earth* the Roes had been among the first to respond to every appeal for help. When I informed Gilbert that Sasha's manuscript had been turned down by many publishers, and that we wanted the *Mother Earth* Publishing Association to have the honour of giving the book to the American public, my good friend said simply: " All right. We will arrange an evening in our apartment and invite some people to hear you read parts of the manuscript. Then we will make an appeal for subscriptions." " Read Sasha's work?" I cried in alarm; "I'll never be able to do it. It is too vital a part of my own life. I shall be sure to break down." Gilbert scoffed at the idea of my being nervous at a small private gathering, considering that I had so often faced thousands in my public work.

When I arrived with the manuscript, the guests were already at Roe's. I felt myself growing faint and covered with a cold sweat. Gilbert took me to the dining-room and handed me a stiff drink. " To give strength to your weak knees," he teased. We returned to a darkened room, with only one light for me at the desk. I began to read. Soon the assembled people seemed to vanish, and Sasha emerged. Sasha at the Baltimore and Ohio Station, Sasha as I saw him in convict clothes in prison, and then Sasha resurrected at the railroad station in Detroit. All the agony, all the hope and despair I had shared with him, leaped up in my throat as I read.

"Whether it is the manuscript or your reading," Gilbert presently remarked, "it is a tremendous piece of work."

Five hundred dollars was pledged that evening towards the expense of publication. A few days later Gilbert took me to see Lincoln Steffens, who contributed two hundred dollars. We now had enough on hand to start setting up the book, but we were advised against putting out such a work in the spring. Besides, Sasha wanted to go over the manuscript once more. Our flat was a beehive, with people coming and going all day long. The *Mother Earth* office was not much quieter. Matters relating to the movement kept us engaged all the time. Not before the summer was Sasha able to get away to our little shack on the Hudson for the final revision of his *Prison Memoirs.*

CHAPTER XXXVIII

THE MCNAMARA DRAMA, STAGED IN THE COURTS OF LOS ANGELES, held the entire country in tense anticipation and then came to a sudden farcical end. The McNamaras confessed! Unexpectedly, to everyone's amazement, they pleaded guilty to the charges on which they were being tried. The reactionary press was jubilant; the Merchants' and Manufacturers' Association, Harrison Grey Otis, William J. Burns, and their crew of spies, whose mission it was to send these men to their death, now offered fervent thanks for the lucky turn affairs had taken. Had they not from the first proclaimed the McNamara brothers anarchists and dynamiters?

The prosecution and the informers had reason to be grateful to the circumstances that had induced the plea of guilty. It was a blow to Labour that even Detective Burns had never dreamed of being able to deliver. Alas, those responsible for the confession came not from the enemy's ranks, but from the camp of Labour itself, from the circle of "well-intentioned" friends.

It would be unfair to lay upon any one person the entire responsibility for the ludicrous end of what had begun as an epoch-making event in the history of the industrial war in the United States. The ignorance of John J. and James B. McNamara about the social significance of their case must share the blame for the irreparable blunder they had made. Had the McNamaras had revolutionary spirit and the intellectual powers of Sasha and other social rebels, there would have been a proud avowal of their acts and an intelligent analysis of the causes that had compelled them to resort to violence. In such a case there could have been neither the feeling nor the admission of guilt. But the McNamara brothers were only trade-unionists who saw in their struggle no more than a feud between their organization and the steel interests.

Yet, however unfortunate the limitations of these two victims, the timidity of their counsel and the credulity of the reformers among their friends were far more blame-worthy. Such people never seem to learn from experience. No matter how often they had seen the lion devour the lamb, they continued to cling to the hope that the nature of the beast might change. If only the lion could get to know the lamb better, they argued, or talk matters over, he would surely learn to appreciate his gentle brother and thereby grow gentle himself. It was therefore not difficult for the prosecutors of the McNamaras to say to them: "Now, gentlemen, induce the prisoners to plead guilty. Get them to confess and we give you our word of honour that their lives will be saved and there will be no further man-hunt, no more arrests, no prosecution of anybody in the labour ranks connected with their acts. Believe us, gentlemen. We may roar like lions, but we have soft hearts. We feel with the poor lambs in the Los Angeles County Jail. Get them to confess and they shall not be doomed. This is a gentlemen's agreement. Now shake, and let's all be lambs."

And those infants believed. They accepted the promise of the sly and cunning beasts. They went forth inspired by the great mission fate had placed before them to bring the lion and the lamb together. But it was not long before the taste of the tender mutton helped to whet the lion's appetite for more of it. A renewed man-hunt followed, arrests upon arrests, indictments by the score, and savage persecution of the victims caught in the dragnet.

Now J. J. and J. B. McNamara were hurled from their pedestal into the dust. They were dragged through the mire, reviled, and branded by the very supporters who had recently strewn roses in their path. The wretched apostates now beat their chests and cried: "We have been deceived, we did not know that the McNamaras were guilty, and that they had used violence. They are criminals."

The collapse of the trial disclosed the appalling hollowness of radicalism in and out of the ranks of labour, and the craven spirit of so many of those who presume to plead its cause.

A few clear minds and staunch souls remained, all too few when compared with the pack that were calling down anathema upon the two victims. These refused to be swayed by the panic which followed on the heels of the McNamara confession. Among the small minority in the United States most anarchists stood by the deserted labour leaders because they were victims of a system supported by violence and un-yielding to any other method in the industrial struggle.

The *Mother Earth* group registered its protest in our magazine and on the platform against the cheap apology of those who claimed to have been "deceived in thinking the McNamaras innocent." We held that if such excuses were sincere, then the trade-unionists and the reformers, as well as the political socialists, were fools and not competent to be teachers of the people. We pointed out that he who remains ignorant of the causes of the class conflict makes himself responsible for its existence.

Every time I lectured on the McNamara case, police and detectives were on my trail, but I did not care. In fact, I should have welcomed arrest. Prison seemed preferable to the world of cowardice and impotence. Nothing happened, however, and I went on with our work. The next job was already at hand, the Lawrence strike.

Twenty-five thousand textile workers, men, women, and children, were involved in the struggle for a fifteen-per-cent increase in their wage. For years they had toiled fifty-six hours a week for an average weekly pay of eight dollars. Out of the strength of these people the mill-owners had grown immensely rich. Poverty and misery had at last driven the Lawrence textile workers to strike. The struggle was hardly under way when the mill lords began to show their teeth. In this they had the support of the State, and even of the college authorities. The Governor of Massachusetts, himself a mill-owner, sent the militia to protect his interests and those of his mill-owning colleagues. The president of Harvard was, as one of the stockholders, equally interested in dividends from the Lawrence mills. The result of this unity between State, capitalism, and seats of learning in Massachusetts was a horde of police, detectives, soldiers, and collegiate ruffians let loose on the helpless strikers. The first victims of the reign of military terror were Anna Lapezo and John Ramo. During a skirmish the girl was shot and the young man bayoneted to death by a soldier. Instead of apprehending the perpetrators of the crime, the State and local authorities arrested among others, Joseph Ettor and Arturo Giovannitti, the two foremost strike leaders. These men were conscious rebels, backed by the Industrial Workers of the World and by the other revolutionary elements in the country. Labour in the East rallied with particular generosity to the support of the Lawrence strikers and to the defence of the two men. The gap left by the arrest of Ettor and Giovannitti was immediately filled by Bill Haywood and Elizabeth Gurley Flynn. Haywood's years of experience in the labour struggle, his determination and tact, made him a distinctive power in the Lawrence situation. On the other hand, Elizabeth's youth, charm, and eloquence easily won everybody's heart. The names of the two and their reputation gained for the strike country-wide publicity and support.

I had known and admired Elizabeth since I had first heard her, years before, at an open-air gathering. She could not have been more than fourteen years of age at the time, with a beautiful face and figure and a voice vibrant with earnestness. She made a strong impression on me. Later I used to see her in the company of her father at my lectures. She was a fascinating picture with her black hair, large blue eyes, and lovely complexion. I often found it hard to take my eyes off her, sitting in the front row at my meetings.

The splendid free-speech fight she had made in Spokane with other members of the I.W.W., and the persecution she had endured, brought Elizabeth Gurley Flynn very near to me. And when I heard she was ill, after the birth of her child, I felt great sympathy for this young rebel, one of the first American women revolutionists of proletarian background. My interest in her had served to increase my efforts in raising funds, not only for the Spokane fight, but for Elizabeth's own use during her first months of young motherhood.

Since she had returned to New York we were often thrown together, in meetings and in more intimate ways. Elizabeth was not an anarchist, but neither was she fanatical or antagonistic, as were some of her comrades who had emerged from the Socialist Labor Party. She was accepted in our circles as one of our own, and I loved her as a friend.

Bill Haywood had but recently come to live in New York. We had met almost immediately and became very friendly. Bill also was not an anarchist, but, like Elizabeth, he was free from narrow sectarianism. He frankly admitted that he felt much more at home with the anarchists, and especially with the *Mother Earth* group, than with the zealots in his own ranks.

The most notable characteristic of Bill was his extraordinary sensitiveness. This giant, outwardly so hard, would wince at a coarse word and tremble at the sight of pain. On one occasion, when he addressed our eleventh-of-November commemoration, he related to me the effect the crime of 1887 had had on him. He was but a youngster at the time, already working in the mines. "Since then," he told me, "our Chicago martyrs have been my greatest inspiration, their courage my guiding star." The apartment at 210 East Thirteenth Street became

Bill's retreat. Frequently he spent his free evenings at our place. There he could read and rest to his heart's content, or drink coffee " black as the night, strong as the revolutionary ideal, sweet as love."

At the height of the Lawrence strike I was approached by Mr. Sol Fieldman, a New York socialist, in regard to two debates on the difference in theory and tactics between socialism and anarchism. I had debated with socialists all through the United States, but never in my own city. I was glad of the opportunity, and the proposal caught Ben's fancy. Nothing but Carnegie Hall would do, he declared; he was sure we could jam it, and off he went to rent the place. But he returned with a sad face; the hall was free for one evening only. For the second date he had to be content with the Republic Theatre.

It occurred to me that the debates presented a splendid occasion to raise a substantial sum for the Lawrence strike, and Mr. Fieldman agreed. Nothing was said as to who should make the appeal, but I set my heart upon having Big Bill do it. He, in the very thick of the battle, was the most appropriate person for the purpose.

Mr. Fieldman wanted to supply the chairman from his own ranks. I made no objections, because it was of no moment to me who presided. On the day of the debate my opponent informed me that he was still without a chairman and that he had been severely censured by his socialist comrades for having proposed the debate. "Very well, we'll wire for Bill Haywood," I said; " he'll be glad to preside and he is the man to make the appeal." But Mr. Fieldman refused. He would prefer even an anarchist, he said, to Haywood. I insisted that it must be Bill for the appeal, no matter who presided. In the evening, when I came to Carnegie Hall, Fieldman was still without a chairman, nor would he consent to Bill. "All right, there will be no debate," I announced; "but I myself will tell the audience the reason for it." The categorical imperative frightened him into submission.

The audience knew that Bill came straight from the Lawrence scene. The feeling the strike had aroused now broke out in an ovation for Bill. His simple appeal for the heroic men and women of Lawrence moved everybody to response. Within a few minutes the platform was strewn with money, and Mr. Fieldman was on all fours gathering in the harvest of Bill's appeal. The amount contributed was five hundred and forty-two dollars, a very large sum from an audience of working people who had already paid admission to the debate.

Then the bull-fight began, but, alas, the bull turned out to be a very tame animal. Mr. Fieldman knew his catechism. He recited his Marxist rosary with the fluency and precision which comes from practice, but not one original or independent thought did he advance. In roseate colours he painted the marvellous achievements of social democracy in Germany, dwelling on its party strength of four million votes and its even greater number of adherents in trade-union ranks, consisting of eight millions. "Think of what those twelve million socialists can do," he cried triumphantly; "stop wars, take possession of the means of production and distribution. Not by violence, but by their political power! As to the State, did not Engels say that it will die of itself?" It was a grand socialist speech, ably delivered. But it was no debate.

The historic data and the current facts I advanced to prove the deterioration of socialism in Germany, the betrayal on the part of most socialists who had achieved power, the tendency in their ranks everywhere towards petty reforms — all that Mr. Fieldman conveniently ignored. Each time he rose to reply, he repeated verbatim what he had said in his opening round.

Our debate on political versus direct action, at the Republic Theatre, was more spirited. Many I.W.W. boys were present and gave the proceedings heightened colour. The Lawrence strike served me as an illuminating example of direct action. My opponent did not feel quite so sure of himself as when he had presented the socialist theory with such finality. He was especially nonplussed by the questions hurled at him from the gallery by an I.W.W. boy: "How would political action serve the mass of migratory workers, who are never long enough in one place to be able to register for voting, or the millions of boys and girls under age and without right to the ballot? Is not direct mass action their only medium, and the most effective to gain economic redress? The textile workers in Lawrence, for instance; should they have waited until they had voted their socialist comrades into the Massachusetts legislature?"

My opponent sweated trying to wriggle out of a definite answer. When he did finally meet the issue, it was to say that the socialists do believe in strikes, but that when they should gain the majority and come into political power, there would be no further need of such methods. This was too much for the overall brigade. They howled with laughter, stamped their feet, and intoned I.W.W. songs.

Our activities did not leave us much leisure for sociability or intellectual enjoyment. The return to America of Paul Orleneff with a new company came as a great surprise and brought joy to all of us who had known the man from his first visit. Paul looked older; his face was more lined, and his eyes had more *Weltschmerz* in them. But he remained the same naïve, unworldly creature, living only in the realm of his art.

The people who could help him to some success were the men of the Yiddish press, particularly Abe Cahan and the other Jewish writers. Orleneff would not listen to my suggestion that he seek them out. It was not resentment, he said, at the unkind treatment during the latter part of his visit in 1905. "You see, Miss Emma," he explained, "for almost a year I have been living Ibsen's Brand. You know what his motto is: 'No compromise; all or nothing.' Can you imagine Brand going about knocking at the door of the editors? If I should do what Brand would scorn to do, I'd ruin my conception of the character."

Before long, Orleneff left America. He could not acclimatize himself in this country or accept its attitude to art. The realization also that the tie which had bound him to Alla Nazimova was definitely broken excluded his continued stay. They were separated now by the gap which must always exist between a truly creative artist and one interested mainly in material success.

In Chicago I had the opportunity of meeting the famous Russian revolutionary Vladimir Bourtzeff. I was greatly interested in his recital of the arduous mission that had come to him of unmasking Azeff as a police spy. Azeff was undoubtedly a most exceptional phenomenon in revolutionary annals. Not that there had not been before, or since, traitors in revolutionary ranks. But Azeff was no ordinary spy, and even today the psychology of the man remains an unsolved enigma. For years he had not only been a member of the Fighting Organization of the Socialist-Revolutionary Party of Russia, but also the all-powerful head of that terrorist body. He had planned and had successfully executed numerous acts against the highest dignitaries of the Tsarist Government, and he enjoyed the absolute confidence of all his co-workers. When Bourtzeff charged Azeff, the ultra-terrorist, with being an agent of the Russian Secret Service, even the nearest friends of the accuser thought him demented. The mere suggestion of such a possibility was considered treason to the revolution, for Azeff personified the very spirit of the Russian revolutionary movement. Bourtzeff, however, was a man of dogged tenacity who possessed an unerring intuition in such matters. He had exposed a number of spies previously, and his sources of information had always proved to be entirely reliable. Yet even he underwent a long inner struggle before he could bring himself to believe in the guilt of the trusted head of the Fighting Organization. The data Bourtzeff secured were incontrovertible and damned Azeff as a man who had during a period of twenty years managed to dupe the Russian Secret Service and the revolutionists at the same time. Bourtzeff succeeded in proving Azeff a traitor to both sides, and both resolved to punish Azeff by death for his monumental deceit. Yet even at the eleventh hour Azeff tricked them, by escaping without leaving a trace.

Except for the good-fellowship of my comrades in Denver, the city had always been a disappointment to me. There even Ben's energy had failed to arouse interest in our work. This time the number of my friends was augmented by Lillian Olf, Lena and Frank Monroe, John Spiss, May Courtney, and other American anarchists, as well as by new comrades among the Yiddish element. But the public at large remained away from our meetings. Then it happened that the Denver *Post* asked me to write a series of articles on the growing social unrest. At the same time several newspaper women I knew offered to arrange a special lecture at the Brown Palace Hotel. The subject they chose was Rostand's *Chantecler*.

I had long since become convinced that the modern drama is a fruitful disseminator of new ideas. My first experience in that regard was in 1897, when I had talked to a group of miners on George Bernard Shaw's plays. It was during their lunch-hour, and we were four hundred feet below the ground. My audience clustered around me, their black faces lit up now and then by the gleam of their lamps. Their eyes, deep-sunken, looked dull at first, but as I continued speaking, they began glowing with understanding of the social significance of Shaw's works. My well-dressed audience in the luxurious ballroom of the Brown Palace Hotel reacted in the same manner as the miners had. They, too, saw themselves reflected in the dramatic mirror. Several teachers of the university and of the high school urged me to deliver a drama course. Among them one woman particularly attracted my attention, Miss Ellen A. Kennan, who had a very scholarly mind. She offered to maintain the class until I returned. Thus my visit to Denver for five lectures lengthened into fourteen and resulted also in five articles for the *Post*.

Among the interesting features of my stay in the city was the opening performance of *Chantecler,* with Maud Adams in the title rôle, which I attended by request to review the play in the press. I had liked Miss Adams in her demure parts, but in stature and voice she impressed me as miscast in the rôle of Chanticler.

San Diego, California, had always enjoyed considerable freedom of speech. Anarchists, socialists, I.W.W. men, as well as religious sects, had been in the habit of speaking out of doors to large crowds. Then the city fathers of San Diego passed an ordinance doing away with the old custom. The anarchists and I.W.W.'s initiated a free-speech fight, with the result that eighty-four men and women were thrown into jail. Among them was E. E. Kirk, who had defended me in San Francisco in 1909; Mrs. Laura Emerson, a well-known woman rebel; and Jack Whyte, one of the most intelligent I.W.W. boys in California.

When I arrived with Ben in Los Angeles in April, San Diego was in the grip of a veritable civil war. The patriots, know as Vigilantes, had converted the city into a battle-field. They beat, clubbed, and killed men and women who still believed in their constitutional rights. Hundreds of them had come to San Diego from every part of the United States to participate in the campaign. They travelled in box cars, on the bumpers, on the roofs of trains, every moment in danger of their lives, yet sustained by the holy quest for freedom of speech, for which their comrades were already filling the jails.

The Vigilantes raided the I.W.W. headquarters, broke up the furniture, and arrested a large number of men found there. They were taken out to Sorrento to a spot where a flag-pole had been erected. There the I.W.W.'s were forced to kneel, kiss the flag, and sing the national anthem. As an incentive to quicker action one of the Vigilantes would slap them on the back, which was the signal for a general beating. After these proceedings the men were loaded into automobiles and sent to San Onofre, near the county line, placed in a cattle-pen with armed guards over them, and kept without food or drink for eighteen hours. The following morning they were taken out in groups of five and compelled to run the gauntlet. As they passed between the double line of Vigilantes, they were belaboured with clubs and blackjacks. Then the flag-kissing episode was repeated, after which they were told to "hike" up the track and never come back. They reached Los Angeles after a tramp of several days, sore, hungry, penniless, and in deplorable physical condition.

In this struggle, in which the local police were on the side of the Vigilantes, several I.W.W. men lost their lives. The most brutal murder was that of Joseph Mikolasek, who died on May 7. He was one of the many rebels who had attempted to fill the gap caused by the arrest of their speakers. When he ascended the platform, he was assaulted by the police. With difficulty he dragged himself to the socialist headquarters and thence home. He was followed by detectives, who attacked him in his house. One officer fired and severely wounded him. In self-defence Mikolasek had picked up an ax, but his body was riddled with bullets before he had a chance to lift it against his assailants.

On every tour to the Coast I had lectured in San Diego. This time we were also planning meetings there after the close of our Los Angeles engagements. Reports from San Diego and the arrival of scores of wounded Vigilante victims decided us to go at once. Especially after the killing of Mikolasek we felt it imperative to take up the free-speech fight waged there. First, however, it was necessary to organize relief for the destitute boys who had escaped their tormentors and had reached us alive. With the help of a group of women we organized a feeding-station at the I.W.W. headquarters. We raised funds at my meetings and collected clothing and food-stuffs from sympathetic store-keepers.

San Diego was not content with the murder of Mikolasek; it would not permit him even to be buried in the city. We therefore had his body shipped to Los Angeles, and prepared a public demonstration in his honour. Joseph Mikolasek had been obscure and unknown in life, but he grew to country-wide stature in his death. Even the police of the city were impressed by the size, dignity, and grief of the masses that followed his remains to the crematorium.

Some comrades in San Diego had undertaken to arrange a meeting, and I chose a subject which seemed to express the situation best — Henrik Ibsen's *An Enemy of the People.*

On our arrival we found a dense crowd at the station. It did not occur to me that the reception was intended for us; I thought that some State official was being expected. We were to be met by our friends Mr. and Mrs. E. E. Kirk, but they were nowhere to be seen, and Ben suggested that we go to the U. S. Grant Hotel. We passed unobserved and got into the hotel autobus. It was hot and stuffy inside and we climbed up on top. We had barely taken our seats when someone shouted: "Here she is, here's the Goldman woman!" At once the cry was taken up by the crowd. Fashionably dressed women stood up in their cars screaming: "We want that anarchist murderess!" In an instant there was a rush for the autobus, hands reaching up to pull me down. With unusual presence of mind, the chauffeur started the car at full speed, scattering the crowd in all directions.

At the hotel we met with no objections. We registered and were shown to our rooms. Everything seemed normal. Mr. and Mrs. Kirk called to see us, and we quietly discussed final arrangements for our meeting. In the afternoon the head clerk came to announce that the Vigilantes had insisted on looking over the hotel register to secure the number of our rooms; he would therefore have to transfer us to another part of the house. We were taken to the top floor and assigned to a large suite. Later on, Mr. Holmes, the hotel manager, paid us a visit. We were perfectly safe under his roof, he assured us, but he could not permit us to go down for our meals or leave our rooms. He would have to keep us locked in. I protested that the U. S. Grant Hotel was not a prison. He replied that he could not keep us incarcerated against our will, but that, as long as we remained the guests of the house, we should have to submit to his arrangement for our safety. "The Vigilantes are in an ugly mood," he warned us; "they are determined not to let you speak and to drive you both out of town." He urged us to leave of our own account and volunteered to escort us. He was a kindly man and we appreciated his offer, but we had to refuse it.

Mr. Holmes had barely left when I was called on the telephone. The speaker said that his name was Edwards, that he was at the head of the local Conservatory of Music, and that he had just read in the papers that our hall-keeper had backed out. He offered us the recital hall of the conservatory. "San Diego still seems to have some brave men," I said to the mysterious person at the other end of the telephone, and I invited him to come to see me to talk over his plan. Before long a fine-looking man of about twenty-seven called. In the course of our conversation I pointed out to him that I might cause him trouble by speaking in his place. He replied that he did not mind; he was an anarchist in art and he believed in free speech. If I were willing to take a chance, so was he. We decided to await developments.

Towards evening a bedlam of auto horns and whistles filled the street. "The Vigilantes!" Ben cried. There was a knock at the door, and Mr. Holmes came in, accompanied by two other men. I was wanted downstairs by the city authorities, they informed me. Ben sensed danger and insisted that I ask them to send the visitors up. It seemed timid to me. It was early evening and we were in the principal hotel of the city. What could happen to us? I went with Mr. Holmes, Ben accompanying us. Downstairs we were ushered into a room where we found seven men standing in a semicircle. We were asked to sit down and wait for the Chief of Police, who arrived before long. "Please come with me," he addressed me; "the Mayor and other officials are awaiting you next door." We got up to follow, but, turning to Ben, the Chief said: "You are not wanted, doctor. Better wait here."

I entered a room filled with men. The window-blinds were partly drawn, but the large electric street light in front disclosed an agitated mass below. The Mayor approached me. "You hear that mob," he said, indicating the street; "they mean business. They want to get you and Reitman out of the hotel, even if they have to take you by force. We cannot guarantee anything. If you consent to leave, we will give you protection and get you safely out of town."

"That's very nice of you," I replied, "but why don't you disperse the crowd? Why don't you use the same measures against these people that you have against the free-speech fighters? Your ordinance makes it a crime to gather in the business districts. Hundreds of I.W.W.'s, anarchists, socialists, and trade-union men have been clubbed and arrested, and some even killed, for this offence. Yet you allow the Vigilante mob to congregate in the busiest part of the town and obstruct traffic. All you have to do is to disperse these law-breakers."

"We can't do it," he said abruptly; "these people are in a dangerous mood, and your presence makes things worse."

"Very well, then, let me speak to the crowd," I suggested. "I could do it from a window here. I have faced infuriated men before and I have always been able to pacify them."

The Mayor refused.

"I have never accepted protection from the police," I then said, "and I do not intend to do so now. I charge all of you men here with being in league with the Vigilantes."

Thereupon the officials declared that matters would have to take their course, and that I should have only myself to blame if anything happened.

The interview at an end, I went to call Ben. The room I had left him in was locked. I became alarmed and pounded on the door. There was no answer. The noise I made brought a hotel clerk. He unlocked the door, but no one was there. I ran back to the other room and met the Chief, who was just coming out.

"Where is Reitman?" I demanded. "What have you done with him? If any harm comes to him, you will pay for it if I have to do it with my own hands."

"How should I know?" he replied gruffly.

Mr. Holmes was not in his office, and no one would tell me what had become of Ben Reitman. In consternation I returned to my room. Ben did not appear. In dismay I paced the floor, unable to decide what steps to take or whom to approach to help me find Ben. I could not call any person I knew in the city without endangering his safety, least of all Mr. Kirk; he was already under indictment in connexion with the free-speech fight. It had been brave of him and his wife to meet us; it was sure to aggravate his situation. The circumstance that the Kirks did not return as they had promised proved that they were being kept away.

I felt helpless. Time dragged on, and at midnight I dozed off from sheer fatigue. I dreamed of Ben, bound and gagged, his hands groping for me. I struggled to reach him and woke up with a scream, bathed in sweat. There were voices and loud knocking at my door. When I opened, the house detective and another man stepped in. Reitman was safe, they told me. I looked at them in a daze, hardly grasping their meaning. Ben had been taken out by the Vigilantes, they explained, but no harm had come to him. They had only put him on a train for Los Angeles. I did not believe the detective, but the other man looked honest. He reiterated that he had been given absolute assurance that Reitman was safe.

Mr. Holmes came in. He corroborated the man and begged me to consent to leave. There was no object in my remaining any longer in town, he urged. I would not be allowed to lecture and I was only endangering his own position. He hoped I would not take undue advantage because I was a woman. If I remained, the Vigilantes would drive me out of town anyhow.

Mr. Holmes seemed genuinely concerned. I knew there was no chance of holding a meeting. Now that Ben was safe, there was no sense in harassing Mr. Holmes any further. I consented to leave, planning to take the Owl, the 2:45 A.M. train, for Los Angeles. I called for a taxi and drove to the station. The town was asleep, the streets deserted.

I had just purchased my ticket and was walking towards the Pullman car when I caught the sound of approaching autos — the fearful sound I had first heard at the station and later at the hotel. The Vigilantes, of course.

"Hurry, hurry!" someone cried; "get in quick!"

Before I had time to make another step, I was picked up, carried to the train, and literally thrown into the compartment. The blinds were pulled down and I was locked in. The Vigilantes had arrived and were rushing up and down the platform, shouting and trying to board the train. The crew was on guard, refusing to let them on. There was mad yelling and cursing — hideous and terrifying moments till at last the train pulled out.

We stopped at innumerable stations. Each time I peered out eagerly in the hope that Ben might be waiting to join me. But there was no sign of him. When I reached my apartment in Los Angeles, he was not there. The U. S. Grant Hotel men had lied in order to get me out of town!

"He's dead! He's dead!" I cried in anguish. "They've killed my boy!"

In vain I strove to drive the terrible thought away. I called up the Los Angeles *Herald* and the San Francisco *Bulletin* to inform them about Ben's disappearance. Both papers were unequivocal in their condemnation of the Vigilante reign of terror. The guiding spirit of the *Bulletin* was Mr. Fremont Older, perhaps the only man on a capitalist paper brave enough to plead labour's cause. He had made a valiant fight for the McNamaras. Mr. Older's enlightened humanity had created on the Coast a new attitude towards the social offender. Since the San Diego fight he had kept up a fearless attack on the Vigilantes. Mr. Older and the editor of the *Herald* promised to do their utmost to unearth Ben.

At ten o'clock I was called on the long-distance phone. A strange voice informed me that Dr. Reitman was boarding the train for Los Angeles and that he would arrive in the late afternoon. "His friends should bring a stretcher to the station." "Is he alive?" I shouted into the receiver. "Are you telling the truth? Is he alive?" I listened breathlessly, but there was no response.

The hours dragged on as if the day would never pass. The wait at the station was more excruciating still. At last the train pulled in. Ben lay in a rear car, all huddled up. He was in blue overalls, his face deathly pale, a terrified look in his eyes. His hat was gone, and his hair was sticky with tar. At the sight of me he cried: "Oh, Mommy, I'm with you at last! Take me away, take me home!"

The newspaper men besieged him with questions, but he was too exhausted to speak. I begged them to leave him alone and to call later at my apartment.

While helping him to undress, I was horrified to see that his body was a mass of bruises covered with blotches of tar. The letters I.W.W. were burned into his flesh. Ben could not speak; only his eyes tried to convey what he had passed through. After partaking of some nourishment and sleeping several hours, he regained a little strength. In the presence of a number of friends and reporters he told us what had happened to him.

"When Emma and the hotel manager left the office to go into another room," Ben related, "I remained alone with seven men. As soon as the door was closed, they drew out revolvers. 'If you utter a sound or make a move, we'll kill you,' they threatened. Then they gathered around me. One man grabbed my right arm, another the left; a third took hold of the front of my coat, another of the back, and I was led out into the corridor, down the elevator to the ground floor of the hotel, and out into the street past a uniformed policeman, and then thrown into an automobile. When the mob saw me, they set up a howl. The auto went slowly down the main street and was joined by another one containing several persons who looked like business men. This was about half past ten in the evening. The twenty-mile ride was frightful. As soon as we got out of town, they began kicking and beating me. They took turns at pulling my long hair and they stuck their fingers into my eyes and nose. 'We could tear your guts out,' they said, 'but we promised the Chief of Police not to kill you. We are responsible men, property-owners, and the police are on our side.' When we reached the county line, the auto stopped at a deserted spot. The men formed a ring and told me to undress. They tore my clothes off. They knocked me down, and when I lay naked on the ground, they kicked and beat me until I was almost insensible. With a lighted cigar they burned the letters I.W.W. on my buttocks; then they poured a can of tar over my head and, in the absence of feathers, rubbed sage-brush on my body. One of them attempted to push a cane into my rectum. Another twisted my testicles. They forced me to kiss the flag and sing *The Star Spangled Banner*. When they tired of the fun, they gave me my underwear for fear we should meet any women. They also gave me back my vest, in order that I might carry my money, railroad ticket, and watch. The rest of my clothes they kept. I was ordered to make a speech, and then they commanded me to run the gauntlet. The Vigilantes lined up, and as I ran past them, each one gave me a blow or a kick. Then they let me go."

Ben's case was but one out of many since the struggle in San Diego had begun, but it helped to focus greater attention on the scene of savagery. A number of labour and radical journalists went to that city to gather material at first hand. The Governor of California appointed Colonel H. Weinstock as special commissioner to investigate the situation. Guarded and cautious as his subsequent report was, it yet substantiated every charge made by the victims of Vigilante rule. It aroused indignation even among the conservative elements of the country.

In Los Angeles the tide of sympathy rose very high and we drew unusually large crowds. On the evening of our protest meeting we had to address our audience in two halls. We could have filled several more if we had had them and enough speakers to go round.

San Francisco, fruitful for years, turned out an enormous crowd this time. Our comrades were spared the labour and expense of advertising; the Vigilantes had done that for us. Their action inspired the San Francisco city officials to give us a glad welcome. The Mayor, the Chief of Police, and hordes of detectives came to meet us at the station, though not to interfere. Our halls, larger than in Los Angeles, yet proved not big enough to hold the masses who came to the lectures, while the rush on our literature floored even Ben, who was seldom content with sales.

The climax was reached with our meeting in the Trade Council Hall. Our friend Anton Johannsen, a well-known labour man, presided. He urged a boycott against the approaching fair in San Diego, "until its citizens are cured of their rabies." Ben recounted the details of the Vigilante attack upon him. I gave a brief report of my experience and then delivered the treasonable lecture, "The Enemy of the People."

Before we left for Portland, we were able to turn over a substantial fund to the San Diego free-speech fight, send money for the Ettor-

Giovannitti defence, and also free *Mother Earth* for a while from a considerable debt.

Mainly responsible for the madness of San Diego were two newspapers. They started the cry of "Anarchist and I.W.W. peril!" The inhabitants were kept in constant fear of dynamite and bombs, which were said to have been smuggled in on barges to blow up the town. The evil spirit of the Vigilante activities was a certain reporter on one of these newspapers. Such fame and glory as his must needs arouse envy in the hearts of other capitalist sheets. A Seattle newspaper set to work to emulate its San Diego colleagues. Long before our arrival it began a campaign calling on the good American patriots to protect the flag and save Seattle from anarchy. Some senile Spanish War veterans suddenly discovered their lost manhood and offered to do their duty. "Five hundred brave soldiers will meet Emma Goldman at the station," the newspaper announced, "and drive her back."

The story, whether true or invented, put everybody in a panic. Our friends in Portland begged us not to proceed to Seattle. Our comrades in Seattle, anxious for our safety, offered to call off the meetings. But I insisted on going through with our program.

Arriving in Seattle, we learned that Mayor Cotteril was a staunch single-taxer. He announced that he would not interfere with free speech, and that he would send the police to protect our meetings. The courage of the tottering veterans evidently caved in at the last moment; they did not appear to give us the promised reception, but the police were on hand. They crowded the hall and stationed themselves on the roofs. They even searched the people who came to my lectures for weapons. The lurid articles in the *Times* and the array of blue-coats naturally did much to intimidate a great many people. I had to request the Mayor to be less solicitous about our safety and call off our protectors. He did, whereupon the audiences took heart to attend my meetings.

On the Sunday of my first lecture a sealed note was left at my hotel for me. The anonymous writer warned me of a plot against my life : I was going to be shot when about to enter the hall, he assured me. Somehow I could give no credence to the story. Not wishing to cause my comrades any anxiety, however, I did not mention the matter to my friend C. V. Cook, who came to escort me to the hall. I told him that I preferred to go alone.

I was never more calm than as I walked leisurely from the hotel to the meeting-place. When within half a block of it I instinctively raised to my face the large bag I always carried. I got safely into the hall and walked towards the platform still holding the bag in front of my face. All through the lecture the thought persisted in my brain: "If I could only protect my face!" In the evening I repeated the same performance, holding my bag to my face all the way to the hall. The meetings went off well, without any sign of the plotters.

For days after, I tried to find some plausible explanation for my silly action with the bag. Why had I been more concerned about my face than about my chest or any other part of my body? Surely no man would think of his face under such circumstances. Yet I, in the presence of probable death, had been afraid to have my face disfigured! It was a shock to discover in myself such ordinary female vanity.

A CATALOG OF SELECTED
DOVER BOOKS
IN ALL FIELDS OF INTEREST

A CATALOG OF SELECTED
DOVER BOOKS
IN ALL FIELDS OF INTEREST

DRAWINGS OF REMBRANDT, edited by Seymour Slive. Updated Lippmann, Hofstede de Groot edition, with definitive scholarly apparatus. All portraits, biblical sketches, landscapes, nudes. Oriental figures, classical studies, together with selection of work by followers. 550 illustrations. Total of 630pp. 9⅛ × 12¼.
21485-0, 21486-9 Pa., Two-vol. set $29.90

GHOST AND HORROR STORIES OF AMBROSE BIERCE, Ambrose Bierce. 24 tales vividly imagined, strangely prophetic, and decades ahead of their time in technical skill: "The Damned Thing," "An Inhabitant of Carcosa," "The Eyes of the Panther," "Moxon's Master," and 20 more. 199pp. 5⅜ × 8½. 20767-6 Pa. $4.95

ETHICAL WRITINGS OF MAIMONIDES, Maimonides. Most significant ethical works of great medieval sage, newly translated for utmost precision, readability. Laws Concerning Character Traits, Eight Chapters, more. 192pp. 5⅜ × 8½.
24522-5 Pa. $5.95

THE EXPLORATION OF THE COLORADO RIVER AND ITS CANYONS, J. W. Powell. Full text of Powell's 1,000-mile expedition down the fabled Colorado in 1869. Superb account of terrain, geology, vegetation, Indians, famine, mutiny, treacherous rapids, mighty canyons, during exploration of last unknown part of continental U.S. 400pp. 5⅜ × 8½. 20094-9 Pa. $7.95

HISTORY OF PHILOSOPHY, Julián Marías. Clearest one-volume history on the market. Every major philosopher and dozens of others, to Existentialism and later. 505pp. 5⅜ × 8½. 21739-6 Pa. $9.95

ALL ABOUT LIGHTNING, Martin A. Uman. Highly readable nontechnical survey of nature and causes of lightning, thunderstorms, ball lightning, St. Elmo's Fire, much more. Illustrated. 192pp. 5⅜ × 8½. 25237-X Pa. $5.95

SAILING ALONE AROUND THE WORLD, Captain Joshua Slocum. First man to sail around the world, alone, in small boat. One of great feats of seamanship told in delightful manner. 67 illustrations. 294pp. 5⅜ × 8½. 20326-3 Pa. $4.95

LETTERS AND NOTES ON THE MANNERS, CUSTOMS AND CONDITIONS OF THE NORTH AMERICAN INDIANS, George Catlin. Classic account of life among Plains Indians: ceremonies, hunt, warfare, etc. 312 plates. 572pp. of text. 6⅛ × 9¼. 22118-0, 22119-9, Pa., Two-vol. set $17.90

THE SECRET LIFE OF SALVADOR DALÍ, Salvador Dalí. Outrageous but fascinating autobiography through Dalí's thirties with scores of drawings and sketches and 80 photographs. A must for lovers of 20th-century art. 432pp. 6½ × 9¼. (Available in U.S. only) 27454-3 Pa. $9.95

CATALOG OF DOVER BOOKS

THE BOOK OF BEASTS: Being a Translation from a Latin Bestiary of the Twelfth Century, T. H. White. Wonderful catalog of real and fanciful beasts: manticore, griffin, phoenix, amphivius, jaculus, many more. White's witty erudite commentary on scientific, historical aspects enhances fascinating glimpse of medieval mind. Illustrated. 296pp. 5⅜ × 8¼. (Available in U.S. only) 24609-4 Pa. $7.95

FRANK LLOYD WRIGHT: Architecture and Nature with 160 Illustrations, Donald Hoffmann. Profusely illustrated study of influence of nature—especially prairie—on Wright's designs for Fallingwater, Robie House, Guggenheim Museum, other masterpieces. 96pp. 9¼ × 10¾. 25098-9 Pa. $8.95

FRANK LLOYD WRIGHT'S FALLINGWATER, Donald Hoffmann. Wright's famous waterfall house: planning and construction of organic idea. History of site, owners, Wright's personal involvement. Photographs of various stages of building. Preface by Edgar Kaufmann, Jr. 100 illustrations. 112pp. 9¼ × 10. 23671-4 Pa. $8.95

YEARS WITH FRANK LLOYD WRIGHT: Apprentice to Genius, Edgar Tafel. Insightful memoir by a former apprentice presents a revealing portrait of Wright the man, the inspired teacher, the greatest American architect. 372 black-and-white illustrations. Preface. Index. vi + 228pp. 8¼ × 11. 24801-1 Pa. $10.95

THE STORY OF KING ARTHUR AND HIS KNIGHTS, Howard Pyle. Enchanting version of King Arthur fable has delighted generations with imaginative narratives of exciting adventures and unforgettable illustrations by the author. 41 illustrations. xviii + 313pp. 6⅛ × 9¼. 21445-1 Pa. $6.95

THE GODS OF THE EGYPTIANS, E. A. Wallis Budge. Thorough coverage of numerous gods of ancient Egypt by foremost Egyptologist. Information on evolution of cults, rites and gods; the cult of Osiris; the Book of the Dead and its rites; the sacred animals and birds; Heaven and Hell; and more. 956pp. 6⅛ × 9¼. 22055-9, 22056-7 Pa., Two-vol. set $21.90

A THEOLOGICO-POLITICAL TREATISE, Benedict Spinoza. Also contains unfinished *Political Treatise*. Great classic on religious liberty, theory of government on common consent. R. Elwes translation. Total of 421pp. 5⅜ × 8½. 20249-6 Pa. $7.95

INCIDENTS OF TRAVEL IN CENTRAL AMERICA, CHIAPAS, AND YUCATAN, John L. Stephens. Almost single-handed discovery of Maya culture; exploration of ruined cities, monuments, temples; customs of Indians. 115 drawings. 892pp. 5⅜ × 8½. 22404-X, 22405-8 Pa., Two-vol. set $17.90

LOS CAPRICHOS, Francisco Goya. 80 plates of wild, grotesque monsters and caricatures. Prado manuscript included. 183pp. 6⅝ × 9⅝. 22384-1 Pa. $6.95

AUTOBIOGRAPHY: The Story of My Experiments with Truth, Mohandas K. Gandhi. Not hagiography, but Gandhi in his own words. Boyhood, legal studies, purification, the growth of the Satyagraha (nonviolent protest) movement. Critical, inspiring work of the man who freed India. 480pp. 5⅜ × 8½. (Available in U.S. only) 24593-4 Pa. $6.95

ILLUSTRATED DICTIONARY OF HISTORIC ARCHITECTURE, edited by Cyril M. Harris. Extraordinary compendium of clear, concise definitions for over 5,000 important architectural terms complemented by over 2,000 line drawings. Covers full spectrum of architecture from ancient ruins to 20th-century Modernism. Preface. 592pp. 7½ × 9⅜. 24444-X Pa. $15.95

THE NIGHT BEFORE CHRISTMAS, Clement Moore. Full text, and woodcuts from original 1848 book. Also critical, historical material. 19 illustrations. 40pp. 4⅝ × 6. 22797-9 Pa. $2.50

THE LESSON OF JAPANESE ARCHITECTURE: 165 Photographs, Jiro Harada. Memorable gallery of 165 photographs taken in the 1930's of exquisite Japanese homes of the well-to-do and historic buildings. 13 line diagrams. 192pp. 8⅜ × 11¼. 24778-3 Pa. $10.95

THE AUTOBIOGRAPHY OF CHARLES DARWIN AND SELECTED LETTERS, edited by Francis Darwin. The fascinating life of eccentric genius composed of an intimate memoir by Darwin (intended for his children); commentary by his son, Francis; hundreds of fragments from notebooks, journals, papers; and letters to and from Lyell, Hooker, Huxley, Wallace and Henslow. xi + 365pp. 5⅜ × 8. 20479-0 Pa. $6.95

WONDERS OF THE SKY: Observing Rainbows, Comets, Eclipses, the Stars and Other Phenomena, Fred Schaaf. Charming, easy-to-read poetic guide to all manner of celestial events visible to the naked eye. Mock suns, glories, Belt of Venus, more. Illustrated. 299pp. 5¼ × 8¼. 24402-4 Pa. $7.95

BURNHAM'S CELESTIAL HANDBOOK, Robert Burnham, Jr. Thorough guide to the stars beyond our solar system. Exhaustive treatment. Alphabetical by constellation: Andromeda to Cetus in Vol. 1; Chamaeleon to Orion in Vol. 2; and Pavo to Vulpecula in Vol. 3. Hundreds of illustrations. Index in Vol. 3. 2,000pp. 6⅛ × 9¼. 23567-X, 23568-8, 23673-0 Pa., Three-vol. set $41.85

STAR NAMES: Their Lore and Meaning, Richard Hinckley Allen. Fascinating history of names various cultures have given to constellations and literary and folkloristic uses that have been made of stars. Indexes to subjects. Arabic and Greek names. Biblical references. Bibliography. 563pp. 5⅜ × 8½. 21079-0 Pa. $8.95

THIRTY YEARS THAT SHOOK PHYSICS: The Story of Quantum Theory, George Gamow. Lucid, accessible introduction to influential theory of energy and matter. Careful explanations of Dirac's anti-particles, Bohr's model of the atom, much more. 12 plates. Numerous drawings. 240pp. 5⅜ × 8½. 24895-X Pa. $5.95

CHINESE DOMESTIC FURNITURE IN PHOTOGRAPHS AND MEASURED DRAWINGS, Gustav Ecke. A rare volume, now affordably priced for antique collectors, furniture buffs and art historians. Detailed review of styles ranging from early Shang to late Ming. Unabridged republication. 161 black-and-white drawings, photos. Total of 224pp. 8⅜ × 11¼. (Available in U.S. only) 25171-3 Pa. $13.95

VINCENT VAN GOGH: A Biography, Julius Meier-Graefe. Dynamic, penetrating study of artist's life, relationship with brother, Theo, painting techniques, travels, more. Readable, engrossing. 160pp. 5⅜ × 8½. (Available in U.S. only) 25253-1 Pa. $4.95

HOW TO WRITE, Gertrude Stein. Gertrude Stein claimed anyone could understand her unconventional writing—here are clues to help. Fascinating improvisations, language experiments, explanations illuminate Stein's craft and the art of writing. Total of 414pp. 4⅝ × 6⅜.   23144-5 Pa. $6.95

ADVENTURES AT SEA IN THE GREAT AGE OF SAIL: Five Firsthand Narratives, edited by Elliot Snow. Rare true accounts of exploration, whaling, shipwreck, fierce natives, trade, shipboard life, more. 33 illustrations. Introduction. 353pp. 5⅜ × 8½.   25177-2 Pa. $8.95

THE HERBAL OR GENERAL HISTORY OF PLANTS, John Gerard. Classic descriptions of about 2,850 plants—with over 2,700 illustrations—includes Latin and English names, physical descriptions, varieties, time and place of growth, more. 2,706 illustrations. xlv + 1,678pp. 8½ × 12¼.   23147-X Cloth. $75.00

DOROTHY AND THE WIZARD IN OZ, L. Frank Baum. Dorothy and the Wizard visit the center of the Earth, where people are vegetables, glass houses grow and Oz characters reappear. Classic sequel to *Wizard of Oz*. 256pp. 5⅜ × 8.
24714-7 Pa. $5.95

SONGS OF EXPERIENCE: Facsimile Reproduction with 26 Plates in Full Color, William Blake. This facsimile of Blake's original "Illuminated Book" reproduces 26 full-color plates from a rare 1826 edition. Includes "The Tyger," "London," "Holy Thursday," and other immortal poems. 26 color plates. Printed text of poems. 48pp. 5¼ × 7.   24636-1 Pa. $3.95

SONGS OF INNOCENCE, William Blake. The first and most popular of Blake's famous "Illuminated Books," in a facsimile edition reproducing all 31 brightly colored plates. Additional printed text of each poem. 64pp. 5¼ × 7.
22764-2 Pa. $3.95

PRECIOUS STONES, Max Bauer. Classic, thorough study of diamonds, rubies, emeralds, garnets, etc.: physical character, occurrence, properties, use, similar topics. 20 plates, 8 in color. 94 figures. 659pp. 6⅛ × 9¼.
21910-0, 21911-9 Pa., Two-vol. set $15.90

ENCYCLOPEDIA OF VICTORIAN NEEDLEWORK, S. F. A. Caulfeild and Blanche Saward. Full, precise descriptions of stitches, techniques for dozens of needlecrafts—most exhaustive reference of its kind. Over 800 figures. Total of 679pp. 8⅛ × 11. Two volumes.   Vol. 1 22800-2 Pa. $11.95
Vol. 2 22801-0 Pa. $11.95

THE MARVELOUS LAND OF OZ, L. Frank Baum. Second Oz book, the Scarecrow and Tin Woodman are back with hero named Tip, Oz magic. 136 illustrations. 287pp. 5⅜ × 8½.   20692-0 Pa. $5.95

WILD FOWL DECOYS, Joel Barber. Basic book on the subject, by foremost authority and collector. Reveals history of decoy making and rigging, place in American culture, different kinds of decoys, how to make them, and how to use them. 140 plates. 156pp. 7⅞ × 10¾.   20011-6 Pa. $8.95

HISTORY OF LACE, Mrs. Bury Palliser. Definitive, profusely illustrated chronicle of lace from earliest times to late 19th century. Laces of Italy, Greece, England, France, Belgium, etc. Landmark of needlework scholarship. 266 illustrations. 672pp. 6⅛ × 9¼.   24742-2 Pa. $14.95

ILLUSTRATED GUIDE TO SHAKER FURNITURE, Robert Meader. All furniture and appurtenances, with much on unknown local styles. 235 photos. 146pp. 9 × 12. 22819-3 Pa. $8.95

WHALE SHIPS AND WHALING: A Pictorial Survey, George Francis Dow. Over 200 vintage engravings, drawings, photographs of barks, brigs, cutters, other vessels. Also harpoons, lances, whaling guns, many other artifacts. Comprehensive text by foremost authority. 207 black-and-white illustrations. 288pp. 6 × 9. 24808-9 Pa. $9.95

THE BERTRAMS, Anthony Trollope. Powerful portrayal of blind self-will and thwarted ambition includes one of Trollope's most heartrending love stories. 497pp. 5⅜ × 8½. 25119-5 Pa. $9.95

ADVENTURES WITH A HAND LENS, Richard Headstrom. Clearly written guide to observing and studying flowers and grasses, fish scales, moth and insect wings, egg cases, buds, feathers, seeds, leaf scars, moss, molds, ferns, common crystals, etc.—all with an ordinary, inexpensive magnifying glass. 209 exact line drawings aid in your discoveries. 220pp. 5⅜ × 8½. 23330-8 Pa. $4.95

RODIN ON ART AND ARTISTS, Auguste Rodin. Great sculptor's candid, wide-ranging comments on meaning of art; great artists; relation of sculpture to poetry, painting, music; philosophy of life, more. 76 superb black-and-white illustrations of Rodin's sculpture, drawings and prints. 119pp. 8⅜ × 11¼. 24487-3 Pa. $7.95

FIFTY CLASSIC FRENCH FILMS, 1912–1982: A Pictorial Record, Anthony Slide. Memorable stills from Grand Illusion, Beauty and the Beast, Hiroshima, Mon Amour, many more. Credits, plot synopses, reviews, etc. 160pp. 8¼ × 11. 25256-6 Pa. $11.95

THE PRINCIPLES OF PSYCHOLOGY, William James. Famous long course complete, unabridged. Stream of thought, time perception, memory, experimental methods; great work decades ahead of its time. 94 figures. 1,391pp. 5⅜ × 8½. 20381-6, 20382-4 Pa., Two-vol. set $23.90

BODIES IN A BOOKSHOP, R. T. Campbell. Challenging mystery of blackmail and murder with ingenious plot and superbly drawn characters. In the best tradition of British suspense fiction. 192pp. 5⅜ × 8½. 24720-1 Pa. $4.95

CALLAS: PORTRAIT OF A PRIMA DONNA, George Jellinek. Renowned commentator on the musical scene chronicles incredible career and life of the most controversial, fascinating, influential operatic personality of our time. 64 black-and-white photographs. 416pp. 5⅜ × 8¼. 25047-4 Pa. $8.95

GEOMETRY, RELATIVITY AND THE FOURTH DIMENSION, Rudolph Rucker. Exposition of fourth dimension, concepts of relativity as Flatland characters continue adventures. Popular, easily followed yet accurate, profound. 141 illustrations. 133pp. 5⅜ × 8½. 23400-2 Pa. $4.95

HOUSEHOLD STORIES BY THE BROTHERS GRIMM, with pictures by Walter Crane. 53 classic stories—Rumpelstiltskin, Rapunzel, Hansel and Gretel, the Fisherman and his Wife, Snow White, Tom Thumb, Sleeping Beauty, Cinderella, and so much more—lavishly illustrated with original 19th century drawings. 114 illustrations. x + 269pp. 5⅜ × 8½. 21080-4 Pa. $4.95

SUNDIALS, Albert Waugh. Far and away the best, most thorough coverage of ideas, mathematics concerned, types, construction, adjusting anywhere. Over 100 illustrations. 230pp. 5⅜ × 8½. 22947-5 Pa. $5.95

PICTURE HISTORY OF THE NORMANDIE: With 190 Illustrations, Frank O. Braynard. Full story of legendary French ocean liner: Art Deco interiors, design innovations, furnishings, celebrities, maiden voyage, tragic fire, much more. Extensive text. 144pp. 8⅞ × 11¾. 25257-4 Pa. $10.95

THE FIRST AMERICAN COOKBOOK: A Facsimile of "American Cookery," 1796, Amelia Simmons. Facsimile of the first American-written cookbook published in the United States contains authentic recipes for colonial favorites—pumpkin pudding, winter squash pudding, spruce beer, Indian slapjacks, and more. Introductory Essay and Glossary of colonial cooking terms. 80pp. 5⅜ × 8½. 24710-4 Pa. $3.50

101 PUZZLES IN THOUGHT AND LOGIC, C. R. Wylie, Jr. Solve murders and robberies, find out which fishermen are liars, how a blind man could possibly identify a color—purely by your own reasoning! 107pp. 5⅜ × 8½. 20367-0 Pa. $2.95

ANCIENT EGYPTIAN MYTHS AND LEGENDS, Lewis Spence. Examines animism, totemism, fetishism, creation myths, deities, alchemy, art and magic, other topics. Over 50 illustrations. 432pp. 5⅜ × 8½. 26525-0 Pa. $8.95

ANTHROPOLOGY AND MODERN LIFE, Franz Boas. Great anthropologist's classic treatise on race and culture. Introduction by Ruth Bunzel. Only inexpensive paperback edition. 255pp. 5⅜ × 8½. 25245-0 Pa. $7.95

THE TALE OF PETER RABBIT, Beatrix Potter. The inimitable Peter's terrifying adventure in Mr. McGregor's garden, with all 27 wonderful, full-color Potter illustrations. 55pp. 4¼ × 5½. (Available in U.S. only) 22827-4 Pa. $1.75

THREE PROPHETIC SCIENCE FICTION NOVELS, H. G. Wells. *When the Sleeper Wakes, A Story of the Days to Come* and *The Time Machine* (full version). 335pp. 5⅜ × 8½. (Available in U.S. only) 20605-X Pa. $8.95

APICIUS COOKERY AND DINING IN IMPERIAL ROME, edited and translated by Joseph Dommers Vehling. Oldest known cookbook in existence offers readers a clear picture of what foods Romans ate, how they prepared them, etc. 49 illustrations. 301pp. 6⅛ × 9¼. 23563-7 Pa. $7.95

SHAKESPEARE LEXICON AND QUOTATION DICTIONARY, Alexander Schmidt. Full definitions, locations, shades of meaning of every word in plays and poems. More than 50,000 exact quotations. 1,485pp. 6½ × 9¼. 22726-X, 22727-8 Pa., Two-vol. set $31.90

THE WORLD'S GREAT SPEECHES, edited by Lewis Copeland and Lawrence W. Lamm. Vast collection of 278 speeches from Greeks to 1970. Powerful and effective models; unique look at history. 842pp. 5⅜ × 8½. 20468-5 Pa. $12.95

THE BLUE FAIRY BOOK, Andrew Lang. The first, most famous collection, with many familiar tales: Little Red Riding Hood, Aladdin and the Wonderful Lamp, Puss in Boots, Sleeping Beauty, Hansel and Gretel, Rumpelstiltskin; 37 in all. 138 illustrations. 390pp. 5⅜ × 8½. 21437-0 Pa. $6.95

THE STORY OF THE CHAMPIONS OF THE ROUND TABLE, Howard Pyle. Sir Launcelot, Sir Tristram and Sir Percival in spirited adventures of love and triumph retold in Pyle's inimitable style. 50 drawings, 31 full-page. xviii + 329pp. 6½ × 9¼. 21883-X Pa. $7.95

THE MYTHS OF THE NORTH AMERICAN INDIANS, Lewis Spence. Myths and legends of the Algonquins, Iroquois, Pawnees and Sioux with comprehensive historical and ethnological commentary. 36 illustrations. 5⅜ × 8½.
25967-6 Pa. $8.95

GREAT DINOSAUR HUNTERS AND THEIR DISCOVERIES, Edwin H. Colbert. Fascinating, lavishly illustrated chronicle of dinosaur research, 1820s to 1960. Achievements of Cope, Marsh, Brown, Buckland, Mantell, Huxley, many others. 384pp. 5¼ × 8¼. 24701-5 Pa. $7.95

THE TASTEMAKERS, Russell Lynes. Informal, illustrated social history of American taste 1850s–1950s. First popularized categories Highbrow, Lowbrow, Middlebrow. 129 illustrations. New (1979) afterword. 384pp. 6 × 9.
23993-4 Pa. $8.95

DOUBLE CROSS PURPOSES, Ronald A. Knox. A treasure hunt in the Scottish Highlands, an old map, unidentified corpse, surprise discoveries keep reader guessing in this cleverly intricate tale of financial skullduggery. 2 black-and-white maps. 320pp. 5⅜ × 8½. (Available in U.S. only) 25032-6 Pa. $6.95

AUTHENTIC VICTORIAN DECORATION AND ORNAMENTATION IN FULL COLOR: 46 Plates from "Studies in Design," Christopher Dresser. Superb full-color lithographs reproduced from rare original portfolio of a major Victorian designer. 48pp. 9¼ × 12¼. 25083-0 Pa. $7.95

PRIMITIVE ART, Franz Boas. Remains the best text ever prepared on subject, thoroughly discussing Indian, African, Asian, Australian, and, especially, North-ern American primitive art. Over 950 illustrations show ceramics, masks, totem poles, weapons, textiles, paintings, much more. 376pp. 5⅜ × 8. 20025-6 Pa. $7.95

SIDELIGHTS ON RELATIVITY, Albert Einstein. Unabridged republication of two lectures delivered by the great physicist in 1920–21. *Ether and Relativity* and *Geometry and Experience*. Elegant ideas in nonmathematical form, accessible to intelligent layman. vi + 56pp. 5⅜ × 8½. 24511-X Pa. $3.95

THE WIT AND HUMOR OF OSCAR WILDE, edited by Alvin Redman. More than 1,000 ripostes, paradoxes, wisecracks: Work is the curse of the drinking classes, I can resist everything except temptation, etc. 258pp. 5⅜ × 8½. 20602-5 Pa. $4.95

ADVENTURES WITH A MICROSCOPE, Richard Headstrom. 59 adventures with clothing fibers, protozoa, ferns and lichens, roots and leaves, much more. 142 illustrations. 232pp. 5⅜ × 8½. 23471-1 Pa. $4.95

PLANTS OF THE BIBLE, Harold N. Moldenke and Alma L. Moldenke. Standard reference to all 230 plants mentioned in Scriptures. Latin name, biblical reference, uses, modern identity, much more. Unsurpassed encyclopedic resource for scholars, botanists, nature lovers, students of Bible. Bibliography. Indexes. 123 black-and-white illustrations. 384pp. 6 × 9. 25069-5 Pa. $8.95

FAMOUS AMERICAN WOMEN: A Biographical Dictionary from Colonial Times to the Present, Robert McHenry, ed. From Pocahontas to Rosa Parks, 1,035 distinguished American women documented in separate biographical entries. Accurate, up-to-date data, numerous categories, spans 400 years. Indices. 493pp. 6½ × 9¼. 24523-3 Pa. $10.95

THE FABULOUS INTERIORS OF THE GREAT OCEAN LINERS IN HISTORIC PHOTOGRAPHS, William H. Miller, Jr. Some 200 superb photographs capture exquisite interiors of world's great "floating palaces"—1890s to 1980s: *Titanic, Ile de France, Queen Elizabeth, United States, Europa,* more. Approx. 200 black-and-white photographs. Captions. Text. Introduction. 160pp. 8⅞ × 11¾. 24756-2 Pa. $9.95

THE GREAT LUXURY LINERS, 1927–1954: A Photographic Record, William H. Miller, Jr. Nostalgic tribute to heyday of ocean liners. 186 photos of *Ile de France, Normandie, Leviathan, Queen Elizabeth, United States,* many others. Interior and exterior views. Introduction. Captions. 160pp. 9 × 12. 24056-8 Pa. $12.95

A NATURAL HISTORY OF THE DUCKS, John Charles Phillips. Great landmark of ornithology offers complete detailed coverage of nearly 200 species and subspecies of ducks: gadwall, sheldrake, merganser, pintail, many more. 74 full-color plates, 102 black-and-white. Bibliography. Total of 1,920pp. 8⅝ × 11¼. 25141-1, 25142-X Cloth., Two-vol. set $100.00

THE SEAWEED HANDBOOK: An Illustrated Guide to Seaweeds from North Carolina to Canada, Thomas F. Lee. Concise reference covers 78 species. Scientific and common names, habitat, distribution, more. Finding keys for easy identification. 224pp. 5⅜ × 8½. 25215-9 Pa. $6.95

THE TEN BOOKS OF ARCHITECTURE: The 1755 Leoni Edition, Leon Battista Alberti. Rare classic helped introduce the glories of ancient architecture to the Renaissance. 68 black-and-white plates. 336pp. 8⅜ × 11¼. 25239-6 Pa. $14.95

MISS MACKENZIE, Anthony Trollope. Minor masterpieces by Victorian master unmasks many truths about life in 19th-century England. First inexpensive edition in years. 392pp. 5⅜ × 8½. 25201-9 Pa. $8.95

THE RIME OF THE ANCIENT MARINER, Gustave Doré, Samuel Taylor Coleridge. Dramatic engravings considered by many to be his greatest work. The terrifying space of the open sea, the storms and whirlpools of an unknown ocean, the ice of Antarctica, more—all rendered in a powerful, chilling manner. Full text. 38 plates. 77pp. 9¼ × 12. 22305-1 Pa. $4.95

THE EXPEDITIONS OF ZEBULON MONTGOMERY PIKE, Zebulon Montgomery Pike. Fascinating firsthand accounts (1805–6) of exploration of Mississippi River, Indian wars, capture by Spanish dragoons, much more. 1,088pp. 5⅜ × 8½. 25254-X, 25255-8 Pa., Two-vol. set $25.90

A CONCISE HISTORY OF PHOTOGRAPHY: Third Revised Edition, Helmut Gernsheim. Best one-volume history—camera obscura, photochemistry, daguerreotypes, evolution of cameras, film, more. Also artistic aspects—landscape, portraits, fine art, etc. 281 black-and-white photographs. 26 in color. 176pp. 8⅜ × 11¼.
25128-4 Pa. $14.95

THE DORÉ BIBLE ILLUSTRATIONS, Gustave Doré. 241 detailed plates from the Bible: the Creation scenes, Adam and Eve, Flood, Babylon, battle sequences, life of Jesus, etc. Each plate is accompanied by the verses from the King James version of the Bible. 241pp. 9 × 12. 23004-X Pa. $9.95

WANDERINGS IN WEST AFRICA, Richard F. Burton. Great Victorian scholar/adventurer's invaluable descriptions of African tribal rituals, fetishism, culture, art, much more. Fascinating 19th-century account. 624pp. 5⅜ × 8½. 26890-X Pa. $12.95

HISTORIC HOMES OF THE AMERICAN PRESIDENTS, Second Revised Edition, Irvin Haas. Guide to homes occupied by every president from Washington to Bush. Visiting hours, travel routes, more. 175 photos. 160pp. 8¼ × 11.
26751-2 Pa. $9.95

THE HISTORY OF THE LEWIS AND CLARK EXPEDITION, Meriwether Lewis and William Clark, edited by Elliott Coues. Classic edition of Lewis and Clark's day-by-day journals that later became the basis for U.S. claims to Oregon and the West. Accurate and invaluable geographical, botanical, biological, meteorological and anthropological material. Total of 1,508pp. 5⅜ × 8½.
21268-8, 21269-6, 21270-X Pa., Three-vol. set $29.85

LANGUAGE, TRUTH AND LOGIC, Alfred J. Ayer. Famous, clear introduction to Vienna, Cambridge schools of Logical Positivism. Role of philosophy, elimination of metaphysics, nature of analysis, etc. 160pp. 5⅜ × 8½. (Available in U.S. and Canada only) 20010-8 Pa. $3.95

MATHEMATICS FOR THE NONMATHEMATICIAN, Morris Kline. Detailed, college-level treatment of mathematics in cultural and historical context, with numerous exercises. For liberal arts students. Preface. Recommended Reading Lists. Tables. Index. Numerous black-and-white figures. xvi + 641pp. 5⅜ × 8½.
24823-2 Pa. $11.95

HANDBOOK OF PICTORIAL SYMBOLS, Rudolph Modley. 3,250 signs and symbols, many systems in full; official or heavy commercial use. Arranged by subject. Most in Pictorial Archive series. 143pp. 8⅛ × 11. 23357-X Pa. $7.95

INCIDENTS OF TRAVEL IN YUCATAN, John L. Stephens. Classic (1843) exploration of jungles of Yucatan, looking for evidences of Maya civilization. Travel adventures, Mexican and Indian culture, etc. Total of 669pp. 5⅜ × 8½.
20926-1, 20927-X Pa., Two-vol. set $13.90

DEGAS: An Intimate Portrait, Ambroise Vollard. Charming, anecdotal memoir by famous art dealer of one of the greatest 19th-century French painters. 14 black-and-white illustrations. Introduction by Harold L. Van Doren. 96pp. 5⅜ × 8½.
25131-4 Pa. $4.95

PERSONAL NARRATIVE OF A PILGRIMAGE TO AL-MADINAH AND MECCAH, Richard F. Burton. Great travel classic by remarkably colorful personality. Burton, disguised as a Moroccan, visited sacred shrines of Islam, narrowly escaping death. 47 illustrations. 959pp. 5⅜ × 8½.
21217-3, 21218-1 Pa., Two-vol. set $19.90

PHRASE AND WORD ORIGINS, A. H. Holt. Entertaining, reliable, modern study of more than 1,200 colorful words, phrases, origins and histories. Much unexpected information. 254pp. 5⅜ × 8½.
20758-7 Pa. $5.95

THE RED THUMB MARK, R. Austin Freeman. In this first Dr. Thorndyke case, the great scientific detective draws fascinating conclusions from the nature of a single fingerprint. Exciting story, authentic science. 320pp. 5⅜ × 8½. (Available in U.S. only)
25210-8 Pa. $6.95

AN EGYPTIAN HIEROGLYPHIC DICTIONARY, E. A. Wallis Budge. Monumental work containing about 25,000 words or terms that occur in texts ranging from 3000 B.C. to 600 A.D. Each entry consists of a transliteration of the word, the word in hieroglyphs, and the meaning in English. 1,314pp. 6⅜ × 10.
23615-3, 23616-1 Pa., Two-vol. set $35.90

THE COMPLEAT STRATEGYST: Being a Primer on the Theory of Games of Strategy, J. D. Williams. Highly entertaining classic describes, with many illustrated examples, how to select best strategies in conflict situations. Prefaces. Appendices. xvi + 268pp. 5⅜ × 8½.
25101-2 Pa. $6.95

THE ROAD TO OZ, L. Frank Baum. Dorothy meets the Shaggy Man, little Button-Bright and the Rainbow's beautiful daughter in this delightful trip to the magical Land of Oz. 272pp. 5⅜ × 8.
25208-6 Pa. $5.95

POINT AND LINE TO PLANE, Wassily Kandinsky. Seminal exposition of role of point, line, other elements in nonobjective painting. Essential to understanding 20th-century art. 127 illustrations. 192pp. 6½ × 9¼.
23808-3 Pa. $5.95

LADY ANNA, Anthony Trollope. Moving chronicle of Countess Lovel's bitter struggle to win for herself and daughter Anna their rightful rank and fortune—perhaps at cost of sanity itself. 384pp. 5⅜ × 8½.
24669-8 Pa. $8.95

EGYPTIAN MAGIC, E. A. Wallis Budge. Sums up all that is known about magic in Ancient Egypt: the role of magic in controlling the gods, powerful amulets that warded off evil spirits, scarabs of immortality, use of wax images, formulas and spells, the secret name, much more. 253pp. 5⅜ × 8½.
22681-6 Pa. $4.95

THE DANCE OF SIVA, Ananda Coomaraswamy. Preeminent authority unfolds the vast metaphysic of India: the revelation of her art, conception of the universe, social organization, etc. 27 reproductions of art masterpieces. 192pp. 5⅜ × 8½.
24817-8 Pa. $6.95

CHRISTMAS CUSTOMS AND TRADITIONS, Clement A. Miles. Origin, evolution, significance of religious, secular practices. Caroling, gifts, yule logs, much more. Full, scholarly yet fascinating; non-sectarian. 400pp. 5⅜ × 8½.
23354-5 Pa. $7.95

THE HUMAN FIGURE IN MOTION, Eadweard Muybridge. More than 4,500 stopped-action photos, in action series, showing undraped men, women, children jumping, lying down, throwing, sitting, wrestling, carrying, etc. 390pp. 7⅞ × 10⅝.
20204-6 Cloth. $24.95

THE MAN WHO WAS THURSDAY, Gilbert Keith Chesterton. Witty, fast-paced novel about a club of anarchists in turn-of-the-century London. Brilliant social, religious, philosophical speculations. 128pp. 5⅜ × 8½.
25121-7 Pa. $3.95

A CÉZANNE SKETCHBOOK: Figures, Portraits, Landscapes and Still Lifes, Paul Cézanne. Great artist experiments with tonal effects, light, mass, other qualities in over 100 drawings. A revealing view of developing master painter, precursor of Cubism. 102 black-and-white illustrations. 144pp. 8¾ × 6⅝.
24790-2 Pa. $6.95

AN ENCYCLOPEDIA OF BATTLES: Accounts of Over 1,560 Battles from 1479 B.C. to the Present, David Eggenberger. Presents essential details of every major battle in recorded history, from the first battle of Megiddo in 1479 B.C. to Grenada in 1984. List of Battle Maps. New Appendix covering the years 1967–1984. Index. 99 illustrations. 544pp. 6½ × 9¼.
24913-1 Pa. $14.95

AN ETYMOLOGICAL DICTIONARY OF MODERN ENGLISH, Ernest Weekley. Richest, fullest work, by foremost British lexicographer. Detailed word histories. Inexhaustible. Total of 856pp. 6½ × 9¼.
21873-2, 21874-0 Pa., Two-vol. set $19.90

WEBSTER'S AMERICAN MILITARY BIOGRAPHIES, edited by Robert McHenry. Over 1,000 figures who shaped 3 centuries of American military history. Detailed biographies of Nathan Hale, Douglas MacArthur, Mary Hallaren, others. Chronologies of engagements, more. Introduction. Addenda. 1,033 entries in alphabetical order. xi + 548pp. 6½ × 9¼. (Available in U.S. only)
24758-9 Pa. $13.95

LIFE IN ANCIENT EGYPT, Adolf Erman. Detailed older account, with much not in more recent books: domestic life, religion, magic, medicine, commerce, and whatever else needed for complete picture. Many illustrations. 597pp. 5⅜ × 8½.
22632-8 Pa. $9.95

HISTORIC COSTUME IN PICTURES, Braun & Schneider. Over 1,450 costumed figures shown, covering a wide variety of peoples: kings, emperors, nobles, priests, servants, soldiers, scholars, townsfolk, peasants, merchants, courtiers, cavaliers, and more. 256pp. 8⅜ × 11¼.
23150-X Pa. $9.95

THE NOTEBOOKS OF LEONARDO DA VINCI, edited by J. P. Richter. Extracts from manuscripts reveal great genius; on painting, sculpture, anatomy, sciences, geography, etc. Both Italian and English. 186 ms. pages reproduced, plus 500 additional drawings, including studies for *Last Supper*, *Sforza* monument, etc. 860pp. 7⅞ × 10¾. (Available in U.S. only) 22572-0, 22573-9 Pa., Two-vol. set $35.90

THE ART NOUVEAU STYLE BOOK OF ALPHONSE MUCHA: All 72 Plates from "Documents Decoratifs" in Original Color, Alphonse Mucha. Rare copyright-free design portfolio by high priest of Art Nouveau. Jewelry, wallpaper, stained glass, furniture, figure studies, plant and animal motifs, etc. Only complete one-volume edition. 80pp. 9⅜ × 12¼. 24044-4 Pa. $9.95

ANIMALS: 1,419 COPYRIGHT-FREE ILLUSTRATIONS OF MAMMALS, BIRDS, FISH, INSECTS, ETC., edited by Jim Harter. Clear wood engravings present, in extremely lifelike poses, over 1,000 species of animals. One of the most extensive pictorial sourcebooks of its kind. Captions. Index. 284pp. 9 × 12.
23766-4 Pa. $9.95

OBELISTS FLY HIGH, C. Daly King. Masterpiece of American detective fiction, long out of print, involves murder on a 1935 transcontinental flight—"a very thrilling story"—NY Times. Unabridged and unaltered republication of the edition published by William Collins Sons & Co. Ltd., London, 1935. 288pp. 5⅜ × 8½. (Available in U.S. only) 25036-9 Pa. $5.95

VICTORIAN AND EDWARDIAN FASHION: A Photographic Survey, Alison Gernsheim. First fashion history completely illustrated by contemporary photographs. Full text plus 235 photos, 1840–1914, in which many celebrities appear. 240pp. 6½ × 9¼. 24205-6 Pa. $8.95

THE ART OF THE FRENCH ILLUSTRATED BOOK, 1700–1914, Gordon N. Ray. Over 630 superb book illustrations by Fragonard, Delacroix, Daumier, Doré, Grandville, Manet, Mucha, Steinlen, Toulouse-Lautrec and many others. Preface. Introduction. 633 halftones. Indices of artists, authors & titles, binders and provenances. Appendices. Bibliography. 608pp. 8⅜ × 11¼. 25086-5 Pa. $24.95

THE WONDERFUL WIZARD OF OZ, L. Frank Baum. Facsimile in full color of America's finest children's classic. 143 illustrations by W. W. Denslow. 267pp. 5⅜ × 8½. 20691-2 Pa. $7.95

FOLLOWING THE EQUATOR: A Journey Around the World, Mark Twain. Great writer's 1897 account of circumnavigating the globe by steamship. Ironic humor, keen observations, vivid and fascinating descriptions of exotic places. 197 illustrations. 720pp. 5⅜ × 8½. 26113-1 Pa. $15.95

THE FRIENDLY STARS, Martha Evans Martin & Donald Howard Menzel. Classic text marshalls the stars together in an engaging, non-technical survey, presenting them as sources of beauty in night sky. 23 illustrations. Foreword. 2 star charts. Index. 147pp. 5⅜ × 8½. 21099-5 Pa. $3.95

FADS AND FALLACIES IN THE NAME OF SCIENCE, Martin Gardner. Fair, witty appraisal of cranks, quacks, and quackeries of science and pseudoscience: hollow earth, Velikovsky, orgone energy, Dianetics, flying saucers, Bridey Murphy, food and medical fads, etc. Revised, expanded In the Name of Science. "A very able and even-tempered presentation."—The New Yorker. 363pp. 5⅜ × 8.
20394-8 Pa. $6.95

ANCIENT EGYPT: ITS CULTURE AND HISTORY, J. E Manchip White. From pre-dynastics through Ptolemies: society, history, political structure, religion, daily life, literature, cultural heritage. 48 plates. 217pp. 5⅜ × 8½. 22548-8 Pa. $5.95

SIR HARRY HOTSPUR OF HUMBLETHWAITE, Anthony Trollope. Incisive, unconventional psychological study of a conflict between a wealthy baronet, his idealistic daughter, and their scapegrace cousin. The 1870 novel in its first inexpensive edition in years. 250pp. 5⅜ × 8½. 24953-0 Pa. $6.95

LASERS AND HOLOGRAPHY, Winston E. Kock. Sound introduction to burgeoning field, expanded (1981) for second edition. Wave patterns, coherence, lasers, diffraction, zone plates, properties of holograms, recent advances. 84 illustrations. 160pp. 5⅜ × 8¼. (Except in United Kingdom) 24041-X Pa. $3.95

INTRODUCTION TO ARTIFICIAL INTELLIGENCE: Second, Enlarged Edition, Philip C. Jackson, Jr. Comprehensive survey of artificial intelligence—the study of how machines (computers) can be made to act intelligently. Includes introductory and advanced material. Extensive notes updating the main text. 132 black-and-white illustrations. 512pp. 5⅜ × 8½. 24864-X Pa. $10.95

HISTORY OF INDIAN AND INDONESIAN ART, Ananda K. Coomaraswamy. Over 400 illustrations illuminate classic study of Indian art from earliest Harappa finds to early 20th century. Provides philosophical, religious and social insights. 304pp. 6⅜ × 9⅜. 25005-9 Pa. $11.95

THE GOLEM, Gustav Meyrink. Most famous supernatural novel in modern European literature, set in Ghetto of Old Prague around 1890. Compelling story of mystical experiences, strange transformations, profound terror. 13 black-and-white illustrations. 224pp. 5⅜ × 8½. (Available in U.S. only) 25025-3 Pa. $6.95

PICTORIAL ENCYCLOPEDIA OF HISTORIC ARCHITECTURAL PLANS, DETAILS AND ELEMENTS: With 1,880 Line Drawings of Arches, Domes, Doorways, Facades, Gables, Windows, etc., John Theodore Haneman. Sourcebook of inspiration for architects, designers, others. Bibliography. Captions. 141pp. 9 × 12. 24605-1 Pa. $8.95

BENCHLEY LOST AND FOUND, Robert Benchley. Finest humor from early 30s, about pet peeves, child psychologists, post office and others. Mostly unavailable elsewhere. 73 illustrations by Peter Arno and others. 183pp. 5⅜ × 8½. 22410-4 Pa. $4.95

ERTÉ GRAPHICS, Erté. Collection of striking color graphics: *Seasons, Alphabet, Numerals, Aces* and *Precious Stones*. 50 plates, including 4 on covers. 48pp. 9⅜ × 12¼. 23580-7 Pa. $7.95

THE JOURNAL OF HENRY D. THOREAU, edited by Bradford Torrey, F. H. Allen. Complete reprinting of 14 volumes, 1837–61, over two million words; the sourcebooks for *Walden*, etc. Definitive. All original sketches, plus 75 photographs. 1,804pp. 8½ × 12¼. 20312-3, 20313-1 Cloth., Two-vol. set $130.00

CASTLES: Their Construction and History, Sidney Toy. Traces castle development from ancient roots. Nearly 200 photographs and drawings illustrate moats, keeps, baileys, many other features. Caernarvon, Dover Castles, Hadrian's Wall, Tower of London, dozens more. 256pp. 5⅜ × 8¼. 24898-4 Pa. $7.95

CATALOG OF DOVER BOOKS

AMERICAN CLIPPER SHIPS: 1833–1858, Octavius T. Howe & Frederick C. Matthews. Fully-illustrated, encyclopedic review of 352 clipper ships from the period of America's greatest maritime supremacy. Introduction. 109 halftones. 5 black-and-white line illustrations. Index. Total of 928pp. 5⅜ × 8½.
25115-2, 25116-0 Pa., Two-vol. set $17.90

TOWARDS A NEW ARCHITECTURE, Le Corbusier. Pioneering manifesto by great architect, near legendary founder of "International School." Technical and aesthetic theories, views on industry, economics, relation of form to function, "mass-production spirit," much more. Profusely illustrated. Unabridged translation of 13th French edition. Introduction by Frederick Etchells. 320pp. 6⅛ × 9¼.
(Available in U.S. only) 25023-7 Pa. $8.95

THE BOOK OF KELLS, edited by Blanche Cirker. Inexpensive collection of 32 full-color, full-page plates from the greatest illuminated manuscript of the Middle Ages, painstakingly reproduced from rare facsimile edition. Publisher's Note. Captions. 32pp. 9⅜ × 12¼. (Available in U.S. only) 24345-1 Pa. $5.95

BEST SCIENCE FICTION STORIES OF H. G. WELLS, H. G. Wells. Full novel *The Invisible Man*, plus 17 short stories: "The Crystal Egg," "Aepyornis Island," "The Strange Orchid," etc. 303pp. 5⅜ × 8½. (Available in U.S. only)
21531-8 Pa. $6.95

AMERICAN SAILING SHIPS: Their Plans and History, Charles G. Davis. Photos, construction details of schooners, frigates, clippers, other sailcraft of 18th to early 20th centuries—plus entertaining discourse on design, rigging, nautical lore, much more. 137 black-and-white illustrations. 240pp. 6⅛ × 9¼.
24658-2 Pa. $6.95

ENTERTAINING MATHEMATICAL PUZZLES, Martin Gardner. Selection of author's favorite conundrums involving arithmetic, money, speed, etc., with lively commentary. Complete solutions. 112pp. 5⅜ × 8½. 25211-6 Pa. $3.50

THE WILL TO BELIEVE, HUMAN IMMORTALITY, William James. Two books bound together. Effect of irrational on logical, and arguments for human immortality. 402pp. 5⅜ × 8½. 20291-7 Pa. $8.95

THE HAUNTED MONASTERY and THE CHINESE MAZE MURDERS, Robert Van Gulik. 2 full novels by Van Gulik continue adventures of Judge Dee and his companions. An evil Taoist monastery, seemingly supernatural events; overgrown topiary maze that hides strange crimes. Set in 7th-century China. 27 illustrations. 328pp. 5⅜ × 8½. 23502-5 Pa. $6.95

CELEBRATED CASES OF JUDGE DEE (DEE GOONG AN), translated by Robert Van Gulik. Authentic 18th-century Chinese detective novel; Dee and associates solve three interlocked cases. Led to Van Gulik's own stories with same characters. Extensive introduction. 9 illustrations. 237pp. 5⅜ × 8½.
23337-5 Pa. $5.95

Prices subject to change without notice.

Available at your book dealer or write for free catalog to Dept. GI, Dover Publications, Inc., 31 East 2nd St., Mineola, N.Y. 11501. Dover publishes more than 175 books each year on science, elementary and advanced mathematics, biology, music, art, literary history, social sciences and other areas.